The
Shelly Cashman
Series®

Discovering Computers

Digital Technology, Data, and Devices

17th Edition

Jennifer T. Campbell

✳️ Cengage

Australia • Brazil • Canada • Mexico • Singapore • United Kingdom • United States

Discovering Computers: Digital Technology, Data, and Devices, 17th Edition

Jennifer T. Campbell

SVP, Product: Erin Joyner

VP, Product: Thais Alencar

Portfolio Product Director: Mark Santee

Senior Portfolio Product Manager: Amy Savino

Product Assistant: Ciara Horne

Learning Designer: Zenya Molnar

Content Manager: Grant Davis

Digital Project Manager: Jim Vaughey

Developmental Editor: Lyn Markowicz

VP, Product Marketing: Jason Sakos

Director, Product Marketing: Danaë April

Executive Product Marketing Manager: Jill Staut

Content Acquisition Analyst: Ann Hoffman

Production Service: Lumina Datamatics

Designer: Erin Griffin

Cover Image Source: MirageC/Getty Images

ID: 669263934

For product information and technology assistance, contact us at Cengage **Customer & Sales Support, 1-800-354-9706 or support. cengage.com.**

For permission to use material from this text or product, submit all requests online at **www.copyright.com.**

Library of Congress Control Number: 2022911675

Student Edition ISBN: 978-0-357-67536-6
Looseleaf ISBN: 978-0-357-67537-3*
*Looseleaf available as part of a digital bundle

Cengage

200 Pier 4 Boulevard

Boston, MA 02210

USA

Cengage is a leading provider of customized learning solutions with employees residing in nearly 40 different countries and sales in more than 165 countries around the world. Find your local representative at **www.cengage.com.**

To learn more about Cengage platforms and services, register or access your online learning solution, or purchase materials for your course, visit **www.cengage.com.**

Notice to the Reader

Publisher does not warrant or guarantee any of the products described herein or perform any independent analysis in connection with any of the product information contained herein. Publisher does not assume, and expressly disclaims, any obligation to obtain and include information other than that provided to it by the manufacturer. The reader is expressly warned to consider and adopt all safety precautions that might be indicated by the activities described herein and to avoid all potential hazards. By following the instructions contained herein, the reader willingly assumes all risks in connection with such instructions. The publisher makes no representations or warranties of any kind, including but not limited to, the warranties of fitness for particular purpose or merchantability, nor are any such representations implied with respect to the material set forth herein, and the publisher takes no responsibility with respect to such material. The publisher shall not be liable for any special, consequential, or exemplary damages resulting, in whole or part, from the readers' use of, or reliance upon, this material.

Printed in the United States of America

Print Number: 02   Print Year: 2022

Table of Contents at a Glance

Table of Contents

Module **4**

Programs and Apps: Using Apps for Productivity, Graphics, and Security 4-1

Module **5**

Digital Security, Ethics, and Privacy: Avoiding and Recognizing Threats   5-1

Module **6**

Input and Output: Entering Data and Producing Information   6-1

Module **7**

Digital Storage: Preserving Your Content 7-1

Module **8**

Operating Systems: Managing, Coordinating, and Monitoring Resources 8-1

Module **9**

Networks and Network Devices: Communicating and Connecting 9-1

Module **13**

**Technology Careers:
Exploring and Preparing for
Opportunities   13-1**

Preface

About the Author

Jennifer T. Campbell has written and co-authored several other leading technology texts, including Technology for Success, Discovering Computers, Discovering the Internet, Web Design: Introductory, Microsoft Expression Web Introductory Concepts and Techniques, Computer Literacy Basics: Microsoft Office 2007 Companion, and Microsoft Office Quick Reference Pocket Guide. For over 25 years Ms. Campbell has served integral roles in computer educational publishing as an editor, author, and marketing manager. She holds a B.A. in English from The College of William and Mary.

Introduction/Preface for the Instructor

This text was revised using careful analysis from surveyed digital literacy and computer concepts instructors. The conceptual approach to text development included focus on the most relevant and up-to-date introductory technology topics along with emphasizing the responsibility that goes along with being a digital citizen. Discovering Computers presents the key content that students need for success using an inviting approach that encourages critical thinking, problem solving, and hands-on application. Its in-depth and relevant content, use of diagrams to depict complex concepts, and practical activities set students up for success in the real world. Each module includes a How To, Ethics and Issues, and Secure IT topic. Woven throughout the modules are Consider This? boxes, which introduce additional topics and encourage critical thinking. No prerequisites are required for this introductory-level text, and no prior knowledge of technology and computer concepts is assumed

The Target market for this title is introductory computing learners, along with entry-level learners for any discipline interested in understanding computer technology basics and digital literacy.

New to This Edition

- All new Module 1, which introduces the concepts of Digital Literacy and how to be a Digital Citizen, including contextual history.
- The Ethics & Issues, Secure IT, and How To content is woven into the chapter narrative, presenting module topics with these critical lenses.
- Databases, System and Application Development, and Web Development now are full individual modules.

Organization of the Text

COVERAGE INTRODUCES TODAY'S WEB AND CLOUD APPS, VIRTUAL AND AUGMENTED REALITY, AND CROWDSOURCING. Students become familiar with the latest computer advancements as this edition's timely coverage and online support address emerging issues and reflect the most recent applications and tools available.

CONVERGENCE, DEVICE, AND PLATFORM AGNOSTIC. The content and exercises do not assume students are using a specific device or platform, and the idea of convergence among device capabilities is addressed.

TIMELY, FOCUSED MODULES HIGHLIGHT TOPICS MOST IMPORTANT FOR STUDENT SUCCESS. All content is structured using a proven approach to enhance the reader's learning experience and highlight key information students need to know at home, at school, and at work.

END-OF-MODULE ASSIGNMENTS PROVIDE CRITICAL HANDS-ON PRACTICE. The author has carefully designed all assignments to help students develop the skills that are most important for their success in your course and in their future coursework and employment.

CRITICAL THINKING SKILLS. Consider This boxes and questions posed throughout the book challenge students to critically evaluate and determine solutions for contemporary technology dilemmas.

Ancillary Package

Test Banks: Questions written by the author are tightly aligned with each module's learning objectives.

Instructor Manual: The module outline corresponds directly with the content in each module, and additional discussion questions and activities are aligned to headings in the book.

PowerPoints: The icebreaker activity relates to the module topic, and the module objectives and content slides align with the book. Activities and the self-assessment align with module learning objectives and supplement the content in the book.

Solution and Answer Guide: The answers provided are written by the author and correspond to the end of module activities.

Transition Guide: The guide is written by the author and provides information on what has changed in this edition so that instructors know what to expect.

Acknowledgments

I wish to thank my editor, Lyn Markowicz, for her expertise in crafting this book. I also thank the team at Cengage: Grant Davis, Amy Savino, Zenya Molnar, and Ciara Horne for their support.

Cengage would like to thank Kacie Rea, M.S.Ed. for her contributions to the Technology Timeline.

Being a Digital Citizen:
At Home, School, and Work

1

iStock.com/istocksdaily

Objectives

After completing this module, you will be able to:

1 Define digital literacy
2 Explain society's reliance on technology
3 Describe how to protect your personal information
4 Explain the role of technology in the professional world
5 Use technology to find a career
6 Define convergence
7 Describe the legal and ethical responsibilities of a digital citizen
8 Identify the uses of assistive technologies

How Technology Impacts You

Digital literacy, also known as **computer literacy**, means having a current knowledge and understanding of computers, mobile devices, the web, and related technologies. A **digital citizen** is a person familiar with how to use technology to become an educated and productive member of the digital world. Aspects of being a digital citizen include the ethical, legal, and productive use of technology.

Even if you consider yourself a technology user and are familiar with many of the important basic concepts that are the backbone of digital literacy, a basic review is helpful. A **computer** is an electronic device, operating under the control of instructions stored in its own memory, that can accept data, process the data to produce information, and store the information for future use. **Memory** consists of electronic components that store instructions waiting to be executed by the processor, data needed by those instructions, and the results of processing the data into information. The **Internet** is a global collection of millions of computers linked together to share information. A **network** is a collection of two or more computers connected together to share resources. **Wi-Fi** (short for wireless fidelity) is a wireless data network technology that provides high-speed data connections that do not require a physical connection; it is used for mobile devices. A **server** is a powerful, high-capacity computer you access using the Internet or other network; it stores files and "serves" them, that is, makes the files available to, users; usually grouped at a location called a data center. An **online social network** (Figure 1-1) is an online community where users can share their interests, ideas, stories, photos, music, and videos with other registered users via a social networking website, such as Facebook, Google Plus, Twitter, Instagram, or Snapchat. Digital literacy is an evolving area that includes many other important topics, such as big data. **Big Data** is a term that refers to the large and complex data sources that defy easy management with traditional data processing methods.

The following are examples of how you, a digital citizen, might use your digital literacy to interact with technology, including embedded computers and the Internet, in your daily life.

Figure 1-1 Knowledge of online social networks is a key component of digital literacy.

iStock.com/Scyther5

A Day in the Life of a Digital Citizen

The sound of the alarm you asked your smart speaker to set last night wakes you up. You can smell the coffee brewing from the coffeemaker you programmed to go off five minutes before your alarm. Once you leave for work, your thermostat will adjust the temperature by five degrees and then readjust to a more comfortable temperature by the time you arrive home.

On your way to and from work, you check the public transportation app on your phone (Figure 1-2) to locate and get directions to the nearest subway station. Once there, you scan your phone to pay your fare and access the terminal. A screen in the station displays an alert when the train is incoming. As the subway speeds toward the next station, it relies on sensors to determine any oncoming traffic and report delays, changes in routes, and the next available stop.

Figure 1-2 You can use apps to find out information about public transit options.

Rawpixel.com/Shutterstock.com

After work, you decide to take your car and go shopping. You program your vehicle's GPS to direct you to the nearest mall. As you drive, your car senses the space between you and the car ahead and slows your speed to keep a safe distance. Outside the mall, you use a parking app to locate a parking spot near the front door and use your car's cameras to safely navigate into the spot.

Before heading into the store, you decide to check your balance on your debit card. Your banking app tells you how much money is in your checking account. You tap to transfer $40 to your smartphone's payment app, then you head to the store.

You walk into a clothing store, searching for a new sweater. You talk to a sales associate, who uses a tablet to look up your personal profile, including past purchases, based on your phone number. The sales associate tells you what size you wear and what colors you have bought in the past few years. Together, you find a sweater that fits and that is not similar to anything in your wardrobe. Before using the store's self-checkout, you check your store loyalty app on your smartphone to see what coupons are available.

Later, back at home, you sign in to your school's network to access your assignments. You use videoconferencing to discuss a group project with your classmates and complete a research paper using credible online sources, giving proper citations to the facts and quotes you find. You turn in your paper using the school's plagiarism checker and then shut down your laptop for the night. You make sure your alarm is set on your phone for tomorrow, and then you call it a night.

❓ Consider This

What is digital distraction?

Digital distraction is the practice of using and relying on technology so much that you do not pay enough attention to normal, everyday activities. Digital distraction might be characterized by using your smartphone while having dinner with others instead of interacting with them, or checking your social media during class. Digital distraction can lead to negative effects, such as lower grades, strained relationships, or danger of an injury or accident because of your lack of awareness of your surroundings. Have you ever been with or witnessed someone being digitally distracted? What occurred? What dangers might you encounter? How can you avoid this happening?

How Technology Impacts Society

If you think you cannot make it through a day without using technology, you are probably right. Even if you set aside your smartphone, you could still end up interacting with a database while making a purchase at your grocery store, watching a video during a class lecture, or using an ATM to get cash. The fact is you are likely to live a digital lifestyle, using a variety of technologies for work and play.

Over the last quarter century or so, technology has revolutionized our lives. Because of advances in technology, you can more quickly and effectively than ever before access, search for, and share information. You can manage your finances, calendars, and tasks. You can play games and watch videos on your phone or computer for entertainment and relaxation. Being digitally literate is essential for acquiring a job, using and contributing to global communications, and participating effectively in the international community.

Society as a whole has changed significantly, as well. Our devices connect us to a variety of other users and to other devices because of the evolution of technology. This can be both positive and negative and can create a division between those who have access to technology and those who do not.

The History of Computers

People have relied on tools and machines to count and manipulate numbers for thousands of years. These tools and technologies have evolved from the abacus in ancient times, to the first computing machines in the nineteenth century, to today's powerful handheld devices, such as smartphones and tablets.

The first generation of computers used **vacuum tubes** (Figure 1-3), which are cylindrical glass tubes that controlled the flow of electrons. The ENIAC (Electronic Numerical Integrator and Computer) and UNIVAC (Universal Automatic Computer) are examples of these expensive machines. Their use and availability were limited due to their large size, the amount of power they consumed, the heat they generated, and how quickly they wore out.

Figure 1-3   Electronic digital computer with vacuum tubes.

Emkaplin/Shutterstock.com

The next generation of computers replaced vacuum tubes with **transistors**, which were smaller, cheaper, and more reliable. These computers contained many components still in use today, including tape and disk storage, memory, operating systems, and stored programs.

In the 1960s, computer engineers developed **integrated circuits**, which packed the equivalent of thousands of vacuum tubes or transistors into a silicon chip about the size of your thumb. In 1971, Ted Hoff and a team of engineers at Intel and IBM introduced the microprocessor. A **microprocessor** is the "brains" of a computer, a chip that contains a central processing unit. Microprocessors were even faster, smaller, and less expensive than integrated circuits. Today, microprocessors often are called **processors** for short.

In the 1970s and 1980s, computers meant for personal use started to gain popularity. In 1978, Steve Jobs and Steve Wozniak of Apple Computer Corporation introduced the Apple II (Figure 1-4), a preassembled computer with color graphics and popular spreadsheet software called VisiCalc.

Figure 1-4   Apple II computer.

Anton_Ivanov/Shutterstock.com

IBM followed Apple's lead in 1981, introducing its **personal computer** (**PC**) intended for individual use instead of commercial or industrial. Other manufacturers also started making similar machines, and the market grew. Since 1981, the number of PCs in use has grown to the billions; however, many people today use tablets and smartphones in addition to or instead of PCs.

Today's computers have evolved into connected devices that can share data using the Internet or wireless networks. They are smaller, faster, and have far greater capabilities than previous computers. In fact, your smartphone probably has more computing power than the computer that guided the Apollo mission to the moon in 1969!

The Internet of Things

The **Internet of Things** (**IoT**) is an environment in which processors are embedded in every product imaginable (things), and these things, in turn, communicate with one another via the Internet or wireless networks. Alarm clocks, coffeemakers, thermostats, streetlights, navigation systems, and much more are enhanced by the growth of IoT. IoT-enabled devices often are referred to as smart devices (Figure 1-5) because of their capability of communicating, locating, and predicting. Smart devices often have associated apps to control and interact with them.

Figure 1-5 Smart devices use IoT to control home functions, such as a thermostat.

Andrey_Popov/Shutterstock.com

The basic premise of IoT is that objects can be tagged, tracked, and monitored through a local network or across the Internet. Communication technologies, such as Bluetooth, RFID tags, near-field communications (NFC), and sensors, have become readily available, more powerful, and less expensive. Sensors and tags can transmit data to a server on the Internet over a wireless network at frequent intervals for analysis and storage.

Developments in big data have made it possible to efficiently access, store, and process the mountain of data reported by sensors. Mobile service providers offer connectivity to a variety of devices so that transmitting and receiving data can take place quickly.

Embedded computers are a part of IoT. An **embedded computer** is a computer that functions as one component in a larger product and has a specific purpose. Embedded computers usually are small and have limited hardware on their own but enhance the capabilities of everyday devices. Embedded computers perform a specific function based on the requirements of the product in which they reside. For example, an embedded computer in a printer monitors the ink levels, detects paper jams, and determines if the printer is out of paper.

Embedded computers seem to be everywhere. This technology enables computers and devices to connect with one another over the Internet using IoT. You encounter examples of embedded computers multiple times a day, perhaps without being aware of it.

Today's vehicles have many embedded computers. These enable you to use a camera to guide you when backing up, warn you if a vehicle or object is in your blind spot, or alert you to unsafe road conditions. Recently, all new cars were required to include backup cameras and electronic stability control, which can assist with steering the car in case of skidding. All this technology is intended to make driving safer (Figure 1-6).

Figure 1-6 Some of the embedded computers designed to improve safety, security, and performance in today's vehicles.

Nir Levy/Shutterstock.com; Santiago Cornejo/Shutterstock.com; iStock.com/Narvikk; iStock.com/Kenneth-Cheung; iStock.com/Marcin Laska; iStock.com/pagadesign; Source: OnStar, LLC

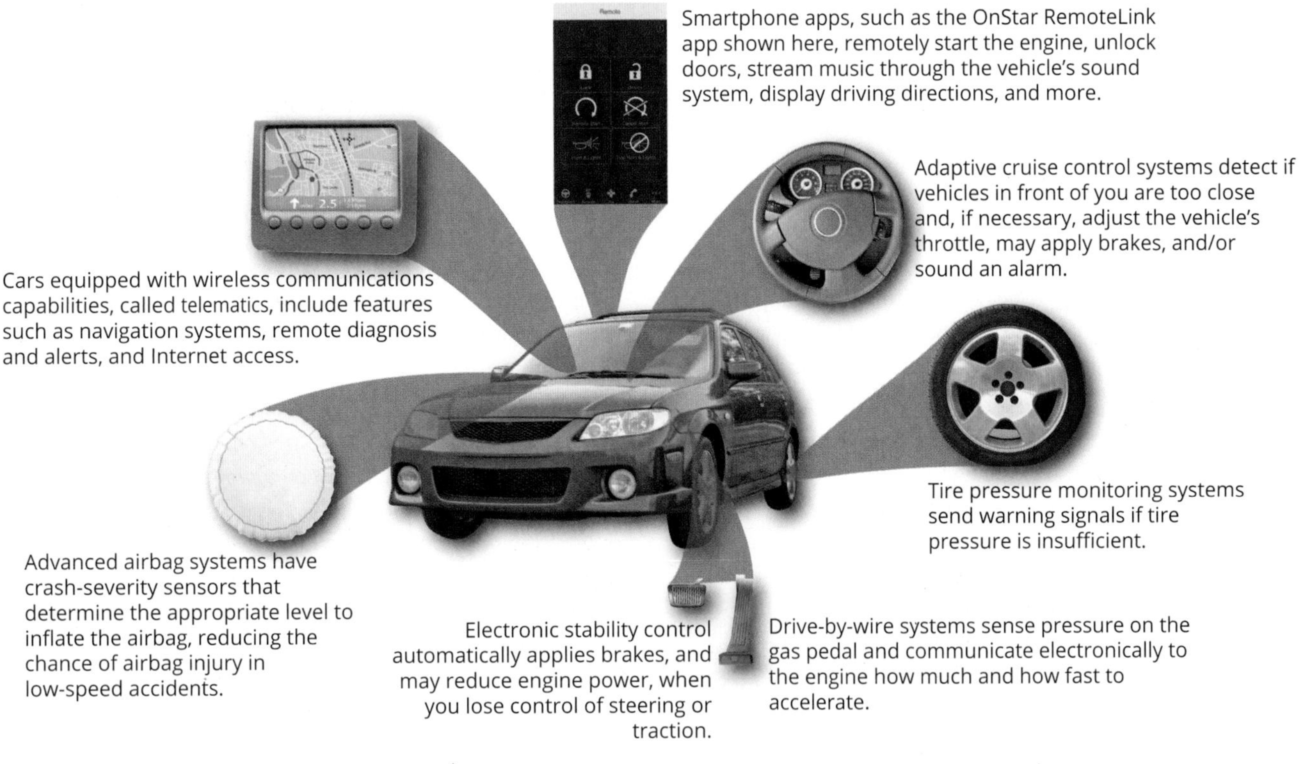

Smartphone apps, such as the OnStar RemoteLink app shown here, remotely start the engine, unlock doors, stream music through the vehicle's sound system, display driving directions, and more.

Adaptive cruise control systems detect if vehicles in front of you are too close and, if necessary, adjust the vehicle's throttle, may apply brakes, and/or sound an alarm.

Cars equipped with wireless communications capabilities, called telematics, include features such as navigation systems, remote diagnosis and alerts, and Internet access.

Tire pressure monitoring systems send warning signals if tire pressure is insufficient.

Advanced airbag systems have crash-severity sensors that determine the appropriate level to inflate the airbag, reducing the chance of airbag injury in low-speed accidents.

Electronic stability control automatically applies brakes, and may reduce engine power, when you lose control of steering or traction.

Drive-by-wire systems sense pressure on the gas pedal and communicate electronically to the engine how much and how fast to accelerate.

Critics of in-vehicle technology claim that it can provide drivers with a false sense of security. If you rely on a sensor while backing up, parking, or changing lanes, you may miss other obstructions that can cause a crash. Reliance on electronic stability control may cause you to drive faster than conditions allow or to pay less attention to the distance between your vehicle and others.

ATMs and Kiosks   **Automated teller machines (ATMs)** are one of the more familiar uses of IoT. You can use your ATM card to withdraw cash, deposit checks, and interact with your bank accounts. Recent innovations are improving card security, such as **chip-and-pin technology** that stores data on an embedded chip instead of a magnetic stripe.

ATMs are a type of kiosk. A **kiosk** is a freestanding booth usually placed in a public area that can contain a display device used to show information to the public or event attendees. Kiosks enable self-service transactions in hotels and airports, for example, to permit users to check in for a flight or room. Health care providers also use kiosks for patients to check in and enter information, such as their insurance card number.

IoT at Home   IoT enables you to manage devices remotely in your home, such as starting the washing machine at a certain time, preparing a grocery shopping list (Figure 1-7), viewing potential intruders via a webcam, or adjusting the room temperature. Personal IoT uses include wearable fitness trackers that record and send data to your smartphone or computer about your physical activity, the number of steps you take in a day, and your heart rate.

IoT continues to advance its capabilities and can help you maintain a secure, energy-efficient, connected, voice-activated, remotely accessible home.

IoT in Business   All businesses and areas of business can take advantage of IoT. Manufacturing can use sensors to monitor processes and increase quality of finished goods. Robotic arms can help ensure precision during the manufacturing process (Figure 1-8). Retail can use sensors to track inventory or send coupons to customers' phones while they shop. Shipping companies can track mileage and location of their trucks and monitor driving times to ensure the safety of their drivers.

Figure 1-8   Manufacturers can use a tablet to control a robotic arm.

Zapp2Photo/Shutterstock.com

A health care provider can use IoT to:

- Connect to a patient's wearable blood pressure or glucose monitor
- Send prescription updates and changes to a pharmacy, and alert the patient of the prescription
- Track and store data provided by wearable monitors to determine necessary follow-up care
- Send the patient reminders about upcoming appointments or tests

The uses of IoT are expanding rapidly, and connected devices continue to impact and enhance business practices at all levels.

The Digital Divide

All this technology has many uses for both personal and business needs; however, it is not available to everyone. The **digital divide** is the gap between those who have access to technology and its resources and information, especially on the Internet, and those who do not. Socioeconomic and demographic factors, such as age, income, location, and education, contribute to the digital divide, which can impact individuals, households, businesses, or geographic areas.

Figure 1-7   IoT devices can help you with daily tasks, such as grocery shopping.

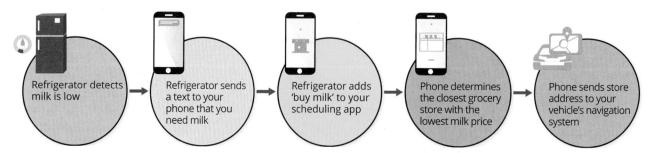

Refrigerator detects milk is low → Refrigerator sends a text to your phone that you need milk → Refrigerator adds 'buy milk' to your scheduling app → Phone determines the closest grocery store with the lowest milk price → Phone sends store address to your vehicle's navigation system

Imagine the educational opportunities when you have access to high-speed, unfiltered Internet content; your own laptop, tablet, or smart device; and software to create, track, and process data and information. Then compare these opportunities with the opportunities available to students who live in countries where the government restricts access to Internet content, and economics prevent them from owning their own devices and the software or apps used on them. These inequalities affect learning, knowledge, and opportunities and can have a lasting impact on the future of those affected.

Corporations, nonprofits, educational institutions, and governments are working on solutions to narrow the digital divide so that all learners can become digitally literate.

❓ Consider This

Does the Internet of Things discriminate?

Advantages of the IoT include comfort, safety, and efficiency. Individuals who can access IoT-enabled devices can find accurate data quickly, use GPS to have a shorter commute, collect and communicate health data using wearable devices, and reduce costs when grocery shopping by knowing what items are needed and when they expire. Individuals in areas in which these technologies are not available, or those who cannot afford them, are at a disadvantage. It is likely that the divide between the more and less fortunate will increase. What can you do to prevent IoT discrimination? What should you expect companies and governments to do?

Secure IT: Protect Your Privacy

Privacy is defined as the state or condition of being free from public attention to the degree that you determine. That is, privacy is freedom from attention, observation, or interference, based on your decision. Privacy is the right to be left alone to the level that you choose.

Prior to the current age of technology, many individuals generally were able to choose the level of privacy that they desired. Those who wanted to have very open and public lives in which anyone and everyone knew everything about them were able to freely provide that information to others. Those who wanted to live a very quiet or even anonymous life could limit what information was disseminated.

Today, however, that is virtually impossible. Data is collected on almost all actions and transactions that individuals perform. This includes data collected through web surfing, purchases (online and in stores), user surveys and questionnaires, and a wide array of other sources. It also is collected on benign activities, such as the choice of movies streamed through the Internet, the location signals emitted by a smartphone, and even the path of walking as recorded by a surveillance camera. This data is then aggregated by data brokers. **Data brokers** hold thousands of pieces of information on hundreds of millions of consumers worldwide. These brokers then sell the data to interested third parties, such as marketers or governments. While data brokers are legitimate and operate within the law, be aware that data collection also can be used to gather your personal information for misuse (Figure 1-9).

Attackers target your personal information because with your information, they can steal your hard-earned money or ruin your ability to receive a loan. In many ways, the theft and manipulation of your personal information for financial fraud is one of the most harmful types of attacks.

Figure 1-9   Ways your data can be accessed, collected, and sold.

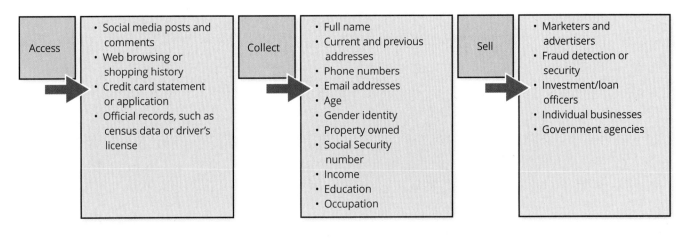

Table 1-1   How Personal Information Is Stolen

Technique	Explanation
Dumpster diving	Personal information from discarded credit card statements, charge receipts, and bank statements can be retrieved after being discarded in the trash.
Phishing	In phishing, attackers attempt to deceive you into revealing personal or financial information when you respond to an email message or visit a website.
Change of address form	Using a standard change-of-address form, the attackers divert all mail to a post office box so that the victim never sees the charges made.
Pretexting	An attacker who pretends to be from a legitimate research firm asks for personal information.
Stealing	Stolen wallets and purses contain personal information that can be used in identity theft.
Data mining	Attackers attempt to guess your passwords or password security questions by soliciting a response to a query on an online social media site that prompts you to enter information such as a pet's name, home state, and more.

Identity theft involves using someone's personal information, such as their name, Social Security number, or credit card number, to commit financial fraud (Table 1-1). Using this information to obtain a credit card, set up a cellular telephone account, or even rent an apartment, thieves can make excessive charges in the victim's name. The victim is charged for the purchases and suffers a damaged credit history that can lead to being denied loans for school, cars, and homes.

To Protect Your Privacy

Many technologies exist to help you protect your data from unauthorized access, including protecting your devices, apps, and individual files with passwords or encryption. You can and should use several ways to prevent your information from falling into the hands of attackers. It is especially important to protect your personal and financial data. Consider the following safeguards to protect your privacy:

- Shred financial documents and paperwork that contains personal information before discarding it.
- Do not carry a Social Security number in a wallet or write it on a check.
- Do not provide personal information either over the phone or through an email message.
- Keep personal information in a secure location in a home or apartment.

- Be cautious about what information is posted on social networking sites and who can view your information. Show "limited friends," such as casual acquaintances and business associates, a reduced version of a profile.
- Keep only the last three months of the most recent financial statements and then shred older documents instead of tossing them in the trash or a recycling bin. For paper documents that must be retained, use a scanner to create a PDF of the document and then add a strong password to the PDF file that must be entered before it can be read.
- Give cautious consideration before giving permission to a website or app request to collect data.
- Use common sense. Websites that request more personal information than would normally be expected, such as a username and password to another account, should be avoided.
- Be alert to signs that may indicate unusual activity in an account, such as a bill that did not arrive at the normal time or a large increase in unsolicited credit cards or account statements.
- Follow up on calls regarding purchases you did not make.
- Carefully review financial and billing statements each month as soon as they arrive.

? **Consider This**

How can you create a strong password?

Do not use your personal information, such as your name, or the name of your pet or family members, your birth date, schools attended, and other information that may be found online. Although requirements vary, in general, use at least eight characters, and mix upper- and lowercase letters, numbers, punctuation marks, and allowed symbols (note that systems sometimes prohibit the use of certain symbols, such as @). Change your password frequently. Do not use the same password for all websites or apps. Avoid common sequences or patterns, such as 12345678, and avoid spelling words backwards or using common abbreviations. Lastly, manage your passwords using an app. Have you ever had an account accessed by someone using your password? Why do you think this did/could occur?

How Technology Impacts the Professional World

Nearly every job requires you to interact with technology to complete projects, exchange information with coworkers, and meet customers' needs. Whether you are looking for a job in a technology field or other area, you can use technology to prepare for and search for a job.

Technological advances, such as the personal computer (PC), enabled workers to do their jobs more efficiently while at their desks. Today's workers can use smartphones, the Internet, the cloud, and more to work remotely, whether they are **telecommuting** (working from home), or traveling halfway around the world.

An **intelligent workplace** uses technology to enable workers to connect to the company's network, communicate with one another, use productivity software and apps, meet via web conferencing, and more. Some companies provide employees with computers and devices that come with the necessary software and apps, network connectivity, and security. Other workplaces have a **BYOD (bring your own device)** policy, enabling employees to use their personal devices to conduct business. Companies use online collaborative productivity software to allow employees to share documents, such as reports or spreadsheets, and to make edits or comments.

Technology in K-12 Education

Schools use social networking tools to promote school events, work cooperatively on group projects, and teach concepts such as anti-bullying. Online productivity software enables students to work collaboratively on projects and send the finished assignment to the teacher using email, reducing the need for paper printouts. **Interactive white boards** enable teachers to project from a computer or device to a screen that they can use to enter, add, or manipulate data or content (Figure 1-10). These factors and more create an **intelligent classroom**, in which technology is used to facilitate learning and communication.

Figure 1-10 Interactive white boards allow teachers to use a mouse or touch to manipulate, edit, or add data to a screen.
iStock.com/Gorodenkoff

Technology in Higher Education

A college or university might use a learning management system (LMS) to set up web-based training sites where students can check their progress in a course, take practice tests, and exchange messages with the instructor or other students. Students also can view instructor lectures online and take classes or earn a degree online. Ebooks let students read and access content from their tablet or device and access digital assets like videos associated with the content.

Technology in Health Care

Physicians use computers to monitor patients' vital signs and research symptoms and diagnoses. The mobile health (mHealth) trend refers to health care professionals using smartphones or tablets to access health records stored on the cloud, and patients using digital devices to monitor their conditions and treatments, thereby reducing the need for visits to the doctor's office. For example, mHealth apps can track prescription information, text reminders to take medication, or refill the prescription. Medical monitoring devices, such as electronic bracelets, collect vital signs and send the data to a specialist. Patients can ingest smart pills that contain sensors to monitor medication or that contain tiny cameras to enable a physician to view the patient's internal organs without invasive procedures. Health care also uses 3-D printers to manufacture skin for burn patients, as well as prosthetic devices and casts. Telemedicine (Figure 1-11) is the use of telecommunications technology, including secure web-based videoconferencing, to diagnose and treat patients remotely, which provides rural or remote patients access to doctors in other areas, or when an in-person medical visit is not possible.

Technology in the Transportation Industry

Transportation workers use handheld computers to scan codes on packages or containers of products before loading them on a vehicle, train, ship, or plane. You then can track the progress of your package as it makes its way to you. Computers find an efficient route for the packages and track their progress (Figure 1-12). Drivers use GPS to navigate quickly and safely, avoiding traffic and hazardous conditions. Soon, self-driving trucks will use robotics for mechanical control. Automated vehicles increase independent transportation options for people with disabilities.

Technology in Manufacturing

Manufacturers use computer-aided manufacturing (CAM) to streamline production and ship products more quickly. With CAM, robots perform work that is too dangerous, detailed, or monotonous for people. In particular, they play a major role in automotive manufacturing. For example, robots typically paint the bodies of cars because painting is complex, difficult, and hazardous. Pairing robotic systems with human workers also improves quality, cost efficiency, and competition. Computers and mobile devices make it possible to order parts and materials from the warehouse to assemble custom products. A company's computers monitor assembly lines and equipment using machine-to-machine (M2M) communications to communicate among machines, equipment, and devices to perform tasks.

Figure 1-11   Telemedicine appointments can be useful when in-person medical visits are not possible.
iStock.com/Geber86

Figure 1-12 The transportation industry uses code scanning to track packages.
Pro_Vector/Shutterstock.com

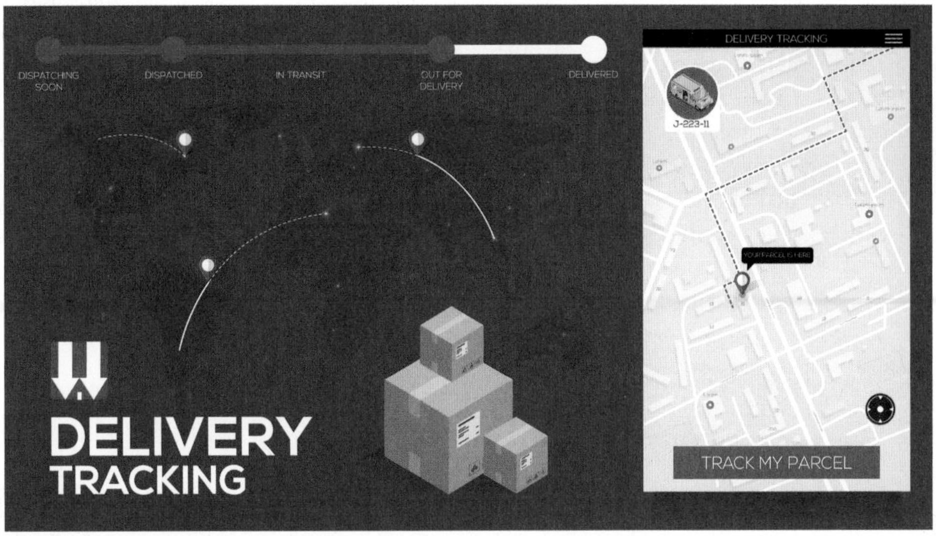

❓ Consider This

How can you set up a home office for telecommuting?

When employees telecommute, they save money on transportation (gas, bus or train fares, and parking). Recent events have forced many individuals to work from home for extended periods. To set up a home office, choose a location that is free from noise and distractions. If you are sharing a room with others who also are telecommuting, consider turning your desk to face the wall and using noise-cancelling headphones. If you participate in videoconferences, make sure your background is professional, or use a filtered background provided by your conferencing app. Invest in a comfortable chair and a desk that has adequate space for your work. Your company may be able to reimburse you for such costs in order to ensure your efficiency. Make sure to put limits in place as you would if you were working in your office — take breaks, and set a specific time when you "leave the office" for the day. Resist the temptation to extend your hours beyond what works for you and your family. Do you telecommute for school or work? What is your workspace like? How might you improve it?

How To: Use Technology in Your Job Search

You can use both social media and job search websites to learn about technology careers and to promote yourself to potential employers. By creating a profile on a career networking site or creating a personal website or blog that showcases your talents, hiring managers can learn more about you beyond what you can convey in a traditional, one-page paper resume. To further demonstrate your skills and abilities, you can consider pursuing a technology certification.

Create a Professional Online Presence

Your professional online presence often is the first thing a recruiter or interviewer will see. They may use your online resume or social networking profiles to determine whether to even contact you for an interview. It also can be a determining factor in getting you hired, so make sure you present yourself as a professional person who would be an asset to any organization or company. Consider the following tips when creating an online presence:

- Do not use humorous or informal names for your account profiles, blog, or domain name.
- Include a photo that shows your best self.
- Upload a PDF of your resume.
- Include links to videos, publications, or digital content you have created.
- Proofread your resume, blog, website, or profile carefully to avoid spelling and grammar mistakes.
- Enable privacy settings on your personal social media accounts, and never post anything online that you would not want a potential employer to see.

Online social networks for professionals can help you keep up with former coworkers, instructors, potential employers, and others with whom you have a professional connection. You can use these networks to search for jobs, learn about a company before interviewing, join groups of people with similar interests or experiences, share information about your career, and communicate with contacts.

Figure 1-13   LinkedIn is a career-based online social networking site.
Source: LinkedIn

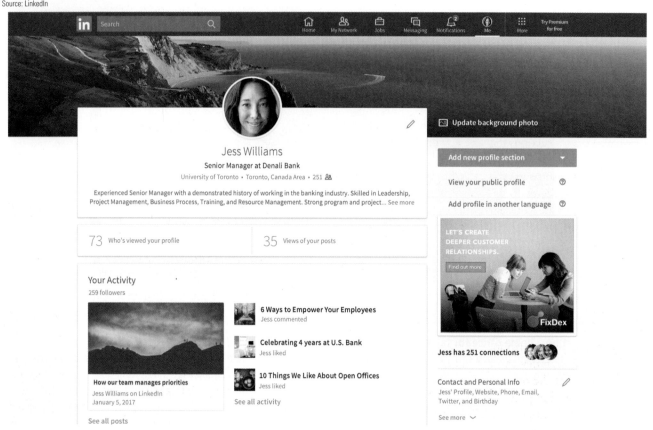

LinkedIn (Figure 1-13) is a social networking site designed to provide business and employment-oriented services. LinkedIn and other professional networking websites also offer online training courses to keep your skills up to date.

Achieve Technology Certifications

Some technology careers require you to have certain certifications. A **certification** in an industry or program demonstrates your knowledge in a specific area to employers and potential employers. Online materials and print books exist to help you prepare for a certification exam. Most certifications do not require coursework assignments, but instead require you to pass an exam that demonstrates your proficiency in the area. Tests typically are taken at an authorized testing center. Some tests are multiple choice, while others are skills-based. You likely will have to pay a fee to take the exam. Some areas that offer certifications include:

- Application software
- Data analytics, database, and web design
- Hardware
- Networking
- Operating systems
- Programming
- Cybersecurity

Obtaining a certification requires you to spend time and money. Certifications demonstrate your commitment to your chosen area and can help you land a job.

? Consider This

How can you use LinkedIn and other professional online social networking tools to help you in your career?

Whether you are looking for a first job or are employed in a career in your field, there are many reasons to use LinkedIn and other sites. Add current and former classmates and coworkers to your network. Do not hesitate to reach out to contacts that might be helpful to you, such as a fellow alumna of your school, or someone in your same position at another company, even if you do not know them personally. Follow companies and join industry groups to stay aware of job opportunities and developments in your field. Keep your profile updated, use a professional photo, and share links to relevant articles or your own achievements. Recommend your colleagues, and ask for recommendations that endorse your skills and provide references for your work or abilities. Have you set up a LinkedIn account? How might you find contacts that will be useful for you? What would you do if you received a request to connect with someone you do not know?

How Convergence Impacts Technology

As you learned, a computer is an electronic device, operating under the control of instructions stored in its own memory. Computers can accept data (input), process the data according to specified rules, produce information (output), and store the information for future use. Electronic components in computers process data using **instructions**, which are the steps that tell the computer how to perform a particular task. A set of coded instructions that tell a computer or device what tasks to perform is referred to as **software**, a **program**, or an **app**. Using software, you can complete a variety of activities, such as search for information, type a paper, balance a budget, create a presentation, or play a game.

Although you might think of a computer as a laptop or desktop, some consider computers to be any devices that perform all or some of those functions. **Convergence** is the increasing integration of technological capabilities on a growing number of previously unrelated devices. For example, you can access some of the same email, social network, and gaming apps and accounts on your laptop, tablet, and smartphone (Figure 1-14). The exact capabilities of each device vary, but the convergence trend means that the overlap in capability is increasing.

The following computers and devices have many overlapping capabilities, but differ in size, initial purpose, and how data is input and output.

Computer Devices

A **laptop** is a thin, lightweight mobile computer with a screen in its lid and a keyboard in its base (Figure 1-15). **Notebook** is another term for laptop. Designed to fit on your lap and for easy transport, most laptops weigh up to 7 pounds (varying by manufacturer and specifications). A laptop that is less than one inch thick and weighs about three pounds or less sometimes is referred to as an ultra-thin laptop. Most laptops can operate on batteries or a power supply or both.

Figure 1-15   Laptops are portable computers that you can use for school or work.
iStock.com/PeopleImages

Figure 1-14   Size comparison of a laptop, tablet, and smartphone.
iStock.com/UnitedPhotoStudio1

A **desktop**, or **desktop computer**, is a personal computer designed to be in a stationary location, where all its components fit on or under a desk or table. On many desktops, the screen is housed in a display device (or simply display) that is separate from a tower, which is a case that contains the processing circuitry. Another type of desktop called an **all-in-one** does not contain a tower and instead uses the same case to house the display and the processing circuitry.

With PCs, desktops, and laptops, keyboards, hand-held devices such as a mouse, and touch screens are the main input methods. Output is displayed visually on the screen, printed as a hard copy, or can be heard as audio.

Mobile Devices

A **mobile device** is a portable or handheld computing device, such as a smartphone or tablet, small enough to hold in your hand. Most mobile devices are Internet capable, meaning that they can connect to the Internet wirelessly. You often can exchange information between the Internet and a mobile device or between a computer or network and a mobile device.

Usually smaller than a laptop but larger than a phone, a **tablet** is a thin, lightweight mobile device that has a touch screen. Tablets often are associated with ebook readers. An **ebook reader**, or **e-reader**, is a mobile device that is used primarily for reading digital media, such as books or magazines.

A **smartphone** is an Internet-capable phone that usually also includes a calendar, an address book, and games, in addition to apps. Smartphones typically communicate wirelessly with other devices or computers. With most smartphone models, you also can listen to music, take photos, and record videos. Users often purchase a set of **earbuds** (Figure 1-16), which are

Figure 1-16 Earbuds enable you to listen to your devices without disturbing others.
iStock.com/PeopleImages

small speakers that rest inside each ear canal, in order to listen to phone calls or media without disturbing those around them.

Mobile devices use a variety of input methods, including touch screen, an on-screen keyboard, and voice. Some mobile devices come with a physical keyboard or use a stylus or pen. Output is displayed on a screen.

Media and Gaming Devices

While many users still purchase separate media and gaming devices, many of the capabilities of these devices, in particular, overlap with computers and mobile devices. You might use your smartphone or tablet to take, edit, and share pictures. You can use your laptop or mobile device to download, stream, and play videos or music.

A **digital camera** is a camera that creates a digital image of an object, person, or scene. With many digital cameras, you also can communicate wirelessly with other devices; many also include apps similar to those on a smartphone. Digital cameras typically allow you to review, and sometimes modify, images while they are in the camera. You also can transfer images from a digital camera to a computer or device, so that you can review, modify, share, organize, or print the images. Some also can record videos.

A **digital media player** is an application that lets you play audio and video files; most tablets and smartphones include media players. **Digital media** includes music, photos, videos, and virtual reality. Thus, portable media players enable you to listen to music, view photos, and watch videos, movies, and television shows. You can download digital media to your device, or you can play the media while it streams. **Streaming** is a way of receiving audio and video content on your device as it is being downloaded from the web.

A **wearable device**, or **wearable**, is a small, mobile computing consumer device designed to be worn. These devices often communicate with a mobile device or computer. Two popular wearable devices are activity trackers and smartwatches. An **activity tracker** is a device that monitors heart rate, measures pulse, counts steps, and tracks sleep patterns. In addition to keeping time, a **smartwatch** can communicate with a smartphone to make and answer phone calls, read and send messages, access the web, play music, work with apps, such as activity trackers and GPS, and more.

A **game console** is a hardware device that allows you to play video games, either single-player or multiplayer. A **handheld game device** is small enough to fit in one hand, making it more portable than a game console. The difference between the two is that game consoles typically require you to connect the console to a television or other screen to view the game, while handheld gaming devices include a small screen. Both types of devices are Internet capable and allow you to listen to music and watch TV or movies or view photos.

❓ Consider This

Are digital cameras, portable media players, ebook readers, and handheld game devices becoming obsolete as more and more smartphones and tablets include their functionality?
Smartphones and tablets enable you to take and store photos; store, organize, and play or view your digital media; read ebooks; and play games. Due to convergence, consumers may need fewer devices for the functionality that they require. Still, consumers may purchase separate stand-alone devices, such as a separate digital camera and portable media player, for a variety of reasons. The stand-alone device (i.e., a digital camera) may have more features and functionality than the combined device offers, such as a smartphone. You might want to be able to use both devices at the same time; for example, you might send text messages on the phone while reading a book on an ebook reader. Or, you might want protection if your combined device breaks. For example, you still can listen to music on a portable media player if your smartphone becomes nonfunctional. How many devices do you possess? What programs or activities do you do that can be done with other devices? Do you own any devices that are for specific purposes? If so, why?

What Does It Mean to Be a Digital Citizen?

You can be digitally literate without necessarily being a responsible digital citizen. For example, digitally literate people know how to copy and paste information from one source into another. Digital citizens, however, know when it is appropriate to copy and paste information, how to properly credit the source, and the ramifications of violating copyright restrictions. Other aspects of digital citizenship include adhering to the relevant laws, abiding by commonly accepted etiquette guidelines, staying aware of your rights and the rights of others, keeping your information secure, and taking care not to adopt unhealthy technology habits.

Digital ethics is a challenging and ever-changing landscape. Being a responsible digital citizen involves being aware of your legal and ethical obligations as you use technology to avoid breaking the law or causing harm to others or yourself. Using available technologies in a way that respects the laws and others' privacy, protects your identity, and safeguards your behavioral and physical health is at the core of being a digital citizen (Figure 1-17).

Netiquette is a term that describes the rules of Internet etiquette. Netiquette includes the code of acceptable behaviors users should follow while on the Internet; that is, it is the conduct expected of individuals while online. Netiquette includes rules for all aspects of the Internet, including the web, social media, Internet messaging, chat rooms, online discussions, and methods to transfer or store files.

Legal and Ethical Responsibilities of a Digital Citizen
Digital ethics is the set of legal and moral guidelines that govern the use of technology, including computers, mobile devices, information systems, databases, and more. A digital citizen is anyone who uses or interacts with technology at work or in daily life for productivity or entertainment. All digital citizens are responsible for educating themselves about their obligations, as well as their own rights.

Figure 1-17   Determining how to use technology involves several gray areas.

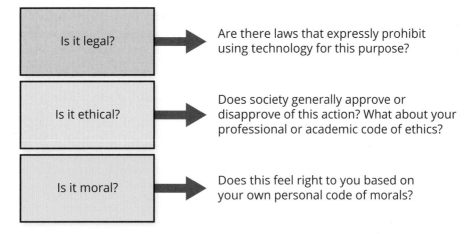

Is it legal? → Are there laws that expressly prohibit using technology for this purpose?

Is it ethical? → Does society generally approve or disapprove of this action? What about your professional or academic code of ethics?

Is it moral? → Does this feel right to you based on your own personal code of morals?

Figure 1-18 Technology raises many ethical and legal questions.

> ✓ Is it ever acceptable to use a fake name online?
>
> ✓ Can I throw my old smartphone in the trash?
>
> ✓ Who is responsible for validating information before sharing it online?
>
> ✓ Can I use a company-issued device for personal communications?
>
> ✓ Why is digital inclusion an important ethical issue?
>
> ✓ What should I do to protect my privacy when using IoT-enabled devices? Is it ever acceptable to copy and paste webpage content?
>
> ✓ Should I do a regular digital detox?
>
> ✓ Can I use a wiki for research?
>
> ✓ How can I make sure my website is accessible?

Like many ethical questions, digital ethical questions do not always have easy answers and can involve complex issues related to privacy and protecting the identity, rights, and behavioral health of individuals (Figure 1-18).

Many laws are being debated, revised, and passed to deal with how technology complicates problems like harassment, abuse of or attacks on free speech, invasions of privacy, copyright infringement, and bullying. Online activity allows for some level of anonymity, making it challenging to identify the perpetrators. Because it is so easy to distribute material widely on the Internet, finding effective solutions to these problems is difficult. States' laws, which vary widely, are being adapted to address these problems.

Cyberbullying is a form of bullying that involves digital devices and platforms, such as social media sites, online forums, messaging apps, and email. Missouri is one state that has attempted to define and enact punishment for cyberbullying, which a Missouri statute defines as bullying "through the transmission of a communication including, but not limited to, a message, text, sound, or image by means of an electronic device." The law states that schools are required to report any instances of cyberbullying and that perpetrators can be convicted of a felony.

Other states, such as Massachusetts, are enacting "hands-free" laws to prevent distracted drivers from causing accidents. Distracted driving means driving a vehicle while focusing on other activities, typically involving an electronic device, such as a cell phone. The law prohibits texting and all other activities while driving. Whether or not your state laws prohibit distracted driving, you can protect yourself and others on the road by taking precautions (Figure 1-19).

How Companies and Schools Can Protect Themselves

Schools, businesses, and organizations have an obligation to protect themselves, their employees, their customers, and their information. One method organizations use to lay out their expectations and rules for digital citizenship is by enacting acceptable use policies. An acceptable use policy (AUP) is a document that lists guidelines and repercussions of use of the Internet and other digital company resources, including network storage and email servers (Figure 1-20).

An AUP is distributed in part to reduce an organization's liability and to clarify what is and is not a fireable offense. For example, if employees use their company's email server to send harassing email or use the company's network resources to hack into another website, and those employees have signed an AUP forbidding such behavior, then the company would clearly have the right to terminate the employees. AUPs typically cover not only illegal or unethical behavior but also actions that waste company resources or time. Companies also use AUPs to protect company data, such as customer

Figure 1-19 Tips for avoiding distracted driving.

What should I do with my device while driving?	What if I remember that I need to text or call someone?	What else can I do?
• Turn it off or silence it. • Set up an automated response that tells people when you are driving. • Set up your GPS or maps app before you start driving.	• Pull over and park in a safe location before reaching for your device. • Ask your passengers to call or text for you.	• Keep kids safe with car seats or seat belts, as appropriate for their age and size. • Secure your pets. • Do not eat or drink, and definitely do not read texts or emails.

Figure 1-20   Acceptable use policies outline rules for using technology.
Source: U.S. Department of Justice

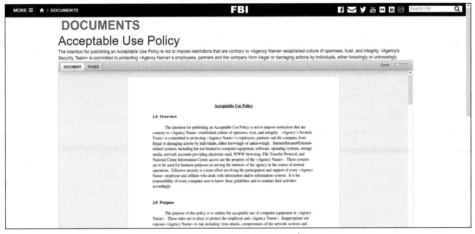

contact information, from being misused. For example, an AUP would forbid an employee from sharing contact information acquired at work for personal or nonbusiness use.

Within an AUP, the details of acceptable behavior often are listed in a code of conduct. Included in a code of conduct are rules against causing harm to others, misuse or unauthorized access of another person's files or data, protection of intellectual property, stealing, software piracy, and social considerations.

Schools typically also have sections in an AUP on how to address behavior such as plagiarism and cyberbullying.

The Internet makes it easier to **plagiarize**, which is copying or using someone else's work and claiming it as your own. Professional writers, such as journalists, are expected to follow strict ethical guidelines when copying or citing content from other sources. As a student, you need to hold yourself to similar standards. If you are not sure exactly what constitutes plagiarism, your school probably has a webpage explaining specific rules of plagiarism. You might even have been asked to sign a document indicating that you understand those rules when you first enrolled. Beware of websites that entice students to cheat intentionally by providing papers for purchase. Most schools will expel a student for such a serious infraction. To help discourage theft of other peoples' work, teachers often require students to submit papers using a service, such as turnitin, that automatically checks for plagiarized passages; turnitin also can help students check for uncited passages and more before submitting. This website, and others like it, also give resources to students to educate them about what plagiarism is and how to avoid it (Figure 1-21).

Figure 1-21   Schools use technology to predict and prevent plagiarism.
Source: Turnitin, LLC.

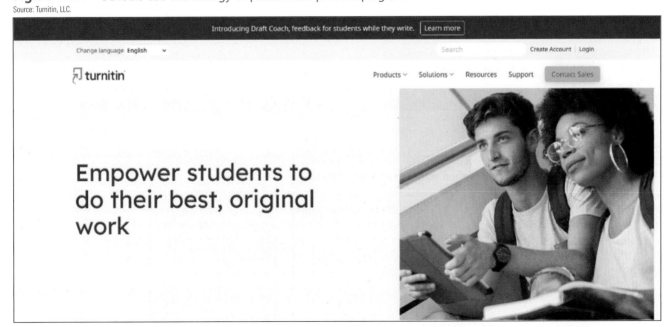

Cyberbullying, which is known to be extremely harmful to its victims, is an issue that schools, students, families, and communities are struggling to deal with. Examples of cyberbullying include sending, posting, or sharing negative and harmful content about another person or group. It is difficult for schools to address and monitor cyberbullying, as much of it takes place off school grounds, outside of regular school hours, and on devices and platforms that do not belong to the school. Yet it often affects the victim at school. Schools are adopting policies that include consequences for any form of student-to-student bullying that contributes to a hostile environment for a student or group.

Green Computing

People use and often waste resources, such as electricity and paper, while using technology. The practice of **green computing** involves reducing electricity consumed and environmental waste generated when using computers, mobile devices, and related technologies.

Personal computers, displays, printers, and other devices should comply with guidelines of the **ENERGY STAR program** (Figure 1-22). The U.S. Department of Energy (DOE) and the U.S. Environmental Protection Agency (EPA) developed the ENERGY STAR program to help reduce the amount of electricity used by computers and related devices. This program encourages manufacturers to create energy-efficient devices. For example, many devices switch to sleep or power-save mode after a specified amount of inactive time.

Electronic waste and trash have a negative effect on the environment where they are discarded. You can avoid electronic waste by not replacing devices every time a new version is released and by recycling devices and products, such as ink and toner cartridges, when they no longer provide value.

Your personal green computing efforts should include:

- Purchasing and using products with an ENERGY STAR label
- Shutting down your computers and devices overnight or when not in use
- Donating computer equipment
- Using paperless communication
- Recycling paper, toner and ink cartridges, computers, mobile devices, and printers
- Telecommuting and using videoconferencing for meetings

Organizations can implement a variety of measures to reduce electrical waste, such as:

- Consolidating servers
- Purchasing high-efficiency equipment
- Using sleep modes and other power management features for computers and devices
- Buying computers and devices with lower power consumption processors and power supplies
- Recycling or disposing of out-of-date or discarded technology properly
- Using outside air, when possible, to cool the data center or computer facility
- Allowing employees to telecommute to save gas and reduce emissions from vehicles

Green computing practices are usually easy to implement and can make a huge impact on the environment.

Figure 1-22   Look for the ENERGY STAR logo when purchasing appliances or devices.
US Environmental Protection Agency/Energy star program

? Consider This

What should you do with your devices when you no longer need them?

Computers, monitors, and other devices and equipment contain toxic materials and potentially dangerous elements, including lead or mercury. You should never store obsolete technology for this reason. Disposing of devices in a landfill can release materials into the environment and cause air, land, or water pollution. Recycling and refurbishing are safer alternatives. Many manufacturers will accept unusable devices and then repurpose them into new devices that can be donated or create new products from the waste. Before you dispose of, sell, donate, or otherwise get rid of any device, be sure to erase and remove any data or information stored on it. Have you ever donated or recycled a device? Have you ever or would you consider purchasing a device that had been donated or recycled? Why or why not?

Ethics & Issues: Who Is Responsible for Providing Assistive Technologies?

The ever-increasing presence of computers in everyone's lives has generated an awareness of the need to address computing requirements for those with limitations, such as intellectual disabilities, mobility issues, and hearing and visual disabilities. **Accessibility** is the practice of removing barriers that may prevent individuals with disabilities from interacting with data, a website, or an app. Many technologies provide adaptive measures to address individuals' needs.

Assistive Technologies

Visually impaired people can change screen settings, such as increasing the size or changing the color of the text to make the words easier to read. Changing the color of text also can address the needs of users with certain types of color blindness. Instead of using a monitor, users with visual challenges can work with voice input and output. That is, the computer speaks out loud the information that appears on a screen or it interprets and converts the user's speech to text form. A Braille printer prints information on paper in Braille (Figure 1-23).

A **screen reader** is technology that uses audio output to describe the contents of the screen. Screen readers can read aloud webpages and documents or provide narration of the computer or device's actions. **Alternative text (alt text)** is descriptive text added to an object, such as a picture or drawing (Figure 1-24). A screen reader will read the alt text aloud so that the user understands the image and its purpose. Webpages and documents should include alt text for all images. Alt text can be as simple as the name of a famous individual shown in a photograph, or more complex, such as interpreting the results of a chart or graph. Productivity applications, such as Microsoft Office,

Figure 1-23 Individuals with visual challenges can use a Braille printer.
iStock.com/Inside-Studio

and webpage creation apps prompt users to add alt text and sometimes provide suggested alt text content.

Hearing impaired people can instruct programs or apps to display words or other visual clues instead of sounds, such as for a notification from an app. **Captioning software** displays scrolling text for dialogue in a video. Cameras can interpret sign language gestures into text.

Mobility issues can impact a user's ability to interact with hardware, such as a keyboard or a mouse. Users with limited hand mobility can use an on-screen keyboard, a keyboard with larger keys, or a hand-mounted pointer to control the pointer or insertion point. Alternatives to mouse buttons include a hand pad, a foot pedal, a receptor that detects facial motions, or a pneumatic instrument controlled by puffs of air. Users with conditions that cause hands to move involuntarily can purchase input devices,

Figure 1-24 Screen readers use alt text to describe an image.
Miki Studio/Shutterstock.com

Alt text

Colorful hot air balloons flying over champagne vineyards at sunset, Montagne de Reims, France

such as a keyboard or mouse, that are less sensitive to accidental interaction due to unintentional movements.

Users with intellectual disabilities might struggle with reading words on a screen, handwriting, or retaining information. Technologies that help these users learn or perform tasks include:

- Speech recognition programs so that the user can input data or information verbally
- Graphic organizers to enable a user to create an outline or structure of information
- Audio books to read information aloud to the user instead of reading on a printed page or on the screen

The basic premise of assisted technology is to improve accessibility for all users and provide the same opportunities to learn, work, and play, no matter what limitations a user has.

Legal Requirements

The **Americans with Disabilities Act (ADA)** is a law that requires any company with 15 or more employees to make reasonable attempts to accommodate the needs of physically challenged workers. The **Individuals with Disabilities Education Act (IDEA)** is a law that requires that public schools purchase or acquire funding for adaptive technologies. These laws were put in place to ensure that people with disabilities can access resources, information, and services using the appropriate technology.

Regardless of legal requirements, companies and schools should be aware of discriminatory practices that may preclude capable individuals from working or learning productively. A fair environment means providing solutions both proactively and when made aware of them.

 Consider This ─────────────────────────────────────

How can you advocate for yourself when you are in need of assistive technology?
Technological advances in assistive technology have opened up career and educational opportunities for many. If you are in a situation where your needs are not met or you could use more assistance, you need to know your rights and how to address them. First, you can research the legal requirements your company or school is obligated to follow. These requirements should specify who pays for any equipment or apps that will help you. Bring these requirements, along with any research you have on your specific technology needs, to your supervisor or a school administrator. Bring a supportive person if you feel more comfortable. Ask to participate in the choice of technology purchase so as to meet your specific needs. Your school or employer may not be aware of your needs or how to meet them without your participation. If these methods do not work, contact a rights' advocacy group that can work on your behalf to ensure that you have the opportunities to fulfill your potential as a student or employee. Are you or is anyone you know in need of assistive technologies? What does your school provide? What other resources are available in your area?

Study Guide

Instructions: The Study Guide exercise reinforces material you should know after reading this module. Answer the questions below using the format that helps you remember best or that is required by your instructor. Possible formats may include one or more of these options: write the answers; create a document that contains the answers; record answers as audio or video using a webcam, smartphone, or portable media player; post answers on a blog, wiki, or website; or highlight answers in the book/ebook.

1. Define the term, digital literacy. What does it mean to be a digital citizen?

2. Define the terms, computer, Internet, and online social network.

3. ___ refers to large and complex data sources that defy easy handling with traditional data processing methods.

4. What are the negative effects of digital distraction?

5. Explain the role of vacuum tubes, transistors, and integrated circuits in computer development.

6. How did the microprocessor contribute to the development of the PC?

7. Define the Internet of Things.

8. Explain the role of embedded computers in IoT. List examples.

9. ___ technology stores data on a credit card's embedded chip instead of a magnetic stripe.

10. Define kiosk. Describe its uses.

11. How does IoT affect home and business users?

12. Describe the digital divide, and how it is harmful.

13. Explain how privacy has been impacted by technology.

14. What privacy risks are involved with using technology?

15. What is a data broker, and how do they access, collect, and sell your data?

16. Describe the effects of identity theft on the victim. How does identity theft occur, and what can you do to prevent it?

17. A(n) ___ attack attempts to deceive you into revealing personal or financial information when you respond to an email message or visit a website.

18. List guidelines for creating a strong password.

19. Define telecommuting and intelligent workplace. Explain how these and other technologies impact the professional world.

20. How has technology impacted K-12 education? How do instructors use an interactive white board?

21. What is the purpose of a learning management system? How else has technology impacted higher education?

22. Describe the mHealth trend. How does telemedicine help patients?

23. Explain how technology has impacted the transportation industry.

24. Define M2M communication. What other ways has technology impacted the manufacturing industry?

25. List guidelines for creating a professional online presence. Why is this important?

26. Describe how achieving a technology certification might help you in your job search or career.

27. Define the term, software. Software also is called a(n) ___ or ___.

28. Explain the role of instructions as they are used in software.

29. Define convergence, and give examples.

30. A(n) ___ is anyone who interacts with a computer or mobile device or utilizes the information it generates.

31. Differentiate among the following computing devices: laptop, desktop, and all-in-one. A laptop also is known as a(n) ___ computer.

32. What are the typical input and output methods for computer devices?

33. List types of mobile devices, and describe the purpose of each.

34. Explain whether or not a mobile device is a computer.

35. How does convergence affect media and gaming devices?

36. What questions might you ask when determining whether something is ethical, legal, or moral?

37. Define netiquette. What behaviors does it provide rules for?

38. Give examples of states' attempts to regulate digital ethical behavior.

39. A(n) ___ is a document that lists guidelines and repercussions of use of the Internet and other digital company resources, including network storage and email servers.

40. What is cyberbullying? Give examples.

41. List ways you can practice green computing. How can you dispose of devices responsibly?

42. Define accessibility.

43. Give examples of assistive technologies. Describe the purpose of alt text.

44. Explain the legal ramifications of the ADA and IDEA.

Key Terms

You should be able to define the Key Terms listed below.

acceptable use policy (AUP) (1-16)
accessibility (1-19)
activity tracker (1-14)
all-in-one (1-14)
alternative text (alt text) (1-19)
Americans with Disabilities Act (ADA) (1-20)
app (1-13)
automated teller machines (ATMs) (1-6)
Big Data (1-2)
BYOD (bring your own device) (1-9)
captioning software (1-19)
certification (1-12)
chip-and-pin technology (1-6)
computer (1-2)
computer-aided manufacturing (CAM) (1-10)
computer literacy (1-2)

convergence (1-13)
cyberbullying (1-16)
data brokers (1-7)
desktop (1-14)
desktop computer (1-14)
digital camera (1-14)
digital citizen (1-2)
digital distraction (1-3)
digital divide (1-6)
digital literacy (1-2)
digital media (1-14)
digital media player (1-14)
distracted driving (1-16)
earbuds (1-14)
ebook reader (1-14)
embedded computer (1-5)
ENERGY STAR program (1-18)
e-reader (1-14)
game console (1-14)
green computing (1-18)
handheld game device (1-14)
identity theft (1-8)

Individuals with Disabilities Education Act (IDEA) (1-20)
instructions (1-13)
integrated circuits (1-4)
intelligent classroom (1-9)
intelligent workplace (1-9)
interactive white boards (1-9)
Internet (1-2)
Internet of Things (IoT) (1-4)
kiosk (1-6)
laptop (1-13)
learning management system (LMS) (1-10)
LinkedIn (1-12)
machine-to-machine (M2M) (1-10)
memory (1-2)
microprocessor (1-4)
mobile device (1-14)
mobile health (mHealth) (1-10)
netiquette (1-15)

network (1-2)
notebook (1-13)
online social network (1-2)
personal computer (PC) (1-4)
phishing (1-8)
plagiarize (1-17)
privacy (1-7)
processor (1-4)
program (1-13)
screen reader (1-19)
server (1-2)
smartphone (1-14)
smartwatch (1-14)
software (1-13)
streaming (1-14)
tablet (1-14)
telecommuting (1-9)
telemedicine (1-10)
transistors (1-4)
vacuum tubes (1-4)
wearable (1-14)
wearable device (1-14)
Wi-Fi (1-2)

Extend Your Knowledge

Instructions: The Extend Your Knowledge exercise expands on subjects covered in the module and encourages you to find the latest developments on these topics. Use a search engine or another search tool to locate news articles, blog entries, videos, expert discussions, or other current sources on the listed topics. List your sources, and write 3-4 sentences describing what you have learned to submit in the format required by your instructor.

- Big Data
- Internet of Things
- Laws governing digital ethics
- Assistive technologies

What did you learn that helped you better understand the concepts in this module? Did anything surprise you? How will what you learned impact you?

Checkpoint

The Checkpoint exercises test your knowledge of the module concepts.

True/False   Mark T for True and F for False. If False, rewrite the statement so that it is True.

_____ 1. A computer is an electronic device, operating under the control of instructions stored in its own memory, that can accept data, process the data to produce information, and store the information for future use.

_____ 2. The basic premise of IoT is that objects can be tagged, tracked, and monitored through a local network or across the Internet.

_____ 3. With phishing, an attacker who presents to be from a legitimate research firm asks for personal information.

_____ 4. A company's computers monitor assembly lines and equipment using modem-to-modem (M2M) communications to communicate between machines, equipment, and devices to perform tasks.

_____ 5. Use humorous or informal names for your account profiles, blog, or domain name to show potential employers that you have a sense of humor.

_____ 6. Electronic components in computers process data using apps, which are the steps that tell the computer how to perform a particular task.

_____ 7. A user is anyone who interacts with a computer or mobile device or utilizes the information it generates.

_____ 8. Designed to fit on your lap and for easy transport, most desktops weigh less than 7 pounds.

_____ 9. Handheld gaming devices typically require you to connect to a television or other screen to view the game.

_____ 10. Netiquette includes the code of acceptable behaviors users should follow while on the Internet.

_____ 11. The Internet makes it easier to pirate, or copy or use someone else's work and claim it as your own.

_____ 12. Captioning software displays scrolling text for dialogue in a video.

Matching   Match the terms with their definitions.

_____ 1. all-in-one

_____ 2. convergence

_____ 3. processor

_____ 4. Internet of Things

_____ 5. kiosk

_____ 6. BYOD

_____ 7. app

_____ 8. LMS

_____ 9. tablet

_____ 10. AUP

a. term that describes the trend of computers and devices with technologies that overlap

b. a freestanding booth usually placed in a public area that can contain a display device used to show information to the public or event attendees

c. series of related instructions, organized for a common purpose, that tells the computer what tasks to perform and how to perform them

d. web-based training site where students can check their progress in a course, take practice tests, and exchange messages with the instructor or other students

e. a document that lists guidelines and repercussions of use of the Internet and other digital company resources, including network storage, and email servers

f. an environment where processors are embedded in every product imaginable, and the products communicate with one another via the Internet or wireless networks

g. thin, lightweight mobile computer that has a touch screen

h. type of desktop computer that does not contain a tower and instead uses the same case to house the display and the processing circuitry

i. a policy enabling employees to use their personal devices to conduct business

j. a chip that contains a central processing unit

Problem Solving

Instructions: The Problem Solving exercises extend your knowledge of module concepts by seeking solutions to practical problems with technology that you may encounter at home, school, or work. The Collaboration exercise should be completed with a team. You often can solve problems with technology in multiple ways. Determine a solution to the problems in these exercises by using one or more resources available to you (such as a computer or mobile device, articles on the web or in print, blogs, podcasts, videos, television, user guides, other individuals, electronics or computer stores, etc.). Is this a real issue you've encountered? Do you think you would be able to solve the situation if you encounter it? Describe your solution, along with the resource(s) used, in the format requested by your instructor (brief report, presentation, discussion, blog post, video, or other means).

Personal

1. **Bad Directions**   Your friend is driving you, and you are using your smartphone for directions. While approaching your destination, you realize that your smartphone app instructed you to turn the wrong way. How could this have happened?

2. **Digital Distraction**   While eating lunch with a friend, you notice your friend is looking at their phone a lot. What kinds of rules can you two agree on so that you can enjoy each other's company without getting distracted? How have you solved this issue with your friends in the past? How might you approach it differently in the future?

3. **Smart Thermostat**   You programmed your apartment's thermostat to turn down the heat during the day while you and your roommates are not home. Because everybody gets home around 5:00 p.m., you used your app to instruct the thermostat to increase the heat by five degrees starting at 4:30 p.m. You walk in the apartment, and it is still colder. How can you make sure the app is connecting to your thermostat?

4. **Unauthorized Charges**   You get a notification from your credit card company that you made several expensive charges that you do not recognize. How might this have happened? What are your next steps? What steps can you take to protect yourself?

5. **Gaming with Friends**   You have a weekly date with several friends to play a multiplayer video game together. An hour before your date, you decide to warm up with a few single-player games. Your game is not showing up on your television screen. What might be wrong with your game console, and how can you fix it?

Professional

6. **Discarding Old Computer Equipment**   Your company has given you a new laptop. Because of the negative environmental impact of discarding the old computer in the trash, your supervisor asked you to suggest options for its disposal. How will you respond? Is it important to you to follow environmentally friendly practices? Why or why not?

7. **Acceptable Use Policy**   During a quick break at work, you attempt to sign in to an online social network on your work desktop. You get a message from your supervisor asking you to see them regarding a violation of the company's AUP. What did you do wrong? How can you explain your actions to your boss? Does the company have a right to limit your activities? How might you apply what you have learned to your current job?

8. **Colleague Needs Help**   You notice your new colleague has had difficulty taking notes during a presentation that had many important visuals. Later, they confide that they have some visual challenges. At their old job they had access to assistive technologies. What are their rights? What are the company's responsibilities? Where can you find information that they can share with their supervisor?

9. **Professional Online Presence**   You have had several first interviews lately, but no job offers. You decide to look at your online presence to see if it contains any red flags. Your social media settings are public, and you do not have a separate account on a professional network. What can you do to make your online presence help you in your job hunt?

10. **Synchronization Error**   You added appointments to the calendar on your computer, but they are not showing up on your smartphone. Your calendar has synchronized with your smartphone in the past. What are your next steps?

Collaboration

11. **Technology in Health Care**   Your primary care physician is opening their own practice. They would like to use technology in the new office that not only will improve the patient experience but also make the job easier. In addition, many appointments use secure web conferencing software to treat patients remotely. Form a team of three people. One team member should research ways that technology can help improve patient check-in and billing. Another team member should research technology your physician can use while working with patients remotely, and the third team member should research technology that can be used in the office to improve the patient experience. What concerns do you and your classmates have about telemedicine security?

How To: Your Turn

Instructions: This exercise presents general guidelines for fundamental skills when using a computer or mobile device and then requires that you determine how to apply these general guidelines to a specific program or situation. You often can complete tasks using technology in multiple ways. Figure out how to perform the tasks described in these exercises by using one or more resources available to you (such as a computer or mobile device, articles on the web or in print, online or program help, user guides, blogs, podcasts, videos, other individuals, trial and error, etc.). Summarize your 'how to' steps, along with the resource(s) used, in the format requested by your instructor (brief report, presentation, discussion, blog post, video, or other means).

1 Sign Up for a LinkedIn Account

A LinkedIn account provides access to contacts, networking opportunities, industry groups, and a wealth of information. Establishing a LinkedIn account gives you a place for your professional online presence. You can add a link to your account on your resume or in an email message expressing interest in a job. Even if you already have an account, follow the steps below to ensure your online presence will help you in your career or job search. The following steps guide you through the process of signing up for a LinkedIn account.

a. Start a browser and navigate to www.linkedin.com.

b. Sign in if you have an account or follow the on-screen instructions to sign up for a free = account.

c. Allow LinkedIn to provide a list of suggested contacts using your contacts list in your email account, social network, current school, and current or past employers. Send connection requests to those with whom you feel comfortable. Try to find a current classmate doing the same assignment, and send them a direct message.

d. Upload a professional head shot if you have one, or ask a friend to take a picture of you with a blank background.

e. Add your contact, school, and work information.

Exercises

1. Read and reply to any direct messages you have received, or send one to a classmate asking for a reply. What can you see yourself using this feature for with potential employers, contacts of contacts, or current colleagues?

2. Perform a search for jobs that interest you. Apply several filters to narrow down your choices by salary, location, qualifications, and more. Are you interested in any of the positions you find in your search?

3. Choose one article online pertaining to your preferred industry that you can share with your new contacts, and add a sentence or two with your opinions about the article.

4. Read through your news feed. Like or respond to at least one post by a contact. What made you react to that post? How can you get others to interact with your posts?

5. Follow at least two companies in your industry. What types of posts do they make? Choose one that interests you to include in your response to your instructor.

6. Join a network of your choice. Possible choices include alumni from your school, persons with similar interests, or anything that you think might be helpful in your career. Which network did you select, and why?

7. Ask a colleague or classmate to view your LinkedIn account and your overall online presence. What suggestions do they have? How will you implement them?

Internet Research

Instructions: These exercises broaden your understanding of module concepts by requiring that you search for information on the web. Use a search engine or another search tool to locate the information requested or answers to questions presented in the exercises. Describe your findings, along with the search term(s) you used and your web source(s), in the format requested by your instructor (brief report, presentation, discussion, blog post, video, or other means). Additionally, reflect on the process you used to complete this activity. How did you go about choosing the tool that you did and why? Would you do anything differently next time?

1 Social Media: Online Social Networks

Online social networks are a central communications tool and the primary source of news and information for many people. Historians place the birth of online social networking with the BBS (Bulletin Board System), where users communicated with a central computer and sent messages to other BBS members and also downloaded files and games. The next phase of online social networks evolved when CompuServe, AOL (America Online), and Prodigy were among the services linking people with similar interests. Today's online social networks share many of the same basic principles by allowing members to communicate common interests, play games, and share photos, videos, and music. Some of these online social networks are for personal use, while others are for entrepreneurs, business owners, and professionals to share job-related topics.

Research This: Compare the features of the top personal online social networks, and create a table listing the number of active members in the United States and worldwide, the number of years the sites have existed, the more popular features, and the amount of content, such as photos, news stories, and links, that is shared each month. What types of advertisements are featured at each of these sites? Which sites are marketed toward younger and older users? Then, research the online social networks used for business. How does their content differ from that found on the personal online social networks? How many companies use these sites as a recruiting tool? How many native languages are supported? How are professionals using these websites to find potential clients and business partners?

2 Security: Passwords

A Consider This in this module offers advice about creating secure passwords. Despite suggestions and constant reminders from security experts to develop and then periodically change passwords, users continue to create weak passwords. These common passwords are broken easily and, therefore, never should be used. For many years, the most common passwords have been the word, password, and the number sequences, 123456 and 12345678.

Research This: Use a search engine to locate at least two different companies' lists of the ten most common passwords in the past two years. Which passwords appear on both lists? Find a password-strength checking website and type three passwords to determine how easy or difficult they are to crack. Why do you think consumers continue to use these passwords despite repeated warnings to avoid them? Do you have accounts using one or more of these passwords? What advice is given for developing strong passwords? What other security measures should you take? How do the companies gather data to determine common passwords? What changes should you make to your passwords?

3 Search Skills: Solving the Digital Divide

The issue of the digital divide is not going to go away any time soon. Its impact is felt locally, nationally, and globally. Within your own school or city, you likely can identify areas that contribute to inequities. The question of how to address the digital divide brings up many ethical concerns. Whose responsibility is it to address? What is the role of the tech industry? How can schools assist? Many organizations are working on this issue and attempting to make digital access available to all.

Research This: Select one scope of the digital divide to explore (local, state, national, or worldwide). List the top areas of inequity that need to be addressed (for example, Internet access, censorship, outdated devices, etc.). Determine the key areas that are stopping these from being addressed. Find at least one organization that is working to address the gap, and describe the efforts they are making. List ways you can work to narrow the gap between students without reliable access to educational software, the Internet, and the hardware on which to run both. Discuss the ethical ramifications of not addressing the digital divide. How can it benefit everyone to have equal access? How are you personally impacted by the digital divide?

Critical Thinking

Instructions: These exercises challenge your assessment and decision-making skills by presenting real-world situations associated with module concepts. The Collaboration exercise should be completed with a team. Evaluate the situations below, using personal experiences and one or more resources available to you (such as articles on the web or in print, blogs, podcasts, videos, television, user guides, other individuals, electronics or computer stores, etc.). Perform the tasks requested in each exercise and share your deliverables in the format requested by your instructor (brief report, presentation, discussion, blog post, video, or other means).

1. The Digital Divide

You work in the educational software industry. Your boss asks you to give a brief lecture to other employees about the digital divide. You research the following questions: What are the advantages and disadvantages to being on either side of the digital divide? What factors create or contribute to the digital divide? Who is affected? What organizations exist that are trying to overcome the digital divide? How are they attempting to do this?

Do This: Create a one-page document in which you define and give examples of the impact of the digital divide, and list ways your company can work to narrow the gap among students without reliable access to educational software, the Internet, and the hardware on which to run both. Discuss the ethical ramifications of not addressing the digital divide — what is your role as a company? What is your role as an individual? What more can be done to address the digital divide? How might you partner with organizations looking to overcome this obstacle?

2. Energy Efficiency

Increases in energy prices lead many individuals to look at purchasing energy-efficient computers and devices. Energy-efficient models often look and perform similarly to equivalent computers or devices that use more energy.

Do This: Find two computers or devices of identical configuration, where the only difference is energy consumption. How much energy does the energy-efficient model save? Are energy-efficient computers and devices more or less expensive? Will the difference in cost (if any) affect your purchasing decision? How else might you be able to change your settings on your existing computer or device to save energy? Use the web to locate articles that recommend energy-efficient products and that provide tips about additional ways to save energy. How can you apply what you learned to other situations?

3. Case Study

Cooperative-Owned Farm Stand You are the new manager for a farm stand that is a cooperative effort, jointly owned by several local farmers. The previous manager tracked all the data on paper. You realize that using technology will increase your efficiency and enable you to communicate better with the owners, employees, and customers. At the next business meeting, you will share ideas about how you will use technology.

Do This: To prepare for the meeting, you compile the following: differences between input and output, a list of the types of data you can use as input, and a list of the types of information you can produce as output. You include the types of computers, mobile devices, and other technologies you will use to enter data and produce the information. Incorporate your own experiences and user reviews of the devices.

Collaboration

4. BYOD Policies

Research the trend of BYOD in workplaces. Compare the advantages to any potential disadvantages. What advantages and disadvantages exist for companies? What advantages and disadvantages exist for employees? What rights and responsibilities do companies have regarding the data, usage, and costs for employees' devices?

Do This: Form a three-member team and choose a field in which you all are interested. Divide responsibilities to answer the specific privacy needs of the chosen industry, locate published policies that affect users and employers, and legal restrictions for both the employer and employee. Locate blog posts or other opinion content that supports and discredits BYOD policies. Each team member should develop a list of questions and facts based on their research. After the research, create a hypothetical BYOD policy for your industry. Be specific about what devices are allowed and what restrictions exist on both sides. Be sure to summarize your investigations, describe the hypothetical business or organization, and outline and support your recommendations.

The Internet:
Connecting and Communicating Online

iStock.com/Vit_Mar

Objectives

After completing this module, you will be able to:

1 Discuss the evolution of the Internet
2 Describe how to use the web
3 Identify techniques for connecting to the Internet
4 Explain various online activities and services
5 Identify considerations for staying safe online
6 Discuss ways to use social networks
7 Describe how to conduct and evaluate online searches
8 Identify considerations for using online content

The Internet Evolution

You probably use the web dozens or hundreds of times a day to find a place for lunch, keep track of scores, shop for a new phone, post a comment on a blog or message board, and search for photos you need to complete a project at school or at work. The **web**, originally known as the **world wide web**, is a service consisting of websites located on computers around the world, connected through the Internet. As a vast library of content, the web is where you go for entertainment, bargains, news, and information of all kinds.

Since its introduction, the web has changed the way you access information, conduct business transactions, and communicate. The **Internet** is a global collection of millions of computers linked together to share information. The linked computers form a worldwide collection of networks that connects millions of businesses, government agencies, educational institutions, and individuals (Figure 2-1). Each of the networks on the Internet provides resources that add to the abundance of goods, services, and information accessible via the Internet. The more you understand about the web and how to access its content, the more you can get out of it.

History of the Internet and the Web

To be digitally literate about the role of the Internet and the web today, you should understand its origins. The Internet has its roots in a networking project started by the Pentagon's Advanced Research Projects Agency (ARPA), an agency of the U.S. Department of Defense. ARPA's goal was to build a network that (1) allowed scientists at different physical locations to share information and work together on military and scientific projects and (2) could function even if part of the network were disabled or destroyed by a disaster, such as a nuclear attack. That network, called **ARPANET**, became functional in September 1969, linking scientific and academic researchers across the United States.

The original ARPANET consisted of four main computers, one each located at the University of California at Los Angeles, the University of California at Santa Barbara, the Stanford Research Institute, and the University of Utah. Each of these computers served as a host on the network. A **host** is any computer or device that provides services and connections to other computers or devices on a network. By 1984, ARPANET had more than 1,000 individual computers linked as hosts. Today, millions of hosts connect to this network, which now is known as the Internet (Figure 2-2).

Figure 2-1   People around the world use the Internet in daily activities, such as viewing media, communicating with others, and accessing information.

iStock.com/Metamorworks

Figure 2-2   ARPANET network map from 1974.
Yngvar

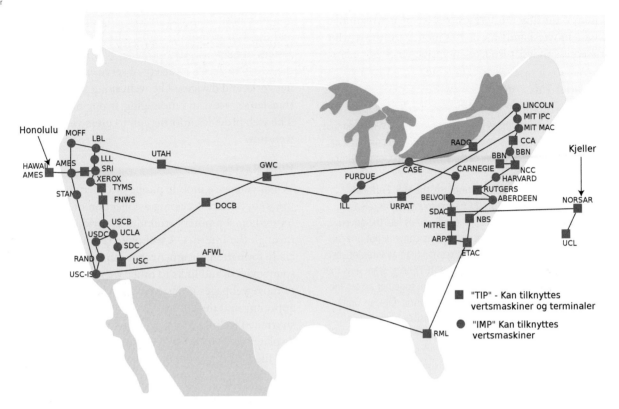

The Internet consists of many local, regional, national, and international networks. Both public and private organizations own networks on the Internet. These networks, along with phone companies, cable and satellite companies, and the government, all contribute toward the internal structure of the Internet and enable you to access web services.

While the Internet was developed in the late 1960s, the web emerged in the early 1990s as an easier way to access online information using a browser. Since then, it has grown phenomenally to become one of the more widely used services on the Internet. Each decade, the landscape and impact of the web has grown and changed dramatically. Think about how differently you might go about your day fifty years ago? What about twenty, ten, or even five years ago? What can you do now that you could not do then?

Net Neutrality   With all the growth, many issues have arisen. A commonly disputed idea today is the idea of net neutrality. **Net neutrality** is the concept that one website has the same value or priority as other websites, resulting in equal, unrestricted access to each site. When net neutrality is enforced, an **Internet service provider (ISP)**, which is a company that sells Internet access, must provide the same level of service to all websites, regardless of their content or purpose. Net neutrality supports the concept that the Internet should be neutral, and all traffic should be treated equally.

Networks transmit data over a communications channel, which can be wired or over the air (wireless). Each type of communications channel can support a certain amount of data being transferred at a given time. **Bandwidth** is a common term used to describe the capacity of a communications channel. When a communications medium or connection supports transferring a large amount of data at one time, it is said to be a high-bandwidth connection. High-bandwidth connections (also called broadband connections) support capacity for transferring content such as videos, music, and other large files; it also can support online gaming. Low-bandwidth connections (also called narrowband connections) support only slower transfer speeds, as they have less capacity. These connections are suitable for performing functions such as sending and receiving email messages, transferring small files, and viewing basic websites. **Email** (short for electronic mail) is the transmission of messages and files via a computer network.

Supporters of net neutrality like the fact that access to websites and other Internet services cannot be restricted based on factors such as content or bandwidth requirements. Those who oppose net neutrality argue that the ability for users to access certain types of high-bandwidth content, such as music and movies, might result in slower Internet speeds for others who are also connecting to the Internet using the same ISPs. Without net neutrality, ISPs could charge more money for those wanting access to content requiring more resources (such as streaming music and movies) and charge less money for those who require access to less resource-intensive services.

❓ Consider This

Who owns the Internet?

Have you ever wondered who is in charge of the web? Who maintains the webpages? Who makes sure all the parts of the complex system work together? No single person, company, institution, or government agency owns the Internet.

Although the Internet is a global resource, the **U.S. Federal Communication Commission** (**FCC**) is responsible for releasing rules surrounding Internet access. Some individuals feel the government should not control Internet access and its content, but one primary goal of the FCC is to guarantee accessibility to all Internet users.

The **Internet Engineering Task Force** (**IETF**) sets standards that allow devices, services, and applications to work together across the Internet. For example, the IETF sets rules for routing data, securing websites, and developing guidelines for responsible Internet use.

Another leading organization is the **World Wide Web Consortium** (**W3C**), which consists of hundreds of organizations and experts that work together to write web standards. The W3C publishes standards on topics ranging from building webpages, to technologies for enabling web access from any device, to user-friendly browser and webpage design. Net neutrality is an issue that the W3C argues should be the standard for all ISPs and web services. The W3C also supports accessibility for all users, the web as a dynamic communications tool, and enhanced web security measures.

What rules and guidelines do you wish existed for the Internet and the web? How do the standards set by these organizations affect your user experience?

Using the World Wide Web

You may hear them used interchangeably, but the Internet and the web are not the same. The Internet is a global system of networks that provides billions of users around the world to access a variety of services by connecting networks and devices. The web, along with email, file transfer services, and messaging, is one of those services. The web provides information to users via webpages and websites.

Web Basics

When you use a mobile phone or other device to access the web, you are accessing a collection of webpages located on computers around the world, connected through the Internet. A **webpage** (Figure 2-3) is a specially formatted document that can contain text, graphics, sound, video, and links to other webpages. The content of most webpages is designed to make them visually appealing and the content easy to find. **Hyperlinks**, often shortened to **links**, are words or graphics you can click to display a webpage or other resources on the Internet, such as a file. Links make it possible to jump to other pages or other locations on the same page in order to find information quickly.

Webpages are either static or dynamic. When you visit a **static webpage**, you see the same content each time. With a **dynamic webpage**, by contrast, the content of the webpage is regenerated each time you display it. Dynamic webpages may contain customized content, such as the current date and time of day, desired stock quotes, weather for a region, or ticket availability for flights. The time

Figure 2-3   Webpage.

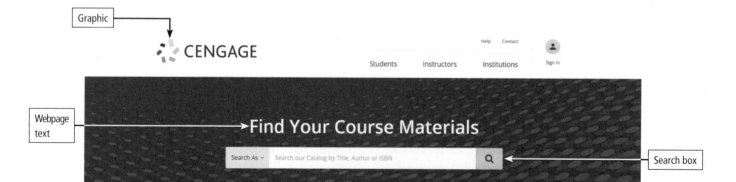

required to download a webpage varies depending on the speed of the Internet connection and the amount of graphics and other media involved.

A collection of related webpages (often shortened to "pages") and associated items, such as documents and photos, stored on a web server makes up a **website**. A **web server** is a computer that delivers requested webpages to your computer or mobile device. The same web server can store multiple websites. In general, websites focus on a specific topic, business, or purpose. A company, institution, group, or person creates and maintains a website.

Webpages may include all or some of these five major areas: header or banner, navigation bar or menu, body, sidebar, and footer. Each area can include text, graphics, links, and media, such as audio and video.

Web Design Basics   Because users view websites on a variety of computers and devices, many website developers use an approach called **responsive web design** (**RWD**) that adapts the layout of the website to fit the screen on which it is being displayed. **HTML (Hypertext Markup Language)** is a set of code that developers use to specify the headings, paragraphs, images, links, and other content elements that a webpage contains (Figure 2-4). HTML is one of the core technologies for developing webpages, along with CSS. HTML specifies a webpage's layout. **CSS (cascading style sheets)** is used to specify the content's design and appearance.

Figure 2-4   HTML code.

iStock.com/Photovibes

Accessing Web Content

To access content on the web, you use a **browser**, which is an app such as Google Chrome, Apple Safari, Mozilla Firefox, or Microsoft Edge (Table 2-1), designed to display webpages. You use the tools in a browser to navigate the web, or move from one webpage to another. The webpage that appears when you start a browser is called the home page or the start page. The main page in a website is also called its home page.

As you navigate websites, your browser keeps a copy of each page you view in a holding area called the **cache**, so that the next time you go to a webpage, it

Table 2-1   Popular Browsers

	Apple Safari	Preinstalled on Apple computers and devices, Safari has been the default browser for macOS since 2003 and is relatively new to Windows. The browser has built-in sharing with online social networks, fast performance, parental controls, and ease of use.
	Google Chrome	Google's Chrome was first released in 2008. This free browser is available for Windows, macOS, and Linux, and it must be downloaded and installed. Chrome has independent tabbed browsing; if one tab experiences a problem, the other tabs continue to function.
	Microsoft Edge	Edge is a Microsoft browser included in the Windows operating system. It is the default browser for Windows on most devices and is not compatible with prior versions of Windows. Features include integration with Cortana and OneDrive, along with annotation and reading.
	Mozilla Firefox	Developed by the Mozilla Corporation for Windows, macOS, and Linux, Firefox is known for its extensive array of plug-ins (discussed later in the module). This free browser was first released in 2004 and must be downloaded and installed. It has enhanced privacy and security features, a spelling checker, tabbed browsing, and a password manager.

(top to bottom) Apple; Google; Microsoft; Mozilla Firefox

loads more quickly. Websites often use **cookies**, which are small text files generated by a web server to store information, such as items you view or purchase on an e-commerce site. The browser also keeps track of pages you have viewed in sequence by tracking **breadcrumbs** — the path you followed to display a webpage. The **navigation bar** in a browser includes buttons, such as Back and Forward, that you can use to revisit webpages along the breadcrumb path.

To keep track of billions of webpages, the Internet assigns each one a **web address** or **uniform resource locator (URL)**, an address that identifies the location of the page on the Internet (Figure 2-5), including its host web server. When the URL for a webpage starts with http://, the browser uses the **Hypertext Transfer Protocol (HTTP)**, the most common way to transfer information around the web, to retrieve the page; when the URL for a webpage starts with http://, the browser uses this protocol for transferring the information. If you can interpret a URL, you can learn about the sponsor, origin, and location of the webpage and catch a glimpse of how the web works. In the server address *www.cengage.com*, the *www* indicates that the server is a web server, *cengage* is the name the Cengage company chose for this website, and *.com* means that a commercial entity runs the web server.

Figure 2-5 The IPv4 and IPv6 addresses, along with the domain name, for Google's website.

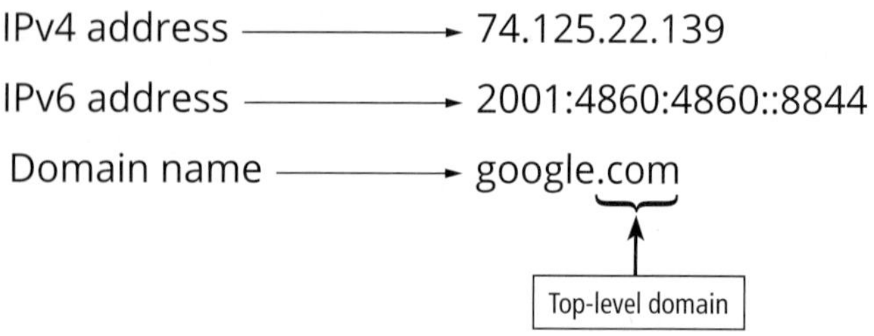

IPv4 address ⟶ 74.125.22.139

IPv6 address ⟶ 2001:4860:4860::8844

Domain name ⟶ google.com

Top-level domain

Many browsers and websites do not require that you enter the http:// or the host name www in the web address. For example, you could enter nps.gov instead of http://www.nps.gov. As you begin typing a web address or if you enter an incorrect web address, browsers often display a list of similar addresses or related websites from which you can select. If, however, the host name is not www, you will need to type the host name as part of the web address.

Internet Protocols Computers and devices communicating with one another on a network must do so while following a **protocol**, which is a common set of rules for exchanging information.

The Internet relies on an addressing system much like the postal service to send data to a computer or device at a specific destination. The server address in a URL corresponds to an Internet Protocol (IP) address, which identifies every computer on the Internet. An **IP address** is a unique number that consists of four sets of numbers from 0 to 255 separated by periods, or dots, as in 69.32.132.255. The Internet uses two IP addressing schemes: IPv4 and IPv6 (Figure 2-5). Due to the growth of the Internet, the original IPv4 addresses began dwindling in availability. The IPv6 scheme increased the available number of IP addresses exponentially.

TCP/IP (Transmission Control Protocol/Internet Protocol) is a set of protocols that is used by all computers and devices on the Internet. TCP defines how data is routed through a network, and IP specifies that all computers and devices connected to a network have a unique IP address.

Domain Names and URLs Although computers can use IP addresses easily, they are difficult for people to remember, so domain names were created. A **domain name** is the portion of a URL that identifies one or more IP addresses, such as cengage.com. URLs use the domain name in the server address part of the URL to identify a particular website.

Each file stored on a web server has a unique pathname (Figure 2-6), just like files stored on a computer. The pathname in a URL includes the names of the folders containing the file, the file name, and its extension. A common file name extension for webpages is .html, sometimes shortened to .htm. For example, the pathname might be student/index.html, which specifies a file named index.html stored in a folder named student.

Figure 2-6 Parts of a URL.

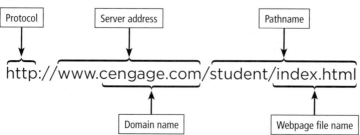

Figure 2-7   URL and pathway display in the address bar.

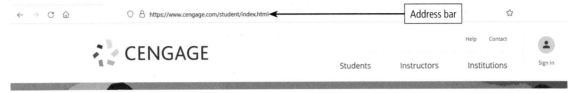

Not all URLs include a pathname. If you do not specify a pathname or file name in a URL, most web browsers open the website's main page, which sometimes is called index.html. A browser displays the URL for the current webpage in its **address bar** (Figure 2-7), the part of a browser window that displays the location of the current webpage. You can also use the address bar to type the URL of the webpage you want to display.

In a web address, the three-letter extension after the period indicates a **top-level domain (TLD)**, such as the "com" in "cengage.com". The TLD identifies the type of organization associated with the domain. As you visit websites, you might notice some that have TLDs other than .com, such as .edu for educational institutions and .gov for U.S. government agencies. The TLD provides a clue about the content of the website.

An organization called Public Technical Identifiers (PTI) approves and controls TLDs, such as those in Table 2-2, which lists popular TLDs in the United States. For websites outside the United States, the suffix of the domain name often includes a two-letter country code TLD, such as .au for Australia and .uk for the United Kingdom.

How Data Travels the Internet

Computers and devices connected to the Internet work together to transfer data around the world using servers and clients and various wired and wireless transmission media. On the Internet, your computer or device is a client that can access data and services on a variety of servers.

The inner structure of the Internet works much like a transportation system. Just as interstate highways connect major cities and carry the bulk of the automotive traffic across the country, several main transmission media carry the heaviest amount of **traffic**, or communications activity, on the Internet. These major carriers of network traffic are known collectively as the **Internet backbone**.

In the United States, the transmission media that make up the Internet backbone exchange data at several different major cities across the country. That is, they transfer data from one network to another until it reaches the final destination.

The **domain name system (DNS)** is the method that the Internet uses to store domain names and their corresponding IP addresses. When you enter a domain name (i.e., google.com) in a browser, a DNS server translates the domain name to its associated IP address so that the request can be routed to the correct computer. A **DNS server** is a server on the Internet that usually is associated with an ISP.

Table 2-2   Popular TLDs

TLD	Intended Purpose
.biz	Businesses
.com	Commercial organizations, businesses, and companies
.edu	Educational institutions
.gov	Government agencies
.mil	Military organizations
.museum	Museums and individual museum professionals
.name	Individuals
.net	Network providers or commercial companies
.org	Nonprofit organizations
.pro	Licensed professionals
.technology	Technology information
.travel	Entities whose primary area of activity is in the travel industry

? **Consider This**

How do you select and customize a browser?

A browser typically is included with the operating system of a computer or mobile device. You can access additional browsers by visiting their websites and downloading the files to install or by selecting a browser app from your device's app store. Use a search engine to locate the browser you want to install, then visit its website to download the most recent version. A **search engine** is software designed to locate relevant webpages by creating a simple query based on your search criteria and storing the collected data in a search database. Most browsers are available for download at no cost. Keep your browser up to date to prevent security gaps. You can set your browser to perform updates automatically. Do research and make a decision based on your computer or device's available memory and operating system, as well as the tasks you want the browser to perform.

You can customize settings to improve your browsing experience by adding favorites (also called bookmarks). A **favorite** is a preferred website that you can access with a click or by selecting an icon from a folder. Browsers include built-in security features, such as filters and secure connections, which protect you from malicious or unsecure websites by blocking access or asking for verification. These features also can block websites you do not want to be displayed and can instruct the browser to save passwords. Privacy features help prevent thieves from accessing information about your browsing history, such as websites you have visited, data about your browsing session, and content you have seen on specific webpages.

Which browser or browsers have you used? Have you ever chosen to use a browser that did not come with your computer or device? If so, why did you make this choice? When browsers were first invented, their only function was to browse the web. Can you recommend a more descriptive name for today's browsers?

How To: Connect to the Internet

You can connect your computers and mobile devices to the Internet through wired or wireless network technology and then access its services free or for a fee. With wired connections, a computer or device physically attaches via a cable or wire to a communications device, such as a modem, that transmits data and other items over transmission media to the Internet. Wireless connections use a wireless modem or other communications device to transmit data and other items wirelessly. Wireless communications can use technologies that include cellular radio, satellite, or Wi-Fi to connect to the Internet. Many devices automatically connect to the Internet through a mobile service provider, such as Verizon.

ISPs use hardware such as cables, satellites, and fiber-optic lines for these connections. Most of today's Internet connections are broadband connections, which are capable of transmitting large amounts of data across the network. Broadband connections usually are "always-on" connections, which means that the computers and devices on the network are always connected to the Internet.

Before you can connect to the Internet, you need to select an ISP. Methods to connect to the Internet include cellular networks, Wi-Fi hot spots, and mobile hot spots. A **hot spot** is a wireless network device that provides Internet connections to mobile computers and devices. A **mobile hot spot** enables you to connect a phone, computer, or other device to the Internet through the cellular network (Figure 2-8).

Selecting an Internet Service Provider

ISPs often charge a fixed amount for an Internet connection, offering customers a variety of plans based on desired speeds, bandwidth, and services. In addition to Internet access, ISPs may include additional services, such as email and online storage.

Figure 2-8 Verizon mobile hot spot.
Source: Verizon Media

Before selecting an ISP, take a look at your personal needs, and ask yourself the following:

- **What types of activities will I be doing?** This affects your bandwidth needs. Data sizes typically are stated in terms of megabytes and gigabytes. A **megabyte (MB)** is equal to approximately one million characters, and a **gigabyte (GB)** is equal to approximately one billion characters. Bandwidth affects the rate at which you can access or upload data. Low bandwidth is not good for streaming media or accessing online software suites.

- **How many devices do I need to connect?** Your needs may change depending on your activities on a given day, long-term decisions such as adding a roommate to your plan, and seasonally, such as if you are a student who does not take classes during the summer. Consider a provider that offers reasonable service to meet your highest needs, can handle multiple devices at once, and possibly enables you to scale back your access during times in which will not need as much access.

- **Do I need access if I travel?** Make sure that the ISP not only offers service in the area in which you live but also can provide reliable access to areas to which you travel frequently.
- **What is my budget?** All the above questions impact the budget of your plan. Look for deals or packages that offer the best value.

Choosing a Network Type

The use of mobile phones to access the Internet has become so popular that providers of mobile phone services continuously have to expand network capacity and support the latest cellular standards to keep up with demand. You also can set up your own hot spot when you need to.

Cellular Networks   Various types of cellular networks, including 4G and 5G, are available. 4G (fourth generation) cellular networks can provide Internet services in most locations where cellular service is offered. 5G networks provide higher-speed data transmission, making them more appealing to those requiring access to high-bandwidth content. As cellular standards evolve, home users use cellular providers for their Internet service, as opposed to relying on wired connections offered by cable and DSL providers. Figure 2-9 illustrates how a cellular network might work.

Many homes and businesses use Wi-Fi networks to provide network and Internet connectivity to computers and devices. When a device that supports Wi-Fi is within range of one or more wireless networks, you can view the list of networks and choose the one to which you want to connect.

Using Wi-Fi Hot Spots   Although most hot spots enable unrestricted or open access, some require that users agree to terms of service, obtain a password (for example, from the hotel's front desk), or perform some other action in order to connect to the Internet. Wireless networks that are available in public places, such as hotels, restaurants, and coffee shops, are known as **Wi-Fi hot spots**.

If you need to connect to the Internet where no wireless networks or Wi-Fi hot spots are available, you can consider using a mobile hot spot. Many smartphones contain mobile hot spot functionality, although cellular service providers may charge an extra fee to use it, and any data transmitted or received through the hot spot will be added to your overall data usage. In addition, separate hot spot devices, about the size of a deck of cards, can provide Internet connectivity to computers and devices using the cellular network. The mobile hot spot creates a wireless network to which nearby computers and devices can connect. The mobile hot spot will display the name of the wireless network you should enter or select to

Figure 2-9   How a cellular network might work.
iStock.com/alexey_boldin

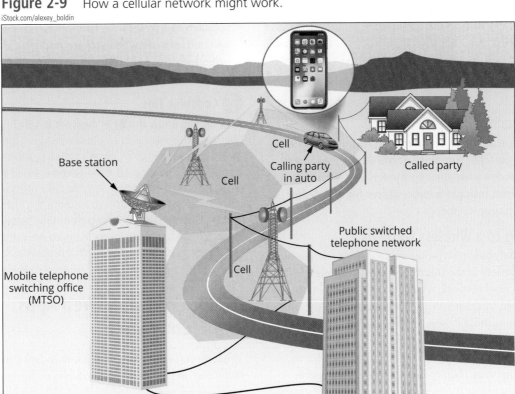

connect (Figure 2-10). You may be required to enter a network key, which is a password required to log into a wireless network. If you are using a mobile hot spot in a busy location, you can also monitor the number of devices that are connecting. If you notice connections that you did not initiate, you should consider changing the wireless network key. Internet connections using a mobile hot spot typically are not as fast as Wi-Fi networks.

Figure 2-10   Available wireless networks.
Campbell

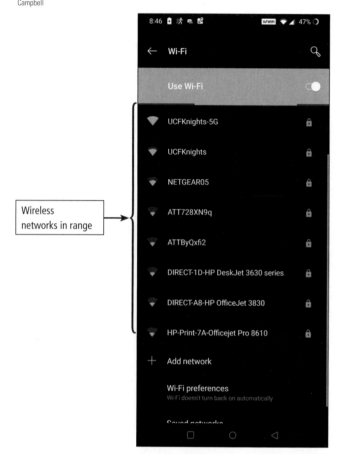

Wireless networks in range →

Tethering transforms a smartphone or Internet-capable tablet into a portable communications device that shares its Internet access with other computers and devices wirelessly. Users may pay additional fees for mobile hot spot and tethering services.

Connecting to a Wireless Network

Employees and students typically connect their computers and mobile devices to the Internet wirelessly through a business or school network, which, in turn, usually connects to a high-speed Internet service. When away from the office, home, or school, mobile users often access the Internet using Wi-Fi, mobile hot spots, or tethering services. A **wireless access point (WAP)** allows a Wi-Fi compliant device to connect to a network (Figure 2-11). Hotels and airports often provide wireless Internet connections as a free service. The exact steps for connecting to a wireless network will depend on your device, connection type, and the network.

Figure 2-11   Netgear wireless access point.
Source: Netgear

When connecting to a wireless network, keep the following in mind:

- Before you can connect to the Internet, you must identify the network using its **service set identifier** (**SSID**), which is the unique address of the wireless network.
- Select the name of the network to which you want to connect.
- After you have selected the network to which you want to connect, tap or click the appropriate button or link to connect to the network.
- If you are connecting to a secure network that requires a wireless network key or authentication with a username and password, you will be prompted to enter the required information. Once the correct information has been supplied, you should automatically be connected to the wireless network.
- Some wireless networks in public places require you to start a browser and agree to terms of service before connecting you to the Internet.
- Because of the risks associated with constant Internet connectivity, you should turn off computers and devices on your network when you are not using them for extended periods of time.

? Consider This

How do you know if a Wi-Fi network is safe?
Often network owners select easy-to-identify names, such as a business name (i.e., Downtown Diner), owner's name (i.e., Jasper's Phone), or address (i.e., 45 Speen Street). If you are connecting to a network in a restaurant or hotel, for example, verify the name of the wireless network with an employee to make sure you are connecting to the correct network. Verifying the network name will help prevent you from inadvertently connecting to a fraudulent network. Have you ever connected to public Wi-Fi? How did you ensure your data and device were secure?

Explore Websites, Web Apps, and E-Commerce

What do you want to do on the web today? Chances are good that a certain type of website provides many options to find what you are seeking. Besides displaying information and other content, websites can be interactive. You can contribute ideas, comments, images, and videos to an online conversation.

Website Categories

You can visit various categories of websites and webpages to accomplish online tasks (Figure 2-12). In addition, you can use websites to play games; access news, weather, and sports information; download or read books; participate in online training; attend classes; and more.

Informational and Research Websites An informational and research website contains factual information. Examples include libraries, encyclopedias, dictionaries, directories, guides (Figure 2-13), and other types of reference. You can find guides on numerous topics, such as health and medicine, research paper documentation styles, and grammar rules. Many of the other types of websites identified in this section also are used to research information.

Figure 2-12 Types of websites.

banking and finance

entertainment

portals

blogs

government or organization

retail and auctions

bookmarking

health and fitness

science

business

information and research

search sites

carrers and employment

travel and tourism

mapping

content aggregation

media sharing

website creation and management

e-commerce

news, weather, sports, and other mass media

web apps and software as a service (SaaS)

educational

online social networks

wikis and collaboration

Figure 2-13 You can research your symptoms and find health information on a medical website, such as WebMD.
Source: WebMD, LLC

Bookmarking   A **bookmarking site** is a website that enables members to organize, tag, and share links to media and other online content (Figure 2-14). A **tag** is descriptive text used to categorize media and invite comments. You can assign tags to webpages, photos, videos, blog posts, email messages, social media messages, and other digital content so that it is easier locate at a later time. (**Social media** refers to the many ways individuals and businesses share information and interact using the Internet.)

News, Weather, Sports, and Other Mass Media   News, weather, sports, and other mass media websites contain stories and articles relating to current events, life, money, politics, weather, technology trends (Figure 2-15), and sports. You often can customize these websites so that you can receive local news or news about specific topics. Some provide a means to send you alerts, such as weather updates or sporting event scores, via text or email messages.

Figure 2-14   Pinterest is an example of a bookmarking site.
Source: Pinterest

Figure 2-15   USA Today is an example of a news site that provides news about many topics, including technology.
Source: USA Today

News on the web enhances newspapers and reaches different populations. Although some exist solely online, many magazines and newspapers sponsor websites that provide summaries of printed articles, as well as articles not included in the printed versions. Newspapers, magazines, and television and radio stations often have corresponding news, weather, or sports websites and apps that include video and updated, extended coverage beyond the information available in a printed newspaper or daily television newscast.

Educational An educational website offers formal and informal teaching and learning. The web contains thousands of tutorials where you can learn how to build a website or cook a meal. For a more structured learning experience, companies provide online training to employees, and colleges offer online classes and degrees. Instructors often use the web to enhance classroom teaching by publishing course materials, grades, and other pertinent class information.

Business, Governmental, and Organizational A business website contains content that increases brand awareness, provides company background or other information, and/or promotes or sells products or services. Government agencies' websites providing citizens with information, such as census data (Figure 2-16), or assistance, such as filing taxes. Many other types of organizations use the web for a variety of reasons. For example, nonprofit organizations raise funds for a cause, and advocacy groups present their views or opinions.

Blogs A **blog** (originated from the term, web log) is an informal website consisting of time-stamped articles, or posts, in a diary or journal format, usually listed in reverse chronological order. The term **blogosphere** refers to the worldwide collection of blogs. A blog that contains video sometimes is called a video blog, or vlog. A **microblog** (also a type of social media site) allows users to publish short messages, usually less than 10,000 characters, for others to read. The collection of a user's Tweets, or posts on Twitter, for example, forms a microblog.

Similar to an editorial section in a newspaper, blogs reflect the interests, opinions, and personalities of the author, called the **blogger**. Some blogs allow readers to add comments on blog posts, which then are published on the blog for all visitors to see. Businesses create blogs to communicate with employees, customers, and vendors. Teachers create blogs to collaborate with other teachers and students. Other bloggers create blogs to share aspects of their personal lives with family, friends, and others.

A blog is more efficient than older publishing forms because a writer can communicate directly and immediately with an audience, without traditional gatekeepers who select and edit content. The audience for a public blog needs only its web address to access it. For a private blog, they need permission from the blogger to read entries. Visitors can read and comment on blog entries, but they cannot edit them.

A popular blog creation site is WordPress, a free, easy-to-use site that lets you create a blog containing text and media, or a complete website. A blogging network is a blogging site that uses the tools of social networking. For example, Tumblr

Figure 2-16 The U.S. Census Bureau website provides population data.
Source: U.S. Department of Commerce

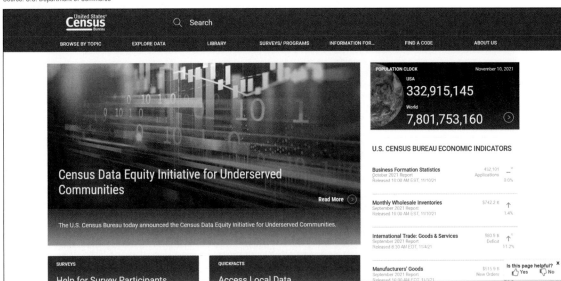

lets users post not only text but also photos, quotations, links, audios, and videos. Bloggers can tag their entries and chat with other bloggers. Bloggers can share one another's posts on Tumblr or on other social networks.

Wikis and Collaboration   As the web becomes more interactive, an increasing amount of content is supplied by users. You can contribute comments and opinions to informational sites such as news sites, blogs, and wikis. A wiki (from the Hawaiian word for "quick") is a collaborative website where you and your colleagues can modify and publish content on a webpage. A wiki enables users to organize, edit, and share information. Some wikis are public, accessible to everyone (Figure 2-17). Others are private so that content is accessible only to certain individuals or groups. Many companies, for example, set up wikis for employees to collaborate on projects or access information, procedures, and documents.

Contributors to a wiki typically must register before they can edit content or add comments. Wikis usually hold edits on a webpage until an editor or content manager can review them for accuracy. Unregistered users typically can review the content but cannot edit it or add comments.

Other types of collaboration websites enable users to share and edit any type of project — including documents, photos, videos, designs, prototypes, calendars, and more,

often at the same time. On these websites, comments or edits are seen by other connected users. Most of these websites also enable users to communicate via text chat, and some provide a whiteboard capability for sharing drawings or sketches. **Chatting** refers to holding real-time typed conversations by two or more people who are online at the same time.

Health and Fitness   Many websites provide up-to-date medical, fitness, nutrition, or exercise information for public access. Some offer users the capability of listening to health-related seminars and discussions. Consumers, however, should verify the online medical information they read with a personal physician. Health service organizations store your personal health history, including prescriptions, lab test results, doctor visits, allergies, and immunizations. Doctors use the web to assist with researching and diagnosing health conditions.

Science   Science websites contain information about space exploration, astronomy, physics, earth sciences, microgravity, robotics, and other branches of science. Scientists use online social networks to collaborate on the web. Nonprofit science organizations use the web to seek public donations to support research.

Figure 2-17   Wikipedia is an example of a user-contributed wiki.
Source: Wikimedia Foundation, Inc.

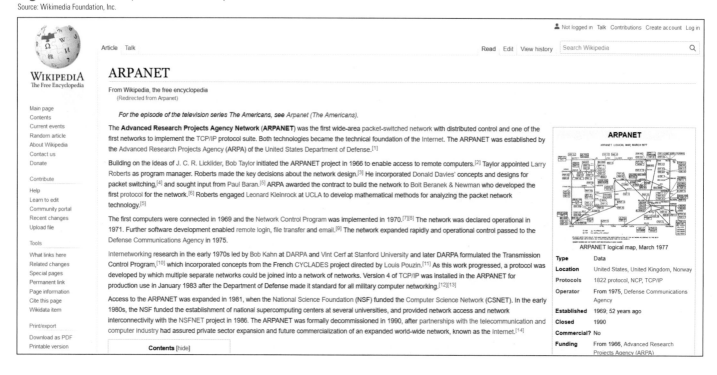

Entertainment An entertainment website offers music, videos, shows, performances, events, sports, games, and more in an interactive and engaging environment. On entertainment websites, you can view or discuss activities ranging from sports to videos. For example, you can cast a vote on a topic for a television show.

Many entertainment websites support streaming media, which allows users to access and use a file while it is transmitting. You can listen to streaming audio or watch streaming video, such as a live performance or broadcast, as it downloads to your computer, mobile device, or an Internet-connected television.

Banking and Finance Online banking and online trading enable users to access their financial records from anywhere in the world, provided they have an Internet connection. Using online banking, users can access accounts, pay bills, transfer funds, calculate mortgage payments, and manage other financial activities from their computer or mobile device (Figure 2-18). With online trading, users can invest in stocks, options, bonds, treasuries, certificates of deposit, money market accounts, annuities, mutual funds, and so on, without using a broker.

Travel and Tourism Travel and tourism websites enable users to research travel options and make travel arrangements. On these websites, you typically can read travel reviews, search for and compare flights and prices, order airline tickets, book a room, or reserve a rental car.

Mapping Several mapping websites and web apps exist that enable you to display up-to-date maps by searching for an address, postal code, phone number, or point of interest (such as an airport, lodging, or historical site). The maps can be displayed in a variety of views, including terrain, aerial, maps, streets, buildings, traffic, and weather. These websites also provide directions when a user enters a starting and destination point. Many work with GPS to determine where a user is located, eliminating the need for a user to enter the starting point and enabling the website to recommend nearby points of interest.

Retail and Auctions You can purchase just about any product or service on the web. To purchase online, you visit the business's **electronic storefront**, which contains product descriptions, images, and a shopping cart. A **shopping cart** allows the customer to collect items to purchase. When ready to complete the sale, the customer enters personal data and the method of payment, which should be through a secure Internet connection.

Figure 2-18 You can manage your bank account, make transfers, and more with a banking website, such as Bank of America.
Source: Bank of America

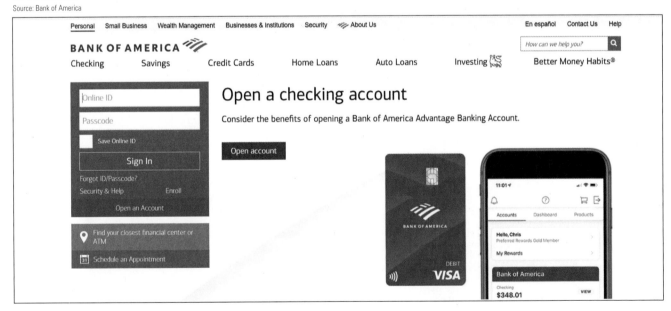

With an **online auction**, users bid on an item being sold by someone else (Figure 2-19). The highest bidder at the end of the bidding period purchases the item. eBay is one of the more popular online auction websites.

Careers and Employment

You can search the web for career information and job openings. Job search websites list thousands of openings in hundreds of fields, companies, and locations. This information may include required training and education, salary data, working conditions, job descriptions, and more. In addition, many organizations advertise careers on their websites.

Portals

A **portal** is a website that combines pages from many sources and provides access to those pages. Most web portals are customized to meet your needs and interests. For example, your bank might create a web portal that includes snapshots of your accounts and access to financial information. Portals exist that offer a selection of services, including the following: search engine; news, sports, and weather; web publishing; yellow pages; stock quotes; maps; shopping; and email and other communications services.

Content Aggregation

A **content aggregator** site, sometimes called a **curation website**, such as News360 or Flipboard, gathers, organizes, and then distributes web content (Figure 2-20). As a subscriber, you choose the type of content you want and receive updates when new content is available.

Figure 2-19   Online auction sites enable you to bid on and pay for items sold by users.
Source: eBay

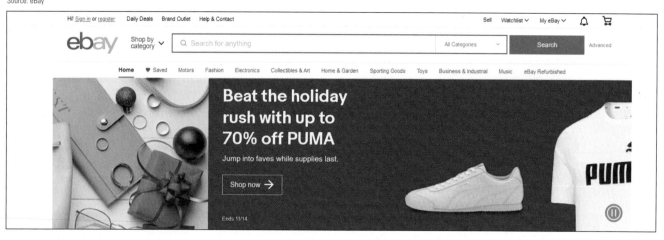

Figure 2-20   Flipboard is an example of a content aggregator.
Source: Flipboard

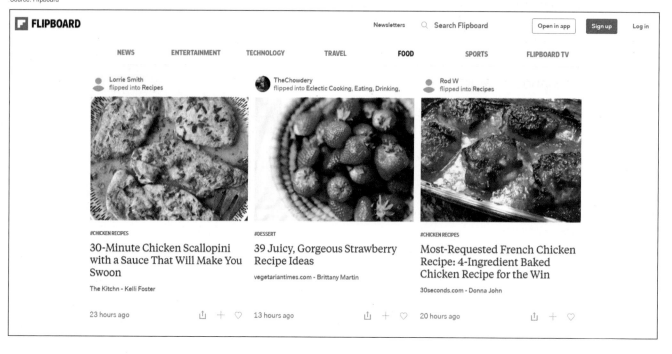

Types of content that may be compiled include news, reviews, images, videos, blogs, and more. Content aggregation websites save users time because they need to visit only one source to obtain information.

Web Apps

In addition to using a browser to visit websites and display webpages, you can use it to access **web apps**, which are apps you can run entirely in a browser. Most of the website types and examples described in this module have a corresponding app that has similar functionality. A web app resides on a server on the Internet, rather than on your computer or mobile device. For example, Microsoft Office provides Excel, PowerPoint, and Word as web apps, and Google offers a suite of online productivity apps. Other popular web apps include Slack (for group collaboration), Trello (for project management), and Google Docs (for word processing).

Other examples include Box (which lets you store and exchange files on the cloud) and Skype (which lets you communicate with others using video and voice). Many web apps also have mobile versions, which you operate from your mobile device. The apps sync data between them, enabling you to access your account information, or perform actions, using either version of the app. Table 2-3 summarizes the pros and cons of using web apps.

E-Commerce

E-commerce, short for electronic commerce, is a business transaction that occurs over an electronic network, such as the Internet (Figure 2-21). Anyone with access to a computer or mobile device, an Internet connection, and a means to pay for purchased goods or services can participate in e-commerce. Popular uses of e-commerce by consumers include shopping and auctions, finance, travel, entertainment, and health.

Consumers use e-commerce because it is convenient, and businesses use e-commerce because it can increase revenue. E-commerce has reshaped the modern marketplace. Business analysts say that physical retail stores are in decline, while e-commerce websites such as Amazon are more popular than ever.

Three types of e-commerce websites are business-to-consumer, consumer-to-consumer, and business-to-business.

- **Business-to-consumer (B2C) e-commerce** consists of the sale of goods and services to the general public, such as at a shopping website.
- **Consumer-to-consumer (C2C) e-commerce** occurs when one consumer sells directly to another, such as in an online auction.
- **Business-to-business (B2B) e-commerce** occurs when businesses provide goods and services to other businesses, such as online advertising, recruiting, credit, sales, market research, technical support, and training.

Figure 2-21 E-commerce transactions have outpaced traditional shopping.
iStock.com/Filadendron

Table 2-3 Pros and Cons of Web Apps

Pros	Cons
Access web apps from any device with a browser and Internet connection.	You must be online to use web apps.
Collaborate with others no matter their location.	Your files are more vulnerable to security and privacy violations.
Store your work on the app's website so you can access it anytime and anywhere.	If the web app provider has technical problems, you might not be able to access your work.
Save storage space on your device.	If the web app provider goes out of business, you can lose your files.
Access the latest version of the app without installing updates.	Web apps often offer fewer features and may run more slowly than installed apps.

Use E-commerce in Business Transactions

Most e-commerce actually is between businesses. B2B services include advertising, technical support, and training. B2B products include raw materials, tools and machinery, and electronics. For B2B purchases, pricing can vary based on the level of service provided, negotiated terms, and other factors. At B2C websites, the consumer is the decision maker. In a B2B transaction, a team of people often need to review and make a purchasing decision. They usually must follow company procedures, which can lengthen or complicate the transaction.

Use E-commerce in Personal Transactions

You can purchase just about any product or service at a B2C e-commerce website. To purchase online, you visit an electronic storefront, which contains product descriptions, images, and a shopping cart to collect items you want to purchase. To complete the sale, you enter personal data and the method of payment, which should be through a secure Internet connection. A B2C website tracks your selected items using cookies. Cookies store shopping cart item numbers, saved preferences, and other information. B2C websites are usually designed to be easy to use so that you can find what you want quickly. They include reviews from other customers to help you make purchasing decisions, special offers for web customers only, and wish lists to encourage you to return to the site. Many B2C websites let you research online and then pick up the purchased item in a physical store.

Online classified ads and online auctions are examples of C2C e-commerce websites. An online auction works much like a real-life auction or yard sale. You bid on an item being sold by someone else. The highest bidder at the end of the bidding period purchases the item. eBay is one of the more popular online auction websites.

C2C sites have many sellers promoting the goods, rather than a single merchant hosting a B2C site. Many C2C sites use email forwarding, which hides real email identities, to connect buyer with seller and still protect everyone's privacy. You pay a small fee to the auction site if you sell an item.

❓ Consider This

How can you ensure you are getting a good price when shopping online?
You can find online deals in at least two ways: visiting comparison shopping sites and using digital deals. Websites such as BizRate and PriceGrabber are comparison shopping websites that save you time and money by letting you compare prices from multiple vendors.

Digital deals come in the form of gift certificates, gift cards, and coupons. Groupon and NewEgg are examples of deal-of-the-day websites, which help you save money on restaurant meals, retail products, travel, and personal services. Digital coupons consist of promotional codes that you enter when you check out and pay for online purchases. Sites such as RetailMeNot and browser extensions such as Honey provide coupon codes and offer alerts for discounts. Have you ever used Groupon or other coupon websites or apps? What types of deals did you find? Was it worth it?

Secure IT: Stay Safe Online

A secure website uses encryption to safeguard transmitted information. **Encryption** is a security method that scrambles or codes data as it is transmitted over a network so that it is not readable until it is decrypted.

An encrypted website connection displays https instead of http in the URL. The "s" in https stands for "secure," so https means **Hypertext Transfer Protocol Secure**. Websites, such as banks and retail stores, use the https protocol to make a secure connection to your computer. Secure websites often use a **digital certificate** to verify a user's identity with a digital key that has been "signed" by a trusted third party (Figure 2-22). This third party verifies the owner and that the key belongs to that owner.

Figure 2-22 Digital certificates provide security when visiting websites.
iStock.com/Anyaberkut

An insecure website does not include indicators such as a lock icon. In addition, the URL starts with "http," indicating an unprotected protocol for transmitting information. The address bar in the Chrome browser identifies such websites as "Not secure."

Online Safety Tips

It is important to keep the following in mind when using the web:

- **Verify the website is safe.** Type the website address of your email, banking, online social network, and other personal accounts directly in a browser; never visit these websites merely by clicking links found in email messages. Before you sign in, double-check the web address to verify it is correct. Browsers may change the color of some of the text in the address bar to verify the website is legitimate. Also, check that the web address begins with https instead of the less secure http, and look for a closed padlock symbol beside it.

- **Turn off location sharing.** At times, you may want to allow location sharing, which gives websites access to your current location. This feature is handy when you want to obtain current weather conditions or use a navigation app. This information could be misused by dishonest individuals, however, so it is recommended you turn off location sharing.
- **Clear your browsing history.** A copy of every website you visit is stored in the browser's cache. If you perform online banking or view your credit card transactions, the cache could contain personal information, such as passwords and account numbers. You can specify to clear the cache automatically each time you exit a browser.
- **Never store passwords.** Many browsers can store your passwords so that you do not need to type them each time you visit the same websites. Although you may consider this feature a convenience, keep in mind that anyone who accesses your computer can view these secure websites easily using your account information.
- **Use a phishing filter.** Many browsers include a phishing filter, which is a program that warns or blocks you from potentially fraudulent or suspicious websites.
- **Enable a pop-up or pop-under blocker.** Malicious software creators can develop pop-up ads or pop-under ads, which are Internet advertisements that suddenly appear in a new window on top of or behind a webpage displayed in a browser. A **pop-up blocker** is a filtering program that stops pop-up ads from displaying on webpages; similarly, a pop-under blocker stops pop-under ads. Many browsers include these blockers. You also can download them from the web at no cost.

- **Use private browsing.** Prevent people using your computer or mobile device from seeing the websites you viewed or searches you conducted by using private browsing. The browser discards passwords, temporary Internet files, data entered into forms, and other information when you exit the browser.
- **Use a proxy server.** To protect your online identity, use a proxy server, which is another computer that screens all your incoming and outgoing messages. The proxy server will prevent your browsing history, passwords, usernames, and other personal information from being revealed.

Make Secure E-Commerce Payments

Before you make a payment on a website or provide sensitive information such as a credit card number, make sure the website is secure. Otherwise, an unauthorized web user could intercept the payment or information and steal your funds or identity.

To make e-commerce payments in an e-commerce transaction, you can provide a credit card number. Be sure the B2C website uses a secure connection. **3D Secure** is a standard protocol for securing credit card transactions over the Internet. Using both encryption and digital certificates, 3D Secure provides an extra layer of security on a website.

Besides the https protocol, e-commerce sites also use **Transport Layer Security (TLS)** to encrypt data. This helps protect consumers and businesses from fraud and identity theft when conducting commerce on the Internet. Using an online payment service, such as PayPal, Square Cash, Venmo (Figure 2-23), and Zelle is another layer of protection.

Figure 2-23   Venmo enables you to pay contacts directly from your account to theirs.
Source: PayPal

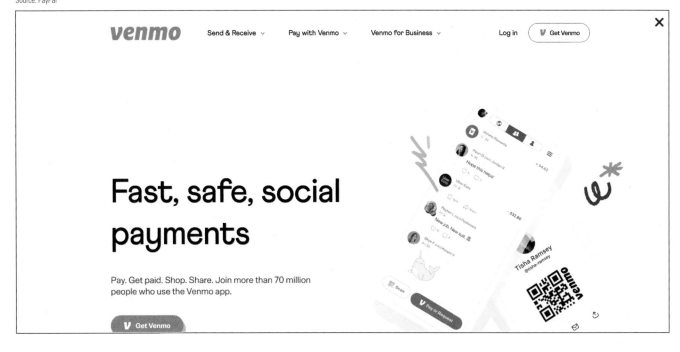

You can also use smartwatches and smartphones to make e-commerce payments. ApplePay and Google Wallet are two of several mobile payment and digital wallet services available on smartphones. Scan the watch or phone over a reader, often available in stores, to make the electronic payment.

Another payment method is to use a one-time or virtual account number, which lets you make a single online payment without revealing your actual account number. These account numbers are good only at the time of the transaction; if they are stolen, they are worthless to thieves.

❓ Consider This

Is it safe to enter financial information online?
As an alternative to entering credit card, bank account, or other financial information online, some shopping and auction websites allow consumers to use an online payment service, such as PayPal. To use an online payment service, you create an account that is linked to your credit card or funds at a financial institution. When you make a purchase, you use your online payment service account, which manages the payment transaction without revealing your financial information. These services include an app, which can be used to transfer funds to any person or entity that also uses the same service.

Communicating Online

As with other aspects of convergence, where capabilities of devices, apps, and services overlap, many online communication tools have similar features to one another. Blogs and wikis are also considered online communication tools. Online conferencing tools have chat and messaging features. Many social networking apps have options to message and bookmark or share content. Digital communications you should be familiar with include email, messaging, podcasts, online conferencing, VoIP, and FTP.

Email
Email was one of the original services on the Internet, enabling scientists and researchers working on government-sponsored projects to communicate with colleagues at other locations (Figure 2-24).

Figure 2-24 You can send email to anyone, anywhere in the world.
iStock.com/Anyaberkut

You use an **email app** to create, send, receive, forward, store, print, and delete email messages. An email message can be simple text or can include an attachment, such as a document, a graphic, an audio clip, or a video clip. A **clip** is a media file, such as a graphic, sound, animation, or movie, that you can add to documents and webpages.

Just as you address a letter when using the postal system, you address an email message with the email address of your intended recipient. Likewise, when someone sends you a message, the sender must have your email address.

An **email address** is a combination of a username and a domain name that identifies a user so that the user can receive Internet email. A **username** is a unique combination of characters, such as letters of the alphabet and/or numbers, that identifies a specific user. Your username must be different from the other usernames in the same domain.

Sometimes, organizations decide the format of usernames for new users so that the usernames are consistent across the company. In many cases, however, users choose their own usernames, often selecting a nickname or any other combination of characters for their username. Many users select a combination of their first and last names so that others can remember it easily.

In an Internet email address, an @ (pronounced at) symbol separates the username from the domain name. Your service provider supplies the domain name. A possible email address for Rick Claremont would be rclaremont@esite.com, which would be read as follows: R Claremont at e site dot com. Most email programs allow you to create a contacts list or address book, which contains names, addresses, phone numbers, email addresses, and other details about people with whom you communicate.

When you send an email message, an outgoing mail server determines how to route the message through the Internet and then sends the message (Figure 2-25). As you receive email messages, an incoming mail server holds the messages in your mailbox until you use your email program to retrieve them. Most email programs have a mail notification alert that informs you via a message and/or sound when you receive a new email message(s).

Email Lists An **email list**, or electronic mailing list, is a group of email addresses used for mass distribution of a message. When a message is sent to an email list, each person on the list receives a copy of the message in their mailbox. Users may elect to receive the messages immediately or in a digest form sent at a specified interval, such as daily or after a number of messages have accumulated. You subscribe to an email list by adding your email address to the mailing list, which is stored on a list server. To remove your name, you unsubscribe from the mailing list. Many companies and organizations subscribe to an email marketing and mailing

Figure 2-25   How an email message may travel from a sender to a receiver.

Oleksiy/Shutterstock.com; iStock.com/luismmolina; Courtesy of Juniper Networks; Courtesy of Juniper Networks; © iStock.com/hocus-focus

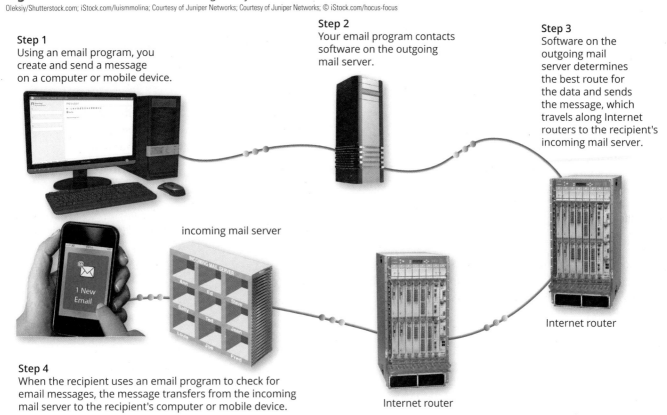

Step 1
Using an email program, you create and send a message on a computer or mobile device.

Step 2
Your email program contacts software on the outgoing mail server.

Step 3
Software on the outgoing mail server determines the best route for the data and sends the message, which travels along Internet routers to the recipient's incoming mail server.

incoming mail server

Internet router

Step 4
When the recipient uses an email program to check for email messages, the message transfers from the incoming mail server to the recipient's computer or mobile device.

Internet router

service, such as Constant Contact. Email marketing services allow organizations to create campaigns and then send them by email to everyone whose name is on a list for distribution. These services allow users to opt out from receiving future messages, forward messages to others, and track the number of people who opened the message.

Messaging Apps

Internet messaging services, which often occur in real-time, are communications services that notify you when one or more of your established contacts are online and then allow you to exchange messages or files or join a private chat room with them. Real-time means that you and the people with whom you are conversing are online at the same time. Some Internet messaging services support voice and video conversations, allow you to send photos or other documents to a recipient, listen to streaming music, and play games with another online contact.

For real-time Internet messaging to work, both parties must be online at the same time. Also, the receiver of a message must be willing to accept messages. To use an Internet messaging service, you may have to install messenger software or an app on the computer or mobile

device, such as a smartphone, you plan to use. Many online social networks include a messaging feature (Figure 2-26). To ensure successful communications, all individuals on the friend list need to use the same or a compatible messenger.

Figure 2-26   Facebook Messenger is an example of a messaging app.

Source: Facebook

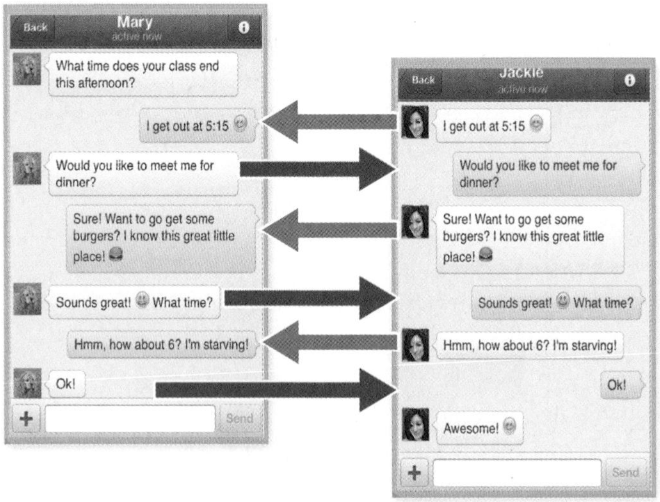

Most messaging apps include the following features, which allow for a variety of communication types:

- **Text messaging**, or sending short text messages, allows you to send messages to a person or group quickly. Participants do not have to be online at the same time.
- Chatting is similar to text messaging but takes place in real-time between users, like a conversation. Chat features may require you to identify yourself or register with the service in order to participate.
- **Multimedia messaging**, or sending photos, videos, or links to websites, allows participants to quickly share content. Messaging apps can even include custom animated characters you can create, using apps such as Animoji, which feature face-tracking technology to apply your voice and facial expressions to animated characters. These are best used in personal rather than business communications.
- **Voice messaging** refers to recording and posting digital messages for another person. Often referred to as a voice mail, it is a message recorded using digital technology. Once digitized, the voice mail is stored in the phone's voice mailbox. With visual voice mail, users can view message details, such as the length of a call and a time stamp showing when the message arrived.
- **Voice-to-text** (also called speech-to-text) converts incoming or outgoing voice messages to written text (Figure 2-27). Some users rely on it for everyday convenience, while others use it only in situations where typing messages is impractical and hand-free operation is required. Voice-to-text technology also can be used in visual voice mail, where it can translate voice messages into typed text.
- An **online discussion**, or discussion forum, is an online area in which users have written discussions about a particular subject. To participate in a discussion, a user posts a message, called an article, and other users

Figure 2-27   Voice-to-text translates your speech into words.

iStock.com/PonyWang

read and reply to the message. A **thread**, or threaded discussion, consists of the original article and all subsequent related replies.

Podcasts

If you miss a lecture or your favorite business news program, or if you are just looking for entertainment, chances are you will find them on a podcast, a popular way to distribute audio or video content on the web. A **podcast** is recorded media that users can download or stream to a computer or mobile device and listen to at any time (Figure 2-28). Examples include lectures, radio shows, news stories, and commentaries. Podcasts are also useful tools that can help you learn more about practically any field, such as sports, music, politics, personal development, or investments. A **video podcast** is a file that contains video and audio; it is usually offered as part of a subscription to a podcasting service.

Figure 2-28   Dell provides many technology-related podcasts.

Source: Dell Technologies

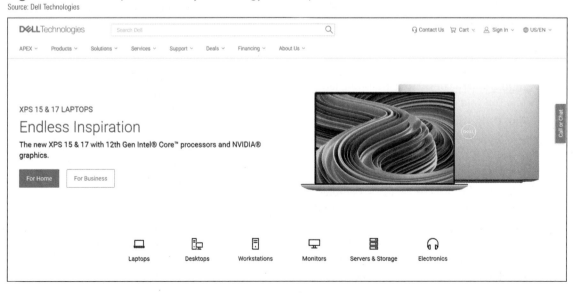

Online Conferencing

Suppose you are working on a business project with a team that includes people in different cities or countries. To collaborate on the project, you can have a **web conference** (also called a **videoconference**), which is a meeting among several geographically separated people who use a network or the Internet to transmit audio and video data (Figure 2-29). During the COVID-19 pandemic, web conferencing became an essential tool for schools and businesses to teach and work without being face to face.

Figure 2-29   Web conferences enable users to have conferences without being in the same location.
iStock.com/VioletaStoimenova

Web conferences typically are held on computers or mobile devices. Participants use web conferencing software to sign in to the same webpage. To communicate with one another, participants can either join a conference phone call or use their computer microphones and speakers. One user acts as the host and shares their desktop with the group. During the online session, the host can display a document that participants see at the same time. Most web conferencing software features a whiteboard that the presenter and participants can annotate. If the host edits the document, everyone sees the changes as they are made. Participants can use chat features to send typed messages to one another during the meeting. Participants also can share files. Conferencing programs may also feature automatic language translation, instant captioning for people with hearing loss, and Braille translation for those who are blind or Deaf-Blind.

A **webinar**, short for web-based seminar, is a presentation an audience accesses over the web that shows a shared view of the presenter's screen and may also include audio and video of the presenter and allow for audience participation. It is often used to present lectures, demonstrations, workshops, or other types of instructional activity.

Talking over a live video connection with a person at another physical location used to exist only in futuristic science fiction. **Video chat**, also called **video calling**, is a face-to-face conversation held over a network, such as the Internet.

Video chat is used in businesses and education for **webcasts** (video broadcasts of an event transmitted across the Internet).

You can use smartphones for video chatting as well as desktop, laptop, and tablet computers with an Internet connection, microphone, and webcam. Video chatting software lets you control the images that appear onscreen, voice and sound volume, and other features. Chatters without a webcam can participate in the chat but will not be seen on screen by other chatters.

Some video chat applications are now going beyond flat 2-D displays to develop holographic images, using beams of light to create patterns that appear as 3-D images. Such advancements will bring the tools of virtual reality into everyday communications.

Popular video chat apps include Skype, FaceTime, Facebook Messenger, WhatsApp, and Amazon Alexa. Some apps also allow **video messaging**, which allows you to leave a video message for a recipient to retrieve later.

Voice over Internet Protocol (VoIP)

Voice over Internet Protocol (VoIP) refers to voice communications over the Internet and is sometimes called **Internet telephony**. In the past, voice communications travelled only along phone lines. Communications or telephone companies charged for phone calls. With the Internet, voice can travel through the same network lines that carry webpages and other Internet services. Many ISPs now offer phone services; if you have a phone number through your ISP, you are using VoIP.

To place an Internet phone call, you need a broadband network connection, a microphone and speaker, both of which are included with a standard computer or mobile device, and VoIP software, such as Skype. Some VoIP services require that you purchase a separate phone and VoIP router and that you subscribe to their service. Others offer certain services free and require a subscription for additional services. Often calls from one country to another are included in your monthly Internet fee.

VoIP allows you to receive calls on your computer from home or cell phones and to place calls from your computer to these phones. You can use different devices to make VoIP calls, including smartphones, landline phones, laptops, tablets, and even desktop computers. If you have a webcam, VoIP technology lets you include video in your calls.

FTP

FTP (File Transfer Protocol) is an Internet standard used to upload or download files between your local computer and a remote web server. Uploading is the process of transferring files from a computer or mobile device to a server on the Internet. Downloading is the process of transferring files from a server on the Internet to your computer or mobile device. Webpage developers, for example, often use FTP to upload their webpages to a web server.

Many operating systems include FTP capabilities. If yours does not, you can download FTP programs from the web, sometimes for a small fee.

An FTP server is a computer that allows users to upload and/or download files using FTP. An FTP site is a collection of files that reside on an FTP server. Many FTP sites have anonymous FTP, whereby anyone can transfer some, if not all, available files. Some FTP sites restrict file transfers to those who have authorized accounts (usernames and passwords) on the FTP server.

? Consider This ————————————————————

What are good practices to follow when using email?

- Keep messages brief.
- Respond to most messages in a timely manner.
- Consider the consequences of sending messages or responses that may contain controversial or negative words; hold off formulating a reply so that anger or other emotions will not result in an unprofessional response.
- Use proper grammar, spelling, and punctuation.
- Never respond to unsolicited messages.
- Use meaningful subject lines.
- Read the message before you send it.
- Do not use the "reply all" feature unless it is critical that your response goes to all original recipients.
- Use email when you want a written record of a communication.
- To manage the number of messages you receive, unsubscribe from unwanted mailing lists, delete unneeded messages, and move important messages to an appropriate folder.

What other strategies have you used when working with email? Have you encountered issues with other users that you wish they would correct?

Use Social Networks

A **social network**, also called a social networking site, is a website that encourages members in its online community to share their interests, ideas, stories, photos, music, and videos with other registered users. Social networking was made possible by the growth of social media. Popular online social networks include Facebook, Twitter, Instagram, Snapchat, and LinkedIn. A news or activity **feed** on the site provides a listing of the most recent content posted to the network.

People you know through personal and professional circles form your social networks. You share common interests, work or spend leisure time together, and know many of one another's friends. Online social networks allow you to manage your social networks online.

Your account on an online social network includes profile information, such as your name, location, photos, and personal and professional interests. You might create accounts on several online social networks to separate your personal and professional activities. Online social networks allow you to view the profiles of other users and designate them as your friends or contacts. Some sites, such as Facebook and LinkedIn, require friends to confirm a friendship, while others, such as Twitter and Google+, allow users to follow one another without confirmation.

Social Media and Social Networks

Individuals and businesses rely on social media to connect and provide information to their contacts or followers. Social media differs from other forms of communication because it is immediate, interactive, and widespread. Estimates say that more than 2.5 billion people use social media worldwide.

Social media helps us form online communities with users who share similar interests around the world. Table 2-4 lists the most common types of social media used today:

Business Uses of Online Social Networks

Businesses use social networking to learn more about their customers by collecting their feedback in the form of comments and experiences. A company's social networking site might advertise its products, services, and events. Non-profit organizations use social networking to promote their activities, accept donations, and connect with volunteers.

Businesses create blogs to communicate with employees, customers, and vendors. Personal blogs often focus on family life, social life, or a personal interest or project, such as building a house or planting a garden. Other blogs can include commentary on news and politics and are an outlet for citizen journalists. Citizen journalists, members of the public who report on current events, often produce blogs that comment on an event while it is taking place, usually in the form of frequent short updates.

Personal Uses of Online Social Networks

Personal uses of online social networks include sharing photos and videos, greetings, or status updates. A status update informs friends what you are doing. You can like, or show appreciation for, online content, such as photos or videos on online social networks, such as Facebook and Google+. When you do, people who see the same content will know that you liked it, and the person who posted it is notified. All your updates, likes, posts, and events appear in the activity stream associated with your account. Activity updates from friends may appear on a separate page associated with your account, often called a news feed.

Table 2-4 Types of Social Media

Type	Lets You	Includes	Examples
Social networking	Share ideas, opinions, photos, videos, websites	Personal and business networking, chat, video chat and videoconferencing, instant messaging, online dating, social memorials	Facebook, LinkedIn, Instagram, Snapchat, Microsoft Skype, Google Hangouts
Blogging and microblogging	Create and update an online journal that you share with readers	Personal journals, expert advice, information on special areas of interest	Twitter, Blogger, WordPress, Tumblr, Pinterest
Media sharing and content sharing	View and distribute pictures, videos, audio files	Photo and video sharing, podcasting, news sites, online learning, distance learning	YouTube, Break, Dailymotion, Flickr, Photobucket, Picasa
Collaborative projects	Read, add, and discuss articles about topics of interest	Online encyclopedias, forums, wikis, message boards, news groups,	Wikipedia, WikiAnswers, Wikia
Social curation, bookmarking, and social news	Tag (mark) and search websites; share websites, articles, news stories, media	Tagging; knowledge management	Delicious, Reddit, Digg
File sharing	Send and receive files from others on an Internet location	Free or paid access to file storage locations on the Internet	Egnyte, ShareFile, Hightail, Dropbox, WeTransfer
Virtual social worlds	Play games with others; create a simulated environment	Virtual reality games	World of Warcraft, Xbox, Steam
Crowdfunding	Raise funds for a project, cause, or business	Websites that let anyone contribute; site takes a percentage of funds raised	GoFundMe, Indiegogo, Kickstarter, Startsomegood

You can expand your online social network by viewing your friends' friends and then, in turn, designating some of them as your friends. Friends of your friends and their friends form your extended contacts. Extended contacts on a personal online social network, such as Facebook, can introduce you to others at your college or from your hometown, connect you with long-distance friends or relatives, or enable you to stay in touch with those who have interests similar to yours.

In many online social networks, you can communicate through text, voice, and video chat, and play games with other members. Facebook, Twitter, Whatsapp, Instagram, Pinterest, and Tumblr are some websites classified as online social networks. You interact with an online social network through a website or mobile app on your computer or mobile device (Figure 2-30).

When accessing an online social network with a GPS-enabled mobile device, the location where you check in may be revealed as part of a status update. An online social network's mobile app can share your location with friends, find others nearby, and alert you to promotional deals from nearby businesses.

Figure 2-30   Social media apps are available on your smartphone or other device.
iStock.com/Stnazkul

Types of Social Networks
Some online social networks have no specialized audience; others are more focused. You have probably viewed an online video, and chances are it was posted to YouTube.

Figure 2-31   YouTube provides videos and playlists of videos.
Source: YouTube, LLC

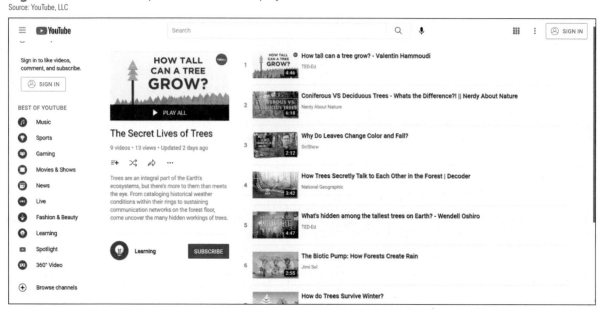

With a media sharing site, such as YouTube or Flickr, you can manage media such as photos, videos, and music and share them with other site members. Use a media sharing site to post, organize, store, and download media (Figure 2-31). With photo sharing sites, such as Instagram, Flickr, Photobucket, and Shutterfly, you can post photos and then organize them into albums, add descriptive tags to categorize them, and invite comments. Photos and other posts on social network sites also include information that generally does not appear to site users, called metadata, which is data that describes other data. Metadata for a picture includes the GPS location coordinates where it was taken, when it was posted, and who posted it.

Privacy and Security Risks with Online Social Networks

Online social networks can be excellent places to share messages, photos, and videos. They can, however, be risky places to divulge personal information. Follow these tips to help protect against thieves who are following the network traffic and attempting to invade private facets of your life.

- **Register with caution.** During the registration process, provide only necessary information. Do not disclose your birthdate, age, place of birth, or the city where you currently are living. If an email address is required, consider using a new address so that the online social network cannot access your email address book. Online social networks occasionally ask users to enter their email address and password to determine if their friends also are members of the network. In turn, the network obtains access to contacts in your address book and can send spam (unsolicited email messages) to your friends.

- **Manage your profile.** Check for privacy settings, usually found on the Settings or Options tabs, to set permissions so that you can control who can review your profile and photos, determine how people can search for you and make comments, and if desired, block certain people from viewing your page. Be aware that online social networks may change privacy settings. Periodically check your settings to ensure you have the most up-to-date settings.

- **Choose friends carefully.** You may receive a friend request that appears to be from someone you know. In reality, this message may originate from an identity thief who created a fake profile in an attempt to obtain your personal information. Confirm with the sender that the request is legitimate.

- **Limit friends.** While many online social networks encourage the practice, do not try to gather too many friends in your social network. Some experts believe that a functional online social network should not exceed 150 people. Occasionally review what your friends are posting about you.

- **Divulge only relevant information.** Write details about yourself that are relevant to the reasons you are participating in an online social network. When posting information, be aware that the message may be accessible publicly and associated with your identity permanently. Do not post anything you would not want to be made public.

- **Be leery of urgent requests for help.** Avoid responding to emergency pleas for financial assistance from alleged family members. In addition, do not reply to messages concerning lotteries you did not enter and fabulous deals that sound too good to be true.

- **Read the privacy policy.** Evaluate the website's privacy policy, which describes how it uses your personal information. For example, if you watch a video while signed in to your account, an external website or app may have access to this information and post this activity as an entry in both your activity stream and your friends' news feeds.

Video sharing sites, such as YouTube and Vimeo, let users post clips. Clips can be user-created, or they can be short portions of published digital media from other sources. You can set up a post so that anyone, or only people you invite, can view or comment on your clip. On Instagram, followers "like" (show approval of or appreciation for) photos.

With the growth of online shopping, users need a way to evaluate products before they buy. **Consumer review networks** let purchasers post online ratings and reviews of practically any product or service. For example, TripAdvisor helps travelers choose accommodations, flights, experiences, and restaurants by providing price and feature comparisons, as well as customer ratings and reviews. Yelp helps consumers find professionals of all kinds, such as dentists, hair stylists, or mechanics, while Angi helps people search for service professionals, such as contractors or plumbers, in their area (Figure 2-32). Shopping sites such as Amazon also feature review capabilities to help users decide which products to buy.

Discussion forum networks let you have online conversations on any topic. For example, Quora features discussions in 10 areas, including literature, technology, science, writing, health, and books. You can follow topics you select, and post questions, opinions, and links. You can also receive notifications when others post to a topic that interests you. The site lets you **upvote**, or promote, answers that you find useful.

Business Uses of Social Media

Businesses use online social networks to connect with their customers, provide promotional offers, and offer targeted advertising. For example, users who recommend online content about travel services may see travel-related advertising on their online social network's webpage.

Businesses also use data from online social networks to better connect with and understand customers. They can review comments from customers about their experiences using companies' products or services. Monitoring these feeds continuously gives companies immediate feedback from customers.

Nonprofit organizations use online social networks to promote activities and causes, accept donations, and allow volunteers to contact one another online.

Figure 2-32   Angi is an example of a consumer review website.
Source: Angi

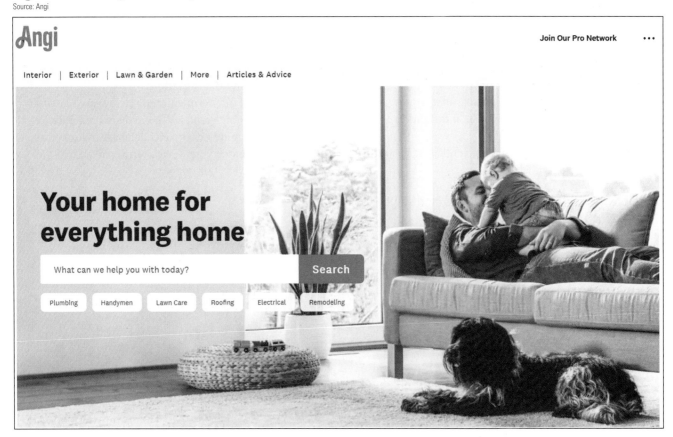

Consider This ─────────────────────────────────────

How do you use hashtags?

On Twitter and other online social networks, a **hashtag** is a descriptive word or phrase (without spaces between words) that starts with the hash symbol (#). Hashtags allow users to classify posts related to a particular topic. Some online social networks list trending topics based on popular hashtags. Many television broadcasts, advertisements, and businesses post hashtags to encourage viewers and customers to share comments on Twitter or Facebook. Have you ever added hashtags to a social media post? For what purpose? Have you searched for topics by hashtags? What were the results?

Apply Information Literacy Standards to Web Searches

Using a search site, such as Google, you can find websites, webpages, images, videos, news, maps, and other information related to a specific topic. Search sites use search engines to enable users to pose queries that return a list of websites or webpages that may provide the information the user needs. You also can use a search engine to solve mathematical equations, define words, find flights, and more.

Of the billions of webpages you can access using Google or another search site, some are valuable and some are not. Telling the difference is a skill you need to succeed in work and life.

Define Information Literacy

How you find, evaluate, use, and communicate online information depends on your **information literacy**, which is the ability to find, evaluate, use, and communicate online information. If you have information literacy, you can do the following:

- Navigate many sources of information, including the Internet, online libraries, and popular media sites.
- Select the right tool for finding the information you need.
- Recognize that not all information is reliable, accurate, or from reputable sources.

- Evaluate whether information is misleading, biased, or out of date.
- Manage information to become a knowledgeable decision maker.

You become information literate by understanding and selecting the tools, techniques, and strategies for locating and evaluating information (Figure 2-33).

How Search Engines Work

Suppose you are working on a presentation about mobile phone technology and need to know about current innovations. How can you find this information quickly?

You probably would use a general search engine and enter a search term or phrase, such as *mobile phone innovations*. Within seconds, the first page of search results lists a dozen webpages that might contain the information you need.

How does a general search engine choose the results you see? When you perform a search, a general search engine does not search the entire Internet. Instead, it compiles a database of information about webpages. It uses programs called spiders or crawlers. A **spider** or **crawler** is software that combs the web to find webpages and add new data about them to the database, thereby building an **index**, or listing of terms and their locations.

A **query** is a search term entered into a search engine on the web to obtain results. When you enter a query, a general search engine refers to its database index and then lists pages that match your search term, ranked by how closely they answer your query.

Figure 2-33   Search tools, techniques, and strategies.

Jeramey Lende/Shutterstock.com

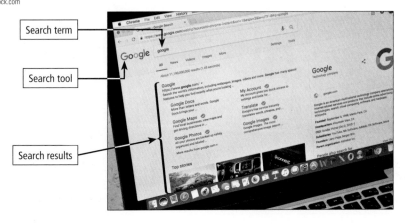

Search term

Search tool

Search results

Figure 2-34 Library search directory.
Source: Georgia tech library

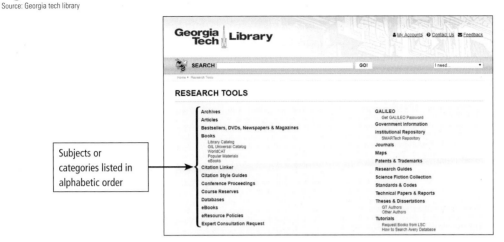

Subjects or categories listed in alphabetic order

Each search engine uses a different method to retrieve webpage information from an index and create a ranked list of results. The ranking depends on how often and where a search term appears on the webpage, how long the webpage has been published, and the number of other webpages that link to it.

Use Search Tools and Strategies

A **search tool** finds online information based on criteria you specify or selections you make. Search tools include search engines and search boxes on webpages. The more effectively you use search tools, the more quickly you can find information and the more relevant that information will be.

Another type of search tool is a **web directory**, or **subject directory**, which is an online guide to subjects or websites, usually arranged in alphabetic order (Figure 2-34).

Search engines and web directories take different approaches to searching for information. Instead of using an index created by digital spiders, a human editor creates the index for a web directory, selecting categories that make sense for the information the web directory provides. The editor usually reviews sites that are submitted to the directory and can exclude those that do not seem credible or reliable. For this reason, a web directory is often a better choice than a search engine if you are conducting research online.

Specialized search tools concentrate on specific resources, such as scholarly journals or the United States Congress. Examples include the Directory of Open Access Journals, Congress.gov Legislative Search, and Google Books. If you need to research the latest academic studies or look up the status of a bill, using a specialized search tool is more efficient than using a general search engine.

To get the most out of a web search, develop a search strategy (Figure 2-35), which involves performing the following tasks before you start searching:

- State what kind of information you are seeking, as specifically as possible.
- Phrase the search term as a question, as in "How do businesses use augmented reality?"
- Identify the keywords or phrases that could answer the question.
- Select an appropriate search tool.

Figure 2-35 Steps in a search strategy.
Bloomicon/Shutterstock.com

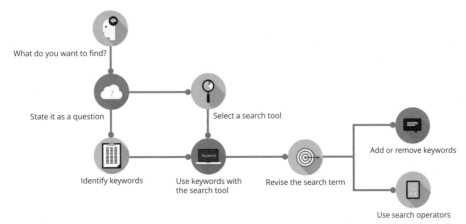

What do you want to find?

State it as a question

Select a search tool

Identify keywords

Use keywords with the search tool

Revise the search term

Add or remove keywords

Use search operators

Next, perform the search. For example, if you want to know about how businesses use augmented reality, you could search using *augmented reality* as the **keywords**, the descriptive word or phrase you enter to obtain a list of results, and produce a list of results that include the words or phrase. If you find the results you need, you can stop searching.

If the term you use is too general, you are likely to find millions of webpages that mention the term. If the term you use is too specific, you might miss useful webpages related to your term. In either case, you need to refine the web search to narrow or broaden the results.

Refine Web Searches

Suppose you are interested in the next generation of the mobile Internet, called 5G Internet, and how it can make you more productive when you are on the go. Enter *5g internet* in a search engine, and the results could include millions of webpages about 5G products, news, definitions, and research.

Many search engines follow practices when listing search results, such as:

- Search engines list the most relevant results, or **hits**, on the first page.
- Results labeled as an "Ad" or "Sponsored link" are from advertisers.
- Each type of filter offers related features. For example, if you filter Google search results to show only images, you can filter the images by size, color, and usage rights, which indicate when you can use, share, or modify the images you find online.
- In addition to listing related links at the bottom of the results page, Google displays a "People also search for" list below a link you visited.

You can also refine a web search by using a **search operator**, also called a **Boolean operator**. Search operators are characters, words, or symbols that refine the search (Table 2-5).

Many search sites have advanced search operators, which are special terms followed by a colon (:). For example, *site:* means to search only the specified site, as in *site:www.cengage.com sam*, which finds information about SAM on the cengage.com website. You can find the advanced search operators by referring to the site's help pages.

To broaden a search, you can use a **word stem**, which is the base of a word. For example, instead of using *businesses* as a keyword, use *business*. You can also combine the word stem with an asterisk (*), as in *tech** to find technology, technician, and technique.

Conduct Online Research

When you need to conduct online research for an assignment or project, look beyond general search engines. Using search engines designed for research yields more reliable results, saving you time and effort.

Use Specialty Search Engines   Where do you go to find academic information for your research? Searching databases is usually a good idea when conducting research, because much of the information on the web is stored in databases. To access this database information, you need to use a special search form and may need to enter a username and password. For example, Google Scholar searches scholarly literature from many disciplines and includes articles, books, theses, and abstracts.

Other specialty search tools let you find information published on certain types of sites. For example, use Google News or Alltop to find news stories and Podcast Search Service to search for podcasts on specific topics or by certain individuals.

Table 2-5   Common Search Operators

Operator	Means	Example
" " (quotation marks)	Find webpages with the exact words in the same order	"augmented reality" in business
| (vertical bar)	OR	augmented | virtual
- (hyphen)	NOT	augmented reality -virtual
*	**Wildcard** (placeholder for any number of characters)	augment* reality
#..#	Find webpages within a range of numbers	augmented reality 2017..2022

? Consider This ——————————————————————————————

Can you assume that content on a website is correct and accurate?

No. Any person, company, or organization can publish a webpage on the Internet. No one oversees the content of these webpages. Use the criteria below to evaluate a website or webpage before relying on its content.

- Affiliation: A reputable institution should support the website without bias in the information.
- Audience: The website should be written at an appropriate level.
- Authority: The website should list the author and the appropriate credentials.
- Content: The website should be well organized and the links should work.
- Currency: The information on the webpage should be current.
- Design: The pages at the website should download quickly, be visually pleasing, and be easy to navigate.
- Objectivity: The website should contain little advertising and be free of bias.

Have you encountered inaccurate information on the web? How did you know it was inaccurate? Would you use a wiki for research for a school assignment?

Ethics & Issues: Using Online Content Responsibly

On the Internet, anyone can publish anything to a website, a blog, or a social media site, regardless of whether the information is true. How can you tell if a website is worth your time? In general, look for sites from trusted, expert institutions or authors. Avoid sites that show bias or contain outdated information.

If you use the Internet for research, be skeptical about the information you find online. Evaluate a webpage before you use it as an information source. One way to evaluate a webpage is to use the CARS checklist and determine whether the online information is credible, accurate, reasonable, and supportable. The CARS criterion includes:

Credibility: When someone is providing you information face to face, you pay attention to clues such as body language and voice tone to determine whether that information is credible, or believable. Obviously, you can not use that same technique to evaluate the credibility of a webpage.

To determine the credibility of a website:

- Identify the author of the webpage and check their credentials. This information is often listed on the Contact Us page or the About page.
- If you find biographical information, read it to learn whether the author has a degree or other expertise in a field related to the topic.
- Use a search engine such as Google or the professional networking site LinkedIn to search for the author's name and see whether the author is an expert on the subject.

Accuracy: To check the accuracy of a website, do the following:

- Verify its facts and claims. Consult an expert or use fact-checking sites, such as snopes.com and factcheck .org, to find professionally researched information.

- Evaluate the information source. Be wary of web addresses that contain slight modifications of legitimate sites, use unusual domain names, or have long URLs.
- Find out more about an organization that seems to have no apparent activity, physical location, or staff, and may exist only to provide information from a seemingly reliable source.
- Check to see if the source has a bias, and evaluate the information with the bias in mind.
- Check the webpage footer for the date the information was published or updated. For many topics, especially technology, you need current information.

Reasonableness: Along with credibility and accuracy, consider how reasonable an online information source is. Reasonable means fair and sensible, not extreme or excessive.

To check how reasonable a website is:

- Identify the purpose of the webpage. Is the page designed to provide facts and other information, sell a product or service, or express opinions?
- Evaluate whether the webpage offers more than one point of view.
- Look for emotional, persuasive, or biased language, which is often a sign that the author is not being fair or moderate. Even opinions should be expressed in a moderate tone.
- Look for a conflict of interest. For example, if the page reviews a certain brand of smartphone and the author sells those types of phones, they have a conflict of interest.

Support: Suppose a webpage refers to a study concluding that most people consider computer professionals to be highly ethical. But the page does not link to the study itself or mention other sources that support this claim. The page is failing the final criterion in the CARS checklist: support.

To evaluate a webpage's support:

- Look for links or citations to reputable sources or authorities. A **citation** is a formal reference to a source, such as a published work. Test the links to make sure they work.
- Check other webpages and print material on the topic to see if they cite the same sources.
- Look for quotations from experts.
- For photos or other reproduced content, a credit line should appear somewhere on the page that states the source and any necessary copyright information.

Gather Content from Online Sources

As you conduct research online, you gather content from webpages, including text, photos, and links to resources. Follow ethical guidelines and be aware of ownership rights to avoid legal, academic, and professional sanctions, and be a responsible member of the online community.

If you copy a photo from the Internet and use it in a report, you might be violating the photographer's **intellectual property rights**, which are legal rights protecting those who create works such as photos, art, writing, inventions, and music.

A **copyright** gives authors and artists the legal right to sell, publish, or distribute an original work. A copyright goes into effect as soon as the work exists in physical form.

If you want to use a photo in your report, you need to get permission from the photo's owner. Contact the photographer by email, and explain what you want to use and how you plan to use it. If a copyright holder gives you permission, keep a copy of the message or document for your records. The holder may also tell you how a credit line should appear. Acquiring permission protects you from potential concerns over your usage and protects the copyright holder's intellectual property rights.

Some online resources, such as ebooks, newspapers, magazines, and journals, are protected by **digital rights management (DRM)**, which is a collection of technologies used by software publishers and trade groups to fight software piracy (theft) and prevent unauthorized copying of digital content; includes authentication, certificates of authenticity, encryption, and digital watermarks. It is a violation of copyright law to circumvent these protections to obtain and then use the materials. To avoid legal challenges, use only those materials to which you have legal access, and then follow accepted usage laws for any information you obtain.

Some work is in the **public domain**, which means that the item, such as a photo, is available and accessible to the public without requiring permission to use; therefore, it is not subject to copyright. This applies to material for which the copyright has expired and to work that has been explicitly released to the public domain by its owner. Many websites provide public domain files free for you to download. Much information on U.S. government sites is in the public domain, although you must attribute the information and be aware that the sites might contain other copyrighted information.

For any online source, if you do not see a copyright symbol, look for a statement that specifically defines the work as being in the public domain. For quotations and other cited material, the U.S. **fair use doctrine** allows you to use a sentence or paragraph of text without permission if you include a citation to the original source.

If the discussion about rights and legal trouble makes you nervous, you are not alone. Clearly, it can be hard to know what is acceptable to use and what is not. Most people are not legal experts, so how can you know what you can use and how you can use it? If you make your writing, photographs, or artwork available online, how do you specify to others how they can use that content?

Creative Commons (CC) is a nonprofit organization that helps content creators keep copyright to their materials while allowing others to use, copy, or distribute their work. CC allows for licensing of online content where owners specify conditions for reusing or adapting it, such as with attribution or modification. As a creator, you select a CC license that explains how others can use your work. For example, you can choose whether to allow commercial use of your poem, or allow derivative works, such as translations or adaptations. People who use content that carries a Creative Commons license must follow CC license rules on giving credit for works they use and displaying copyright notices.

CC licenses are based on copyright law and are legal around the world. The CC organization is helping to build a large and ever-growing digital commons, shown in (Figure 2-36).

Apply Information Literacy Standards

Part of information literacy involves the ethical use of the information you find on the web. When you use the Internet for research, you face ethical decisions. Ethics is the set of moral principles that govern people's behavior. Many schools and other organizations post codes of conduct for computer use, which can help you make ethical decisions while using a computer.

Ethically and legally, you can use other people's ideas in your research papers and presentations, provided you cite the source for any information that is not common knowledge.

Thorough research on technology and other topics usually involves books, journals, magazines, and websites. Each type of information source uses a different citation style. Instructors often direct you to use a particular citation style, such as MLA, APA, or Chicago. You can find detailed style guides for each style online. Some software, such as Microsoft Word, helps you create and manage citations and then produce a bibliography, which is an alphabetical collection of citations (Figure 2-37).

Figure 2-36   Creative Commons website.
Source: Creative Commons

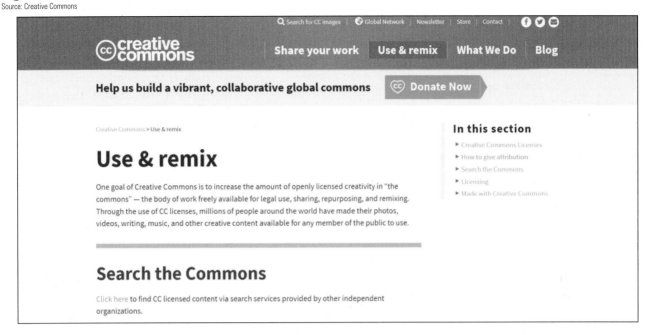

Figure 2-37   Citing sources in Microsoft Word.
Creative Commons

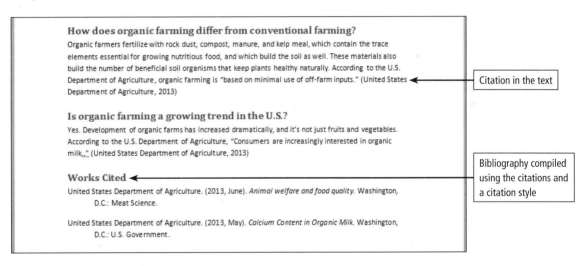

If you use the content from a Wikipedia article but change some of the words, do you have to cite the source for that material? Yes, you do. Otherwise, you are guilty of plagiarism.

To avoid plagiarism, cite your sources for statements that are not common knowledge. Even if you paraphrase, which means to restate an idea using words different from those used in the original text, you are still trying to claim someone else's idea as your own. Cite sources when you borrow ideas or words to avoid plagiarism.

❓ Consider This ──

How do you know if your search content is filtered?

Have you ever done research or made a query using a public network or a computer at a public space, such as a library or university, and found that the results seemed limited? The use of content filtering software used by some libraries controls the type of information you can access. Free speech advocates argue that this violates the First Amendment because it restricts library patrons from viewing certain websites and content. Critics of content filtering software argue that the programs do not always work as intended. They may overfilter content, blocking information or education websites based on a single word. Conversely, they can underfilter content, which could result in access to websites with inaccurate or inappropriate content. Is it fair for governments to require public schools and libraries to use content filtering software? Why or why not? Who does it protect, and who does it hurt?

Study Guide

Instructions: The Study Guide exercise reinforces material you should know after reading this module. Answer the questions below using the format that helps you remember best or that is required by your instructor. Possible formats may include one or more of these options: write the answers; create a document that contains the answers; record answers as audio or video using a webcam, smartphone, or portable media player; post answers on a blog, wiki, or website; or highlight answers in the book/ebook.

1. Define the terms, web and Internet.

2. Explain the contributions of ARPANET.

3. Describe the role of a host on a network.

4. Explain the concept of net neutrality, and the role ISPs play.

5. _____ is a common term used to describe the capacity of a communication channel.

6. Identify the roles of the FCC, IETF, and W3C in setting Internet standards.

7. Differentiate between the web and the Internet.

8. Describe how a hyperlink works.

9. What is a webpage? Differentiate between static and dynamic webpages.

10. A(n) _____ is a computer that delivers requested webpages to your computer or mobile device.

11. Why do web designers use the RWD approach?

12. Describe the uses of HTML and CSS.

13. Define the terms, browser, navigate, and cache.

14. Explain the relationship between a URL, a domain name, and an IP address.

15. Define the term, web address. Name a synonym.

16. What does HTTP stand for?

17. Name the components of a web address.

18. Describe the purpose and composition of an IP address. Differentiate between IPv4 and IPv6.

19. List popular TLDs.

20. Describe how data and information travel the Internet.

21. What is the purpose of a favorite when browsing the web?

22. State the purpose of a hot spot.

23. List considerations before selecting an ISP.

24. State the purpose of a DNS server.

25. Explain the types of cellular networks.

26. _____ transforms a smartphone or Internet-capable tablet into a portable communications device that shares its Internet access with other computers and devices.

27. Briefly explain how to connect to a wireless network.

28. List types of websites and describe the purpose of each.

29. Describe the uses of tags.

30. Define the terms: blog, blogosphere, and microblog. For what purposes do businesses use blogs?

31. Define the term, wiki. What is the role of an editor or content manager on a wiki?

32. What does an electronic storefront typically display?

33. Explain the purpose of a portal.

34. List considerations when using web apps.

35. Define the term, e-commerce. Differentiate among B2C, C2C, and B2B e-commerce.

36. How do e-commerce sites use cookies?

37. _____ is a security method that scrambles or codes data as it is transmitted over a network.

38. List ways you can stay safe online.

39. _____ is a scam where a perpetrator claims to be from a legitimate enterprise in an attempt to trick the user.

40. Explain how to be safe during e-commerce purchases.

41. Describe the purpose of these Internet services and explain how each works: email, email lists, Internet messaging, podcasts, online conferencing VoIP, and FTP.

42. Describe the components of an email address.

43. List communication types used with messaging apps.

44. Explain how to use an online social network for personal or business use.

45. _____ is data that describes other data.

46. List ways to use online social networks securely.

47. Describe how to use a search engine. What are some ways to develop a search strategy?

48. List criteria for evaluating a website's content.

49. Define the following: intellectual property rights, copyright, DRM, and Creative Commons.

50. Explain how to use content responsibly.

Key Terms

You should be able to define the Key Terms listed below.

3D Secure (2-19)
address bar (2-7)
ARPANET (2-2)
bandwidth (2-3)
blog (2-13)
blogger (2-13)
blogosphere (2-13)
bookmarking site (2-12)
Boolean operator (2-30)
breadcrumb (2-6)
browser (2-5)
business-to-business
    (B2B) e-commerce
    (2-17)
business-to-consumer
    (B2C) e-commerce
    (2-17)
cache (2-5)
chatting (2-14)
citation (2-32)
clip (2-20)
consumer review
    network (2-27)
consumer-to-consumer
    (C2C) e-commerce
    (2-17)
content aggregator
    (2-16)
cookie (2-6)
copyright (2-32)
crawler (2-28)
Creative Commons (CC)
    (2-32)
CSS (cascading style
    sheets) (2-5)
curation website (2-16)
digital certificate (2-18)
digital rights
    management (DRM)
    (2-32)
discussion forum
    network (2-27)
DNS server (2-7)

domain name (2-6)
domain name system
    (DNS) (2-7)
dynamic webpage (2-4)
e-commerce (2-17)
electronic storefront
    (2-15)
email (2-3)
email address (2-20)
email app (2-20)
email list (2-20)
encryption (2-18)
fair use doctrine (2-32)
favorite (2-8)
feed (2-24)
FTP (File Transfer
    Protocol) (2-23)
gigabyte (GB) (2-8)
hashtag (2-28)
hit (2-30)
host (2-2)
hot spot (2-8)
HTML (Hypertext
    Markup Language)
    (2-5)
hyperlink (2-4)
Hypertext Transfer
    Protocol (HTTP)
    (2-6)
Hypertext Transfer
    Protocol Secure (2-18)
index (2-28)
information literacy
    (2-28)
intellectual property
    rights (2-32)
Internet (2-2)
Internet backbone (2-7)
Internet Engineering
    Task Force (IETF)
    (2-4)
Internet messaging
    (2-21)

Internet service provider
    (ISP) (2-3)
Internet telephony
    (2-23)
IP address (2-6)
keyword (2-30)
link (2-4)
media sharing site (2-26)
megabyte (MB) (2-8)
metadata (2-26)
microblog (2-13)
mobile hot spot (2-8)
multimedia messaging
    (2-22)
navigation bar (2-6)
net neutrality (2-3)
online auction (2-16)
online discussion (2-22)
podcast (2-22)
pop-up blocker (2-19)
portal (2-16)
protocol (2-6)
public domain (2-32)
query (2-28)
responsive web design
    (RWD) (2-5)
search engine (2-8)
search operator (2-30)
search tool (2-29)
service set identifier
    (SSID) (2-10)
shopping cart (2-15)
social media (2-12)
social network (2-24)
spider (2-28)
static webpage (2-4)
subject directory (2-29)
tag (2-12)
TCP/IP (Transmission
    Control Protocol/
    Internet Protocol) (2-6)
tethering (2-10)
text messaging (2-22)

thread (2-22)
top-level domain (TLD)
    (2-7)
traffic (2-7)
Transport Layer Security
    (TLS) (2-19)
uniform resource locator
    (URL) (2-6)
upvote (2-27)
username (2-20)
U.S. Federal
    Communication
    Commission (FCC)
    (2-4)
video calling (2-23)
video chat (2-23)
videoconference (2-23)
video messaging (2-23)
video podcast (2-22)
voice messaging (2-22)
Voice over Internet
    Protocol (VoIP) (2-23)
voice-to-text (2-22)
web (2-2)
web address (2-6)
web app (2-17)
webcast (2-23)
web conference (2-23)
web directory (2-29)
webinar (2-23)
webpage (2-4)
web server (2-5)
website (2-5)
Wi-Fi hot spot (2-9)
wiki (2-14)
wildcard (2-30)
wireless access point
    (WAP) (2-10)
word stem (2-30)
world wide web (2-2)
World Wide Web
    Consortium (W3C)
    (2-4)

Extend Your Knowledge

Instructions: The Extend Your Knowledge exercise expands on subjects covered in the module and encourages you to find the latest developments on these topics. Use a search engine or another search tool to locate news articles, blog entries, videos, expert discussions, or other current sources on the listed topics. List your sources, and write 3–4 sentences describing what you have learned to submit in the format required by your instructor.

- Net neutrality laws
- Responsive web design techniques
- DNS registration
- Location sharing on social media
- Web conferencing etiquette

What did you learn that helped you better understand the concepts in this module? Did anything surprise you? How will what you learned impact you?

Checkpoint

The Checkpoint exercises test your knowledge of the module concepts.

True/False   Mark T for True and F for False. If False, rewrite the statement so that it is True.

_____ 1. No single person or government agency controls or owns the Internet.

_____ 2. Static webpages may contain customized content, such as the current date and time of day, desired stock quotes, weather for a region, or ticket availability for flights.

_____ 3. Before you can connect to the Internet, you must identify the network using its service set identifier (SSID).

_____ 4. A tag is descriptive text used to categorize media and invite comments.

_____ 5. The "s" in https stands for standardized.

_____ 6. Two users can have the same email address.

_____ 7. A news or activity feed on a social media site provides a listing of the most recent content posted to the network.

_____ 8. Crawlers comb the web to find webpages and add new data about them to the database.

_____ 9. To broaden a search, you can use a Boolean operator, which is the base of a word.

_____ 10. A copyright gives authors and artists the legal right to sell, publish, or distribute an original work.

Matching   Match the terms with their definitions.

_____ 1. Boolean operator

_____ 2. chat

_____ 3. curation website

_____ 4. favorite

_____ 5. domain name

_____ 6. Internet backbone

_____ 7. tag

_____ 8. tethering

_____ 9. web server

_____ 10. wiki

a. real-time typed conversations by two or more people who are online at the same time

b. term used to refer to the major carriers of network traffic

c. characters, words, or symbols that refine a search

d. descriptive text used to categorize media and invite comments

e. preferred websites that you can access with a click or selecting an icon from a folder

f. website or web app that gathers, organizes, and then distributes web content

g. technique that transforms a smartphone or Internet-capable tablet into a portable communications device that shares its Internet access with other computers and devices wirelessly

h. portion of a URL that identifies one or more IP addresses

i. a collaborative website where you and your colleagues can modify and publish content on a webpage

j. computer that delivers requested webpages to your computer or mobile device

Problem Solving

Instructions: The Problem Solving exercises extend your knowledge of module concepts by seeking solutions to practical problems with technology that you may encounter at home, school, work, or with nonprofit organizations. The Collaboration exercise should be completed with a team. You often can solve problems with technology in multiple ways. Determine a solution to the problems in these exercises by using one or more resources available to you (such as a computer or mobile device, articles on the web or in print, blogs, podcasts, videos, television, user guides, other individuals, electronics or computer stores, etc.). Describe your solution, along with the resource(s) used, in the format requested by your instructor (brief report, presentation, discussion, blog post, video, or other means).

Personal

1. **Wi-Fi Log-In**   While sitting at a restaurant, you access a list of available Wi-Fi hot spots. When you try to sign in to the one with the name of the restaurant, you are asked for a password. What are your next steps?

2. **Unsolicited Follower Requests**   You recently signed up for an account on social media. When you sign in periodically, you find that people you do not know are requesting to follow your account. How should you respond?

3. **Unexpected Website**   You are trying to find the website of a local community college. You type the name of the school, using .com as the TLD. Your browser takes you to the website for a company with the same name as the school. What could be wrong?

4. **Suspicious Website Content**   When you navigate to a webpage from your search results, you notice that, while you clicked a hit that looked relevant, the webpage contains several misspellings, along with some inaccurate information. What should you do?

5. **Social Media Password**   Your social media password has been saved on your computer for quite some time, and the browser has been signing you in automatically. After deleting your browsing history and saved information from your browser, the online social network began prompting you again for your password, which you have forgotten. What are your next steps?

Professional

6. **Suspicious Website Visits**   The director of your company's information technology department sent you an email message stating that you have been spending an excessive amount of time viewing websites not related to your job. You periodically visit websites not related to work, but only on breaks, which the company allows. How do they know your web browsing habits? How will you respond to this claim?

7. **Intranet Wiki Errors**   When you sign in to the company's wiki, you notice that some of your important customers' data has been deleted. Other entries have been edited to include inaccurate information. Who should you contact to help fix this problem? What might be the response if the perpetrator is caught?

8. **Suspicious Email Message**   You receive an email message with a link from a friend of yours, who is well-known for sending messages that contain jokes or memes. However, you have not heard from this friend for awhile, and the email message contains only the link. What precautions should you take?

9. **Mobile Hot Spot Not Found**   You use a mobile hot spot while you are traveling to an out-of-state conference. When you attempt to connect to the hot spot, none of your devices is able to find any wireless networks. What might be the problem, and what are your next steps?

10. **Sporadic Email Message Delivery**   The email program on your computer has been displaying new messages only every hour, on the hour. Historically, new email messages would arrive and be displayed immediately upon being sent. Furthermore, your coworkers claim that they sometimes do not receive your email messages until hours after you send them. What might be the problem?

Collaboration

11. **Technology in Transportation**   Your project team has been assigned to present a business proposal to a group in San Antonio, Texas. You need to transport some people and set up a way for others to attend remotely. Form a team of three people and determine how to use technology to make travel arrangements and set up a web conference. One team member should research the steps to make flight and hotel reservations via the web, one team member should determine the steps to set up the webinar and what equipment will be needed both on-site and remotely, and another team member should find options to transport participants from the airport to the hotel.

How To: Your Turn

Instructions: This exercise presents general guidelines for fundamental skills when using a computer or mobile device and then requires that you determine how to apply these general guidelines to a specific program or situation. You often can complete tasks using technology in multiple ways. Figure out how to perform the tasks described in these exercises by using one or more resources available to you (such as a computer or mobile device, articles on the web or in print, online or program help, user guides, blogs, podcasts, videos, other individuals, trial and error, etc.). Summarize your 'how to' steps, along with the resource(s) used, in the format requested by your instructor (brief report, presentation, discussion, blog post, video, or other means).

1 **View and Manage Data Usage**

Many people have limited data plans, so it is important to know how to view the amount of data you have used on your phone or tablet when you are not connected to the Internet using a Wi-Fi connection. If you are using a phone or tablet where Wi-Fi is available, you should strongly consider using the Wi-Fi connection not only to limit data plan usage but also to experience faster speed. If you find that your data usage is high each month, you may be able to see which apps are using the most data and adjust usage of those apps accordingly. The following steps guide you through the process of viewing and managing data usage.

a. Display the settings on your mobile device.

b. Select the option to view data usage.

c. If necessary, tap the option to display a list of apps and how much data each app uses. If necessary, select the time period for which you want to see the data usage.

d. If you notice an app using a large amount of data, tap the icon to see details for that app. If necessary, disable background data transfer for the app. Background data transfer is data the app downloads and uploads even while you are not actively using the app.

e. If you want your mobile device to notify you when you are approaching your monthly data limit, set the necessary notification option and select a value below your monthly data limit in the appropriate area.

f. If you want your mobile device to turn off data (this does not include Wi-Fi) when you reach a certain limit, set the necessary option and then select a value that is just less than your monthly data limit to ensure you never reach or exceed the limit.

g. Save all changes.

Exercises

1. Do you have a data limit on your mobile data plan? If so, what is it?

2. When you enter an area with Wi-Fi, do you configure your mobile device to connect to the Wi-Fi? Why or why not?

3. Review the mobile data usage on your mobile device. Which app uses the most data? Which app uses the least data?

Internet Research

Instructions: These exercises broaden your understanding of module concepts by requiring that you search for information on the web. Use a search engine or another search tool to locate the information requested or answers to questions presented in the exercises. Describe your findings, along with the search term(s) you used and your web source(s), in the format requested by your instructor (brief report, presentation, discussion, blog post, video, or other means). Additionally, reflect on the process you used to complete this activity. How did you go about choosing the tool that you did and why? Would you do anything differently in your research next time?

❶ App Producers: Funding and Generating Income

App developers invest large amount of money to create and market their apps. One source of funding, especially for start-up companies, is venture capitalists' funding. These investors scrutinize business plans and market trends in an effort to locate app developers with the potential to generate substantial returns. Once the businesses are operational, additional monies are needed to maintain and improve the apps. At this point, the app might be able to charge other companies to display advertisements. The charge for companies to place an advertisement generally increases as the number of users grows. Another method of generating income is to charge users for accessing premium content. Online dating services use this tactic successfully, for they allow people to browse online profiles free of charge but require them to pay to contact a potential dating match.

Research This: Locate venture capitalists who are seeking app developers with new products. Which criteria do they use to make investment decisions? Who are the successful venture capitalists, and which companies have they funded? Which types of advertisements are displayed? How does the content of these ads pertain to the demographics and interests of users?

❷ Search Skills: Understand Search Results

Search results display the most relevant results first. Search results may include links to websites, news stories, images, videos, maps, and information from Wikipedia and other online databases. Results also may show links to similar searches, related people, or posts from online social networks or social media sites.

Because many search engines rely on advertising for revenue, some search results are paid advertisements. Companies and organizations may pay search providers to display links to their websites prominently in the search results when search text contains words relevant to their products and services. Paid ads often appear at the top or along the side of a search results page. A search results page may display an icon or use shading to specify that the search result is an advertisement.

When evaluating the reliability of search results, consider the sources of the information provided. Specialized information, such as medical advice or stock performance, should come from recognizable sources, while you might rely on reviews from customers when selecting a restaurant or purchasing a smartphone.

Research This: Type each search text phrase listed in the paragraph below into the search boxes in Bing, Google, and Yahoo! and then take a screenshot of the first webpage of search results from each. Compare them, identifying ads, news, images, videos, social media results, information from online databases, search tools, and common links that both search engines returned. Which search engine's results do you find more useful in each case? Why?

Type the following search text: (1) internet service providers, (2) google corporate headquarters, (3) flights from boston to los angeles, and (4) identity theft.

❸ Security: Thermal Heat Signatures

Cybercriminals may be on the lookout for customers entering their PINs at keypads near cash registers or at ATMs. Body heat and oils from fingers touching the keys remains for a short time. A device with infrared-scanning capabilities can detect which keys are warmer than others. This device, which is readily available for purchase on websites that sell electronics, snaps on the back of a phone. It captures the thermal heat signatures, with the most recently touched keys glowing red and the cooler keys glowing light green. The thief, therefore, knows which keys comprise the PIN, and can narrow down the sequence of numbers by looking at the intensity of colors on the infrared scan. Even if they have to try a few different combinations of numbers, they may be able access your account using the bank's website using your PIN.

Research This: How much does a thermal imaging phone case cost? Which brand of phone is more commonly used to capture thermal imaging? What steps can consumers take to thwart thieves using infrared scanning? Which key materials are less apt to retain the thermal signatures: metal, rubber, or plastic? How can you protect your account and other information even if a cybercriminal is able to determine your PIN?

Critical Thinking

Instructions: These exercises challenge your assessment and decision-making skills by presenting real-world situations associated with module concepts. The Collaboration exercise should be completed with a team. Evaluate the situations below, using personal experiences and one or more resources available to you (such as articles on the web or in print, blogs, podcasts, videos, television, user guides, other individuals, electronics or computer stores, etc.). Perform the tasks requested in each exercise and share your deliverables in the format requested by your instructor (brief report, presentation, discussion, blog post, video, or other means).

1. **Mobile Browser Comparison**

   Although most mobile devices include a mobile browser, users have the option of downloading and installing other browsers.

   Do This: Evaluate and compare reviews of at least four mobile browsers, such as Google Chrome, Firefox, Mercury, Opera, or Safari. Discuss the major differences among the browsers you researched, including number and types of features, which devices are compatible, how they display webpages, security features, and the speed at which they perform. Discuss any experiences you or your classmates have had with various browsers. Include in your discussion which mobile browser you would recommend and why.

2. **Creative Commons Licenses**

   Creative Commons (CC) is a public copyright license that allows creators to share their work for free distribution. Creators can put limitations on the use of their work; for example, they can specify that it can be used only for noncommercial purposes or that the work cannot be edited or manipulated. Users must abide by the specifications in the license but otherwise can redistribute or use the creator's work for free. Licenses can be applied to all work that can receive a copyright, including books, plays, movies, blogs, and software.

   Do This: Locate sources for accessing CC content. Find three different types of work that have CC licenses. How do the licenses differ? How does the media type affect the license specifications? What consequences might you receive if you misuse content under a CC license?

3. **Case Study**

   Cooperative-Owned Farm Stand You are the new manager for a farm stand that is a cooperative effort, jointly owned by several local farmers. The previous manager tracked all the data on paper. You realize that creating a social media presence will enable you to share information about current crop availability, special events, farmer spotlights, and more.

   Do This: First, you decide which social media platforms will be best for your use. You plan to mostly create events and share photographs. Research popular social media platforms and choose two that will best meet your needs. Explain your choices. Describe the types of content you would post on each. Give specific examples, and describe the purpose of each post. Do the platforms you selected enable you to post to both at once? If so, will you do so? Why or why not? Describe the standard content you will include on each platform, including logos, addresses, and more. What special features of each platform can you take advantage of? How will you acquire the content you need? What costs are associated with each?

Collaboration

4. **Website Evaluation**

   You and three teammates want to start a food truck business selling gourmet sandwiches. You envision a website that includes a menu, nutritional options, and allergy information, as well as an option to preorder for pickup.

   Do This: With your teammates, evaluate existing food truck websites by comparing the advantages and disadvantages of each. Assign each member the task of evaluating one business. Team members should evaluate each vendor's website. Pay particular attention to the following areas: (1) design, (2) ease of use, (3) menu, (4) nutritional information, (5) allergy information, (6) online ordering, (7) location information and directions, (8) hours and contact information, and (9) whether the business also has an app. Summarize your evaluations and rank the websites in terms of their effectiveness. Be sure to include brief explanations supporting your rankings.

Evaluating Hardware:
For Home and Work

iStock.com/lsti2

Objectives

After completing this module, you will be able to:

1 Explain considerations when purchasing technology devices
2 Describe the characteristics and uses of input and output devices
3 Evaluate hardware
4 Prevent and troubleshoot hardware theft or failure
5 Distinguish among internal, external, and cloud-based storage
6 Describe network hardware
7 Explain the uses of cases, motherboard components, system clock, processor cooling, the ALU, the machine cycle, and registers
8 Discuss ways to prevent health-related injuries and disorders caused from technology use
9 Identify responsible e-waste and technology disposal techniques

How Do You Select a Device?

If you use a smartphone, tablet, or computer, you depend on computer hardware, the physical components that allow your device to operate properly. Hardware refers to the device itself and its components, such as wires, cases, switches, and electronic circuits. Computer hardware can include internal components that you cannot see, or they can be externally connected devices.

Computers include a variety of hardware types, including the central processing unit, RAM, ROM, and peripheral devices. Before you can evaluate your hardware needs, you should learn about hardware components and be able to categorize the various types of computer hardware.

Define Each Component of Computer Hardware

Computers contain various types of hardware, such as memory, storage devices, a central processing unit, input and output devices, and communication devices. When using a computer or requesting help, you should understand how the hardware works and how components interact with one another.

The central processing unit (CPU) is a complex integrated circuit consisting of millions of electronic parts and is primarily responsible for converting input (data) into meaningful output (information). Data travels in and out of the CPU through embedded wires called a bus. Figure 3-1 illustrates the approximate locations of CPUs in various types of computers and mobile devices.

When you purchase a computer, you might notice that processors can be advertised as having one or more cores. A processor core is a unit on the processor with the circuitry necessary to execute instructions. Processors with more cores typically perform better and are more expensive than processors with fewer cores. A processor with multiple cores is referred to as a multi-core processor.

If a processor uses specific data frequently, it can store that data in a processor cache. A processor cache stores this data next to the processor so that it can easily and quickly be retrieved.

When a CPU executes instructions as it converts input into output, it does so with the control unit and the arithmetic logic unit. The control unit manages the flow of instructions within the processor, and the arithmetic logic unit (ALU) is responsible for performing arithmetic operations in the CPU.

Computer memory is responsible for holding data and programs as they are being processed by the CPU. Different types of memory exist, including random access memory, read-only memory, and virtual memory.

Random access memory (RAM) is the storage location that is part of every computer and that temporarily stores running apps and document data while a computer is on. RAM is stored on one or more chips connected to the main circuit board of the computer (also referred to as the motherboard), and temporarily stores data needed by the operating system and apps you use. The motherboard is a circuit board inside a computer that contains the microprocessor, the computer memory, and other internal devices. When you start an app on your computer, the app's instructions are transferred from the hard drive to RAM. Although accessing an app's instructions from RAM

Figure 3-1   Central processing units.

Shahreen/Shutterstock.com; Raw Group/Shutterstock.com; Source: Ford Motor Company; Aarrows/Shutterstock.com; Ververidis Vasilis/Shutterstock.com

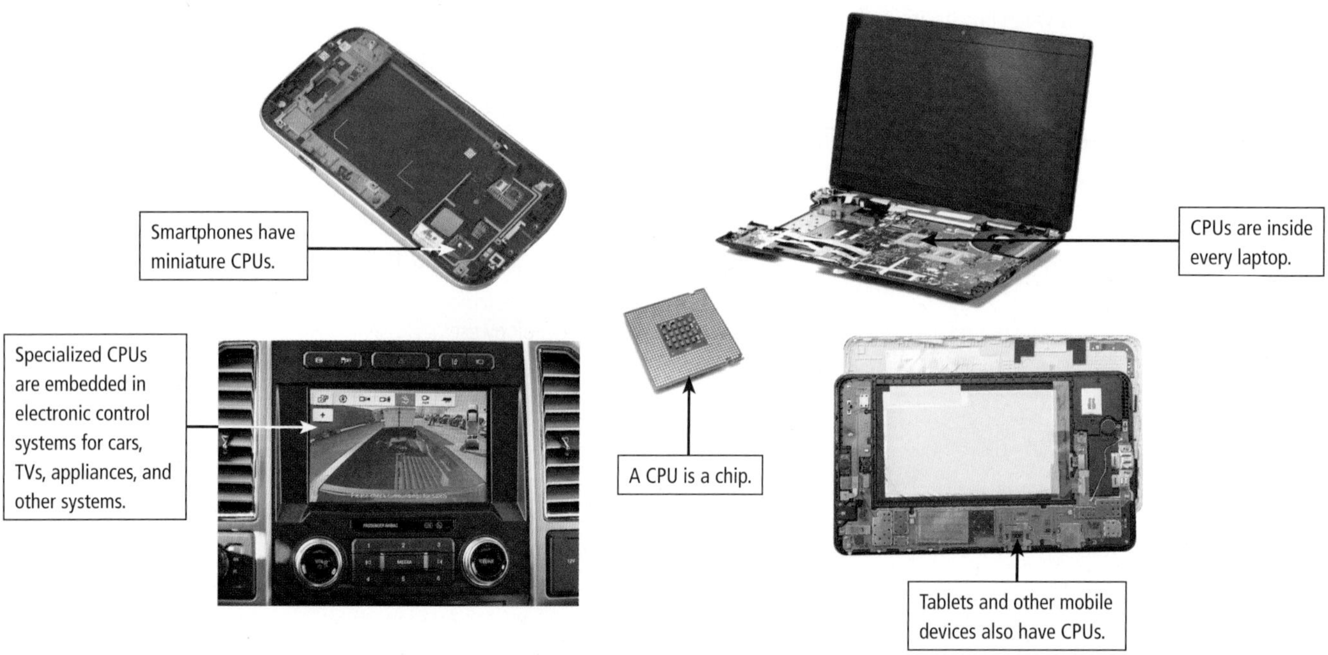

Smartphones have miniature CPUs.

CPUs are inside every laptop.

Specialized CPUs are embedded in electronic control systems for cars, TVs, appliances, and other systems.

A CPU is a chip.

Tablets and other mobile devices also have CPUs.

results in increased performance, the contents of RAM are lost when power is removed. Memory that loses its contents when power is removed is said to be volatile. Memory that is nonvolatile does not lose its contents when power is removed.

Read-only memory (ROM) is permanently installed on your computer and is attached to the motherboard. The ROM chip contains the BIOS (basic input/output system), which tells your computer how to start. The BIOS also performs a power-on self test (POST), which is a sequence at startup that tests all computer components for proper operation. The ROM also provides the means of communication between the operating system and hardware devices. Computer manufacturers often update the instructions on the ROM chip, which are referred to as firmware. These updated instructions, or firmware version, can enable your computer to perform additional tasks or fine-tune how your computer communicates with other devices.

When you run your operating system and other apps on your computer, the operating system and each app will require a certain amount of RAM to function properly. As you run more apps simultaneously, more RAM will be required. If your computer runs low on RAM, it may need to swap the contents of RAM to and from the hard drive. When this takes place, your computer is said to be using virtual memory, which is the capability of an operating system to temporarily store data on a storage medium until it can be "swapped" into RAM. The area of the hard drive temporarily used to store data that cannot fit in RAM is called a swap file, or paging file. Depending on the type of hard drive installed on your computer, using virtual memory may decrease your computer's performance. Figure 3-2 illustrates how a computer might use virtual memory.

Various types of random access memory exist, and the different types vary in cost, performance, and whether or not they are volatile. Table 3-1 describes common types of RAM.

Figure 3-2   How a computer might use virtual memory.
kastianz/Shutterstock.com; TungCheung/Shutterstock.com

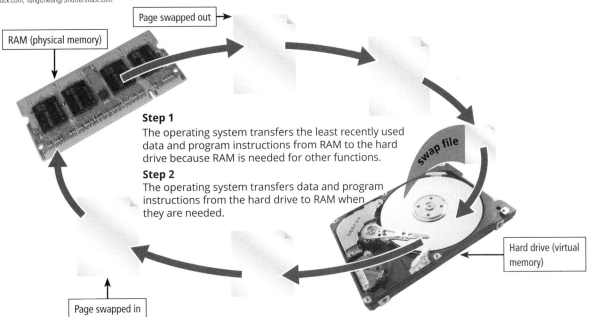

RAM (physical memory)

Page swapped out

swap file

Step 1
The operating system transfers the least recently used data and program instructions from RAM to the hard drive because RAM is needed for other functions.

Step 2
The operating system transfers data and program instructions from the hard drive to RAM when they are needed.

Hard drive (virtual memory)

Page swapped in

Table 3-1   Types of RAM

Type of RAM	Description	Volatile or Nonvolatile
Dynamic RAM (DRAM)	Memory needs to be constantly recharged or contents will be erased	Volatile
Static RAM (SRAM)	Memory can be recharged less frequently than DRAM, but can be more expensive than DRAM	Volatile
Magnetoresistive RAM (MRAM)	Memory uses magnetic charges to store contents, and can retain its contents in the absence of power	Nonvolatile
Flash memory	Fast type of memory that typically is less expensive than some other types of RAM, and can retain its contents in the absence of power	Nonvolatile

Figure 3-3 Computer memory.
Jultud/Shutterstock.com; iStock.com/darval; 1989studio/Shutterstock.com; Gregory Gerber/Shutterstock.com

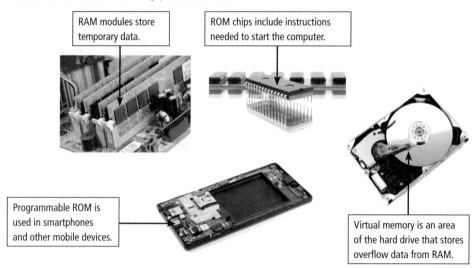

RAM modules store temporary data.

ROM chips include instructions needed to start the computer.

Programmable ROM is used in smartphones and other mobile devices.

Virtual memory is an area of the hard drive that stores overflow data from RAM.

While RAM is used to temporarily store instructions used by apps, storage devices are designed to store data and information for extended periods of time (Figure 3-3). The type and amount of data you want to store will help you determine the most appropriate storage device to use. Some examples of storage devices include internal and external hard drives, solid-state drives, and optical media.

What Hardware Features Should You Consider?

When purchasing a computer, understanding your needs will help you to select the most appropriate device. For example, if you plan to use the computer to check your email and browse the web, the type of computer you purchase might be different from one you might purchase for creating and editing video content. When choosing a computer, you should select one with the platform, hardware, form factor, and add-on devices that best meet your needs. Table 3-2 identifies factors to consider when buying a computer, as well as questions that will help lead you to making the most appropriate choices.

A computer's **platform** refers to the software, or operating system, it uses. When two computers use the same platform, it typically is easier to transfer files between the computers. If you are purchasing a computer to do schoolwork, for example, consider purchasing one that uses the same operating system as the computers at your school. If you have a job and want the ability to do some work both on your office and home computers, consider purchasing a computer that uses the same operating system as your work computer. The operating systems used elsewhere in your home, both on computers and mobile devices, also might play a role in the selection. For example, if you own an iPhone or iPad, you might choose to purchase an Apple computer for maximum compatibility between the devices. Two of the most common operating systems on today's computers are Windows and macOS. Chromebooks are types of laptops that run the ChromeOS operating system. While these are budget friendly, they often do not have the same features or support the same apps as computers running Windows or macOS. Other operating systems include UNIX, Linux, Google Android, and Apple iOS.

Table 3-2 Factors to Consider in Buying a Computer

Consideration	Questions
Platform	• Do I need to use software that requires a specific platform? • Does the computer need to be compatible with other devices I own that use a particular platform?
Hardware	• Do I require specific hardware to perform intended tasks? • How much data and information do I plan to store on the computer?
Hardware specifications	• Will the tasks I perform or software I want to run require certain hardware specifications?
Form factor	• Will I be using this computer in one location, or will I need to be mobile?
Add-on devices	• What additional devices will I need to perform my intended tasks?

Figure 3-4   Computer specifications on a retailer's website.
Source: Bestbuy.com

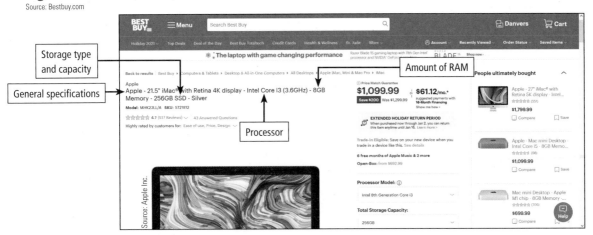

When you buy a computer, you should review the computer's hardware specifications so that you purchase one that meets your needs. Computers are available in a variety of brands. Each brand might include models that have varying types of processors, amounts of memory, storage devices, and form factors. You can find specifications about a computer on the computer's packaging, on signage next to the computer's display in a store, or on the manufacturer's or retailer's website (Figure 3-4).

Depending on how you plan to use the computer, you also may have additional requirements such as a certain number of USB ports, touchscreen, Bluetooth compatibility, or an optical drive. When reviewing hardware specifications online, you may need to explore the product's webpage to identify all hardware specifications. In Figure 3-4, for example, general specifications are listed at the top of the product page; however, scrolling the page will reveal additional features and more detailed hardware specifications.

While your budget will play a big role in the computer you purchase, many computers might be available in the same price range. It is important to evaluate what each computer has to offer so that you can select the device that best meets your needs.

If you plan to use the computer to create and edit video content, you might select a desktop computer with a large monitor and the best available processor. However, if you plan to use a computer just to check your email messages and perform research on the Internet, you might select a laptop with a lower-end processor. The processor most affects a computer's speed.

A great way to determine the required hardware specifications for your computer is to evaluate the minimum hardware requirements, also called system requirements, for the software you plan to use. For example, if you plan to use a software suite, such as Microsoft Office, Microsoft's website outlines the minimum processor, operating system, amount and type of RAM, and storage capacity required to properly run the software (Figure 3-5).

Figure 3-5   System requirements for Microsoft Office.
Source: Microsoft Corporation

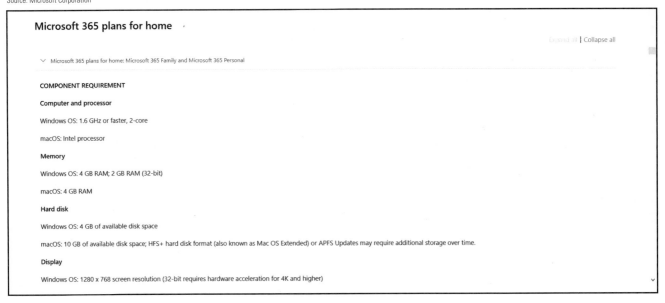

Table 3-3 Evaluating System Requirements

Specification	Recommended Solution
Different processor requirements	Identify the program or app with the greater processor requirement and select a computer with a processor that meets or exceeds the requirement.
Different memory requirements	Identify the program or app with the greater memory requirement and select a computer with a memory type and capacity that meets or exceeds this requirement.
	Computers with as little as 4 GB of memory are great for basic web browsing and very basic productivity tasks, while computers with as much as 32 GB are often used for virtual reality applications, high-end gaming, and other intensive tasks.
Different storage requirements	Add the storage requirements for each program or app you want to use, and select a computer with the storage capacity that exceeds the sum of all storage requirements.
Other differing hardware requirements	In most cases, identify the program or app with the greater requirement and select a computer that at least meets or exceeds this requirement.

Each program or app has its own system requirements. The system requirements for one program or app might conflict with the system requirements of the other(s), so you will need to select the computer with the hardware specifications that can accommodate both programs or apps. Table 3-3 describes how to evaluate conflicting system requirements.

You may want the computer to meet your needs for the next three to five years. If you select a computer that exactly meets the system requirements for the present software you intend to use, you might not be able to install or use additional programs or apps in the future. With the reliance of online software and cloud storage, this may be less of a deterrent than in the past, but still is an important consideration for those times when you are unable to access online apps or storage. While purchasing the most expensive computer you can afford might meet your needs, you might not ever use all available resources. If you intend to use a computer to play games, you might consider a computer built specifically for gaming applications. These computers typically have a large amount of RAM, as well as other supporting hardware to support an immersive gaming experience. Evaluate your options carefully and seek advice from professionals if you are unsure of your exact needs.

Which Type of Computer Is Right for You?

After you have determined the platform and hardware requirements for the computer you want to purchase, you will select a form factor. The form factor refers to the shape and size of the computer. Not all form factors may support the hardware you need. For example, a tablet might not contain adequate hardware specifications for editing videos. Various types of computers exist, including desktop computers, all-in-one computers, laptops, tablets, and other mobile devices.

Desktops A desktop computer (Figure 3-6) typically consists of the system unit, monitor, keyboard, and mouse. The system unit (or chassis) refers to the case on a desktop that contains and protects the motherboard, hard drive, memory, and other electronic components. Desktop computers are designed to be in a stationary location, where all of its components fit on or under a desk or table. Components that typically occupy space outside of a desktop include peripheral devices, such as a keyboard, mouse, webcam, speakers, and printer. Depending on the form factor, it may also require an external monitor. Towers and all-in-one desktops are two types of desktop form factors, both of which can vary in size.

Because desktop computers consist of multiple separate components, they are not very portable; however, these computers often can be more powerful and contain more storage than their mobile equivalents, such as laptops and tablets. Hardware components, such as the hard drive and RAM, can be more easily upgraded in desktop computers than in other types of computers. You might use a desktop computer at an office where users do not need the ability to move their computer from place to place.

All-in-Ones An all-in-one computer is similar to a desktop computer, but the monitor and system unit are housed together. All-in-one computers take up less space than a desktop computer and are easier to transport but are typically more difficult to service or upgrade because the components are housed in a very limited space. All-in-one computers sometimes are more expensive than a desktop computer with equivalent hardware specifications.

Figure 3-6   Desktop and all-in-one form factors.

George Dolgikh/Shutterstock.com; Source: Apple Inc

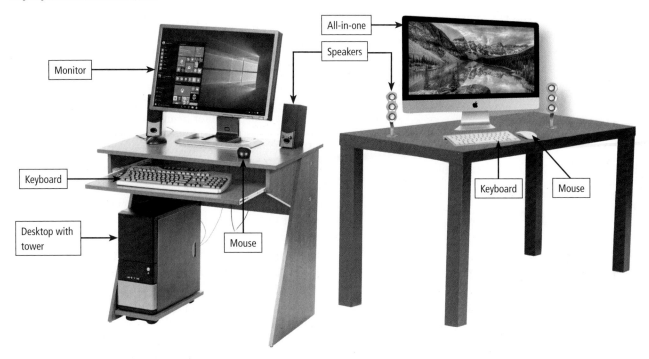

Laptops   Laptops have input devices, such as a keyboard, touchpad, and webcam; output devices, such as a screen and speakers; one or more storage devices, such as a hard drive; and communication capabilities. Many of today's laptops also have touchscreens. Figure 3-7 shows a traditional laptop and an ultrathin laptop.

Ultrathin laptops weigh less than traditional laptops and usually are less powerful. Ultrathin laptops have fewer parts in order to minimize the thickness of the device but may also have a longer battery life and be more expensive.

Figure 3-7   Laptop form factors.

Julia Nikitina/Shutterstock.com; Source: Apple Inc

Tablets   Two popular form factors of tablets are slate and convertible (Figure 3-8). A slate tablet resembles a letter-sized pad and does not contain a physical keyboard. A convertible tablet is a tablet that has a screen in its lid and a keyboard in its base, with the lid and base connected by a swivel-type hinge. You can use a convertible tablet like a traditional laptop, or you can rotate the display and fold it down over the keyboard so that it looks like a slate tablet.

Figure 3-8   Slate and convertible tablets.
iStock.com/Rasslava

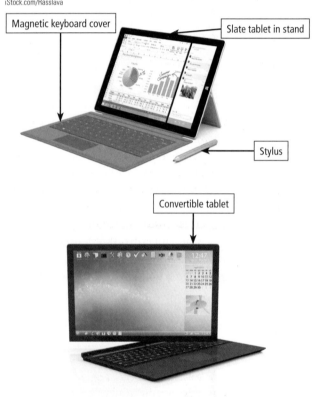

Tablets often are less powerful than other types of computers, but they provide an easy, convenient way to browse the web, read and respond to emails, and create simple documents. Tablets also are easy to transport, making them ideal to take to classes and meetings to take notes. Tablets are used in a variety of professions, such as the medical profession, to easily collect data from patients for storage in their permanent medical records. While the primary method of input on a tablet is by using a digital pen, stylus, or fingertip, you also may be able to connect a wireless Bluetooth keyboard to make it easier to type. It often is not possible to upgrade a tablet; if your tablet's performance begins to deteriorate or cannot keep up with the latest operating systems and apps, it may be necessary to replace the device.

Peripheral Devices   An add-on device, also referred to as a **peripheral device**, is a device such as a keyboard, mouse, printer, or speakers that can connect to and extend the capability of a computer. For example, if you need to share hard copies of documents you create, you should purchase a printer. If you plan to work in a quiet location but still would like to hear audio, you might consider purchasing a headset or earbuds. If you will need to regularly bring files from one computer to another and are unsure about accessing cloud storage between the two computers or devices, you might purchase an external storage device that you can connect to various computers.

A peripheral device may be compatible with only a specific operating system, such as Windows. In addition to making sure that the device is compatible with the software on your computer, you also should make sure you have the necessary ports to connect the device. A **port** is a slot on the computer where you can attach a peripheral device. For example, if a peripheral device is designed to connect to a USB port on the computer, you should make sure that you have an available USB port. If all USB ports on your computer are in use, you might consider purchasing a USB hub. A **USB hub** is an external device that contains several USB ports (Figure 3-9). Finally, consider purchasing an extended warranty or service plan if one is available.

Figure 3-9   USB hub.
iStock.com/jordanchez

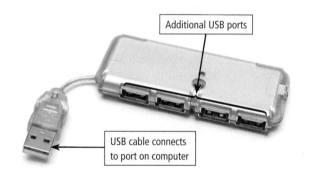

Mobile Computer Buyer's Guide

With the abundance of mobile computer manufacturers, research each before making a purchase. The following are purchasing considerations unique to mobile computers.

1. **Determine which mobile computer form factor fits your needs.** Consider a tablet or ultrathin laptop if you require a lightweight device and the most mobility. If you require additional ports or want the computer's capabilities to be more comparable to a desktop, consider purchasing a traditional laptop.

2. **Consider a mobile computer with a sufficiently large screen.** Laptops and tablets are available with various screen sizes. For example, most traditional and ultrathin laptop screens range in size from 11 to 17 inches, while most tablet screens range in size from 7 to 12 inches.

3. **Experiment with different keyboards and pointing devices.** Mobile computers often vary in size, and for that reason have different keyboard layouts. Familiarize yourself with the keyboard layout of the computer you want to purchase, and make sure it is right for you. If you have large fingers, for example, you should not purchase a computer with a small, condensed keyboard. Laptops typically include a touchpad to control the pointer. Tablets have a touch screen and an on-screen keyboard.

4. **Consider processor, memory, and storage upgrades at the time of purchase.** As with a desktop, upgrading a mobile computer's memory and internal storage may be less expensive at the time of initial purchase. Some internal storage is custom designed for mobile computer manufacturers, meaning an upgrade might not be available in the future.

5. **The availability of built-in ports and slots is important.** Determine which ports and slots (discussed later in this module) you require on the mobile computer. If you plan to transfer photos from a digital camera using a memory card, consider a mobile computer with a built-in card slot compatible with your digital camera's memory card. If you plan to connect devices such as a printer or USB flash drive to your mobile computer, consider purchasing one with a sufficient number of USB ports. In addition, evaluate mobile computers with ports enabling you to connect an external monitor.

6. **If you plan to use your mobile computer for a long time without access to an electrical outlet, or if the battery life for the mobile computer you want to purchase is not sufficient, consider purchasing a second battery.** Some mobile computers, such as most tablets and ultrathin laptops, have built-in batteries that can be replaced only by a qualified technician. In that case, you might look into options for external battery packs or power sources.

7. **Purchase a well-padded and well-designed carrying case that is comfortable and ergonomic.** An amply padded carrying case will protect your mobile computer from the bumps it may receive while traveling. A well-designed carrying case will have room for accessories such as USB flash drives, pens, and paperwork. Although a mobile computer may be small enough to fit in a handbag, make sure that the bag has sufficient padding to protect the computer. Test the carrying case with the laptop inside to ensure it is comfortable and ergonomic.

8. **If you plan to connect your mobile computer to a video projector, make sure the mobile computer is compatible with the video projector.** You should check, for example, to be sure that your mobile computer will allow you to display an image on the screen and projection device at the same time. Also, ensure that the mobile computer has the ports required or that you have the necessary cables and equipment to connect to the video projector.

Desktop Buyer's Guide

If you have decided that a desktop is most suited to your technology needs, the next step is to determine specific software, hardware, peripheral devices, and services to purchase, as well as where to buy the computer. The following considerations will help you determine the appropriate desktop to purchase.

1. **Determine the specific software to use on the desktop.** Decide which software contains the features necessary for the tasks you want to perform. Your hardware requirements depend on the minimum requirements of the software you plan to use on the desktop.

2. **Know the system requirements of the operating system.** Determine the operating system you want to use because this also dictates hardware requirements. If, however, you purchase a new desktop, chances are it will include the latest version of your preferred operating system.

3. **Look for bundled software.** Purchasing software at the same time you purchase a desktop may be less expensive than purchasing the software at a later date.

4. **Avoid purchasing the least powerful desktop available.** Technology changes rapidly, which means a desktop that seems powerful enough today may not serve your computing needs in the future. Purchasing a desktop with the most memory, largest hard drive capacity, and fastest processor you can afford will help delay obsolescence.

5. **Consider upgrades to the keyboard, mouse, monitor, printer, microphone, and speakers.** You use these peripheral devices to interact with the desktop, so make sure they meet your standards.

6. **Consider a touch screen monitor.** A touch screen monitor will enable you to interact with the latest operating systems and apps using touch input.

7. **Evaluate all-in-ones, which may be less expensive than purchasing a tower and monitor separately.** In addition, all-in-ones take up less space and often look more attractive than desktops with separate towers.

8. **If you are buying a new desktop, you have several purchasing options.** You can buy directly from a school bookstore, a local computer dealer, or a large retail store, or you can order from a vendor by phone or the web. Each purchasing option has its advantages. Explore each option to find the best combination of price and service.

9. **Be aware of additional costs.** Along with the desktop itself, you also may need to make extra purchases. For example, you might purchase computer furniture, an uninterruptible power supply (UPS) or surge

protector (discussed later in the module), an external hard drive, a printer, a router, or a USB flash drive.

10. **If you use your computer for business or require fast resolution of major computer problems, consider purchasing an extended warranty or a service plan through a local dealer or third-party company.** Most extended warranties cover the repair and replacement of computer components beyond the standard warranty.

❓ Consider This

How does convergence affect your hardware choices?
Convergence concepts — such as web apps enabling availability across multiple devices and cloud storage of data — affect your need for multiple devices for specific purposes. For example, you may need to access your work or school apps and files from home. Where you may have, in the past, needed a laptop that you could take from the office or school to home, you may be able to use your personal tablet, eliminating or reducing the need to carry your larger devices back and forth. What devices do you own or use? What types of activities can you do that are not device specific? What advantages does convergence give you when selecting and using hardware?

Input and Output Devices

Input and output devices are necessary to provide information to and receive information from a computer. **Information** is data that has been processed to become meaningful. **Data** is raw facts, such as text or numbers. **Input** is any data and instructions entered into the memory of a device. **Output** is information processed into a useful form, such as text, graphics, audio, video, or any combination of these (Figure 3-10).

An **input device** communicates instructions and commands to a computer. On a computer, the most common input device might be a keyboard, which can communicate text and instructions. On a mobile phone, the most common input device might be its touchscreen. Additional types of input devices include, but are not limited to, a mouse, stylus, scanner, webcam, microphone, and game controller.

An **output device** conveys information from the computer to the user. On a computer or mobile device, the most common output device might be its display device. Other types of output devices include speakers, headphones, projectors, and printers.

How Computers Represent Data

Most computers are digital and use a binary system to operate. A **binary system** is a number system that has two digits, 0 and 1. The digit 0 indicates the absence of an electronic charge, and a 1 indicates the presence of an electronic charge. These electronic charges (or absence thereof), when grouped together, represent data. Each 0 or 1 is called a bit. A **bit** (short for binary digit) is the smallest unit of data a computer can process. When 8 bits are grouped together, they form a **byte**. A byte can represent a single character in the computer or mobile device. Figure 3-11 illustrates various bytes, their corresponding bits, and what they represent.

When you type numbers, letters, and special characters on your keyboard, the computer translates them into the corresponding bits and bytes that it can understand. This translation spares you from having to manually type the bits for each number, letter, or special character. When

Figure 3-10 A computer processes data (input) into information (output).

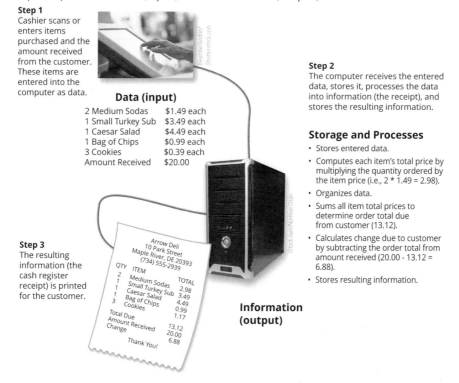

Step 1
Cashier scans or enters items purchased and the amount received from the customer. These items are entered into the computer as data.

Data (input)

2 Medium Sodas	$1.49 each
1 Small Turkey Sub	$3.49 each
1 Caesar Salad	$4.49 each
1 Bag of Chips	$0.99 each
3 Cookies	$0.39 each
Amount Received	$20.00

Step 2
The computer receives the entered data, stores it, processes the data into information (the receipt), and stores the resulting information.

Storage and Processes
- Stores entered data.
- Computes each item's total price by multiplying the quantity ordered by the item price (i.e., 2 * 1.49 = 2.98).
- Organizes data.
- Sums all item total prices to determine order total due from customer (13.12).
- Calculates change due to customer by subtracting the order total from amount received (20.00 - 13.12 = 6.88).
- Stores resulting information.

Step 3
The resulting information (the cash register receipt) is printed for the customer.

Arrow Deli
10 Park Street
Maple River, DE 20393
(734) 555-2939

QTY	ITEM	TOTAL
2	Medium Sodas	2.98
1	Small Turkey Sub	3.49
1	Caesar Salad	4.49
1	Bag of Chips	0.99
3	Cookies	1.17

Total Due 13.12
Amount Received 20.00
Change 6.88

Thank You!

Information (output)

Figure 3-11   A group of eight bits form a byte.

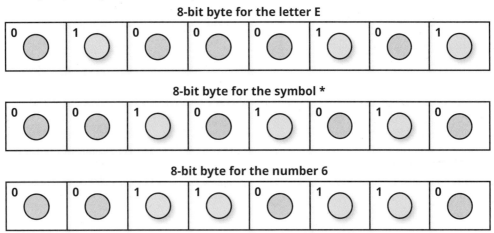

8-bit byte for the letter E

| 0 | 1 | 0 | 0 | 0 | 1 | 0 | 1 |

8-bit byte for the symbol *

| 0 | 0 | 1 | 0 | 1 | 0 | 1 | 0 |

8-bit byte for the number 6

| 0 | 0 | 1 | 1 | 0 | 1 | 1 | 0 |

you display text on an output device, such as a computer monitor, the computer translates the various bits back to numbers, letters, and special characters that you can understand. Figure 3-12 shows how a letter is converted to binary form and back.

When a computer translates a character into bits and bytes, it uses a text coding scheme. Two popular text coding schemes are ASCII and Unicode. **ASCII** (American Standard Code for Information Interchange) is an 8-bit coding scheme, which means that 8 bits are used to represent uppercase and lowercase letters, mathematical operators, and logical operations. **Unicode** is a 16-bit coding scheme that is an extension of ASCII and can support more than 65,000 symbols and characters, including Chinese, Japanese, Arabic, and other pictorial characters.

Figure 3-12   Converting a letter to binary form and back.

Chiyacat/Shutterstock.com; Kitch Bain/Shutterstock.com; iStock.com/Sweetym

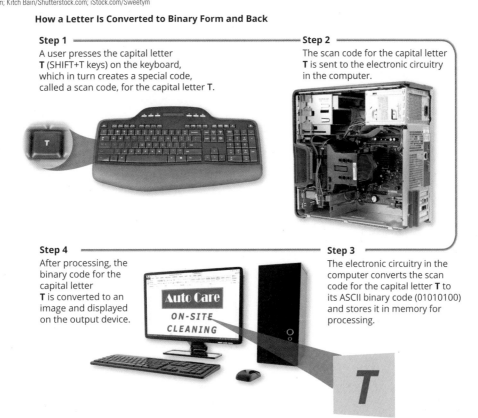

How a Letter Is Converted to Binary Form and Back

Step 1 — A user presses the capital letter **T** (SHIFT+T keys) on the keyboard, which in turn creates a special code, called a scan code, for the capital letter **T**.

Step 2 — The scan code for the capital letter **T** is sent to the electronic circuitry in the computer.

Step 4 — After processing, the binary code for the capital letter **T** is converted to an image and displayed on the output device.

Step 3 — The electronic circuitry in the computer converts the scan code for the capital letter **T** to its ASCII binary code (01010100) and stores it in memory for processing.

Input Devices

As mentioned previously, an input device is used to communicate instructions or commands to a computer. Various types of input devices are available, including keyboards, pointing devices, touchscreens, microphones, cameras, scanners, and game controllers.

A **keyboard** is an input device that contains keys you can press to enter letters, numbers, and symbols (Figure 3-13), as well as keys that can issue commands. Desktop computers have keyboards connected either wired or wirelessly, and laptop computers have a keyboard built-in. Mobile devices, such as tablets and smartphones, typically have an on-screen keyboard; that is, an image of a keyboard displays on the screen, and you touch the appropriate keys to enter letters, numbers, and symbols.

Another widely used type of input device is a pointing device. A **pointing device** is used to point to and select specific objects on the computer screen. Examples of pointing devices include a mouse, touchpad, and track-ball. Pointing devices can be used to select objects, move objects, and position or draw items on the screen.

Figure 3-13   Typical computer keyboard.
iStock.com/Tarik Kizilkaya

A **mouse** is the most common pointing device used with computers. A mouse fits under your hand and can connect to your computer either with a wire or wirelessly (Figure 3-14). Moving the mouse on a flat surface, such as a desk, moves a pointer on the screen. When the pointer is positioned over an object you want to select, you can press a button on the mouse to select the object. This action is referred to as clicking the mouse.

Figure 3-14   Typical mouse.
iStock.com/leventince

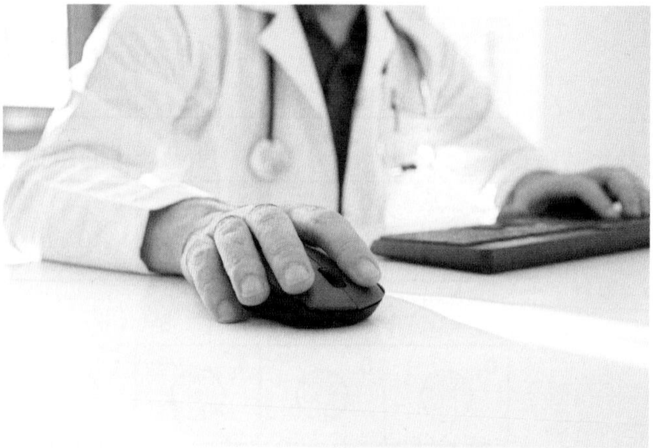

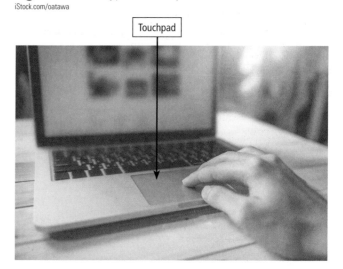

A touchpad is a pointing device that is commonly used on laptops. A **touchpad** is a touch-sensitive flat surface on which you drag your finger to move the pointer on the screen (Figure 3-15). When the pointer is over an item on the screen you wish to select, you can tap the touchpad with your finger to select the object.

Figure 3-15   Typical touchpad.
iStock.com/oatawa

Touchpad

A **trackball** is a stationary pointing device with a ball anchored inside a casing, as well as two or more buttons (Figure 3-16). Moving the ball moves the pointer on the screen, and pressing the buttons issues the commands to the computer.

A **touchscreen** is a display that lets you touch areas of the screen to interact with software. In addition to responding to the touch of your fingers, touchscreens also

Figure 3-16 Typical trackball.
iStock.com/pengpeng

may be able to respond to a stylus or digital pen to enter commands. Tablets and smartphones typically have touchscreens. **Multitouch screens** can respond to multiple fingers touching the screen simultaneously. This is useful when you are performing a gesture such as pinching or stretching an object to resize it.

Pen input is used to make selections or draw on a touchscreen with more precision than a finger. Common pen input devices include a stylus and a digital pen. A **stylus** is a pen-shaped digital tool for making selections and entering information on a touchscreen. A **digital pen** is a small pen-shaped device, that you can use to draw, tap icons, or tap keys on an on-screen keyboard, similar to a stylus, but is more capable because it has programmable buttons. Some digital pens can also capture your handwriting as you write on paper or on the screen (Figure 3-17).

An option for issuing instructions to your computer without using your hands is using your voice. A **microphone** is used to enter voice or sound data into

Figure 3-17 Digital pen.
iStock.com/Yuri_Arcurs

Digital pen

a computer. Examples of activities that might require a microphone include videoconferencing, voice recognition, and recording live music. Many laptops and tablets have built-in microphones, but you can connect a microphone to other types of computers either using a wire or wirelessly. Using a microphone, you can record audio, issue commands to the computer, or speak while the computer translates your words to text in a document. Microphones are also essential if you are using the computer to have an audio or video conversation with one or more other people.

Cameras are input devices because they support you adding pictures or videos to a computer. Most computers come with built-in cameras called webcams. A **webcam** is a type of digital video camera that captures video and still images as well as audio input; often built into a desktop, laptop, or tablet computer, webcams can be used for videoconferencing, chatting, or online gaming (Figure 3-18). If your computer does not have a built-in webcam, or you would like to connect a different type of camera to your computer, you can do so either via a wired or wireless connection.

Figure 3-18 Webcam.
iStock.com/innovatedcaptures

Webcam

A **scanner** is an input device that converts an existing paper image into an electronic file that you can open and work with on your computer. For example, if you want to convert a printed logo to digital form so that you can edit and duplicate it, you could use a scanner to convert the printed logo to a format a computer can understand. In addition to scanning printed materials such as logos and documents, 3-D scanners can scan three-dimensional objects, which then can be manipulated and possibly printed using a 3-D printer. You also can use a scanner to scan a printed document so that you can edit it using an app on your computer.

Gaming Devices A **game controller** is an input device you use when playing a video game. Various types of game controllers exist, including joysticks, gamepads, dance pads, wheels, and motion-sensing controllers.

- A **joystick** has a handheld vertical lever, mounted on a base, that you move in different directions to control the actions of the simulated vehicle or player.
- A **gamepad** is held in both hands and controls the movement and actions of players or objects. On gamepads, users press buttons with their thumbs or move sticks in various directions to trigger events (Figure 3-19).
- A **dance pad** is a flat, electronic device divided into panels that users press with their feet in response to instructions from the video game.
- A **wheel** is a type of game controller that mirrors the functionality of a steering wheel in an automobile. Turning the wheel will turn the vehicle you are driving in the game.
- A **motion-sensing controller** allows users to guide on-screen elements with air gestures.

Figure 3-19 Gamepad.

iStock.com/Pekic

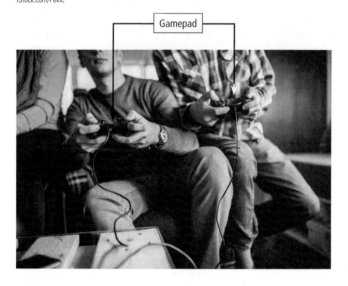

Gamepad

Output Devices

Commonly used output devices include display devices, speakers, headphones, printers, projectors, and voice output.

Computers use display devices as output devices to communicate information to the users. Display devices are connected to desktop computers via a cable, while all-in-one computers, laptops, tablets, and smartphones have built-in display devices. Display devices come in a variety of sizes. If you are simply using a computer to browse the web and check your email, you might consider a smaller display device. If you are working with graphics or large spreadsheets, however, you might use a larger display device. If you want to present to a group of individuals, you might consider using a projector. If you often refer to multiple documents or apps at once, you might consider adding a second monitor or display device.

Speakers are used to convey audio output, such as music, voice, sound effects, or other sounds. While speakers often are built into computers, tablets, and smartphones, you can also connect speakers via a wired or wireless connection. For example, if you want to play music in a small office setting and would like others to hear it, you might connect a separate speaker to your computer so that it can play more loudly. If you prefer to listen to audio in a public space without disturbing others, consider using headphones. **Headphones** consist of a pair of small listening devices that go over your ears and are attached to a band that you place on your head. As an alternative to headphones, **earbuds** are speakers that are small enough to place in your ears. If you prefer a device that provides audio output while being able to accept voice input, consider a headset. **Headsets** include one or more headphones for output, and a microphone for input.

A printer creates hard copy output on paper, film, and other media. A printer can be connected to a computer via a cable, a network, or wirelessly. Table 3-4 describes the various types of printers.

Table 3-4 Types of Printers

Type of Printer	Description
Ink-jet printer	Prints by spraying small dots of ink onto paper
Laser printer	Uses a laser beam and toner to print on paper
Multifunction device (MFD)	Also called an all-in-one printer; can serve as an input device by copying and scanning, as well as an output device by faxing and printing
Mobile printer	Small, lightweight printer that is built into or attached to a mobile device for mobile printing
Plotter	Large-format printer that uses charged wires to produce high-quality drawings for professional applications such as architectural blueprints; plotters draw continuous lines on large rolls of paper
3-D printer	Creates objects based on computer models using special plastics and other materials

Figure 3-20   Projector and screen.
iStock.com/EricFerguson

Projectors can display output from a computer on a large surface, such as a wall or screen (Figure 3-20). Projectors often are used in classroom or conference room environments where individuals give presentations. Projectors are connected to computers using a cable or wirelessly and can either duplicate what is on the computer's monitor or act as an extension of the monitor (the monitor might display one image while the projector displays another). Some projectors are small and easy to transport, while others are larger and may be permanently mounted in a room.

In addition to output being displayed or printed, computers can also provide voice output. A **voice synthesizer** converts text to speech. Some apps and operating systems have a built-in voice synthesizer. In addition to this form of output being convenient for some, it is also helpful for those with visual impairments.

❓ Consider This ─────────

Is it safe to use a webcam?
Webcams are a necessary feature for many, especially those who learn or work remotely. Built-in webcams enable you to use your device to project yourself on-screen, but are they safe? Unauthorized access to your webcam can leave you vulnerable to video or photographs being taken without your consent. This may happen if you are a victim of a virus that installs spy tools, or with misuse of software whose purpose is to take photos to prevent hardware theft. Experts recommend disabling or covering your webcam when not in use. Many devices come with a simple sliding block that covers the webcam. Have you used a webcam for work or school? Have you ever been concerned that others have access to your webcam? What can you do to protect yourself?

Install and Evaluate Hardware

Before you turn on your computer or device for the first time, make sure that all necessary components are included. You should also inspect the computer to make sure it is free from damage. Read the manual to ensure you are following the setup instructions (Figure 3-21).

Carefully unpack all components from the box and place them in their desired locations. Connect all components and accessories, such as your keyboard, and then connect the power. It is a good idea to fully charge the battery before using the device for the first time. Finally, you can turn on the computer or device and follow all remaining steps on the screen.

Figure 3-21   User manuals provide safe setup instructions.
iStock.com/Energyy

While you likely will use any peripheral devices, such as a printer or scanner, over your wireless network, you may need to install some peripheral devices directly to your device through a port. Some devices, called **Plug-and-Play** devices, will begin functioning properly as soon as you connect them to your computer. Other devices might require that you manually install special software, called a device driver, to work properly. A **device driver** is a program that allows your computer or device to issue controls to a separate device, such as a printer, monitor, or video card. To connect a wireless device to your computer, follow the installation instructions that come with the device. If you have to install an app for your device to work, make sure you are signed in with a user account that has the necessary permission to install programs and apps.

Evaluate the Performance of Computer Hardware

When searching for a computer to purchase, you should be able to evaluate the hardware specifications so that you can select the computer that best meets your needs. If you are using a computer for basic tasks, such as browsing the web or checking your email, you might not require the same specifications as someone who uses a computer for more computer-intensive tasks, such as graphic design or other media development. The processor's **clock speed** measures the speed at which it can execute instructions. A **cycle** is the smallest unit of time a process can measure. The efficiency of a CPU is measured by instructions per cycle (IPC).

The bus speed and width is another factor that affects a computer's performance. As mentioned earlier, a bus is an electronic channel that allows the CPU and various devices inside or attached to a computer to communicate. The **bus width** determines the speed at which data travels and is also referred to as the **word size**. The wider the bus, the more data that can travel on it. A 64-bit bus, for example, transfers data faster than a 32-bit bus. If you have a fast CPU but the bus speed is slow, that can cause a condition called bottlenecking.

While computer manufacturers advertise performance factors such as clock speed and bus speed, other factors can affect processor performance. For this reason, you should research benchmark test results for the processor(s) you are considering. A **benchmark** is a test run by a laboratory or other organization to determine processor speed and other performance factors. Benchmarking tests compare similar systems performing identical tasks. You typically can find benchmarking information online.

Secure IT: Reducing Hardware Risks

The primary advantage of a mobile device like a laptop computer, tablet, or smartphone is that it can be easily transported from one location to another. This mobility, however, is also one of its greatest weaknesses: a thief can easily grab an unattended device. In addition, risks to your device include **malware** (malicious software, such as viruses and spyware, that can delete or corrupt files and gather personal information), dust and other debris, environmental irregularities, and power fluctuations. You can take steps to avoid each of these risks, but also should ensure you can access your data in case of theft or destruction of your device.

Avoid Hardware Theft

To prevent laptops from being stolen, you can use a cable lock. Most portable devices (as well as many expensive computer monitors) have a special security slot built into the case. A cable lock can be inserted into the security slot and rotated so that the cable lock is secured to the device (Figure 3-22). The cable can then be connected to an immovable object.

Figure 3-22 Laptop cable lock.
iStock.com/Khosrownia

To reduce the risk of theft or loss:

- Keep mobile devices out of sight when traveling in a high-crime area.
- Avoid becoming distracted by what is on the device, and limit your use of headphones and earbuds so that you can maintain an awareness of your surroundings.
- When holding a device, use both hands to make it more difficult for a thief to snatch.
- Do not use the device on escalators or near transit train doors.
- If a theft does occur, do not resist or chase the thief. Instead, take note of the suspect's description, including any identifying characteristics and clothing, and then call the authorities. Also contact the wireless carrier and change all passwords for accounts accessed on the device.

If a mobile device is lost or stolen, several security features can be used to locate the device to recover it. If a lost or stolen device cannot be recovered, it might be necessary to perform remote wiping, which erases the sensitive data stored on the mobile device. This ensures that even if a thief is able to access the device, no sensitive data will be compromised.

Maintain Computer Hardware

You should perform tasks periodically to keep your computer hardware in good condition and the software functioning properly. Failure to properly maintain a computer can result in decreasing its lifespan and/or its performance.

Hardware maintenance involves performing tasks to keep the computer's physical components in good working order. Before performing hardware maintenance, you should properly turn off the computer or device and remove it from its power source. If you are performing hardware maintenance on a laptop, if possible you should remove the battery. Failure to do so might result in damaging the computer's physical components. Recommendations that will help keep your computer and devices functioning properly include:

- Use a damp cloth to clean the screen gently. Do not use any special cleaners to clean the display.
- If you have a keyboard, use a can of compressed air to free the keyboard from any dirt and debris. Always hold the can of compressed air upright to avoid damaging the keyboard.
- If an air vent where a fan removes heat is present, make sure the vent is free of dust and debris. If the air vent is dirty, contact a trained professional to have it cleaned properly. Do not attempt to clean the air vent yourself, as it is possible that dirt and debris can enter the computer or device.

- Make sure any media you insert into the computer is clean and free from debris.
- Extreme temperatures or humidity can damage electronics. As a rule of thumb, if you are uncomfortable because of temperatures that are too high or low, your computer or device likely should not be operating in that location.
- Computers and devices that are plugged in should not be subject to power fluctuations such as power spikes or power surges. To protect from power fluctuations, consider purchasing and connecting an uninterruptible power supply or a surge suppressor. An **uninterruptible power supply (UPS)** is a device that maintains power to computer equipment in case of an interruption in the primary electrical source (Figure 3-23). A **surge suppressor** is a device that prevents power fluctuations from damaging electronic components.
- Make sure you have enough free space on your device. When you run low on available storage space, performance can quickly deteriorate. If you are unable to free enough space, consider deleting files or apps from the computer or device and storing them on the cloud.
- Keep your computer away from dusty or cluttered areas.
- Regularly back up your data, and keep your hard drive away from extreme temperatures.
- Handle removable media with care and, if possible, use protective cases when transporting the media.

Figure 3-23   Uninterruptible power supply.
iStock.com/Fahroni

Protect Computer Equipment

Protecting a computer from a cyberattack is important, but all that effort is useless if the computer has been damaged by dropping it or by a lightning strike, if the hard drive has failed, or if the computer itself is stolen. This means that an overall protection scheme should include the necessary steps to protect the computer equipment.

Protecting Computers from Electrical Problems   Although the electrical power that comes into your home, school, or place of work is generally constant in its "force" (voltage), there may be occasional increases or decreases that can impact sensitive electrical devices, particularly computers. These electrical changes are listed in Table 3-5.

Table 3-5   Electrical Changes

Electrical Change	Explanation
Blackout	Total loss of power
Brownout	Drop in voltage lasting minutes or hours
Spike	Very short duration of voltage increase
Surge	Short duration of voltage increase
Noise	Unwanted high-frequency energy

A **surge protector** can defend computer equipment from spikes, surges, and noise. **Noise** is an electrical disturbance that can degrade communications. A surge protector lies between the computer and the electrical outlet and absorbs any electrical change so that it does not reach the computer equipment.

Restore a Device

If you are experiencing a problem with your computer or device, you might need to take corrective actions such as restoring the operating system or correcting display problems.

If you are experiencing a problem with your operating system, often characterized by programs and apps not properly starting, persistent error messages, or slow performance, you should consider restoring the operating system. Before you attempt to restore the operating system, you should copy all personal files to a separate storage device, such as a USB flash drive or external hard drive. When you **restore** an operating system, you are reverting all settings back to their default, or migrating back to the operating system's previous version. To restore your operating system, review the help documentation and follow the specified steps (Figure 3-24). You should still back up your files as a preventative measure.

If you experience problems with your display device, such as it not displaying video output properly, make sure any external monitor or display device is properly connected. If you still experience problems, the video card

Figure 3-24   Windows includes a feature to restore your operating system.

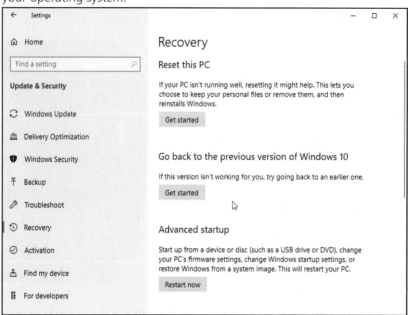

might be defective. The **video card** is a circuit board that processes image signals. Consider taking the computer to a professional for repair.

If you are experiencing issues with other accessories or peripheral devices, you may need to update the device driver.

Perform Data Backups

One of the most important preventative measures is to create data backups on a regular basis. Creating a **data backup** means copying files from a device, such as a computer's hard drive, that are then stored in a remote location, such as the cloud. Data backups can protect against hardware malfunctions, user error, software corruption, and natural disasters. They can also protect against cyberattacks because they can restore your data after an attack or malfunction.

Online backup services use special software on the computer to monitor what files have changed or have been created; these then are automatically uploaded to a cloud server. Because these backups are performed automatically and stored at a remote location, these online backup services provide the highest degree of protection to most users. You can schedule your online backup service to run at certain times of the day, such as overnight, so as not to slow down your device during work or school hours.

Sometimes, however, situations arise when an online backup service may not be the right choice, such as when only a slow Internet connection is available. In that case, you can perform your own backup from the hard drive to another medium and then store that medium in a remote location. Modern operating systems can perform these backups, and third-party software is also available.

Protect Mobile Devices   Numerous types of attacks are directed toward mobile devices. Several of the most common attacks are directed toward wireless networks that support these devices.

A Wi-Fi network is technically known as a wireless local area network (WLAN). Devices such as tablets, laptop computers, smartphones, and wireless printers that are within range of a centrally located connection device can send and receive information using radio frequency (RF) transmissions at high speeds.

The central connection devices needed for a home-based Wi-Fi network usually are called **wireless routers** (Figure 3-25). The wireless router acts as the "base station" for the wireless devices, sending and receiving wireless signals between all devices, as well as providing the

Figure 3-25   Wireless router.

iStock.com/Towfiqu Ahamed

"gateway" to the external Internet. The router connects the user's modem to the Internet.

Wi-Fi networks are vulnerable to several risks, such as:

- Reading wireless transmissions. Usernames, passwords, credit card numbers, and other information sent over the Wi-Fi network could be easily seen by an attacker.
- Viewing or stealing computer data. An attacker who can connect to a home Wi-Fi network could access any folder that has file sharing enabled on any computer on the network. This essentially provides an attacker full access to view or steal sensitive data from all computers on the network.
- Injecting malware. Attackers could inject trojans, viruses, and other malware onto the user's computer.
- Downloading harmful content. In several instances, attackers have accessed a home computer through an unprotected Wi-Fi network, downloaded child pornography to the computer, and then turned that computer into a file server to distribute the content. When authorities traced the files back to that computer, the unsuspecting owner was arrested and their equipment confiscated.

Security concerns also arise when using a public Wi-Fi network in a coffee shop, airport, or school campus. First, these networks are rarely protected (to allow easy access by users), so attackers can read any wireless transmissions sent to and from the user's device. In addition, an attacker may set up what is referred to as an evil twin, which is another computer designed to mimic an authorized Wi-Fi device. A user's mobile device may unknowingly connect to this evil twin instead of the authorized device so that attackers can receive the user's transmissions or directly send malware to the user's computer.

When using any public Wi-Fi, be sure you are connecting to the approved wireless network. Also limit the type of activity you do on public networks to simple web surfing or watching online videos. Accessing online banking sites or sending confidential information that could be intercepted is not a good idea.

Configuring your own Wi-Fi wireless router to provide the highest level of security is an important step.

❓ Consider This

How can you safely use mobile devices in public areas?
Cognitive psychologists have studied the effects of inattentional blindness, which occurs when a person's attention is diverted while performing a natural activity, such as walking. Diverted attention is particularly pronounced when people are using a mobile device, especially with headphones or earbuds. Technology-related inattentional blindness is also called digital distraction. Using technology responsibly and safely can prevent theft and injuries. Emergency room reports indicate that distracted walking accidents are on the rise, especially when people trip over cracks in sidewalks or run into fixed objects, such as parked cars and telephone poles. Keep your head up and stay aware of your surroundings. Have you ever fallen or run into anything while using a device? What other steps can you take to ensure this does not happen to you?

Internal, External, and Cloud-Based Storage Solutions

When using a computer, you inevitably will need to store files that you either download or create. Various storage solutions exist, each with its own set of strengths and weaknesses.

When using a computer, the most common storage medium is the internal **hard drive** (Figure 3-26). Hard drives either can store data magnetically, or they can use solid-state storage. Internal hard drives are installed in the computer you are using. For example, if you are creating a file on your work computer and store it on an internal hard drive, you will not be able to access the file from a different computer unless you copy the file to the other computer either by using an external hard drive, USB flash drive, or sending it electronically. Magnetic hard disk drives (HDDs) typically have greater storage capacity and are less expensive than their solid-state equivalents but have several moving parts, making it inadvisable to move the computer while they are running. A **solid-state drive** (SSD) is a hard drive without moving parts and is faster and more durable than magnetic drives. Solid-state drives often are used on mobile devices, such as laptops and tablets, and are available in various physical sizes.

In addition to storing data and information on an internal hard drive, you also can store it on an external hard drive.

Figure 3-26 Hard disk drive.
iStock.com/Gilmanshin

An **external hard drive** can add storage capacity to your computer, is housed in a separate case, and typically connects to your computer using a USB cable (Figure 3-27). Similar to internal hard drives, external hard drives can use either magnetic or solid-state technology. External hard drives also can be transported from one computer to another, so if you are working on a file and save it to the external hard drive, you can connect the drive to a different computer to continue working on that same file.

Optical media use laser technology for storage and playback, and include CDs, DVDs, and Blu-ray discs (BDs), but their use as storage media is declining. Optical media were once widely used to distribute installation files for programs and apps, but saving files to optical media required special software or capabilities within the operating system. While optical media is easy to transport, if the discs get damaged, you might not be able to access your stored files. Instead of optical discs, many individuals now use USB flash drives, external hard drives, and cloud storage to transport files.

Cloud storage involves storing electronic files on a remote server connected to the Internet, not on a local computer, a practice that is called storing data on the

Figure 3-27 USB cable.
iStock.com/Valeriy Lushchikov

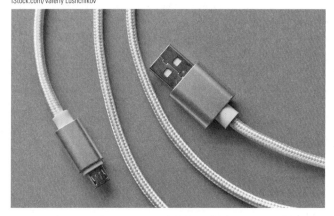

Figure 3-28 Cloud storage.
iStock.com/Lvcandy

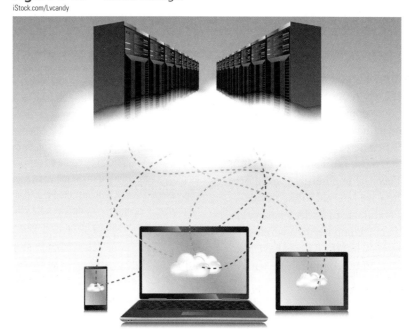

cloud. Cloud storage enables you to store your files remotely on servers that could be in a different city, state, or part of the world. Storing files to and retrieving files from cloud storage typically requires only a computer or mobile device with an Internet connection (Figure 3-28). With cloud storage, you might not require as much storage on your computer because you can store your files remotely. Cloud storage companies host and maintain the servers and provide access to your files.

 Consider This

What are some advantages of cloud storage?
Reasons users subscribe to cloud storage include accessing files on the Internet from any computer or device. Cloud-based files can be shared with others easily by providing them a link to the location. You also can store large audio files without downloading them, as well as store off-site backups of your data. What data do you keep on the cloud? How do you ensure its security? Have you shared files over the cloud with others? What issues did/could arise from file sharing?

Network Hardware

Wherever you go, you most likely will encounter and interact with some type of network. Whether it be a network that supports your cell phone, a wireless network at home or in a coffee shop that lets you browse the web and check your email, or an enterprise network connecting thousands of users, all networks have the same basic characteristics and hardware.

Networks allow computers to share resources, such as hardware, software, data, and information. A network requires a combination of hardware and software to operate. Smaller networks usually require simple hardware and can rely on the operating system's features to connect to other devices on the network, while larger networks typically require more sophisticated hardware and software.

Network Connection Components

Devices on a network, also called **nodes**, might include computers, tablets, mobile phones, printers, game consoles, and smart home devices. Most networks also include additional components, such as hubs, switches, and routers. These devices help connect multiple devices and facilitate the connections among the devices that are communicating. A **hub** is a device that provides a central point for cables in a network and transfers all data to all devices. A **switch** is similar to a hub in that it provides a central point for cables in a network; however, it transfers data only to the intended recipient. Switches are used more frequently today than hubs. A **router** is a device that connects two or more networks and directs, or routes, the flow of information along the networks. Routers also can be used to connect computers to the Internet, so that multiple users can share a connection. For example, you might have a router installed at your house to which all devices connect, and the router is typically connected with a wire or cable to a device called a modem, which provides the Internet connectivity. Many routers used at home are wireless routers, which provide wireless network access to compatible devices. A **modem** is a communications device that connects a communications channel, such as the Internet, to a sending or receiving device, such as a computer. The modem connects your network to the Internet through an Internet Service Provider (ISP). Most ISPs offer broadband connectivity capable of transmitting large amounts of data at high speeds.

Network Communication Devices

Creating a network requires two or more devices that need to communicate, a way to communicate, and the infrastructure necessary to facilitate the communication. For a computer to connect to a network, it should have a network interface card. A **network interface card (NIC)** is a circuit board that connects a computer to a wired or wireless network. NICs often are internal to the device. Some NICs can connect a computer to a wired network, while other NICs can connect a computer to a wireless network. Some wireless network interface cards have a visible antenna that is used to better communicate with the wireless network.

As discussed previously, a modem connects a network to the Internet. Most of today's modems are digital, which means that they send and receive data to and from a digital line. Cable and DSL (digital subscriber line) are two common types of digital modems. The type of modem required for your network will depend on your ISP. A cable modem sends and receives digital data over a cable TV connection. The cable modem may be part of a set-top cable box, or it may be a separate device. A DSL modem uses existing standard copper telephone wiring to send and receive digital data.

Some modems also function as a wired and/or wireless router. For example, if you have a cable modem that you connect to your home's cable television lines, you might also be able to connect multiple wired and wireless devices if the cable modem also functions as a router (Figure 3-29).

Figure 3-29 Modems can connect many devices to the Internet.
iStock.com/Pictafolio

What are the ethical responsibilities of a network administrator?
Network administrators control the functions of, provide access to, and maintain a network. This means that they may have access to every file and email message that exists on a company or organization's server. In some cases, the company may request the administrator to monitor network activity to ensure that employees are following rules, such as not sharing sensitive company information or visiting unauthorized websites during company time. The ethical line between following these requests and respecting employees' privacy can be difficult to manage. At times, a network administrator may come across personal information about an employee and will need to decide what their role in reporting this is. If you were a network administrator, would you feel comfortable monitoring employees' activities? Why or why not? What would you do if you found out something disturbing about another person while doing your job?

Inside the Case

Whether you are a home user or a business user, you most likely will purchase a new computer or mobile device or upgrade an existing computer at some time in the future. Thus, you should understand the purpose of each component in a computer or mobile device.

Cases

Computers and mobile devices include components that are used for input, processing, output, storage, and communications. Many of these components are inside the case that contains and protects the electronics of the computer or mobile device from damage. These cases, which are made of metal or plastic, are available in a variety of shapes and sizes. Desktop cases are separate from the monitor. On most laptops, the case is under the keyboard. With tablets and smartphones, the case is behind the display. The case on wearable devices (such as smartwatches), portable media players, digital cameras, and handheld game devices typically consumes the entire device and houses the display and input devices.

At some point, you might have to open the case on a desktop or access panels on a laptop to replace or install a new electronic component; otherwise, you will need to hire a professional to assist with this task. For this reason, you should be familiar with the electronic components inside the case (Figure 3-30).

Motherboard Components   Many electronic components, such as the processor and memory, attach to the motherboard; others are built into it (Figure 3-31). On desktop and laptop computers, the circuitry for the processor, memory, and other components reside on a computer chip(s). A computer **chip** is a

Figure 3-30   Typical components of a higher-end desktop and laptop.

Saiko3p/Shutterstock.com; Phoopanotpics/Fotolia LLC; iStock.com/Maisarau; Gilmanshin/Shutterstock.com; iStock.com/RAW_group; Jiri Pavlik/Shutterstock.com; Raw Group/Shutterstock.com; iStock.com/RAW_group; iStock.com /smuay; iStock.com/Tatiana Popova; iStock.com/lolik; iStock.com/PeterPal; iStock.com/vetkit

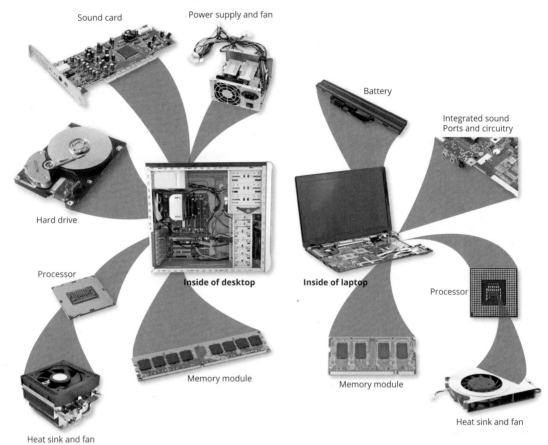

Figure 3-31   A desktop and laptop motherboard.

Courtesy of Gigabyte; iStock.com/RAW_group

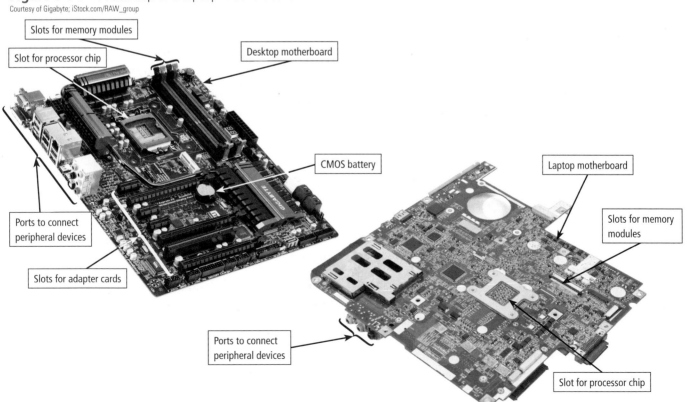

small piece of semiconducting material, usually silicon, on which integrated circuits are etched. An **integrated circuit** contains many microscopic pathways capable of carrying electrical current. Each integrated circuit can contain millions or even billions of elements such as resistors, capacitors, and transistors. A **transistor** can act as an electronic switch that opens or closes the circuit for electrical charges.

Most chips are no bigger than one-half-inch square. Manufacturers package chips so that the chips can be attached to a circuit board, such as a motherboard.

The System Clock   The processor relies on a small quartz crystal circuit called the **system clock** to control the timing of all computer operations. Just as your heart beats at a regular rate to keep your body functioning, the system clock generates regular electronic pulses, or ticks, that set the operating pace of components of the system unit.

Each tick equates to a **clock cycle**. Processors today typically are **superscalar**, which means they can execute more than one instruction per clock cycle.

Current personal computer processors have clock speeds in the gigahertz range. Giga is a prefix that stands for billion, and a **hertz** is one cycle per second. Thus, one **gigahertz (GHz)** equals one billion ticks of the system clock per second. A computer that operates at 3 GHz has 3 billion (giga) clock cycles in one second (hertz).

The faster the clock speed, the more instructions the processor can execute per second. The speed of the system clock is just one factor that influences a computer's performance. Other factors, such as the type of processor chip, amount of cache, memory access time, bus width, and bus clock speed, are discussed later in this module.

Processor Cooling   Processor chips for laptops, desktops, and servers can generate quite a bit of heat, which could cause the chip to malfunction or fail. Although the power supply on some computers contains a main fan to generate airflow, today's personal computer processors often require additional cooling. Some computer cases locate additional fans near certain components, such as a processor, to provide additional cooling. Heat sinks, liquid cooling technologies, and cooling pads often are used to help further dissipate processor heat.

A **heat sink** is a small ceramic or metal component with fins on its surface that absorbs and disperses heat produced by electrical components, such as a processor. Many heat sinks have fans to help distribute air dissipated by the heat sink. Some heat sinks are packaged as part of a processor chip. Others are installed on the top or the side of the chip.

Some computers use liquid cooling technology to reduce the temperature of a processor. **Liquid cooling technology** uses a continuous flow of fluid(s), such as water and glycol, in a process that transfers the heated fluid away

from the processor to a radiator-type grill, which cools it, and then returns the cooled fluid to the processor.

Laptop users sometimes use a cooling pad to help further reduce the heat generated by their computer. A **cooling pad** rests below a laptop and protects the computer from overheating; it also protects the user's lap from excessive heat. Some cooling pads contain a small fan to transfer heat away from the laptop. These types of cooling pads often draw power from a USB port. Instead of using power, other pads absorb heat through a conductive material inside the pad.

The Arithmetic Logic Unit

The arithmetic logic unit (ALU) performs arithmetic, comparison, and other operations. Arithmetic operations include basic calculations, such as addition, subtraction, multiplication, and division. Comparison operations involve comparing one data item with another to determine whether the first item is greater than, equal to, or less than the other item.

Depending on the result of the comparison, different actions may occur. For example, to determine if an employee should receive overtime pay, software instructs the ALU to compare the number of hours an employee worked during the week with the regular time hours allowed (e.g., 40 hours). If the hours worked exceed 40, for example, software instructs the ALU to perform calculations that compute the overtime wage.

Machine Cycle

For every instruction, a processor repeats a set of four basic operations, which comprise a **machine cycle** (Figure 3-32).

- **Fetching** is the process of obtaining a program or an application instruction or data item from memory.
- **Decoding** refers to the process of translating the instruction into signals the computer can execute.
- **Executing** is the process of carrying out the commands.
- **Storing**, in this context, means writing the result to memory (not to a storage medium).

In some computers, the processor fetches, decodes, executes, and stores only one instruction at a time. With others, the processor fetches a second instruction before the first instruction completes its machine cycle, resulting in faster processing. Some use multiple processors simultaneously to increase processing times.

Registers   A processor contains small, high-speed storage locations, called **registers**, that temporarily hold data and instructions. Registers are part of the processor, not part of memory or a permanent storage device. Processors have many different types of registers, each with a specific storage function. Register functions include storing the location from where an instruction was fetched, storing an

Figure 3-32   The steps in the machine cycle.

iStock.com/sweetym; iStock.com/manley099

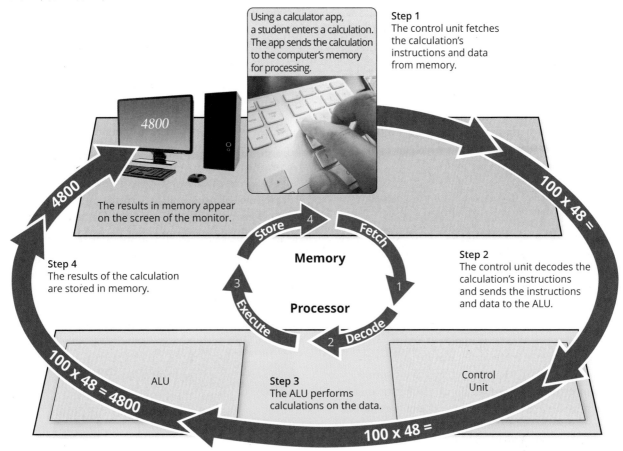

Using a calculator app, a student enters a calculation. The app sends the calculation to the computer's memory for processing.

Step 1
The control unit fetches the calculation's instructions and data from memory.

Step 4
The results of the calculation are stored in memory.

The results in memory appear on the screen of the monitor.

Step 2
The control unit decodes the calculation's instructions and sends the instructions and data to the ALU.

Step 3
The ALU performs calculations on the data.

Memory

Processor

Store   Fetch   Execute   Decode

ALU   Control Unit

100 x 48 =

100 x 48 = 4800

4800

instruction while the control unit decodes it, storing data while the ALU calculates it, and storing the results of a calculation.

❓ Consider This

Why is it important to know the inner components of your devices?

You many not embark on a career in hardware repair, but every user should have a basic knowledge of the parts of a computer or device, as well as understand how they work together. Troubleshooting, selecting, upgrading, and disposing of hardware all requires you to understand what goes on under the device's case. Have you ever explored the inside of a computer or device? If so, for what purpose? What have you learned that will help you when you go to select your next device?

How To: Protect Yourself When Using Devices

In addition to the hazards related to the safety of your information and hazards to the environment from toxic electronic components, another type of hazard exists. This is the hazard of technology to your physical health as well as your behavioral and social well-being.

Define and Prevent Risks to Physical Health

How frequently do you use your smartphone? It is probably more often than you think. Although it varies by age, according to some estimates younger users check their smartphone 86 times each day. And most of the time users are on their smartphones, they are doing something else as well.

Although people might not use a personal computer with the same frequency or in the same way as they do a smartphone, nevertheless the amount of time spent on a computer for most people is measured in the thousands — or even tens of thousands — of hours per year. And any activity at which a person spends that much time is very likely to put a strain on the physical body.

Many users of technology devices report aches and pains associated with repeated and long-term usage of the devices, known as **repetitive strain injury (RSI)**. RSI impacts your muscles, nerves, tendons, and ligaments. RSI most often affects the upper parts of the body, including:

- Elbows
- Forearms
- Hands
- Neck
- Shoulders
- Wrists

Table 3-6   Causes and Examples of RSI

Cause	Description	Example
Repetitive activity	Repeating the same activity over a lengthy time period	Typing on a keyboard for multiple hours every day over several years
Improper technique	Using the wrong procedure or posture	Slouching in a chair
Uninterrupted intensity	Performing the same high-level activity without frequent periods of rest	Working at a computer all day with no breaks

RSI has a variety of symptoms, including the following:

- Aching
- Cramp
- Numbness
- Pain
- Stiffness
- Tenderness
- Throbbing
- Tingling
- Weakness

RSI most often is caused by three factors. Table 3-6 lists the causes, descriptions, and examples of RSI.

Most computer users suffer from RSI that is brought about through using an improper technique for sitting at a computer. Incorrect posture indicators include users not sitting up straight in the chair, users being too close to the computer screen, and glare from the window behind them reflecting off the screen. Being too close to a screen or looking at screens without regular breaks can cause eyestrain.

To prevent RSI, your workplace should be arranged correctly. **Ergonomics** is an applied science that specifies the design and arrangement of items that you use so that you and the items interact efficiently and safely. Figure 3-33 shows the correct ergonomic posture and techniques for sitting while working on a computer. These include:

- Arms. The arms are parallel to the floor at approximately a 90-degree angle.
- Eyes. The distance to the screen is 18–28 inches from the eyes, and the viewing angle is downward at about 20 degrees to the center of the screen.
- Feet. The feet are flat on the floor. Use a proper chair with adjustable height and multiple legs for stability.

Many users opt for standing desks to eliminate some of the health risks from sitting all day (Figure 3-34).

Figure 3-34   Standing at your desk can reduce RSIs and neck strain.
istock.com/wavebreakmedia

Figure 3-33   Ergonomic sitting setup.
Science Photo Library/Alamy Stock Photo

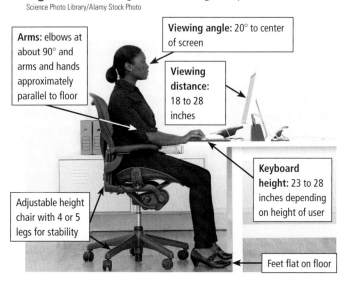

Arms: elbows at about 90° and arms and hands approximately parallel to floor

Viewing angle: 20° to center of screen

Viewing distance: 18 to 28 inches

Keyboard height: 23 to 28 inches depending on height of user

Adjustable height chair with 4 or 5 legs for stability

Feet flat on floor

Define and Prevent Risks to Behavioral Health

Just as there are hazards to physical health from using digital devices, there also are behavioral health hazards. These hazards are sometimes more difficult to observe but are every bit as serious as RSI and other physical hazards.

One behavioral hazard is **technology addiction**, which occurs when a user is obsessed with using a technology device and cannot walk away from it without feeling extreme anxiety. Because near-constant use of technology has become the norm, whether it is a toddler playing a game on a tablet, a teenager locked away in a bedroom tied to a laptop, or an adult buried in a phone at a party, technology addiction can be difficult to identify in a friend or companion, much less in yourself.

In addition to technology addiction, other behavioral risks are associated with using technology, including:

- Sedentary lifestyle. Too much time spent using a technology device often results in too little time for physical activity and can contribute to an overall sedentary lifestyle.
- Psychological development. Excessive use of technology has been associated with several psychological mental health concerns such as poor self-confidence, anxiety, depression, lower emotional stability, and even lower life satisfaction.
- Social interaction. Users who spend excessive amounts of time using technology often resist face-to-face interaction with others, and this may hinder social skill development or even cause social withdrawal.

Define and Prevent Risks to Social Health

The scientific study of how people's thoughts, feelings, and social behaviors are influenced by other people is called social psychology. While many positive factors influence your social behavior and resulting social health, negative impacts can cause serious harm to your social health.

One negative impact that can result in serious emotional harm is cyberbullying. **Doxxing** is a form of cyberbullying in which documents (dox) are shared digitally that give private or personal information about a person, such as their contact information or medical records, or information about their family. Cyberbullying is considered more harmful than general bullying for several reasons. Table 3-7 compares features of bullying to cyberbullying to show why it is so harmful.

Another social health risk is cyberstalking. In the animal kingdom, the term, stalking, is often used to describe an animal hunting its prey. Among humans, stalking is unwanted and obsessive attention or harassment directed toward another person. **Cyberstalking** involves the use of technology to stalk another person through email, text messages, phone calls, and other forms of communication.

Cyberbullying and cyberstalking are serious intrusions into a person's life. If you suspect that someone you know may be a victim or if you yourself are, you should contact local law enforcement agencies.

❓ Consider This

Is doxxing legal?

Like many technology-based crimes, doxxing laws are difficult to define and enforce. Because the Internet provides some anonymity, it can be hard to determine who the perpetrator is. No federal law specifically addresses doxxing, but laws against stalking often are used in prosecution. Also, because often the intent is to harass or intimidate the victim, harassment laws can be applied. The perpetrator also can be charged if the information is obtained illegally. Have you ever known anyone who was doxxed? What information was published? What was the intent of the crime? How was the perpetrator punished? What was/might be the impact on a doxxed individual?

Ethics & Issues: Dispose of Hardware Responsibly

E-waste is electronic waste from discarded digital devices. It often contains toxic metals, such as lead and mercury. According to the Environmental Protection Agency (EPA), Americans generate over 9.4 million tons of e-waste each year. Not only does this increase the need for more and larger landfill sites, but also discarded computer equipment can harm the environment. Computer parts contain valuable materials such as gold, palladium, platinum, and copper; however, they also contain other metals that are toxic, such as lead and mercury. These toxic metals may eventually contaminate the ground and water supply, causing harm to the environment.

When upgrading to a new smartphone or computer, a digital citizen responsibly disposes of or recycles the old, unwanted device. Before you dispose of or recycle a device, make sure all your data, communications, pictures, videos, contacts, and anything else you will need is stored on the cloud or backed up to another device so that you

Table 3-7 Harmful Features of Cyberbullying

Feature	Bullying	Cyberbullying
Seems to never end	A child may be bullied at school, but once the child goes home the bullying ceases.	Because cyberbullying comments posted online are visible all the time, to the victim the bullying never ends.
Everyone knows about it	Mean-spirited words spoken to a victim may be heard only by those who are nearby.	A cyberbully can post comments online that can be read by everyone.
May follow for a lifetime	Bullying usually stops when the person or victim leaves.	Posted cyberbullying comments may remain visible online for years and even follow the victim through life, impacting college admissions and employment.

can transfer it to your new device, then delete the backup. Methods for doing this vary by device, but most offer tools to encrypt the device's contents and reset the device to its factory settings.

Three responsible methods for disposing of your devices include the following:

- Take or send it a recycling facility or designated drop-off center, where it will be refurbished or recycled (Figure 3-35).
- Donate it to a charity, senior organization, homeless or domestic violence shelter, or other nonprofit organization that can lend or give the device to someone who may not otherwise have access to one.
- Bring it to a technology store or firm, where they will often give you credit toward a newer device in exchange for the old one, which they can then recycle or refurbish.

Figure 3-35   Electronic recycling center.

iStock.com/Baranozdemir

Evaluate the organization or facility to which you will bring the device to ensure that it follows health code regulations for the workers who disassemble and sort the materials from a recycled device. Ensure that the e-waste generated from disposing of the unwanted electronic devices and materials will not simply be sent to a developing country or underprivileged area that accepts e-waste for a profit, in spite of the negative environmental impact.

An initiative called Sustainable Electronics Management (SEM) promotes the reduction of e-waste. Table 3-8 outlines the action steps of SEM. All users should consider how they can reduce their e-waste.

Table 3-8   SEM Action Steps

Step	Action	Description
1	Buy green	When purchasing new electronic equipment, buy only products that have been designed sustainably.
2	Donate	Donate used but still functional equipment to a school, charity, or nonprofit organization.
3	Recycle	Send equipment to a verified used electronics recycling center.

❓ Consider This

Why should you care about e-waste?

Recycling a device can be inconvenient — you may have to conduct research to find a responsible recycling service or wait for an electronic recycling event to happen, but it is worth it. The potential for contamination of water and soil if you dispose of electronics locally can impact you and your community. Many developing countries, however, have become disposal sites for e-waste by illegitimate recycling companies that illegally import the devices for destruction or dismantling. The risk to the employees who work at these facilities is high, and the environmental impact can last for decades. Have you ever recycled or donated a device? What research did you do beforehand? Why do you think it is important to ensure your e-waste is ethically and responsibly disposed of?

Study Guide

The Study Guide reinforces material you should know after reading this module.

Instructions: Answer the questions below using the format that helps you remember best or that is required by your instructor. Possible formats may include one or more of these options: write the answers; create a document that contains the answers; record answers as audio or video using a webcam, smartphone, or portable media player; post answers on a blog, wiki, or website; or highlight answers in the book/ebook.

1. Define the term, hardware.
2. Describe the role of the CPU.
3. Differentiate between RAM, ROM, and virtual memory.
4. Define the term, motherboard.
5. What is a computer's platform, and how does it factor into the computer decision-making process?
6. List factors to consider when purchasing a computer or device.
7. Differentiate among desktops, all-in-ones, laptops, and tablets.
8. What is the role of a peripheral device? List examples.
9. Explain how a port and a USB hub help you connect your peripheral devices.
10. List considerations when purchasing a mobile computer.
11. List considerations when purchasing a desktop computer.
12. Differentiate between information and data, and explain how they relate to input and output.
13. Define the terms, input and output.
14. List examples of input and output devices.
15. The _____ system has two digits, 0 and 1.
16. Define ASCII and Unicode.
17. Explain how the following game controllers are used: joystick, gamepad, dance pad, wheel, and motion-sensing controller.
18. List considerations for installing hardware.
19. What is the purpose of a device driver?
20. Explain how the following are used to evaluate performance: clock speed, cycle, bus width, and word size.
21. Define the term, malware.
22. Explain how to prevent hardware theft.
23. How can you protect your hardware from damage or debris?
24. For what purposes would you use a UPS or a surge suppressor?
25. When you _____ an operating system, you are reverting all settings back to their default, or migrating back to the operating system's previous version.
26. Explain why it is important to perform a data backup.
27. Explain how Wi-Fi is used for mobile devices.
28. Describe risks from attacks on Wi-Fi networks.
29. Describe digital distraction.
30. Differentiate among internal, external, and cloud-based storage solutions.
31. List advantages of cloud storage.
32. Explain how a network relies on nodes, hubs, switches, and routers.
33. What ethical considerations does a network administrator have?
34. Describe the components inside a computer's case, and how to find the case on different device types.
35. Define the following terms: chip, integrated circuit, and transistor.
36. What is the role of a register? What is the role of a system clock?
37. How does a computer cool itself?
38. Describe the role of the ALU.
39. List and describe the four steps of the machine cycle.
40. List symptoms of RSI. What factors cause RSI, and how can you prevent it?
41. Define the term, technology addiction. List other examples of behavioral risks associated with using technology.
42. Define the term, doxxing. Describe the legal complexities with prosecuting doxxing.
43. Explain the damaging effects that can be caused by cyberbullying and cyberstalking.
44. Explain the risks associated with improper e-waste disposal.
45. How can you responsibly dispose of e-waste?

Key Terms

You should be able to define the Key Terms listed below.

all-in-one computer (3-6)
arithmetic logic unit (ALU) (3-2)
ASCII (3-11)
benchmark (3-16)
binary system (3-10)
bit (3-10)
bus (3-2)
bus width (3-16)
byte (3-10)
central processing unit (CPU) (3-2)
chassis (3-6)
chip (3-22)
clock cycle (3-24)
clock speed (3-16)
cloud storage (3-20)
control unit (3-2)
cooling pad (3-24)
cyberstalking (3-27)
cycle (3-16)
dance pad (3-14)
data (3-10)
data backup (3-19)
decoding (3-24)
desktop computer (3-6)
device driver (3-16)
digital pen (3-13)
doxxing (3-27)
earbud (3-14)
ergonomics (3-26)

e-waste (3-27)
executing (3-24)
external hard drive (3-20)
fetching (3-24)
firmware (3-3)
form factor (3-6)
game controller (3-14)
gamepad (3-14)
gigahertz (GHz) (3-24)
hard drive (3-20)
hardware (3-2)
headphone (3-14)
headset (3-14)
heat sink (3-24)
hertz (3-24)
hub (3-21)
information (3-10)
input (3-10)
input device (3-10)
integrated circuit (3-24)
joystick (3-14)
keyboard (3-12)
liquid cooling technology (3-24)
machine cycle (3-24)
malware (3-16)
microphone (3-13)
modem (3-21)
motherboard (3-2)
motion-sensing controller (3-14)
mouse (3-12)

multi-core processor (3-2)
multitouch screen (3-13)
network interface card (NIC) (3-22)
node (3-21)
noise (3-18)
nonvolatile (3-3)
optical media (3-20)
output (3-10)
output device (3-10)
paging file (3-3)
peripheral device (3-8)
platform (3-4)
Plug-and-Play (3-16)
pointing device (3-12)
port (3-8)
power-on self test (POST) (3-3)
processor cache (3-2)
projector (3-15)
random access memory (RAM) (3-2)
read-only memory (ROM) (3-3)
register (3-24)
repetitive strain injury (RSI) (3-25)
restore (3-18)
router (3-21)
scanner (3-13)

solid-state drive (SSD) (3-20)
speaker (3-14)
storing (3-24)
stylus (3-13)
superscalar (3-24)
surge protector (3-18)
surge suppressor (3-17)
swap file (3-3)
switch (3-21)
system clock (3-24)
system unit (3-6)
technology addiction (3-26)
touchpad (3-12)
touchscreen (3-12)
trackball (3-12)
transistor (3-24)
Unicode (3-11)
uninterruptible power supply (UPS) (3-17)
USB hub (3-8)
video card (3-19)
virtual memory (3-3)
voice synthesizer (3-15)
volatile (3-3)
webcam (3-13)
wheel (3-14)
wireless router (3-19)
word size (3-16)

Extend Your Knowledge

Instructions: The Extend Your Knowledge exercise expands on subjects covered in the module and encourages you to find the latest developments on these topics. Use a search engine or another search tool to locate news articles, blog entries, videos, expert discussions, or other current sources on the listed topics. List your sources, and write 3–4 sentences describing what you have learned to submit in the format required by your instructor.

- Cyberstalking laws
- Webcam safety
- E-waste recycling
- Safe volume for headphones

What did you learn that helped you better understand the concepts in this module? Did anything surprise you? How will what you learned impact you?

Checkpoint

The Checkpoint exercises test your knowledge of the module concepts.

True/False Mark T for True and F for False. If False, rewrite the statement so that it is True.

_____ **1.** Data travels in and out of the CPU through embedded wires called a motherboard.

_____ **2.** Input is information processed into a useful form, such as text, graphics, audio, video, or any combination of these.

_____ **3.** Doxxing is a form of cyberbullying in which documents (dox) are shared digitally that give private or personal information about a person, such as their contact information or medical records.

_____ **4.** A cycle is the smallest unit of time a process can measure.

_____ **5.** Volatility is an electrical disturbance that can degrade communications.

_____ **6.** A benchmark is a test run by a laboratory or other organization to determine processor speed and other performance factors.

_____ **7.** A surge suppressor is a device that maintains power to computer equipment in case of an interruption in the primary electrical source.

_____ **8.** Cloud storage involves storing electronic files on the Internet, not on a local computer.

_____ **9.** A switch is a device that connects two or more networks and directs the flow of information along the networks.

_____ **10.** The four steps in the machine cycle are fetching, decoding, executing, and storing.

Matching Match the terms with their definitions.

_____ **1.** volatile

_____ **2.** data

_____ **3.** ergonomics

_____ **4.** bus width

_____ **5.** surge protector

_____ **6.** solid-state drive

_____ **7.** e-waste

_____ **8.** modem

_____ **9.** integrated circuit

_____ **10.** joystick

a. used to defend equipment from spikes, surges, and noise

b. raw facts, such as text or numbers

c. memory that loses its power when power is removed

d. specifies the design and arrangement of items that you use so that you interact with the items efficiently and safely

e. determines the speed at which data travels

f. contains many microscopic pathways capable of carrying electrical current

g. a hard drive without moving parts

h. game controller with a handheld vertical lever, mounted on a base, that you move in different directions to control the actions of the simulated vehicle or player

i. often contains toxic metals such as lead and mercury

j. a communications device that connects a communications channel, such as the Internet, to a sending or receiving device, such as a computer

Problem Solving

Instructions: The Problem Solving exercises extend your knowledge of module concepts by seeking solutions to practical problems with technology that you may encounter at home, school, or work. The Collaboration exercise should be completed with a team. You often can solve problems with technology in multiple ways. Determine a solution to the problems in these exercises by using one or more resources available to you (such as a computer or mobile device, articles on the web or in print, blogs, podcasts, videos, television, user guides, other individuals, electronics or computer stores, etc.). Describe your solution, along with the resource(s) used, in the format requested by your instructor (brief report, presentation, discussion, blog post, video, or other means).

Personal

1. **Slow Smartphone Performance**   Your smartphone is running exceptionally slow. Not only does it take the device a long time to start, but apps also are not performing as well as they used to perform. How might you resolve this?

2. **Doxxing**   Your address and other personal information was posted on a website without your permission. What can you do to get the situation resolved?

3. **Webcam Not Working**   You are signing in to a video call with your friend, but your tablet is not recognizing your webcam. What might be wrong, and what are your next steps?

4. **Battery Draining Quickly**   Although the battery on your smartphone is fully charged, it drains quickly. In some instances when the phone shows that the battery has 30% remaining, it shuts down immediately. What might be wrong?

5. **Potential Virus Infection**   While using your laptop, a message is displayed stating that your computer is infected with a virus and instructs you to click a link to download a program designed to remove the virus. How will you respond?

Professional

6. **Excessive Phone Heat**   While using your smartphone, you notice that throughout the day it gets extremely hot, making it difficult to hold up to your ear. What steps can you take to correct this problem?

7. **Server Not Connecting**   While traveling on a business trip, your phone suddenly stops synchronizing your email messages, calendar information, and contacts. Upon further investigation, you notice an error message stating that your phone is unable to connect to the server. What are your next steps?

8. **Incompatible Device Driver**   You install a network printer to use in your small office. During the setup process, however, you get a notification that the device driver is incompatible with your network server. What might be the problem?

9. **Cloud Service Provider**   Your company uses a cloud service provider to back up the data on each employee's computer. Your computer recently crashed, and you need to obtain the backup data to restore to your computer; however, you are unable to connect to the cloud service provider's website. What are your next steps?

10. **Connecting to a Projector**   Your boss asked you to give a presentation to your company's board of directors. When you enter the boardroom and attempt to connect your laptop to the projector, you realize that the cable to connect your laptop to the projector does not fit in any of the ports on your laptop. What are your next steps?

Collaboration

11. **Technology in Energy Management**   Your science instructor is teaching a lesson about how technology has advanced the energy management field. Form a team of three people to prepare a brief report about how technology and energy management are connected. One team member should research how computers play a role in conserving energy. Another team member should research other types of technology present in today's homes and buildings that can conserve energy, and the third team member should research other benefits (such as cost savings) resulting from proper energy management.

How To: Your Turn

Instructions: These exercises present general guidelines for fundamental skills when using a computer or mobile device and then requires that you determine how to apply these general guidelines to a specific program or situation. You often can complete tasks using technology in multiple ways. Figure out how to perform the tasks described in these exercises by using one or more resources available to you (such as a computer or mobile device, articles on the web or in print, online or program help, user guides, blogs, podcasts, videos, other individuals, trial and error, etc.). Summarize your 'how to' steps, along with the resource(s) used, in the format requested by your instructor (brief report, presentation, discussion, blog post, video, or other means).

① Manage Power for Mobile Computers and Devices

Configuring power management settings on mobile computers and devices will help ensure your battery life is maximized. The following steps guide you through the process of configuring power management features on mobile computers and devices.

a. Display the settings on your mobile computer or device.

b. Click the option to display power management or battery settings.

c. If necessary, select a power plan setting to view or modify.

d. Make the necessary adjustments to the settings that affect power consumption. For example, configure the display to dim or turn off after 30 seconds of inactivity. This will allow you enough time to read what is on the screen without having to touch the screen or move the mouse.

e. Research other recommendations specific to your device, such as screen brightness or closing apps while not in use. Apply one of these changes to your device.

f. Save all changes.

Exercises

1. What power management settings have you configured on your mobile computer or device?

2. Compare battery life on your device before and after configuring power management settings. Have you noticed an improvement in battery life? If so, how much?

3. What other power management setting did you configure on your mobile computer or device? Name the source of the recommendation. Did that change make a difference in your performance?

Internet Research

Instructions: These exercises broaden your understanding of module concepts by requiring that you search for information on the web. Use a search engine or another search tool to locate the information requested or answers to questions presented in the exercises. Describe your findings, along with the search term(s) you used and your web source(s), in the format requested by your instructor (brief report, presentation, discussion, blog post, video, or other means). Additionally, reflect on the process you used to complete this activity. How did you go about choosing the tool that you did and why? Would you do anything differently in your research next time?

1 Social Media: Product Ratings and Reviews

Businesses know that using social media is an efficient and effective method of building brand loyalty and promoting the exchange of ideas. The informal communication between consumers and company representatives can help maintain credibility and promote trust. Consumers rely on social media accounts that they follow, and they are presented with ads that can help them discover information about or to purchase a brand's products or services. Twitter, Facebook, Instagram, and other social media often are used to befriend customers, give a positive feeling about services and goods, engage readers, and market new ideas. Subscribers share their opinions, thoughts, and experiences, either positive or negative, through product and service reviews.

Research This: Visit at least three similar businesses' (for example, car detailing or custom framing) online social network profiles and review the content. How many followers does each business have on each platform? Which posts are engaging and promote positive attitudes about the company and the products or services offered? How many user-generated reviews and product ratings are shown? Do any of the user-generated reviews have links within them to make purchases? How do the online social networks encourage sharing opinions? In which ways do the companies respond to and interact with followers and fans? If negative posts are written, does the company respond professionally and positively?

2 Security: Surge Protection

Surge protectors and uninterruptible power supplies offer protection from electrical power surges while your computer or device is plugged in. Since you likely have your desktop or laptop computer plugged in most, if not all, of the time, these devices are particularly vulnerable. While these surges are part of everyday life, they are more likely to occur during thunderstorms and peak energy consumption periods. These unavoidable occurrences can damage or ruin sensitive electronic equipment. The processor in a computer is particularly sensitive to the fluctuations in current. When shopping for a surge protector, purchase the best product you can afford. Typically, the amount of protection offered by a surge protector is proportional to its cost. That is, the more expensive the surge protector, the more protection it offers.

Research This: Visit an electronics store or view websites with a variety of surge protectors from several manufacturers. In addition to finding information on the seller or manufacturer's website, find independent reviews from users. Compare at least three surge protectors by creating a table using these headings: manufacturer, model, price, Joule rating (a Joule is the unit of energy the device can absorb before it can be damaged; the higher the Joule rating, the better the protection), warranty, energy-absorption rating, response time, and other features. Which surge protector do you recommend? Do each of them work with your particular computer or device? What other recommendations did you find to support your decision? Why?

3 Cloud Services Data: Providers and Mashups (DaaS)

The web has made it possible for many information providers to make business, housing, weather, demographic, and other data available on demand to third parties. Accessing online data on demand is an example of DaaS (data as a service), a service of cloud computing that provides current data over the Internet for download, analysis, or use in new applications.

Mashups are apps that combine data from one or more online data providers. Mapping mashups are popular because users can visualize locations associated with data originating from a variety of online sources, including real estate listings, crime statistics, current Tweets, live traffic conditions, or digital photos.

Research This: (1) Use a search engine to find two different online data markets. Write a report sharing the sources or focus of information each provides, the availability of visualization tools to preview data, and how developers can access or incorporate the data into their own apps and websites. (2) Use a search engine to find a popular mapping mashup based on data from one of the sources listed above, or another topic. Identify the provider of the data and the provider of the maps on which the data is displayed. What could this data be used for? (3) Use a search engine to find an app or website that will help you create your own map mashup showing locations of your online data: Facebook friends, Instagram photos, or Tweets. Take a screenshot of the mashup you made. Did anything surprise you about the mashup?

Critical Thinking

Instructions: The Critical Thinking exercises challenge your assessment and decision-making skills by presenting real-world situations associated with module concepts. The Collaboration exercise should be completed with a team. Evaluate the situations below, using personal experiences and one or more resources available to you (such as articles on the web or in print, blogs, podcasts, videos, television, user guides, other individuals, electronics or computer stores, etc.). Perform the tasks requested in each exercise and share your deliverables in the format requested by your instructor (brief report, presentation, discussion, blog post, video, or other means).

1. Technology Purchases

You are the director of information technology at a company that creates digital and print marketing materials for clients. Your graphic artists and other employees require new computers and devices. You need to evaluate the requirements of individual employees so that you can order replacements.

Do This: Determine the type of computer or mobile device that might be most appropriate for the following employees: a graphic designer who exclusively works in the office, a customer service rep who is responsible for assisting clients and often communicates using video-conferencing, and a client representative who travels to various locations and needs wireless communications capabilities. Consider the varying requirements of each, including mobility, security, and processing capabilities. Discuss various options that might work for each user, and considerations when purchasing each type of device.

2. Game Devices

You manage a youth recreation center and have been given a grant to purchase a game console and accessories, along with fitness games, for use at the center. You especially are interested in games that multiple users can play at the same time.

Do This: Use the web to research three popular recent game consoles. Choose five characteristics to compare the game consoles, such as Internet capabilities, multiplayer game support, storage capacity, television connection, and game controllers. Research fitness games for each console and what accessories are needed to run the games. Determine the goals of each game, such as skill-building, weight loss, or entertainment. Read user reviews of each game, as well as professional reviews by gaming industry experts. If possible, survey your friends and classmates to learn about their experiences with each game, such as heart rate while playing the games, any fitness goals reached, and their enjoyment of the game. Select one game to purchase, and list the costs, technical requirements, and controllers needed.

3. Case Study

Cooperative-Owned Farm Stand   You are the new manager for a farm stand that is a cooperative effort, jointly owned by several local farmers. You realize that purchasing a tablet will enable you to access information, take pictures and video, and more while visiting the fields and other farms.

Do This: You need to prepare information about tablet options to present to the owners. First, identify tablets that include a camera with video capabilities. Research the cost and quality differences among the various models. Make a list of additional features, such as video editing capabilities, as well as storage space. Explore whether apps are included with the tablet that can be used to edit, store, or organize images and transfer them to the cloud or be used on social media. Compare your findings with the camera capabilities of a recent model smartphone. Identify reasons why a tablet might be a better option than a stand-alone camera. Determine which type of tablet would be best for the farm stand's needs and the capabilities that are most important.

Collaboration

4. National Security Uses for Technology   Technology is an integral part of military operations. Many military research projects use simulators that resemble civilian computer games. Your company has been contacted by the Department of Defense for a research project.

Do This: Form a four-member team, and then form two two-member groups. Assign each group one of the following topics to research: (1) How have mobile computers and cloud computing affected issues of national security? (2) How can the utilization of biometric devices or wearable computers be integrated into civilian use? Meet with your team and discuss your findings. Determine any advantages or disadvantages, as well as any legal ramifications that may arise.

Programs and Apps: Using Apps for Productivity, Graphics, and Security

4

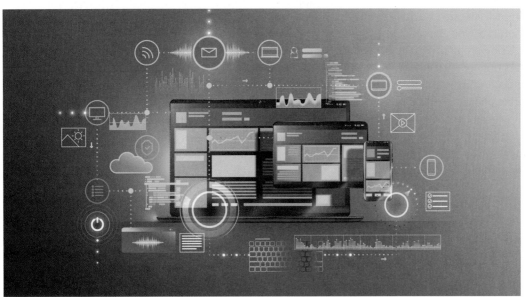

Objectives

After completing this module, you will be able to:

1 Identify the general categories of programs and apps
2 Differentiate among the ways you can acquire programs and apps
3 Identify the key features of productivity applications
4 Identify the key features of graphics and media applications
5 Explain how digital media is used online
6 Describe augmented reality, virtual reality, and artificial intelligence
7 Identify the uses of personal interest applications
8 Identify the key features of security tools
9 Identify the key features of file, disk, and system management tools

How Do You Use Programs and Apps?

Everything you do with your smartphone, computer, or tablet requires a program or app. Whether you are sending messages, watching videos, browsing the web, or checking the news, programs and apps help you accomplish these tasks. Businesses and home users use productivity apps to manage documents, spreadsheets, presentations, and databases. With graphics software, you can edit and enhance digital images and videos. Using programs and apps, you can accomplish a variety of tasks (Figure 4-1), including productivity (such as creating documents or databases), graphics and media (such as editing photos or videos), personal interest (such as getting directions or collecting recipes), and device or system management (such as organizing your folders and files or running diagnostic tools). The terms, software, program, and app are used interchangeably.

Types of Apps

Many categories of apps exist, including productivity, graphics and media, personal interest, and communications (Table 4-1). While all apps allow you to accomplish a task, the device on which you access them and the way you obtain the app can determine its capabilities. For example, **local apps** are apps that you install on your computer's hard drive; Microsoft Office is a suite of applications for word processing, spreadsheets, databases, email, and presentations that you can install locally on your computer.

Portable apps run from a removable storage device such as an external hard drive or flash drive or from the cloud. When using an external hard drive or flash drive, you connect the storage device to your computer and then run the application. When installed in the cloud, you can access portable apps from a folder in your cloud storage. Portable apps are useful when you have limited storage space on your computer.

A **native app** is an app written for a specific operating system and installed on a computer or mobile device. Native apps can take advantage of specific features of the devices on which they are installed, such as a smartphone's camera, microphone, or contacts list. Many native apps require an Internet connection to provide full functionality. Some apps can run offline and will store information on your device until they can synchronize with the cloud.

Web apps are programs that you access via the Internet using a browser on a computer or mobile device. Because these programs run over the Internet, web apps often offer collaboration features and store the files or documents you create in the cloud. Microsoft Office 365 and Google's G Suite are web-based productivity applications for creating documents, spreadsheets, presentations, email, and calendars.

Apps that you access on a smartphone or tablet are called **mobile apps**. Usually you download and install these from your device's app store. Many people use

Figure 4-1   People use a variety of apps.

GoSource: Google, Inc.; Source: Flipboard; Source: Canva

Table 4-1   Programs and Apps by Category

Category	Types of Programs and Apps	
Productivity (business and personal)	• Word processing • Presentation • Spreadsheet • Database • Note taking • Calendar and contact management • Project management	• Accounting • Personal finance • Legal • Tax preparation • Document management • Support services • Enterprise computing
Graphics and media	• Computer-Aided Design (CAD) • Desktop publishing • Paint/Image editing • Photo editing and photo management • Clip Art/Image gallery	• Video and audio editing • Multimedia and website authoring • Media player • Augmented and virtual reality
Personal interest	• Lifestyle • Mapping • Medical	• Entertainment • Convenience • Education
Communications	• Blog • Browser • Chat Room • Online discussion • Email	• File transfer • Internet phone • Internet messaging • Mobile messaging • Videoconference
Security	• Personal firewall • Antivirus	• Malware removers • Internet filters
File, disk, and system management	• File manager • Search • Image viewer • Uninstaller • Disk cleanup	• Screen saver • File compression • PC maintenance • Backup and Restore • Power Management

mobile apps to increase their personal productivity while on the go: using mobile apps, you can check email, maintain an online calendar and contact lists, and obtain maps and travel directions on your mobile device without having to use a desktop or laptop computer. Because screens on mobile devices tend to be small, mobile apps usually focus on a single task, such as checking email, searching the web, or sending a text message. Figure 4-2 compares mobile and web apps.

Figure 4-2   Mobile and web apps.

Dny3d/Fotolia LLC; Mipan/Fotolia LLC

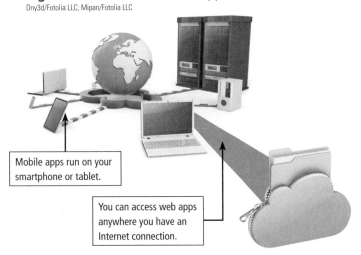

Mobile apps run on your smartphone or tablet.

You can access web apps anywhere you have an Internet connection.

Figure 4-3   Amazon's native app (left) and web app (right).
Source: Amazon.com.Inc.

A native web app can access your phone's camera or microphone to help you specify items to purchase.

A mobile web app runs in a mobile browser. The web address appears in the address bar.

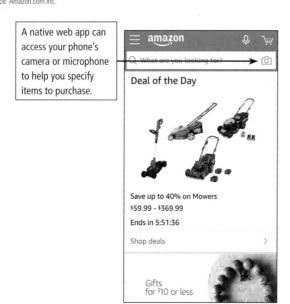
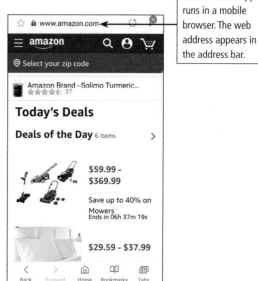

Some apps are available as both native and web apps. Figure 4-3 shows native and web versions of Amazon's mobile shopping app. The native app allows you to search for an item to purchase by taking a photo of a product or its bar code with your device's camera or tapping the microphone to speak the names of items to add to your shopping cart. The mobile web app runs in a browser, as shown by the web address in the search bar. Both versions of the app display the same product information.

When you use a productivity app in a browser as a web app, or on your mobile device, you generally store the documents and files you create in the cloud using the provider's cloud storage service. Storing the files in the cloud makes them available to access from many devices. You can collaborate with others who can view or edit the same document.

Desktop- or laptop-installed versions of the apps generally provide the most complete and advanced capabilities. Web and mobile versions are often simpler, or lightweight, and contain the more basic and popular features.

Common Features of Apps

Apps have many common features, regardless of whether they run on a computer or mobile device. They:

- are usually represented on your computer's desktop or smartphone's home screen by an icon or tile;
- can be run by double-clicking or tapping the icon or tile;
- open in a window on your desktop or smartphone;
- have menus that give you options to access different features of the program or app; and
- have buttons to click or tap to issue commands or perform actions.

Some apps are available as both a web app and a mobile app. In this case, you typically can **synchronize** the data and activity between the web app and the mobile app so that your actions, data, information, and settings will be consistent across all your devices. For example, you might look at your Gmail account on your smartphone or tablet, and access Gmail on your computer via its website, as shown in Figure 4-4. In both cases, the email messages displayed in your inbox are the same. If you delete an email message using the email app on your mobile device, it will not appear when you check email using the email application on your laptop later.

Figure 4-4   Mail apps synchronize data between mobile and web-based versions.
Alexey Boldin/Shutterstock.com

Email app installed from device's app store

Email web app on laptop runs in a browser

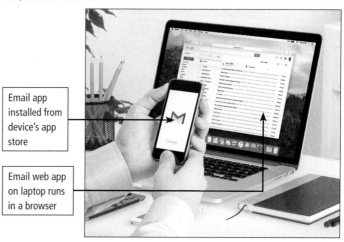

Use Mobile Apps

You touch or tap the screen to interact with mobile apps. You also can use an on-screen keyboard, which is a keyboard displayed on the screen that includes keys for typing text, numbers, and symbols, to enter information in an app on your mobile device either by tapping or swiping over the keys to type. Many on-screen keyboards assist you by predicting words and phrases you might want to type based on context, or by providing automatic corrections. Some on-screen keyboards include voice recognition capabilities so that you can speak the words to be typed. Users who need to type significant amounts of information may opt for a portable keyboard that they can connect to their smartphones using Bluetooth (Figure 4-5).

Many mobile devices come with preinstalled apps for managing email, contacts, calendars, a photo gallery, a browser, sending and receiving text messages, a camera, a voice recorder, mobile payments, and more. You can organize apps into groups by category, such as Games or Social Media, to make them easier to find. Apps are represented by icons on your screen.

The Pros and Cons of Mobile Apps
Although mobile apps are popular and convenient, they have limitations, as shown in Table 4-2.

Many mobile apps require the capability to connect to the Internet, either over Wi-Fi or using your carrier's

Table 4-2   Pros and Cons of Mobile Apps

Pros	Cons
Mobile web apps can be created quickly compared to native apps.	Mobile web apps are not as fast and have fewer features than native web apps or desktop apps.
You can access your information on the go.	Poorly designed apps can turn people away.
Voice input and smart on-screen keyboard simplify interactions.	Typing using a small on-screen keyboard can be cumbersome.

mobile network. Connectivity is crucial to today's mobile user; people want to stay connected to their office, home, and friends all the time, no matter where they are. Files that the apps use or create often are compatible between your desktop or laptop computer and your mobile device.

Most mobile apps are **platform specific**; that is, if you have an Android phone, you need to install the Android version of your app; if you have an iPhone, you need to download the iPhone version of your app. In most cases, the capabilities of different versions of the same app are comparable; each device's app has a consistent look and feel with that device's user interface and is built to run with that device's mobile operating system.

Figure 4-5   You can enter information in mobile apps using a Bluetooth keyboard or an on-screen keyboard.
Sorapop Udomsri/Shutterstock.com

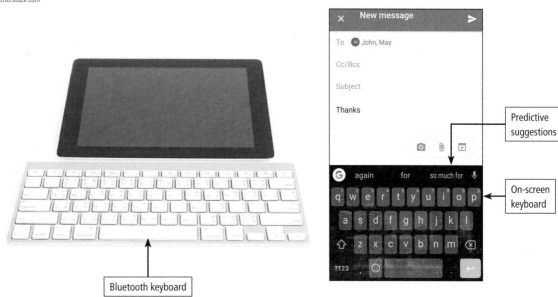

Current Trends in App Development

With the growth and popularity of mobile devices, today more people access apps on mobile devices than on laptop or desktop computers. This increased usage requires designers and developers to design apps with mobile devices in mind first and to take advantage of the connectivity and new business opportunities that mobile devices offer.

Mobile first design means that designers and developers start building apps to work on mobile devices first because these typically have more restrictions, such as smaller screens. Then, they develop expanded features for a tablet or desktop version. This approach causes app designers and developers to prioritize the most important parts of their websites and apps and implement them first. Mobile first design requires designers to streamline how people interact with their apps by placing content first and providing a simplified user experience.

Mobile web apps often have a **responsive design**, which means the app is optimized for display in a browser on a mobile device, regardless of screen size or orientation. Many app developers prefer web apps because they run on all devices. Web apps rely on HTML (Hypertext Markup Language) 5 to display information, JavaScript to manage the app's performance, and CSS (Cascading Style Sheets) to format information.

By using **cross-platform** development tools, developers can build apps that work on multiple platforms, rather than writing different code for Android or iOS devices. Some cross-platform development tools rely on HTML 5, JavaScript, and CSS to create a common web app that runs on multiple platforms. Other cross-platform development tools provide a compiler that can translate code into the different native formats for iOS and Android devices.

As the Internet of Things (IoT) continues to become more relevant, many apps can report data. Fitness trackers have sensors to track your heart rate; digital cameras have sensors for remote controls; smart home devices such as a Nest Thermostat have temperature sensors; and Google Home or Amazon Alexa smart speakers have sensors that detect the sound of a voice. All these IoT objects send or receive data that you can examine using apps on your smartphone or tablet.

When you shop online, you can use Internet banking in mobile apps. **Mobile commerce**, or **m-commerce**, apps let you use your mobile device to make online purchases of goods and services. Mobile payment capabilities are built into apps, such as Uber or Lyft for rides (Figure 4-6), and online retailers, such as Amazon or Walmart.

Figure 4-6   M-commerce allows apps such as Uber to provide payment methods for services.
Alex Ruhl/Shutterstock.com

---

❷ Consider This —————————————————————————————————

How does the convergence trend influence programs and apps?

Just as convergence affects your need for multiple devices for specific purposes, it also enables you to use apps across multiple platforms. For example, you can use the same app for email across multiple devices. Your account enables synchronization across the devices, so, for example, you can read, reply to, and sort emails from one email account from your phone and laptop. Convergence enables this type of convenience when using programs and apps. What apps do you own or use on multiple devices? What issues, if any, have you encountered with apps that you access among devices? How did/might you solve them? What advantages does convergence give you when selecting and using programs and apps?

Ethics and Issues: Acquire Programs and Apps Responsibly

Like art, music, or literature, programs and apps are protected by copyright laws. This is because programs and apps are the intellectual property of the software developer. Copyright laws protect the exclusive legal right of the software developer to reproduce, publish, or sell the program or app. Unless the creator has designated the product as public domain, it is subject to all rules and regulations regarding copyrights. Knowing the responsible way to download, install, and use programs and apps, as well as the different methods of accessing programs and apps, will help you demonstrate digital literacy.

Legal Protections for Programs and Apps

As with any copyrighted product, when you copy, distribute, download, or otherwise use without permission or payment programs and apps, you are violating the law. Punishments range from fines of a few hundred to hundreds of thousands of dollars. You also can be sent to prison. The laws apply to both individuals and large corporations, and the punishments depend on the intent and severity of the unauthorized use. For example, individuals who use an unauthorized copyrighted image on their personal greeting cards or a corporation that uses an artist's work on its website without obtaining permission are violating copyright law. These might seem like harmless acts, but they still are against the law unless you obtain permission, pay any licensing fees, and give proper credit.

Many areas are not clear-cut with respect to the law, because copyright law gives the public fair use to copyrighted materials. Fair use is only vaguely defined, legally, and raises many questions. These issues with copyright law led to the development of digital rights management (DRM). DRM for programs and apps defines restrictions regarding their use, modification, and distribution. For example, a program that you download for a fee to your computer may have restrictions on the number of devices on which you can install the program. **Access controls** are security measures that define who can use a program or app, as well as what actions they can perform within the program or app. Developers include access controls to regulate use of programs and apps, such as requiring users to verify themselves using passwords, biometrics, or other identifying techniques (Figure 4-7).

Distributing Programs and Apps

Programs and apps are distributed in a variety of forms: retail, custom, software as a service (SaaS), shareware, freeware, open source, and public domain.

- Retail programs and apps are mass-produced and copyrighted and meet the needs of a wide variety of users, not just a single user or company. Some retail software, such as an operating system, is preinstalled on new computers and mobile devices. You also can purchase retail software from local stores and on the web. With online purchases, you may be able to download purchased programs immediately instead of having to visit a retail store.
- Custom programs and apps perform functions specific to a business or industry. Sometimes a company cannot locate retail software that meets its unique requirements. In this case, the company may hire software developers to create specialized custom software. Custom programs and apps usually cost more than retail. When a company requires custom software, they must hire a developer to modify an existing program or app to meet its specific purposes, or in some cases to start from scratch.

Figure 4-7 Passwords and biometrics are types of access controls.
Mangpor2004/Shutterstock.com; Oatawa/Shutterstock.com

- **Software as a service (SaaS)** is distributed online for a monthly subscription or an annual fee (Figure 4-8). Instead of releasing a new complete version of the program or app to purchase, the company will provide updates to its subscribers that include fixes for issues or additional functionality. These updates are free to subscribers. If your subscription lapses, you no longer can access the software or receive updates.

- **Shareware** is copyrighted and distributed at no cost for a trial period. To use shareware beyond that period, you send payment to the developer, or you might be billed automatically unless you cancel within a specified period of time. Some developers trust users to send payment if software use extends beyond the stated trial period. Others render the software useless if no payment is received after the trial period expires. In some cases, a scaled-down version of the software is distributed free, and payment entitles the user to the fully functional product.

- **Freeware** is copyrighted and provided at no cost by an individual or a company that retains all rights; thus, developers typically cannot incorporate freeware in applications they intend to sell. The word, free, in freeware indicates the software has no charge.

- **Open source** programs and apps have no restrictions from the copyright holder regarding modification and redistribution; users can add functionality and sell or give away their versions to others. They may have restrictions from the copyright holder regarding modification of the software's internal instructions and its redistribution. For example, developers may be required to provide the source code when distributing an application and may be restricted from charging a fee to those who use it. Open source programs and apps usually can be downloaded from a web server on the Internet, often at no cost. Promoters of open source methods state two main advantages: a community of developers contributes enhancements to the software for all to use, and customers can personalize the software to meet their needs.

- **Public domain** programs and apps have been donated for public use and have no copyright restrictions. Anyone can copy or distribute public domain software to others at no cost.

Figure 4-8   SaaS providers such as DocuSign offer plans for subscription-based use.
Source: DocuSign

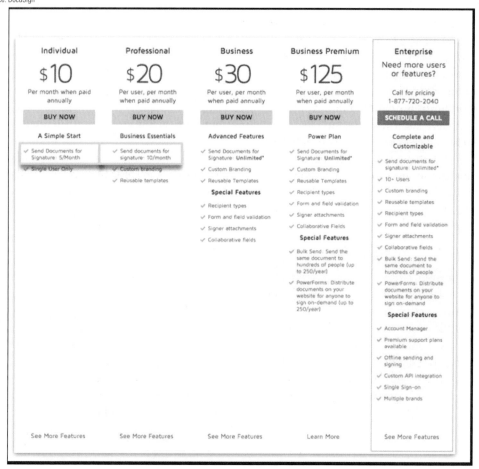

Install, Update, and Uninstall Programs and Apps

Some programs and apps are preinstalled on your computer or device by the manufacturer. You can buy additional programs and apps from a variety of sources, including your device's app store, the developer's website, online resellers, or brick-and-mortar stores. Packaged programs you get from a physical store may be stored on a CD or DVD, from which you install the program, but more likely will be a printed access code that you use to download the program or app from a website. If you purchase or access the program or app from a digital location, the software typically downloads and installs automatically.

Consider the source from which you purchase the program or app. A manufacturer's website or a well-known reseller typically provides guarantees of the program or app's legitimacy and safety. Other sources, such as unfamiliar websites or a link in an email or pop-up window, may sell programs and apps that have been modified to contain elements that may endanger your system or data, or they may be selling the product illegally.

No matter the source, be sure to check the fine print when installing any new programs or apps. Many include clauses that authorize the collection of your personal data or browsing activities (Figure 4-9). This may include sending the developer data, accessing your personal contacts (such as their phone numbers, email addresses, and social media profiles), or reporting on your browser searches or purchasing history.

During installation of software or before the first use, a program or app may ask you to register and/or activate the software. **Registration** typically is optional and usually involves submitting your name and other personal information to the software manufacturer or developer. Registering the software often entitles you to product support. **Activation** is a technique that some software manufacturers use to ensure that you do not install the software on more computers than the number for which it is legally licensed. Activation usually is required upfront, or after a certain trial period, after which the program or app has limited functionality or stops working. Thus, activation is a required process for programs that request it. Some software allows multiple activations; for example, you can install it and run it on a laptop and a desktop at the same time. Registering and/or activating software also usually entitles you to free program updates for a specified time period, such as a year.

Figure 4-9   Instagram's data policy.
Source: Instagram

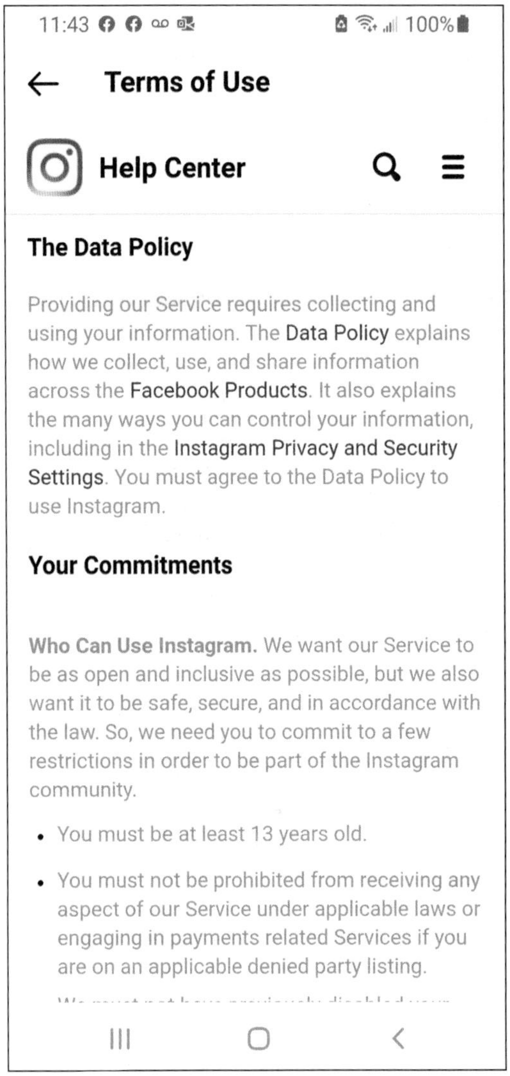

Use an App Store to Download and Install Apps   Most of the time you will visit an online store called an **app store** to locate and download apps for your mobile device. App stores offer many free apps; other apps are usually available for between $1 and $5. iPhone users can obtain apps from Apple's App Store; Google Play and Amazon's App Store are popular app stores for Android users.

Developers publish updates to their apps to app stores, along with a description of changes made. Your app store can notify you when updates are available. A good practice is to review the individual updates before you download and install them. Many people, however, opt to have their phones or tablets update apps automatically as updates become available. Usually your mobile device should be charging and connected to a Wi-Fi source before updating apps. When operating system updates are available, typically your device will send a notification, so that you can install it at a convenient time. Table 4-3 lists common mobile apps and the tasks they can help you accomplish.

When you purchase a program or app, you are purchasing a license to use the product under the terms specified in the license agreement. A **license agreement** specifies the number of devices on which you can install the product, any expiration dates, and other restrictions. Table 4-4 shows different types of license agreements.

Table 4-3   Popular Types of Mobile Apps

Type of App	Helps You To	Examples
Banking and payment	Manage bank accounts, pay bills, deposit checks, transfer money, make payments	Your bank's mobile app, Venmo, PayPal
Calendar	Maintain your online calendar, schedule appointments	Google Calendar, Outlook Calendar
Cloud storage	Store your files on the cloud	Box, Dropbox, OneDrive, Google Drive, iCloud, Amazon Drive
Contact management	Organize your address book	Contacts
Device maintenance	Optimize storage, delete unused or duplicate files, optimize device performance	CCleaner, PhoneClean
Email	Send and receive email messages from your mobile device	Outlook, Gmail
Fitness	Track workouts; set weight-loss goals; review stats from fitness tracking devices	Fitbit, MyFitnessPal
Games	Play games on your mobile device	Words with Friends
Location sharing	Share your location with friends	Find My friends, Find My Family, Google Maps
Mapping/GPS	View maps; obtain travel directions based on your location	Google Maps, Waze
Messaging	Send text messages, photos, or short videos, or make voice or video calls to your friends	Facebook Messenger, FaceTime, WhatsApp, GroupMe
News and information	Stay up-to-date on current affairs of interest to you	Flipboard, Google News, Weather Channel, CNN
Personal assistant	Search the Internet, set timers, add appointments to your calendar, make hands-free calls by speaking commands	Siri, Cortana, Google Home, Amazon Alexa
Personal productivity	View and make minor edits to documents received by email or stored on your device or in the cloud	Microsoft Word, Excel, PowerPoint, and Outlook; Google Docs, Spreadsheets, Slides, and Email
Photo and video editing and sharing	Modify photos and videos by cropping, adding filters, adjusting brightness and contrast	Fotor, Canva, Adobe Premiere Clip
Shopping	Make online retail purchases	Amazon.com
Social media	Share status updates, photos, or videos on social networking sites or view friends' posts	Facebook, Instagram, LinkedIn, Twitter
Travel	Make airline, hotel, and restaurant reservations; read and post reviews	Airbnb, Kayak, Priceline, Yelp, TripAdvisor
Web browsing	View websites on your mobile devices	Chrome, Edge, Firefox, Safari

Table 4-4 Types of License Agreements

Type	Description
Single-user or **end-user license agreement** (**EULA**)	Grants permission for one installation
Multiple-user license agreement	Lets a specified number of users access the program or app
Site license	Allows an organization to provide access to as many users as they want, either by individual installations or providing network access or Internet passwords

Update Programs and Apps   Periodically, developers make updates to programs and apps. **Updates** can prevent or repair problems, provide additional functionality, or address any security or other issues. Mobile apps typically update automatically, without requiring any action on your part. Programs you run on a desktop or laptop may require you to download updates from the manufacturer's website. Many desktop and mobile apps use an **automatic update** feature that provides the latest system software and security updates automatically. With web apps, by contrast, you always access the latest version when you run it in a browser. Updates that address a single issue are called **patches**. A **service pack** is a collection of updates combined in one package. Registering your programs and apps enables the developer to deliver and install updates automatically. **Upgrades** are new releases of the program or app and may require an additional fee to enable the upgrade to install. Upgrades might include additional features not available in the version you currently are using.

Use Programs and Apps   Once you install a program or app, you can run the program. Some run, or start, automatically when you turn on your computer or device. Others you will need to prompt to run, by double-clicking or tapping an icon on your screen. When you start a program or app, your computer or device loads, or reads and transfers into memory, all the necessary files and instructions to use it. When you finish working with a program or app, you should save any files or documents, if necessary, then close it to free up memory.

Uninstall Programs and Apps   After you no longer need a program or app, you can uninstall it. On your computer, you might be tempted to use your system's file management program to delete the folder containing the program's files. Instead, you should always use the uninstaller that is included with your operating system to ensure that all related files are removed, even if they are located in different folders; it also ensures that no files that other applications rely on are removed. An **uninstaller** is a tool that removes the program files, as well as any associated entries in the system files. Mobile devices make uninstallation easy, typically by providing an option to uninstall an app when you press and hold its icon on your screen (Figure 4-10). Uninstalling frees up storage space on your computer or device.

Figure 4-10   Tap and hold an icon on a smartphone to access the uninstall option.

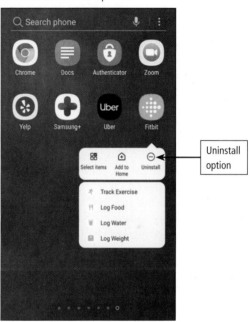

Acquire Legitimate Programs and Apps

A common infringement on copyrights is **piracy**, where people illegally copy software, movies, music, and other digital materials. Piracy is common in software, where the code and files are digital. Piracy is illegal, and you can be fined or otherwise punished if you purchase or sell pirated programs and apps. Fines typically are assigned for each act of piracy — if you illegally copy or distribute hundreds of songs, you could be fined thousands of dollars for each song.

Piracy affects the pricing and availability of programs and apps to the everyday user who follows the rules. Developers put in time and money to produce, market, and distribute programs and apps. They expect to profit from each program or license sold When you purchase or use pirated software, the developer does not get any money, and they may be forced to discontinue or increase the price of the program or app. Piracy also impacts innovation in program development. If developers do not make all expected profits, they are not motivated to keep creating new products.

To ensure you are not contributing to piracy, buy from only legitimate resellers or directly from the manufacturer, register your product to ensure it cannot be installed on another device without your knowledge, and report any illegal sale or purchase of programs or apps.

❓ Consider This

Why update or upgrade your programs and apps?
If your program or app is working without issues, why do you need updates or upgrades? The benefit of enabling automatic updates is that you ensure that you have all the latest features and security settings of a product. Many programs and apps continue to add functionality after the initial release. This enables developers to release a stable, tested version of a product and then continue to add new features and release them as they become finalized. Because hackers and distributors of malware continue to find new ways to access and manipulate programs and apps, you should make sure to accept all changes by the developer to address security. Typically, you are notified of any available updates by a pop-up window or other notification from within the program or app. Beware of an email message or pop-up window that occurs when using a browser, as those may not come from the manufacturer and could include malware. If you get such a notification, verify it by checking the developer's website before clicking any links or otherwise enabling updates. How do you ensure that your apps are updated? Have you ever received notification that updates are required? What type of functionality change have you experienced when updating apps?

Productivity Apps

Productivity apps are apps for personal use that you may use to create documents, develop presentations, track appointments, or stay organized. They can assist you in becoming more effective and efficient while performing daily activities at work, school, and home and enable you to create and modify complex projects. Productivity applications include word processing, spreadsheet, presentation, database, productivity suites, and enterprise computing.

A variety of manufacturers offer productivity apps in each of these areas, ranging from desktop to mobile to web and cloud apps. Many have a desktop version and a corresponding mobile version adapted for smaller screen sizes and/or touch screens.

Using Productivity Apps for Projects   With productivity applications, users often create, edit, format, save, and share projects.

During the process of developing a project, you likely will switch back and forth among the following activities.

1. When you create a project, you enter text or numbers, insert images, add contacts, schedule appointments, and perform other tasks using a variety of input methods, such as a keyboard, a mouse, touch, or voice.
2. To **edit** is to make a change to the contents of a document, worksheet, or presentation, such as font, spacing, and alignment, among others. Common editing tasks include inserting, deleting, cutting, copying, and pasting.
   a. Inserting adds text, images, or other content.
   b. Deleting removes text, images, or other content.
   c. Cutting removes content and stores it in a temporary storage location, called a **clipboard**.
   d. Copying places content on a clipboard, while leaving the content in the project.
   e. Pasting transfers content from a clipboard to a specific location in a project.
3. When users **format** a project, they change the appearance of its text and objects. Formatting is important because the overall look of a project significantly can affect its capability to communicate information clearly. Examples of formatting tasks are changing the font, font size, and font style (Figure 4-11).
   a. A **font** is a name assigned to a specific design of characters. Cambria and Calibri are examples of fonts.

Figure 4-11   The Cambria and Calibri fonts are shown in two font sizes and a variety of font styles.

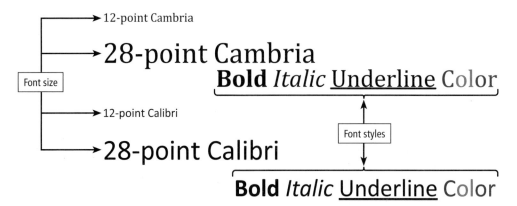

b. **Font size** indicates the size of the characters in a particular font. Font size is gauged by a measurement system called points. A single point is about 1/72 of an inch in height.

c. A **font style** adds emphasis to a font. Bold, italic, underline, and color are examples of font styles.

4. During the process of creating, editing, and formatting a project, the computer or mobile device holds it in memory. To keep the project for future use requires that you save it. When you **save** a project, the computer transfers the project from memory to a local storage medium, such as a USB flash drive or hard drive, or the cloud, so that you can retrieve it later.

5. You can distribute a project as a hard copy or electronically. A **hard copy** is information that exists on a physical medium, such as paper. To generate a hard copy, you print a project. Sending electronic files via email or posting them for others to view, on websites for example, saves paper and printer supplies. Many users opt for electronic distribution because it contributes to green computing.

Word Processing

A **word processing app**, sometimes called a word processor, includes tools for entering, editing, and formatting text and graphics. Word processors are among the more widely used types of app. You can use them to create documents and reports, mailing labels, flyers, brochures, newsletters, resumes, letters, and more (Figure 4-12). You can change font and font sizes, change the color of text and backgrounds, add photos and shapes, and use provided templates to give a professional appearance to your documents.

Key Features of Word Processing Software Although the user interface and features of word processing programs may differ, all word processors share some common key features. The files you create are called **documents**, and each document is a collection of one or more pages. When you start a word processing program, a blank document opens on the screen. The screen displays an **insertion point**, a blinking vertical line to mark your place, and **scroll bars** along the edges that let you navigate to view parts of a document that is too large to fit on the screen all at once. The word processing program offers a variety of commands and options you can use to create and format the document, such as specifying fonts, sizes, colors, and margins.

Figure 4-12 Word processing apps, such as Microsoft Word, enable you to create many different types of documents.

Source: Microsoft Corporation

Table 4-5   Uses of Word Processing

Who Uses Word Processing	To Create
Business executives, office workers, medical professionals, politicians	Agendas, memos, contracts, proposals, reports, letters, email, newsletters, personalized bulk mailings and labels
Personal users	Letters, greeting cards, notes, event flyers, check lists
Students	Essays, reports, stories, resumes, notes
Conference promoters and event planners	Business cards, postcards, invitations, conference tent cards, name tags, gift tags, stickers
Web designers	Documents for publishing to the web after converting them to HTML

With some word processing programs, you can speak the text into a microphone connected to your computer or mobile device, and the program will convert your speech to text and type it for you. As you type or speak text, when you reach the end of one line, the word processing software automatically "wraps" words to a new line. When the text fills the page, the new text automatically flows onto a new page.

Formatting features modify the appearance of a document. Editing, review, reference, and graphics capabilities enhance document content. **Document management tools** protect and organize files and let you share your document with others. Word processing programs have both business and personal uses, as summarized in Table 4-5 and Figure 4-13.

Common Word Processing Tasks   With a word processing program, you can make text easier to read and manage complex documents. Some of the tools to accomplish this include:

- **Formatting:** Formatting a document improves its appearance and readability by adding columns, borders, page breaks, and spacing.
- **Styles:** A **style** is a named collection of formats that are stored together and can be applied to text or objects.

- **Templates:** A **template** is similar to a form with prewritten text; the word processing program will prepare the requested document with text and/or formatting common to all documents of this nature.
- **Collaboration:** By storing documents in the cloud, you can share documents with several people who can read, edit, and comment on the same document at the same time.

Spreadsheet

When you want to manipulate numbers or display numerical data, a spreadsheet is a valuable tool. Keeping to-do lists, creating a budget, tracking your personal finances, following the performance of your favorite sports teams, and calculating payments on a loan are all tasks you can accomplish using a spreadsheet. Businesses often use spreadsheets to calculate taxes or payroll. **Spreadsheet apps** allow you to organize data in columns and rows and perform calculations on the data. These columns and rows collectively are called a **worksheet**. Most spreadsheet software has basic features to help users create, edit, and format worksheets. A spreadsheet file also is known as a workbook because it can contain thousands of related individual worksheets. Data is organized vertically in columns and horizontally in rows on each worksheet.

Figure 4-13   Word processing programs have both personal and business uses.

Personal uses of word processors include creating, editing, viewing, printing, publishing, and collaborating on a variety of documents, such as letters, invitations, flyers, reports, and research papers.

Business uses of word processors include creating memos, contracts, invoices, and marketing brochures.

You use spreadsheet software to create, edit, and format worksheets. To create a worksheet, you enter values, labels, and formulas into cells. Worksheets are laid out in a grid of rows and columns; they use letters or pairs of letters, such as A or AB, to identify each column, and consecutive numbers to identify each row. You can see only a small part of the worksheet on your screen at once. Use the scroll bars along the bottom or right side of the spreadsheet app to view other parts of a worksheet. You can insert or delete entire rows and columns.

A **cell** in a worksheet is the location formed by the intersection of a column and a row. For example, cell A9 is located at the intersection of column A and row 9. You can refer to a cell by its **cell address**, or location in the worksheet. A **workbook** is a collection of related worksheets contained in a single file (Figure 4-14).

Identify the Key Features of Spreadsheets   Spreadsheet software often includes many additional features, such as:

- Formatting tools to change a worksheet's appearance
- Page layout and view features to change the zoom level, divide a worksheet into panes, or freeze rows or columns, to make large worksheets easier to read
- Printing features to control whether you want to print entire worksheets or only selected areas
- Web capabilities to share workbooks online, add hyperlinks, and save worksheets as webpages
- Developer tools to add customized functions
- Tools to analyze data in a spreadsheet

Formulas and Functions   Many cells contain numbers, or values that can be used in calculations. Other cells contain **formulas**, or computation rules, to calculate values using cell references, numbers, and arithmetic **operators**, such as +, -, * (multiplication), and / (division). You can type a formula directly in a cell or in the formula bar above the worksheet.

Spreadsheet formulas always begin with an equal sign (=). When you type a formula in a cell that uses values in other cells, that cell will display the result of the calculation. The values in the calculations are **arguments** (information necessary for a formula or function to calculate an answer). If you later change any of the values in the cells referenced in the formula, the spreadsheet app will automatically recalculate the value in the cell to display the updated sum. Formulas use arithmetic operators and functions to perform calculations based on cell values in a worksheet. A **function** is a predefined computation or calculation, such as calculating the sum or average of values or finding the largest or smallest value in a range of cells. Spreadsheet apps contain built-in functions to perform financial, mathematical, logical, date and time, and other calculations.

Common Spreadsheet Tasks   Once you enter data into a worksheet, you can use several tools to make the data more meaningful; you also can apply common formatting options similar to word processing apps.

Figure 4-14   Worksheets can contain data, tables, formulas, and charts.
Source: Microsoft Corporation

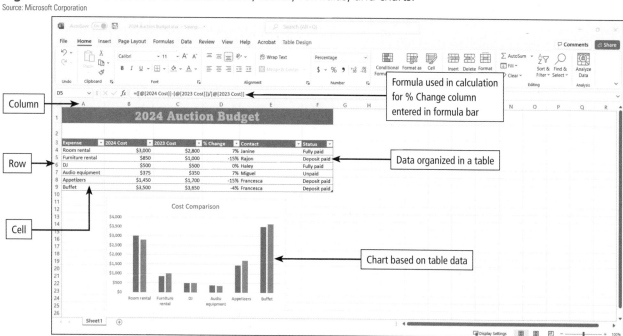

Figure 4-15 Charts help to visualize data in the worksheet.
Source: Microsoft Corporation

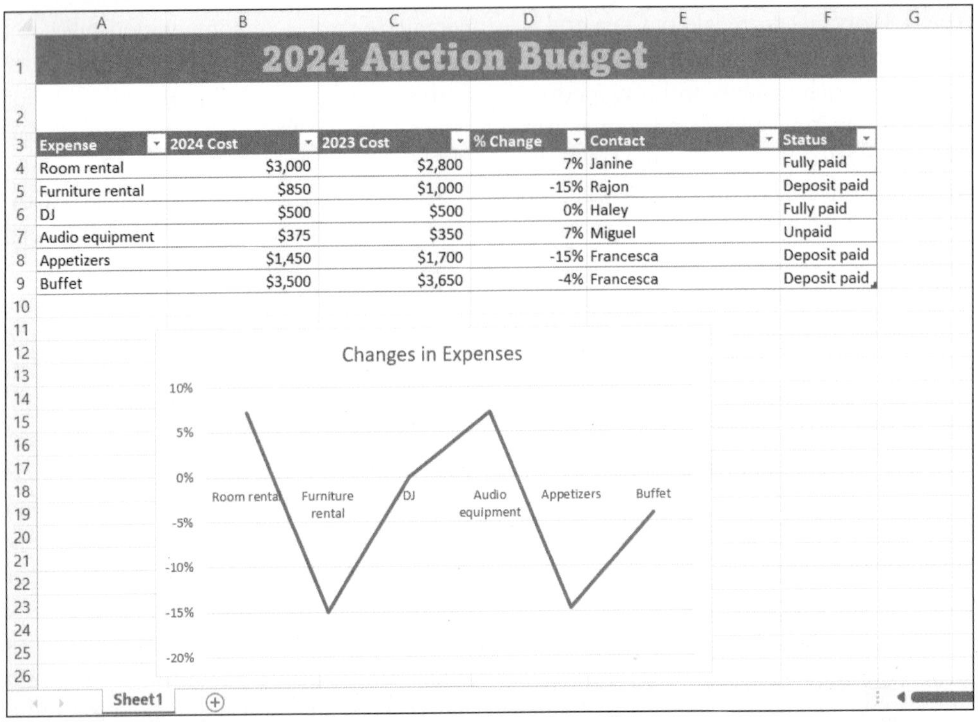

- Use **conditional formatting** to highlight cells that meet specified criteria. For example, in a worksheet containing states and populations, you might use conditional formatting to display all the population values greater than 10,000,000 using bold, red text with a yellow background.
- Sort data by values in a column to arrange them in increasing or decreasing order, or **filter** worksheet data to display only the values you want to see, such as sales associates who brought in more than $100,000 in a month.
- **Charts** (sometimes called graphs) represent data using bars, columns, pie wedges, lines, or other symbols. Charts present data visually and make it easier to see relationships among the data. You can visualize data using pie charts, bar graphs, line graphs, and other chart types (Figure 4-15).

Presentation

When you want to display information in a slide show, **presentation apps** can help you organize your content and create professional-looking digital slide shows. You might create a presentation for work or school, show slides of photos from your vacation to friends, or create digital signs. Slide shows can be printed; viewed on a laptop, desktop, or mobile device; projected on a wall using a multimedia projector connected to a computer; or displayed on large monitors or information kiosks.

A **presentation** contains a series of slides. Each slide has a specific layout based on its content (such as titles, headings, text, graphics, videos, and charts), and each layout has predefined placeholders for these content items (such as title layout, two-column layout, and image with a caption layout).

Key Features of Presentation Software As you work, you can display presentations in different views. Normal view shows thumbnails, or small images of slides, and an editing pane, where you can add or modify content. In Notes view, you can add speaker's notes with talking points for each slide when giving the presentation. You can insert, delete, duplicate, hide, and move slides within your presentation.

You can add main points to a slide as a bulleted list by typing them in a text box on the slide. You also can add graphics or images to illustrate your talking points.

Presentation apps sometimes include a gallery that provides images, photos, video clips, and audio clips to give presentations greater impact. Some presentation apps offer a search tool to help you locate online images or videos to include in your slides. Some presentation apps even offer design ideas to give your slides a more professional appearance, as shown in Figure 4-16.

Presentation apps may also incorporate features such as checking spelling, formatting, researching, sharing, and publishing presentations online.

Figure 4-16   Presentation apps provide you with templates and design ideas.

Source: Microsoft Corporation

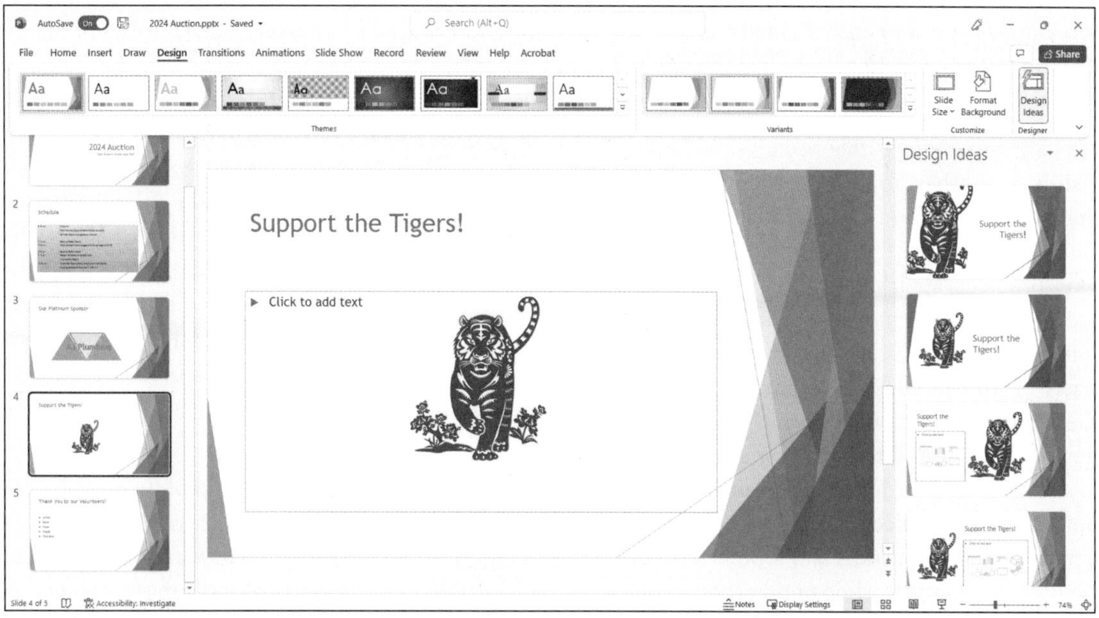

Format Presentation Content   Slides can contain text, graphics, audio, video, links, and other content, as shown in Table 4-6.

You also can select the theme, or design, for the entire presentation, by choosing a predefined set of styles for backgrounds, text, and visual designs that appear on each slide, or modifying predefined elements to make them your own. You can accomplish this by:

- Formatting text using tools like those in word processing software to choose fonts, sizes, colors, and styles, such as bold or italics
- Setting a slide's dimensions, aspect ratio (standard or widescreen), and orientation (portrait or landscape)
- Changing text direction, aligning text on a slide or within a text box, and adding shadows or reflection effects
- Resizing graphics to make them larger or smaller; rotating, mirroring, or cropping images
- Adding SmartArt graphics that display text in predesigned configurations to convey lists, processes, and other relationships
- Formatting charts and worksheets to present numerical data, like that found in spreadsheets
- Moving objects to different locations on a slide, aligning objects, and grouping objects

Table 4-6   Adding Content to Slides

Slide Content	How to Enter	Provides
Text in a paragraph or bulleted list	Click a placeholder and type, or copy and paste text from another file, or insert text from a document file.	Content; most programs offer a variety of bullet styles, including number and picture bullets
Graphics, such as line art, photographs, clip art, drawn objects, diagrams, data tables, and screenshots	Click a content placeholder, draw directly on the slide, or copy and paste a graphic from another file.	Illustrations to convey meaning and information for the slide content
Media clips, such as video and audio, including recorded narrations	Click a content placeholder and choose a file, or insert the file directly onto a slide by recording it.	Media content to enhance a slide show
Links	Click content placeholder, copy and paste links from a website or type the link directly.	Links to another slide, another document, or a webpage
Embedded objects	Click menu commands or a content placeholder.	External files in a slide
Charts	Link or embed a worksheet or chart from a spreadsheet app to a slide in a presentation.	Graphic display of data to support a presentation

Common Presentation Tasks With a presentation program, you can customize your slides by adding visually interesting effects and ensure consistency with the design. Some of the tools to accomplish this include the following:

- **Transitions** are visual effects that occur as you move from one slide to another. You can set many options for transitions, such as sound effects, direction, and duration.
- **Animations**, or effects applied to an object that make the object appear, disappear, or move, can add visual appeal to a presentation when used carefully. Presentation apps offer a variety of animations, such as entrance, exit, and emphasis, each with a variety of options.
- A **slide master** is an overall template for a presentation formatted with a theme, customized title and text fonts, backgrounds, and other objects that appear on slides in the presentation. Adding headers and footers lets you display the presentation title, slide number, date, logos, or other information on a single slide, or on all slides automatically.
- A **slide show** is a display or delivery of the content of your presentation. You might print handouts from your slides so that audience members can take notes or send a link to your slides by email message so that audience members can follow along during the presentation on their own devices.

Databases

A **database** is a collection of data organized in a manner that allows access, retrieval, and reporting of that data. With database software, you can create, access, and manage a database by adding, updating, and deleting data; filter, sort, and retrieve data from the database; and create forms and reports using the data in the database. A relational database management system (RDBMS), or **relational database**, is a database that consists of a collection of tables where items are organized in columns and rows. You can use database software to keep track of contacts, addresses, collections, and more. Large enterprises use databases to store vast quantities of data that enable us to shop online (Figure 4-17), execute web searches, or find friends on social media.

Key Features of Database Apps In a relational database, such as Microsoft Access, data is organized into tables of **records** (rows of data) and is stored electronically in a database. After opening a database, you choose options to view tables, create queries, and perform other tasks.

Each piece of data in a database is entered and stored in an area called a **field**, a column containing a specific property for each record, such as a person, place, object, event, or idea. Each field is assigned a **field name**, which is a column label that describes the field. Fields are defined by their data type, such as text, date, or number. The text data type stores characters that cannot be used in

Figure 4-17 Databases.

Odua Images/Shutterstock.com

If you shop online, you search databases of products to find what you want.

Large databases store billions of pieces of data and handle hundreds or thousands of users at a time.

When you make a purchase, a database stores your transaction information.

mathematical calculations. Logical data types store yes/no or true/false values. Hyperlinks store data as web addresses.

Tables are a collection of records for a single subject, such as all the customer records, organized in grids of rows and columns, much like worksheets in spreadsheet applications. Tables store data for the database. Columns contain fields; rows contain records. A database can contain one or more tables.

Common Database Tasks

Databases have many applications for personal use (tracking schedules or organizing contacts), small business use (process orders or tracking inventory), and large company use (customer relationship management interactions). Common features of databases include:

- Forms: A **form** is a screen used to enter data into a database. A form is made up of **controls**, or elements such as labels, text boxes, list boxes, buttons, and graphics, that specify where content is placed and how it is labeled.
- Queries: A **query** extracts data from a database based on specified criteria, or conditions, for one or more fields.
- Reports: A **report** is a user-designed layout of database content. Like forms, reports have labels to describe data and other controls that contain values.

Manage Databases   Databases are complex files. Databases with multiple users usually need a database administrator to oversee the database. A database administrator has several important responsibilities, including:

- Controlling access to the database by regulating who can use it and what parts they can see; for example, you do not want all employees to view private salary information
- Ensuring data integrity and minimizing data entry errors by controlling how data is entered, formatted, and stored
- Preventing users from inadvertently changing or deleting important data

- Controlling version issues, which arise when multiple users access the same data at the same time, so that changes are not lost or overwritten
- Managing database backup plans regularly to avoid loss or to recover damaged or lost files
- Establishing and maintaining strict database security to protect susceptible data from hacker attacks

The Role of Big Data   When you enter a status update on Facebook, send a tweet on Twitter, purchase an item on Amazon, or download a song from iTunes, each of these activities is stored in a database. These database collections, known as Big Data, can grow very quickly because of the large volume of data that users generate continuously. Amazon, for example, analyzes data from shopping patterns of all its customers to recommend products that you might like to purchase.

New technologies are being developed to manage large quantities of unstructured data, such as status updates, Tweets, and online purchases, which do not fit well into rows and columns. Storing very large data sets, such as all the tweets on Twitter or messages on Facebook sent in a day, typically involves distributing these items among several database servers in the cloud. By storing large databases in the cloud, companies easily can increase storage or processing capabilities as needed to store, access, or query the data.

Productivity Suite

Many vendors bundle their individual apps into a productivity suite. A **productivity suite** is a collection of individual related applications available together as a unit. You can share text, graphics, charts, and other content among projects you create with individual apps; you also can download additional templates for creating specialized projects. For example, you could include a chart created in a spreadsheet app as part of a slide in a presentation or as a figure in a word processing document. Table 4-7 summarizes popular productivity suites available today.

Table 4-7   Popular Productivity Suites

	Microsoft Office	**Apple iWork**	**G Suite**	**OpenOffice**
Operating systems supported	Windows, macOS or web apps	macOS, iOS, or web apps	ChromeOS or web apps	Windows, Linux, macOS
Word processor	Microsoft Word	Pages	Google Docs	Writer
Spreadsheet	Microsoft Excel	Numbers	Google Sheets	Calc
Presentation	Microsoft PowerPoint	Keynote	Google Slides	Impress
Database	Microsoft Access			Base
Email	Microsoft OutLook	Apple Mail	Gmail	
Online version	Office Online	iWork for iCloud	G Suite	
Cloud storage	Microsoft OneDrive	iCloud	Google Drive	

Enterprise Computing

A large organization, commonly referred to as an enterprise, requires special computing solutions because of its size and geographic distribution. **Enterprise computing** refers to the use of technology by a company's employees to meet the needs of a large business. A typical enterprise consists of a wide variety of departments, centers, and divisions — collectively known as functional units. Nearly every enterprise has the following functional units: human resources, accounting and finance, engineering or product development, manufacturing, marketing, sales, distribution, customer service, and information technology.

Software used in functional units is not mutually exclusive; however, each functional unit in an enterprise uses specific software, as outlined below.

- Human resources software manages employee information, such as pay rate, benefits, personal information, performance evaluations, training, and vacation time.
- Accounting software manages everyday transactions, such as sales and payments to suppliers. Finance software helps managers budget, forecast, and analyze.
- Engineering or product development software allows engineers to develop plans for new products and test their product designs.
- Manufacturing software assists in the assembly process, as well as in scheduling and managing the inventory of parts and products.
- Marketing software allows marketing personnel to create marketing campaigns, target demographics, and track campaign effectiveness.
- Sales software enables the salesforce to manage contacts, schedule meetings, log customer interactions, manage product information, and take customer orders.
- Distribution software analyzes and tracks inventory and manages product shipping status.
- Customer service software manages the day-to-day interactions with customers, such as phone calls, email messages, web interactions, and messaging sessions (Figure 4-18).
- Information technology staff use a variety of programs and apps to maintain and secure the hardware and software in an enterprise.

Figure 4-18   Customer service reps track calls and service requests using technology.

iStock.com/Alvarez

Computer-Aided Technology

Computer-aided technology involves using computers to help design, analyze, and manufacture products. In fields such as manufacturing, interior design, and architecture, people use computer-aided technology to bring their products or designs to life.

Architects, scientists, designers, engineers, and others use **computer-aided design (CAD)** apps to create highly detailed and technically accurate drawings (Figure 4-19). With CAD software, you can share, modify, and enhance drawings with speed and accuracy.

Figure 4-19   Computer-aided design helps engineers and manufacturers.

iStock.com/Gorodenkoff

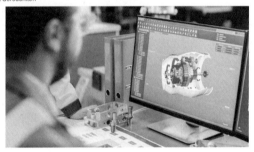

Interior designers use CAD software to model proposed room designs. Clothing designers can experiment with fabrics and patterns. Architects use CAD to prototype buildings and create floor plans. Engineers and scientists use 3-D CAD software to create **wireframe drawings** of objects, which are 3-D objects composed of lines, that they can rotate to view from many angles.

? **Consider This**

When should you use a database instead of a spreadsheet program?

Although databases and spreadsheets both store data, these programs have different purposes and capabilities. Spreadsheet programs are ideal for calculating results or creating charts from values in a worksheet. You should use a database program, however, if want to collect, reorganize and filter data, and/or create reports from the data. What experience do you have with databases and spreadsheets? What features were most useful to you with both? Have you ever tried to use a spreadsheet when you should have used a database?

Graphics and Media Applications

Digital graphics and media include still images, animated images, and audio (Figure 4-20). Digital media apps fall into two categories: those that are used to capture, edit, and create digital media, and those that play digital media. Demonstrating skills and knowledge about graphics and digital media makes you a more attractive job applicant and valuable employee. Digital graphics and media make digital content appealing and entertaining. Digital media is also an essential part of most industries. Entertainment and technology companies create and sell digital media. Educational institutions use it to communicate information and enhance learning. Health care, military, and transportation organizations use it for training. Businesses use digital media to attract and interact with customers. You can add graphics to your documents and presentations to illustrate a point or provide visual context.

In order to understand how digital media apps work, you must understand digital media basics.

Types of Digital Media

The major types of digital media include graphics, animation, video, and audio. Websites, entertainment products, and business marketing efforts often use a combination of digital media to attract, inform, entertain, and persuade viewers and listeners. If you are involved with efforts to promote a product, service, or yourself, you can use digital media to reach your audience and emphasize your message.

A **graphic** is an image or picture. A **digital graphic** is an image you can see, store, and manipulate on a computer, tablet, smartphone, or other digital device. Digital graphics can be as simple as a line drawing or as complex as a highly detailed photo or 3-D illustration (Figure 4-21). Digital media apps can be used to create, edit, and modify digital graphics.

You also can use digital media apps to create an animation. Like animations in a presentation, these types of animations are a series of images displayed in sequence to create the illusion of movement. Each still image is called a frame. Instead of storing moving images, a digital animation stores data about the color and brightness of each frame. Like animation, a video is a series of still

Figure 4-20 Types of digital media.

GaudiLab/Shutterstock.com; Violetkaipa/Shutterstock.com; Sarunyu L/Shutterstock.com; Sitthiphong/Shutterstock.com

Listen to digital music

Create and share digital photos

Watch digital animated movies and TV shows

Figure 4-21 Digital graphics.

Arbi Studio/Shutterstock.com; Brian Kinney/Shutterstock.com

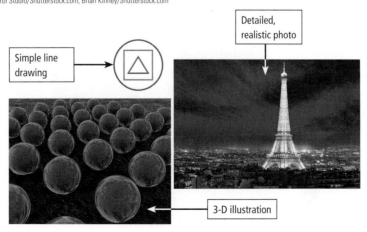

Simple line drawing

Detailed, realistic photo

3-D illustration

images played quickly enough to appear as continuous motion. While you typically create an animation by drawing illustrations, you create a **digital video** by capturing live action with a video camera.

Digital video usually includes **digital audio**, which is sound that is recorded and stored as computer data. Music, speech, and sound effects are types of digital audio.

How Computers Represent Images and Sounds

Cameras, musical instruments, and video projectors are **analog** devices, meaning they read or produce physical signals in their original form. For example, an analog tape recorder captures sound waves directly from a guitar or singer and then plays the sound waves through an analog speaker. Computers are digital devices, meaning they read and produce numeric data as combinations of 1s and 0s. A digital recorder turns the sound it captures into numbers representing tones, and then generates an electronic signal based on those numbers (Figure 4-22).

Digital media translates analog data into digital data so that anyone with a computer can create, edit, and play the media. Converting analog data to digital data also is called **digitizing** the data, which is the process of changing the data into a form that computers and other digital devices can use. That means you no longer need to be a virtuoso musician or talented artist to produce professional-quality audio and video.

Sound is produced when vibrations, such as a drumstick hitting a drum pad, cause pressure changes in the surrounding air, creating analog (continuous) sound waves. A process called **sampling** converts the analog sound waves into digital sound (Figure 4-23). The digitizing process breaks the sound wave into separate segments, or samples, and stores each sample numerically. The more samples taken per second, the higher the sound quality and the larger the file.

The quality of an audio file is also determined by its **bit rate**, which is the number of bits of data processed every second. Bit rates are usually measured as kilobits per second (kbps). As with the sampling rate, the higher the bit rate, the higher the sound quality and the larger the file.

Large files take longer to download from a website or load and play on a webpage. They also require more storage space than smaller files. If you are using an audio file in a project and can choose from varying bit rates (such as 128 kbps and 160 kbps) and sampling rates (such as 22,050, 44,100, and 88,200), choose a file that balances quality and size.

Figure 4-22 Converting analog data into digital data.
Pand P Studio/Shutterstock.com; Rawpixel.com/Shutterstock.com

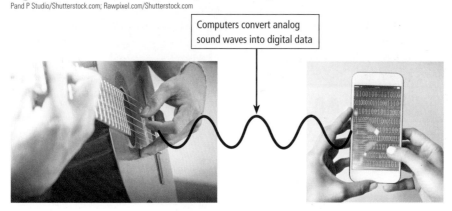

Computers convert analog sound waves into digital data

Figure 4-23 Sampling sound.
Makalo86/Shutterstock.com; Wacpan/Shutterstock.com; Marco Scisetti/Shutterstock.com; Eliks/Shutterstock.com

Microphone picks up analog sound waves and sends them to a computer

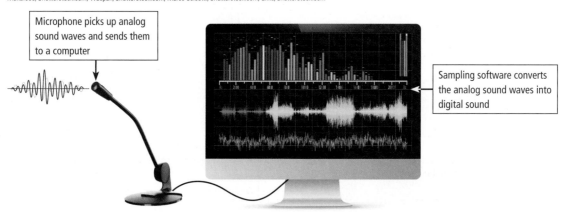

Sampling software converts the analog sound waves into digital sound

File format refers to the organization and layout of data in the file. The file name extension usually reflects the file format. For digital media files, the format determines which programs or devices you can use to open or edit the file. For example, you need a painting program, such as Windows Paint, to edit a bitmap graphic. Digital media playback devices often can play only certain formats of video and audio files. For example, you can play older iTunes songs only on an Apple device, such as an iPhone.

Digital Graphics

Digital graphics fall into two main types. Bitmap graphics (also called raster graphics) assign colors to the smallest picture elements, called pixels. Each color is assigned a binary number, such as 00 for black and 11 for white. To a computer, a bitmap image is a list of the color numbers for all the pixels it contains.

Vector graphics consist of shapes, curves, lines, and text created by mathematical formulas. Instead of storing the color value for each pixel, vector graphics contain instructions that define the shape, size, position, and color of each object in an image.

You create and edit bitmaps using graphics apps, such as Adobe Photoshop and Windows Paint. Bitmap-editing programs are also called painting programs. You use drawing programs, such as Adobe Illustrator, to create and edit vector images.

Resolution and Compression   When using graphics in your work, you should be aware of how certain properties affect quality. Resolution refers to the clarity or sharpness of an image: the higher the resolution, the sharper the image and the larger the file size.

Bitmap graphics are resolution dependent, which means image quality deteriorates as their dimensions increase. If you significantly resize or stretch bitmaps to fit a space they were not designed to fill, the images become blurred and distorted. On the other hand, vector graphics keep the same quality as their dimensions change.

On a digital camera, resolution is typically measured in megapixels, or millions of pixels. The higher the number of megapixels, the higher the resolution of your photos, and the larger the picture files; however, high-resolution photos and other complicated graphics can be difficult to copy, download, or send as email attachments, due to their large file size.

Compression makes digital media files smaller by reducing the amount of data in the files. Some types of bitmap graphics (JPEG files) use lossy compression, which discards some of the original file data during compression. Fortunately, you usually do not notice the lost data. Other types of media files (TIF, PNG, and GIF) can be compressed using lossless compression, which reduces the file size for storage. When opened and viewed, the files are uncompressed and contain all their original data.

Graphics File Formats   You can create and store bitmap and vector graphics in several file formats. Each file format is suited for particular uses. Do you need a two-color button for a webpage; vacation photos for posting on Instagram; or a highly detailed photograph that will appear in print? Each use has different requirements. You can select from the file formats shown in Table 4-8.

Table 4-8   Common Graphics File Formats

Graphic File Format	File Extension	Best Use/Notes
Bitmap graphics		
GIF	.gif (Graphics Interchange Format)	Simple web graphics and short web animations Format is limited to 256 colors; supports transparency; small file size makes it good for websites
JPEG	.jpeg or .jpg (Joint Photographic Experts Group)	Photos on the web Images have rich colors, but discard some data to reduce file size, which can affect quality
PNG	.png (Portable Network Graphics)	Logos, icons, and illustrations Images have good quality even when highly compressed; supports 16 million colors; better quality and smaller file size than GIF
TIF	.tif or .tiff (Tagged Image File Format)	High-quality photos and printed graphics Large file size is better suited for print than web use
Vector graphics		
EPS	.eps (Encapsulated PostScript)	Logos and other illustrations that are frequently resized A standard format for exporting vector graphics without data loss
SVG	.svg (Scalable Vector Graphics)	Illustrations on the web Developed by the World Wide Web Consortium (W3C); allows interactivity and animation

Table 4-9 Common Audio File Formats

File Format	File Extension	Compression	Notes
AAC and M4P	.aac and .m4p	Lossy	Apple uses these formats for iTunes downloads
AIFF (Audio Interchange File Format)	.aiff or .aif	None	Files are large; good to excellent sound quality
MP3	.mp3	Lossy	Common format for music and audio books; most digital audio devices can play MP3 files
WAVE or WAV (Waveform Audio)	.wav	None	Files are large; good to excellent sound quality
WMA (Windows Media Audio)	.wma	Lossless	Played using windows media player; also copy-protected

Digital Audio As with graphics, you can store audio files in a variety of formats, each with a specific purpose. For example, some types of audio formats are for storing music, others are for audio recordings such as Audible books, and others are for podcasts. Some formats use lossy or lossless compression to reduce file size. You can identify an audio file format by looking at the file extension. Table 4-9 summarizes common audio file formats.

To create uncompressed audio files, such as WAV and AIFF files, you convert real sound waves directly to digital form without additional processing, resulting in accurate sound quality, but very large files. Choose uncompressed audio files to capture and edit pure audio and then save them in a compressed format.

Audio files lose data when they are compressed with lossy compression, sacrificing quality and fidelity for file size. Most people, however, cannot detect any difference between uncompressed and lossy compressed audio files. Choose audio files with lossy compression (MP3 or M4P) when you are listening to sound other than music or when you want to conserve disk space.

Audio files with lossless compression have good audio quality and smaller file sizes than uncompressed audio files, but they still are larger than files with lossy compression. Choose audio files with lossless compression (WMA) if you want to listen to music with accurate audio representation.

Record and Play Sounds and Music You may want to record yourself performing a song, creating a podcast episode, or reading a voice-over (voice narration) to add to a slide presentation. To record voice-overs and save the recordings for playback on a computer, you need the following hardware and software:

- An audio input device, such as a microphone or headset
- Sound recorder software to capture the sound from the input device
- Software that can digitize the captured sound

As shown in Figure 4-24, many smartphones have built-in sound recording tools, including microphones and software, for capturing your own voice memos and narrations or the speech of other people.

After you capture and digitize sound, you can save it as an audio file and then play it back or add it to a video or presentation, for example. To play music files you download or record yourself, you also need special hardware and software, including a sound card, which is a circuit board that computers use to process sound.

Speakers play sound and can be built-in or attached as peripheral hardware to your device, either by a cable or wirelessly. Add-on speakers, which often offer higher-quality sound than built-ins, used to have bulky profiles. Today's portable micro speakers come in a range of sizes, some as small as an inch or two in height and width. They connect to your smartphone, tablet, or other devices using a wireless Bluetooth connection and can double as speakerphones for phone calls or similar audio communications. If you are in an environment such as an office or library where speakers are not practical, you can use a headset or headphones to keep the sound private.

Figure 4-24 Recording sound.
Jet Cat Studio/Shutterstock.com

You can start recording a podcast using the sound recording tools in a smartphone

You also need software to play sound. When playing certain types of audio files on a desktop or laptop, such as MP3 files, you need a stand-alone player. **Audio apps**, such as those found on tablets and smartphones, have features such as file shuffling and volume control. Some audio software has **skins**, which are visual images to accompany with the sounds.

Synthesized Music   Some digital audio files are recordings of actual sounds converted to a digital format. Another type is **synthesized music**, which is created as a digital file from the start using electronic instruments called synthesizers, or synths for short. As shown in Figure 4-25, musicians play synthesizers, which look like piano keyboards, to mimic sounds from acoustic or electric instruments or to produce unusual sounds that other instruments cannot generate. Many contemporary music compositions use some synthesized music.

To play a synthesizer, you press a key on the keyboard, generating an electrical current that becomes sound when it passes through an amplifier and speakers. A technology called **MIDI (Musical Instrument Digital Interface)** converts the electric current to digital form so that you can store and play the synthesized music on a computer or mobile device.

In addition to synthesizers, you can create MIDI files using other instruments connected to a computer, such as guitars, violins, and drums. MIDI files do not contain sound; rather, they contain instructions for generating the components of sounds, including pitch, volume, and note duration.

MIDI technology also lets synthesizers and other electronic musical instruments communicate with one another. For example, you can play a certain note on a MIDI synthesizer to trigger a beat on a drum machine. If you are a solo performer, you can use connected MIDI devices to produce the effect of a larger musical ensemble. Because the music you create is digital audio, you can edit the files to change the key or tempo, reorder sections, and add instrumentation, meaning you can produce, record, and modify synthesized music in a home studio.

Speech and Voice Recognition   **Speech recognition** enables a device or software to identify the words and phrases you speak and then convert them to a format the device can read. Using speech recognition software, you can talk to your laptop to have the words appear on the screen. You also can speak commands that your device will perform and even write a report by speaking into the microphone on your device.

Basic or older speech recognition software has a limited vocabulary and is usually accurate only if you speak very clearly. More advanced software such as Apple Siri, Windows Cortana, and Amazon Alexa digital assistants can interpret natural speech (Figure 4-26).

Figure 4-25   Musician playing a synthesizer.
Media Whalestock/Shutterstock.com

Figure 4-26   Speech recognition in digital assistants.
Source: Apple Computer

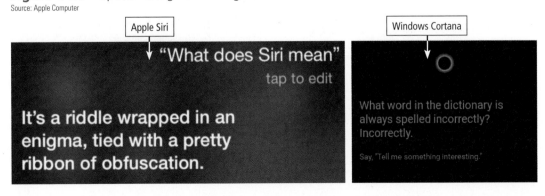

Speech recognition is part of most new computers and mobile devices, making the software easy to access and use. The drawbacks include dropping spoken words because of variations in pronunciation and difficulty screening out background noise. Most speech recognition software understands English, but not many other languages.

Voice recognition once meant the same thing as speech recognition, but it is coming to mean speaker recognition, or determining who is speaking rather than what is being said. Voice recognition software is used as a security measure to allow access to only authorized people the software recognizes by voice.

Whereas speech recognition software translates spoken words into text a computing device can understand, a text-to-speech app, also called read aloud technology, does the opposite. It accepts text as input and then generates speech as output. To do so, it breaks words into individual sound units called phonemes, and then strings them together to create words and phrases, or synthesized speech. A digital assistant uses synthesized speech to respond to your questions.

Businesses and call centers use synthesized speech for routine communications. Assistive software uses synthesized speech to narrate on-screen text, making computers accessible to blind people. Applications are increasingly using this technology to provide read-aloud features for all users. Developers can include the code in their software to synthesize speech in different voices, including multiple languages.

You can also use text-to-speech software to type text in an application, create a sound file, and then play it back, post it on a website as a podcast, or send the sound file via an email message.

Digital Video Are you recording a video of an event to post on YouTube? Maybe you are inserting a video in a PowerPoint presentation or downloading a movie trailer to play on your phone. Each purpose requires a different video file format. Fast Internet connections have made watching videos on computers and mobile devices almost as popular as watching television. You can find videos on many websites, whether the videos are posted by individuals, by web developers, or as advertising. People use websites such as YouTube, Vimeo, and Instagram to share personal videos; you can also watch commercial movies and TV through YouTube. If you post a video that is shared millions of times over social media in a short period, it is called a viral video.

Digital video files have two parts: a codec and a container. A codec (short for compressor/decompressor) is software that encodes and usually compresses data for storage and then decompresses the data for playback. Video files typically use lossy compression.

A video container bundles the video, audio, codec, and other parts (such as subtitles) into a single package. Most digital video file formats are named after their container. Video codecs are compatible with only some containers. Table 4-10 describes common video codecs, and Table 4-11 describes common video containers.

Video File Resolutions Video file formats are one way to describe a video file. Resolution is another. If you have seen videos available for download on the web described as 720p, HD, or 4K, those descriptions refer to resolution.

Table 4-10 Common Video Codecs

Name	Compatible With	Best Use/Notes
DivX	AVI video container	Commercial video production Provides the highest video quality at the expense of file size
H.264	MP4 video container	Playing on playback devices or streaming services Common, efficient codec; preferred for YouTube videos
H.265	MP4 video container	Very high resolution videos New video codec; also called HEVC
MPEG-2	MP4 and Quicktime containers	DVDs, Blu-ray discs, professional-grade cameras Not used for streaming services
MPEG-4	Wide range of compatibility	Online streaming services Common codec providing good quality

Table 4-11   Common Video Containers

Name	File Size and Quality	Best Use/Notes
AVI (.avi)	Files are often larger than others	Videos to store on a computer One of the oldest and most accepted formats
MP4 (.mp4)	Relatively small files and high quality	Nearly universal Websites such as YouTube and Vimeo prefer MP4 files
Quicktime (.mov)	Large files with high quality	Playback on Apple devices Developed by Apple
Windows Media (.wmv)	Small file size with reduced quality	Sharing with others and posting on the web Developed by Microsoft

Digital video resolution is given as width × height. The higher the resolution, the sharper the video, and the larger the file size. Video resolutions can be organized into three categories:

- Standard Definition (SD): Resolutions of 640 × 360 and 720 × 480
- High Definition (HD): Resolutions of 1280 × 720 (called 720p) and 1920 × 1080 (called 1080p or Full HD)
- Ultra High Definition (UHD): The 4K standard provides a resolution of 3840 × 2160 (called 2160p), while the 8K standard provides a resolution of 7840 × 4320 (called 4320p)

Although 8K videos provide the highest resolution, that does not mean you should download the 8K version of a video when an SD or HD video is available. An 8K video file is 16 times larger than a Full HD video. Files that large take a long time to download and require significant storage space.

In addition, only some devices can play UHD files. If you want to watch a 4K video on a 720p display screen, your computer or TV converts the high-resolution video to 720p because that is the best the screen can offer.

In most cases, Full HD videos balance high-quality playback with smaller file sizes that download quickly, making them ideal for sharing and posting on websites.

Digital Animation

When you view a webpage and objects move, you are viewing animation. Films, games, training videos, business presentations, and websites are the most popular venues for animation. Animation can teach medical students to perform a procedure or advise novice pilots how to maneuver through bad weather. **Simulations** are sophisticated computer animations that are useful for training and teaching in many fields, particularly in areas in which learning can be dangerous or difficult (Figure 4-27).

Animation on the Web   Ads, films, television shows, computer games, and promotional videos use 2-D animation. Websites frequently use it to enhance content. One popular animation method on the web is an **animated GIF**, a series of slightly different GIF images displayed in sequence to achieve animation effects.

Currently, most web animations are created with **HTML 5**, the latest version of HTML that is built into browsers. HTML 5 features high-quality playback without the need for additional plug-in software and is the standard for web animation development.

Animation in Entertainment   The most popular uses of 3-D animation are in ads, films, and computer games. 3-D animation in films is done during the production phase, while the film is being shot, and then incorporated into the final footage.

Figure 4-27   Using animation and simulations in training.
Aleksandra Suzi/Shutterstock.com

Screens show an animated environment

Flight simulator for pilot training

In computer games like the one shown in Figure 4-28, 3-D animation is produced as you are playing, because you are in control of the characters' movements. This technology is called **real-time animation**.

Figure 4-28   Real-time 3-D animation.
© Electronic Arts Inc.

Real-time animation consumes an enormous amount of computer resources. At 60 frames per second (fps), your computer must handle more than 1 billion bits of information every second to display a 3-D image. The computer also has to track the movements of each player, using even more resources. Because of these requirements, you need a computer with a powerful processor to play games with 3-D animation.

2-D and 3-D Animations   A 2-D animation displays 2-D images in rapid sequence to create the illusion of lifelike motion, as in a classic animated cartoon (Figure 4-29). To create a 2-D animation, you draw one image in a frame, followed by another in a slightly different pose, and so on until the motion is complete. Not surprisingly, this technique is called in-betweening, shortened to **tweening**. You can create the in-between images manually or let a computer create them. A 2-D animated video requires 24 fps.

Similar to 2-D animation, a 3-D animation displays 3-D objects or models in rapid sequence to create the illusion of

natural motion. Unlike 2-D objects, 3-D objects have volume and can rotate 360 degrees, making them more lifelike.

Three-dimensional animation is more complex than 2-D animation because you must first create the 3-D graphic, and then create 24 to 60 versions of the graphic for each second of animation. A 3-D animation in a computer game or film displays 24–60 fps.

To create a 3-D animation, you create a digital 3-D object, ranging from a simple ball to a complex character, and then add shadows and light. You define the texture of each surface on the object, which determines how it reflects the light. One way to create a solid 3-D image is to apply highlights and shadows to a wireframe drawing (a 3-D object composed of individual lines) in a process called rendering (Figure 4-30).

After creating a 3-D object, you define how it moves. For example, a ball compresses slightly when it bounces. To make the object move, you set its starting position in a keyframe, which is a location on the animation timeline that marks the beginning of a given movement. For example, frame 1 of the animation might be a keyframe. Move the object to a later position on the timeline, such as frame 100, which becomes the next keyframe. You use animation software to generate images of the changes in the object as it transitions from one keyframe to the next, creating the illusion of movement.

Another type of 3-D animation is stop motion animation, in which animators move real-life objects through a sequence of poses and capture the movements one frame at a time. When you play the frames in sequence, the objects seem to move.

Although 3-D animation is more complex and realistic than 2-D animation, one form of animation is not necessarily better than the other. Each type produces a different effect, with 2-D animation providing clear, simple expressions of concepts and stories, and 3-D animation creating a more immersive, dynamic experience.

Figure 4-29   2-D and 3-D animation.
Sangmesh Desai Sarkar/Shutterstock.com; Amnaj Tandee/Shutterstock.com

Classic cartoons use 2-D animation

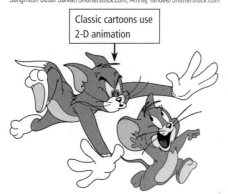

3-D animation uses 3-D objects and characters

Figure 4-30   3-D rendering.

Mikhail Bakunovich/Shutterstock.com

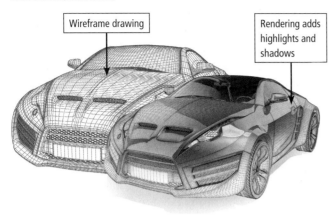

Wireframe drawing

Rendering adds highlights and shadows

Digital Media Creation and Editing Apps

In addition to capturing images with hardware devices, you can use **graphics apps** to create, view, manipulate, and print digital images such as photos, drawings, clip art, and diagrams. You can create bitmap images with painting apps using brush tools and paint palettes that simulate watercolors, pastels, and oil paints. **Image-editing apps** let you modify existing images. For example, you can rotate an image on its axis, change its colors, or modify lines and other shapes.

Drawing apps let you create simple vector images. In some programs, you layer graphics to create collages. You can use more advanced programs to create sketches, logos, typography, and complex illustrations for web or print use.

Use **photo editing apps** to enhance and retouch photographs. For example, you can add special effects, such as reflections or sepia tones; correct problems, such as red-eye or poor lighting; or remove unwanted parts of an image. You can also edit photos on a smartphone using free mobile apps, such as Snapseed, VSC, and Adobe Lightroom.

Capture Videos   You probably use video often for entertainment, school, and work, especially on a mobile device. You can capture video using a smartphone or digital video camera, as shown in Figure 4-31, and then play it back on a computing device or post it on a video sharing website.

You can use a **digital video camera**, **camcorder**, tablet, or smartphone to capture full-motion images and store them in a file on the camera or phone. Action camcorders are compact, waterproof, and weather-resistant, making them ideal for live action. You might use them for activities such as sailing, surfing, skiing, and extreme sports.

Figure 4-31   Uses for digital video.

LDprod/Shutterstock.com; Siarhei Dzmitryienka/Shutterstock.com; Olena Hromova/Shutterstock.com; Casimiro PT/Shutterstock.com

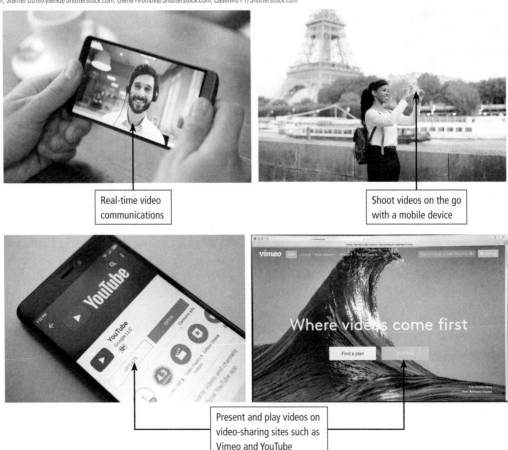

Real-time video communications

Shoot videos on the go with a mobile device

Present and play videos on video-sharing sites such as Vimeo and YouTube

Digital video files are large: when you transfer a video from a digital video camera to your computer or storage media, you could need 1 to 30 GB of storage for each hour of video, with HD video requiring storage space in the upper end of the range.

To watch video on a computer, you need special hardware and software. The hardware is built into computers, tablets, or smartphones and includes a screen, speakers, and a **video card** — a circuit board that lets your device process video. You also need software called a **media player**. Most laptops, tablets, and smartphones come with media players. Video technology changes so quickly that you may need to update your media player and related software frequently.

Animation Apps   With a personal computer and readily available animation apps, all you need is a little training and some skill to create animations. With animation apps, you can add animation to digital graphics and videos. For example, you can add a simulated snowfall to a skiing video, create scrolling 3-D titles, or animate a logo or character. Figure 4-32 shows 3-D text you might create and animate to show the text sinking in the water.

Figure 4-32   Text animation.

Jörg Röse-Oberreich/Shutterstock.com

Use animation software to add animated text to videos and other digital content

You also can create animated content, including cartoons, ads, and games, from scratch or by adapting images provided with the software. Professional-level animation software is expensive and has a steep learning curve. Film studios and special effects departments use specialized software to animate movies, television shows, and games.

? Consider This

How do you legally download and use digital media?
Like other intellectual property, digital media is subject to copyright laws and restrictions. Illegal downloads or publication of copyrighted media can subject you to fines or imprisonment. When downloading media, consider the source. With a subscription-based service that enables you to play media or listen to music, the artist or copyright owner has authorized the service. Other sites enable you to download media but typically have restrictions on the usage of that media. For example, personal listening or viewing may be acceptable, but charging others for access or using it for commercial purposes is not. Have you downloaded or accessed digital media online? For what purpose? How did you access the content? What payment, if any, did you incur?

Digital Media on the Web

To watch videos or listen to audio, such as audio books, podcasts, and music on your computer, you can download the media files the same way you download graphics files. However, you must transfer the entire video or audio file to your computer, which can take a long time and require a great deal of storage space.

As an alternative, you can **stream** the media, which means you receive the audio or video content on your computer from a server and then can watch or listen to the media as it arrives.

For **on-demand content**, such as television shows, the original media file is stored on the media distributor's server. If you subscribe to the streaming service, it sends the media to your computer for viewing. Because the file is stored online, you can watch it more than once. Examples of subscription video streaming services include Netflix, Hulu, Amazon Prime Video, HBO Max, Chromecast, Roku, and YouTube. With **live video streaming**, often used for sports events, the content is sent out live, as it happens, and is available only once.

Smart TVs and Streaming Devices
In addition to viewing streaming video on your computer or mobile device, you can view it on your television set. **Smart TVs** connect to a Wi-Fi network and let you view Internet content, including television shows, movies, games, and photos. If you do not have a smart TV, you can connect hardware to your television, such as a TV stick or a set-top box, which lets you stream television shows and movies from subscription services (Figure 4-33).

Because streaming video is more convenient and less expensive than traditional cable and satellite television content, many people are "cutting the cord" to their cable and satellite television subscriptions. Instead of watching scheduled content, you can create a personal entertainment hub with a smart TV and streaming video service to watch your favorite shows, movies, news, and sports at your convenience.

Stream Digital Audio
You can also stream digital audio in the form of audio books, using sites such as Audible, and as audio podcasts, which may include news stories, music, lectures, or radio shows. To stream music, you can use a music streaming service, such as Pandora, Spotify, SoundCloud, Groove Music, or iHeartRadio. Some streaming services are free and others are paid; the free services usually feature advertisements. As with streaming video, streamed music is not stored on your computer.

You can play audio directly from the Internet by connecting to live audio feeds for live sports events, shows, or even police, fire department, and air traffic control feeds using a browser or a media player.

Figure 4-33   Streaming video devices.
Rasulov/Shutterstock.com; Source: Amazon.com, Inc.; Source: Apple Computer; Source: Amazon.com

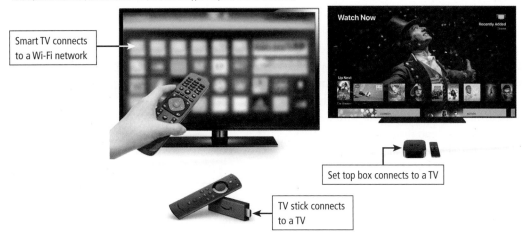

Smart TV connects to a Wi-Fi network

Set top box connects to a TV

TV stick connects to a TV

Figure 4-34   AR game Pokemon Go on a smartphone.
Matthew Corley/Shutterstock.com

Augmented reality superimposes digital media in a real environment

---

❓ Consider This

How do you select a streaming service?

Subscription-based streaming services, such as Netflix and Hulu, allow you to access a variety of on-demand content, including original programming unavailable on other platforms. These subscriptions can be expensive, and they do restrict the number of users and devices that can access content. Other streaming services can be accessed with a library card, depending on your local library's availability. Student discounts apply to some streaming services, so make sure to do your research to determine the best deal. Some streaming access is given with the purchase of a new phone, a cable package, or other purchases.

Virtual and Augmented Reality and Artificial Intelligence

Although digital video can be convincingly realistic, you are still aware of being a viewer watching the video content. Virtual reality, augmented reality, and artificial intelligence are areas that often are used in gaming and go beyond traditional video capabilities.

Virtual and Augmented Reality

Virtual reality (VR), a computer-simulated, 3-D environment that you can explore and manipulate, attempts to remove the barrier between the viewer and the media. With special headsets to display 3-D images that create the illusion of limitless space and depth, VR immerses you in an artificial world. **Augmented reality (AR)** apps overlay information and digital content on top of physical objects or locations. Some augmented reality mobile apps overlay media or other digital content over an image on the screen (Figure 4-34). For example, a user can scan an image of the human body using an augmented reality app, and the app overlays 3-D graphics onto the body. By changing the angle, or zooming in and out, the user can visualize various muscles, organs, and systems of the human body.

A virtual world is different from other simulations, such as video games or movies, because it is believable, interactive, and immersive. In a virtual world, a 3-D computer model creates a convincing illusion of depth and space to make you feel you are part of a real scene you can explore. Sensors detect your movements, and a head-mounted display adjusts what you see and hear. For example, if you are visiting a virtual version of Paris and enter a café, the sights and sounds in the virtual world change as you move, just as they would in the real world.

A virtual world is also different from augmented reality, mixed reality, and some types of virtual reality. If you had an augmented reality app on your phone, for example, and were roaming real-world Paris, you could point the phone at a landmark to display its image overlaid with details about it, including its name and history. The app enhances, or augments, the reality, while a virtual world replaces it.

Like augmented reality, mixed reality maintains a connection to the physical world. The goal of mixed reality is to produce an environment where physical and digital objects interact.

Many games, such as flight and racing simulators, have elements of virtual reality. For example, you could use a wide screen display, headphones with surround sound, and a realistic joystick in a flight simulation game to experience piloting a jet; however, the game does not fully immerse you in a virtual world. If you turn your head away from the screen, you break the illusion of flying a plane.

AR and VR in Gaming   Today's video games use high-end graphics, powerful processors, and the Internet to create environments that rival reality and bring together players from around the world. Most games are played on video consoles with special game controllers. These systems use hand-held controllers as input devices, speakers and a television screen or computer monitor as output devices, a hard drive, and memory cards or optical discs for storage (Figure 4-35).

On consoles that connect to the Internet, you can interact with other players online and watch TV or movies. Large-scale multiplayer games, such as Halo, Doom, Overwatch,

Figure 4-35   Gaming system.

Source: Samsung.com

Minecraft, and World of Warcraft, operate on many Internet servers, with each one accommodating thousands of players.

For a more immersive experience, you can set up a **VR gaming system** using hardware (Figure 4-36). These systems run on customized desktops and include a headset, controllers, and sensors to track your movements. Augmented reality gaming integrates

Figure 4-36   VR gaming system.

© Oculus VR

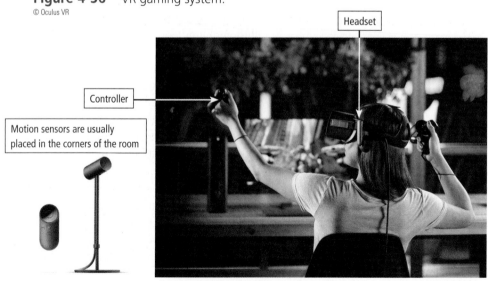

visual and audio game content with your environment. Unlike VR gaming, which often requires a separate room to create an immersive experience, AR gaming superimposes digital game elements in the real world. You usually play AR games on smartphones, tablets, and portable consoles.

Microsoft offers the HoloLens headsets, which use **holograms**, projected images that appear three-dimensional, to allow you to superimpose virtual objects and characters onto scanned images of real objects in the room, and then interact with the virtual and real objects. Instead of purchasing special hardware for gaming, you can also play games on computers, tablets, or smartphones. Simple games may come with the operating system of a computer or mobile device; you can also download them from an app store. Many of these games use 2-D animation. People use game consoles for activities other than entertainment. For example, doctors can practice their fine motor skills on surgery simulators using **motion-sensing game consoles**, which allow you to interact with the system through body movements (Figure 4-37). Physical therapists use these consoles along with virtual reality gaming techniques to challenge and motivate patients doing rehabilitation.

Figure 4-37   Using a motion-sensing game console.

Artificial Intelligence

Artificial intelligence (AI) is the technological use of logic and prior experience to simulate human intelligence. In broad terms, AI lets computers perform tasks that require human-level intelligence. **Machine learning** is a branch of AI that trains machines to learn from data, identify patterns, and make decisions to progressively improve their performance without much human intervention.

Some of the practical uses of AI include strategic gaming, military simulations, statistical predictions, and self-driving cars. For example, meteorologists use AI to analyze weather data patterns to create a list of possible outcomes for an upcoming weather event. The predictions made by the AI software then need to be interpreted, reviewed, and prioritized by people.

Some of the ways you might interact with AI on a daily basis include:

- Virtual assistants, which use voice recognition and search engines to answer, react, or reply to user requests
- Social media and online ads, which track your data, such as websites visited, and provide ads targeted to your personal interests
- Video games that provide information to your virtual opponents based on your skill level and past actions
- Music and media streaming services, which recommend options based on your past listening and viewing choices
- Smart cars, which automate many driving tasks such as managing speed and avoiding collisions
- Navigation apps, which provide you with information about traffic and the best routes, along with preferred stops along your way
- Security, such as using your fingerprint to access your phone, or facial recognition and motion-detection cameras that alert you to unusual or unauthorized visitors

Another use of AI is natural language processing. **Natural language processing** is a form of data input in which computers interpret and digitize spoken words or commands. In some cases, users must train the software to recognize the user's speech patterns, accent, and voice inflections. **Digital assistants** like Amazon's Alexa or Apple's Siri use natural language processing to respond to your verbal commands or questions, using search technology to provide answers or perform a task, such as adding an item to a grocery list (Figure 4-38).

Robotics is the science that combines engineering and technology to create and program robots. Robots are useful in situations where it is impractical, dangerous, or

Figure 4-38   Smart devices provide you with assistance, answers, and more.
Denys Prykhodov/Shutterstock.com

inconvenient to use a human, such as cleanup of hazardous waste and materials; for domestic uses, such as vacuuming; and in agricultural and manufacturing applications (Figure 4-39).

Figure 4-39   Robot used to detect weeds and spray chemicals.

Zapp2Photo/Shutterstock.com

Robots also can assist surgeons. A robotic arm or instrument can be more precise, flexible, and controlled than a human hand. 3-D cameras enable the surgeon to see inside the body. Robotic surgeries often take less time to heal and can prevent risk of infection because they require a smaller incision site; however, robots require a surgeon to control and direct the operation. Surgeons must not only be trained medically, but also trained to use the robot.

Self-driving cars use cameras to change speed due to traffic. They rely on GPS to navigate the best and fastest route. The proponents say that they reduce dangers related to human error. One of the biggest concerns about self-driving cars is that they may contribute to accidents caused by distracted driving.

Outside of gaming, science and medicine use VR for training and research. For example, medical students can use VR to practice their emergency medicine skills. NASA uses VR to simulate space flight and the environments of other planets. Other commercial uses include enabling potential home buyers to visually move through a home's various rooms or allowing construction companies to show a preview of the completed building.

When you make a decision based on observation, or answer a question, your brain and senses prompt you to use your past experiences, knowledge base, and visual and other sensory clues to generate with a response. AI and other technologies that mimic human action use some of the same processes. Computers learn from past interactions to predict likely outcomes or responses. They use databases and Internet searches to determine answers to questions. Cameras can read faces and analyze voices to recognize users.

 Consider This

How much can you rely on artificial intelligence?
The science fiction genre has always been fascinated with exploring the uses of AI and robotics, sometimes with disastrous results. In reality, it is unlikely that robots will overtake humans. Benefits of using AI and robotics include efficient and safe manufacturing, especially when the work needed is too intricate for human hands or requires the use of chemicals that can be harmful to humans. One downside is that often jobs that traditionally were done by humans are being replaced by robotic or automated devices. Another downside is that when an error or malfunction occurs, the technology is useless, and often it is difficult to replace its function easily or cheaply. For what purposes have you or would you use AI or robotics to enhance your life? What tasks would you ask the devices to perform for you? Why?

Personal Interest Applications

Countless desktop, mobile, and web apps are designed specifically for lifestyle, medical, entertainment, convenience, education, or financial activities. Most of the programs in this category are relatively inexpensive; many are free or open source and are available for download from websites or a device's app store. Some applications focus on a single service, while others provide several services in a single application.

- Lifestyle applications: Access the latest news or sports scores, check the weather forecast, compose music, research genealogy, find recipes, meet or chat with friends online near you, or locate nearby restaurants, gas stations, or points of interest.
- Medical applications: Research symptoms, establish a fitness or health program, track exercise activity, refill prescriptions, count calories, or monitor sleep patterns.
- Entertainment applications: Listen to music or the radio, view photos, watch videos or shows, read a book or other publication, organize and track fantasy sports teams, and play games individually or with others.
- Convenience applications: Obtain driving directions or your current location, convert speech to text instead of typing, set an alarm or timer, check the time, calculate a tip, use your phone as a flashlight, manage a shared online calendar with your family, or use a personal assistant that acts on your voice commands.
- Education applications: Access how-to guides, learn or fine-tune a particular skill, follow a tutorial, run a simulation, assist children with reading and other elementary skills, attend and participate in online courses, or support academics.
- Financial applications: Prepare your taxes, manage your bank accounts, pay bills, make investments, exchange money with others, and track your budget (Figure 4-40).

Figure 4-40 Using a financial app.
iStock.com/Vgajic

❓ Consider This

How can educational apps and services benefit you?
Until a few years ago, remote learning systems were used on a limited basis to provide degree or certificate programs or classes to nonlocal participants or to enhance the communication outside of the classroom between instructors and classmates. Chances are, you participated in remote learning for several months to a year or more due to the pandemic. Teachers had to pivot their instruction to webinars and the use of online platforms, such as Zoom and Teams, instead of being able to interact with students face to face. While this was a reaction to the circumstances, some of what was necessary is being adopted as a permanent method. The continued development of educational apps and services means enhanced opportunities for you to participate in classes that are not local to you and may even enable you to earn a degree or certification while remaining at home. Asynchronous learning, or learning not done in real time, provides even more flexibility as you can choose when to listen to recorded lectures. How did you react to having to learn remotely? What was the impact on your education? What technology did you use to participate in class and interact with your classmates?

Secure IT: Security Tools

To protect your computers and mobile devices against malware, you can use one or more security tools. These security tools include personal firewalls, antivirus programs, malware removers, and Internet filters. Although some of these tools are included with the operating system, you also can purchase stand-alone programs that offer improvements or added functionality.

Personal Firewall A **firewall** is a protective barrier between a computer or network and others on the Internet. A personal firewall is a security tool that detects and protects a personal computer and its data from unauthorized intrusions. Personal firewalls constantly monitor all transmissions to and from a computer or mobile device and may inform a user of attempted intrusions. When connected to the Internet, a computer or mobile device is vulnerable to attacks from hackers who try to access a computer or network illegally. These attacks may destroy data, steal information, damage a computer, or carry out some other malicious action.

Antivirus Apps A **virus** is malicious computer code that reproduces itself on the same computer. Almost all viruses "infect" by inserting themselves into a computer file. When the file is opened, the virus is activated. An **antivirus app** protects a computer against viruses by identifying and removing any computer viruses found in memory, on storage media, or on incoming files. To protect a computer or mobile device from virus attacks, users should install an antivirus program and keep it updated by purchasing revisions or upgrades to the software. Antivirus programs scan for programs that attempt to modify a computer's start-up files, the operating system, and other programs that normally are read from but not modified. In addition, many antivirus programs automatically scan files downloaded from the web, email attachments, opened files, and all types of removable media inserted in the computer or mobile device.

If an antivirus program identifies an infected file, it attempts to remove the malware. If the antivirus program cannot remove the infection, it often quarantines the infected file. A quarantine is a separate area of a hard drive that holds the infected file until the infection can be removed. This step ensures other files will not become infected. Quarantined files remain on a computer or mobile device until the user deletes them or restores them.

Most antivirus programs also include protection against other malware, such as worms, trojan horses, and spyware. When you purchase a new computer, it may include a trial version of antivirus software. Many email servers also have antivirus programs installed to check incoming and outgoing email messages for viruses and other malware.

Spyware, Adware, and Other Malware Removers
Spyware is a type of program placed on a computer or mobile device without the user's knowledge that secretly collects information about the user and then communicates the information it collects to some

outside source while the user is online. Some vendors or employers use spyware to collect information about program usage or employees. Internet advertising firms often collect information about users' browsing habits. Spyware can enter your computer when you install a new program, through a graphic on a webpage or in an email message, or through malware.

Adware is a type of program that displays an online advertisement in a banner or pop-up or pop-under window on webpages, email messages, or other Internet services. Sometimes, Internet advertising firms hide spyware in adware. A spyware remover is a type of program that detects and deletes spyware and similar programs. An adware remover is a program that detects and deletes adware. Malware removers detect and delete spyware, adware, and other malware.

Internet Filters   **Filters** are programs that remove or block certain items from being displayed. Five widely used Internet filters are anti-spam programs, web filters, phishing filters, pop-up and pop-under blockers, and ransomware apps. **Spam** is an unsolicited email message or posting sent to many recipients or forums at once. Spam is considered Internet junk mail. The content of spam ranges from selling a product or service, to pro-moting a business opportunity, to advertising offensive material. Spam also may contain links or attachments that contain malware.

An anti-spam program is a filtering program that attempts to remove spam before it reaches your inbox or forum. If your email program does not filter spam, many anti-spam programs are available at no cost on the web. ISPs often filter spam as a service for their subscribers.

Web filtering software is a program that restricts access to certain material on the web. Some restrict access to specific websites; others filter websites that use certain words or phrases. Many businesses use web filtering software to limit employees' web access. Some schools, libraries, and parents use this software to restrict access to websites that are not educational.

Phishing is a scam in which a perpetrator sends an official-looking email message that attempts to obtain your personal and/or financial information (Figure 4-41). Some phishing messages ask you to reply with your information; others direct you to a phony website or a pop-up or pop-under window that looks like a legitimate website, which then collects your information. A phishing filter is a program that warns or blocks you from potentially fraudulent or suspicious websites. Some browsers include phishing filters.

Figure 4-41   Phishing email message.
Source: Email sent to Dr. Mark Revels

A **pop-up ad** is an Internet advertisement that suddenly appears in a new window on top of a webpage. Similarly, a **pop-under ad** is an Internet advertisement that is hidden behind the browser window so that it will be viewed when users close their browser windows. A pop-up blocker or pop-under blocker is a filtering program that stops pop-up or pop-under ads from displaying on webpages. Many browsers include these blockers. You also can download pop-up and pop-under blockers from the web at no cost.

Ransomware is a type of attack that affects your files and personal data. Some attacks encrypt your data and files, or otherwise restrict access, unless you pay for an access key to release them (Figure 4-42). Some ransomware threatens to publish your personal data, or in the case of a corporation, sensitive company files, unless a payment is made.

Figure 4-42   Ransomware attacks affect your data and files until you pay.
Rawf8/Shutterstock.com

? Consider This —————————————————————

What are virus hoaxes, and how can you avoid them?
Computer hoaxes spread across the Internet in record time and often are the source of urban legends. These hoaxes take several forms and often disappear for months or years at a time, only to resurface some time later.

Most alarming to some users are the computer virus hoaxes that warn a computer is infected and needs immediate attention. Some warnings state the problem is so severe that the computer or device will explode or that the entire hard drive will be erased in a matter of seconds. These messages claim to offer a solution to the problem, generally requesting a fee for a program to download.

In reality, these fake messages are generated by unscrupulous scammers preying upon gullible people who panic and follow the directions in the message. These users divulge credit card information and then often download files riddled with viruses.

If you receive one of these virus hoaxes, never respond to the message. Instead, delete it. Most importantly, never forward it to an unsuspecting friend or coworker. If you receive the virus hoax from someone you know, send them a separate email message with information about the hoax. Have you ever received a virus hoax? How did you know it was a hoax? What damage, if any, did it cause you? What action did you, or could you, take?

How To: Use System Management Tools

Many issues that arise when using programs and apps have simple fixes using tools installed with your operating system. Knowing how to fix issues can save you not only frustration, but time and money. Being able to troubleshoot can save you from hiring outside technology consultants and get you back to using your programs and apps quickly.

A **crash** occurs when the program or app stops functioning correctly. This can be caused by an issue with the hardware, the software, a virus or other malware, or using invalid data or commands. Recovery from a crash can be as simple as rebooting your computer or device. Many resources exist online, such as Help forums or free IT support chat rooms.

Troubleshooting refers to the steps you take to identify and solve a problem, such as a crash. When a crash occurs, you should do the following:

- Make a note of any error messages that display. Sometimes error messages include an error number, which can help identify what went wrong.
- Try to save any data or information on which you are working, if possible, so that you do not lose it.
- Restart the program to see if it recovers from the crash.
- Reboot your computer or device and try running the program again.

- Visit the website of the software development company to see if any updates to the software are available that you may need to install.
- Conduct an Internet search to see if any known solutions to the issue exist. Verify the reliability of the source before attempting any fixes.
- Scan your computer for viruses or malware and resolve any issues.

If none of the above steps works, you also can uninstall and reinstall the software. You can avoid some of the pitfalls associated with a crash by regularly backing up the files on your computer, saving your work frequently, and running a verified malware detector at all times.

Many tools exist to help you troubleshoot issues and manage programs and apps, including the following:

- Process managers track the memory usage, status, and errors of currently running software.
- System information lists keep track of license numbers and installation keys in case you need to reinstall software.
- Auditing tools analyze security, performance, and network connections.
- Patch finders compare the software versions you are running with the latest versions available on the developers' websites and identify any updates, or patches, you need to install.
- Restorers allow you to restore your computer or software settings. These are helpful if you made an update that seems to have caused issues with your system or a specific program.
- File managers perform functions such as displaying a list of files on a storage medium; organizing files in folders; and copying, renaming, deleting, moving, and sorting files. A **folder** is a specific named location on a storage medium that contains related files. Most operating systems typically include a file manager.
- Search tools allow you to locate a file, contact, calendar event, app, or any other item stored on your computer or mobile device based on criteria you specify. An *index* stores a variety of information about a file, including its name, date created, date modified, author name, and so on. When you enter search criteria, instead of looking through every file and folder on the storage medium, the search tool looks through the index first to find a match. Each entry in the index contains a link to the actual file on the storage media for easy retrieval.
- Image viewers allow users to display, copy, and print the contents of a graphics file, such as a photo. With an image viewer, users can see images without having to open them in a paint or image editing program. Many image viewers include some photo editing capabilities.

- Uninstaller tools remove an app, as well as any associated entries in the system files. When you install a program, the operating system records the information it uses to run the software in the system files.
- Disk **cleanup** tools search for and remove unnecessary files on computers and mobile devices. Unnecessary files may include downloaded program files, temporary Internet files, deleted files, and unused program files. Disk cleanup tools for mobile devices often locate duplicate files or photos, or large files that a user might want to delete or upload to the cloud.
- File compression tools shrink the size of a file(s). A compressed file, also called a zipped file, takes up less storage space than the original file. When you select multiple files or folders to include in a compressed file, the file compression tool will group all of them into one compressed file. Sending a compressed file as an attachment to an email message is often preferable to attaching several files individually. When you receive or download a compressed file, you must uncompress it by restoring the file(s) or folder(s) it contains to their original form.
- Power management tools monitor battery usage, showing apps that consume the most battery power, displaying battery usage data since the device was last charged, and estimating usage time remaining. Power management apps can enable power saving mode automatically when a device's battery runs low so that the battery will last longer until charged.

❓ Consider This

What happens when you cannot fix your programs and apps?

Sometimes, despite all these tools and techniques, your device is no longer functioning well and needs to be replaced. Unrecoverable crashes not only affect your device and any programs or apps you have purchased but also your data and files. You can always purchase a new computer or device and reinstall programs and apps, but unless you have a backup of your files, they are lost forever. One advantage of using cloud-based web apps, such as Google Docs, is that your files are stored in the cloud, so you still can access them from another computer or device even if your device fails. You also should install or enable a cloud-based backup program that periodically saves your files and settings to a cloud server. Cloud backup ensures that you can recover your files if you are unable to restore your computer or device. Other backup programs use removable or other media, such as an external hard drive, to store the backed-up files. If the issue with your computer or device is caused by flooding, fire, or other disaster, however, the backup media may also be destroyed.

Study Guide

The Study Guide reinforces material you should know after reading this module.

Instructions: Answer the questions below using the format that helps you remember best or that is required by your instructor. Possible formats may include one or more of these options: write the answers; create a document that contains the answers; record answers as audio or video using a webcam, smartphone, or portable media player; post answers on a blog, wiki, or website; or highlight answers in the book/ebook.

1. Differentiate among local, portable, native, web, and mobile apps. From where do you typically get mobile apps?

2. List common features of apps.

3. You typically can _____ data between web and mobile apps.

4. Describe how to interact with a mobile app.

5. List pros and cons to mobile apps. Define the term, platform-specific.

6. Explain the trends in mobile first design, responsive design, and cross-platform development tools.

7. Describe the purpose of m-commerce apps.

8. Explain legal protections for programs and apps.

9. Define the term, access control.

10. Differentiate between the following app distribution types: retail, custom, SaaS, shareware, freeware, open source, and public domain.

11. Why is it important to consider the source of a program or app? Define the term, registration.

12. _____ is a technique that manufacturers use to ensure that you do not install the software on more computers than legally licensed.

13. Explain how you can use an app store.

14. Describe specifications of a license agreement.

15. Define these terms: update, patch, and service pack. _____ are new releases of the program or app.

16. Why is it important to use an uninstaller?

17. Describe the effects of piracy.

18. List types of productivity apps.

19. Describe the activities that occur during project development. When users _____ a project, they change the appearance of its text and objects.

20. Differentiate among font, font size, and font style.

21. Identify tools word processing programs provide.

22. Define the following terms: worksheet and function.

23. List ways to format a presentation. A(n) _____ is an overall template for a presentation formatted with a theme and customized title and text fonts.

24. Explain the uses of databases for the following: individuals, small businesses, and large companies.

25. Define the terms, field, record, table, query, report, and form. What is the role of Big Data?

26. List advantages of using a productivity suite.

27. Define the term, enterprise computing. Name the types of software used by functional units in an enterprise.

28. Explain the uses of CAD technology. Define the term, wireframe drawing.

29. List and differentiate among four major types of digital media.

30. Define the terms, digitizing and sampling, and explain how they are used with digital media.

31. Differentiate between bitmap and vector graphics. _____ refers to the clarity or sharpness of an image.

32. Explain how compression affects graphics quality.

33. List types of graphics file formats.

34. Describe types of audio file formats.

35. List the equipment you need to record and play sounds and music. Define the term, synthesized music.

36. Explain how speech and voice recognition are used.

37. What is found in a video container? Differentiate among the categories of video resolution.

38. How is animation used on the web and in entertainment? Describe the tweening technique.

39. Identify types of digital media creation and editing apps. How do you capture video?

40. Define the terms, stream and on-demand. What is a smart TV?

41. Differentiate between virtual and augmented reality. Explain how gaming uses both.

42. List ways in which you might interact with AI on a daily basis. How can robotics be used?

43. List and describe types of personal interest applications.

44. Define these terms: malware, virus, firewall, spyware, adware, phishing, and ransomware.

45. A(n) _____ occurs when the program or app stops functioning correctly. List steps to troubleshoot programs and apps.

46. List types of system management tools.

Key Terms

You should be able to define the Key Terms listed below.

access control (4-7)
activation (4-9)
adware (4-36)
analog (4-22)
animated GIF (4-27)
animation (4-18)
antivirus app (4-35)
app store (4-9)
argument (4-15)
artificial intelligence (AI)
   (4-33)
audio app (4-25)
augmented reality (AR)
   (4-31)
automatic update (4-11)
bit rate (4-22)
bitmap graphic (4-23)
camcorder (4-29)
cell (4-15)
cell address (4-15)
chart (4-16)
clipboard (4-12)
codec (4-26)
compression (4-23)
computer-aided design
   (CAD) (4-20)
conditional formatting
   (4-16)
container (4-26)
control (4-19)
crash (4-37)
cross-platform (4-6)
database (4-18)
digital assistant (4-33)
digital audio (4-22)
digital graphic (4-21)
digital video (4-22)
digital video camera (4-29)
digitizing (4-22)
document (4-13)
document management
   tool (4-14)

drawing app (4-29)
edit (4-12)
end-user license
   agreement (EULA)
   (4-11)
enterprise computing
   (4-20)
field (4-18)
field name (4-18)
file format (4-23)
filter (4-16), (4-36)
firewall (4-35)
folder (4-37)
font (4-12)
font size (4-13)
font style (4-13)
form (4-19)
format (4-12)
formula (4-15)
freeware (4-8)
function (4-15)
graphic (4-21)
graphics app (4-29)
hard copy (4-13)
hologram (4-33)
HTML 5 (4-27)
image-editing app (4-29)
insertion point (4-13)
license agreement (4-10)
live video streaming (4-30)
local app (4-2)
lossless compression
   (4-23)
lossy compression (4-23)
machine learning (4-33)
m-commerce (4-6)
media player (4-30)
megapixel (4-23)
micro speaker (4-24)
MIDI (Musical
   Instrument Digital
   Interface) (4-25)

mobile app (4-2)
mobile commerce (4-6)
mobile first design (4-6)
motion-sensing game
   console (4-33)
native app (4-2)
natural language
   processing (4-33)
on-demand content
   (4-30)
open source (4-8)
operator (4-15)
patch (4-11)
phishing (4-36)
photo editing app (4-29)
piracy (4-11)
pixel (4-23)
platform specific (4-5)
pop-under ad (4-36)
pop-up ad (4-36)
portable app (4-2)
presentation (4-16)
presentation app (4-16)
productivity app (4-12)
productivity suite (4-19)
query (4-19)
ransomware (4-36)
real-time animation (4-28)
record (4-18)
registration (4-9)
relational database (4-18)
report (4-19)
resolution (4-23)
responsive design (4-6)
robotics (4-33)
sampling (4-22)
save (4-13)
scroll bar (4-13)
service pack (4-11)
shareware (4-8)
simulation (4-27)
skin (4-25)

slide master (4-18)
slide show (4-18)
smart TV (4-30)
software as a service
   (SaaS) (4-8)
sound card (4-24)
spam (4-36)
speech recognition
   (4-25)
spreadsheet app (4-14)
spyware (4-35)
stream (4-30)
style (4-14)
synchronize (4-4)
synthesized music (4-25)
synthesized speech
   (4-26)
table (4-19)
template (4-14)
text-to-speech app (4-26)
transition (4-18)
troubleshooting (4-37)
tweening (4-28)
uninstaller (4-11)
update (4-11)
upgrade (4-11)
vector graphic (4-23)
video card (4-30)
viral video (4-26)
virtual reality (VR)
   (4-31)
virus (4-35)
voice recognition (4-26)
voice-over (4-24)
VR gaming system (4-32)
web app (4-2)
wireframe drawing
   (4-20)
word processing app
   (4-13)
workbook (4-15)
worksheet (4-14)

Extend Your Knowledge

Instructions: The Extend Your Knowledge exercise expands on subjects covered in the module and encourages you to find the latest developments on these topics. Use a search engine or another search tool to locate news articles, blog entries, videos, expert discussions, or other current sources on the listed topics. List your sources, and write 3–4 sentences describing what you have learned to submit in the format required by your instructor.

- Mobile first app design
- Augmented reality
- Ransomware attacks
- SaaS subscriptions

What did you learn that helped you better understand the concepts in this module? Did anything surprise you? How will what you learned impact you?

Checkpoint

The Checkpoint exercises test your knowledge of the module concepts.

True/False   Mark T for True and F for False. If False, rewrite the statement so that it is True.

_____ 1. A local app is an app written for a specific operating system.

_____ 2. Mobile first design means that designers and developers start building apps to work on mobile devices first because these typically have more restrictions.

_____ 3. Freeware is copyrighted and distributed at no cost for a trial period.

_____ 4. Cutting is the process of removing content and storing it in a temporary storage location, called a clipboard.

_____ 5. A process called sampling converts analog sound waves into digital sound.

_____ 6. When you stream media, you receive the audio or video content on your computer from a server and can watch or listen to the media as it arrives.

_____ 7. Virtual reality apps overlay information and digital content on top of physical objects or locations.

_____ 8. You can use convenience applications to obtain driving directions or your current location, set an alarm or timer, and use your phone as a flashlight.

_____ 9. Malware is an unsolicited email message or posting sent to many recipients or forums at once.

_____ 10. A troubleshoot occurs when the program or app stops functioning correctly.

Matching   Match the terms with their definitions.

_____ 1. augmented reality

_____ 2. access control

_____ 3. tweening

_____ 4. personal firewall

_____ 5. phishing

_____ 6. hologram

_____ 7. lossless compression

_____ 8. shareware

_____ 9. SaaS

_____ 10. query

a. security measures that define who can use a program or app, and what actions they can do within the program or app

b. copyrighted software that is distributed at no cost for a trial period

c. an app that overlays information and digital content on top of physical objects or locations

d. technique that reduces graphic file size for storage, but when opened and viewed, the files are uncompressed and contain all of their original data

e. apps distributed online for a monthly subscription or an annual fee

f. security tool that detects and protects a personal computer and its data from unauthorized intrusions

g. technique to create a 2-D animation in which you draw one image in a frame, followed by another in a slightly different pose, and so on until the motion is complete

h. scam in which a perpetrator sends an official-looking email message that attempts to obtain your personal and/or financial information

i. extracts data from a database based on specified criteria, or conditions, for one or more fields

j. projected images that appear three-dimensional

Problem Solving

Instructions: The Problem Solving exercises extend your knowledge of module concepts by seeking solutions to practical problems with technology that you may encounter at home, school, work, or with nonprofit organizations. The Collaboration exercise should be completed with a team. You often can solve problems with technology in multiple ways. Determine a solution to the problems in these exercises by using one or more resources available to you (such as a computer or mobile device, articles on the web or in print, blogs, podcasts, videos, television, user guides, other individuals, electronics or computer stores, etc.). Describe your solution, along with the resource(s) used, in the format requested by your instructor (brief report, presentation, discussion, blog post, video, or other means).

Personal

1. **Antivirus Program Not Updating**   You are attempting to update your antivirus program with the latest virus definitions, but you receive an error message. What steps will you take to resolve this issue?

2. **Unwanted Programs**   When you displayed a list of programs installed on your computer so that you could uninstall one, you noticed several installed programs that you do not remember installing. Why might these programs be on your computer?

3. **Apps Not Syncing**   You checked your email on your phone last night, and deleted several messages. When you view your email on your computer this morning, the messages you deleted still appear. Why might the apps not be syncing? What are your next steps?

4. **Incompatible App**   You are using your Android tablet to browse for apps in the Google Play store. You found an app you want to download, but you are unable to download it because a message states it is incompatible with your device. Why might the app be incompatible with your device?

5. **Possible Phishing**   Scam You receive an email message that appears to be from your bank, asking you to click a link that will take you to a webpage to verify your account information and password. How can you determine if this email message is legitimate? What can you do if you acted upon the steps in the email message but then later figure out it is a scam?

Professional

6. **Presentation Feedback**   You recently prepared a presentation for your colleagues about a project you have been developing. You spent a lot of time adding bright colors, funny animations, and transitions between the bullets and slides. When you give your presentation, you notice that your colleagues seem confused and are not paying attention to the content you prepared. What might you do to fix your presentation and redeliver it?

7. **License Agreement**   You are planning to work from home for several days, but you are unsure of whether you are allowed to install a program you use at work on your home computer. What steps will you take to determine whether you are allowed to install the software on your home computer?

8. **Low on Space**   The computer in your office is running low on free space. You have attempted to remove as many files as possible, but the remaining programs and files are necessary to perform your daily job functions. What steps might you take to free enough space on the computer?

9. **Unacceptable File Size**   Your boss has asked you to design a new company logo using a graphics app installed on your computer. When you save the logo and submit it , the response is that the file size is too large and that you must find a way to decrease the file size. What might you do to make the image file size smaller without reducing the quality?

10. **Spreadsheet Data Not Accurate**   You are working with a worksheet that contains functions. You notice that the calculations present results that are much larger than seems logical based on your assumptions. What might be wrong? How can you fix it?

Collaboration

11. **Technology in Video Production**   The admissions office at a local college is considering creating a promotional video and has asked for your help. The director of admissions would like to incorporate technology wherever possible, in hopes that it would decrease the cost of the video's production. Form a team of three people to determine what technology can be used to assist in producing the video. One team member should research the type of technology that can be used to record the video. Another team member should research software options available for video editing and the types of computers or mobile devices necessary to run those applications, and the third team member should research the alternatives for publishing and distributing the video online.

How To: Your Turn

Instructions: This exercise presents general guidelines for fundamental skills when using a computer or mobile device and then requires that you determine how to apply these general guidelines to a specific program or situation. You often can complete tasks using technology in multiple ways. Figure out how to perform the tasks described in these exercises by using one or more resources available to you (such as a computer or mobile device, articles on the web or in print, online or program help, user guides, blogs, podcasts, videos, other individuals, trial and error, etc.). Summarize your 'how to' steps, along with the resource(s) used, in the format requested by your instructor (brief report, presentation, discussion, blog post, video, or other means).

1 Compress/Uncompress Files and Folders

You may want to compress files if your hard drive is running out of available space. While the operating system may be able to compress some files by 50 percent or more, other files' sizes may not decrease significantly when they are compressed. Compressed files typically are stored by default in a file with a .zip file extension. The following steps describe how to compress a file or folder and then uncompress (expand or extract) the compressed file on a laptop or desktop computer.

a. Right-click the file(s) or folders you wish to compress to display a shortcut menu.

b. Click the option to compress the file(s) or folder(s). (You may need to select a Send to or other command to display the compression options.)

c. If necessary, type the desired file name for the compressed file.

Uncompressing (or expanding) compressed files or folders returns them to their original form. The following steps uncompress a compressed file.

a. Double-click the compressed file.

b. If necessary, click the option to uncompress (expand or extract) the file.

or

a. Right-click the compressed file to display a shortcut menu.

b. Click the option to uncompress (expand or extract) the file.

Exercises

1. In addition to the operating system's built-in functionality to compress files and folders, what other programs and apps exist that can compress files and folders?

2. In addition to trying to free space on your storage device, for what other reasons might you want to compress files and folders? Would you compress files you are storing on the cloud? Why or why not?

3. Try compressing various types of files on your hard drive, such as a Word document and an image. Compare the file sizes before and after compression. What did you notice with each type of file?

Internet Research

Instructions: The Internet Research exercises broaden your understanding of module concepts by requiring that you search for information on the web. Use a search engine or another search tool to locate the information requested or answers to questions presented in the exercises. Describe your findings, along with the search term(s) you used and your web source(s), in the format requested by your instructor (brief report, presentation, discussion, blog post, video, or other means). Additionally, reflect on the process you used to complete this activity. How did you go about choosing the tool that you did and why? Would you do anything differently in your research next time?

1 **Social Media: Online Gaming**

Gaming via social media has seen explosive growth in recent years. Exponential gaming growth has spawned companion businesses that facilitate and manage the gaming experience. Some mobile and desktop apps provide gamers with a portal for tracking all their online gaming results in a central location that can be shared with friends and others with similar game interests. These apps integrate with the major Internet messaging services, have personalized news feeds, and incorporate a "suggestion" engine for new game discoveries. Many gaming blogs offer game tricks, work-arounds, and hidden features. Beginning gamers can engage their minds during downtime and expand their circle of online friends.

Research This: Visit at least two online social networks for gamers. How many games are shown? Which topics are featured in community discussions and live chats? Are rewards available? If so, what are they? Which online leagues and tournaments are offered? What are some of the latest news articles about specific games and the gaming industry? Have you participated in gaming online social networks? If so, which ones? What information might be collected about you that you would want to protect? What steps can you take to participate in these social networks safely?

2 **Security: Virus Hoaxes**

Virus hoaxes are widespread and sometimes cause panic among Internet users. Many fact-checking websites, such as Factcheck.org, exist. Fact-checking websites offer insight on the sources and variations of a wide variety of rumors, deceptions, and folklore.

Research This: Use a browser to search for trustworthy fact-checking sites, and pick two. Explain why you chose the websites you used. Visit each fact-checking website, and type the search text phrase, virus hoaxes & realities, in the Search box. For each site, make a list of three recent real rumors and three recent false rumors circulating on the Internet. Explain the origin of each, and what the impact of each rumor or threat might be. Compare the list from each website. What conclusions did you reach about current threats or hoaxes?

3 **Cloud Services: Photo Editing (SaaS)**

Online photo editing apps provide browser-based capabilities to modify digital images and often contain many similar features as their desktop counterparts. They are an example of SaaS (software as a service), a service of cloud computing that provides access to software solutions accessed through a browser. In addition to drawing shapes, touching up colors, and adding filters to images, online photo editing apps allow users to access, store, and share their photos in the cloud. Online photo editing apps often include the capability to share photos with friends easily by sending a link or by posting the photo to online social networks.

Research This: (1) Use a search engine to research various online photo editing apps. Compare the features of two of them as you explore their capabilities. Summarize your findings in a table that should show image formats you can import or save, sharing capabilities, special editing features, and ways to organize photos online. Which features take advantage of the fact that the app is cloud based? (2) If you have access to computers running two different operating systems, such as Windows and Mac, or two devices, such as a laptop and a tablet or smartphone, try running the photo editing app in a browser on both computers or devices. What similarities and differences do you notice between the two versions?

Critical Thinking

Instructions: The Critical Thinking exercises challenge your assessment and decision-making skills by presenting real-world situations associated with module concepts. The Collaboration exercise should be completed with a team. Evaluate the situations below, using personal experiences and one or more resources available to you (such as articles on the web or in print, blogs, podcasts, videos, television, user guides, other individuals, electronics or computer stores, etc.). Perform the tasks requested in each exercise and share your deliverables in the format requested by your instructor (brief report, presentation, discussion, blog post, video, or other means).

1. **Graphics and Media**

   You are the marketing director at a company that frequently hires student interns to produce marketing materials. The interns tend to need direction in figuring out how to use graphics and media best to produce both print and online materials. As part of your job, you lead workshops that teach the interns about the different types of media and graphics, as well as the formats and apps they can use.

   Do This: Choose one category of graphics or media, such as audio, video, or animations. Use the web to research popular tools or apps for each category and then determine if they are able to produce both print and digital content, along with the costs for each. Choose one program from each category, and read user reviews and articles by industry experts. Describe situations where you would use each type of tool. Share any experiences you have with using the tools.

2. **Web and Mobile App Comparison**

   You recently purchased a new smartphone and want to research mobile apps that also have accompanying web apps.

   Do This: Choose three categories of apps, and find an example for each that has both a free web and mobile version. Read user reviews of each app, and search for articles by industry experts. Research any known safety risks for the apps. If you determine the app is safe, have access to the appropriate device, and would like to test the mobile app, you can download it to a smartphone or other mobile device. Try accessing the web app on a computer. Using your experience or research, note the differences in functionality between the web and mobile app. Is one or the other easier to use? Why or why not?

3. **Case Study**

   Cooperative-Owned Farm Stand   You are the new manager for a farm stand that is a cooperative effort, jointly owned by several local farmers. The farm stand needs productivity software in order to keep track of sales and expenses and use that information in documents and presentations for the board. You prepare a report to present about productivity software options to improve their business processes.

   Do This: Use the web to research popular productivity suites. List common features of each, find pricing information, and note any feedback or ratings by users. Which suites would you recommend? Why? Describe the steps involved in developing a project, and how to include data from one app in the suite to another. Identify additional possible uses the farm stand may have for the suite.

Collaboration

4. **Augmented and Virtual Reality in Interior Design**

   The manager of a home furnishings business is researching ways to use augmented or virtual reality apps to provide an enhanced customer experience at home, on their website, and in the store.

   Do This: Form a three-member team and research the use of augmented or virtual reality apps. Each member of your team should choose a different type of app, such as taking panoramic photos, using virtual reality tools for interior design, and enhancing photos or maps with additional information. List ways that a home furnishings or interior design business might use each type of app as part of their business, in the store, in a mobile app, or on their website. If possible, download or access a free version of an augmented or virtual reality app from each category and spend some time using it. Read user reviews of popular apps, and search for articles by industry experts. Meet with your group to discuss your findings, and prepare a report and demonstration showing how a home furnishings business might make use of these apps.

Digital Security, Ethics, and Privacy:
Avoiding and Recognizing Threats

5

Objectives

After completing this module, you will be able to:

1 Identify risks associated with technology use
2 Identify cybercrimes and criminals
3 Recognize issues related to information accuracy, intellectual property rights, and green computing
4 Describe ways to safeguard against various types of Internet and network attacks
5 Discuss techniques to prevent unauthorized computer access and use
6 Identify risks and safeguards associated with wireless communications
7 Discuss issues surrounding information privacy
8 Describe how schools and businesses protect themselves
9 Explain the importance of inclusivity and digital access

Risks Associated with Technology Use

Warning: Using This Device Could Be Hazardous to Your Health and Safety is a label you would never see on a computer. But that does not mean that using a computer is entirely safe. A risk is any possibility that something might occur resulting in an injury or a loss. You often hear warnings about risks, such as a thunderstorm approaching or that a floor is wet. You probably take some type of action to protect yourself when you become aware of risks, such as going indoors to avoid the storm or walking carefully so that you do not slip and fall.

Although we do not often think about it, using technology can also introduce risks. A **digital security risk** is any event or action that could cause a loss of or damage to computer or mobile device hardware, software, data, information, or processing capability. Types of digital security risks include threats to our information, physical health, mental health, and the environment (Figure 5-1). And as with a storm or wet floor you should take precautions with these digital risks.

You likely use your phone or computer hundreds of times a day to message with friends, search for a restaurant, work on a school assignment, play games, shop, or check your bank balance. You rely on technology to create, store, and manage your critical information, whether on your own devices or on devices that are used by companies or organizations that have access to your data. Thus, it is important that computers and mobile devices, along with the data and programs they store, are accessible and available when needed. It also is crucial

that all users take measures to protect or safeguard their computers, mobile devices, data, and programs from loss, damage, and misuse. For example, organizations must ensure that sensitive data and information, such as credit records, employee and customer data, and purchase information, is secure. Home users must ensure that their credit card numbers are secure when they make online purchases.

While some breaches to digital security are accidental, many are intentional. Attackers are always watching for any openings to steal your information or infect your devices. They often trick you into doing things that make it easy for them to steal your data, identity, and more. Some intruders do not disrupt a computer or device's functionality; they merely access data, information, or programs on the computer or mobile device before signing out. Other intruders indicate some evidence of their presence either by leaving a message or by deliberately altering or damaging data.

Cybercrime

An intentional breach of digital security often involves a deliberate act that is against the law. Any illegal act involving the use of a computer or related devices generally is referred to as a **computer crime**. The term **cybercrime** refers to online or Internet-based illegal acts, such as distributing malicious software or committing identity theft. Software used by cybercriminals sometimes is called **crimeware**. Today, combating cybercrime is one of the FBI's top priorities. **Cybersecurity** is the practice of protection against digital threats, including unauthorized or illegal access of data.

Figure 5-1   You can protect yourself from digital security risks.
Wavebreakmedia/Shutterstock.com

Jada positions her computer screen at the right height and makes sure she does not have a glare from the window that might cause eye strain.

Jada considers a digital detox periodically.

Jada is concerned that the hazardous toxic elements in her computer are properly recycled when her computer is discarded.

Jada is careful to protect the information she enters from attackers.

Digital forensics, also called cyberforensics, is the discovery, collection, and analysis of evidence found on computers and networks. Digital forensics involves the examination of media, programs, data and log files on computers, mobile devices, servers, and networks. Many entities use digital forensics, including law enforcement, criminal prosecutors, military intelligence, insurance agencies, and information security departments in the private sector.

A digital forensics examiner must have knowledge of the law, technical experience with many types of hardware and software products, superior communication skills, familiarity with corporate structures and policies, a willingness to learn and update skills, and a knack for problem solving.

You have learned about some of the risks and preventions, including cyberbullying, cyberstalking, malware, and phishing. This module covers these in more depth, as well as additional topics. As a digital citizen, you have a responsibility to be aware of how digital security and safety affect yourself and others.

Digital Detox

Mental health concerns, including technology addiction, are part of digital safety. Experts recommend taking occasional breaks from digital devices. A **digital detox** is a period of time during which an individual refrains from using technology. Participation in a digital detox has behavioral health benefits, including better sleep, less anxiety, and more productive thoughts. A break from devices also can help alleviate physical problems such as eye strain and repetitive stress injuries. Understanding the effects of technology on time management is another way to protect your behavioral and social health. Keep a log for several days about how much time you spend using devices in ways that are productive or unproductive. Analyze how your technology use affects your productivity. Be accountable for managing your time using apps that prohibit specific technology uses, such as gaming or social media, during work or school hours.

Cybercrimes and Criminals

Today, one of the more dangerous risks of using a computer is that someone will steal important information. Although the technical term for these thieves is **threat actor**, a more general and common term used to describe individuals who launch attacks against other users and their computers is simply attackers. These attackers may work individually, but more often they belong to organized gangs of young attackers who meet in hidden online dark web forums to trade information, buy and sell stolen data and attacker tools, and even coordinate their attacks. The **dark web** is a part of the web that is accessed using specialized software, where users and website operators can remain anonymous while performing illegal actions.

Who are these attackers? **Script kiddies** are individuals who want to attack computers but lack the knowledge of computers and networks needed to do so. Script kiddies instead do their work by downloading freely available automated attack software (*scripts*) from websites and using it to perform malicious acts.

A **hacker** is a person who intends to access a computer system without permission. Although originally a complimentary word for a computer enthusiast, hacker now has a derogatory meaning and refers to someone who accesses a computer or network illegally. Some hackers claim the intent of their security breaches is to improve security. A **cracker** also is someone who accesses a computer or network illegally but has the intent of destroying data, stealing information, or other malicious action. Both hackers and crackers have advanced computer and network skills. **Hacktivists** are attackers who are strongly motivated by principles or beliefs. Attacks by hacktivists can involve breaking into a website and changing the contents on the website as a means of making a political statement.

Cyberterrorists attack a nation's computer networks, like the electrical power grid, to cause disruption and panic among citizens. Instead of using an army to strike at an adversary, governments are now employing

 Consider This

What if you cannot remove malware?

Malware infections are one of the more common types of cybercrimes and security risks. In extreme cases, in order to remove malware from a computer or mobile device, you may need to erase, or reformat, an infected computer's hard drive, or reset a mobile device to its factory settings. For this reason, it is critical you have uninfected (clean) backups of all files. A **backup** is a duplicate of a file, program, or media that can be used if the original is lost, damaged, or destroyed. Consider creating recovery media when you purchase a new computer, and be sure to keep all installation media in the event you need to reinstall the computer's operating system and your apps. Seek advice from a technology specialist before performing a format or reformat procedure on your media. Have you ever had a malware infection? What steps did/could you take? How would you make the decision between resetting or reformatting your device or trying to remove the malware?

state-sponsored attackers to launch computer attacks against their enemies through **nation state actors**. The term, **cyberwarfare**, describes an attack whose goal ranges from disabling a government's computer network to crippling a country. Cyberterrorism and cyberwarfare usually require a team of highly skilled individuals, millions of dollars, and several years of planning.

Another serious security threat to companies can come from insiders, who can be the company's own employees, contractors, or business partners. For example, a health care worker upset about being passed over for a promotion might illegally gather health records on celebrities and sell them to the media, or securities traders who lose billions of dollars on bad stock bets could use their knowledge of the bank's computer security system to conceal the losses through fake transactions.

Once, the reason for launching computer attacks was for the attackers to show off their technology skills (fame). Today, that is no longer the case. Attackers are more focused on financial gain, desiring to steal personal information so that they can generate income (fortune).

These attackers try to steal and then use your credit card numbers, online financial account information, or Social Security numbers using data mining. **Data mining** is the process of sifting through Big Data to find the important questions that will yield fruitful results. With this information, they can pretend to be you and buy expensive items online while charging them to your credit card or break into your bank account to transfer your money to another account.

A **cyberextortionist** is an individual who attacks a nation's computer networks, like the electrical power grid, to cause disruption and panic among citizens. These perpetrators threaten to expose confidential information, exploit a security flaw, or launch an attack that will compromise the organization's network — if they are not paid a sum of money.

Social engineering is a category of attacks that attempts to trick the victim into giving valuable information to the attacker. Examples include hoaxes and phishing. At its core, social engineering relies on an attacker's clever manipulation of human nature in order to persuade the victim to provide information or take actions. Several basic principles of psychology make social engineering highly effective. These are listed in Table 5-1, with the example of an attacker pretending to be the chief executive officer (CEO) calling the organization's help desk to have a password reset.

Table 5-1   Social Engineering Principles

Principle	Description	Example
Authority	Directed by someone impersonating authority figure or falsely citing their authority	"I'm the CEO calling."
Intimidation	To frighten and coerce by threat	"If you don't reset my password, I will call your supervisor."
Consensus	Influenced by what others do	"I called last week and your colleague reset my password."
Scarcity	Something is in short supply	"I can't waste time here."
Urgency	Immediate action needed	"My meeting with the board starts in five minutes."
Familiarity	Victim well-known and well-received	"I remember reading a good evaluation on you."
Trust	Help a person known to you	"You know who I am."

 Consider This

Why would anyone hire a hacker?

Some organizations hire individuals previously convicted of computer crimes to help identify security risks and implement safeguards because these individuals know how criminals attempt to breach security. It may seem counterintuitive to hire a person who has experience breaking into networks to prove or find flaws in your company's security system. On the other hand, what better person than someone who understands the methods and motivations of a hacker? Companies often hire white hat hackers, who are hackers who hack in order to expose flaws and recommend fixes. Black hat hackers is the term used to refer to those who hack for their own personal gain or to cause distress. If you were a network administrator, would you hire a hacker? Why or why not? What precautions might you take?

Figure 5-2 Indicate whether you think the situation described is ethical or not.

Your Thoughts?	Ethical	Unethical
1. A person designing a webpage finds one on the web with similar requirements, copies it, modifies it, and publishes it as their own webpage.	☐	☐
2. A student researches using only the web to write a report.	☐	☐
3. Someone copies a well-known novel to the web and encourages others to read it.	☐	☐
4. A company uses recycled paper to print a 50-page employee benefits manual that is distributed to 425 employees.	☐	☐
5. An employee uses data from a nonprofit's published report in a brochure without citing the source.	☐	☐
6. A newspaper uses anonymous sources when researching an article.	☐	☐
7. A company requires permission from managers for employees to print documents longer than two pages.	☐	☐
8. A student finds a numerical fact listed in several reliable sources and uses it without citing the source.	☐	☐
9. Unable to find the owner of a photograph found on a website, an employee uses it in marketing materials without permission.	☐	☐
10. A publisher issues a new version of a book that is in the public domain.	☐	☐

Ethics and Society

As with any powerful technology, computers and mobile devices can be used for both good and bad intentions. The standards that determine whether an action is good or bad are known as ethics.

Technology ethics are the moral guidelines that govern the use of computers, mobile devices, information systems, and related technologies. Frequently discussed areas of computer ethics include information accuracy, intellectual property rights, and green computing. The questionnaire in Figure 5-2 raises issues in each of these areas.

Information Accuracy

Information accuracy is a concern today because many users access information maintained by other people or companies, such as on the Internet. Do not assume that because the information is on the web that it is correct. Be aware that the organization providing access to the information may not be the creator of the information.

In addition to concerns about the accuracy of computer input, some individuals and organizations raise questions about the ethics of using computers to alter output, primarily graphic output, such as a retouched photo. With graphics equipment and software, users easily can digitize photos and then add, change, or remove images. The altered photo in Figure 5-3 could be used for entertainment purposes, but other types of alterations may be made to mislead or confuse the audience.

Intellectual Property Rights

As previously discussed, intellectual property (IP) rights are the rights to which creators are entitled for their work. Certain issues arise surrounding IP today because many of these works are available digitally and easily can be redistributed or altered without the creator's permission. A copyright protects any tangible form of expression. Creative Commons is another source for finding content that may or may not be used, along with any restrictions or payment needed to use it.

A common infringement of copyright is piracy, where people illegally copy software, movies, and music. Many areas are not clear-cut with respect to the law, because copyright law gives the public fair use to copyrighted

Figure 5-3 A digitally edited photo that shows a fruit that looks like an apple on the outside and an orange on the inside.
Giuliano20/Dreamstime.com

Figure 5-4   Answer questions related to copyright usage.

Your Thoughts?	Yes	No
1. Should individuals be able to download contents of your website, modify it, and then put it on the web again as their own?	☐	☐
2. Should a faculty member have the right to print material from an ebook or a website and distribute it to all members of the class for teaching purposes only?	☐	☐
3. Should someone be able to scan photos or pages from a book, publish them on the web, and allow others to download them?	☐	☐
4. Should a blogger or website creator be able to include any photos they find on the web in their blogs or websites, even with attribution?	☐	☐
5. Should someone be able to put the lyrics of a song on the web?	☐	☐
6. Should students be able to take term papers they have written and post them on the web, making it tempting for other students to download and submit them as their own work?	☐	☐

material. The issues surround the phrase, fair use, which allows use for educational and critical purposes. This vague definition is subject to widespread interpretation and raises many questions (Figure 5-4).

These issues with copyright law led to the development of the digital rights management (DRM) strategy that aims to prevent illegal distribution of movies, music, and other digital content.

Green Computing

Recall that green computing involves reducing the electricity and environmental waste while using computers, mobile devices, and related technologies. Figure 5-5 summarizes measures users can take to contribute to green computing.

Enterprise data centers and computer facilities consume large amounts of electricity from computer hardware and associated devices and utilities, such as air conditioning, coolers, lighting, and so on. Organizations can implement

a variety of measures to reduce electrical waste, including the following:

- Consolidate servers by using **virtualization**, which involves sharing computing resources, such as servers or storage devices, among computers and devices on a network.
- Purchase high-efficiency equipment.
- Use sleep modes and other power management features for computers and devices.
- Buy computers and devices with low power consumption processors and power supplies.
- When possible, use outside air to cool the data center or computer facility.

Some organizations continually review their **power usage effectiveness** (**PUE**), which is a ratio that measures how much power enters the computer facility or data center against the amount of power required to run the computers and devices.

Figure 5-5   A list of suggestions to make computing healthy for the environment.

© US Environmental Protection Agency, ENERGY STAR program/The Cadmus Group, Inc; Roman Sotola/Shutterstock.com

Green Computing Tips

1. Conserve Energy
   a. Use computers and devices that comply with the ENERGY STAR program.
   b. Do not leave a computer or device running overnight.
   c. Turn off the monitor, printer, and other devices when not in use.
2. Reduce Environmental Waste
   a. Use paperless methods to communicate.
   b. Recycle paper and buy recycled paper.
   c. Recycle toner and ink cartridges, computers, mobile devices, printers, and other devices.
   d. Telecommute.
   e. Use videoconferencing and VoIP for meetings.

? Consider This

What are the risks associated with inaccurate data?

Data entry errors can lead to lost business, lawsuits, and expense. For example, if you enter measurements in kilometers for one data column but in miles for a different column, without conversion, any calculations or comparisons using this unconverted data would be useless, as well as misleading. Other examples of inaccurate data entry include data entered in the wrong field, missing data, or duplicate data entries. Businesses risk their reputations if they present inaccurate information to customers or investors due to faulty data; they also can be fined if the error results in misrepresentation of profits or assets or if they miscalculate taxes owed. Have you ever entered data inaccurately? What did/could occur as the result? What did/could you do to ensure this does not happen again?

Internet and Network Attacks

Information transmitted over networks has a higher degree of security risk than information kept on an organization's premises. In an organization, network administrators usually take measures to protect a network from security risks. On the Internet, where no central administrator is present, the security risk is greater. Internet and network attacks that jeopardize security include malware, botnets, denial of service attacks, back doors, and spoofing. These types of attacks can affect your privacy, personal information, finances, and more.

Malware

Recall that malware, short for malicious software, consists of programs that act without a user's knowledge and deliberately alter the operations of computers and mobile devices. Table 5-2 summarizes common types of malware. Some malware contains characteristics in two or more classes. For example, a single threat could contain elements of a virus, worm, and trojan horse.

Malware can deliver its **payload**, or destructive event or prank, on a computer or mobile device in a variety of ways, such as when a user opens an infected file, runs an infected program, connects an unprotected computer or mobile device to a network, or when a certain condition or event occurs, such as the computer's clock changing to a specific date. A common way that computers and mobile devices become infected with viruses and other malware is through users opening infected email attachments (Figure 5-6) or clicking links that link to websites that contain viruses.

Table 5-2   Common Types of Malware

Type	Description
Adware	A program that displays an online advertisement in a banner, pop-up window, or pop-under window on webpages, email messages, or other Internet services
Ransomware	A program that blocks or limits access to a computer, phone, or file until the user pays a specified amount of money
Rootkit	A program that hides in a computer or mobile device and allows someone from a remote location to take full control of the computer or device
Spyware	A program placed on a computer or mobile device without the user's knowledge that secretly collects information about the user and then communicates the information it collects to some outside source while the user is online
Trojan horse	A program that hides within or looks like a legitimate program. Unlike a virus or worm, a trojan horse does not replicate itself to other computers or devices
Virus	A potentially damaging program that affects, or infects, a computer or mobile device negatively by altering the way the computer or device works without the user's knowledge or permission
Worm	A program that copies itself repeatedly, for example in memory or on a network, using up resources and possibly shutting down the computer, device, or network

Figure 5-6   How a virus can spread via an email message.
iStockcom/Steve Cukrov; iStock.com/Casarsa

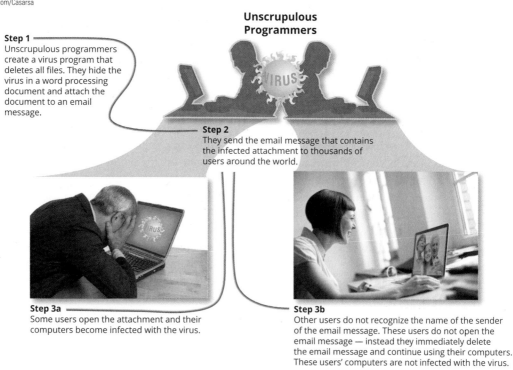

Unscrupulous Programmers

Step 1
Unscrupulous programmers create a virus program that deletes all files. They hide the virus in a word processing document and attach the document to an email message.

Step 2
They send the email message that contains the infected attachment to thousands of users around the world.

Step 3a
Some users open the attachment and their computers become infected with the virus.

Step 3b
Other users do not recognize the name of the sender of the email message. These users do not open the email message — instead they immediately delete the email message and continue using their computers. These users' computers are not infected with the virus.

Botnets

A compromised computer or device, known as a **zombie**, is one whose owner is unaware the computer or device is being controlled remotely by an outsider. A **botnet**, or zombie army, is a group of compromised computers or mobile devices connected to a network, such as the Internet, that are used to attack other networks, usually for nefarious purposes.

A **bot** is a program that performs a repetitive task on a network. Cybercriminals install malicious bots on unprotected computers and devices to create a botnet. The perpetrator then uses the botnet to send spam via email, spread viruses and other malware, or commit other attacks.

Denial of Service Attacks

A **denial of service attack (DoS attack)** is a type of attack, usually on a server, that is meant to overload the server with network traffic so that it cannot provide necessary services, such as the web or email. Perpetrators carry out a DoS attack in a variety of ways, including using bots. Or, they may use an unsuspecting computer to send an influx of confusing data messages or useless traffic to a computer network. The victim computer network slows down considerably and eventually becomes unresponsive or unavailable, blocking legitimate visitors from accessing the network.

A more devastating type of DoS attack is the **distributed DoS attack (DDoS attack)** in which multiple computers, such as a zombie army, are used to attack a server or other network resource. DDoS attacks have been able to stop operations temporarily at numerous large websites and companies.

The damage caused by a DoS or DDoS attack usually is extensive. During the outage, retailers lose sales from customers, news websites and search engines lose revenue from advertisers, and time-sensitive information may be delayed. Repeated attacks could tarnish reputations, causing even greater losses.

Back Doors

A **back door** is a program or set of instructions in a program that allows users to bypass security controls when accessing a program, computer, or network. Once perpetrators gain access to unsecure computers, they often install a back door or modify an existing program to include a back door, which allows them to continue to access the computer remotely without the user's knowledge. A rootkit can be a back door. Some worms leave back doors, which have been used to spread other worms or to distribute spam from the unsuspecting victim computers.

Programmers often build back doors into programs during system development. These back doors save development time because the programmer can bypass security controls while writing and testing programs. Similarly, a computer repair technician may install a back door while troubleshooting problems on a computer. If a programmer or computer repair technician fails to remove a back door, a perpetrator could use the back door to gain entry to a computer or network.

Spoofing

Spoofing is a technique intruders use to make their network or Internet transmission appear legitimate to a victim computer or network. Two common types of spoofing schemes are IP and address spoofing.

- IP spoofing occurs when an intruder computer fools a network into believing its IP address is associated with a trusted source. Perpetrators of IP spoofing trick their victims into interacting with the phony website. For example, the victim may provide confidential information or download files containing viruses, worms, or other malware.
- Address spoofing occurs when the sender's email address or other components of an email header are altered so that it appears that the email message originated from a different sender. Address spoofing commonly is used in virus hoaxes, spam, and phishing scams (Figure 5-7).

Protection from Viruses and Other Malware

It is impossible to ensure a virus or malware never will attack a computer, but you can take steps to protect your computer by following these practices:

- **Use virus protection software.** Install a reputable antivirus program and then scan the entire computer to be certain it is free of viruses and other malware. Update the antivirus program and the virus signatures (known specific patterns of viruses) regularly.
- **Use a firewall.** Set up a hardware firewall or install a software firewall that protects your network's resources from outside intrusions.
- **Be suspicious of all unsolicited email and text messages.** Never open an email message unless you are expecting it, *and* it is from a trusted source. When in doubt, ask the sender to confirm the message is legitimate before you open it. Be especially cautious when deciding whether to click links in email and text messages or to open attachments.
- **Disconnect your computer from the Internet.** If you do not need Internet access, disconnect the computer from the Internet. Some security experts recommend disconnecting from the computer network before opening email attachments.

Figure 5-7 Spoofers alter the components and header of an email message so that it appears the message originated from a different sender.
Source: Privacy Rights Clearinghouse

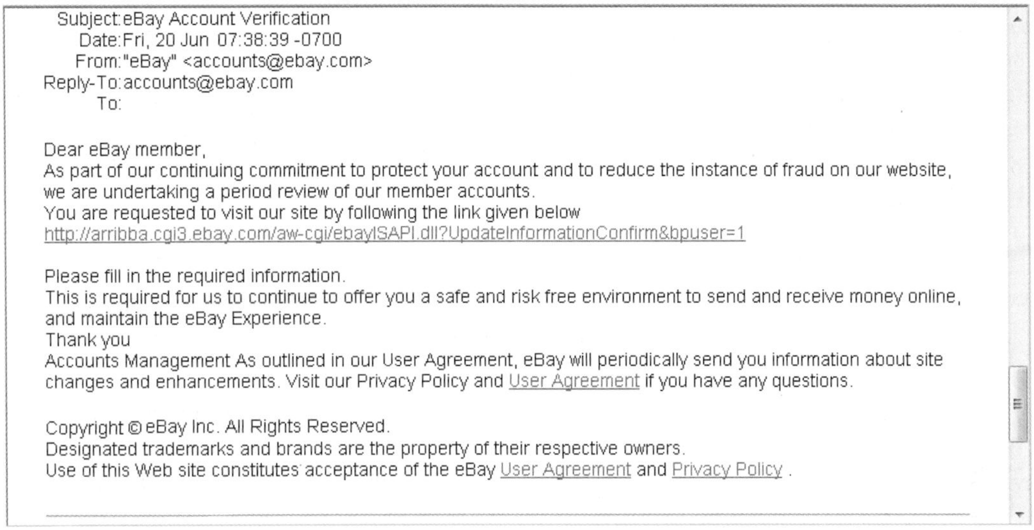

> Subject: eBay Account Verification
> Date: Fri, 20 Jun 07:38:39 -0700
> From: "eBay" <accounts@ebay.com>
> Reply-To: accounts@ebay.com
> To:
>
> Dear eBay member,
> As part of our continuing commitment to protect your account and to reduce the instance of fraud on our website, we are undertaking a period review of our member accounts.
> You are requested to visit our site by following the link given below
> http://arribba.cgi3.ebay.com/aw-cgi/ebayISAPI.dll?UpdateInformationConfirm&bpuser=1
>
> Please fill in the required information.
> This is required for us to continue to offer you a safe and risk free environment to send and receive money online, and maintain the eBay Experience.
> Thank you
> Accounts Management As outlined in our User Agreement, eBay will periodically send you information about site changes and enhancements. Visit our Privacy Policy and User Agreement if you have any questions.
>
> Copyright © eBay Inc. All Rights Reserved.
> Designated trademarks and brands are the property of their respective owners.
> Use of this Web site constitutes acceptance of the eBay User Agreement and Privacy Policy .

- **Download software with caution.** Download programs or apps only from websites you trust, especially those with music and video sharing software.
- **Close spyware windows.** If you suspect a pop-up or pop-under window may be spyware, close the window. Never click an Agree or OK button in a suspicious window.
- **Before using any removable media, scan it for malware.** Follow this procedure even for shrink-wrapped software from major developers. Some commercial software has been infected and distributed to unsuspecting users. Never start a computer with removable media inserted in the computer unless you are certain the media are uninfected.
- **Keep current.** Install the latest updates for your computer software. Stay informed about new virus alerts and virus hoaxes.
- **Back up regularly.** In the event your computer becomes unusable due to a virus attack or other malware, you will be able to restore operations if you have a clean (uninfected) backup.

❓ Consider This

How can you tell if your computer or mobile device is functioning as a zombie?
Your computer or mobile device may be a zombie if you notice an unusually high drive activity, a slower than normal Internet connection, or connected devices becoming increasingly unresponsive. The chances of your computer or devices becoming part of a botnet greatly increase if your devices are not protected by an effective firewall. Have you ever suspected your device is a zombie? How might this have occurred? What steps can you take to fix it and to prevent it from happening again?

Secure IT: Protect Yourself and Your Data

Your digital footprint is the record of everything you do online. A digital footprint can be nearly impossible to completely erase, which is why you need to ensure you are protecting your identity and data. You have learned about some of the methods that protect your data and information, computers, mobile devices, and networks from attacks, including using firewalls and access controls. Additional information about these and other methods is included in this section.

Information Theft

For most computer users, the greatest risk comes from attackers who want to steal their information for their own financial gain.

The risks you face online when using the Internet or email include:

- **Online banking:** Attackers try to steal your password to access your online bank account and transfer your money overseas.
- **E-commerce shopping:** When you enter your credit card number to make an online purchase, an attacker can try to intercept your card number as it is transmitted over the network.
- **Fake websites:** Attackers can set up an imposter website that looks just like the website where you pay your monthly credit card bill. This fake website tricks you into entering your username and password, and that information then falls into the hands of the attackers. Because the fake website looks very similar to the real website, it can be hard to identify these unsafe websites.

- **Social media sites:** Attackers can ask to be a "friend" on your social media site by pretending to be someone you met or went to school with. Once you accept this new friend, the attacker may be able to see personal information about you, such as your pet's name or your favorite vacation spot. This information could be used to reset your password on another website that requires the answer to the security question that asks you to enter the name of your pet. Also, smartphone apps that are linked to social media sites have been known to gather user information without proper notification.

Gathering your personal information is not something that is done only by attackers. Many organizations collect and store your personal information for legitimate means. This information should be accessible only to those who are authorized to use it. But some organizations might secretly share your confidential information without your consent. Table 5-3 lists some of the valid and invalid uses of your personal information by organizations.

Most organizations will attempt to prevent information theft by implementing user identification and authentication controls. These controls are best suited for protecting information on computers located on an organization's premises. To further protect information on the Internet and networks, organizations and individuals use a variety of encryption techniques.

Mobile users today often access their company networks through a virtual private network. A **virtual private network** (**VPN**) is a private, secure path across a public network that allows authorized users secure access to a company or other network. When a mobile user connects to a main office using a standard Internet connection, a VPN provides the mobile user with a secure connection to the company network server, as if the user has a private line. VPNs help ensure that data is safe from being intercepted by unauthorized people by encrypting data as it transmits from a laptop, smartphone, or other mobile device.

Firewalls

In addition to personal firewall uses, organizations use firewalls to protect network resources from outsiders and to restrict employees' access to sensitive data, such as payroll or personnel records. They can implement a firewall solution themselves or outsource their needs to a company specializing in providing firewall protection.

Large organizations often route all their communications through a proxy server, which typically is a component of the firewall. A **proxy server** is a server outside the organization's network that controls which communications pass in and out of the organization's network. That is, a proxy server carefully screens all incoming and outgoing messages. Proxy servers use a variety of screening techniques. Some check the domain name or IP address of the message for legitimacy.

Personal firewalls constantly monitor all transmissions to and from the computer and may inform a user of any attempted intrusions. Both Windows and Mac operating systems include firewall capabilities, including monitoring Internet traffic to and from installed applications. Some small/home office users purchase a hardware firewall, such as a router or other device that has a built-in firewall, in addition to or instead of a personal firewall. Hardware firewalls stop malicious intrusions before they attempt to affect your computer or network (Figure 5-8).

Unauthorized Access and Use

Unauthorized access is the use of a computer or network without permission. Unauthorized use is the use of a computer or its data for unapproved or possibly illegal activities.

Home and business users can be a target of unauthorized access and use. Unauthorized use includes a variety of activities: an employee using an organization's computer to send personal email messages, an employee using the organization's word processing software to track their child's soccer league scores, or a perpetrator gaining access to a bank computer and performing an unauthorized transfer.

Table 5-3 Uses of Personal Information

Organization	Information	Valid Use	Invalid Use
School	Telephone number	Call you about an advising appointment	Give to credit card company who calls you about applying for a new credit card
Hospital	Medical history	Can refer to past procedures when you are admitted as a patient	Sell to drug company who sends you information about its drugs
Employer	Personal email address	Will send to you the latest company newsletter	Provide to a local merchant who is having a holiday sale

Figure 5-8 How a firewall works.

© Netgear; Courtesy of CheckPoint Software Technologies Ltd; iStock.com/Skodonnell; Source: Nutrition Blog Network; iStock.com/123Render; Source: Microsoft Corporation; Natalia Siverina/Shutterstock.com; iStock.com/Scanrail; Source: Microsoft Corporation; iStock.com/Arattansi

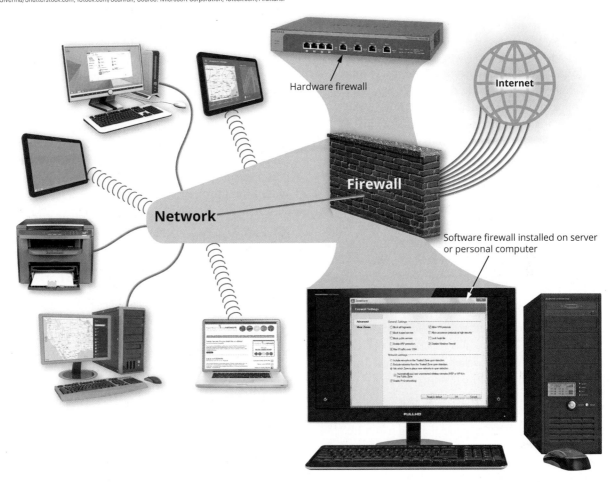

Organizations take several measures to help prevent unauthorized access and use. At a minimum, they should have a written acceptable use policy (AUP) that outlines the activities for which the computer and network may and may not be used. An organization's AUP should specify the acceptable use of technology by employees for personal reasons. Some organizations prohibit such use entirely. Others allow personal use on the employee's own time, such as a lunch hour. Whatever the policy, an organization should document and explain it to employees. The AUP also should specify the personal activities, if any, that are allowed on company time. For example, can employees check personal email messages or respond to personal text messages during work hours?

To protect your personal computer from unauthorized intrusions, you should disable file and printer sharing in your operating system. This security measure attempts to ensure that others cannot access your files or your printer. You also should be sure to use a firewall. The following sections address other techniques for protecting against unauthorized access and use. The technique(s) used should correspond to the degree of risk that is associated with the unauthorized access.

Access Controls

Many organizations use access controls to minimize the chance that a perpetrator intentionally may access or an employee accidentally may access confidential information on a computer, mobile device, or network. In addition, the computer, device, or network should maintain an **audit trail** that records in a file both successful and unsuccessful access attempts. An unsuccessful access attempt could result from users mistyping their password, or it could result from a perpetrator trying thousands of passwords.

Organizations should investigate unsuccessful access attempts immediately to ensure they are not intentional breaches of security. They also should review successful access for irregularities, such as use of the computer after normal working hours or from remote computers. The security program can be configured to alert a security administrator whenever suspicious or irregular activities are suspected. In addition, an organization regularly should review users' access privilege levels to determine whether they still are appropriate.

Backing Up

To protect against data loss caused by hardware/software/information theft or system failure, users should back up computer and mobile device files regularly. To back up a file means to make a copy of it. In the case of system failure or the discovery of corrupted files, you restore the files by copying the backed up files to their original location on the computer or mobile device.

Online backup services use special software on the computer to monitor what files have changed or have been created; these are then automatically uploaded to a cloud server. Because these backups are performed automatically and stored at a remote location, these online backup services provide the highest degree of protection to most users.

Sometimes, however, situations occur when an online backup service may not be the right choice, such as when only a slow Internet connection is available. In that case, you can perform your own backup from the hard drive to another medium and then store that medium in a remote location. Modern operating systems can perform these backups, and third-party software also is available. Cloud backup services can save you the cost of maintaining hardware.

You can perform four types of backup: full, differential, incremental, or selective. A fifth type, continuous data protection, often is used only by large enterprises to back up data to an in-house network storage device purchased and maintained by the enterprise. Table 5-4 summarizes the purpose, advantages, and disadvantages of each of these backup methods.

Some users implement a three-generation backup policy to preserve three copies of important files. In a grandparent-parent-child backup scheme, full backups are made at regular (daily or weekly) intervals on removable media, such as a flash drive. The oldest saved backup is called the grandparent, the next oldest is the parent, and the current backup is the child. When a new child backup is made, the previous child backup is retained as the parent backup, the parent backup becomes the grandparent backup, and the oldest grandparent backup is discarded, and its media often is reused for a future backup.

❓ Consider This

Should you use a lock screen?

A lock screen is a screen that restricts access to a computer or mobile device until a user performs a certain action. Some simply require a user to swipe the screen to unlock the screen. Others verify a user's identity by requiring entry of a password, PIN, or passcode; a fingerprint scan; or a gesture swipe. Gestures are motions users make on a touch screen with the tip of one or more fingers or their hand. For example, to unlock the screen on a phone, a user could connect the dots on the screen using a pattern previously defined by the user. A picture password allows the user to select an image that appears on the lock screen. The user selects a pattern of taps or gestures on the photo that the computer stores and then must repeat the pattern to unlock the screen. Others use face recognition to ensure that only the recognized owner of the device can access it. Have you used a lock screen? What protections does a lock screen provide? What complications might occur with using a lock screen?

Table 5-4 Various Backup Methods

Type of Backup	Description	Advantages	Disadvantages
Full backup	Copies all of the files on media in the computer.	Fastest recovery method. All files are saved.	Longest backup time.
Differential backup	Copies only the files that have changed since the last full backup.	Fast backup method. Requires minimal storage space to back up.	Recovery is time-consuming because the last full backup plus the differential backup are needed.
Incremental backup	Copies only the files that have changed since the last full or incremental backup.	Fastest backup method. Requires minimal storage space to back up. Only most recent changes saved.	Recovery is most time-consuming because the last full backup and all incremental backups since the last full backup are needed.
Selective backup	Users choose which folders and files to include in a backup.	Fast backup method. Provides great flexibility.	Difficult to manage individual file backups. Least manageable of all the backup methods.
Continuous data protection (CDP)	All data is backed up whenever a change is made.	The only real-time backup. Very fast recovery of data.	Very expensive and requires a great amount of storage.

Wireless Security

In addition to protecting your mobile device from theft, you also should protect it from attackers who want to steal information stored on it or transmitted to and from the device. It also is necessary to protect the privacy of your information.

Protect Mobile Devices

Several types of attacks are specifically directed toward mobile devices. Some of the more common attacks are directed toward wireless (Wi-Fi) networks that support these devices.

Some risks from attacks on Wi-Fi networks include the following:

- **Reading wireless transmissions:** Usernames, passwords, credit card numbers, and other information sent over the Wi-Fi network could be easily seen by an attacker.
- **Viewing or stealing computer data:** An attacker who can connect to a home Wi-Fi network could access any folder that has file sharing enabled on any computer on the network. This essentially provides an attacker full access to view or steal sensitive data from all computers on the network.
- **Injecting malware:** Attackers could inject trojan horses, viruses, and other malware in to the user's computer.

- **Downloading harmful content:** In several instances, attackers have accessed a home computer through an unprotected Wi-Fi network, downloaded child pornography to the computer, and then turned that computer into a file server to distribute the content. When authorities traced the files back to that computer, the unsuspecting owner was arrested and their equipment confiscated.

Using a public Wi-Fi network in a coffee shop, airport, or school campus also involves security concerns. First, these networks are rarely protected (to allow easy access by users), so attackers can read any wireless transmissions sent to and from the user's device. In addition, an attacker may set up an **evil twin**, a normal-looking yet fraudulent Wi-Fi network that allows hackers to capture personal information users transmit. A user's mobile device may unknowingly connect to this evil twin instead of the authorized device so that attackers can receive the user's transmissions or directly send malware to the user's computer.

When using any public Wi-Fi, be sure you are connecting to the approved wireless network. Also limit the type of activity you do on public networks to simple web surfing or watching online videos. Accessing online banking sites or sending confidential information that could be intercepted is not a good idea.

Configuring your own Wi-Fi wireless router to provide the highest level of security is an important step. Configuration settings for wireless routers are listed in Table 5-5.

Table 5-5   Configuration Settings for Wireless Routers

Wireless Router Setting	Explanation	Recommended Configuration
Access password	This requires a password to access the configuration settings of the device.	Create a strong password so that attackers cannot access the wireless router and turn off the security settings.
Remote management	Remote management allows the configuration settings to be changed from anywhere through an Internet connection.	Turn off remote management so that someone outside cannot access the configuration settings.
Service Set Identifier (SSID)	The SSID is the name of the local wireless network.	Change this from the default setting to a value that does not reveal the identity of the owner or the location of the network (such as MyWireNet599342).
Wi-Fi Protected Access 2 (WPA2) Personal	WPA2 encrypts the wireless data transmissions and also limits who can access the Wi-Fi network.	Turn on WPA2 and set a strong preshared key (PSK), which must also be entered once on each mobile device.
Wi-Fi Protected Setup (WPS)	WPS simplifies setting up the security on a wireless router.	Turn off WPS due to its security vulnerabilities.
Guest access	Guest access allows temporary users to access the wireless network without any additional configuration settings.	Turn on Guest Access when needed and turn it back off when the approved guests leave.
Disable SSID broadcasts	This prevents the wireless router from advertising the wireless network to anyone in the area.	Leave SSID broadcasts on; turning them off only provide a very weak degree of security and may suggest to an attacker that your network has valuable information.

Secure Your Wireless Network

When you set up a wireless network, it is important to secure the network so that only your computers and mobile devices can connect to it. Unsecured wireless networks can be seen and accessed by neighbors and others nearby, which may make it easier for them to connect to and access the data on the computers and mobile devices on your network. The following list provides suggestions for securing your wireless network.

- Immediately upon connecting your wireless access point and/or router, change the password required to access administrative features. If the password remains at its default setting, others may possibly be able to connect to and configure your wireless network settings.
- Change the SSID (service set identifier), or network name, from the default to something that uniquely identifies your network, especially if you live in close proximity to other wireless networks.
- Do not broadcast the SSID. This will make it more difficult for others to detect your wireless network. When you want to connect a computer or mobile device to your wireless network, it will be necessary to enter the SSID manually.
- Enable an encryption method, and specify a password or passphrase that is difficult for others to guess. The most secure passwords and passphrases contain more than eight characters, uppercase and lowercase letters, numbers, and special characters.
- Enable and configure the Media Access Control (MAC) address control feature. A **MAC address** is a unique hardware identifier for your computer or device. The MAC address control feature specifies which computers and mobile devices can connect to your network. If a computer or device is not specified, it will not be able to connect.
- Choose a secure location for your wireless router so that unauthorized people cannot access it. Someone who has physical access to a wireless router can restore factory defaults and erase your settings.

Cloud Data Privacy

Privacy and security concerns arise when consumers and businesses consider moving their data to an online storage service. While the cloud offers a tremendous amount of storage space at a relatively low cost, the security of data and the reliability of cloud companies trigger concerns.

Personal Risks with Cloud Computing When people register for a cloud computing service, they sign a written contract or click an online OK or Agree button to affirm they read and understand the terms of the agreement. Any data stored in the cloud is entrusted to the third-party provider, which has a legal obligation to protect the data from security breaches. The company also must guard against data loss due to physical disasters, such as power outages, cooling failures, and fire. When data has been compromised, many states require the company to disclose the issue to the data owner promptly.

One concern arises when transferring data over a network to the cloud. When the data is traveling to or from a computer and the cloud service, it is subject to interception. To minimize risk, security experts emphasize that the web address of the website you are visiting must begin with https, and the data should be encrypted and authenticated.

Law enforcement's access to the data raises another security issue. Email messages stored on a private server belong to the company or individual who owns the computer, so law enforcement officials must obtain a search warrant to read a particular user's messages. In contrast, law enforcement officials can access email messages stored on the cloud by requesting the information from the company that owns the cloud service. The user might not be notified of the search until up to 90 days after the search occurred; moreover, the search may occur without limitations and may include continuous monitoring of an individual's email communications.

International laws and industry regulations protect sensitive and personal data. The education, health care, and financial services industries in the United States have strict data privacy regulations that affect cloud storage. For example, the Family Educational Rights and Privacy Act (FERPA) regulates the confidentiality of students' educational records, so colleges must obtain students' consent to share data with cloud storage providers and other third parties.

The Cloud Security Alliance (CSA) points out another risk — that of hackers who register for a cloud service with a credit card or for a free trial period and then unleash malware in an attempt to gain access to passwords. Because the registration and validation procedure for accessing the cloud is relatively anonymous, authorities can have difficulty locating the abusers.

Cloud storage companies have increased their privacy and security features in recent years. Many allow consumers and businesses to protect files with passwords or require two-step authentication to access files, to delete data if a mobile device has been stolen or lost, and to delete data that has been stored past an expiration date.

Business Risks with Cloud Computing   Businesses often contract with cloud storage providers for data storage. Many businesses also use cloud storage providers to store customer data. This data could include contact information, credit card numbers, and ordering history.

Ownership of cloud data becomes an issue when a cloud storage provider or the business using the cloud services closes. Other issues include what happens if the business fails to pay the cloud storage provider, or when a contract ends. Many feel that it is the responsibility of the business owner to remove and destroy company data before a contract ends. Supporters of this argument believe that cloud storage providers should not be accessing data they host. Others contend that if a business fails to remove and destroy its data before its cloud storage contract ends, cloud storage providers should return the data, or remove the data permanently.

An ongoing debate exists related to who is responsible for cloud data security. Many experts put the responsibility of securing data in the hands of the data owner. Others advocate for a shared security model, in which the cloud storage provider includes security tools, but the company provides additional security as needed.

Ownership and security of data should be included in any contract between a business and cloud storage provider. Contracts also should specify what happens in a variety of scenarios, including if either party stops its operations or if hackers access the data.

 Consider This ⎯⎯⎯⎯⎯⎯⎯⎯⎯⎯⎯⎯⎯⎯

How do you know if someone is accessing your home network?
If you notice the speed of your wireless connection is slower than normal, it may be a sign that someone else is accessing your network. You also may notice indicator lights on your wireless router flashing rapidly when you are not connected to your wireless network. Most wireless routers have a built-in utility that allows you to view the computers and devices currently connected to your network. If you notice a computer or device that does not belong to you, consult your wireless router's documentation to determine how to remove it from the network. Have you ever had an intruder use your network? What are the risks to having unauthorized users accessing your network? How can you prevent this from happening?

Information Privacy

Protection of your information should be at the forefront of every decision you make with technology. You should assume that everything you post online, every link you click, every web search you conduct, and all your other actions can be tracked and used, not only for legitimate purposes, such as for targeted advertisements, but for malicious purposes, such as to steal your identity. Beyond considering your actions, however, you can take several steps to protect unauthorized access to your devices and accounts, including authorization, biometrics, and more, to ensure that you (and only you) have access to your private information.

Use Strong Authentication

Authentication is the process of ensuring that the person requesting access to a computer or other resources is authentic and not an imposter. Different types of authentication or proof of genuineness can be presented; some of these are discussed in the following sections.

Use Strong Passwords   A username — also called a user ID (identification), log on name, or sign in name — is a unique combination of characters, such as letters of the alphabet or numbers, that identifies one specific user. In most computer systems, users signing in would be asked to identify themselves. This is done by entering an identifier known as the username, such as MDenton. Yet because anyone could enter this username, the next step is for a user to authenticate themselves by proving that they actually are MDenton. This is often done by providing information that only the user would know, namely, a password (Figure 5-9). A **password** is a secret combination of letters, numbers, and/or characters that only the user should know.

Passwords are by far the most common type of authentication today. Yet despite their widespread use, passwords provide only weak protection. The weakness of passwords is due to human memory: you can memorize only a limited number of items. Passwords place heavy loads on human memory in multiple ways:

- The most effective passwords are long and complex; however, these usually are difficult to memorize and then accurately recall when needed.
- Users must remember multiple passwords for many different accounts. You have accounts for different computers and mobile devices at work, school, and home; multiple email accounts; online banking; website accounts; and so on.
- For the highest level of security, each account password should be unique, which further strains a user's memory.
- Many security policies require that passwords expire after a set period of time, such as every 45–60 days, at which time a new one must be created. Some security policies even prevent a previously used password from being used again, forcing the user to repeatedly memorize new passwords.

Figure 5-9   User sign in requiring password.
Iurii Stepanov/Shutterstock.com

Because of the burdens that passwords place on human memory, most users take shortcuts to help them memorize and recall their passwords. One shortcut is to create and use a weak password. Weak passwords use a common word as a password, a short password, a predictable sequence of characters, or personal information in a password.

Several recent attacks have stolen hundreds of millions of passwords, which then are posted on the Internet. The 10 most common passwords are very weak and are listed in in Table 5-6.

Table 5-6   Ten Most Common Passwords

Rank	Password
1	123456
2	123456789
3	qwerty
4	password
5	1111111
6	12345678
7	abc123
8	password1
9	1234567
10	12345

Attackers can easily break weak passwords using sophisticated hardware and software tools. They often focus on breaking your passwords because, like the key to a door, once the password is compromised it opens all the contents of your computer or account to the attacker.

It is important that you create and manage secure, strong passwords. A strong password is a longer combination of letters, numbers, and/or symbols that unlocks access to protected electronic data. Most security experts recommend that a secure password should be a minimum of 15–20 characters in length. A longer password is always more secure than a shorter password, regardless of complexity. The longer a password is, the more attempts an attacker must make to break it.

Table 5-7 illustrates the number of possible passwords for different password lengths using a standard 95-key keyboard along with the average attempts needed to break a password. Obviously, a longer password takes significantly more time to attempt to break than a short password.

In addition to having long passwords, consider these other general recommendations when creating passwords:

- Do not use passwords that consist of dictionary words or phonetic words.
- Do not repeat characters (xxx) or use sequences (abc or 123).
- Do not use birthdays, family member names, pet names, addresses, or any personal information.

You might be wondering how you possibly can apply all these recommendations and memorize long, complex, and unique passwords for all your accounts. Instead of relying on human memory for passwords, security experts universally recommend that you use a **password manager**, which is a program that helps you create and store multiple strong passwords in single user vault file that is protected by one strong master password. You can then retrieve individual passwords as needed from the vault file, thus freeing you from the need to memorize multiple passwords. The value of using a password manager is that unique strong passwords, such as WUuAôxB$2aWøBnd&Tf7MfEtm, can be created easily and used for any of your accounts.

The first time you view a password-protected website and enter your username and password, the password manager saves this information. The next time you visit one of these websites or apps, the software supplies the account information automatically. Password managers use two-step verification and advanced encryption techniques to ensure information is stored securely.

Some managers offer the option to generate random passwords, which have a unique combination of jumbled numbers and letters that are difficult for criminals to steal, for each account. Other features include the capability to auto-fill information, such as your name, address, and phone number, on forms and to provide a hint if you have forgotten your master password.

Table 5-7   Number of Possible Passwords

Password Length	Number of Possible Passwords	Average Attempts to Break Password
2	9025	4513
3	857,375	428,688
4	81,450,625	40,725,313
5	7,737,809,375	3,868,904,688
6	735,091,890,625	367,545,945,313

Password manager services can be free to use or may require a small annual fee. Some security experts recommend using a service that charges a fee, stating that these companies may provide more features. Before using any manager, call the company and ask about security measures, the capability to sync with multiple mobile devices, 24-hour customer service via live chat or phone, and limits on the number of passwords that can be saved.

Passphrase Instead of passwords, some organizations use passphrases to authenticate users. A passphrase is a private combination of words, often containing mixed capitalization and punctuation, associated with a username that allows access to certain computer resources. Passphrases, which often can be up to 100 characters in length, are more secure than passwords, yet can be easy to remember because they contain words.

Pin A PIN (personal identification number), sometimes called a passcode, is a numeric password, either assigned by a company or selected by a user. PINs provide an additional level of security. Select PINs carefully and protect them as you do any other password. For example, do not use the same four digits, sequential digits, or dates others could easily determine, such as birth dates.

Possessed Objects A possessed object is any item that you must possess, or carry with you, in order to gain access to a computer or computer facility. Examples of possessed objects are badges, cards, smart cards, and keys. The card you use in an ATM (automated teller machine), for example, is a possessed object that allows access to your bank account.

Biometrics

In addition to using passwords for authentication based on what you know, another category rests on the features and characteristics of you as an individual. This type of authentication, something you are, is called biometric security. Biometric security uses the unique characteristics of your face, hands, or eyes to authenticate you. Some of the different types of biometrics that are used today for authentication include:

- **Retina:** The retina is a layer at the back of the eye. Each person's retina is unique, even if you have an identical twin. A retinal scanner maps the unique patterns of a retina as you look into the scanner's eyepiece.
- **Fingerprint:** Your fingerprint consists of a unique pattern of ridges and valleys. A static fingerprint scanner requires you to place your entire thumb or finger on a small oval window on the scanner, which takes an optical picture of the fingerprint and compares it with the fingerprint image on file. Another type of scanner is a dynamic fingerprint that requires you to move your finger across a small slit or opening.

- **Voice:** Voice recognition, using a standard computer microphone, can be used to authenticate users based on the unique characteristics of a person's voice.
- **Face:** A biometric authentication that is becoming increasingly popular on smartphones is facial recognition. Every person's face has several distinguishable landmarks called nodal points, illustrated in Figure 5-10. Using a standard computer webcam, facial recognition software can measure the nodal points and create a numerical code (faceprint) that represents the face.

Figure 5-10 Facial recognition.
Metamorworks/Shutterstock.com

- **Iris:** Your iris is a thin, circular structure in the eye. An iris scanner, which can use a standard computer webcam, uses the unique characteristics of the iris for identification.
- **Hand:** A hand geometry system measures the shape and size of a person's hand (Figure 5-11). Because hand geometry systems can be expensive, they often are used in larger companies to track workers' time and attendance or as security devices. Colleges use hand geometry systems to verify students' identities. Daycare centers and hospital nurseries use them to identify parents who pick up their children.

Figure 5-11 Hand geometry system.
Courtesy of Ingersoll Rand Security Technologies

• **Signature:** A signature verification system recognizes the shape of a handwritten signature; it also measures the pressure exerted and the motion used to write the signature. Signature verification systems use a specialized pen and tablet. Signature verification systems often are used to reduce fraud in financial institutions.

Biometric devices are gaining popularity as a security precaution because they are a virtually foolproof method of identification and authentication. For example, some grocery stores, retail stores, and gas stations use biometric payment, where the customer's fingerprint is read by a fingerprint reader that is linked to a payment method, such as a checking account or credit card. Users can forget their usernames and passwords. Possessed objects can be lost, copied, duplicated, or stolen. Personal characteristics, by contrast, are unique and cannot be forgotten or misplaced.

Biometric devices do have disadvantages. If you cut your finger, a fingerprint reader might reject you as a legitimate user. Hand geometry readers can transmit germs. If you are nervous, a signature might not match the one on file. If you have a sore throat, a voice recognition system might reject you. Many people are uncomfortable with the thought of using an iris scanner.

Two-Factor Authentication

A growing trend in authentication is to combine multiple types of authentication. This is most often used with passwords (something you know) and the approved user having a specific item in his possession (something you have) that no one else would have. This is called **two-factor authentication (2FA)**, and it makes authentication stronger.

The most common authentication elements that are combined are passwords and codes sent to a cell phone using a text message. After correctly entering your password, a four- to six-digit code is sent to your cell phone. The code must then be entered as the second authentication method (Figure 5-12).

Figure 5-12 Two-factor authentication.
Selinofoto/Shutterstock.com

Users may be able to specify a computer or mobile device as a trusted device during a 2FA so that future sign-in attempts on that same computer or mobile device will bypass the two-factor verification. The trusted device they choose should be one they use frequently, such as their personal laptop or smartphone.

As an alternative to 2FA, when you enter your username in a single sign-in account, such as for Microsoft, Google, Twitter, and Facebook, you automatically are signed in to other accounts and services. Many also recognize your information to provide additional customized content.

CAPTCHAs

Sometimes, when submitting a form or creating an account on a website, you will be asked to enter a series of characters or click objects in an image. These websites use a CAPTCHA, which stands for Completely Automated Public Turing test to tell Computers and Humans Apart. A **CAPTCHA** is a program developed at Carnegie Mellon University that displays an image containing a series of distorted characters for a user to identify and enter in order to verify that user input is from humans and not computer programs such as bots (Figure 5-13).

Figure 5-13 CAPTCHAs verify human usage.
iStock.com/Milindri

A CAPTCHA is effective in blocking computer-generated attempts to access a website, because it is difficult to write programs for computers to detect distorted characters, while humans generally can recognize them. For blind users or if words are too difficult to read, the CAPTCHA text can be read aloud; you also have the option of generating a new CAPTCHA.

Encryption

If you were the only one who had your information, it would be a much easier job to keep it safe. Unfortunately, our personal information is transmitted and stored on remote servers many times each day. Think about the last time you made an online purchase: your credit card number was transmitted from you to the online retailer to your credit card provider to your bank to your smartphone — and that is just part of the journey. Yet despite the risks to our data, we have technology to significantly strengthen the security of our information, whether it is sitting on our computer or being transmitted around the world.

Imagine that an attorney had a set of documents that needed to be kept safe. The attorney could hire guards and add outside lighting to deter a thief. But what if the thief were still able to avoid these protections and break into the attorney's office? Now suppose that the attorney had also placed the documents in a safe that required a key to open it. This extra level of protection would thwart even the most sophisticated thief because it would require a very specialized set of skills to even attempt to open a locked safe.

This is the idea behind encryption. Encryption is the process of scrambling information in such a way that it cannot be read unless the user possesses the key to unlock so that it is returned to a readable format (decryption). This provides an extra level of protection: if attackers were somehow able to get to the information on your computer, they still could not read the scrambled (encrypted) information because they would not have the key to unlock it.

And encryption can be applied to data on your hard drive (data-at-rest) just as it can be used to protect data being transmitted across the Internet (data-in-transit). A company employee traveling to another country carrying a laptop that contains sensitive company information would encrypt that data to protect it in case the laptop was lost or stolen. The employee also would encrypt a signed contract to send over the Internet back to the home office so that nobody else could intercept and read the contract.

It is essential that the key for encryption/decryption be kept secure. If someone were able to access your key, that person then could read any encrypted documents sent to you or impersonate you by encrypting a false document with your key and sending it in your name. The receiver of the document would assume that you were the sender because they were able to decrypt the document using your key.

Recall that a digital certificate is used to verify a user's identity and key that has been signed by a trusted third party. This third party verifies the owner and that the key belongs to that owner. Digital certificates make it possible to verify the identity of a user and the user's key to prevent an attack from someone impersonating the user. A digital signature is an electronic, encrypted, and secure stamp of authentication on a document.

A certificate authority (CA) is an organization that issues digital certificates and signatures. Each CA is a trusted third party that takes responsibility for verifying the sender's identity before issuing a certificate or signature. The cost varies depending on the desired level of data encryption, with the strongest levels recommended for financial and e-commerce transactions.

Protect Yourself while Online

Like most users, you probably spend most of your time online when you are on your computer or smartphone. Because people spend so much time online, it is good to consider ways they can protect themselves while online. This also includes protecting online profiles while using social media.

Today, all browsers support dynamic content that can change, such as animated images or customized information. This can be done through browser additions called extensions, plug-ins, and add-ons.

These browser additions, however, introduce a new means for attackers to exploit security weaknesses and gain access to the user's computer through the browser. For example, an add-on might allow a computer to download a script, or series of instructions that commands the browser to perform specific actions. An attacker could exploit a security weakness in the add-on to download and execute malware on the user's computer. Cookies can pose both security and privacy risks. Some can be stolen and used to impersonate a user, while others can be used to track browsing or buying habits.

Browser Security   Although all browsers are different, each can be configured for stronger security through different settings. Some of the important security settings include:

- **Cookies:** You can accept or deny cookies. Also, you can specify that cookies be deleted once the browser is closed. In addition, exceptions can be made for specific websites, and all existing cookies can be viewed and selectively removed.
- **Scripting:** Websites can be allowed to run scripting languages or be blocked from running them, and exceptions can be made for specific websites.
- **Plug-ins:** You can block all plug-ins or selective plug-ins. Another option prompts you when a plug-in requests to run. A plug-in validation will examine the plug-ins that are being used and alert you to any out-of-date or known vulnerable plug-ins.
- **Pop-ups:** You also can block all pop-up messages, permit all pop-ups, or selectively choose which websites to run pop-ups.
- **Clear browsing data:** All accumulated history of web browsing can be cleared from a computer's hard drive. This is important to do when using a public computer.

Protect Your Personal and Financial Information   Your personal information includes not only your identity, but your financial information. Attackers can impersonate you, either to cause distress or for their own financial gain. Often, months or years can go by without you being aware that your information is being misused, which can cause irreparable damage to your credit and reputation.

You can, and should, take several steps to prevent your information from being stolen and having your information falling into the hands of attackers. It is especially important to protect your financial data.

The following are some of the actions that can be taken by identity thieves:

- Produce counterfeit checks or debit cards and then remove all money from the bank account.
- Establish phone or wireless service in the victim's name.
- File for bankruptcy under the person's name to avoid eviction.
- Go on spending sprees using fraudulently obtained credit and debit card account numbers.
- Open a bank account in the person's name and write bad checks on that account.
- Open a new credit card account, using the name, date of birth, and Social Security number of the victim. When the thief does not pay the bills, the delinquent account is reported on the victim's credit report.
- Obtain loans for expensive items, such as cars and motorcycles.

One of the growing areas of identity theft involves identity thieves filing fictitious income tax returns with the U.S. Internal Revenue Service (IRS). Identity thieves steal a filer's Social Security number and then file a falsified income tax return claiming a large refund — often larger than the victim is entitled to — that is sent to the attacker. Because the IRS has been sending refunds more quickly than in the past, thieves can receive the refund and disappear before the victim files a legitimate return and the fraud is detected.

The United States has laws in place to help users monitor and protect their financial information that is stored by a credit reporting agency. You can request one free credit report annually to review your credit history and determine if an attacker has secretly taken out a credit card or even a loan in your name. You can also have a credit freeze (as well as a thaw) put on your credit information so that it cannot be accessed without your explicit permission. These are also free. It is a good idea to monitor your credit information regularly.

Protecting Your Online Profile   Social-networking sites contain a treasure trove of information for attackers. An attacker might view your Facebook page to find answers to security questions that are used for resetting passwords (such as, What is your mother's maiden name?). With so much valuable information available, social networking sites should be at the forefront of security today; sadly, that is not always the case. Social networking sites have a history of providing lax security, of not giving users a clear understanding of how security features work, and of changing security options with little or no warning.

Several general defenses can be used for any social networking site. First and foremost, you should be cautious about what information you post. Posting that you are going to Florida on Friday for two weeks could be a tempting invitation for a burglar. Other information posted could later prove embarrassing. Asking yourself whether your boss would approve or what your mother might think of this before posting may provide an incentive to rethink the material before posting.

Second, be cautious regarding who can view your information. Certain types of information could prove to be embarrassing if read by certain parties, such as a prospective employer. Other information should be kept confidential. You should consider carefully who is accepted as a friend on a social network. Once a person has been accepted as a friend, that person will be able to access any personal information or photographs.

Finally, because security settings in social networking sites are often updated frequently by the website with little warning, pay close attention to information about new or updated security settings. New settings often provide a much higher level of security by allowing you to fine-tune your account profile options.

Online Gaming Risks   Gamers often understand general security issues regarding online behavior, but they may not be aware of a different set of technology and social risks they may encounter as they interact in the online world. Anyone experiencing the joys of playing games online or playing games with others through online services should realize that thieves and hackers lurking behind the scenes may take advantage of security holes and vulnerabilities that can turn a gaming session into a nightmare.

Viruses, worms, and malware can be hidden in downloaded game files, mobile apps, email message attachments, and messaging software. In addition, messages on online social networks may encourage gamers to visit fraudulent websites filled with malware. If the game requires a connection to the Internet, then any computer connected to the game's server is subject to security cyberthreats. Thieves can take control of a remote computer that does not have a high level of security protection and use it to control other computers, or they could break into the computer and install malware to discover personal information.

Malicious users know that the gaming community uses social media extensively, so they also create accounts and attempt to mislead uninformed users into revealing personal information. The thieves may claim to have software updates and free games, when they really are luring users to bogus websites that ask users to set up profiles and accounts.

Gamers should follow these practices to increase their security:

- Before downloading any software or apps, including patches to games, or disclosing any private details, check the developer to be certain the website or the person making the request is legitimate.
- Read the permissions notices to learn what information is being requested or being collected. Avoid games requiring passwords to be saved to an online account on a smartphone.
- Exercise extreme caution if the game requires ActiveX or JavaScript to be enabled or if it must be played in administrator mode.
- Use a firewall, and make exceptions to allow only trusted individuals to access your computer or mobile device when playing multiplayer online games.
- Do not share personal information with other gamers who you meet online.

Privacy Laws

The concern about privacy has led to the enactment of federal and state laws regarding the storage and disclosure of personal data, some of which are shown in Table 5-8. Common points in some of these laws are as follows:

1. Information collected and stored about individuals should be limited to what is necessary to carry out the function of the business or government agency collecting the data.

2. Once collected, provisions should be made to protect the data so that only those employees within the organization who need access to it to perform their job duties have access to it.
3. Personal information should be released outside the organization collecting the data only when the person has agreed to its disclosure.
4. When information is collected about an individual, the individual should know that the data is being collected and have the opportunity to determine the accuracy of the data.

❓ Consider This

Do cookies pose risks?

Some websites sell or trade information stored in your cookies to advertisers — a practice many believe to be unethical. If you do not want personal information distributed, you should limit the amount of information you provide to a website or adjust how your browser handles cookies. You can regularly clear cookies or set your browser to accept cookies automatically, prompt if you want to accept a cookie, or disable all cookie use. Keep in mind if you disable cookie use, you may not be able to use some e-commerce websites. As an alternative, you can purchase software that selectively blocks cookies. What signs might indicate that a company has sold your cookie data? How do you weigh the convenience of cookies with the risks? Would you ever disable cookies? Why or why not?

Table 5-8 Some U.S. Privacy Laws

Law	Purpose
Children's Internet Protection Act	Protects minors from inappropriate content when accessing the Internet in schools and libraries
Children's Online Privacy Protection Act (COPPA)	Requires websites to protect personal information of children under 13 years of age
Digital Millennium Copyright Act (DMCA)	Makes it illegal to circumvent antipiracy schemes in commercial software; outlaws sale of devices that copy software illegally
Freedom of Information Act (FOIA)	Enables public access to most government records
HIPAA (Health Insurance Portability and Accountability Act)	Protects individuals against the wrongful disclosure of their health information
PATRIOT (Provide Appropriate Tools Required to Intercept and Obstruct Terrorism)	Gives law enforcement the right to monitor people's activities, including web and email habits
Privacy Act	Forbids federal agencies from allowing information to be used for a reason other than that for which it was collected
Fair and Accurate Credit Transactions Act (FACTA)	Provides rules for financial institutions, including lenders and credit reporting agencies, to protect consumers from fraud and identity theft

How To: Establish Policies to Ensure Safety

Companies, schools, and organizations have obligations to protect their data, network, and employees. Some areas have already been discussed, including cyberbullying and network security. In addition, companies need to ensure employees know which activities using company-issued devices are acceptable and understand how to recover from a disaster, such as a tornado or data breach.

Establishing Policies

Employees of a company, school, or organization sometimes are given devices on which to perform their work, as well as access to a network. During the course of a day, it can be tempting to use the company-issued device or network to check social media, respond to a personal email message, or conduct other personal activities. While this might seem like it is not an issue, many companies restrict or forbid personal activities due to concerns about liability if an employee does something illegal or unethical, or because of concerns related to privacy of company information. Companies establish guidelines for use, occasionally limit access, and possibly oversee employees' activities for unacceptable actions.

Codes of Conduct   A **code of conduct** is a written guideline that helps determine whether a specification is ethical/unethical or allowed/not allowed. An IT code of conduct focuses on acceptable use of technology. Employers and schools often specify standards for the ethical use of technology in an IT code of conduct and then distribute these standards to employees and students (Figure 5-14). You also may find codes of conduct online that define acceptable forms of communications for websites where users post commentary or other communications, such as blogs, wikis, online discussions, and so on.

Content Filtering   One of the more controversial issues that surround the Internet is its widespread availability of objectionable material, such as prejudiced literature, violence, and obscene photos. Some believe that such materials should be banned. Others believe that the materials should be filtered; that is, they should be restricted.

Content filtering is the process of restricting access to certain material. Many businesses use content filtering to limit employees' web access. These businesses argue that employees are unproductive when visiting inappropriate or objectionable websites. Some schools, libraries, and parents use content filtering to restrict access to minors. Content filtering opponents argue that banning any materials violates constitutional guarantees of free speech and personal rights.

Web filtering software are programs that restrict access to specified websites. Some also filter websites that use specific words (Figure 5-15). Others allow you to filter email messages, chat rooms, and programs. Many Internet security programs include a firewall, antivirus program, and filtering capabilities combined. Browsers also often include content filtering capabilities.

Figure 5-15   Web filtering software restricts access to websites and content.
Source: TitanHQ

Employee Monitoring   Employee monitoring involves the use of computers, mobile devices, or cameras to observe, record, and review an employee's use of a technology, including communications, such as email messages, keyboard activity (used to measure productivity), and websites visited. Many programs exist that easily allow employers to monitor employees. Further, it is legal for employers to use these programs.

Figure 5-14   Sample IT code of conduct.
Source: Google

Sample IT Code of Conduct

1. Technology may not be used to harm other people.
2. Employees may not meddle in others' files.
3. Employees may use technology only for purposes in which they have been authorized.
4. Technology may not be used to steal.
5. Technology may not be used to bear false witness.
6. Employees may not copy or use software illegally.
7. Employees may not use others' technology resources without authorization.
8. Employees may not use others' intellectual property as their own.
9. Employees shall consider the social impact of programs and systems they design.
10. Employees always should use technology in a way that demonstrates consideration and respect for fellow humans.

Some organizations declare that they will review email messages regularly, and others state that email messages are private. In some states, if a company does not have a formal email policy, it can read email messages without employee notification.

Disaster Recovery

A **disaster recovery plan** is a written plan that describes the steps an organization would take to restore its computer operations in the event of a disaster. A disaster can be natural (tornadoes, fires, or floods) or man-made (hackers, viruses, etc.). Creating a disaster recovery plan depends on the disaster type and should include the first steps, possible occurrences, and equipment or actions to include (Table 5-9). Each company and each department or division within an organization usually has its own disaster recovery plan. The following scenario illustrates how an organization might implement a disaster recovery plan.

Rosewood Associates is a consulting firm that helps clients use social media for marketing and customer outreach. Last week, a fire broke out in the office suite above Rosewood. The heat and smoke, along with water from the sprinkler system, caused extensive damage. As a result, Rosewood must replace all computers, servers, and storage devices. Also, the company lost all the data it had not backed up.

Rosewood currently backs up its systems daily to an internal server and weekly to a remote cloud server. Because of damage to the internal server, the company lost several days of data. Rosewood does not have a plan for replacing hardware. Thus, they will lose several additional days of productivity while purchasing, installing, and configuring new hardware.

To minimize the chance of this type of loss in the future, the company hired you as a consultant to help create a disaster recovery plan. You first discuss the types of disasters that can strike, as shown in the table. You then explain that the goal of a disaster recovery plan is to prevent, detect, and correct system threats, and to restore the most critical systems first.

A disaster recovery plan typically contains these four components: emergency plan, backup plan, recovery plan, and test plan.

Emergency Plan: An emergency plan specifies the steps Rosewood will take as soon as a disaster strikes. The emergency plan is organized by type of disaster, such as fire, flood, or earthquake, and includes:

1. Names and phone numbers of people and organizations to notify (company management, fire and police department, clients, etc.)
2. Computer equipment procedures, such as equipment or power shutoff, and file removal; employees should follow these procedures only if it is safe to do so
3. Employee evacuation procedures
4. Return procedures (who can enter the facility and what actions they are to perform)

Backup Plan: The backup plan specifies how Rosewood will use backup files and equipment to resume computer operations, and includes:

1. The location of backup data, supplies, and equipment
2. Who is responsible for gathering backup resources and transporting them to an alternate computer facility
3. The methods by which data will be restored from cloud storage
4. A schedule indicating the order and approximate time each application should be up and running

Table 5-9 Considerations for Disaster Recovery

Disaster Type	What to Do First	What Might Occur	What to Include in the Plan
Natural (earthquake, hurricane, tornado, etc.)	Shut off power Evacuate, if necessary Pay attention to advisories Do not use phone lines if lightning occurs	Power outage Phone lines down Structural damage to building Road closings, transportation interruptions Flooding Equipment damage	Generator Satellite phone, list of employee phone numbers Alternate worksite Action to be taken if employees are not able to come to work/leave the office Wet/dry vacuums Make and model numbers and vendor information to get replacements
Man-made (hazardous material spill, terrorist attacks, fire, hackers, malware, etc.)	Notify authorities (fire departments, etc.) of immediate threat Attempt to suppress fire or contain spill, if safe to do so Evacuate, if necessary	Data loss Dangerous conditions for employees Criminal activity, such as data hacking and identity theft Equipment damage	Backup data at protected site Protective equipment and an evacuation plan Contact law enforcement Make and model numbers and vendor information to obtain replacements

Recovery Plan: The recovery plan specifies the actions Rosewood will take to restore full computer operations. As with the emergency plan, the recovery plan differs for each type of disaster. You recommend that Rosewood set up planning committees. Each committee would be responsible for different forms of recovery, such as replacing hardware or software.

Test Plan: The test plan includes simulating various levels of disasters and recording Rosewood's ability to recover. You run a test in which the employees follow the steps in the disaster recovery plan. The test uncovers a few needed recovery actions not specified in the plan, so you modify the plan. A few days later, you run another test without giving the employees any advance notice to test the plan again.

 Consider This

Can you install software on work computers or work-issued smartphones?
Many organizations and businesses have strict written policies governing the installation and use of software and enforce their rules by checking networked or online computers or mobile devices periodically to ensure that all software is licensed properly. If you are not completely familiar with your school's or employer's policies governing installation of software, check with the information technology department or your school's technology coordinator. Are there cases in which it would be acceptable for you to install software or apps on a nonpersonal device? Explain. Does your school or workplace have guidelines?

Ethics and Issues: Inclusivity and Digital Access

Chances are you have access to a computer, a smartphone, and a network. Inclusion concerns arise when others do not have the same access as you. Some access and inclusivity issues are related to ensuring that technology is available to and usable for those with disabilities, as previously discussed. Others occur because of economic disparities, geographic restrictions, and more.

Digital Inclusion

IoT access has many advantages; however, people (or entire countries) who cannot afford IoT technologies may experience a negative impact as IoT users are able to gain advantages, such as information access, enhanced security, and convenience. Recall that the digital divide is the gap between those who have access to technology and its resources and information, especially on the Internet, and those who do not.

Digital inclusion is the movement to ensure that all users, regardless of economic or geographic constraints, have access to the devices, data, and infrastructure required to receive high-speed, accurate, reliable information. The goal of digital inclusion is to ensure that everyone has access to all the resources offered online, including education, participation in local and national government, employment listings and interviews, and health care access. Some barriers to digital inclusion include:

- Geographic areas that lack the infrastructure necessary to provide reliable Internet access
- Government restrictions or censorship
- Affordable devices or connections
- Lack of education
- Lack of understanding of the value of technology

Another issue regarding IoT is its effect on users' privacy. Smart technology, such as electric meters, smart TVs, wearable technology, and GPS devices, submit data about your usage to companies which then use it for their own purposes — often to sell you more products or track your whereabouts. To protect yourself and limit your exposure to data collection, be sure to enable privacy settings on your IoT devices. Watch the news for companies or products that experience a data breach, which is any unauthorized collection or distribution of data. If you become aware of a company with which you do business that has been hacked, contact them to see if your data was accessed, change your passwords, and keep an eye on any suspicious activity.

 Consider This

What if you are at a digital disadvantage?
If you are on the wrong side of the digital divide compared to others around you, you may have disadvantages to getting your schoolwork done, accessing job opportunities, and making connections with your peers. Many schools offer Chromebooks, laptops, or tablets free to all students to ensure access for all. In addition, refurbished or recycled devices are a lower-cost option to consider. If you find yourself with fewer resources than your classmates or peers, contact your school. Some schools have grants or other opportunities to ensure that all students have an equal opportunity for success. Do you know anyone who has been without the same access as others? What other resources might someone in this situation have? What might you do to help?

Study Guide

Instructions: The Study Guide exercise reinforces material you should know after reading this module. Answer the questions below using the format that helps you remember best or that is required by your instructor. Possible formats may include one or more of these options: write the answers; create a document that contains the answers; record answers as audio or video using a webcam, smartphone, or portable media player; post answers on a blog, wiki, or website; or highlight answers in the book/ebook.

1. Define the term, digital security risk.

2. Define the terms, computer crime, cybercrime, and crimeware.

3. ___ is the practice of protection against digital threats, including unauthorized or illegal access of data.

4. List users of digital forensics.

5. Explain the importance of a digital detox.

6. Define the term, dark web. Explain who uses it and why.

7. Differentiate among script kiddies, hackers, crackers, hactivists, cyberterrorists, and cyberextortionists.

8. Explain how attackers use data mining.

9. Define the term, social engineering.

10. Explain concerns related to information accuracy and intellectual property rights.

11. List measures organizations can take to reduce electrical waste.

12. Malware can deliver its ___, or destructive event or prank, on a computer or mobile device in a variety of ways.

13. Differentiate among zombie, botnet, and bot.

14. Describe the damages caused by and possible motivations behind DoS and DDoS attacks.

15. What is the purpose of a back door? How do attackers use it to infect your computer?

16. Explain what happens during IP and address spoofing.

17. List steps to protect yourself from viruses and other malware.

18. Your digital ___ is the record of everything you do online.

19. List risks you face when u sing the Internet or email.

20. Explain why companies use a VPN to provide network access to mobile users.

21. Explain the uses of a firewall and a proxy server.

22. Explain how an AUP can prevent unauthorized use of technology.

23. Explain the importance of an audit trail.

24. List and differentiate among the types of backup.

25. List common attacks directed towards Wi-Fi networks.

26. Explain how attackers use evil twins.

27. List steps you can take to secure your wireless router.

28. A(n) ___ address is a unique hardware identifier for your computer or device.

29. Explain how law enforcement's access to cloud data raises security concerns. Describe laws and practices to protect cloud data.

30. Define the term, authentication.

31. Explain the role of usernames and passwords.

32. How can you ensure that your password is strong?

33. Describe the role of a password manager.

34. Explain how the following can provide or deny access: passphrases, PINs, and possessed objects.

35. List and describe types of biometric security measures. Explain advantages and disadvantages of biometric devices.

36. Explain how 2FA and CAPTCHAs are used for verification.

37. Explain the importance of encryption, digital certificates, and digital signatures. What is the role of a CA?

38. List actions that identity thieves may take.

39. Explain steps to protect your financial information.

40. List settings that you can specify on your browser to provide stronger security.

41. Explain how and why you should protect your online profile.

42. Describe common points in privacy laws.

43. Identify risks and safety measures when gaming.

44. Explain the role of a code of conduct. What should a code of conduct include?

45. Describe the purpose of content filtering. Explain controversies regarding content filtering.

46. Explain ways companies monitor employee activities.

47. List considerations when creating a disaster recovery plan. What should you include in a disaster recovery plan?

48. Describe considerations regarding digital inclusion.

49. List barriers to digital inclusion.

Key Terms

You should be able to define the Key Terms listed below.

audit trail (5-11)
authentication (5-15)
back door (5-8)
backup (5-3)
biometric security (5-17)
bot (5-8)
botnet (5-8)
CAPTCHA (5-18)
code of conduct (5-22)
computer crime (5-2)
content filtering (5-22)
cracker (5-3)
crimeware (5-2)
cybercrime (5-2)
cyberextortionist (5-4)
cybersecurity (5-2)
cyberterrorist (5-3)

cyberwarfare (5-4)
dark web (5-3)
data mining (5-4)
decryption (5-19)
denial of service attack
    (DoS attack) (5-8)
digital detox (5-3)
digital footprint (5-9)
digital forensics (5-3)
digital inclusion (5-24)
digital security risk
    (5-2)
digital signature (5-19)
disaster recovery plan
    (5-23)
distributed DoS attack
    (DDoS attack) (5-8)

evil twin (5-13)
hacker (5-3)
hactivist (5-3)
MAC address (5-14)
nation state actor (5-4)
passcode (5-17)
passphrase (5-17)
password (5-15)
password manager (5-16)
payload (5-7)
PIN (personal
    identification number)
    (5-17)
power usage
    effectiveness (PUE)
    (5-6)
proxy server (5-10)

script kiddie (5-3)
social engineering
    (5-4)
spoofing (5-8)
technology ethics
    (5-5)
threat actor (5-3)
two-factor
    authentication (2FA)
    (5-18)
virtualization (5-6)
virtual private network
    (VPN) (5-10)
web filtering software
    (5-22)
zombie (5-8)

Extend Your Knowledge

Instructions: The Extend Your Knowledge exercise expands on subjects covered in the module and encourages you to find the latest developments on these topics. Use a search engine or another search tool to locate news articles, blog entries, videos, expert discussions, or other current sources on the listed topics. List your sources, and write 3–4 sentences describing what you have learned to submit in the format required by your instructor.

- White hat hackers
- Biometric devices
- 2FA
- Digital detox

What did you learn that helped you better understand the concepts in this module? Did anything surprise you? How will what you learned impact you?

Checkpoint

The Checkpoint exercises test your knowledge of the module concepts.

True/False   Mark T for True and F for False. If False, rewrite the statement so that it is True.

_____ 1. Digital forensics involves the examination of media, programs, data and log files on computers, mobile devices, servers, and networks.

_____ 2. Hackers are individuals who want to attack computers but lack the knowledge of computers and networks needed to do so.

_____ 3. Inclusion is the practice of sharing computing resources, such as servers or storage devices, among computers and devices on a network.

_____ 4. A bot is a program that performs a repetitive task on a network.

_____ 5. A proxy server is a server outside the organization's network that controls which communications pass in and out of the organization's network.

_____ 6. An evil twin is a normal-looking yet fraudulent Wi-Fi network that allows hackers to capture personal information users transmit.

_____ 7. A URL is a unique hardware identifier for your computer or device.

_____ 8. A CAPTCHA displays an image containing a series of distorted characters for a user to identify and enter in order to verify that user input is from humans.

_____ 9. Content filtering is the process of ensuring equal access to certain material.

_____ 10. The goal of digital inclusion is to ensure that everyone has access to all the resources offered online.

Matching   Match the terms with their definitions.

_____ 1. digital detox

_____ 2. botnet

_____ 3. FERPA

_____ 4. cyberextortionist

_____ 5. PUE

_____ 6. 2FA

_____ 7. code of conduct

_____ 8. cracker

_____ 9. digital inclusion

_____ 10. VPN

a. a ratio that measures how much power enters the computer facility or data center against the amount of power required to run the computers and devices

b. someone who accesses a computer or network illegally with the intent of destroying data, stealing information, or other malicious action

c. a private, secure path across a public network that allows authorized users secure access to a company or other network

d. regulates the confidentiality of students' educational records

e. movement to ensure that all users, regardless of economic or geographic constraints, have access to the devices, data, and infrastructure required to receive high-speed, accurate, reliable information

f. a group of compromised computers or mobile devices connected to a network used to attack other networks, usually for nefarious purposes

g. a written guideline that helps determine whether a specification is ethical/unethical or allowed/not allowed

h. a combination of multiple types of authentication

i. an individual who attacks a nation's computer networks, like the electrical power grid, to cause disruption and panic among citizens

j. a period of time during which an individual refrains from using technology

Problem Solving

Instructions: The Problem Solving exercises extend your knowledge of module concepts by seeking solutions to practical problems with technology that you may encounter at home, school, work, or with nonprofit organizations. The Collaboration exercise should be completed with a team. You often can solve problems with technology in multiple ways. Determine a solution to the problems in these exercises by using one or more resources available to you (such as a computer or mobile device, articles on the web or in print, blogs, podcasts, videos, television, user guides, other individuals, and electronics or computer stores). Describe your solution, along with the resource(s) used, in the format requested by your instructor (brief report, presentation, discussion, blog post, video, or other means).

Personal

1. **Digital Detox**   You have been feeling anxious lately when not using your smartphone. Your friends and family are complaining that you do not pay attention to them, but you do not think you have a problem. How might you determine if you need a digital detox?

2. **Zombie**   Your device has been running slowly and acting erratically. You believe your device might be a zombie. How might you determine if your device is a zombie? What steps can you take to protect your device from further intrusions?

3. **Two-Step Verification Problem**   A website you are attempting to access requires two-step verification. In addition to entering your password, you also have to enter a code that it sends to you as a text message. You no longer have the same phone number, so you are unable to receive the text message. What are your next steps?

4. **Antivirus Software Outdated**   After starting your computer and signing in to the operating system, a message is displayed stating that your virus definitions are out of date and need to be updated. What are your next steps? How can you ensure that the message is legitimate?

5. **Problems with CAPTCHA**   You are signing up for an account on a website and encounter a CAPTCHA. You attempt to type the characters you see on the screen, but an error message appears stating that you have entered the incorrect characters. You try two more times and get the same result. You are typing the characters to the best of your ability but think you still might be misreading at least one of the characters. What are your next steps?

Professional

6. **Corporate Firewall Interference**   You installed a new browser on your work computer because you no longer wish to use the default browser provided with the operating system. When you run the new browser, an error message appears stating that a username and password are required to configure the firewall and allow this program to access the Internet. Why has this happened?

7. **Digital Inclusion**   Your company is in an area that has a diverse economic population. As part of its commitment to the community, it wants to help combat the digital divide that exists. What actions can you recommend your company to take?

8. **Unclear Acceptable Use Policy**   You read your company's acceptable use policy, but it is not clear about whether you are able to use the computer in your office to visit news websites on your lunch break. How can you determine whether this type of activity is allowed?

9. **Disaster Recovery Plan**   Your boss has asked you to review the company's disaster recovery plan to make sure it covers risks for flooding. What are some possible occurrences? What should the company's first steps be?

10. **Server Virtualization**   You are working at a medium-sized company that has many servers and computers, many of which perform similar duties. You think that virtualization will help your company's security, as well as reduce environmental effects. How can you convince your managers that this is a good idea?

Collaboration

11. **Technology in National and Local Security**   National and local security agencies often use technology to protect citizens. For example, computers are used to maintain a No Fly List, which contains a list of individuals not cleared to board a commercial aircraft. Form a team of three people to create a list of the various ways technology helps to keep the public safe. One team member should research how local agencies, such as police departments, use technology to ensure security. Another team member should research ways national security agencies use technology to protect the public from threats, and the last team member should research ways that private businesses use technology to enhance security. Compile these findings into a report and submit it to your instructor.

How To: Your Turn

Instructions: This exercise presents general guidelines for fundamental skills when using a computer or mobile device and then requires that you determine how to apply these general guidelines to a specific program or situation. You often can complete tasks using technology in multiple ways. Figure out how to perform the tasks described in these exercises by using one or more resources available to you (such as a computer or mobile device, articles on the web or in print, online or program help, user guides, blogs, podcasts, videos, other individuals, and trial and error). Summarize your 'how to' steps, along with the resource(s) used, in the format requested by your instructor (brief report, presentation, discussion, blog post, video, or other means).

1 **Evaluate Your Electronic Profile**

When you make purchases online, click advertisements, follow links, and complete online forms requesting information about yourself, you are adding to your electronic profile. While an electronic profile may help businesses guide you toward products and services that are of interest to you, some people view them as an invasion of privacy. The following steps guide you through the process of locating online information about yourself and taking steps to remove the information, if possible.

a. Start a browser.

b. Navigate to a search engine of your choice.

c. Perform a search for your full name.

d. In the search results, follow a link that you feel will display a webpage containing information about you. If the link's destination does not contain information about you, navigate back to the search results and follow another link.

e. Evaluate the webpage that contains information about you. If you wish to try removing the information, locate a link that allows you to contact the site owner(s) or automatically request removal of the information.

f. Request that your information be removed from the website. Some websites may not honor your request for removal. If you feel that the information must be removed, you may need to solicit legal advice.

g. If the search results display information from an account you have on an online social network, such as Facebook or LinkedIn, you may need to adjust your privacy settings so that the information is not

public. If the privacy settings do not allow you to hide your information, you may need to consider deleting the account.

h. Repeat Steps d–g for the remaining search results. When you no longer see relevant search results for the search engine you used, search for other variations of your name (use your middle initial instead of your middle name, exclude your middle name, or consider using commonly used nicknames instead of your first name).

i. Use other search engines to search for different variations of your name. Some search engines uncover results that others do not.

j. If you have an account on an online social network, navigate to the website's home page and, without signing in, search for your name. If information appears that you do not want to be public, you may need to adjust your privacy settings or remove your account.

k. Follow up with requests you have made to remove your online information.

Exercises

1. What personal information have you uncovered online? Did you have any idea that the information was there?

2. What additional steps can you take to prevent people and businesses from storing information about you?

3. What steps might you be able to take if you are unsuccessful with your attempts to remove online information that identifies you?

Internet Research

Instructions: The Internet Research exercises broaden your understanding of module concepts by requiring that you search for information on the web. Use a search engine or another search tool to locate the information requested or answers to questions presented in the exercises. Describe your findings, along with the search term(s) you used and your web source(s), in the format requested by your instructor (brief report, presentation, discussion, blog post, video, or other means). Additionally, reflect on the process you used to complete this activity. How did you go about choosing the tool that you did and why? Would you do anything differently in your research next time?

❶ Social Media: Unauthorized Access

Sharing photos on your social media sites of yesterday's visit to the ballpark might be at the top of today's to-do list, but these images might be just the clues cyberthieves need to access your account. Facebook, in particular, is one website that scammers and advertisers use to gather information regarding your whereabouts and your personal life. Their malicious attacks begin with a visit to your timeline or other record of your activities. Searching for keywords on your page, they send targeted messages appearing to originate from trusted friends. If you open their attachments or click their links, you have given these unscrupulous individuals access to your account. In addition, you may think you have crafted a password no one could guess. With your page open for others to view, however, the thieves scour the contents in hopes of locating starting clues, such as children's names, anniversary dates, and pet breeds, which could be hints to cracking your password.

Research This: In the Help section of an online social network you use, search for information about changing your profile's security and privacy settings. What steps can you take to mitigate the chance of becoming the victim of a hack? For example, can you adjust the connection settings to restrict who can see stories, send friend requests and messages, or search for you by name or contact information? Can you hide certain posts or block people from posting on your page? Can you report posts if they violate the website's terms? What are other potential threats to someone accessing your account? How do your settings compare to the suggestions? Would you change anything? Why or why not?

❷ Security: Digital Certificates and Signatures

Digital certificates and signatures detect a sender's identity and verify a document's authenticity. In this module you learned that many e-commerce companies use them in an attempt to prevent digital eavesdroppers from intercepting confidential information. The online certificate authority (CA) vendors generate these certificates using a standard, called X.509, which is coordinated by the International Telecommunication Union and uses algorithms and encryption technology to identify the documents.

Research This: Visit websites of at least two companies that issue digital certificates. Compare products offered, prices, and certificate features. What length of time is needed to issue a certificate? What is a green address bar, and when is one issued? What business or organization validation is required? Then, visit websites of at least two companies that provide digital signatures. Compare signing and sending requirements, types of supported signatures, and available security features. Which documents are required to obtain a digital signature? When would a business need a Class 2 rather than a Class 3 digital signature?

❸ Cloud Services: Cloud Security (SecaaS)

Antivirus software offers regular, automatic updates in order to protect a server, computer, or device from viruses, malware, or other attacks. Antivirus software is an example of cloud security, or security as a service (SecaaS). SecaaS is a service of cloud computing that delivers virus definitions and security software to users over the Internet as updates become available, with no intervention from users. SecaaS is a special case of software as a service (SaaS) but is limited to security software solutions.

Individuals and enterprise users take advantage of antivirus software and security updates. Enterprise cloud users interact with cloud security solutions via a web interface to configure apps that provide protection to email servers, preventing spam before it arrives, keeping data secure, and watching for online threats and viruses. As the use of cloud-based resources continues, the market for SecaaS solutions is expected to increase significantly in coming years.

Research This: (1) Use a search engine to find two different providers of SecaaS solutions. Research the different solutions they provide and then report your findings. (2) How are enterprise security requirements different from those of individual users? What strategies did you learn about that you might employ with your own security methods?

Critical Thinking

Instructions: The Critical Thinking exercises challenge your assessment and decision-making skills by presenting real-world situations associated with module concepts. The Collaboration exercise should be completed with a team. Evaluate the situations below, using personal experiences and one or more resources available to you (such as articles on the web or in print, blogs, podcasts, videos, television, user guides, other individuals, and electronics or computer store). Perform the tasks requested in each exercise and share your deliverables in the format requested by your instructor (brief report, presentation, discussion, blog post, video, or other means).

1. **Online Gaming Safety**

   You and your friend frequently play a popular online role-playing game. Your friend's computer had a virus recently, which was traced back to a malware-infected website. Your friend tells you about visiting the website after following a link while playing the game. What risks are involved when playing online games?

   Do This: Use the web to find articles about incidents of malware infections associated with online gaming. Research tips for increasing security when playing online games. Is malware still a threat if you do not download updates? Why or why not? What are the disadvantages to not downloading updates? Have you ever downloaded updates to a game? If so, how did you ensure the updates were safe? Locate a list of games that are known to cause malware infections. Share your findings and any online gaming security problems you have experienced with the class.

2. **Ensuring Safety and Security Online**

   You work in the information technology department for a large enterprise. An increasing number of users are contacting the help desk complaining about slow computer performance. Help desk representatives frequently attribute the decreased performance to malware. Although the help desk has installed security software on each computer, users also must practice safe computing. Your manager asked you to prepare information that teaches employees how to guard against malware and other security threats.

   Do This: Include information such as how to determine if a website is safe, how to identify email and other spoofing schemes, guidelines for downloading programs and apps, email attachment safety, and how to avoid phishing scams. Create a list of how organizations use common safeguards to protect other users on the network, such as firewalls, proxy servers, usernames and passwords, access controls, and audit trails.

3. **Case Study**

   Cooperative-Owned Farm Stand You are the new manager for a farm stand that is a cooperative effort, jointly owned by several local farmers. The farm stand has asked you to develop a disaster recovery plan for its headquarters. The space consists of two back rooms: one room is the office, with all of the electronic equipment and paper files; the other is for storage of non-electronic equipment. You and two other employees, one of whom is graduating with a bachelor's degree in information technology (IT), work in the office. The electronic equipment in the office includes a desktop, a laptop, an external hard drive for backups, a wireless router, and two printers. In addition, each employee has been issued a smartphone.

   Do This: Choose either a natural or man-made disaster. Create a disaster recovery plan that outlines emergency strategies, backup procedures, recovery steps, and a test plan. Assign each employee a role for each phase of the disaster recovery plan.

Collaboration

4. **Implementing Biometric Security**

   You are the new assistant to the chief technology officer of a large company. You have been reading an article about computer security that discussed several examples of security breaches, including thieves breaking into an office and stealing expensive equipment, and a recently terminated employee gaining access to the office after hours and corrupting data. Because of these incidents, your company would like to start using biometric devices to increase its security. Your boss has asked you to come up with some proposals.

   Do This: Form a three-member team and research the use of biometric devices to protect equipment and data. Each member of your team should choose a different type of biometric device, such as fingerprint readers, face recognition systems, and hand geometry systems. Find products for each device type, and research costs and user reviews. Search for articles by industry experts. Would you recommend using the biometric device for security purposes? Why or why not? Meet with your team, discuss and compile your findings, and then share with the class.

Technology Timeline

1937 Dr. John V. Atanasoff and Clifford Berry design and build the first electronic digital computer. Their machine, the Atanasoff-Berry-Computer, or ABC, provides the foundation for advances in electronic digital computers.

AP Images/Frederick News-Post (2)

1945 John von Neumann poses in front of the electronic computer built at the Institute for Advanced Study. This computer and its von Neumann architecture served as the prototype for subsequent stored program computers worldwide.

Alan Richards, photographer. From the Shelby White and Leon Levy Archives Center at the Institute for Advanced Study, Princeton (N.J.).

© Photographer unknown. From the Shelby White and Leon Levy Archives Center, Institute for Advanced Study, Princeton, NJ, USA

1947 William Shockley, John Bardeen, and Walter Brattain invent the transfer resistance device, eventually called the transistor. The transistor would revolutionize computers, proving much more reliable than vacuum tubes.

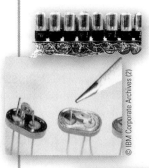

© IBM Corporate Archives (2)

1952 Dr. Grace Hopper considers the concept of reusable software in her paper, "The Education of a Computer." The paper describes how to program a computer with symbolic notation instead of detailed machine language.

Courtesy of Hagley Museum and Library

1937 · 1941 · 1943 · 1945 · 1946 · 1947 · 1951 · 1952 · 1953

Silver Screen Collection/Moviepix/Getty Images

1941 American film star, Hedy Lamarr, files a patent for technology involving frequency-hopping methods, which eventually led to the development of Wi-Fi, Bluetooth, and GPS systems.

Portrait de Alan Mathison Turing (1912-1954), mathematicien, cryptologue et informaticien britannique/UIG (SSPL)/ Bridgeman Images

1943 During World War II, British scientist Alan Turing designs the Colossus, an electronic computer created for the military to break German codes. The computer's existence is kept secret until the 1970s.

FLHC 20216/Alamy Stock Photo

1946 Dr. John W. Mauchly and J. Presper Eckert, Jr. complete work on the first large-scale electronic, general-purpose digital computer. The ENIAC (Electronic Numerical Integrator And Computer) weighs 30 tons, contains 18,000 vacuum tubes, occupies a 30 × 50 foot space, and consumes 160 kilowatts of power.

University of Pennsylvania Archives

Courtesy Unisys Corporation

1951 The first commercially available electronic digital computer, the UNIVAC I (UNIVersal Automatic Computer), is introduced by Remington Rand. Public awareness of computers increases when the UNIVAC I correctly predicts that Dwight D. Eisenhower will win the presidential election.

© IBM Corporate Archives

1953 Core memory, developed in the early 1950s, provides much larger storage capacity than vacuum tube memory.

1953 The IBM model 650 is one of the first widely used computers. The computer is so successful that IBM manufactures more than 1,000. IBM will dominate the mainframe market for the next decade.

1957 The IBM 305 RAMAC computer is the first to use magnetic disk for external storage. The computer provides storage capacity similar to magnetic tape that previously was used but offers the advantage of semi-random access capability.

© IBM Corporate Archives; Courtesy of the Department of the Navy

1959 Annie Easley, one of four Black employees at NASA, completes vital work on the Centaur rocket project, focusing on energy-conversion systems and developing and running code.

Interim Archives/Archive Photos/Getty Images

1965 Dr. John Kemeny of Dartmouth leads the development of the BASIC programming language.

Courtesy of Dartmouth College

1968 In a letter to the editor titled, "GO TO Statements Considered Harmful," Dr. Edsger Dijkstra introduces the concept of structured programming, developing standards for constructing computer programs.

1968 Alan Shugart at IBM demonstrates the first regular use of an 8-inch floppy disk.

© IBM Corporate Archives

1965 Digital Equipment Corporation (DEC) introduces the first microcomputer, the PDP-8. The machine is used extensively as an interface for time-sharing systems.

Courtesy of Hewlett-Packard Company

1968 Computer Science Corporation (CSC) becomes the first software company listed on the New York Stock Exchange.

1957 FORTRAN (FORmula TRANslation), an efficient, easy-to-use programming language, is introduced by John Backus.

© IBM Corporate Archives

1957	1958	1959	1960	1962	1964	1965	1967	1968

1967 Douglas Engelbart applies for a patent for the first computer mouse, which was made of wood.

1964 The number of computers has grown to 18,000. Third-generation computers, with their controlling circuitry stored on chips, are introduced. The IBM System/360 computer is the first family of compatible machines, merging science and business lines.

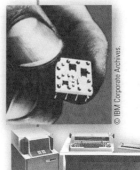

© IBM Corporate Archives.

1958 Jack Kilby of Texas Instruments invents the integrated circuit, which lays the foundation for high-speed computers and large-capacity memory. Computers built with transistors mark the beginning of the second generation of computer hardware.

Courtesy of Texas Instruments (2)

1960 COBOL, a high-level business application language, is developed by a committee headed by Dr. Grace Hopper.

Courtesy of Hagley Museum and Library

1964 IBM introduces the term, word processing, for the first time with its Magnetic Tape/Selectric Typewriter (MT/ST). The MT/ST was the first reusable storage medium that allowed typed material to be edited without requiring that the document be retyped.

1962 Evelyn Boyd Granville, the second Black female to obtain a Ph.D. in mathematics from an American university (Yale), joins the North American Aviation Company (NAA), where she was a research specialist with NASA. Granville's expertise in mathematics and programming made her an ideal candidate to provide technical support for software that analyzed satellite orbits for Project Apollo.

Evelyn Boyd, Lawrence House, Smith College Yearbook, 1945, (Record ID 2294) Photographer unknown. © Smith College Special Collections

© IBM Corporate Archives.

1969 Under pressure from the industry, IBM announces that some of its software will be priced separately from the computer hardware, allowing software firms to emerge in the industry.

© IBM Corporate Archives

1969 The ARPANET network is established, which eventually grows to become the Internet.

1975 MITS, Inc. advertises one of the first microcomputers, the Altair. The Altair is sold in kits for less than $400, and within the first three months 4,000 orders are taken.

LiPo Ching/MCT/Newscom

1975 Ethernet, the first local area network (LAN), is developed at Xerox PARC (Palo Alto Research Center) by Robert Metcalfe.

iStock.com/LongHa2006

1976 Steve Jobs and Steve Wozniak build the first Apple computer. A subsequent version, the Apple II, is an immediate success. Adopted by elementary schools, high schools, and colleges, for many students, the Apple II is their first contact with the world of computers.

Bettmann/Getty Images

Corbis Premium Historical/Getty Images

1980 IBM offers Microsoft Corporation cofounder, Bill Gates, the opportunity to develop the operating system for the soon-to-be announced IBM personal computer. With the development of MS-DOS, Microsoft achieves tremendous growth and success.

1980 Alan Shugart presents the Winchester hard disk, revolutionizing storage for personal computers.

Courtesy of IBM Corporate Archives

| 1969 | 1970 | 1971 | 1975 | 1976 | 1979 | 1980 | 1981 |

1976 Fairchild Channel F system is released. The development team, headed by Jerry Lawson (one of few Black engineers who worked in gaming at this time), Ron Smith, and Nick Talesfore, created a system that utilized the first removable cartridge gaming system. This allowed users to play a variety of games by simply inserting a new game cartridge in the same system and was the precursor to modern gaming systems.

© IBM Corporate Archives

1970 Fourth-generation computers, built with chips that use LSI (large-scale integration) arrive. While the chips used in 1965 contained up to 1,000 circuits, the LSI chip contains as many as 15,000.

Courtesy of Intel Corporation (2)

1971 Dr. Ted Hoff of Intel Corporation develops a microprocessor, or microprogrammable computer chip, the Intel 4004.

1979 VisiCalc, a spreadsheet program written by Bob Frankston and Dan Bricklin, is introduced.

1979 The first public online information services, CompuServe and the Source, are founded.

1981 The IBM PC is introduced, signaling IBM's entrance into the personal computer marketplace. The IBM PC quickly garners the largest share of the personal computer market and becomes the personal computer of choice in business.

Courtesy of IBM Corporate Archives

1981 The first computer virus, Elk Cloner, is spread via Apple II floppy disks, which contained the operating system. A short rhyme would appear on the screen when the user pressed the Reset button after the 50th boot of an infected disk.

iStock.com/Rebekkah_ann

Lane V. Erickson/Shutterstock.com
Courtesy of Microsoft® Corporation

3.275 Million

1982 3,275,000 personal computers are sold, almost 3,000,000 more than in 1981.

1982 Hayes introduces the 300 bps smart modem. The modem is an immediate success.

1982 Compaq, Inc. is founded to develop and market IBM-compatible PCs.

Courtesy of Hewlett-Packard Company

1986 Microsoft has public stock offering and raises approximately $61 million.

San Francisco Chronicle/Hearst Newspapers via Getty Images/ Getty Images

1984 IBM releases the PC/AT computer, developed by Mark Dean and Dennis Moeller, the first to implement Industry Standard Architecture (ISA), allowing users to connect peripheral devices to the computer.

1988 Microsoft surpasses Lotus Development Corporation to become the world's top software vendor.

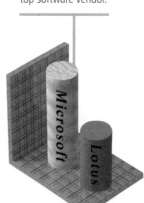

1991 Kodak announces the first digital SLR (single-lens reflex) camera. The Kodak DCS 100 is developed mostly for photojournalism purposes and stores the photos and batteries in a separate unit.

NMPFT/SSPL/ Science and Society

1991 World Wide Web Consortium releases standards that describe a framework for linking documents on different computers.

| 1982 | 1983 | 1984 | 1986 | 1988 | 1989 | 1991 |

1983 Instead of choosing a person for its annual award, TIME magazine names the computer Machine of the Year for 1982, acknowledging the impact of computers on society.

iStock.com/Audioundwerbung

Apple

1984 Apple introduces the Macintosh computer, which incorporates a unique, easy-to-learn, graphical user interface.

Chris Willson/Alamy Stock Photo

1989 Nintendo introduces the Game Boy, its first handheld game console.

© IBM Corporate Archives

1983 Lotus Development Corporation is founded. Its spreadsheet software, Lotus 1-2-3, which combines spreadsheet, graphics, and database programs in one package, becomes the best-selling program for IBM personal computers.

Courtesy of Hewlett-Packard Company

1984 Hewlett-Packard announces the first LaserJet printer for personal computers.

Hank Morgan/Science Source

1989 While working at CERN, Switzerland, Tim Berners-Lee invents the World Wide Web.

Courtesy of Intel Corporation

1989 The Intel 486 becomes the world's first 1,000,000 transistor microprocessor. It executes 15,000,000 instructions per second — four times as fast as its predecessor, the 80386 chip.

Courtesy of Microsoft Corporation

1993 Microsoft releases Microsoft Office 3 Professional, the first version of Microsoft Office for the Windows operating system.

Source: Amazon.com

1994 Amazon is founded and later begins business as an online bookstore. Amazon eventually expands to sell products of all types and facilitates the buying and selling of new and used goods. Today, Amazon employs more than 1.6 million people worldwide.

1995 eBay, an online auction website, is founded. Providing an online venue for people to buy and sell goods, it quickly becomes the world's largest online marketplace as it approaches 100 million active users worldwide.

AP Images/Nigel Treblin/Dapd

1993 Several companies introduce computers using the Pentium processor from Intel. The Pentium chip contains 3.1 million transistors and is capable of performing 112,000,000 instructions per second.

Source: Oracle

1995 Sun Microsystems launches Java, an object-oriented programming language that allows users to write one program for a variety of computer platforms.

Source: Linux

1994 Linus Torvalds creates the Linux kernel, a UNIX-like operating system that he releases free across the Internet for further enhancement by other programmers.

1995 Microsoft releases Windows 95, a major upgrade to its Windows operating system. Windows 95 consists of more than 10,000,000 lines of computer instructions developed by 300 person-years of effort.

Courtesy of Intel Corporation

1992   1993   1994   1995

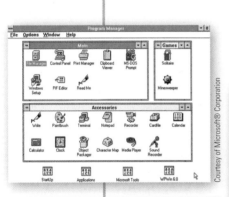
Courtesy of Microsoft® Corporation

1992 Microsoft releases Windows 3.1, the latest version of its Windows operating system. Windows 3.1 offers improvements such as TrueType fonts, multimedia capability, and object linking and embedding (OLE). In two months, 3,000,000 copies of Windows 3.1 are sold.

1993 The U.S. Air Force completes the Global Positioning System by launching its 24th Navstar satellite into orbit. Today, GPS receivers can be found in cars, laptops, and smartphones.

Courtesy of Garmin International

1994 Jim Clark and Marc Andreessen found Netscape and launch Netscape Navigator 1.0, a browser.

Courtesy of Netscape Communications Corporation

1994 Apple introduces the first digital camera intended for consumers. The Apple QuickTake 100 is connected to home computers using a serial cable.

Courtesy of Mark D. Martin

Orhan Cam/Shutterstock.com

1993 The White House launches its website, which includes an interactive citizens' handbook and White House history and tours.

1994 Yahoo!, a popular search engine and portal, is founded by two Stanford Ph.D. students as a way to keep track of their personal interests on the Internet.

AP Images/ Paul Sakuma

1997 Intel introduces the Pentium II processor with 7.5 million transistors. The new processor, which incorporates MMX technology, processes video, audio, and graphics data more efficiently and supports programs such as movie editing, gaming, and more.

Courtesy of Intel Corporation

1999 Intel introduces the Pentium III processor. This processor succeeds the Pentium II and can process 3-D graphics more quickly. The Pentium III processor contains between 9.5 and 44 million transistors.

Courtesy of Intel Corporation

1999 Governments and businesses frantically work to make their computers Y2K (Year 2000) compliant, spending more than $500 billion worldwide.

1997 Microsoft releases Internet Explorer 4.0 and seizes a key place in the Internet arena.

AP Images

1999 Open source software, such as the Linux operating system and the Apache web server created by unpaid volunteers, begins to gain wide acceptance among computer users.

KK Tan/Shutterstock.com

1996   1997   1998   1999

Courtesy of Palm, Inc.

1996 U.S. Robotics introduces the PalmPilot, an inexpensive user-friendly personal digital assistant (PDA).

1996 Microsoft releases Windows NT 4.0, an operating system for client-server networks.

Source: Microsoft Corporation

Courtesy of Google, Inc.

1998 Google files for incorporation and is now the most used search engine, capturing more than 60 percent of the market over other search engines.

iStock.com/Juniorbeep

Brad Cherson/Alamy Stock Photo

1998 E-commerce booms. Companies such as Amazon.com, Dell, and E*TRADE spur online shopping, allowing buyers to obtain a variety of goods and services.

1998 Apple introduces the iMac, the next version of its popular Macintosh computer. The iMac wins customers with its futuristic design, see-through case, and easy setup.

Source: Napster

2000 Shawn Fanning, 19, and his company, Napster, turn the music industry upside down by developing software that allows computer users to swap music files with one another without going through a centralized file server.

Courtesy of Intel Corporation

2001 Intel unveils its Pentium 4 chip with clock speeds starting at 1.4 GHz. The Pentium 4 includes 42 million transistors.

2002 Digital video cameras, DVD burners, easy-to-use video editing software, and improvements in storage capabilities allow the average computer user to create Hollywood-like videos with introductions, conclusions, rearranged scenes, music, and voice-over.

Courtesy of Intel Corporation

2000 E-commerce achieves mainstream acceptance. Annual e-commerce sales exceed $100 billion, and Internet advertising expenditures reach more than $5 billion.

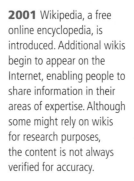

Source: Wikimedia

2001 Wikipedia, a free online encyclopedia, is introduced. Additional wikis begin to appear on the Internet, enabling people to share information in their areas of expertise. Although some might rely on wikis for research purposes, the content is not always verified for accuracy.

2002 After several years of negligible sales, the Tablet PC is reintroduced to meet the needs of a more targeted audience.

Courtesy of ViewSonic Corporation

2000　　　2001　　　2002

2000 Dot-com (Internet based) companies go out of business at a record pace — nearly one per day — as financial investors withhold funding due to the companies' unprofitability.

2002 Microsoft launches its .NET strategy, which is a new environment for developing and running software applications featuring ease of development of web-based services.

Tatiana Popova/ Shutterstock.com

2002 DVD burners begin to replace CD burners (CD-RW). DVDs can store up to eight times as much data as CDs. Uses include storing home movies, music, photos, and backups.

Kenneth Murray/Science Source

2000 Telemedicine uses satellite technology and videoconferencing to broadcast consultations and to perform distant surgeries. Robots are used for complex and precise tasks.

2002 Intel ships its revamped Pentium 4 chip with the 0.13 micron processor and Hyper-Threading (HT) Technology, operating at speeds of 3.06 GHz.

Courtesy of Intel Corporation

2004 Mozilla releases its first version of the Firefox browser. Firefox provides innovative features that enhance the browsing experience for users, including tabbed browsing and a Search box. Firefox quickly gains popularity and takes market share away from Microsoft's Internet Explorer.

AP Images

2004 Facebook, an online social network originally available only to college students, is founded. Facebook eventually opens registration to all people and immediately grows to more than 110 million users.

Courtesy of Facebook

2004 Sony unveils the PlayStation Portable (PSP). This handheld game console is the first to use optical discs.

Issei Kato IK/CP/ Reuters

2004 Companies such as RealNetworks, Microsoft, Sony, and Walmart stake out turf in the online music store business started by Apple.

2004 Flat-panel LCD monitors overtake bulky CRT monitors as the popular choice of computer users.

2004 Linux, an open source operating system, makes major inroads into the server market as a viable alternative to Microsoft Windows Server 2003, Sun's Solaris, and UNIX.

Source: Linux

2004 106 million, or 53 percent, of the 200 million online population in America accesses the Internet via broadband.

2003

2004

Nick Koudis/Getty Images

Mannie Garcia/Reuters/Newscom

2003 In an attempt to maintain their current business model of selling songs, the Recording Industry Association of America (RIAA) files more than 250 lawsuits against individual computer users who offer copyrighted music over peer-to-peer networks.

2003 Wireless computers and devices, such as keyboards, mouse devices, home networks, and wireless Internet access points become commonplace.

Courtesy of Palm Inc.

Wavebreakmedia/Shutterstock.com; Fuse/Getty Images
Sport/Getty Images; iStock.com/hocus-pocus;
StockLite /Shutterstock.com; iStock.com/LifesizeImages

2004 USB flash drives become a cost-effective way to transport data and information from one computer to another.

Courtesy of SanDisk Corporation

2004 Major retailers begin requiring suppliers to include radio frequency identification (RFID) tags or microchips with antennas, which can be as small as one-third of a millimeter across, in the goods they sell.

Courtesy of Intermec Technologies

Courtesy of Palm Inc.

2004 The smartphone overtakes the PDA as the mobile device of choice.

2004 Apple introduces the sleek all-in-one iMac G5. The new computer's display device contains the system unit.

iStock.com/Lpettet

2006 Sony launches its PlayStation 3. New features include a Blu-ray Disc player, high-definition capabilities, and always-on online connectivity.

2005 YouTube, an online community for video sharing, is founded. YouTube includes content such as home videos, movie previews, and clips from television shows. In November 2006, Google acquires YouTube.

Source: YouTube

2006 Apple begins selling Macintosh computers with Intel microprocessors.

2006 Web 2.0, a term coined in 2004, becomes a household term with the increase in popularity of online social networks, wikis, and web applications.

Courtesy of Intel Corporation

iStock.com/Robyvannucci

Video iPod

2005 Apple releases the latest version of its popular pocket-sized iPod portable media player, capable of playing songs, photos, podcasts, and up to 150 hours of music videos and television shows on a 2.5" color display.

HANDOUT/Tribune News Service/USA) Newscom

2006 Nintendo releases the Nintendo DS Lite, a handheld game console with new features such as dual screens and improved graphics and sound.

Toru Hanai/Reuters

2005 ━━━━━━━━ **2006**

2005 Spam, spyware, phishing, and pharming take center stage, along with viruses and other malware, as major nuisances to the 801 million computer users worldwide.

Courtesy of Intel Corporation

2006 IBM produces the fastest supercomputer, Blue Gene/L. It can perform approximately 28 trillion calculations in the time it takes you to blink your eye, or about one-tenth of a second.

2005 Blogging and podcasting become mainstream methods for distributing information via the web.

Blogging
Podcasting

2006
Intel introduces its Core 2 Duo processor family. Boasting record-breaking performance while using less power, the family consists of five desktop computer processors and five mobile computer processors. The desktop processor includes 291 million transistors, yet uses 40 percent less power than the Pentium processor.

Issei Kato (JAPAN)/Reuters

2005 Microsoft releases the Xbox 360, its latest game console. Features include the capability to play music, display photos, and communicate with computers and other Xbox gamers.

Courtesy of Microsoft Corporation

2006 Nintendo Wii is introduced and immediately becomes a leader in game consoles. The Wii is being used in revolutionary ways, such as training surgeons.

2007 Intel introduces Core 2 Quad, a four-core processor made for dual-processor servers and desktop computers. The larger number of cores allows for more energy-efficient performance and optimizes battery performance in laptops.

Courtesy of Intel Corporation

2007 VoIP (Voice over Internet Protocol) providers expand usage to include Wi-Fi phones. The phones enable high-quality service through a Wireless-G network and high-speed Internet connection.

Courtesy of Belkin International

2007 Apple introduces the iPhone and sells 270,000 phones in the first 2 days. iPhone uses iTouch technology that allows you to make a call simply by tapping a name or number in your address book. In addition, it stores and plays music like an iPod. Also, Apple sells its one billionth song on iTunes.

Neville Elder/Corbis Historical/Getty Images

2007 Apple releases its Mac OS X version 10.5 "Leopard" operating system, available in a desktop version and server version. The system includes a significantly revised desktop, with a semitransparent menu bar and an updated search tool that incorporates the same visual navigation interface as iTunes.

Oliver Leedham/Alamy Stock Photo

2008 Smartphones become smarter. Smartphones introduced this year include enhanced features such as touch screens with multi-touch technology, mobile TV, tactile feedback, improved graphics, GPS receivers, and better cameras.

AP Images/Mark Lennihan

2008 Bill Gates retires from Microsoft. He continues as chairman and advisor on key development projects.

Courtesy of Microsoft Corporation

2008 Google releases its new browser. Google Chrome uses an entirely unique interface and offers other features, such as dynamic tabs, crash control, and application shortcuts.

Source: Google

2007

2008

2007 Half of the world's population uses mobile phones. More and more people are using a mobile phone in lieu of a landline in their home.

iStock.com/Sean Locke

2007 Blu-ray Discs increase in popularity, overcoming and replacing HD DVD in less than one year. A Blu-ray Disc can store approximately 9 hours of high-definition (HD) video on a 50 GB disc or approximately 23 hours of standard-definition (SD) video.

Helene Rogers/Art Directors & Trips Photo/AGE Fotostock

2007 Wi-Fi hot spots are popular in a variety of locations. People bring their computers to coffeehouses, fast food restaurants, or bookstores to access the Internet wirelessly, either free or for a small fee.

RTimages/Shutterstock.com

2008 Netflix, an online movie rental company, and TiVo, a company manufacturing digital video recorders (DVRs), make Netflix movies and television episodes available on TiVo DVRs.

Source: Netflix

Source: TiVo

2008 Computer manufacturers begin to offer solid-state drives (SSDs) instead of hard disks, mostly in laptops. Although SSDs have a lower storage capacity, are more expensive, and slightly more susceptible to failure, they are significantly faster.

Norman Chan/Dreamstime.com

2008 WiMAX goes live! The advantage of this technology is the capability to access video, music, voice, and video calls wherever and whenever desired. Average download speeds are between 2 Mbps and 4 Mbps. By year's end, Sprint has approximately 100 million users on its network.

iStock.com

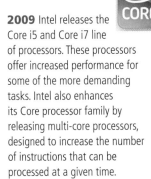

Source: Intel Corporation

2009 Intel releases the Core i5 and Core i7 line of processors. These processors offer increased performance for some of the more demanding tasks. Intel also enhances its Core processor family by releasing multi-core processors, designed to increase the number of instructions that can be processed at a given time.

2009 Online social networks revolutionize communications. Schools, radio stations, and other organizations develop pages on popular online social networks, such as Facebook, creating closer connections with their stakeholders.

2009 In June 2009, federal law requires that all full-power television stations broadcast only in digital format. Analog television owners are required to purchase a converter box to view over-the-air digital programming.

Courtesy of Intel Corporation

2009 Computers and mobile devices promote fitness by offering games and programs to help users exercise and track their progress. These games and programs also are used to assist with physical rehabilitation.

Stuartkey/Dreamstime.com

Google docs
Source: Google

2009 Web apps continue to increase in popularity. Web apps make it easier to perform tasks such as word processing, photo editing, and tax preparation without installing software on your computer.

Courtesy of Coby Electronics

2011 Netbooks offer a smaller, lighter alternative to laptops. Netbooks have screens between seven and ten inches and are used mostly for browsing the web and communicating online.

Source: Verizon Wireless

2011 More than 200 types of mobile devices are using Google Android, an operating system originally designed for mobile devices.

2011 A new generation of browsers is released to support HTML5, enabling webpages to contain more vivid, dynamic content.

HTML 5

HTML5 Logo by World Wide Web Consortium

2011 Ebooks and ebook readers explode in popularity. Many novels, textbooks, and other publications now are available digitally and can be read on an ebook reader, computer, or mobile device.

iStock.com/MichaelJay

iStock.com/Brightrock

iStock.com/EdStock

2011 Steve Jobs, a cofounder of Apple, passes away after a long battle with cancer. Jobs is remembered for revolutionizing the computer and music industries.

2009   2010   2011

Source: Seagate Technology LLC

2010 Hard disk capacity continues to increase at an exponential rate, with the largest hard disks storing more than 2.5 TB of data and information.

Source: AMD

2010 AMD develops a 12-core processor, which contains two 6-core processors, each on an individual chip. Power consumption is similar to that of a 6-core processor but offers reduced clock speed.

2010 Kinect for Xbox 360 changes the way people play video games. Game players now can interact with the game with a series of sensors, as well as a camera, tracking their movements in 3-D.

Courtesy of Microsoft Corporation

2010 Apple releases the iPad, a revolutionary mobile device with a 9.7-inch multi-touch screen. The iPad boasts up to 10 hours of battery life, connects wirelessly to the Internet, and is capable of running thousands of apps.

iStock.com/Hanibaram

g+

Source: Google

2011 Google introduces its Google+ online social network and integrates it across many of its products and services.

Source: Lenovo

2011 Intel introduces Ultrabooks, which are powerful, lightweight alternatives to laptops. Ultrabooks normally weigh three pounds or less, have great performance and battery life, and are usually less than one inch thick.

2012 Microsoft announces the Surface, a tablet designed to compete with Apple's iPad. The Surface has a built-in stand, runs the Windows 8 operating system and its apps, and supports a cover that also can serve as a keyboard.

2013 Twitter users generate more than 500 million Tweets per day.

2012 Apple releases the iPhone 5. This newest iPhone has a four-inch screen, contains a new, smaller connector, and uses Apple's A6 processor.

Source: Apple

2013 Sony releases the PlayStation 4 (PS4) game console and Microsoft releases the Xbox One game console.

2012 Microsoft releases Windows 8, its newest version of the Windows operating system. Windows 8 boasts a completely redesigned interface and supports touch input.

2013 Amazon announces it will use drones to deliver packages to its customers.

2013 Tablet sales grow at a faster rate than personal computer sales ever grew.

Source: Amazon.com

iStock.com/Franckreporter

2012

2013

2012 Google's Android surpasses Apple's iOS as the most popular operating system used on smartphones. Although the iPhone still is the best-selling smartphone, competing products are gaining market share quickly.

Source: Google, Inc.

2013 Samsung releases the Galaxy Gear, a smartwatch that synchronizes with a Samsung Galaxy smartphone using Bluetooth technology.

Ivan Garcia/Shutterstock.com

2013 QR codes rapidly gain in popularity, giving mobile device users an easy way to access web content.

Source: qr-code-generator.com

2013 Windows 8.1, a significant update to Microsoft's Windows 8 operating system, is released.

Source: Windows

Source: Windows

2012 Microsoft releases Office 2013. Office 365, which uses the familiar Office 2013 interface, also is released, allowing users to use their Microsoft accounts to access Office apps from computers that do not have Office installed.

2012 Nintendo releases the Wii U game console.

iStock.com/Mlenny

2013 Apple releases the iPhone 5S, the first iPhone with TouchID. TouchID verifies a user's identity using an integrated fingerprint reader.

2013 Many consumers prefer tablets for their mobile computing needs. Tablets provide ultimate portability while still allowing users to access a vast array of apps, as well as access to the Internet and their email messages.

iStock.com/Mozcann

Green Computing

2014 Individuals and enterprises increase their focus on green computing. Computer manufacturers not only sell more energy-efficient hardware, they also provide easy ways in which customers can recycle their old computers and devices.

2014 Solid-state storage is becoming more popular, with storage capacities increasing and prices decreasing.

Scanrail1/ Shutterstock.com

2014 Apple releases the Apple Watch, a wearable device that runs apps and can monitor various aspects of your health and fitness.

Courtesy of Apple, Inc.

2014 Decreases in storage costs and increases in Internet connection speeds persuade more users to use cloud storage for their data. Cloud storage also provides users with the convenience of accessing their files from almost anywhere.

2015 3-D printing decreases in price and increases in popularity.

Dreamnikon/Fotolia LLC

iStock.com/Nefstock

2015 Microsoft releases Windows 10, which expands on many of the new features introduced in Windows 8 and also brings back popular features, such as the Start menu, from previous versions of Windows.

2015 Individuals and families are increasingly turning to streaming video on the Internet and abandoning their cable companies.

2014

2015

2014 Bitcoin continues to grow as a digital currency and online payment system.

Courtesy of Mark Frydenberg

2014 Apple releases the iPhone 6 and iPhone 6 Plus. Both devices have significantly larger screens than its predecessors.

Courtesy of Apple, Inc.

2014 Televisions with features such as curved screens and Ultra HD displays begin to increase in popularity.

iStock.com/JazzIRT

iStock.com/ Ferrantraite

2014 Google Glass goes on sale to the public in the United States.

2014 Amazon drops the price of its Fire Phone to $0.99, possibly indicating that apps and services are valued more than the device.

iStock.com/Ilya_Starikov

2015 Emerging protocols, such as LTE-A and Wi-Fi 802.11 ac, ad, aq, and ah, increase performance on mobile and wireless networks.

2015 Approximately 91 percent of all Internet traffic is video, including HD and 3-D video.

2015 Microsoft releases Office 2016, which includes new productivity software and application updates.

2017 Intelligent personal assistants, which can help individuals find information or complete tasks, are becoming more prominent and are including more features. Popular intelligent personal assistants include Siri, Samsung S Voice, Microsoft Cortana, Amazon Alexa, and Google Assistant.

George W. Bailey/ Shutterstock.com

2016 Several companies, such as Tesla and Google, are making advances with self-driving cars. These cars not only will be designed to improve safety as they navigate streets and highways, but also to provide flexible transportation for those who otherwise would lack transportation. Tesla announces that all Tesla vehicles produced in their factory will include the necessary hardware for self-driving capability.

iStock.com/Jason Doiy

iStock.com/ Baranozdemir

2016 Virtual Reality (VR) headsets are exploding in popularity, and many game consoles and smartphones are taking advantage by supporting this technology. Popular VR headsets include Google Cardboard, Oculus Rift, Samsung Gear VR, and HTC Vive.

iStock.com/ Christopher Ames

2017 Nintendo releases the Switch, its newest game console. The Nintendo Switch can connect to a dock that is connected to a television, or it can be removed from the dock and used in portable mode. Multiple players also can gather with their devices for multiplayer games.

Barone Firenze/ Shutterstock.com

2017 Payments apps explode in popularity and widely are used by many people to transfer money electronically. In addition, email services, such as Gmail, and online social networks, such as Facebook, provide the capability for users to send money via electronic messages.

2016

2017

Agnormark/iStock/Getty Images

2016 The popularity of drones quickly increases, causing concern for the Federal Aviation Administration (FAA). The FAA introduced regulations limiting who can operate drones, as well as where and when they can be operated.

Paul Stringer/Shutterstock.com

2016 Google introduces two new smartphones, the Pixel and Pixel XL. These phones contain features such as Google Assistant, a fingerprint sensor on the back of the phone, high-quality front and rear cameras, unlimited cloud storage for photos and videos, and support for virtual reality.

iStock.com/Belekekin

2016 Scientists and medical professionals continue the biological and biomedical use of 3-D printing to help patients in need. 3-D printing is becoming more widely used to create body parts, such as hands, arms, and legs, as well as tissue and cells. 3-D printers also can be used to print surgical tools, which cost only a fraction of their stainless steel equivalents.

iStock.com/3alexd

2017 The number of worldwide Internet users exceeds 3.3 billion.

iStock.com/Kasto80

iStock.com/ Audioundwerbung

2017 Home automation becomes less expensive and more popular. An increasing number of individuals are installing hardware in their homes that enable them to control devices such as lights, garage doors, irrigation systems, coffeemakers, alarm systems, surveillance cameras, and air conditioners.

2017 Worldwide sales of electric vehicles inch toward five million. Electric vehicles, which are connected to a power source to charge onboard batteries, provide their owners with significant fuel savings and are much less damaging to the environment. An increasing number of municipalities and businesses are providing charging stations for electric vehicles. These stations can be used for free or for a fee.

Future Publishing/Getty Images

2019 Drone delivery takes off as UPS and Wing Aviation (subsidiary of Google) get Federal Aviation Administration certification, improving the speed and reliability of deliveries while simultaneously lowering costs.

2019 Microsoft announces Azure Quantum, allowing for cloud-based quantum computing. While classic computing relies on binary computing, with bits representing a 1 or a 0, quantum computing uses bits that can represent a 1, 0, or a 1 and 0 at the same time. This allows quantum computers to solve problems exponentially faster than traditional computers.

Smith Collection/Gado/Getty Images

2018 Charmaine Hung, a female technical product manager for Oculus, is one of the key decision makers in the design of the Oculus Go headset. The design focus was to make it user friendly and accessible for all genders.

2018 Babel-fish earbuds, earbuds that sync to your phone and translate words into the user's chosen language, become more affordable and translations come closer to real-time exchanges.

Picture alliance/Getty Images

2018 3-D metal printing becomes more efficient and cheaper, enabling manufacturers to custom design parts instead of holding large inventories.

2018 AI services are now offered on the cloud, enabling greater access, ease of use, and a cheaper way to utilize machine learning models.

2018

2019

2018 Chinese start-up company Royole launches the world's first foldable smartphone, the FlexPai. The flexible phone simulates real-life interactions, such as flipping through pages in a book with a slight bend of the corner. The phone also outputs a slight vibration so that the user can feel the sensation of flipping through real pages. Bendable smartphones use plastic components instead of glass, making them more durable devices.

2019 Social robots, such as Pepper, developed by SoftBank Robotics, can recognize human emotions and can engage in conversations.

2019 Smart watches become more advanced, and multiple products, including the Apple Watch, have FDA-approved electrocardiogram capabilities with a sensor that tracks blood pressure.

The Washington Post/Getty Images

iStock.com/Tarik Kizilkaya

Bloomberg/Getty Images

2020 Computer vision, a field that develops high-level computational understanding from images and videos, continues to expand. Production lines start to use this image-capturing system to check parts for defects. This technology also is used to check for social distancing violations during a pandemic, where social distancing is crucial.

iStock.com/AndreusK

Bloomberg/Getty Images

2020 The first Amazon Go grocery store location is opened. No cashier is required to cash out; shoppers scan a QR code that connects to their Amazon account, place items in their cart, and walk out of the store.

2020 The iPhone 12 is released with many major upgrades, including access to 5G speeds, the capability to shoot 4K video in Dolby Vision, and the capability to take pictures in very low light using the LiDAR scanner. The phone also uses MagSafe, allowing external accessories, such as wireless chargers, car mounts, and battery packs, to be integrated into the phone seamlessly.

iStock.com/Nyc russ

iStock.com/Just_Super

2021 Elon Musk leads a live demonstration that monitors a pig's brain activity with the Neuralink chip. This test was run with and without the chip to demonstrate that no long-term side-effects are associated with the implant.

SOPA Images/LightRocket/ Getty Images

2021 Windows 11 is released, providing improved security and cleaner design, as well as new ways to download apps.

2020

2021

2020 Sony's PlayStation 5 is released. A solid-state drive, faster graphics processor, and a controller with haptic sensors all combine for quick processing and a more immersive gaming experience.

iStock.com/Girts Ragelis

2020 *Coded Bias* documentary is released, following Joy Buolamwini's discovery of racial bias in facial recognition technology and further widespread bias in AI technology.

Suzi Pratt/Getty Images

2020 Arnav Kapur's Alter Ego, developed in MIT's media lab, is named one of the best inventions of the year. Alter Ego translates a person's thoughts into digital text and is being used in limited trials to help people who suffer from conditions that impair speech.

Gary Hershorn/Corbis News/ Getty Images

2021 Google Pixel 6 is released. This is one of the biggest changes to the Pixel that Google has released in years. The model includes a Tensor smartphone chip, which improves machine learning capabilities, including highly accurate speech recognition, real-time language translation, and the capability to clarify blurry faces in pictures.

Misha Friedman/Getty Images News/ Getty Images

2021 IBM implements the Quantum System One in Ehningen, Germany, and Tokyo, Japan. This system allows a person to write and perform algorithms using the quantum programming language, Qiskit. This is a first step to commercially scaling IBM's quantum technology, which can lead to solving computational problems quickly and with more accuracy. Some of these problems include developing drugs and vaccines more quickly, improving climate models, and optimizing transportation systems.

2021 Edge computing is becoming the next step of cloud computing, allowing data to be stored closer to the location where it is being used, instead of a central repository.

2021 RoseTTAFold 2 solves the "protein-folding problem" using deep artificial intelligence learning. The protein-folding problem is the exploration of how a protein's amino acid sequence forms its 3-D structure. If a protein is misfolded, it will not function properly and can lead to diseases, such as Parkinson's Disease. RoseTTAFold 2 predicts the structures of proteins and solves this problem in the most efficient way to date.

Input and Output: Entering Data and Producing Information

Objectives

After completing this module, you will be able to:

1 Differentiate between input and output
2 Identify manual input devices
3 Identify digital input devices
4 Identify physical output methods
5 Identify digital output methods
6 Identify uses of various assistive technology input and output methods
7 Explain how to customize and manage input and output devices
8 Identify e-waste risks and strategies

Input and Output

Recall that computers process data (input) into information (output). When used as a noun, input is any data and instructions entered in the memory of a computer, and output is data that has been processed into a useful form. When used as a verb, input is the action of entering data, and output is the action of producing information.

In this module you will explore input and output methods using hardware, some of which you have been introduced to already.

How Do You Use Input?

Recall that data is a collection of unprocessed items, including text, numbers, images, audio, and video. Once data is in memory, a computer or mobile device interprets and executes instructions to process the data into information. Figure 6-1 shows a variety of options you might use to input data and instructions into a computer.

Instructions that a computer or mobile device processes can be in the form of software (programs and apps), commands, and user responses.

Figure 6-1 Examples of input devices.

iStock.com/MattKay; iStock.com/M-Production; iStock.com/PeopleImages; iStock.com/Peppersmint; iStock.com/PeopleImages; iStock.com/AsiaVision

kiosk touch screen

keyboard and mouse

stylus

Input Devices

NFC technology

game controller

QR code

microphone (in headset)

When software developers write programs or apps, they usually enter the instructions into the computer or mobile device using a keyboard, mouse, or other input method. The software developer then stores the program or app in a file that a user can execute (run). When a user runs a program or app, the computer or mobile device loads the program or app from a storage medium into memory.

A command is an instruction that causes a program or app to perform a specific action. Programs and apps respond to commands that a user issues. Users issue commands in a variety of ways, which include touching an area on a screen, pressing keys on the keyboard, clicking a mouse button to control a pointer on the screen, or speaking into a microphone.

A user response is an instruction a user issues by responding to a message displayed by a program or app. A response to the message instructs the program or app to perform certain actions. For example, when a program or app asks the question, 'Do you want to save the changes made to this file?', and you respond with the instruction of 'Yes', the program or app will save the file with the changes you made. If you respond with the instruction of 'No', the program or app will not save your changes before exiting.

How Do You Use Output?

Output varies in form, depending on the hardware and software being used and the requirements of the user. You can view or watch output on a screen, print it, or hear it through speakers, headphones, or earbuds. While working with a computer or mobile device, a user encounters four basic types of output: text, graphics, audio, and video. Very often, a single form of output, such as a webpage, includes more than one of these types of output.

- **Text:** Examples of output that primarily contain text are text messages, email messages, memos, letters, press releases, reports, classified advertisements, envelopes, and mailing labels. On the web, users read blogs, news and magazine articles, books, stock quotes, speeches, and lectures.
- **Graphics:** Many forms of output include graphics to enhance visual appeal and convey information. Business letters have logos. Reports include charts. Newsletters use drawings, clip art, and photos (Figure 6-2). Users print high-quality photos taken with a digital camera. Users include animations, such as GIFs, in social media posts.
- **Audio:** Users download or stream their favorite songs and listen to the music. Software, such as games, encyclopedias, and simulations, often include musical accompaniments and audio clips, such as narrations and speeches. On the web, users listen to podcasts, sporting events, radio broadcasts, audio clips, news, music, and concerts. They also use VoIP.

Figure 6-2   An electronic newsletter with graphics.
iStock.com/Tolgart

- **Video:** As with audio, software and websites often include video clips and video blogs. Users watch news reports, movies, sporting events, weather conditions, and live performances on a computer or mobile device.

? Consider This

Are storage devices categorized as input or output devices?
When storage devices write on storage media, they are creating output. Similarly, when storage devices read from storage media, they function as a source of input. Nevertheless, they are categorized as storage devices, not as input or output devices. What type of storage device do you use? What type of information is stored on it? Would you agree that it is neither an input nor output device? Why or why not?

Manual Input

A manual input device is one in which you enter data directly to the device by typing or using a pointing device, touching with a pen or finger, with your voice, or using video capture. You have been introduced to several hardware devices used for input, including keyboards, pointing devices, touch screens, and more. This section focuses on the type of input of each.

Typing and Pointing Input

Keyboards and pointing devices are traditional types of manual input devices. Keyboards enable you to type text or commands; pointing devices enable you to make selections on the screen. These device types predate the touch screen capabilities that most devices include now, although some keyboards now are virtual and rely on touch input. Unlike digital-only input devices, they require you to physically manipulate a device to instruct the computer or device to enter or manipulate data or to complete an action.

Figure 6-3 Windows and macOS standard keyboards.
Courtesy of Logitech; GreenLandStudio/Shutterstock.com

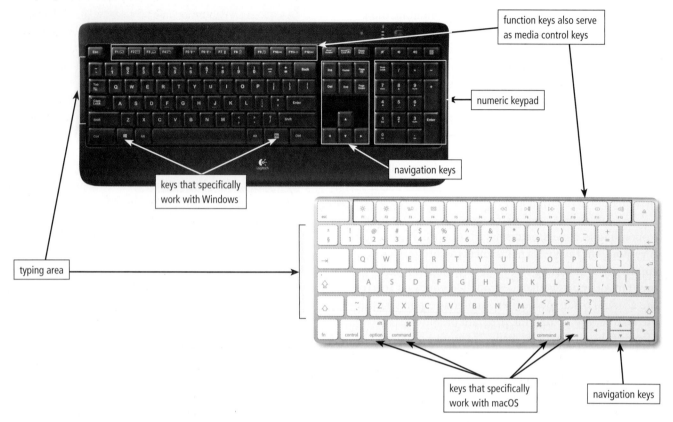

Using Keyboards Most computers and mobile devices include a physical or virtual keyboard or provide the capability to attach a peripheral keyboard. Nearly all keyboards have a typing area, function keys, toggle keys, and navigation keys (Figure 6-3). Many also include media control buttons, Internet control buttons, and other special keys. Others may include a fingerprint reader or a pointing device.

- The typing area includes letters of the alphabet, numbers, punctuation marks, and other basic keys.
- Function keys, which are labeled with the letter F followed by a number, are special keys programmed to issue commands to a computer. The command associated with a function key may vary, depending on the program or app you are using.
- A toggle key is a key that will alternate views or turn a feature on or off each time you press it. Caps Lock and Num Lock are examples of toggle keys. Many mobile devices have keys that toggle the display of alphabetic, numeric, and symbols on touch keyboards in order to display more characters and symbols on a keyboard with fewer keys.
- Users can press the navigation keys, such as arrow keys and Page Up/Pg Up and Page Down/Pg Dn on the keyboard, to move the insertion point in a program or app left, right, up, or down.

- A keyboard shortcut is a key or combination of keys that you press to access a feature or perform a command, instead of using a mouse or touch gestures. Some keyboard shortcuts are unique to a particular application or operating system.
- Media control buttons might allow you to control a media player program or adjust speaker volume.
- Internet control buttons allow you to access an email application, start a browser, and search the web.

Desktops include a standard keyboard. Standard keyboards typically have from 101 to 105 keys, which often include function keys along the top and a numeric keypad on the right. Mobile computers and devices may use a compact keyboard, which is smaller than a standard keyboard and usually does not include the numeric keypad or navigation keys. Some compact keyboards are separate devices that communicate wirelessly or attach to the computer or device with a magnet, clip, or other mechanism. Other users work with on-screen or virtual keyboards instead of a physical keyboard. An ergonomic keyboard has a design that reduces the chance of repetitive strain injuries (RSIs) of the wrist and hand (Figure 6-4). Recall that the goal of ergonomics is to incorporate comfort, efficiency, and safety in the design of the workplace. Even keyboards that are not ergonomically designed attempt to offer a user more comfort by including a wrist rest.

Figure 6-4   An ergonomic keyboard.
iStock.com/Bill Oxford

A **gaming keyboard** is a keyboard designed specifically for users who enjoy playing games on the computer (Figure 6-5). Gaming keyboards typically include programmable keys so that gamers can customize the keyboard to the game being played. The keys on gaming keyboards light up so that the keys are visible in all lighting conditions. Some have small displays that show important game statistics, such as time or targets remaining.

Figure 6-5   Gaming keyboard.
iStock.com/Alberto Case

Using Pointing Devices   In a graphical user interface, a **pointer** is a small symbol on the screen that becomes different shapes depending on the task you are performing, the application you are using, and the pointer's location on the screen. A pointing device can enable you to select text, graphics, and other objects, such as buttons, icons, links, and commands. The following pages discuss a variety of pointing devices.

- **Mouse:** A mouse is a pointing device that fits under the palm of your hand comfortably. As you move a mouse, the pointer on the screen also moves. The bottom of a mouse is flat and contains a mechanism that detects movement of the mouse. Desktop users have an optical mouse or a touch mouse, both of which can be placed on nearly all types of flat surfaces (Figure 6-6). An **optical mouse** uses optical sensors that emit and sense light to detect the mouse's movement.

Similarly, a **laser mouse** uses laser sensors that emit and sense light to detect the mouse's movement. Some mouse devices use a combination of both technologies. The top and sides of an optical or laser mouse may have one to four buttons; some also may have a small wheel. Some are more sensitive than others for users requiring more precision, such as graphic artists, engineers, or game players. A **touch mouse** is a touch-sensitive mouse that recognizes touch, in addition to detecting movement of the mouse and traditional click and scroll operations. For example, you press a location on a touch mouse to simulate a click, sweep your thumb on the mouse to scroll pages, or slide multiple fingers across the mouse to zoom. As with keyboards, you can purchase an ergonomic mouse to help reduce the chance of RSIs or to reduce pain and discomfort associated with RSIs.

Figure 6-6   Laser mouse.
iStock.com/Joel Aguilar

- **Touchpad:** A touchpad is a small, flat, rectangular pointing device that is sensitive to pressure and motion (Figure 6-7). Touchpads are found most often on laptops and convertible tablets. To move the pointer using a touchpad, slide your fingertip across the surface of the pad. Some touchpads have one or more buttons around the edge of the pad that work like mouse buttons; others have no buttons. On most touchpads, you also can tap the pad's surface to imitate mouse operations, such as clicking. Some touchpads also recognize touch gestures, such as swipe, pinch, and stretch motions.

Figure 6-7   Touchpad.
iStock.com/Christian Horz

- **Trackball:** A trackball is a stationary pointing device with a ball on its top or side. The ball in most trackballs is about the size of a Ping-Pong ball. Some devices, called a trackball mouse, combine the functionality of both a trackball and a mouse (Figure 6-8). To move the pointer using a trackball, you rotate the ball with your thumb, fingers, or the palm of your hand. In addition to the ball, a trackball usually has one or more buttons that work like mouse buttons.

Figure 6-8 Trackball.

iStock.com/Epixx

Touch Input

Many computers and devices use touch as a primary method of input. Operating systems enable users to turn touch input on or off. Touch screens are convenient because they do not require a separate device for input. Smartphones, tablets, and many monitors offer touch screens.

Finger Input You can interact with a touch screen by touching areas of the screen with your finger or a stylus to make selections or to begin typing. Many touch screens also respond to gestures. A **gesture** is a motion you make on a touch screen with the tip of one or more fingers or your hand (Table 6-1). For example, you can slide your finger to drag an object or pinch your fingers to zoom out.

Touch screens that recognize multiple points of contact at the same time are known as multi-touch. Because gestures often require the use of multiple fingers (points of contact), touch screens that support gestures are multi-touch.

Table 6-1 Touch screen gestures.

Motion	Description	Common Uses
Tap	Quickly touch and release one finger one time	Activate a link (built-in connection) Press a button Run a program or app
Double-tap	Quickly touch and release one finger two times	Run a program or app Zoom in (show a smaller area on the screen, so that contents appear larger) at the location of the double-tap
Press and hold	Press and hold one finger to cause an action to occur, or until an action occurs	Display a shortcut menu (immediate access to allowable actions) Activate a mode enabling you to move an item with one finger to a new location
Drag, or slide	Press and hold one finger on an object and then move the finger to the new location	Move an item around the screen Scroll
Swipe	Press and hold one finger and then move the finger horizontally or vertically on the screen	Scroll Display a bar that contains commands on an edge of the screen
Stretch	Move two fingers apart	Zoom in (show a smaller area on the screen, so that contents appear larger)
Pinch	Move two fingers together	Zoom out (show a larger area on the screen, so that contents appear smaller)

Devices that utilize touch input include monitors and screens for computers, tablets, and smartphones; wearable devices; portable media players; digital cameras; kiosks; and navigation systems.

- **Monitors and screens:** Touch-enabled monitors and screens allow users to interact with the operating system without a keyboard or pointing device. Instead of using a mouse to click an object on the screen, users simply can tap or double-tap the item they otherwise would have clicked. For example, users can tap or double-tap an icon to start a program or an application, slide their finger to scroll, or use their finger to drag items across the screen.
- **Wearable devices:** Wearable devices, such as smartwatches, do not have room for a physical keyboard, so they mainly rely on touch input. The gestures you might perform on a wearable device include tapping to make a selection and sliding or swiping to scroll through the various screens (Figure 6-9).

Figure 6-9   Using a touch screen on a wearable device.
iStock.com/Urbazon

- **Portable media players:** Portable media players widely use touch as the primary method of input so that the size of the screen on the device is maximized. That is, space on the device does not have to be dedicated to other controls, such as buttons or click wheels. Users slide and swipe to browse their music libraries on their portable media players and then tap to select the song they want to play. While songs are playing, users can tap the screen to display controls so that they can pause or stop the song, navigate to another song, or adjust the volume.
- **Digital cameras:** Touch input helps digital camera users perform gestures such as swiping left and right on the screen to browse photos, tapping the screen to identify the area on which a user wishes to focus when taking a picture, pinching and stretching to zoom while viewing photos, tapping areas of photos to remove red-eye, adding a filter, and dragging borders of photos to crop them.

- **Kiosks:** Kiosks, such as those at an airport allowing you to check in for a flight, can be used by hundreds of people per day. Because kiosks are designed to help you perform a specific function as quickly as possible, touch input is ideal for their user-friendly interfaces. Users typically interact with kiosks by tapping various areas of the screen to select options. If typing is required, an on-screen keyboard is displayed so that users can enter information, such as their name or a confirmation number. Kiosks requiring sensitive or a significant amount of input also might include a separate keyboard and pointing device. For example, ATMs with touch screens often have a separate keypad to enter your PIN so that it is more difficult for others to see what you are typing.
- **Navigation systems:** Typing on a separate keyboard is not wise while operating a vehicle. Navigation systems allow users to perform actions such as tapping to enter a destination address, dragging to display different areas of the map, or pinching and stretching to zoom (Figure 6-10). Operating a navigation system with touch input requires you to take your eyes off the road to interact with the device, so you should operate the touch screen on a navigation system only while your vehicle is parked or stopped. Some navigation and other in-vehicle systems enable voice input as well. To reduce the chances of driver distraction, some built-in navigation systems reduce functionality while the vehicle is in motion.

Figure 6-10   In-car navigation system.
iStock.com/Ryosha

Pen Input

With pen input, you touch a stylus or digital pen on a flat surface to write, draw, or make selections. Pen input devices can be used to input information on a screen or rely on a special device to capture and digitize input.

- **Stylus:** A stylus is a small metal or plastic device that looks like a tiny ink pen but uses pressure instead of ink. Nearly all tablets and mobile devices, some laptop screens, and a few desktop monitors have touch screens that support pen input, in addition to touch input. These computers and devices may include a stylus. Some stylus designs include buttons you can press to simulate clicking a mouse.

- **Digital pen:** A digital pen, which is slightly larger than a stylus, is an input device that captures and converts a user's handwriting or drawings into a digital format, which users can upload (transfer) to a computer or mobile device. Some require the user to write or draw on special paper or a tablet; others can write or draw on any surface. Once uploaded, **handwriting recognition software** on the computer or mobile device translates the handwritten letters and symbols created on the screen into typed text or objects that the computer or device can process. For this reason, digital pens most often are used for taking notes. Some are battery operated or USB powered; others use wireless technology, such as Bluetooth.

- **Signature capture pad:** To capture a handwritten signature, a user writes their name on a **signature capture pad** with a stylus that is attached to the device. Software then transmits the signature to a central computer, where the signature is stored. Retailers use signature capture pads to record purchasers' signatures (Figure 6-11). Signature capture pads often work with POS (point-of-sale) terminals that also enable you to swipe or tap your credit card to complete payment.

Figure 6-11   Customer signing at point-of-sale terminal.

iStock.com/Fotofrog

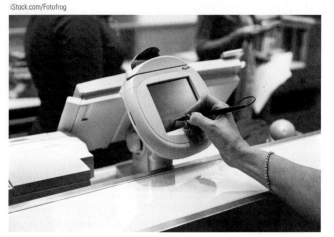

- **Graphics tablet:** To use pen input on a computer that does not have a touch screen, you can attach a graphics tablet to the computer. A **graphics tablet**, also called a digitizer, is a hardware device used to create drawings with a pressure-sensitive pen using an electronic plastic board that detects and converts movements of the stylus or digital pen into digital signals that are sent to the computer (Figure 6-12). Each location on the graphics tablet corresponds to a specific location on the screen. Architects, mapmakers, designers, and artists, for example, use graphics tablets to create images, sketches, or designs.

Figure 6-12   Graphics tablet.

iStock.com/Edwin Tan

❓ Consider This

Is it more efficient to take notes by hand or with a digital device?

When instructors start lectures, they usually look out at the classroom to see some students bent over a tablet, others frantically typing on a laptop, and still others using pen and paper to take notes. Which method is most effective for retaining knowledge? A study concluded that students who used traditional pen and paper to take notes in class and while studying had better understanding and recall of information. The study determined that when taking notes on a laptop, students tended to write down the speaker's exact words. Taking notes longhand required students to process the information, use their own words, and select what information is important enough to write down. Tablet users tended to have a mix of both transcribed and selected content. Regardless of the note-taking method, students performed equally when asked to recall factual information. Laptop users, however, were less able to answer conceptual or interpretive questions than those who took notes longhand. What type of notes do you take? Should instructors require students to use a specific method of note taking? Why or why not?

Digital Input

Digital input devices are devices that enable you to capture and process video, audio, or data. You have been introduced to several hardware devices used for digital input, including webcams, microphones, and more. This section focuses on the type of input associated with each and introduces additional digital input devices that digitize print and other types of data.

Voice Input

Voice input is the process of entering input by speaking into a microphone. The microphone may be built in the computer or device, in a headset, or an external peripheral device that sits on top of a desk or other surface. Some external microphones have a cable that attaches to a port on a computer; others communicate using wireless technology, such as Bluetooth.

Uses of voice input include Internet messaging that supports voice conversations, chat rooms that support voice chats, video calls, videoconferencing, VoIP, and voice recognition. Recall that VoIP enables users to speak to other users via their Internet connection. Voice recognition, also called speech recognition, is the computer or mobile device's capability of distinguishing spoken words. Some computers and mobile devices make use of built-in and third-party voice recognition applications, which have a natural language interface (Figure 6-13). A voice recognition app allows users to dictate text and enter instructions by speaking into a microphone.

Figure 6-13   Siri, Apple's voice recognition application.
iStock.com/Wachiwit

On mobile devices, these applications allow users to speak simple, task-based instructions to the device, such as setting an alarm, entering a calendar appointment, or making a call. Some mobile devices have a **speech-to-text** feature, which recognizes a user's spoken words and enters them into email messages, text messages, or other applications that support typed text entry.

Voice input is part of a larger category of input called audio input. **Audio input** encompasses entering any sound into the computer, such as speech, music, and sound effects. In order to enter high-quality sound into a computer, the computer requires a sound card or integrated sound capability. Users enter sound into computers and mobile devices via equipment such as microphones, CD/DVD/Blu-ray Disc players, or radios, each of which plugs in a port on the computer or device.

Some users also record live music and other sound effects into a computer by connecting external music devices, such as an electronic keyboard, guitar, drums, harmonica, and microphones, to a computer. Music production software allows users to record, compose, mix, and edit music and sounds (Figure 6-14). For example, music production software enables you to change the speed, add notes, or rearrange the score to produce an entirely new arrangement.

Figure 6-14   Using sound mixing software to edit audio.
iStock.com/Kosamtu

Video Input

Video input involves capturing full-motion images and storing them on a computer or mobile device's storage medium or on the cloud. A digital video (DV) camera records video as digital signals, which you can transfer directly to a computer or mobile device with the appropriate connection. A webcam is a type of digital video camera that enables you to capture video and still images, and usually audio input, for viewing or manipulation on a computer or mobile device. Many laptops, tablets, and smartphones have built-in webcams. Some webcams are separate peripheral devices, which usually attach to the top of a desktop monitor. Smartphones and other mobile devices have built-in integrated DV cameras.

Using a webcam or integrated DV camera, you can send email messages with video attachments, broadcast live images or video over the Internet, conduct videoconferences, and make video calls.

You can configure some webcams to display the images they capture remotely on a webpage or via an app on a mobile device. This use of a webcam attracts website visitors by showing images that change regularly. Home or small business users might use webcams to show a work in progress, weather and traffic information, or employees at work; they also might use it as a security system. Some websites have live webcams that display still pictures and update the displayed image at a specified time or time intervals, such as every 15 seconds, or when motion is detected. Others use streaming to distribute video in real-time.

Digital Video Technology   Using **DV technology**, you can input, edit, manage, publish, and share your videos. You can enhance digital videos by adding scrolling titles and transitions, cutting out or adding scenes, and adding background music and voice-over narration. The following steps are involved in the process of using DV technology.

Step 1: Select a DV camera. DV cameras range from inexpensive consumer versions to high-end DV camera models that support Blu-ray or HDV standards. Many mobile devices allow you to record digital video that you later can transmit to your computer or email app from the device. When selecting a DV camera, consider features such as zoom, sound quality, editing capabilities, and resolution.

Step 2: Record a video. With most DV cameras, you have a choice of recording programs that include different combinations of camera settings. These programs enable you to adjust the exposure and other functions to match the recording environment. You also have the ability to select special digital effects, such as fade, wipe, and black and white.

Step 3: Transfer and manage videos. You can connect most video cameras and mobile devices to a computer using a USB port or wirelessly. With many devices, you can transfer the videos to a media sharing website or an online social network. Before doing this, however, consider the frame rate and video file format. The **frame rate** of a video refers to the number of frames per second (fps). A smaller frame rate results in a smaller file size for the video, but playback of the video will not be as smooth as one recorded with a higher frame rate.

Step 4: Edit a video. When editing, you first split the video into smaller pieces, or scenes, that you can manipulate easily (Figure 6-15). Most video editing software automatically splits the video into scenes at locations that you specify. After splitting, you should delete, or prune, unwanted scenes or portions of scenes. You can crop (or resize) scenes, and add logos, special effects, or titles. Special effects include warping, changing from color to black and white, morphing, or zoom motion. **Morphing** transforms one video image into another image over the course of several frames of video.

Figure 6-15   Using video editing software.
iStock.com/Gorodenkoff

Step 5: Enhance a video. The next step is to add audio effects, including voice-over narration and background music. Using many video editing programs, you can add more tracks, or layers, of sound to a video in addition to the sound that the video camera or mobile device recorded. Adding audio tracks enables you to set a mood by providing background music or sounds. In the final step, you use video editing software to combine the scenes into a complete video by ordering scenes and adding transition effects. Transition effect options include fades, wipes, blurs, bursts, ruptures, and erosions.

Step 6: Distribute a video. You can upload video directly from your device to video sharing and online social networks; you also can send a video message. If you have a disc burner (a hardware device that imprints data onto a DVD or CD), you can package media for individual distribution or sale.

Motion Input

Until recently, the idea of controlling a computer by waving your hands was seen only in Hollywood science fiction movies. Today, the entertainment industry (such as for gaming and animating movies), the military, athletics, and the medical field have found uses for motion input. With **motion input**, sometimes called **gesture recognition**, users can guide on-screen elements using air gestures. Air gestures involve moving your body or a handheld input device through the air. With motion input, a device containing a camera detects your gesture and then converts it to a digital signal that is sent to a computer, mobile, or game device. For example, gamers can swing their arm or a controller to simulate rolling a bowling ball down a lane toward the pins.

Motion-sensing devices communicate with a game console or a personal computer using wired or wireless technology. The console or computer translates a player's natural gestures, facial movements, and full-body motion into input.

Motion Input in Entertainment   Motion-sensing game controllers enable a user to guide on-screen elements by moving a handheld input device through the air. Examples include handheld devices that enable gamers to use sweeping arm movements to simulate sports activities, such as a golf swing (Figure 6-16), balance boards that judge stability and motion when holding yoga poses, and remote control attachments, such as a steering wheel used to guide a car along a race course.

Figure 6-16   Using a motion-sensing game controller.
iStock.com/AnthonyRosenberg; iStock.com/Chris Schmidt; Dani McDaniel/Shutterstock.com

Controller translates motion of golf swing to move the golf ball on the screen

Screen shows the position and movements of the avatar

Player moves controller to simulate a golf swing

Some controllers track peripheral motion within a specific area. With these devices, users can move their finger to draw or move their whole body to dance or exercise. Some use a device that can track small finger gestures, enabling users to be more precise in their movements.

Facial motion capture converts people's facial movements into a digital format while they talk, smile, and more. Animators, for example, use the digital data to simulate facial movements to create realistic gaming avatars or computer-generated characters in movies. Facial movements, however, are more subtle and difficult to detect. Thus, the technology used for capturing facial motions requires more precision and a higher resolution than that required by gaming devices.

Motion Input in the Military   The military uses motion input for training, such as flight simulation or weapon usage. To ensure safety, trainees maneuver a helicopter or other device using motion input within a simulated environment or from a remote location. Motion input also aids in physical rehabilitation for wounded soldiers by providing a method for conducting physical therapy exercises outside of a military hospital. Another use of motion input is to assist in recovery from post-traumatic stress disorder (PTSD). People with PTSD can use avatars and simulators to work through scenarios in a comfortable environment.

Motion Input in Sports   Coaches and sports trainers use motion input to improve athletes' performance and to correct inefficient or injury-causing motions. Analyzing the arc of a pitcher's arm and factoring the speed of the motion and the trajectory of the ball can help improve a pitcher's accuracy and speed. Combining the athlete's motion input with complex algorithms can pinpoint areas in which the athlete can improve.

Motion Input in the Medical Field   The medical field also uses motion input for training. For example, surgeons can practice new technologies in a simulated environment. Using motion input that enhances movements, surgeons also can operate less invasively. Surgeons even operate remotely, enabling experts to manipulate surgical devices and share their expertise to save lives around the world. Sports medicine specialists use motion input to assess injuries, determine treatment, and assist in physical therapy.

Scanners and Reading Devices

Some input devices save users time by capturing data directly from a source document, which is the original form of the data. Examples of source documents include time cards, order forms, invoices, paychecks, advertisements, brochures, photos, inventory tags, or any other document that contains data to be processed.

Devices that can capture data directly from a source document include NFC (near field communications), optical scanners, optical readers, bar code readers, QR codes, RFID (radio frequency identification) readers, magstripe (magnetic stripe card) readers, and MICR (magnetic-ink character recognition) readers.

NFC Technology **NFC (near field communication)** is a close-distance network protocol used by smartphones and other devices to read data from another device or an item, such as a credit card or ticket (Figure 6-17). NFC enables the contactless transfer of data by enabling an app to read an electronic tag. NFC-enabled cards can be used for electronic payment, for accessing to your account or rewards at a store or restaurant, and for identification, ticket validation, and entry to your hotel room. Typically, NFC transfers data that is not rewritable, such as an ID tag or special code.

Figure 6-17 Using NFC to make a payment.
iStock.com/Ronstik

Optical Scanners An optical scanner, usually called a scanner, is a light-sensing input device that reads printed text and graphics and then translates the results into a form the computer can process. A flatbed scanner works in a manner similar to a copy machine, except it creates a file of the document in memory instead of a paper copy. Once you scan a picture or document, you can display the scanned object on the screen, modify its appearance, store it on a storage medium, print it, attach it to an email message, include it in another document, or post it on a website or photo community for everyone to see.

The quality of a scanner is measured by its resolution, that is, the number of bits it stores in a pixel and the number of pixels per inch. The higher each number, the better the quality, but the more expensive the scanner.

Many scanners include **OCR (optical character recognition)**, which converts text to digital text so that it can be edited, copied, and searched directly within the program. OCR software converts a scanned image to a text file that can be edited, for example, with a word processing application.

Optical Readers An **optical reader** is a device that uses a light source to read characters, marks, and codes and then converts them into digital data that a computer can process. Two technologies used by optical readers are optical character recognition (OCR) and **optical mark recognition (OMR)**.

- Most OCR devices include a small optical scanner for reading characters and sophisticated software to analyze what is read. OCR devices range from large machines that can read thousands of documents per minute to handheld wands that read one document at a time. OCR devices read printed characters in a special font.
- OMR devices read hand-drawn marks, such as small circles or rectangles. A person places these marks on a form, such as a test, survey, or questionnaire answer sheet.

Bar Code Readers A **bar code reader**, also called a **bar code scanner**, is an optical reader that uses laser beams to read bar codes. A **bar code** is an identification code that often consists of either a set of vertical lines and spaces of different widths or a two-dimensional pattern of dots, squares, and other images. The bar code represents data that identifies the manufacturer and the item.

Manufacturers print a bar code either on a product's package or on a label that is affixed to a product, such as groceries, books, clothing, vehicles, mail, and packages. Each industry uses its own type of bar code.

QR Codes A **QR code** (quick response code) is known as a 2-D bar code because it stores information in both a vertical and horizontal direction in a square-shaped graphic that represents a web address or other content, such as contacts or phone numbers (Figure 6-18). QR codes can be read with a QR bar code reader or a QR code reader app on a smartphone or other mobile device. All types of material, from posters to textbooks to merchandise, include QR codes that consumers scan to obtain additional information, which may be in the form of a website or social media page, or it might display text for the user to read.

Figure 6-18 Using a QR code to access information.
iStock.com/AJ_Watt

RFID Readers   RFID (radio frequency identification) is a technology that uses radio signals to communicate with a tag placed in or attached to an object, an animal, or a person. RFID tags, which contain a memory chip and an antenna, are available in many shapes and sizes. An RFID reader reads information on the tag via radio waves. RFID readers can be handheld devices or mounted in a stationary object, such as a doorway.

Uses of RFID include tagging and updating inventory (as an alternative to bar code identification); tracking times of runners in a marathon; tracking location of people, airline baggage, packages, and misplaced or stolen goods; checking lift tickets of skiers; gauging temperature and pressure of tires on a vehicle; checking out library books; providing access to rooms or buildings (Figure 6-19); managing purchases; and tracking payment as vehicles pass through booths on tollway systems.

Figure 6-19   Using an RFID electronic key system.
iStock.com/Iggy1965

Magstripe Readers   A magstripe reader, short for magnetic stripe card reader, reads the magnetic stripe on the back of credit cards, entertainment cards, bank cards, identification cards, and other similar cards. The stripe contains information identifying you and the card issuer. Some information stored in the stripe may include your name, account number, the card's expiration date, and a country code. As chip-and-pin technology becomes more prevalent, magstripe readers are used less widely.

Most magstripe readers are separate devices that communicate with a POS terminal, such as those in retail stores. Home or small business users, however, may attach a small plastic magstripe reader to a smartphone or tablet so that they can accept payments using a mobile app. When a credit card is swiped through a magstripe reader, it reads the information stored on the magnetic stripe on the card.

MICR Readers   An MICR (magnetic-ink character recognition) device reads text printed with magnetized ink. An MICR reader converts MICR characters into a form the computer can process. The banking industry almost exclusively uses MICR for check processing. When a bank receives a check for payment, it uses an MICR inscriber to print the amount of the check in MICR characters in the lower-right corner. Each check is inserted in an MICR reader, which sends the check information — including the amount of the check — to a computer for processing.

Data Collection Devices   Instead of reading or scanning data from a source document, a data collection device obtains data directly at the location where the transaction or event takes place. For example, employees use bar code readers, handheld computers, or other mobile devices to collect data wirelessly (Figure 6-20). These types of data collection devices are used in restaurants, grocery stores, factories, warehouses, the outdoors, or other locations where heat, humidity, and cleanliness are not easy to control. For example, factories and retail stores use data collection devices to take inventory and order products. Data collection devices have the capability of wirelessly transmitting data over a network or the Internet; however, tablets are replacing many data collection devices.

Figure 6-20   Using a data collection device in a warehouse.
iStock.com/TommL

Consider This

Is your credit card vulnerable to scanning?

RFID technology embedded in credit and debit cards transmits signals with the coded account information to scanners, which thieves place in their coat pockets, purses, and other nonmetallic containers. Some signals have a range as far as 30 feet, so that the electronic pickpockets simply walk among crowds in search of obtaining these radio waves. The RFID technology embedded in the credit cards is approximately the size of a postage stamp. It consists of a coil of wire connected to an electronic circuit that generates a pattern of electrical pulses with coded account information unique to a specific card. An antenna transmits these radio waves to a scanner.

The radio waves do not penetrate metal or water easily. You, consequently, can protect these cards and documents by wrapping them in aluminum foil or placing them near water bottles. Security experts also recommend stacking several credit cards in an attempt to scramble the signals. Place the cards in your wallet with the magnetic stripe facing inside. RFID-blocking wallets also are manufactured to prevent scanners from obtaining the emitted signals. Have you ever had a credit card compromised due to RFID scanning? How did you know that was the cause? What else can you do to protect yourself?

Physical Output

Printed information (hard copy) exists physically and is a more permanent form of output than that presented on a display (soft copy). A hard copy, also called a printout, is either in portrait or landscape orientation. A printout in **portrait orientation** is taller than it is wide, with information printed across the shorter width of the paper. A printout in **landscape orientation** is wider than it is tall, with information printed across the widest part of the paper. Letters, reports, and books typically use portrait orientation. Spreadsheets, slide shows, and graphics often use landscape orientation.

To meet the range of printing needs from home users to enterprise users, many different types and styles of printers exist with varying speeds, capabilities, and printing methods. Figure 6-21 presents a list of questions to help you determine the printer best suited to your needs.

Figure 6-21   Questions to ask before purchasing a printer.

✓ What is my budget?
✓ How fast must my printer print?
✓ Do I need a color printer?
✓ What is the cost per page for printing?
✓ Do I need multiple copies of documents?
✓ Will I print graphics?
✓ Do I want to print photos?
✓ Do I want to print directly from a memory card?
✓ What types of paper does the printer use?
✓ What sizes of paper does the printer accept?
✓ Do I want to print on both sides of the paper?
✓ How much paper can the printer tray hold?
✓ Will the printer work with my computer and software?
✓ How much do supplies such as ink, toner, and paper cost?
✓ Can the printer print on envelopes?
✓ How many envelopes can the printer print at a time?
✓ How much do I print now, and how much will I be printing in a year or two?
✓ Will the printer be connected to a network?
✓ Do I want wireless printing capability?

Nonimpact Printers

A **nonimpact printer** forms characters and graphics on a piece of paper without actually contacting the paper. Some spray ink, while others use heat or pressure to create images. Commonly used nonimpact printers are ink-jet printers, photo printers, laser printers, all-in-one printers, 3-D printers, thermal printers, mobile printers, label printers, and plotters and large-format printers.

Ink-Jet Printers   An **ink-jet printer** is a type of nonimpact printer that forms characters and graphics by spraying tiny drops of liquid ink onto a piece of paper. Ink-jet printers are a popular type of color printer for use in the home.

Ink-jet printers produce text and graphics in both black-and-white and color on a variety of paper types and sizes. These printers normally use individual sheets of paper stored in one or two removable or stationary trays. Most ink-jet printers can print lab-quality photos. Ink-jet printers also print on other materials, such as envelopes, labels, index cards, greeting card paper (card stock), transparencies, and iron-on T-shirt transfers. Many ink-jet printers include software for creating greeting cards, banners, business cards, and letterhead.

The speed of an ink-jet printer is measured by the number of pages per minute (ppm) it can print. Graphics and colors print at a slower rate than text.

Figure 6-22   How an ink-jet printer works.
Almaamor/Dreamstime.com; Boyan Dimitrov/Shutterstock.com

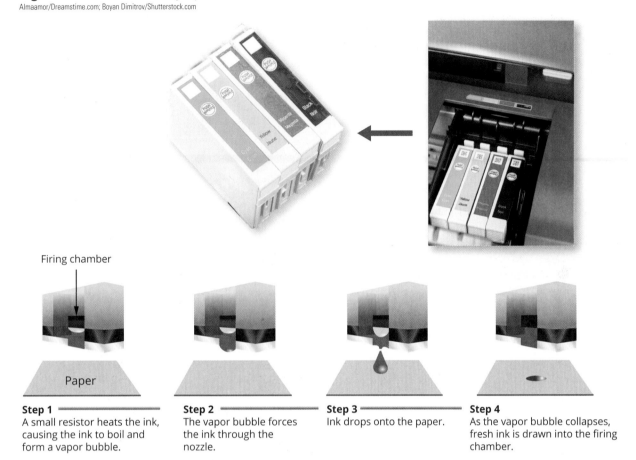

Firing chamber

Paper

Step 1
A small resistor heats the ink, causing the ink to boil and form a vapor bubble.

Step 2
The vapor bubble forces the ink through the nozzle.

Step 3
Ink drops onto the paper.

Step 4
As the vapor bubble collapses, fresh ink is drawn into the firing chamber.

The printhead mechanism in an ink-jet printer contains ink-filled cartridges. Each cartridge has fifty to several hundred small ink holes, or nozzles. The steps in Figure 6-22 illustrate how a drop of ink appears on a page. The ink propels through any combination of the nozzles to form a character or image on the paper.

When the cartridge runs out of ink, you simply replace the cartridge. Most ink-jet printers use two or more ink cartridges, one containing black ink and the other(s) containing colors. Some color cartridges contain a variety of ink colors; others contain only a single color. Consider the number of ink cartridges a printer requires, along with the cost of the cartridges, when purchasing a printer. To reduce the expense of purchasing cartridges and reduce waste, some users opt to purchase refilled cartridges or have empty cartridges refilled by a third-party vendor.

Photo Printers   A **photo printer** is a color printer that produces lab-quality photos (Figure 6-23). Some photo printers print just one or two sizes of photos, for example, 3 × 5 inches and 4 × 6 inches. Others print up to 8 × 10 or larger. Some even print panoramic photos. Generally, the more sizes the printer prints, the more expensive the printer.

Many photo printers use ink-jet technology. With models that can print letter-sized documents, users connect the photo printer to their computer and use it for all their printing needs. For a few hundred dollars, this type of photo printer is ideal for the home or small business user.

Figure 6-23   Photo printer.
iStock.com/Tankist276

Figure 6-24 How a laser printer works.
PaPicasso/Shutterstock.com

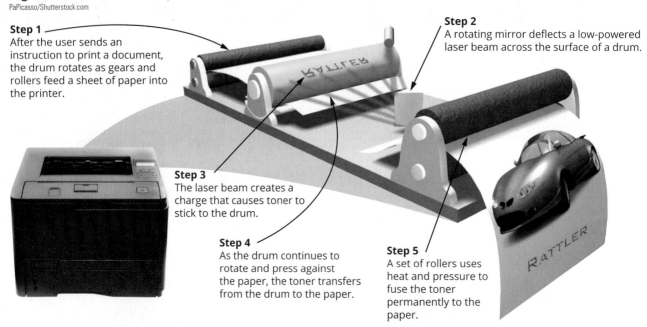

Step 1
After the user sends an instruction to print a document, the drum rotates as gears and rollers feed a sheet of paper into the printer.

Step 2
A rotating mirror deflects a low-powered laser beam across the surface of a drum.

Step 3
The laser beam creates a charge that causes toner to stick to the drum.

Step 4
As the drum continues to rotate and press against the paper, the toner transfers from the drum to the paper.

Step 5
A set of rollers uses heat and pressure to fuse the toner permanently to the paper.

Laser Printers A **laser printer** is a high-speed, high-quality nonimpact printer. Laser printers are available in both black-and-white and color models. A laser printer for personal computers ordinarily uses individual 8 1/2 × 11-inch sheets of paper stored in one or more removable trays that slide in the printer case.

Laser printers print text and graphics in high-quality resolutions. While laser printers usually cost more than ink-jet printers, many models are available at affordable prices for the home user. Laser printers usually print at faster speeds than ink-jet printers.

When printing a document, laser printers process and store the entire page before they actually print it. Storing a page before printing requires that the laser printer has a certain amount of memory in the device. The more memory in the printer, the faster it usually can print.

Operating in a manner similar to a copy machine, a laser printer creates images using a laser beam and powdered ink, called **toner**. The laser beam produces an image on a drum inside the printer. The light of the laser alters the electrical charge on the drum wherever it hits. When this occurs, the toner sticks to the drum and then transfers to the paper through a combination of pressure and heat (Figure 6-24). When the toner runs out, you replace the toner cartridge.

All-in-One Printers An **all-in-one printer**, also called a multifunction printer (MFP), is a single device that looks like a printer or a copy machine but provides the functionality of a printer, scanner, and copy machine. Some use color ink-jet printer technology, while others use laser technology.

3-D Printers A **3-D printer** uses a process called additive manufacturing to create an object by adding material to a three-dimensional object, one horizontal layer at a time. 3-D printers can print solid objects, such as clothing, prosthetics, eyewear, implants, toys, parts, prototypes, and more (Figure 6-25).

Figure 6-25 3-D printer creating a model of a heart.
iStock.com/Devrimb

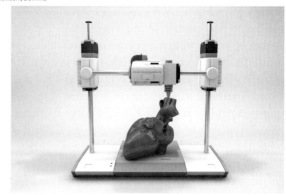

Using a digital model scanned from an existing item or created with CAD (computer-aided design) software, 3-D printers begin creating an object at the bottom and add layers of material to the object until it is complete. Depending on the type of printer, the layers are built and blended seamlessly using a variety of substances including liquid polymer, gel, resin, edible food, ceramics, plastic, nylon, wood, bronze, and copper.

In the past, 3-D printers were quite expensive and used only by large enterprises. Today, consumers work with more affordable desktop 3-D printers to create hundreds of thousands of everyday objects, including custom toys, cups, household tools, kitchen utensils, storage boxes, replacement parts, game pieces, and more. For those users who do not feel comfortable creating a digital model, 3-D printer manufacturers typically provide downloadable patterns, and online community members often share patterns for free.

Small and large businesses use 3-D printing in a variety of fields, including medical, automotive, aerospace, art, architecture, and manufacturing. For example, Boeing uses more than 50,000 parts created with 3-D printing for its civilian and military aircraft, Nike develops prototypes of its shoes, and surgeons implant prosthetic body parts, including ribs and other bones, into patients. The medical field has found many uses for 3-D printers.

Thermal Printers   A **thermal printer** generates images by pushing electrically heated pins against heat-sensitive paper. Basic thermal printers are inexpensive, but the print quality is low, the images tend to fade over time, and thermal paper can be expensive. Self-service gas pumps often print gas receipts using a built-in, lower-quality thermal printer. Many POS terminals in retail and grocery stores also print purchase receipts on thermal paper.

Some thermal printers have high print quality and can print at much faster rates than ink-jet and laser printers. A dye-sublimation printer, sometimes called a digital photo printer, uses heat to transfer colored dye to specially coated paper. Photography studios, medical labs, security identification systems, and other professional applications requiring high image quality use dye-sublimation printers that can cost thousands of dollars. Dye-sublimation printers for the home or small business user, by contrast, typically are much slower and less expensive than their professional counterparts. Some are small enough for the mobile user to carry in a briefcase.

Mobile Printers   A **mobile printer** is a small, lightweight, battery-powered printer that allows a mobile user to print from a laptop, smartphone, or other mobile device while traveling. Barely wider than the paper on which they print, mobile printers fit easily in a briefcase alongside a laptop. Mobile printers mainly use ink-jet or thermal technology. As most computers and mobile devices have wireless capabilities that enable them to connect to a printer over a network, mobile printers are less common.

Label Printers   A **label printer** is a small printer that prints on an adhesive-type material that can be placed on a variety of items, such as envelopes, packages, optical discs, photos, and file folders. Most label printers also print bar codes (Figure 6-26). Label printers typically use thermal technology.

Figure 6-26   Label printer.
iStock.com/Berenika_L

Plotters and Large-Format Printers   A **plotter** is a sophisticated printer used to produce high-quality drawings, such as blueprints, maps, and circuit diagrams. These printers are used in specialized fields such as engineering and drafting and usually are very costly. Current plotters use a row of charged wires (called styli) to draw an electrostatic pattern on specially coated paper and then fuse toner to the pattern. The printed image consists of a series of very small dots, which provides high-quality output.

Using ink-jet printer technology, but on a much larger scale, a **large-format printer** creates photo-realistic-quality color prints. Graphic artists use these high-cost, high-performance printers for signs, posters, and other professional quality displays (Figure 6-27).

Figure 6-27   Large format printer.

iStock.com/Morenosoppelsa

How does resolution affect print quality?

As with many other input and output devices, one factor that determines the quality of an ink-jet printer is its resolution. Printer resolution is measured by the number of dots per inch (dpi) a printer can print. With an ink-jet printer, a dot is a drop of ink. A higher dpi means the print quality is higher because the drops of ink are smaller and more drops fit in an area. The difference in quality becomes noticeable when the size of the printed image increases. That is, a wallet-sized image printed at 1200 dpi may look similar in quality to one printed at 2400 dpi. When you increase the size of the image to 8 × 10, for example, the printout of the 1200 dpi resolution may look grainier than the one printed using a 2400 dpi resolution.

Impact Printers   An **impact printer** forms characters and graphics on a piece of paper by striking a mechanism against an inked ribbon that physically contacts the paper. Impact printers characteristically are noisy because of this striking activity (Figure 6-28). Impact printers are ideal for printing multi-part forms because they print through many layers of paper easily. Factories, warehouses, and retail counters may use impact printers because these printers withstand dusty environments, vibrations, and extreme temperatures.

Digital Output

Unlike physical output, no tangible output is issued with digital output. Common devices that create digital output include displays, DTVs and Smart TVs, and other devices, such as speakers, headphones and earbuds, data projectors, interactive whiteboards, and force-feedback game controllers and tactile output. The following sections discuss each of these output devices.

Figure 6-28   An impact printer produces printed images when tiny pins strike an inked ribbon.

Courtesy of Oki Data Americas, Inc.

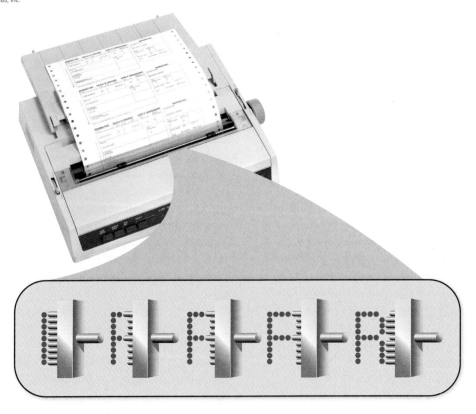

Displays

Recall that a display device, or simply display, is an output device that visually conveys text, graphics, and video information. Sometimes called soft copy, information on a display exists electronically and appears for a temporary period. Displays consist of a screen and the components that produce the information on the screen. Most current displays are a type of flat-panel display, which means they have a shallow depth and a flat screen.

Desktops often use a monitor as their display. Adjustable monitor stands allow you to adjust the height of the monitor to be at eye-level. Monitor controls enable you to adjust the brightness, contrast, positioning, height, and width of images. Some have touch screens, integrated speakers, and/or a built-in webcam. Today's monitors have a small footprint; that is, they do not take up much desk space. For additional space savings, some monitors are wall mountable. Many users set up multiple monitors to display separate screens of information from the same computer or device (Figure 6-29).

Figure 6-29   Using two monitors.
iStock.com/AJ_Watt

Display Technologies

Many desktop monitors, along with the screens on mobile computers and devices, use some type of LCD technology. An **LCD** (**liquid crystal display**) sandwiches a liquid compound between two sheets of material that presents sharp, flicker-free images on a screen when illuminated. The light source, called the backlight, often uses either CCFL (cold cathode fluorescent lamp) or LED (light-emitting diode) technology.

A display that uses LED for the backlight often is called an LED display or an LED LCD display. LED displays consume less power, last longer, and are thinner, lighter, and brighter than a display that uses CCFL technology, but they also may be more expensive. Screens in laptops and mobile devices often use LED backlight technology.

Instead of LCD or traditional LED, some displays use OLED technology. OLED (organic LED) uses organic molecules that are self-illuminating and, thus, do not require a backlight. OLED displays consume less power and produce an even brighter, easier-to-read display than LCD or LED displays, but they can have a shorter life span. OLEDs also can be fabricated on thin, flexible surfaces.

Many mobile computers and devices use either AMOLED or Retina Display technology. An AMOLED (active-matrix OLED) screen uses both active-matrix (a high-quality, lightweight display technology capable of producing a wide range of colors with a fast response time) and OLED technologies, combining the benefits of high-quality viewing from all angles with lower power consumption. Variations of AMOLED provide different levels of viewing quality.

Display Quality

You measure the screen on a monitor, laptop, tablet, smartphone, or other mobile device diagonally from one corner to the other. In addition to screen size, the quality of a display depends on its resolution, response time, brightness, dot pitch, and contrast ratio.

- **Resolution:** A monitor or screen that has a 1600 × 900 resolution displays up to 1600 pixels per horizontal row and 900 pixels per vertical row, for a total of 1,440,000 pixels to create a screen image. A higher resolution uses a greater number of pixels and, thus, provides a smoother, sharper, and clearer image. As the resolution increases, however, some items on the screen appear smaller. Displays are optimized for a specific resolution, called the native resolution. Although you can change the resolution to any setting, for best results, use the monitor or screen's native resolution setting.
- **Response time:** The response time of a display refers to the time in milliseconds (ms) that it takes to turn a pixel on or off. The lower the number, the faster the response time.
- **Brightness:** Brightness of a display is measured in nits. A **nit** is a unit of visible light intensity equal to one candela (formerly called candlepower) per square meter. The **candela** is the standard unit of luminous intensity. The higher the nits, the brighter the images.
- **Dot pitch:** Dot pitch, sometimes called pixel pitch, is the distance in millimeters between pixels on a display. Text created with a smaller dot pitch is easier to read. The lower the number, the sharper the image.
- **Contrast ratio:** Contrast ratio describes the difference in light intensity between the brightest white and darkest black that can be produced on a display. Higher contrast ratios represent colors better.

Graphics Chips, Ports, and Flat-Panel Monitors A graphics chip, called the **graphics processing unit (GPU)**, controls the manipulation and display of graphics on a display device. The GPU either is integrated on the motherboard or resides on a video card in a slot on the motherboard.

Several video standards define the resolution, aspect ratio, number of colors, and other display properties. The **aspect ratio** defines a display's width relative to its height. A 2:1 aspect ratio, for example, means the display is twice as wide as it is tall. Some displays support multiple video standards. For a display to show images as defined by a video standard, both the display and GPU must support the same video standard.

HDTVs and Smart TVs

HDTV (high-definition television) works with digital broadcast signals, transmitting digital sound, supporting wide screens, and providing high resolutions. A Smart TV is an Internet-enabled HDTV from which you can browse the web, stream video from online media services, listen to Internet radio, communicate with others on online social media, play online games, and more — all while watching a television show (Figure 6-30). Using a Smart TV, you can stream content from the TV to other Internet-enabled devices, such as a tablet or smartphone, and use cloud storage services to share content. **UHD** (ultra-high-definition television) expands on HDTV technology to provide even better resolution.

HDTVs often use LCD, LED, or plasma technology. A **plasma display** uses gas plasma technology, which sandwiches a layer of gas between two glass plates. When voltage is applied, the gas releases ultraviolet (UV) light. This UV light causes the pixels on the screen to glow and form an image.

Figure 6-30 Using a Smart TV.
© LG Electronics USA Inc.; Courtesy of LG Electronics USA Inc.

Other Output Devices

In addition to displays and printers, other output devices are available for specific uses and applications. These include speakers, headphones and earbuds, data projectors, interactive whiteboards, and force-feedback game controllers and tactile output.

- **Speakers:** Most personal computers and mobile devices have a small internal speaker that usually emits only low-quality sound. Thus, many users attach surround sound speakers or speaker systems to their computers, game consoles, and mobile devices to generate higher-quality sounds for playing games, interacting with media presentations, listening to music, and viewing movies (Figure 6-31).

Figure 6-31 Computer speakers.
iStock.com/Rouzes

- **Headphones and earbuds:** When using speakers, anyone in listening distance can hear the output. Instead, users can listen through headphones or earbuds so that only the individual wearing the headphones or earbuds hears the sound from the computer. Both headphones and earbuds usually include noise-cancelling technology to reduce the interference of sounds from the surrounding environment. A headset functions as both headphones and a microphone. Users wear a headset to free their hands for typing and other activities while talking or listening to audio output.
- **Data projectors:** A **data projector** is a device that projects the text and images displaying on a computer or mobile device screen on a larger screen so that an audience can see the image clearly. For example, many classrooms use data projectors so that all students easily can see an instructor's presentation on the screen. Interactive whiteboards are replacing data projectors in many instances.

- **Interactive whiteboard:** An **interactive whiteboard** is a touch-sensitive device, resembling a dry-erase board, that displays the image on a connected computer screen, usually via a projector. A presenter controls the program by clicking a remote control, touching the whiteboard, drawing on or erasing the whiteboard with a special digital pen and eraser, or writing on a special tablet. Notes written on the interactive whiteboard can be saved directly on the computer and/or printed. Interactive whiteboards are used frequently in classrooms as a teaching tool (Figure 6-32), during meetings as a collaboration tool, and to enhance delivery of presentations.

Figure 6-33   Gaming wheel.
iStock.com/Pagadesign

Figure 6-32   Interactive whiteboard.
iStock.com/Monkeybusinessimages

- **Gaming and motion-sensing devices:** Joysticks, wheels, gamepads, and motion-sensing game controllers are used to control movements and actions of a player or object in computer games, simulations, and video games. These devices also function as output devices when they include **force feedback**, which is a technology that sends resistance to the device in response to actions of the user (Figure 6-33). For example, as you use the simulation software to drive from a smooth road onto a gravel alley, the steering wheel trembles or vibrates, making the driving experience as realistic as possible. These devices also are used in practical training applications, such as in the military and aviation. Some input devices, such as a mouse, and mobile devices, such as a smartphone, include **tactile output** that provides the user with a physical response from the device. For example, users may sense a bumping feeling on their hand while scrolling through a smartphone's contact list.

? Consider This

Are printers becoming obsolete?
You can share information easily on social media, through cloud-based apps, using email, and more. Why would you need to print anything? Personal users like to print photos to frame. Legal documents often are required to be produced and signed physically, not digitally. Many home users, however, are forgoing purchasing a printer. Libraries and office supply stores enable remote printing for a small fee. You can send your documents or files over the Internet and either pick up the physical copies or have them delivered. The fewer documents you print, the less paper waste you create. Some businesses or organizations include in their email or electronic documents a note to consider the environment before printing. How often do you print? What types of documents do you print? Do you own a printer? If not, what printer services do you use?

Ethics & Issues: Assistive Technology Input and Output

The ubiquitous presence of technology in everyone's lives has generated an awareness of the need to address accessibility requirements for those who have or may develop physical, learning, or processing disabilities. Schools, companies, and organizations have an obligation to provide access to input and output technology, including hardware, databases, and the Internet, to all employees. In addition, publishers of digital output, including ebooks, blogs, and websites, should consider the needs of all users when creating content. The goal of accessible input and output is to enable all users to be independent when working with, being entertained by, or accessing services that use technology.

Adaptive Input Devices

Besides voice recognition, which is ideal for blind or visually impaired users, several other input options are available. Users with limited hand mobility who want to use a keyboard can use an on-screen keyboard or a keyboard with larger keys. Deaf users, for example, can instruct programs to display words instead of sounds. Visually impaired users can change screen settings, such as increasing the size or changing the color of the text to make the words easier to read. Blind users can rely on voice or Braille input. Other adaptive input devices include the following:

- **Eye gaze pointing devices** analyze the area of the screen that the user is looking at. Users can make a selection by blinking or other gesture.
- A **foot mouse** enables users with limited mobility in their arms or hands to control input using their feet; they also include buttons or sections that enable the user to move the insertion point, as well as click or tap the screen to make selections.
- **Sip-and-puff (SNP)** technology enables users to control the mouse or other computer or device functions using a tube that they either inhale (sip) or exhale (puff) to issue commands.

Adaptive Output Devices

Many different types of assistive output options are available, including screen readers that translate text into audio. Other output devices include the following:

- **Refreshable Braille displays** use nylon pins or magnets to translate content into the Braille system that users can read with their fingers. Braille displays typically use an eight-dot character — six dots for the traditional Braille characters and two for formatting or highlighting (Figure 6-34).

Figure 6-34   Refreshable Braille display.

iStock.com/Zlikovec

- Braille printers use embossing techniques to produce hard copies of digital content that can be read by touch.
- OCR readers can scan printed materials and digitize them so that a screen reader can read the content aloud or print on a Braille printer.

Creating Accessible Content

How a user accesses input and output goes beyond hardware. It also involves the creation of content that takes into account the adaptive devices that may be using it, as well as the needs of users with learning or processing challenges. You also should take care to make your language inclusive to all identities, and be sensitive to preferred identifying terms for race, gender, and more. Some considerations when creating accessible content include:

- Use clear, simple language. This not only helps users for whom English is not their first language, but for those with language processing disorders. It also makes it less likely that a screen reader will misinterpret the meaning.
- Use meaningful links when hyperlinking content. Phrases such as "Click Here" do not tell the user the purpose of clicking the link. Instead, use the name of the document, website, or article to which you are linking.
- Always provide alt text to describe the contents of all visuals on a screen. Use simple, concise language, and be consistent when there are many similar graphics or animations.
- Avoid unnecessary graphics, such as shapes or background images that do not add value to your content but that a screen reader or Braille printer may be unable to translate.
- Do not use flashing images that may trigger issues for users with seizure disorders.

❓ Consider This ────────────────

What technology requirements do older adults have?
Older adults often require technologies to address changes in vision, hearing, and mobility due to arthritis or other conditions. Some of the same assistive technologies can be used by older adults to help them keep connected and to access services. Many of today's older adults are comfortable using technology and have access to smartphones, tablets, and more. In-vehicle technology geared towards older adults helps to ensure that they can drive safely, and it is a fast-growing field. Recommendations for older drivers include 360-degree cameras to assist when parking, adaptive headlights that move as you move the steering wheel, automatic high beams, rearview cameras, crash notification systems, and alerts when the driver is suspected to be drowsy. Do you know an older adult who uses assistive devices? What types of devices or modifications do you think are important to meet the needs of this population?

How To: Customize and Manage Input and Output Devices

When you start using a computer or device, the operating system and related software and hardware have default settings. **Default settings** are standard settings that control how the screen is set up and how a document looks when you first start typing. As you continue to work with your computer or device, you may decide to customize the settings to be more productive.

Customize System Software

Every operating system has its own tools for customization. For example, Windows uses the Windows Settings dialog box. Operating systems allow you to make adjustments such as:

- Changing the brightness of the screen
- Adding a desktop theme, which is a predefined set of elements such as background images and colors
- Adjusting the screen resolution, which controls how much content you can see on a screen without scrolling
- Adding a sound scheme, which associates sounds such as a bell chime with an event, such as closing a window
- Pinning frequently used apps to the taskbar for easy access
- Selecting items to appear in the Notification area

You also can use these tools to link your smartphone to your computer, uninstall apps, add accounts, manage your network connections, and adjust privacy settings.

You also can customize the desktop by moving the taskbar, creating and organizing icons for apps and files, and more. In addition, you can create links to files and apps called **shortcuts**. A shortcut does not place the actual file, folder, or app on the desktop — it still remains in the location where it is saved on your computer or device. A shortcut merely allows you to access the object from the desktop without going through a file manager or a program menu, such as the Start menu.

Customize Input and Output Devices Using System Software

On a Windows computer, you use the Windows Settings dialog box (Figure 6-35) to find and click an option to access further choices. For example, if you click System, you can adjust settings such as the display, sounds, power, battery, storage, and more.

You can change the settings of your pointing device, including a mouse or trackball. For example, you can switch the mouse buttons if you are left-handed or adjust the sensitivity of your touchpad. Windows enables you to change these options in the Settings dialog box.

You can adjust the keyboard settings to change the commands associated with certain keys, and other modifications, including:

- Controlling the pointing device with the keyboard by using the arrow and other keys
- Changing the language or dialect associated with the keyboard
- Creating new keyboard shortcuts to commands, or enabling sticky keys, which allow you to press keyboard shortcuts one key at a time instead of simultaneously
- Adjusting the settings for toggle keys, for example the Caps Lock key, which turn a feature on or off each time a user clicks or presses it

Figure 6-35   The Windows Settings dialog box.
Source: Microsoft Corporation

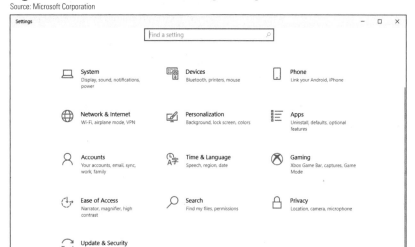

Consider This

Why is your keyboard set up like this?

You might think, logically, that letters on a keyboard would be in alphabetical order. However, the first six keys of your keyboard's top row of letters probably includes the letters Q, W, E, R, T, and Y. This arrangement is called a QWERTY keyboard. The keys originally were arranged on old mechanical typewriters to separate frequently used keys, which caused typists to slow down or cause jams. European keyboards typically replace the Y with Z, as in languages such as German, Z is a more common letter. Other keyboard configurations exist to address language differences, ergonomics, finger strength, and more. In the United States, standard keyboards use the QWERTY format, and keyboarding classes teach how to type using this method. Have you ever used a non-QWERTY keyboard? If so, what was the configuration? Do you find QWERTY easy to use? What might you change?

Secure IT: Reduce E-Waste Risks

When you work on a computer or talk on a mobile phone, could you be at risk from harmful radiation? Every electronic device emits some level of radiation. While the amounts for computers and mobile devices may not be harmful in low doses, some critics argue that constant exposure, such as sitting in an office all day or wearing a Bluetooth headset for several hours at a time, can cause levels of radiation that, over time, may cause cancer or other health concerns.

In addition to the computer itself, peripheral devices, such as printers, along with the wireless or cordless methods to connect the devices, emit radiation. Research is inconclusive about safe levels and long-term risks. Most agree that it is not the level from any one device, but rather the cumulative effect from long-term exposure (several hours a day over many years) to multiple devices simultaneously that causes harm.

The following are some suggestions to help protect yourself and minimize your risks:

- Replace older equipment, such as CRT (cathode-ray tube) monitors, with devices such as LCD monitors, which meet current emission standards.
- Sit back from your monitor as far as possible.
- If you use your device while sitting, protect your lap with a device that shields from radiation.
- Move other electronic sources, such as hard drives and printers, as far away as possible.
- Minimize your wireless connections, such as a wireless keyboard or a wireless mouse.
- Remove your Bluetooth headset when not in use, and frequently switch the headset from one ear to the other.
- Turn off devices when not in use.
- Recycle or donate older, unused devices to eliminate any radiation exposure from older devices, even when they are not in use.
- Take regular breaks from technology use.

 Consider This

What is keyboard monitoring software?

Some employers and parents use keyboard monitoring software, also called keylogging software, to monitor everything that has been entered in a computer. This software runs undetected and stores every keystroke in a file for later retrieval. When used in a positive fashion, employers can measure the efficiency of data entry personnel. This software can verify that employees are not engaging in activities that could subject the company to harassment, hacking, or other similar charges. Parents, likewise, can verify their children are not visiting inappropriate websites. Educators and researchers can gauge students' input to analyze how well they are learning a second language or improving their typing skills. Criminals, on the other hand, use the programs to capture usernames, passwords, credit card numbers, and other sensitive data and then use this data to access financial accounts and private networks. Antivirus programs can help detect the presence of keyboard monitoring software. Do you know anyone who has installed keylogging software or who has found keylogging software installed on their computer? Is keylogging software an invasion of privacy? Should employers inform employees if the software is installed? Why or why not?

Study Guide

Instructions: The Study Guide exercise reinforces material you should know after reading this module. Answer the questions below using the format that helps you remember best or that is required by your instructor. Possible formats may include one or more of these options: write the answers; create a document that contains the answers; record answers as audio or video using a webcam, smartphone, or portable media player; post answers on a blog, wiki, or website; or highlight answers in the book/ebook.

1. ___ is the action of entering data, and ___ is the action of producing information.

2. Define the terms, command and user response. Give an example of a user response.

3. What is the role of memory with regards to how a computer process instructions?

4. List four basic types of output. Give examples of each.

5. Explain whether or not storage devices are categorized as input or output devices.

6. List features that are common to most keyboards. Describe the purpose of a keyboard shortcut.

7. Describe the characteristics of ergonomic and gaming keyboards.

8. List different mouse types.

9. Differentiate between a touchpad and a trackball.

10. Explain how to interact with a touch screen. Define the term, gesture.

11. Describe the uses of the following touch screen types: monitors and screens for computers, tablets, and smartphones; wearable devices; portable media players; digital cameras; kiosks; and navigation systems.

12. List methods and devices for using pen input. Explain how a signature capture pad is used.

13. Explain the uses of a graphics tablet.

14. Explain how hand-writing notes during class could impact your knowledge retention.

15. Name hardware and devices used for voice and audio input.

16. Name hardware and devices used for video input.

17. Outline steps involved in using DV technology.

18. Define the term, motion input. Describe how the entertainment industry, the military, sports, and the medical field use motion input.

19. Describe types of scanners and reading devices.

20. Describe the uses of and data included in a bar code.

21. A(n) ___ code stores information that can correspond to a web address or other content.

22. List uses of RFID technology, and list uses for magstripe readers.

23. Describe how a bank uses MICR technology.

24. Give examples of data collection devices, and describe how they are used.

25. List guidelines to protect your credit card from scanning devices.

26. Differentiate between portrait and landscape orientation of hard copies.

27. Explain how an ink-jet printer works.

28. Describe the following printer types: photo, laser, all-in-one, 3-D, thermal, mobile, label, plotter, and impact.

29. Differentiate between toner and an ink cartridge.

30. Explain how resolution affects printer quality.

31. ___ consist of a screen and the components that produce the information on the screen.. Describe different types of monitors.

32. Differentiate among LCD, CCFL, LED, TFT, OLED, and AMOLED technologies.

33. How is resolution determined?

34. Define these terms: resolution, response time, nit, candela, dot pitch, and contrast ratio.

35. Explain the purpose of the GPU. Define the term, aspect ratio.

36. Explain the capabilities of HDTV and Smart TVs.

37. Differentiate among headphones, earbuds, and headsets.

38. Define the term, data projector.

39. Describe uses of interactive whiteboards and force-feedback game controllers. Define the term, tactile output.

40. Explain the importance of adaptive input and output devices. List examples of each.

41. List considerations when creating accessible content.

42. Define the term, default settings. List adjustments operating systems allow you to make to the system.

43. List ways you can adjust keyboard settings.

44. Why do most keyboards use the QWERTY configuration?

45. Explain risks associated with hardware radiation.

46. List ways to protect yourself from hardware radiation.

47. Explain the criminal and beneficial purposes of keyboard monitoring software.

Key Terms

You should be able to define the Key Terms listed below.

3-D printer (6-16)
all-in-one printer (6-16)
aspect ratio (6-20)
audio input (6-9)
bar code (6-12)
bar code reader (6-12)
bar code scanner (6-12)
candela (6-19)
command (6-3)
contrast ratio (6-19)
data collection device (6-13)
data projector (6-20)
default settings (6-23)
dot pitch (6-19)
DV technology (6-10)
ergonomic keyboard (6-4)
eye gaze pointing device (6-22)
foot mouse (6-22)
force feedback (6-21)
frame rate (6-10)

function key (6-4)
gaming keyboard (6-5)
gesture (6-6)
gesture recognition (6-11)
graphics processing unit (GPU) (6-20)
graphics tablet (6-8)
handwriting recognition software (6-8)
HDTV (6-20)
impact printer (6-18)
ink-jet printer (6-14)
interactive whiteboard (6-21)
keyboard shortcut (6-4)
label printer (6-17)
landscape orientation (6-14)
large-format printer (6-17)
laser mouse (6-5)

laser printer (6-16)
LCD (liquid crystal display) (6-19)
magstripe reader (6-13)
MICR (magnetic-ink character recognition) (6-13)
mobile printer (6-17)
morphing (6-10)
motion input (6-11)
NFC (near field communication) (6-12)
nit (6-19)
nonimpact printer (6-14)
OCR (optical character recognition) (6-12)
optical mark recognition (OMR) (6-12)
optical mouse (6-5)
optical reader (6-12)
photo printer (6-15)
plasma display (6-20)
plotter (6-17)

pointer (6-5)
portrait orientation (6-14)
QR code (6-12)
refreshable Braille display (6-22)
response time (6-19)
RFID (radio frequency identification) (6-13)
shortcut (6-23)
signature capture pad (6-8)
sip-and-puff (SNP) (6-22)
speaker (6-20)
speech-to-text (6-9)
tactile output (6-21)
thermal printer (6-17)
toggle key (6-4)
toner (6-16)
touch mouse (6-5)
UHD (6-20)
user response (6-3)
video input (6-9)

Extend Your Knowledge

Instructions: The Extend Your Knowledge exercise expands on subjects covered in the module and encourages you to find the latest developments on these topics. Use a search engine or another search tool to locate news articles, blog entries, videos, expert discussions, or other current sources on the listed topics. List your sources, and write 3-4 sentences describing what you have learned to submit in the format required by your instructor.

• Webcam safety
• Keyboard shortcuts specific to your platform
• Alternative keyboards to QWERTY
• Radiation risks from hardware

What did you learn that helped you better understand the concepts in this module? Did anything surprise you? How will what you learned impact you?

Checkpoint

The Checkpoint exercises test your knowledge of the module concepts.

True/False   Mark T for True and F for False. If False, rewrite the statement so that it is True.

_____ 1. A command is an instruction that causes a program or app to perform a specific action.

_____ 2. While working with a computer or mobile device, a user encounters four basic types of input: text, graphics, audio, and video.

_____ 3. A function key is a key that will alternate views or turn a feature on or off each time you press it.

_____ 4. A touchpad is a small, flat, rectangular pointing device that is sensitive to pressure and motion.

_____ 5. A graphics tablet also is called a digitizer.

_____ 6. A magstripe is an identification code that represents data that identifies the manufacturer and the item.

_____ 7. The printhead mechanism in an ink-jet printer contains toner.

_____ 8. In terms of response time, the lower the number, the faster the response time.

_____ 9. SNP technology enables users to control the mouse or other computer or device functions using a tube into which they either inhale or exhale to issue commands.

_____ 10. Shortcuts are used to place the actual file, folder, or app on the desktop.

Matching   Match the terms with their definitions.

_____ 1. DV technology

_____ 2. refreshable Braille display

_____ 3. memory

_____ 4. keylogging software

_____ 5. RFID

_____ 6. all-in-one printer

_____ 7. screen resolution

_____ 8. function keys

_____ 9. nit

_____ 10. stylus

a. electronic components that store instructions waiting to be executed by the processor

b. special keys programmed to issue commands to a computer

c. a small metal or plastic device that looks like a tiny ink pen but uses pressure instead of ink

d. used to input, edit, manage, publish, and share your videos

e. uses include tagging and updating inventory

f. also called an MFP

g. a unit of visible light intensity equal to one candela

h. typically use an eight-dot character — six dots for the traditional characters, and two for formatting or highlighting

i. controls how much content you can see on a screen without scrolling

j. used to monitor everything that has been entered into a computer

Problem Solving

Instructions: The Problem Solving exercises extend your knowledge of module concepts by seeking solutions to practical problems with technology that you may encounter at home, school, or work. The Collaboration exercise should be completed with a team. You often can solve problems with technology in multiple ways. Determine a solution to the problems in these exercises by using one or more resources available to you (such as a computer or mobile device, articles on the web or in print, blogs, podcasts, videos, television, user guides, other individuals, electronics or computer stores, etc.). Is this a real issue you've encountered? Do you think you would be able to solve the situation if you encounter it? Describe your solution, along with the resource(s) used, in the format requested by your instructor (brief report, presentation, discussion, blog post, video, or other means).

Personal

1. **Assistive Technologies** You have just purchased a new computer and, because of a visual impairment, you are having trouble reading the information on the screen. What are your next steps?

2. **Smart TV Issues** You are watching a movie on your Smart TV using a streaming media service. Every few minutes, a message is displayed on the TV stating that the Internet connection is not working. Why might this be happening, and what can you do to resolve this issue?

3. **Touch Gestures Not Working** You are using the stretch touch gesture to zoom on your mobile device. Each time you perform the gesture, however, instead of zooming, one of your fingers appears to be dragging an item around the screen. What might be the problem?

4. **Dim Screen** While using your laptop, the screen suddenly becomes dim. You set the brightness to its highest setting before it dimmed and wonder why it suddenly changed. After resetting the brightness to its highest setting, you continue working. What might have caused the screen to dim?

5. **Malfunctioning Earbud** While listening to music on your portable media player, one side of the earbuds suddenly stops working. What might have caused this?

Professional

6. **Printer Problem** You are attempting to print on a wireless printer from your laptop, but each time you click the Print button, you receive an error message that the printer is not connected. What are your next steps?

7. **Projector Resolution Issue** You are preparing for a meeting in your company's conference room and have connected your laptop to the projector. When the projector displays the information from your laptop screen, the resolution drops significantly and not everything fits on the screen. What steps can you take to correct this problem?

8. **Fingerprints Not Recognized** To increase security, your company now requires employees to sign in to their computer accounts using a fingerprint reader instead of entering a username and password. This past weekend, you cut the finger you use to sign in, and your computer now does not recognize your fingerprint. As a result, you are unable to access your computer. What are your next steps?

9. **Access Denied** Your company uses security badges with embedded RFID tags to authenticate the rooms to which employees have access. This badge also grants employees access to the company's parking lot. When arriving at work one morning, you wave your badge in front of the RFID reader, but the gate that allows access to the parking lot does not open. In addition, a red light blinks on the RFID reader. What are your next steps?

10. **Monitors Reversed** You have two monitors on your desk at work: the monitor on the left is your primary monitor and displays the taskbar and the applications you currently are using, and you typically use the monitor on the right to display an email program. When you arrive at work and sign in to your Windows account, you realize that the monitor on the right is now the primary monitor. What might have happened?

Collaboration

11. **Technology in Finance** Technology enables individuals and businesses to conduct transactions in the finance industry with great convenience and speed; however, many individuals do not realize the extent to which technology impacts the industry. Form a team of three people to learn more about the important role that technology plays in today's finance industry. One team member should research the different ways that technology impacts and improves personal financial transactions, such as home banking. Another team member should research how large businesses use technology to manage their finances, and the other team member should research the different ways technology has helped improve the stock market. Write a brief report summarizing your findings.

How To: Your Turn

Instructions: This exercise presents general guidelines for fundamental skills when using a computer or mobile device and then requires that you determine how to apply these general guidelines to a specific program or situation. You often can complete tasks using technology in multiple ways. Figure out how to perform the tasks described in these exercises by using one or more resources available to you (such as a computer or mobile device, articles on the web or in print, online or program help, user guides, blogs, podcasts, videos, other individuals, trial and error, etc.). Summarize your 'how to' steps, along with the resource(s) used, in the format requested by your instructor (brief report, presentation, discussion, blog post, video, or other means).

1 **Record and Edit a Video**

After recording a video, you may want to edit it before sharing it with others. For example, you might want to remove portions of the video, add special effects, or play an audio track instead of the audio recorded with the video. The following steps guide you through the process of recording and editing a video.

Record a Video

a. Verify your camera or phone's battery is charged and that the device has sufficient space available to store the video you are about to record.

b. If you plan to record the video from one location, consider placing the camera on a stable surface or using a tripod.

c. If you intend to record outside where it is sunny, determine what screens might be helpful.

d. Start the recording.

e. If you plan to move the camera during recording, do so with slow, smooth movements.

f. Stop the recording.

Edit a Video

a. Make a copy of the video so that you can revert to the original if you make a mistake.

b. Start a video editing program on your computer and open the video.

c. To trim a video — that is, remove portions from the beginning and/or end of the video — click the command to trim the video. Select the new starting and ending position for the video.

d. To add a special effect or filter to the video, select the location in the video where you want to add the special effect, and then click the command corresponding to the special effect you want to add.

e. To add music that will play while the video is playing, click the command to add a separate audio track to the video. Next, navigate to and select the music file you want to add. Finally, select the starting and ending locations in the video for the music.

f. Preview the video, save your changes, and exit the program.

Exercises

1. What is the purpose of adding special effects or filters?

2. What type of device do you use to record videos? Why?

3. Compare and contrast at least three programs or apps that can be used to edit videos. Which one do you prefer? Why?

Internet Research

Instructions: These exercises broaden your understanding of module concepts by requiring that you search for information on the web. Use a search engine or another search tool to locate the information requested or answers to questions presented in the exercises. Describe your findings, along with the search term(s) you used and your web source(s), in the format requested by your instructor (brief report, presentation, discussion, blog post, video, or other means). Additionally, reflect on the process you used to complete this activity. How did you go about choosing the tool that you did and why? Would you do anything differently next time?

❶ Security: Passwords

The Department of Homeland Security's Office of Cyber and Infrastructure Analysis (DHC/OCIA) strives to thwart and respond to physical or cyber-threats and hazards. Part of the office's role is to create and implement policies designed to strengthen and secure the country's critical physical assets and services, such as air traffic control, natural gas supplies, water treatment, power plants, and finance, which are likely targets of cyberattacks. Federal agencies must comply with and routinely assess privacy standards and civil liberties protections. The government must share information regarding the cyberthreats, such as malicious code found on networks, but not contents of personal email messages. The private companies are urged to adopt the security incentives and increase their security systems, but participation is voluntary.

Research This: Locate and read the latest standards from DHS/OCIA Then, research news articles describing lawmakers' and businesses' support and criticism of these orders. What measures are proposed to increase the nation's cybersecurity? What positions do the Internet Security Alliance and The Internet Association take on this matter? What efforts has Congress made to pass legislation addressing computer security? What has changed since the last orders? Why do you think the changes were implemented?

❷ Cloud Services: Virtualization (IaaS)

An online business' website receives higher traffic during peak holiday shopping times. Purchasing and configuring additional servers to meet this demand for the short term can be an expensive task for companies managing complex computing environments. To minimize cost and maximize performance, companies often use virtualization software rather than purchasing and installing additional memory, storage, or processing power. Virtualization software allows one physical machine to emulate the capabilities of one or more servers. Virtualization is an example of infrastructure as a service (IaaS), a service of cloud computing that allows users to configure a computing environment's hardware, devices, storage, and operating systems using software.

Research This: (1) Use a search engine to find current articles, websites, or reviews of the two popular virtualization offerings. (2) Find a case study about a company using virtualization services, summarize the problem the company was trying to solve, and describe how virtualization played a part in solving it. Why is running a private cloud in a virtualized environment a popular cloud computing solution? What did you learn about companies' advantages and disadvantages to using these programs?

❸ Making Use of the Web: Fitness

Fitness websites, videos, and apps can provide guidance and motivation for all fitness levels and lifestyles. You can seek advice about exercising, maintaining a nutritious diet, and buying equipment. Many free workouts exist to stream, and apps offer free calorie tracking and other services. For more expert advice, such as designing customized workout routines, or nutritionist-created diet plans, apps exist to purchase, or otherwise-free apps offer a fee-based premium version. With both free and paid services, users can set goals and then track their performance and overall progress with logs and detailed graphs.

Research This: (a) Search for streaming fitness routine workouts for an area that interests you, such as barre, boxing, or weight training. What qualifications do the trainers in the videos have? Are the videos free? Do multiple videos exist from the same trainer for the same workout type?

(b) Locate two nutrition-tracking apps available in your app store. What similar features do these apps have, such as fitness tools, effective exercises, and food planners? Which app has the best reviews? Are all of the services offered free, or is there a premium version? Would you pay to use a nutrition planner? Why or why not? Which articles, planners, and tools would you use to start or continue your fitness routines?

Critical Thinking

Instructions: These exercises challenge your assessment and decision-making skills by presenting real-world situations associated with module concepts. The Collaboration exercise should be completed with a team. Evaluate the situations below, using personal experiences and one or more resources available to you (such as articles on the web or in print, blogs, podcasts, videos, television, user guides, other individuals, electronics or computer stores, etc.). Perform the tasks requested in each exercise and share your deliverables in the format requested by your instructor (brief report, presentation, discussion, blog post, video, or other means).

1. **Bar Codes versus RFID**

   You work as an efficiency analyst at one of the largest retail companies in the world, with multiple stores in every state, as well as in many other countries. For the past several years, the company has used bar code readers at checkout counters that scan the bar code on products to determine from a database the price to charge customers and to keep a record of inventory. The company's bar code reader technology is incompatible with the new inventory system and needs to be replaced with RFID.

   Do This: Analyze and discuss the impact such a change will have on the company, its suppliers, and its customers. Include in your discussion any security risks. Find two examples of RFID readers and compare prices, user reviews, and features. Are handheld options for RFID readers available for store clerks to use on the store floor or for customer checkout? Compile your findings. List advantages and disadvantages of implementing RFID. Include information about reliability and costs. If you had to switch between bar code readers and RFID, how might that impact you at work? What training might you need?

2. **Carpal Tunnel Syndrome**

   While attending college for the past two years, you have worked part-time as a data entry clerk. Recently, you began to feel a pain in your right wrist. Your doctor diagnosed the problem as carpal tunnel syndrome, which is the most well-known of a series of musculoskeletal disorders that fall under the umbrella of repetitive strain injuries (RSIs). Your doctor made several recommendations to relieve the pain. You want to learn more about this debilitating injury.

   Do This: Use the web to investigate carpal tunnel syndrome. Research the carpal tunnel syndrome warning signs and risk factors. Find suggestions about proper workstation ergonomics to avoid carpal tunnel syndrome. Evaluate the differences among various treatment options. Does insurance typically cover treatment? Include in your discussion the average length for time of recovery. How should you change your workspace to help heal and prevent further damage? Should the company's insurance pay for changes to your workspace? Why or why not?

3. **Case Study**

   Cooperative-Owned Farm Stand You are the new manager for a farm stand that is a cooperative effort, jointly owned by several local farmers. The board of directors has asked you to assess their current input and output devices and make recommendations for assistive technologies to ensure that new employees, first time farm participants, and all others will be able to adapt the technology to be able to enter data and review on-screen and printed information.

   Do This: Use the web to find information about assistive input devices, such as voice recognition and larger keyboards. Research output devices, such as large-screen monitors and Braille printers. In addition to devices, research assistive software that you can install on existing computers, devices, and POS terminals shared by others. Find reviews from users of these assistive devices. Research costs for implementation, and find information about any grants your company can apply for as a nonprofit to ease the costs. Compile your findings.

Collaboration

4. **Printer Analysis**

   You work for a local real estate agency as an IT consultant. The agency has always used a printer to print high-quality, custom color brochures for the homes it is showing. Each brochure is printed double-sided on glossy paper, and the agency prints an average of 200 brochures per week. Many of the brochures, however, end up in the recycling bin because potential home owners rely more on real estate apps and websites to find the latest information on the market.

   Do This: Form a three-member team. List advantages and disadvantages to having print materials on hand. What technologies, such as QR codes, might you use on printed materials to cut down on the need for full-color, multipage print pieces? What print services are available in your area that a real estate agency could use for high-quality printing instead of doing it in-house? Meet with your team, and discuss and compile your findings. Share information about the print services you researched, describe their services and costs, and evaluate their advantages and disadvantages. Identify any additional recommendations you might have for the management. What do you recommend? Why?

Digital Storage:
Preserving Your Content

7

iStock.com/maxkabakov

Objectives

After completing this module, you will be able to:

1 Differentiate between storage and memory
2 Identify storage hardware types
3 Discuss cloud computing concepts
4 Evaluate cloud storage options
5 Explain how to secure your cloud data
6 Identify enterprise and other storage options
7 Explain how memory relates to storage
8 Identify risks for the Internet of Things

Storage and Memory Uses

Your computer and devices use both storage and memory to access and save data and information; however, storage and memory are not the same thing. Consider this analogy: a storage medium is similar to a filing cabinet that holds file folders, and memory is similar to the top of your desk. When you want to work with a file, you remove it from the filing cabinet (storage medium) and place it on your desk (memory). When you are finished with the file, you remove it from your desk (memory) and return it to the filing cabinet (storage medium) (Figure 7-1).

Figure 7-1   Storage is similar to a file cabinet for digital content.
iStock.com/z_wei

Recall that memory consists of electronic components that store instructions waiting to be executed by the processor, data needed by those instructions, and the results of processing the data into information. **Storage** refers to long-term, permanent access of data and information. Items

on a storage medium remain intact even when you turn off a computer or mobile device. Thus, a storage medium is nonvolatile. Most memory (i.e., RAM), by contrast, holds data and instructions temporarily and, thus, is volatile.

Storage Media

A storage medium, also called **secondary storage**, is the location where a computer keeps data, information, programs, and applications. Examples of storage media include digital storage (cloud), and storage hardware, such as hard disks, solid-state drives (both of which can be internal or external), memory cards, USB flash drives, optical discs, tags, and more.

If you want to completely back up the contents of your computer, you might store those contents on an external hard drive or on cloud storage. Your internal hard drive might store your operating system and apps that you have downloaded. You might access other apps on the cloud. Businesses often use cloud storage for backup but might also use a tape drive, which is a storage device that stores data on magnetic tapes, to create a local backup. If you want to move several files from one computer to another and are not convinced you can access them remotely, consider using a USB flash drive. Finally, you might use a DVD or other type of optical disc to store a movie or other large media files that exceed your cloud storage capacity.

Cloud storage keeps information on servers on the Internet. Because the user accesses files on cloud storage through a browser using an app from the storage provider, the user does not own or have access to the actual media on which the files are stored. Figure 7-2 shows a variety of storage options.

In addition to programs and apps, users store a variety of data and information on storage media in their computers and mobile devices or on cloud storage. For example, many users store digital photos, appointments,

Figure 7-2   Various storage technologies.
iStock.com/Mozcann; iStock.com/Onfokus; iStock.com/Charday Penn; iStock.com/Liangpv; iStock.com/Kuzmik_A; iStock.com/DNY59; iStock.com/Eivaisla

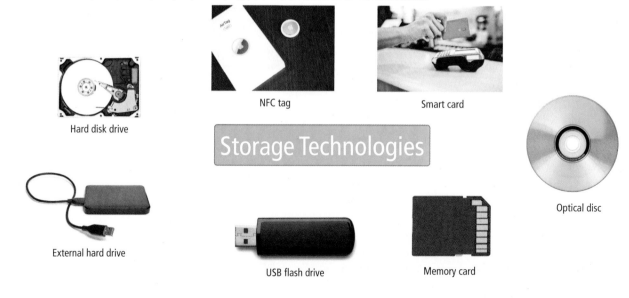

Hard disk drive

NFC tag

Smart card

Storage Technologies

Optical disc

External hard drive

USB flash drive

Memory card

Table 7-1 Terms Used to Define Storage

Storage Term	Approximate Number of Bytes	Exact Number of Bytes
Kilobyte (KB)	1 thousand	2^{10} or 1,024
Megabyte (MB)	1 million	2^{20} or 1,048,576
Gigabyte (GB)	1 billion	2^{30} or 1,073,741,824
Terabyte (TB)	1 trillion	2^{40} or 1,099,511,627,776
Petabyte (PB)	1 quadrillion	2^{50} or 1,125,899,906,842,624
Exabyte (EB)	1 quintillion	2^{60} or 1,152,921,504,606,846,976
Zettabyte (ZB)	1 sextillion	2^{70} or 1,180,591,620,717,411,303,424
Yottabyte (YB)	1 septillion	2^{80} or 1,208,925,819,614,629,174,706,176

schedules, contacts, email messages, and tax records. A home user also might store budgets, bank statements, a household inventory, stock purchase records, homework assignments, recipes, music, and videos. In addition or instead, a business user stores reports, financial records, travel records, customer orders and invoices, vendor payments, payroll records, inventory records, presentations, quotations, and contracts. Business and power users store diagrams, drawings, blueprints, designs, marketing literature, corporate newsletters, and product catalogs.

A **storage device** is the hardware that records and/or retrieves items to and from storage media. **Writing** is the process of transferring data, instructions, and information from memory to a storage medium. **Reading** is the process of transferring these items from a storage medium into memory. When storage devices write on storage media, they are creating output. Similarly, when storage devices read from storage media, they function as a source of input. Nevertheless, they are categorized as storage devices, not as input or output devices.

Storage Capacity

Capacity is the number of bytes (characters) a storage medium can hold. A gigabyte (GB) equals approximately 1 billion bytes. A terabyte (TB) is equal to approximately 1 trillion bytes. Table 7-1 identifies the terms manufacturers may use to define the capacity of storage media. For example, a storage medium with a capacity of 750 GB can hold approximately 750 billion bytes.

Storage requirements among users vary greatly. Home users, small/home office users, and mobile users typically have much smaller storage requirements than enterprise users. Using a mix of cloud-based and local (i.e., stored on your device) storage options can extend the useful life of your device by enabling your storage needs to grow over time without exceeding the device's capacity.

Storage Access Times

The speed of storage devices and memory is defined by access time. **Access time** measures (1) the amount of time it takes a storage device to locate an item on a storage medium or (2) the time required to deliver an item from memory to the processor. The access time of storage devices is slow compared with the access time of memory. Memory (chips) accesses items in billionths of a second (nanoseconds). Storage devices, by contrast, access items in thousandths of a second (milliseconds) or millionths of a second (microseconds).

Instead of, or in addition to, access time, some manufacturers state a storage device's transfer rate because it affects access time. **Transfer rate** is the speed with which data, instructions, and information transfer to and from a device. Transfer rates for storage are stated in KBps (kilobytes per second), MBps (megabytes per second), and GBps (gigabytes per second). Figure 7-3 shows how different types of storage media and memory compare in terms of transfer rates and uses.

Figure 7-3   Relative speed and uses for storage media.

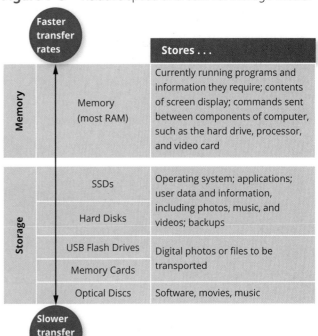

Consider This ───────────────────────────────────

How can you encrypt data and files on storage devices?

Encryption encodes data so that only authorized people can access it. Some operating systems provide a feature allowing users to encrypt individual files, folders, or the entire contents of a hard drive or external storage device. In addition, third-party programs are designed to encrypt data. While each program may use a different method of encrypting files, they all use the process of cryptography. Mathematical functions, called algorithms, scramble the data. A password generally is needed to decrypt, or reassemble, this data. Encrypted files offer security, but users might notice that the operating system may require more time to open and access encrypted files. While no encryption program is infallible, security experts recommend using this process to protect individual files, folders, or entire storage media with personal or sensitive information. What types of files would you encrypt on media in or attached to your computer or mobile device? Would you consider not using encryption in the chance that you might lose the password?

───

Storage Hardware

When using a computer, you inevitably will need to store files that you either download or create. Storage hardware is a physical device that you use to store data and information. It can be part of your device or something that you insert or connect to in order to save or access storage. Storage hardware, some of which has been previously covered, includes hard drives (both hard disks and SSDs) and optical media.

Hard Drives

When using a computer, the most common storage medium is the internal hard drive. Hard drives can store data either magnetically or using solid-state storage. Internal hard drives are installed in the computer you are using. For example, if you are creating a file on your work computer and store it on an internal hard drive, you will not be able to access the file from a different computer unless you copy the file to the other computer either by using an external hard drive or USB flash drive, or by sending it electronically. Magnetic hard disk drives (HDDs) typically have greater storage capacity and are less expensive than their solid-state equivalents, but they have several moving parts, making them more prone to damage, especially if you try to move the computer while it is running.

The term, hard drive, refers collectively to hard disks and SSDs. Hard drives can be internal or external. That is, they can reside inside a computer or mobile device, or they can be an external device that connects to a computer or some mobile devices. An internal hard disk is one that is a part of the computer or device. Internal and external hard drives work similarly.

Internal Hard Disk   A **hard disk**, also called a **hard disk drive (HDD)**, is a storage device that contains one or more inflexible, circular platters that use magnetic particles to store data, instructions, and information. Depending on how the magnetic particles are aligned, they represent either a 0 bit or a 1 bit. Recall that a bit (binary digit) is the smallest unit of data a computer can process. Thus, the alignment of the magnetic particles represents the data.

Desktops and laptops often contain at least one hard disk. The entire hard disk is enclosed in an airtight, sealed case to protect it from contamination (Figure 7-4).

The storage capacity of hard disks is determined by the number of platters the hard disk contains, the composition of the magnetic coating on the platters, whether it uses longitudinal or perpendicular recording, and its density.

Figure 7-4   Typical hard disk.

Kitch Bain/Shutterstock.com; Ludodesign/Fotolia LLC; Gertan/Shutterstock.com

Hard disk mounted
inside a laptop

Close-up of laptop
hard disk

Hard disk mounted
inside a desktop

Close-up of desktop
hard disk

- A **platter** is made of aluminum, glass, or ceramic and has a thin coating of alloy material that allows items to be recorded magnetically on its surface.
- **Longitudinal recording** aligns the magnetic particles horizontally around the surface of the disk. With **perpendicular recording**, by contrast, hard disks align the magnetic particles vertically, or perpendicular to the disk's surface, making much greater storage capacities possible.
- **Density** is the number of bits in an area on a storage medium. A higher density means more storage capacity.

Hard disks are read/write storage media. That is, you can read from and write on a hard disk any number of times. Before any data can be read from or written on a hard disk, however, the disk must be formatted. **Formatting** is the process of dividing the disk into tracks and sectors (Figure 7-5) so that the operating system can store and locate data and information on the disk. A track is one of the series of concentric circles on one of the surfaces of a magnetic hard disk platter. Tracks are narrow recording bands that form a full circle on the surface of the disk. The disk's storage locations consist of wedge-shaped sections, which break the tracks into small arcs called sectors. A **sector** is an individual block of data, or a segment of a track. Several sectors form a cluster. Sometimes, a sector has a flaw and cannot store data. When you format a disk, the operating system marks these bad sectors as unusable. As data is sometimes saved to nonconsecutive segments, a process called defragmentation can be used to reorganize data on the hard drive so that it is in continuous order, which helps to speed up the retrieval process.

On desktops, the platters most often have a form factor (size) of approximately 3.5 inches in diameter. On laptops, mobile devices, and some servers, the form factor is 2.5 inches or less. A typical hard disk has multiple platters stacked on top of one another. Each platter has two read/write heads, one for each side. A **read/write head** is the

Figure 7-5   Tracks and sectors on a hard disk.

Gilmanshin/Shutterstock.com

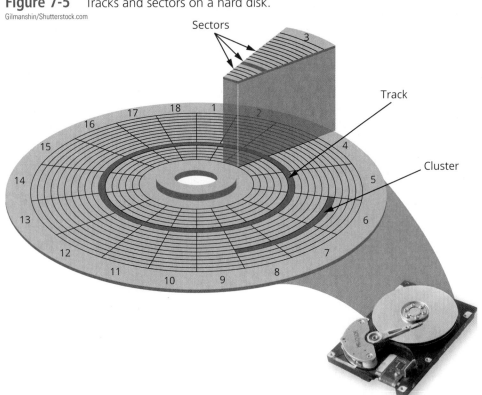

mechanism that reads items and writes items in the drive as it barely touches the disk's recording surface. A head actuator on the hard disk attaches to arms that move the read/write heads to the proper location on the platter (Figure 7-6).

Figure 7-6   How a hard disk works.

Alias Studiot Oy/Shutterstock.com

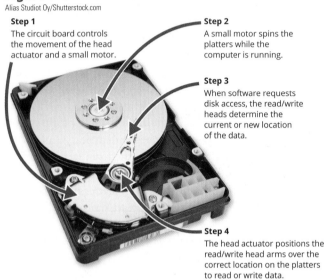

Step 1
The circuit board controls the movement of the head actuator and a small motor.

Step 2
A small motor spins the platters while the computer is running.

Step 3
When software requests disk access, the read/write heads determine the current or new location of the data.

Step 4
The head actuator positions the read/write head arms over the correct location on the platters to read or write data.

While the computer is running, the platters in the hard disk rotate at a high rate of speed. This spinning, which usually is 5,400 to 15,000 revolutions per minute (rpm), allows nearly instant access to all tracks and sectors on the platters. The platters may continue to spin until power is removed from the computer, or more commonly today, the platters stop spinning or slow down after a specified time to save power. The spinning motion creates a cushion of air between the platter and its read/write head. This cushion ensures that the read/write head floats above the platter instead of making direct contact with the platter surface. The distance between the read/write head and the platter is about two-millionths of one inch.

External Hard Drives   An **external hard drive** is a separate, freestanding storage device that connects with a cable to a USB port or other port on a computer or mobile device (Figure 7-7). Both hard disks and SSDs are available as external hard drives.

Sizes and storage capacities of external hard drives vary, with some having greater capacities than internal hard drives. Smaller external hard drives are portable and enable mobile users to transport photos and other files from one computer to another easily. As with an internal hard drive, an entire external hard drive is enclosed in an airtight, sealed case. External hard drive units can include

Figure 7-7   An external hard disk attached to a laptop.

iStock.com/greg801

multiple hard drives that you can use for different purposes, if desired.

SSDs   Recall that an SSD (solid-state drive) is a flash memory storage device that contains its own processor to manage its storage (Figure 7-8). SSDs often are used on mobile devices, such as laptops and tablets, and come in various physical sizes. Flash memory is a type of nonvolatile memory that can be erased electronically and rewritten. Flash memory chips are a type of solid-state media, which means they consist entirely of electronic components, such as integrated circuits, and contain no moving parts (Figure 7-8). The lack of moving parts makes flash memory storage more durable and shock resistant than other types of media, such as magnetic hard disks or optical discs.

Figure 7-8   An SSD.

iStock.com/scanrail; Jules/Fotolia LLC; Jipen/Shutterstock.com

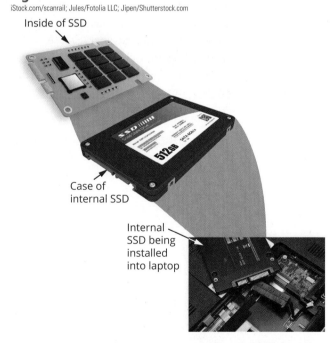

Inside of SSD

Case of internal SSD

Internal SSD being installed into laptop

SSDs may be in the form of flash memory chips installed directly on a motherboard or an adapter card. They also may be housed in a separate casing that attaches to the motherboard and are available in a variety of form factors. SSDs are used in all types of computers, including servers, desktops, laptops, tablets, and a variety of mobile devices, such as portable media players and DV cameras. Some computers have both a hard disk and an SSD.

SSDs have several advantages over traditional (magnetic) hard disks, including the following:

- Faster access times (can be more than 100 times faster)
- Faster transfer rates
- Quieter operation
- Greater durability
- Lighter weight
- Less power consumption (leads to longer battery life)
- Less heat generation
- Longer life (more than 10 times longer)
- Defragmentation is not required

The disadvantages of SSDs are that they typically have lower storage capacities than hard disks, data recovery in the event of failure can be more difficult than for traditional hard disks, and their cost is higher per gigabyte. In order to keep the price of a laptop affordable, laptops with SSDs usually have a lower storage capacity than laptops with a traditional hard disk.

Portable Flash Memory Storage In addition to SSDs, two other widely used types of flash memory storage include memory cards and USB flash drives. Users opt for memory cards and USB flash drives because they are portable. A memory card is a removable flash memory storage device, usually no bigger than 1.5 inches in height or width, that you insert in and remove from a slot in a computer, digital camera, mobile device, or card reader/writer (Figure 7-9). Memory cards enable mobile users easily to transport digital photos, music, videos, or other files to and from mobile devices and computers or other devices. A slot on a computer or device often accepts multiple types of cards.

Figure 7-9 Memory cards often are used with cameras.
iStock.com/nicolas

A **USB flash drive** (universal serial bus) is a removable storage device for folders and files that you plug in a USB port on your computer, making it easy to transport folders and files to other computers (Figure 7-10). Other names for a flash drive are thumb drive, pen drive, jump drive, and keychain drive. USB flash drives are convenient for mobile users because they are small and lightweight enough to be transported on a keychain or in a pocket. With a USB flash drive, users easily transfer documents, photos, music, and videos from one computer to another. Storage capacities of USB flash drives and memory cards vary.

Figure 7-10 USB flash drive.
iStock.com/Vladimir Sukhachev

Optical Media

Optical media include CDs, DVDs, and Blu-ray discs (BDs), but their use as storage media is declining. An optical disc is a type of storage medium that consists of a flat, round, portable disc made of metal, plastic, and lacquer that is written and read by a laser. Optical media were once widely used to distribute installation files for programs and apps, but saving files to optical media required special software or capabilities within the operating system. While optical media is easy to transport, if the discs get damaged, you might not be able to access your stored files. Instead of optical discs, many individuals now use USB flash drives, external hard drives, and cloud storage to transport files.

Many desktops and laptops no longer have an optical disc drive as more users turn to streaming media to play music or videos, and games and apps are available as downloads from the Internet, rather than purchased in disc format and played or installed from the disc.

Different formats of optical discs are available. Some are read only, meaning users cannot write (save) on the media. Others are read/write, which allows users to save on the disc just as they save on a hard drive. Table 7-2 differentiates among the optical disc formats: CD, DVD, and Blu-ray.

Table 7-2   Characteristics of Optical Disk Formats

Disc Type	Format(s)	Typically Use(s)
CD	• CD-ROM (read-only) • CD-R (recordable) • CD-RW(rewritable)	audio, photo
DVD	• DVD-ROM (read-only) • DVD-R, DVD+R (recordable) • DVD-RW, DVD+RW, and DVD+RAM (rewritable)	video
Blu-ray	• Higher-capacity disc than DVD	video

 **Consider This**

Are deleted files gone forever?

If you deleted a file from a hard drive and need to recover it, look in the Recycle Bin (Windows) or Trash (Mac). Several free recovery programs also are available to download, which might help you recover your files. As a last resort, expert commercial data recovery software is available at retail stores or through the storage manufacturer's website. Some cloud services do not allow for users to recover deleted files. Typically, you get a message that files you delete will be permanently gone before you delete a file. If you synchronize your files between your device's hard drive and the cloud, you may be able to recover a version of the file from your hard drive. Your cloud service may be able to recover the file for you, but typically only for a certain time period after the deletion. Have you ever mistakenly deleted a file? What can you do if this happens to you? How can you prevent this from happening?

Cloud Storage

Recall that cloud computing refers to an environment of servers that house and provide access to resources users access via the Internet. Home and business users choose cloud computing for a variety of reasons, including the following:

- **Accessibility:** Data and/or applications are available worldwide from any computer or device with an Internet connection.
- **Cost savings:** The expense of software and high-end hardware, such as fast processors and high-capacity memory and storage devices, shifts away from the user.

- **Space savings:** Floor space required for servers, storage devices, and other hardware is not required from the user.
- **Scalability:** Provides the flexibility to increase or decrease computing requirements as needed.

Cloud computing consists of a front end and a back end, connected to each other through a network. The front end includes the hardware and software with which a user interacts to access the cloud. For example, a user might access a resource on the cloud through a browser on a laptop. The back end consists of the servers and storage devices that manage and store the resources accessed by users.

The purpose of digital storage is the same as using physical storage: to save or back up your work. Cloud storage involves the digital storing of electronic files on the Internet, not on a local computer, a practice referred to as storing data "on the cloud." The advantages of using the cloud to store your files, data, and information digitally include being able to access them from multiple devices, to share or collaborate easily with others, to save storage space on your device, and to take advantage of security options that a cloud storage provider can offer.

One use of cloud storage is to store off-site backups of data. Online backups are popular among both business users and consumers because they can schedule backups to take place automatically and do not need to purchase storage media. Users generally pay for backup services based on the amount of bandwidth or storage they use.

Cloud Storage Advantages

Cloud storage enables you to store your files remotely on servers that could be in a different city, state, or part of the world. Storing files to and retrieving files from cloud storage typically requires only a computer or mobile device with an Internet connection (Figure 7-11). With cloud storage, you might not require as much storage on your computer because you can store your files remotely.

Users subscribe to cloud storage for a variety of reasons:

- To access files on the Internet from any computer or device that has Internet access
- To store large audio, video, and graphics files on the Internet instantaneously, instead of spending time downloading to a local hard drive or other media
- To allow others to access their files on the Internet so that others can listen to an audio file, watch a video clip, or view a photo — instead of sending the file to them via an email message
- To view time-critical data and images immediately while away from the main office or location; for example,

doctors can view X-ray images from another hospital, home, or office or while on vacation
- To provide data center functions, relieving enterprises of this task

Figure 7-11 Cloud storage.

iStock.com/Lvcandy

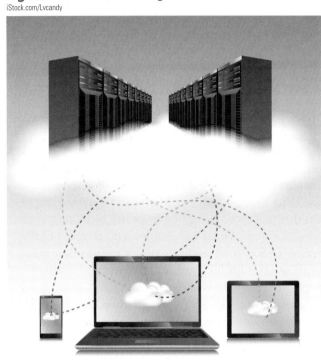

Services Offered by Cloud Storage Providers

Cloud computing allows companies to outsource, or contract to third-party providers, elements of their information technology infrastructure. They pay only for the computing power, storage, bandwidth, and access to applications that they actually use. As a result, companies need not make large investments in equipment or the staff to support it.

Cloud storage providers enable you to synchronize files, write documents, back up files on your computer or mobile device, share project work, stream music, post photos, and play games online. Many offer a limited amount of free storage and make additional storage available for a fee.

In addition to SaaS (software as a service), consumers and organizations rely on cloud computing services to manage IT infrastructure (infrastructure as a service); provide file management tools (storage as a service);

access online data (data as a service); and create, test, and deploy applications using web-based development tools (platform as a service).

- **Infrastructure as a service:** Infrastructure as a service (IaaS) uses software to emulate hardware capabilities, enabling companies to scale, or adjust up or down, storage, processing power, or bandwidth as needed. For example, retailers may need to increase these capabilities to accommodate additional traffic to their websites during busy holiday shopping seasons. When the season ends, retailers easily can reduce these settings.
- **Storage as a service:** Cloud storage providers offer Storage as a service (STaaS) file management services such as storing files online, system backup, and archiving earlier versions of files. Cloud storage is especially useful to tablet and smartphone users because it enables them to access their files from all of their devices. Note that to distinguish these services from SaaS, the first two letters of storage are used in the acronym.
- **Desktop as a Service:** Some companies specify the applications, security settings, and computing resources available to employees on their desktop computers. These images, or configurations, provide a common desktop work environment available to employees across an entire organization. Because the desktop and its applications appear to be installed on the user's own computer, desktop as a service also is known as a virtual desktop.
- **Data as a Service:** Government agencies, companies, and social media sites make data available for developers to incorporate in applications or to use when making business decisions and plans. Data as a service (DaaS) allows users and applications to access a company's data. Mashups are applications that incorporate data from multiple providers into a new application. Displaying homes or crime statistics on a map are examples of mashups that require data from real estate, police records, and mapping providers.
- **Platform as a Service:** Application developers need to maintain computers running specific hardware, operating systems, development tools, databases, and other software. Platform as a service (PaaS) allows developers to create, test, and run their solutions on a cloud platform without having to purchase or configure the underlying hardware and software.

Other Cloud Services

When looking for a cloud service provider, consider the additional services they might offer, and evaluate the provider based on which service(s) are most important to you. Some additional cloud services include:

- **Synchronize Files:** Many cloud storage providers place a folder on your computer with contents you can synchronize across multiple devices. Other providers allow you to upload files for storage online and then download them via a web app or mobile app. Cloud storage providers often retain previous versions of your files, in case you need to revert to an earlier one.
- **Write Documents:** Google Drive (Figure 7-12) and OneDrive provide integrated web apps to edit documents in a browser and store them on the cloud. Some third-party tools, such as Evernote, an online note taking application, synchronize your notes with popular cloud storage providers.
- **Back Up Files:** Storing files on the cloud is an easy way to back them up in case the hard drive on your computer fails or your mobile device is lost, stolen, or damaged. Some cloud backup services, such as Carbonite, automatically copy a computer or mobile device's new or changed files to the cloud, freeing users of performing backups themselves. Backup providers generally do not synchronize files across a user's multiple devices, but only provide capabilities to store and retrieve files on the cloud.
- **Stream Media:** You can play music and videos stored offline (i.e., on your computer or mobile devices) in places without Internet access. Many people also store their media files on the cloud so as not to use up the limited internal storage available on mobile devices. Some services, such as Google Play, support streaming music stored on the cloud to Android, iOS, and other devices.

 **Consider This**

What is a personal cloud?
Some hard drive manufacturers sell networked hard drives that make your data available on a cloud that exists within your home or office. That is, the networked hard drive connects directly to your router, creating a personal cloud that allows you to access its files over the Internet. With a personal cloud, you maintain the storage device on which the files are located versus a cloud storage provider where your files are stored on servers on the Internet that a cloud storage provider configures, maintains, and backs up.

Cloud Storage Options

To use cloud storage, you typically select a platform, such as Google Drive, Microsoft OneDrive, or Box. Some platforms offer a limited amount of storage for free. With Google Drive or Microsoft OneDrive, the files that you save are created by or can be edited or shared using the cloud-based apps that are a part of the service. Other cloud storage options, such as Box, primarily are storage locations and do not provide corresponding apps.

Companies or organizations that rely on cloud storage partner with cloud storage companies that host servers on which the company or organization's files reside. Employees or those to whom the company or organization grants access, can upload, download, or share files stored on the host servers from any location. The files are protected by security measures, including passwords and identification requirements, or encryption, and are backed up to other servers so that outages in which access is limited or denied are rare. One advantage of relying on cloud-based storage

Figure 7-12   Google Drive.
Source: Google

is the flexibility of not having to purchase and maintain servers. This enables companies and organizations to add storage as needed without needing to purchase hardware or employ additional staff to maintain the servers.

Evaluating Providers

With so many providers offering free and paid cloud storage services, it is important to compare features to take advantage of the capabilities that each offers. Criteria to consider include the amount of free storage offered, the cost to purchase more if needed, and the maximum file size that each service allows you to upload. Keep the files you use most on the service on which you have the most storage space; use services that support streaming to store and play media files. Photos, songs, and videos take longer to upload than smaller text or webpage files, so it is important to select a provider whose servers have sufficient bandwidth to support large file transfers.

It also is important to read a cloud storage provider's privacy policy and terms of agreement to which you must consent before using its services. Some cloud storage providers may not guarantee the protection of the files you upload, so you still should keep a backup of the files you stored on the cloud.

Select a Cloud Storage Provider

Many people are choosing to back up data to the cloud in addition to, or instead of, backing up to storage media, such as external hard drives and optical discs. Cloud storage providers enable you to synchronize data on your computers and mobile devices effortlessly to one or more servers in remote locations. Various cloud storage providers exist, and it is important to select one that adequately meets your needs. In addition to selecting a cloud storage provider, you also should decide what to upload to the cloud.

Consider the following guidelines when selecting a cloud storage provider:

- Verify the company is reputable and has been in business for an extended period of time.
- Choose a provider that encrypts your files.
- Make sure the company has not fallen victim to major security breaches.
- Determine whether the provider's service is compatible with your computer(s) and mobile device(s).
- Compare the price of various storage plans and choose a provider that offers competitive pricing.
- Verify the cloud storage provider will support the types of files you want to back up. For example, some cloud storage providers might allow you to back up

only photos, so they would not be useful for backing up your personal files, such as documents and spreadsheets.
- If desired, choose a cloud storage provider that allows you to share selected files with others.
- Consider whether the provider offers a mobile app that you can use to access your files using a mobile device.

❓ Consider This

What should you upload to the cloud?
Consider uploading files that you cannot afford to lose, such as financial documents or scanned copies of insurance paperwork, as well as files that might have sentimental value, such as photos and video. In the unlikely event of a disaster that ruins your computer, mobile device, and backups you possess, the cloud storage provider will retain these files. Do not back up programs and apps if you have access to the installation media or files. If your cloud storage provider offers only a limited amount of storage space, back up only the files you are sure you will need again in the future. Routinely review the files you have stored on the cloud storage provider and remove files you no longer need. What do you upload to the cloud? Have you ever had to make choices about what to upload because of limited space available? How can you solve this problem? What is the most important aspect of cloud computing to you?

Secure IT: Secure Your Data on the Cloud

The amount of information and data about you that exists on the cloud is more extensive than you might imagine. The files you store and share online and the media files you choose to stream or download are a part of your digital footprint.

One area that is growing is the use of cryptocurrency, payment apps, and digital wallets. These digital payment options not only are convenient but also are touchless, which reduces your risk of picking up germs from surfaces, such as money, credit cards, or payment kiosks. **Cryptocurrency** is digital currency that can be used to transfer money or payment between users or corporations. Cryptocurrency is not backed or secured by a government; this differs from a national currency (such as the U.S. dollar), making cryptocurrency vulnerable to volatility as its value rises and falls. **Payment apps**, such as Venmo, enable you to transfer money between your credit card or bank account to another user. A **digital wallet**, such as ApplePay, is an app that is connected to a specific payment card or financial account (Figure 7-13). These methods are convenient, but they can be risky and can increase the amount of financial data available to hackers.

Figure 7-13   Using a digital wallet.

iStock.com/Ridofranz

As you rely more and more on cloud-based storage of data, streaming media, digital payments, and web-based apps, the risk to your data increases dramatically.

Some steps to protect your cloud-based data include:

- Choose your cloud provider(s) carefully, whether you are using a web-based app that also offers storage, such as Google Drive, or using an online backup system, such as Carbonite. Read consumer and industry reviews that discuss security, not only from hackers, but from system downtime that might prevent you from accessing your data when you need it.
- Read the user agreement for your cloud provider. Do they provide encryption services? Do they imply that they have access to your files and can collect data about what you upload, download, or create? Some providers create data profiles that they then sell to marketers or other data collection services.
- Set the most advanced privacy settings that your service allows. Some privacy settings enable you to prevent your account from being searched for or located by others, even your contacts.
- Use strong passwords and two-factor authentication to protect against unauthorized access from hackers.
- Do not store sensitive data, such as financial statements, documents containing your Social Security number or other information, without ensuring that they will be encrypted or that the data is not accessible by the provider.

 Consider This

What are the benefits of using digital payment options?

Using a digital wallet or payment apps is undoubtedly convenient. Suppose you are out to dinner with friends and decide to split the check. To avoid your server having to process multiple credit card payments or to rely on carrying cash, one person can pay for the meal and the others send electronic payment for their portion. Unlike paying in cash, if something happens, such as the need to cancel the transaction or if you believe the payment has been compromised, the digital wallet provider may be able to assist you or the vendor you are trying to pay. Digital wallets also enable those who are unbanked or underbanked (have limited or no access to a bank) to process payments electronically. Some digital wallets or payment apps show transactions made not only by you, but by your friends (including to whom the payment was made, and in some cases a description of the purchase or transaction). Security experts recommend that you make your transactions private. Have you ever used a digital wallet or a payment app? What did you use as the payment source — a bank or credit card? Did anything ever go wrong with one of your transactions? How did/could you rectify the situation if that occurred?

Enterprise and Other Storage Options

Enterprise hardware allows large organizations to manage and store data and information using devices intended for heavy use, maximum efficiency, and maximum availability. The availability of hardware to users is a measure of how often it is online. Highly available hardware is accessible 24 hours a day, 365 days a year. To meet these needs, enterprise hardware often includes levels of **redundancy**, which means that if one component fails or malfunctions, another can assume its tasks. Enterprise storage centers are called data centers. A **data center** is a secure location with many large computers that act as servers, which make files available to users (Figure 7-14).

Figure 7-14   A data center.

iStock.com/EvgeniyShkolenko

Some organizations manage an enterprise storage system in-house. Others elect to outsource all (or at least the backup) storage management to an outside organization or a cloud storage provider. Enterprises use a combination of storage techniques to meet their large-scale needs, including cloud storage and some other methods, along with RAID, network attached storage, storage area networks, and tape.

RAID   For applications that depend on reliable data access, users must have the data available when they attempt to access it. Some manufacturers provide a type of hard drive system that connects several smaller drives into a single unit that acts like a single large hard drive. A group of two or more integrated hard drives is called a RAID (redundant array of independent disks). Although RAID can be more expensive than traditional hard drives, it is more reliable. Computers and enterprise storage devices often use RAID.

RAID may duplicate data, instructions, and information to improve data reliability. RAID implements duplication in different ways, depending on the storage design, or level, being used. The simplest RAID storage design is level 1, called **mirroring**, which writes data on two drives at the same time to duplicate the data. A level 1 configuration enhances storage reliability because, if a drive should fail, a duplicate of the requested item is available elsewhere within the array of drives. Other RAID levels use a technique called **striping**, which splits data, instructions, and information across multiple drives in the array. Striping improves drive access times but does not offer data duplication. For this reason, some RAID levels combine both mirroring and striping. Figure 7-15 illustrates mirroring and striping.

Figure 7-15   Mirroring (a) and striping (b).

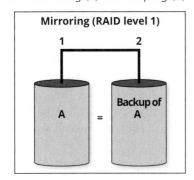

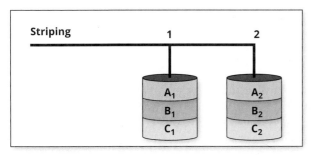

NAS and SAN   **Network attached storage (NAS)** is a server that is placed on a network with the sole purpose of providing storage to users, computers, and devices attached to the network. A network attached storage server, often called a storage appliance, has its own IP address, usually does not have a keyboard or display, and contains at least one hard drive, often configured in a RAID. Administrators can add storage to an existing network quickly by connecting a network attached storage server to a network.

A **storage area network (SAN)** is a high-speed network with the sole purpose of providing storage to other attached servers. In fact, a storage area network includes only storage devices. High-speed fiber-optic cable usually connects other networks and servers to the storage area network, so that the networks and servers have fast access to large storage capacities. A storage area network can connect to networks and other servers that are miles away using high-speed network connections.

Both network attached storage and storage area network solutions offer easy management of storage, fast access to storage, sharing of storage, and isolation of storage from other servers. Isolating the storage enables the other servers to concentrate on performing a specific task, rather than consuming resources involved in the tasks related to storage. Both storage solutions include disk, optical disc, and magnetic tape types of storage.

Other Types of Storage   In addition to the previously discussed types of storage, other options are available for specific uses and applications. These include tape, magnetic stripe cards, smart cards, RFID tags, and NFC chips and tags.

- One of the first storage media used with enterprise computers was tape. **Tape** is a magnetically coated ribbon of plastic that is capable of storing large amounts of data and information at a low cost. Tape no longer is used as a primary method of storage. Instead, businesses use tape most often for long-term storage and backup.
- A **magnetic stripe card** is a credit card, entertainment card, bank card, or other similar card with a stripe that contains information identifying you and the card. The information encoded on the stripe often includes your name, account number, and the card's expiration date.
- A **smart card**, which is an alternative to a magnetic stripe card, stores data on an integrated circuit embedded in the card. Two types of smart cards, also called chip cards, are contact and contactless. When you insert a contact smart card in a specialized card reader, the information on the smart card is read and, if necessary, updated. Contactless smart cards communicate with a reader using a radio frequency, which means the user simply places the card near the reader.

- Recall that RFID is a technology that uses radio signals to communicate with a tag placed in or attached to an object, an animal, or a person. The **RFID tag** consists of an antenna and a memory chip that contains the information to be transmitted via radio waves (Figure 7-16). An RFID reader reads the radio signals and transfers the information to a computer or computing device. RFID tags are either active or passive. An active RFID tag contains a battery that runs the chip's circuitry and broadcasts a signal to the RFID reader. A passive RFID tag does not contain a battery and, thus, cannot send a signal until the reader activates the tag's antenna by sending out electromagnetic waves. Because passive RFID tags contain no battery, these can be small enough to be embedded in skin.

Figure 7-16 RFID image on a box.
iStock.com/nullplus

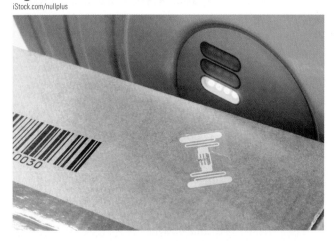

- Recall that NFC is a technology (based on RFID) that uses close-range radio signals to transmit data between two NFC-enabled devices or an NFC-enabled device and an NFC tag. NFC-enabled devices include smartphones, digital cameras, computers, televisions, and terminals. An NFC-enabled device, such as a smartphone, contains an NFC chip. Other objects, such as credit cards and tickets, can contain an NFC chip. An NFC tag, similar to RFID tag, contains a chip and an antenna that contains information to be transmitted. Most NFC tags are self-adhesive, so that they can be attached to any location (Figure 7-17). When a user places the NFC-enabled device close to another NFC-enabled device or an NFC tag, radio waves enable communications between the chips in the NFC-enabled devices or the chip in the NFC-enabled device and the NFC tag. Uses of NFC communications include using a mobile device to pay for goods or services, displaying a webpage, making a phone call, sending a text message, or exchanging contact information.

Figure 7-17 Adhesive NFC tag.
iStock.com/Pierrephoto

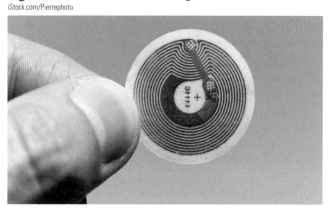

? Consider This

How much data should companies be required to keep?
After a string of corporate scandals, lawmakers enacted the Sarbanes-Oxley (SOX) Act in 2002. SOX provides a myriad of financial reporting requirements and guidelines for publicly traded companies. A main focus of SOX is the retention of business records. Because of SOX, companies have been confronted with massive new data storage requirements. For example, a company must retain all its email messages just as it would other business records. Deleting stored email messages can result in a destruction of evidence infraction. Supporters of SOX state that it is essential to avoid corporate scandals caused by lack of accuracy in financial reporting. They also say that consumer confidence has increased because the financial statements are more transparent. Opponents claim that the law is overreaching and costs too much for the added benefits. Is the Sarbanes-Oxley Act an unfair burden on companies? Why or why not? Are such laws necessary in order to protect the public? Why or why not?

How Memory Relates to Storage

When you turn on a computer or mobile device, it locates the operating system on its storage medium and loads the operating system into its memory (specifically, RAM). When you issue a command to run an application, such as a browser, the operating system locates the application on a storage medium and loads it into memory (RAM). When you are finished using the application, the operating system removes it from RAM, but the application remains on the storage medium.

Memory usually consists of one or more chips on the motherboard or some other circuit board in the computer. Memory stores three basic categories of items:

1. The operating system and other programs that control or maintain the computer and its devices; an **operating system** is a program that manages the complete operation of your computer or mobile device and lets you interact with it

2. Applications that carry out a specific task, such as word processing
3. The data being processed by the applications and the resulting information

This role of memory to store both data and programs is known as the stored program concept.

Bytes and Addressable Memory

A byte (character) is the basic storage unit in memory. When an application's instructions and data are transferred to memory from storage devices, the instructions and data exist as bytes. Each byte resides temporarily in a location in memory that has an address. Simply put, an address is a unique number that identifies the location of a byte in memory. To access data or instructions in memory, the computer references the addresses that contain bytes of data. Figure 7-18 shows how seats in a stadium are similar to addresses in memory: (1) a seat, which is identified by a unique seat number, holds one person at a time, and a location in memory, which is identified by a unique address, holds a single byte, and (2) both a seat, identified by a seat number, and a byte, identified by an address, can be empty.

Types of Memory

Memory is one of the main characteristics users look at when purchasing a computer or device. While it can be upgraded, memory capacity affects the device's operation speed. Users typically are referring to RAM when discussing computer and mobile device memory. RAM is the most common type of volatile memory. Examples of non-volatile memory include ROM, flash memory, and CMOS.

RAM   RAM, also called main memory, consists of memory chips that can be read from and written to by the processor and other devices. When you turn on power to a computer or mobile device, certain operating system files (such as the files that determine how the desktop or home screen appears) load into RAM from a storage device, such as a hard drive. These files remain in RAM as long as the computer or mobile device has continuous power. As additional applications and data are requested, they also load into RAM from storage.

The processor interprets and executes a program or application's instructions while the program or application is in RAM. During this time, the contents of RAM may

Figure 7-18   Similar to seats in a stadium, one location memory (seat) holds a single byte (person) or can be empty.
iStock.com/GeorgePeters

Seat J20 is empty

Seat J21 is occupied

change (Figure 7-19). RAM can accommodate multiple programs and applications simultaneously.

Because most RAM is volatile, you must save any data, instructions, and information you may need in the future. Saving is the process of copying data, instructions, and information from RAM to a storage device or to the cloud. Many applications, including those with cloud-based storage enable automatic saving, meaning that all your changes to your files are saved as you make them, without the need to issue a save instruction.

Most of today's computers improve their processing times with **cache** (pronounced cash), which is a temporary storage area. **Memory cache** helps speed the processes of the computer because it stores frequently used instructions and data.

ROM ROM (read-only memory) refers to memory chips storing permanent data and instructions. The data on most ROM chips cannot be modified — hence, the name read-only. In addition to computers and mobile devices, many peripheral devices contain ROM chips. For example, ROM chips in printers contain data for fonts. Manufacturers of ROM chips often record data, instructions, or information on firmware chips when the chips are manufactured. These chips contain permanently written data, instructions, or information, such as a computer or mobile device's start-up instructions.

Figure 7-19 How program instructions transfer in and out of RAM.
Gilmanshin/Shutterstock.com; TungCheung/Shutterstock.com; Vladyslav Starozhylov/Shutterstock.com; Source: Microsoft Corporation

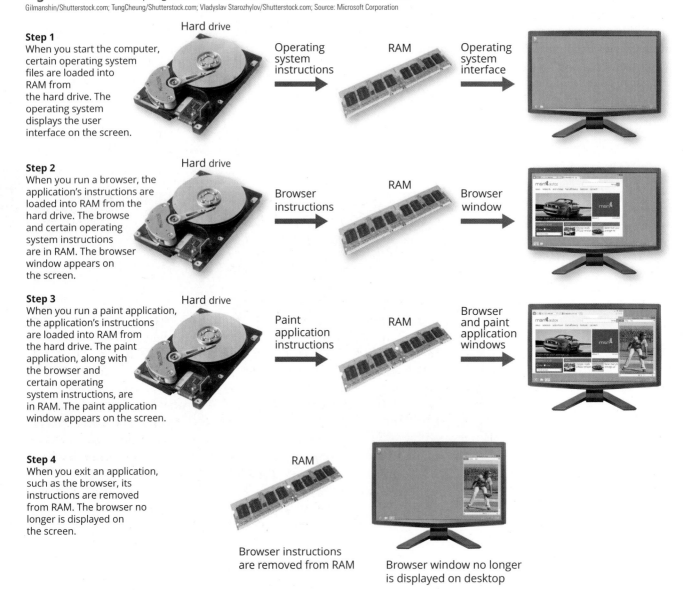

Step 1
When you start the computer, certain operating system files are loaded into RAM from the hard drive. The operating system displays the user interface on the screen.

Hard drive → Operating system instructions → RAM → Operating system interface

Step 2
When you run a browser, the application's instructions are loaded into RAM from the hard drive. The browse and certain operating system instructions are in RAM. The browser window appears on the screen.

Hard drive → Browser instructions → RAM → Browser window

Step 3
When you run a paint application, the application's instructions are loaded into RAM from the hard drive. The paint application, along with the browser and certain operating system instructions, are in RAM. The paint application window appears on the screen.

Hard drive → Paint application instructions → RAM → Browser and paint application windows

Step 4
When you exit an application, such as the browser, its instructions are removed from RAM. The browser no longer is displayed on the screen.

RAM

Browser instructions are removed from RAM

Browser window no longer is displayed on desktop

Flash Memory Flash memory is a type of nonvolatile memory that can be erased electronically and rewritten. Most computers use flash memory to hold their start-up instructions because it allows the computer to update its contents easily. For example, when the computer changes from standard time to daylight savings time, the contents of a flash memory chip (and the real-time clock chip) change to reflect the new time. Flash memory chips also store data and programs on many mobile devices and peripheral devices, such as smartphones, portable media players, printers, digital cameras, automotive devices, and digital voice recorders. When you enter names and addresses in a smartphone, for example, a flash memory chip stores the data. Some portable media players store music on flash memory chips; others store music on tiny hard drives or memory cards. Memory cards contain flash memory on a removable device instead of a chip.

CMOS Some RAM chips, flash memory chips, and other memory chips use **CMOS** (complementary metal-oxide semiconductor) technology because it provides high speeds and consumes little power. CMOS technology uses battery power to retain information even when the power to the computer is off. Battery-backed CMOS memory chips, for example, can keep the calendar, date, and time current even when the computer is off. The flash memory chips that store a computer's start-up information often use CMOS technology.

? Consider This —————————

Should you wipe your device before recycling?

When smartphone or other device users recycle or sell their devices without wiping all their personal records from memory, the person buying or acquiring the device then can access the sensitive data left in memory. A kill switch allows smartphone owners to delete all data or to disable their devices remotely in the event of theft or loss. Each device has its own set of steps described in the owner's manual or online. Mobile phone retailers often can offer help in clearing personal data; if you resort to this measure, be certain to watch the sales associate perform this action. If your mobile phone has a SIM or memory card, remove and destroy it if you are not going to transfer it to another phone. Have you ever wiped the memory of a device? What action would you take if you received or bought a used device and then discovered the previous owner's personal information stored in memory? Should lawmakers require smartphone manufacturers to include a kill switch in their products? Why or why not?

Ethics & Issues: Internet of Things and Privacy

Being digitally observed in the connected world is inescapable. Every day, smart electric meters, wearable technology, and vehicles' black boxes submit data about us as part of the IoT. As watches, thermostats, fitness trackers, appliances, irrigation systems, clothing, and other "things" become equipped with sensors that can transmit data to and from the Internet, keeping every "thing" connected could become one of the world's largest industries. Researchers predict billions of devices will be part of the IoT in the next few years. With all these devices in nearly every facet of our daily lives, data is being accumulated and sold to health care providers, home security businesses, utility companies, and researchers.

Computers and mobile devices are not the only items that connect to the Internet. You can buy a thermostat that allows you to adjust the temperature of your home from anywhere using an app on your smartphone. The thermostat contains a temperature sensor that can send and receive data. A wireless chip attached to your medicine bottle can send text messages to remind you to take your medication and then contact your pharmacy to refill the prescription when it is due. Smart trash cans in public places have sensors that monitor the amount of trash deposited and then send a message that notifies owners when the containers need to be emptied. This saves garbage collectors from checking the containers every day; instead, they can empty the containers only when receiving a message that they are full.

Wearable technology, such as smartwatches and wristbands, can track your pulse and heart rate, as well as accept calls and display notifications from a smartphone. Many public buses and subways have GPS sensors that report their locations so that travelers can track them with mobile apps. Retailers can use **beacons**, which are devices that send low-energy Bluetooth signals to nearby smartphones, to alert customers who use a payment app, such as PayPal, to personalized offers in their stores. Washers and dryers in many college dormitory laundry rooms are connected to sensors that report the availability of an individual machine. Students can visit a website, use a mobile app, or request text message alerts to locate available machines before carrying their laundry to the laundry room.

Savvy consumers can take some steps to attempt to limit exposure to data collection. For example, they can enable privacy settings, but that does not guarantee that data is not being gathered, transmitted, and compiled. A recent report of Smart TVs secretly collecting data about audiences' viewing habits sparked privacy and security concerns. Consumers need to urge companies to design products with built-in privacy protections. These devices could have default settings that prevent the sharing of data until obtaining the consumer's consent. Companies should explain what data is being collected and whether it will be used to help people live more productive lives or to create personal profiles that predict behavior. In addition, companies bear the responsibility of ensuring sensitive data being collected is kept secure and confidential.

Privacy and security concerns abound with the IoT, but many consumers and technology experts believe that the security, health, and productivity benefits of this technology outweigh the potential risks.

 Consider This

Should you use IoT to keep track of your belongings?

NFC devices, such as Apple's AirTag, are IoT devices that enable you to attach or insert a small tracker to your phone, purse, laptop, or other item. The tracker enables you to find the location of the item using an app. This can be beneficial if you misplace your keys or if your bag gets stolen. However, as these types of devices are small, they may be attached or placed without your knowledge, which enables people to track your location or activities. The same apps that detect your device's location also can alert you if an unrecognizable tag is nearby, such as in your car. You then can disable the device from tracking you, or, if the tag belongs to someone known to you, you can ignore the alert. Have you ever used a tag to keep track of your belongings? Were you ever notified that an unfamiliar tag was in your presence? What did/could you do to ensure your safety?

Study Guide

The Study Guide reinforces material you should know after reading this module.

Instructions: Answer the questions below using the format that helps you remember best or that is required by your instructor. Possible formats may include one or more of these options: write the answers; create a document that contains the answers; record answers as audio or video using a webcam, smartphone, or portable media player; post answers on a blog, wiki, or website; or highlight answers in the book/e-book.

1. Differentiate between storage and memory and describe how they interact.
2. Define the term, storage.
3. Define the term, secondary storage. List types of storage media.
4. Differentiate between writing and reading data to storage media.
5. ___ refers to the number of bytes a storage medium can hold. Identify terms manufacturers use to determine this.
6. Explain what access time measures.
7. Explain how transfer rates are stated.
8. In encryption, mathematical functions, called ___, scramble the data.
9. List characteristics and functions of a hard disk.
10. Define the terms, platter and destiny.
11. Differentiate between longitudinal and perpendicular recording.
12. Define the terms, track and sector. ___ is the process of dividing the disk into tracks and sectors.
13. Define the term, read/write head.
14. Explain why you might use an external drive.
15. Define the term, solid state media. List devices that use SSDs.
16. List advantages and disadvantages of SSDs versus magnetic hard disks.
17. List two types of flash memory storage.
18. Describe memory cards and their uses.
19. Explain who might use a USB flash drive, and for what purpose.
20. Define the term, optical disc. List types of optical discs.
21. Explain if and how you can restore deleted files.
22. Explain why home and business users choose cloud computing.
23. List advantages of cloud storage.
24. List and define ways to access services provided by cloud computing companies.
25. Define the term, mashup.
26. Explain how cloud users can do the following: synchronize files, write documents, backup files, and stream media.
27. Explain the uses of a personal cloud.
28. List cloud storage providers.
29. Explain guidelines for selecting a cloud service provider.
30. How do you select what data to store on the cloud?
31. Define these terms: cryptocurrency, payment app, and digital wallet. Explain benefits of using digital payment.
32. List steps to protect your cloud-based data.
33. ___ means that if one component fails or malfunctions, another can assume its tasks.
34. Define the term, data center.
35. Explain the role of RAID in data storage and retrieval. Differentiate between mirroring and striping.
36. Differentiate between a network attached storage (NAS) and a storage area network (SAN).
37. Describe the following storage methods: tape, magnetic stripe card, smart card, RFID, and NFC.
38. Explain the ethical issues surrounding the Sarbanes-Oxley Act.
39. List three basic categories of items stored in memory.
40. Define the term, operating system.
41. A(n) ___ is a unique number that identifies the location of a byte in memory.
42. Give another name for RAM.
43. Define the term, cache. Explain how memory cache helps computer speed.
44. Differentiate between the following nonvolatile memory types: ROM, flash memory, and CMOS.
45. Explain why and how you should wipe your device before recycling or selling it.
46. Explain safety concerns surrounding IoT. Should you use IoT to keep track of your belongings?

Key Terms

You should be able to define the Key Terms listed below.

access time (7-3)
address (7-15)
beacon (7-17)
cache (7-16)
capacity (7-3)
CMOS (7-17)
cryptocurrency (7-11)
data as a service (DaaS) (7-9)
data center (7-12)
density (7-5)
digital wallet (7-11)
external hard drive (7-6)
flash memory (7-17)
formatting (7-5)
hard disk (7-4)

hard disk drive (HDD) (7-4)
infrastructure as a service (IaaS) (7-9)
longitudinal recording (7-5)
magnetic stripe card (7-13)
main memory (7-15)
mashup (7-9)
memory cache (7-16)
memory card (7-7)
mirroring (7-13)
network attached storage (NAS) (7-13)
operating system (7-14)

optical disc (7-7)
optical media (7-7)
payment app (7-11)
perpendicular recording (7-5)
platform as a service (PaaS) (7-9)
platter (7-5)
read/write head (7-5)
reading (7-3)
redundancy (7-12)
RFID tag (7-14)
secondary storage (7-2)
sector (7-5)
smart card (7-13)
solid-state media (7-6)

storage (7-2)
storage area network (SAN) (7-13)
storage as a service (STaaS) (7-9)
storage device (7-3)
striping (7-13)
tape (7-13)
track (7-5)
transfer rate (7-3)
USB flash drive (7-7)
virtual desktop (7-9)
writing (7-3)

Extend Your Knowledge

Instructions: The Extend Your Knowledge exercise expands on subjects covered in the module and encourages you to find the latest developments on these topics. Use a search engine or another search tool to locate news articles, blog entries, videos, expert discussions, or other current sources on the listed topics. List your sources, and write 3-4 sentences describing what you have learned to submit in the format required by your instructor.

- Cryptocurrency volatility
- Cloud storage privacy statements
- SaaS
- Data centers

What did you learn that helped you better understand the concepts in this module? Did anything surprise you? How will what you learned impact you?

Checkpoint

The Checkpoint exercises test your knowledge of the module concepts.

True/False   Mark T for True and F for False. If False, rewrite the statement so that it is True.

_____ 1. Items on a storage medium remain intact even when you turn off a computer or mobile device.

_____ 2. Reading is the process of transferring items from a storage medium into memory.

_____ 3. Density is the number of bits in an area on a storage medium.

_____ 4. A sector is one of the series of concentric circles on one of the surfaces of a magnetic hard disk platter.

_____ 5. SaaS is a cloud-based file management services used for storing files online, system backup, and archiving earlier versions of files.

_____ 6. Cryptocurrency is digital currency that can be used to transfer money or payment between users or corporations.

_____ 7. A group of two or more integrated hard drives is called a SAN.

_____ 8. When an application's instructions and data are transferred to memory from storage devices, the instructions and data exist as bytes.

_____ 9. The flash memory chips that store a computer's start-up information often use CMOS technology.

_____ 10. Retailers can use flares, which are devices that send low-energy Bluetooth signals to nearby smartphones, to alert customers who use a payment app such as PayPal, to personalized offers in their stores.

Matching   Match the terms with their definitions.

_____ 1. transfer rate

_____ 2. IaaS

_____ 3. longitudinal recording

_____ 4. optical disc

_____ 5. PaaS

_____ 6. access time

_____ 7. striping

_____ 8. solid-state media

_____ 9. thumb drive

_____ 10. cache

a. measures the amount of time it takes a storage device to locate an item on a storage medium

b. aligns the magnetic particles horizontally around the surface of the disk

c. uses software to emulate hardware capabilities, enabling companies to scale, or adjust up or down, storage, processing power, or bandwidth as needed

d. splits data, instructions, and information across multiple drives in the array

e. a flash memory storage device that plugs in a USB port on a computer or mobile device

f. allows developers to create, test, and run their solutions on a cloud platform

g. consist entirely of electronic components, such as integrated circuits, and contain no moving parts

h. the speed with which data, instructions, and information transfer to and from a device

i. a temporary storage area

j. storage medium that consists of a flat, round, portable disc made of metal, plastic, and lacquer that is written and read by a laser

Problem Solving

Instructions: The Problem Solving exercises extend your knowledge of module concepts by seeking solutions to practical problems with technology that you may encounter at home, school, or work. The Collaboration exercise should be completed with a team. You often can solve problems with technology in multiple ways. Determine a solution to the problems in these exercises by using one or more resources available to you (such as a computer or mobile device, articles on the web or in print, blogs, podcasts, videos, television, user guides, other individuals, electronics or computer stores, etc.). Describe your solution, along with the resource(s) used, in the format requested by your instructor (brief report, presentation, discussion, blog post, video, or other means).

Personal

1. **Unrecognized Storage Device**   You have connected an external storage device to your new MacBook Pro, but the operating system is not recognizing the device's contents. Instead, it asks whether you want to format the device. Why might this be happening?

2. **Digital Wallet Not Working**   While grocery shopping, you are unable to pay using your digital wallet. When you try, the app says you have insufficient funds, but you know that you have more than enough in your account to cover the expense. What might be wrong, and how can you resolve it?

3. **Upgrading Laptop Memory**   Your laptop has been running sluggishly. After reading about some possible reasons for this, you decide that you need to upgrade your laptop's memory. How can you determine what you need to purchase and how to install it?

4. **Missing Files**   You stored some files on a USB flash drive, but when you attempted to access them you noticed that they no longer were there. What might have happened, and what next steps will you take to attempt to recover these files?

5. **Internet Access Unavailable**   You are using a cloud storage provider to save files you want to use both at work and at home. When you arrive at work, you notice that your Internet connection is unavailable, and you are unable to access the files stored on the cloud. What steps can you take to prevent this in the future?

Professional

6. **Inaccessible Files**   Your company requires you to store your files on a remote server so that you can access the files from any location within the company. When you sign in to another computer using your account, you cannot see your files. What might be causing this?

7. **Encrypted Storage Device**   You have purchased an external storage device so that you can back up files on your office computer. The IT department in your company informs you that you must make sure the data on the device is encrypted. What are your next steps?

8. **Exploring STaaS Options**   Your company needs more storage than its servers can manage. Rather than purchase more expensive servers that need to be maintained, your manager wants to shift to a partial STaaS option for additional storage and to house your backups. What steps will you take to research, locate, and evaluate current storage technologies?

9. **Faulty RFID Card**   You use an RFID card to obtain access to your office. When you attempt to scan your card, the RFID reader appears not to recognize that your card is nearby. What are your next steps?

10. **Files Not Synchronizing**   You have saved files on the cloud from your home computer, but the files are not appearing on the computer in your office. What might have happened, and what steps can you take to retrieve the files?

Collaboration

11. **Technology in the Automotive Industry**   Technology is used in the automotive industry to provide many in-vehicle options to assist drivers with backing up and other safety concerns. Your instructor would like everyone to realize the impact of the developments in this type of technology in this industry. Form a team of three people. One team member should investigate how technology is used to improve a driver's experience. Another team member should investigate how this technology impacts the manufacturing process, and the last team member should research how this technology is used to market and sell cars. Write a brief report summarizing your findings.

How To: Your Turn

Instructions: This exercise presents general guidelines for fundamental skills when using a computer or mobile device and then requires that you determine how to apply these general guidelines to a specific program or situation. You often can complete tasks using technology in multiple ways. Figure out how to perform the tasks described in these exercises by using one or more resources available to you (such as a computer or mobile device, articles on the web or in print, online or program help, user guides, blogs, podcasts, videos, other individuals, trial and error, etc.). Summarize your 'how to' steps, along with the resource(s) used, in the format requested by your instructor (brief report, presentation, discussion, blog post, video, or other means).

1 **Determine Your Device's Storage Capacity**

It may be necessary to determine your device's storage capacity before you decide to install a new operating system, program, or app; if you want to transfer a large number of files to your computer or mobile device; or determine how much data you should store on the cloud. For example, a new program you want to install may state that it requires a certain amount of storage capacity, so you should verify the storage capacity available on your device before deciding to purchase and install the program. To determine a device's total storage capacity, you can review the specifications for your computer or mobile device, either using the documentation that came with your device or on the manufacturer's website. The following steps guide you through the process of determining your device's storage capacity using other methods.

Computers

a. Locate the specifications that list your computer's storage capacity to determine the maximum storage available on your computer.

b. Open the window that shows the available storage devices on the computer.

c. Display the properties of the drive for which you want to determine the total storage capacity.

d. Navigate to the location showing the total storage capacity and available storage space.

e. Note how much space is available, and what categories of data (apps, system files, photos, documents, etc.) take up the most space.

Mobile Devices

a. Locate the specifications that list your device's storage capacity to determine the maximum storage available on your device.

b. Display the device settings.

c. Navigate to the storage settings.

d. If necessary, navigate to the screen showing the total storage capacity and available storage space.

e. Note how much space is available, and what categories of data (apps, system files, photos, documents, etc.) take up the most space.

Exercises

1. Does the total storage capacity displayed on your computer or mobile device match the exact amount advertised when you purchased your computer or mobile device? If not, what might cause the discrepancy?

2. How much storage space is available on your computer or mobile device? How much space is recommended to have available for maximum efficiency? How much space do you need to clear, if any?

3. What categories of data can/should you focus on moving to the cloud? Does your operating system offer any cloud-based storage options? How can you best take advantage of them, even if your device has plenty of storage?

Internet Research

Instructions: These exercises broaden your understanding of module concepts by requiring that you search for information on the web. Use a search engine or another search tool to locate the information requested or answers to questions presented in the exercises. Describe your findings, along with the search term(s) you used and your web source(s), in the format requested by your instructor (brief report, presentation, discussion, blog post, video, or other means). Additionally, reflect on the process you used to complete this activity. How did you go about choosing the tool that you did and why? Would you do anything differently in your research next time?

❶ Social Media: Locating Personal Information

Digital footprints tracking your Internet activity are relatively easy to find. Maintaining online anonymity is difficult to achieve once you have established online social network accounts with your actual name. While deleting an online social network account is a fairly easy process, deleting all remnants of information relating to the account can be a more difficult task. Just because you no longer can sign in to the account does not mean your posts, photos, and personal information do not exist somewhere on a website.

If you desire to remove an Internet presence for security or personal reasons, begin by searching for your name or account usernames. Remove your profiles from any online social network account that is displayed in the search results. Each of the online social network websites has a process to close an account, generally through the account's settings page. Next, contact the websites listed in the search results and ask that your name be removed. Many companies have a form to complete and submit. A third place to hunt for your information is on websites listing public records and people searches. Again, attempt to contact these companies and request that your personal information be removed. As a last resort, some services will perform these tasks for a fee.

Research This: Use a search engine to locate instances of your name or usernames. Did the search results list these names? If so, which online social networks or companies have records of your name? Then, search for your name on at least two websites that have public records or people databases. Did you see your name on these websites? If so, do you want the details, such as a phone number or address, available for anyone to see? If not, attempt to remove this data and write a report of the steps you took and your success in deleting the personal information.

❷ Cloud Services: Storage as a Service (STaaS)

Using the cloud as a primary storage method not only helps you create backups of your files, it also lessens your need for increasing storage capabilities of your computer or device. You also can take advantage of the capability to sign in to your STaaS from another computer or device, which eliminates the need to carry a flash drive.

Cloud storage creates a continuous backup of new and changed files. Like many cloud services, STaaS offers a "pay as you go" pricing model, where customers subscribe to a service for a period and then pay for the features or storage they use. Many cloud storage providers offer web and mobile apps to access and restore files.

Cloud backup services differ from cloud storage services in that cloud backup services offer the software and infrastructure only to back up and restore files. They generally do not support synchronizing files across devices or sharing files with many users, which are common features of cloud storage services.

Research This: (1) Use a search engine to find two different cloud storage providers. Compare their pricing plans, storage offered, app availability, security features, and other services offered. (2) Why are cloud storage services attractive options for small to medium-sized businesses? (3) When is it practical to use cloud backup services, and when is it practical to use cloud storage?

❸ Making Use of the Web: Instructional and How-To Sites

The web offers instructions for just about any topic: home improvement, cooking, arts and crafts, and more. Experts and amateurs provide step-by-step videos and blog posts that can guide you through the process of creating or completing a project. Many of these websites, videos, or blogs, are sponsored by companies from which you can purchase necessary supplies, such as tools or materials.

You can use these resources to perform a variety of tasks, although you should be cautious about any projects that require you to work with electricity, plumbing, heat, or potentially hazardous materials. Use your common sense before attempting any project, and be certain to determine the validity of the source.

Research This: (a) Search for streaming videos for an area that interests you, such as home decorating, cooking, or simple home repair. What qualifications do the makers of the videos have? Are the videos free? What supplies or tools do you need, and are links to products recommended?

(b) Locate two blogs that offer content for the same area. Do the steps in the blog posts differ from the videos? How can you determine which has better advice? What safety tips does the blog post have? Would you attempt the project after reading the post or watching the video? Why or why not?

Critical Thinking

Instructions: The Critical Thinking exercises challenge your assessment and decision-making skills by presenting real-world situations associated with module concepts. The Collaboration exercise should be completed with a team. Evaluate the situations below, using personal experiences and one or more resources available to you (such as articles on the web or in print, blogs, podcasts, videos, television, user guides, other individuals, electronics or computer stores, etc.). Perform the tasks requested in each exercise and share your deliverables in the format requested by your instructor (brief report, presentation, discussion, blog post, video, or other means).

1. **Increasing Storage Capacity**

   You are the office manager at a local boutique. The store needs to increase its storage capacity, and so decides to buy an external hard drive. Your boss asks you to research access times and storage capacities of various external hard drives.

   Do This: Use the web to learn more about available hard drive options. What other factors should you evaluate when determining the appropriate hard drive to purchase? Analyze the advantages and disadvantages of using external hard drives for storage. Include in your discussion backup plans, costs, and alternate options. Recommend two hard drives to your boss. Include user reviews and any information by industry experts in your comparison between the two different hard drives. Which is the best option? Why? Compile your findings.

2. **NFC**

   You have bought an NFC tag to keep track of your smartphone. You are curious about its uses but are concerned about potential risks. Before you enable NFC and install apps that can use this technology, you want to do some research.

   Do This: Use the web to find and then list current and developing uses of NFC. If possible, find reviews or blog posts about these technologies. Describe any safety issues you found in your research. List ways you can protect yourself when using NFC technology. Locate apps that can use NFC. For what purposes can you use this new technology? What disadvantages and risks exist? How can you avoid unauthorized access to your NFC tag? Do any current laws govern or restrict the use of NFC for data collection? What are they? Can you provide additional potential uses for NFC at home, school, or work?

3. **Case Study**

   Cooperative-Owned Farm Stand The owners have asked you to create a backup plan for the stand's computers and devices. The partners in the farm stand have access to multiple shared laptops, a desktop, and a tablet. A few are owned by the co-op, but most are owned by the individual.

   Do This: Use the web to find industry experts' recommendations for backing up data. Write a sample backup plan and schedule for the owners, and include types of backups you will use. Describe each backup type you propose and why you recommend it. Is any special software required to back up the different devices? The owners asked you to present reasons for using cloud storage as part of your backup plan. Research the benefits of using cloud storage over other backup methods. Why would you choose cloud storage? What are the cost differences? Compare three cloud storage providers, ranking them by cost and storage capacity.

Collaboration

4. **Computers in Telemarketing**

   Your team is performing IT research for a magazine-subscription telemarketing company. The company's 150 telemarketers must make a minimum of 100 calls a day. To save money on office space and attract employees who live in other areas, the company is shifting 100 of the 150 workers to work remotely. The company must decide on the type of cloud storage to provide the telemarketers so that they can access the necessary data at home. Management also wants to determine what hardware the remote telemarketers will need.

   Do This: Form a three-member team and assign one member to determine cloud storage requirements, another to determine necessary hardware, and a third to find solutions that meet the storage and hardware needs. Meet with your team, and discuss and compile your findings. Which options would you recommend? Why? What are the advantages of each? Share your findings with the class.

Operating Systems: Managing, Coordinating, and Monitoring Resources

iStock.com/Egor Poprotskii

Objectives

After completing this module, you will be able to:

1 Explain the purpose of an operating system
2 Describe how an operating system works
3 Identify types of operating systems
4 Explain how to select an operating system
5 Explain how to manage files and folders with an operating system
6 Describe the uses of operating system management utilities
7 Identify operating system security features
8 Explain the uses of a virtual machine

Operating Systems

Is your computer or device quick to respond to your instructions? Is it reliable? Do you have utilities that enable you to work productively and efficiently? What type of file storage does your computer or device have? The answers to these questions depend on your system software, specifically your operating system.

When you purchase a computer or mobile device, it usually comes preloaded with system software, including an operating system. **System software** is the software that runs a computer, including the operating system. Recall that an operating system (OS) is a set of programs that coordinates all the activities among computer or mobile device hardware. When you start your computer or device, system software starts running in the background. The operating system and utility programs control the behind-the-scenes operations of a computer or mobile device. An operating system also is called a platform. Most programs and apps you run on your computer come in versions specific to your operating system and are optimized to take advantage of the operating system's features.

Most operating systems perform similar functions that include starting and shutting down a computer or mobile device, providing a user interface, updating operating system software, securing your device and data, managing memory, configuring device settings, establishing an Internet connection, and managing files and folders. Some operating systems also allow users to control a network and administer security (Figure 8-1).

Suppose you are writing a report and want to save the document to your hard drive. Table 8-1 shows the role the OS plays as you perform this task.

Although an operating system can run from a USB flash drive or an external drive, in most cases, an operating system resides inside a computer or mobile device. On mobile devices, the operating system may reside on firmware in the device. Recall that firmware consists of ROM chips or flash memory chips that store permanent instructions.

Figure 8-1   Common operating system functions.

iStock.com/Filo; iStock.com/Egor Suvorov; iStock.com/Bsd555; iStock.com/Shomiz; iStock.com/Yuwnis07; iStock.com/DragonTiger; iStock.com/Golden Sikorka; iStock.com/Grace Maina

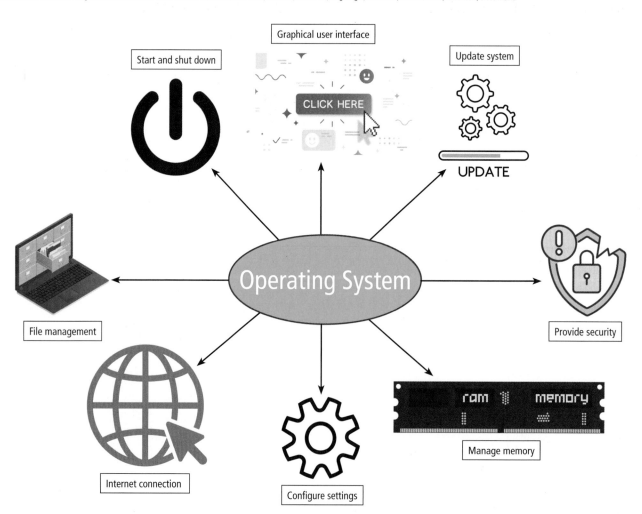

Table 8-1   Interacting with the Operating System

Your Task	Role of Operating System
Start a word processing program and open a document	• Starts the word processing program • Provides tools for you to open the document file
Add information to the document	• Manages memory so the computer can run • Saves your unsaved work to temporary storage
Save the document on the hard drive	• Finds the hard drive • Makes sure the hard drive has enough storage space • Saves the document • Stores the location and file name so that you can access the document later

GUIs

Although operating systems differ in functionality and look, depending on the platform or device, one characteristic that most operating systems today share is that they use a visual interface called a GUI. A **graphical user interface (GUI)** is a collective term for all the ways you interact with the device. A GUI controls how you interact with menus, programs and apps, and visual images, such as icons, by touching, pointing, tapping, or clicking buttons and other objects to issue commands.

GUIs are based on graphical objects, where each object represents a task, command, or object. To interact with a GUI, you tap, click, double-click, or perform some action with icons and buttons (Figure 8-2).

• An **icon** is a small picture that represents a program, file, or hardware device.
• A **button** is a graphic that you click to execute commands you need to work with an app, such as on a toolbar, taskbar, or the ribbon.

Figure 8-2   Graphical user interface.
Source: Microsoft Corporation

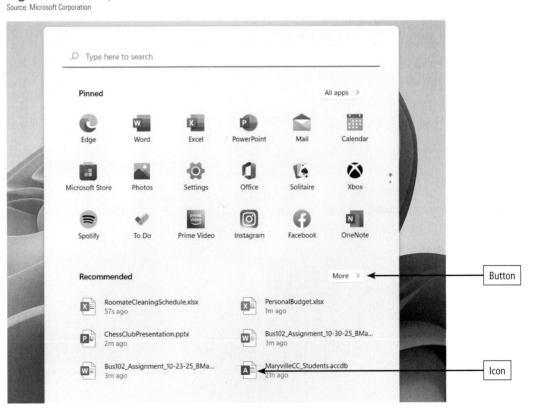

How do you instruct a computer to do what you want it to do? One way is to use a menu. A **menu** is a list of related items, including folders, applications, and commands. Many menus organize commands on a **submenu**, which is a list of additional commands associated with the selected command on a menu. A **shortcut menu** is a list of frequently used commands that relate to an object.

Another feature that enables you to make choices is a dialog box. Some menu commands display a **dialog box**, which is a box with controls that lets you tell the operating system how you want to complete a command (Figure 8-3). Menus and dialog boxes enable you to access a program or app's features.

Dialog box controls include:

- **Option buttons:** round buttons that present one choice; also called a radio button
- **Check boxes:** square boxes that present a yes/no choice and display a check mark or x when selected
- **List boxes:** lists of options that appear when you click arrows in a dialog box; some list boxes allow you to make multiple selections

Operating System Functions

You should be familiar with the functions of your system so that you can take advantage of them to increase your productivity. Standard operating system functions include:

- Starting and shutting down a computer or device
- Managing programs
- Managing memory
- Coordinating tasks
- Configuring devices
- Establishing an Internet connection
- Monitoring performance
- Providing file management
- Updating operating system software
- Monitoring security
- Controlling network access

Operating systems also provide **utilities**, which are apps or programs that enable you to perform maintenance-type tasks related to managing the computer or device. You use utilities, also called tools, to manage files, search for content or programs, view images, install and uninstall programs and apps, compress and back up files, and maintain the computer or device. Screen savers are another type of utility.

Figure 8-3   Dialog box.
Source: Microsoft Corporation

❓ Consider This

Does every operating system use a GUI?

To configure devices, manage system resources, automate system management tasks, and troubleshoot network connections, network administrators and other technical users work with a command-line interface. In a command-line interface, a user types commands represented by short keywords or abbreviations (such as dir to view a directory, or list of files) or presses special keys on the keyboard (such as function keys or key combinations) to enter data and instructions. Some people consider command-line interfaces difficult to use because they require exact spelling, form, and punctuation. Minor errors, such as a missing period, generate an error message. Command-line interfaces, however, give a user more control to manage detailed settings. Have you ever interacted with a command-line interface? Would you prefer to use a GUI or a command-line interface? Why?

How an Operating System Works

An operating system takes care of the technical tasks of running the computer or device while you work on school or professional projects, watch videos, connect with friends, or play games. The operating system is the essential software or app on your computer or device.

A multiuser operating system does not always process tasks on a first-come, first-served basis. If a user or task has been assigned a higher priority than others by the network administrator, the operating system performs higher-priority tasks first. For example, an operating system on a corporate server may process tasks to check for incoming email messages more frequently than it processes tasks to access archived documents.

The Purpose of an Operating System

The operating system is responsible for coordinating the resources and activities on a computer. On a computer system, resources are the components required to perform work, including the processor, RAM, storage space, and connected devices. The operating system is the go-between for you and the computer — it accepts your instructions and data and provides information from the system to you. The operating system also manages interactions between hardware and software. For example, if you want to print a flyer you created in your word processing program, the operating system establishes a connection to the printer, sends the flyer document to the printer, and lets other software know the printer is busy until it finishes printing the flyer. During this process, the operating system directs internal components such as the processor, RAM, and storage space to manage and complete its task.

How an Operating System Manages Memory

The purpose of memory management is to optimize the use of a computer or device's internal memory to allow the computer or device to run more efficiently. RAM is the storage location that temporarily stores open apps and document data while a computer or device is on. The operating system assigns data and instructions to an area of memory while they are being processed. It carefully monitors the contents of memory and releases items when the processor no longer requires them. Frequently used instructions and data are stored in a cache.

Every program or app, including the operating system, requires RAM. The more RAM a device has, the more efficiently it runs. If several programs or apps are running simultaneously, your computer or device might use up its available RAM. When this happens, the computer or device may run slowly. The operating system can allocate a portion of a storage medium, such as a hard disk, to become virtual memory to function as additional RAM.

Virtual memory allows an operating system to temporarily store data on a storage medium until it can be "swapped" into RAM. The swap file, the area of the hard drive used for virtual memory, swaps data, information, and instructions between memory and storage. A page is the amount of data and program instructions that can swap at a given time. The technique of swapping items between memory and storage is called paging. Paging is a time-consuming process. When an operating system spends more of its time paging instead of executing apps, the whole system slows down and it is said to be thrashing. You may be able to adjust the settings on your operating system to free up memory in order to enable your computer or device to run more quickly.

Most laptops and desktop computers have the option to add memory and storage. To increase the memory on a smart phone, you can add flash memory in the form of microSD cards (Figure 8-4). This is something many users take advantage of, especially those users who take many high-resolution photos and videos for professional or personal use.

Figure 8-4   microSD card.
iStock.com/Martvisionlk

How Operating Systems Manage Input and Output

Recall that input is any data and instructions entered in the memory of a device. You can input data and instructions in many ways, including interacting with your touch screen or using a keyboard. Once data is in memory, the computer or device interprets it, and the system software executes instructions to process the data into information. Instructions used for processing data can be in the form of a program or app, commands, and user responses. The information is processed into output. For example, a webpage typically combines text and graphics and may include audio and video as well. Do you want to print the processed information? Do you want to post it to social media or a website or send it electronically as an attachment? Think of output as the goal of input (Figure 8-5). This will help you determine the program, device, or display on which you enter input and instruct the operating system where to direct the output.

Figure 8-5 Screen displays, printers, and speakers are examples of output devices.

Rawpixel.com/Shutterstock.com; Buildiful Media/Shutterstock.com; Moviephoto/Shutterstock.com

Screen display

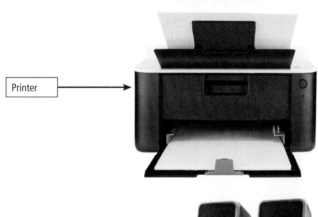

Printer

Speakers

If a computer or device is slow in accepting or providing input or output, the operating system uses buffers. A **buffer** is an area of memory that stores data and information waiting to be sent to an input or output device. Placing data into a buffer is called **spooling**. An example of spooling is when a document is sent to the buffer while it waits for the printer to be available. By sending data to a buffer, the operating system frees up resources to perform other tasks while the data waits to be processed.

How Operating Systems Manage Programs

How an operating system handles programs directly affects your productivity. An operating system can be single-tasking or multitasking:

- A single-tasking operating system allows only one program or app to run at a time. For example, if you are using a browser and want to check email messages, you must exit the browser before you can run the email program. Operating systems on embedded computers and some mobile devices use a single-tasking operating system.
- Most operating systems today are multitasking. A multitasking operating system allows two or more programs or apps to reside in memory at the same time. Using the example just cited, if you are working with a multitasking operating system, you do not have to exit the browser to run the email program. Both programs can run concurrently.

When a computer is running multiple programs concurrently, one program is in the foreground and the others are in the background (Figure 8-6). The one in the **foreground** is the active program, that is, the one you currently are using. The other programs running but not in use are in the **background**. The foreground program typically is displayed on the screen, and the background programs are hidden partially or completely behind the foreground program. A multitasking operating system's user interface easily allows you to switch between foreground and background programs.

In addition to managing applications, an operating system manages other processes. These processes include programs or routines that provide support to other programs or hardware. Some are memory resident. Others run as they are required.

Some operating systems support a single user; others support thousands of users running multiple programs. A multiuser operating system enables two or more users to run programs simultaneously. Networks, servers, and supercomputers allow hundreds to thousands of users to connect at the same time and, thus, use multiuser operating systems.

Figure 8-6 The foreground app is on the screen, and the others are in the background.
iStock.com/Simpson33

Background apps

Foreground app

? Consider This

Do embedded computers use mobile operating systems?
Typically, an embedded computer uses an embedded operating system, sometimes called a real-time operating system (RTOS). Examples of products that use embedded operating systems include digital cameras, ATMs, digital photo frames, HDTV receivers, fuel pumps, ticket machines, process controllers, robotics, and automobile components. Embedded operating systems often perform a single task, usually without requiring input from a user. Several embedded operating systems are available, each intended for various uses. Were you aware that an embedded computer uses an operating system? What features of embedded computers that you typically use would you consider to be part of the operating system? How do you think embedded computers' operating systems might differ from those of computers or mobile devices?

Types of Operating Systems

Operating systems often are written to run on specific types of computers, based on their computing needs and capabilities. That is, servers do not run the same operating system as tablets or laptops because these computers perform different computing tasks. For example, a tablet or laptop operating system might have a feature to turn off the device after a few minutes of inactivity in order to conserve battery power. A server, by contrast, always is plugged in and generally remains on all the time, which means its operating system would not need this power-saving feature. The same types of computers, such as laptops, may run different operating systems. It also is possible to run more than one operating system on the same computer. The three basic categories of operating systems on computers and mobile devices are desktop, server, and mobile (Table 8-2). Operating systems, such as UNIX and Linux, that function as both desktop and server operating systems sometimes are called multipurpose operating systems.

Table 8-2 Examples of Operating Systems by Category

Category	Name
Desktop	Windows
	macOS
	UNIX
	Linux
	Chrome OS
Server	Windows Server
	macOS Server
	UNIX
	Linux
Mobile	Google Android
	Apple iOS
	Windows (Mobile Edition)

Desktop Operating Systems

An operating system installed on a single computer is called a **personal computer (PC) operating system** or a **desktop operating system**. Most are single-user operating systems because only one user interacts with the OS at a time. Desktop operating systems also sometimes are called stand-alone operating systems or client operating systems.

If you receive a laptop or access to a computer through your school or workplace, you likely will not have a choice in operating system. If you purchase one for yourself, though, you should take several factors into consideration. When selecting an operating system, users compare factors such as available programs and apps, hardware and software support, and security. Depending on the computer or device you select, you may not have a choice in operating systems. Certain computers and devices run only those operating systems designed specifically for the computer or device. Before selecting an operating system, be sure to read reviews by experts, as well as user feedback. Determine your needs and priorities to choose the operating system that will help you be productive. Always choose the most updated version of an operating system to take advantage of any new features, as well as security settings and fixes.

Examples of widely used desktop operating systems include Windows, macOS, UNIX, Linux, and Chrome OS (Table 8-3), which are described in more detail in the following sections.

Table 8-3   Examples of Desktop Operating Systems

OS	Used On	Notable Features
Microsoft Windows	Desktop computers, laptops, and some tablets	Supports the Cortana virtual assistant, touchscreen input, HoloLens headsets, and built-in apps, such as the Microsoft Edge browser
macOS	Macintosh desktop computers and laptops	Includes the Siri virtual assistant, coordination with Apple mobile devices, and cloud file storage
UNIX	Most computers and devices	Multitasking operating system with many versions, as the code is licensed to different developers
Linux	Desktop computers, laptops, and some tablets	Distributed under the terms of a General Public License (GPL), which allows you to copy the OS for your own use, to give to others, or to sell
Chrome OS	Chromebook laptops	Based on Linux, uses the Google Chrome browser as its user interface and primarily runs web apps

Microsoft Windows   In the mid-1980s, Microsoft developed its first version of **Microsoft Windows**, which provided a graphical user interface. Since then, Microsoft continually has updated its Windows operating system, incorporating innovative features and functions. The term, PC (personal computer), sometimes is used to describe a computer that runs a Windows operating system. Windows includes a browser (Microsoft Edge), a cloud storage service (Microsoft OneDrive), and the Windows store for app purchases.

macOS   Since its 1984 release with Macintosh (Mac) computers, Apple's Macintosh operating system (now called **macOS**) has earned a reputation for its ease of use and has been the model for most of the new GUIs developed for non-Mac systems. Features of the latest version of macOS include a browser (Safari), cloud storage service (iCloud), and the Mac App Store for app purchases.

UNIX   **UNIX** (pronounced YOU-nix) is a multitasking operating system developed in the early 1970s by scientists at Bell Laboratories. Bell Labs (a subsidiary of AT&T) was prohibited from actively promoting UNIX in the commercial marketplace because of federal regulations. Bell Labs instead licensed UNIX for a low fee to numerous colleges and universities, where UNIX obtained a wide following. In the 1980s, the source code for UNIX was licensed to many hardware and software companies to customize for their devices and applications. As a result, several versions of this operating system exist, each with slightly different features or capabilities. Although some versions of UNIX have a command-line interface, most versions of UNIX offer a graphical user interface. Power users often work with UNIX because of its flexibility and capabilities. An industry standards organization, The Open Group, now owns UNIX as a trademark.

Linux   **Linux** (pronounced LINN-uks), introduced in 1991, is a popular, multitasking UNIX-based operating system that runs on a variety of personal computers, servers, and devices. In addition to the basic operating system, Linux also includes many free utilities and programming languages. Linux is **open source** software, which means its code is provided for use, modification, and redistribution. Linux is available in a variety of forms, known as distributions. Some distributions of Linux are command line. Others are GUI. Some companies market software that runs on their own distribution of Linux. Many application programs, utilities, and plug-ins have Linux distributions.

Chrome OS   **Chrome OS**, introduced by Google, is a Linux-based operating system designed to work primarily with web apps. Apps are available through the Chrome Web Store, and data is stored on Google Drive. The only apps typically installed on the computer are the Chrome browser, a media player, and a file manager. A specialized laptop that runs Chrome OS is called a **Chromebook**, and a specialized desktop that runs Chrome OS is called a **Chromebox**. Because computers running Chrome OS work mostly with web apps, they do not require as much internal storage capacity as other desktop operating systems. Their start-up and shutdown time also is considerably less than other desktop operating systems because Chrome OS uses a streamlined start-up procedure.

Server Operating Systems

A **server operating system** (Table 8-4) is a multiuser operating system because it controls a single, centralized server computer that supports many users on networked computers. A server operating system manages the network. It also controls access to network resources, such as network printers.

Table 8-4 Examples of Server Operating Systems

OS	Used On	Notable Features
Windows Server	The server version of Windows	It includes advanced security tools and a set of programs called Internet Information Services that manage web apps and services
macOS Server	Supports all sizes of networks and servers	One unique feature is that it lets authorized users access servers using their iPhones or other Apple devices
UNIX	A multipurpose operating system that can run on a desktop PC or a server	Many web servers, which are Internet computers that store webpages and deliver them to your computer or device, use UNIX because it is a powerful, flexible operating system

Although desktop operating systems include network capability, server operating systems are designed specifically to support all sizes of networks. Many also enable **virtualization**, which is the practice of sharing computing resources, such as servers or storage devices, among computers and devices on a network. Unless you are a network administrator, you likely will not knowingly interact with a server operating system, but you should be familiar with the capabilities of the operating system being used for this purpose.

Mobile Operating Systems

Smartphones, tablets, and other mobile devices use a **mobile operating system**. A mobile operating system has features similar to those of a desktop operating system but is focused on the needs of a mobile user and the capabilities of the device. A mobile operating system works especially well with mobile device features, such as touch screens, voice recognition, and Wi-Fi networks. They also are designed to run using the limited memory of most mobile devices, and the display works well with smaller screen sizes.

Mobile devices are optimized to perform functions common to mobile users. These include having video and photo cameras, media players, speech recognition, GPS, wireless capabilities, rotating screen displays that adjust when you switch orientation of your device's screen, and text messaging. You likely use all these features on a frequent basis for entertainment, travel, and communication. Table 8-5 shows popular mobile operating systems, and Figure 8-7 shows examples of smartphones running Android and iOS.

Table 8-5 Examples of Mobile Operating Systems

OS	Notable Features
Android	Developed by Google based on Linux, and designed to be run on many types of smartphones and tablets
iOS	Runs only on Apple devices, including the iPhone, iPad, and iPod; derived from macOS

Figure 8-7 Examples of Android and iOS operating systems.
Source: Android/Google; Apple

Android

iOS

Mobile versus Desktop Operating Systems

An operating system has the same role, whether for a desktop or mobile device. It manages operations and provides a user interface. Because of this shared role, many similarities exist between the functions of desktop and mobile operating systems. From a user's perspective, operating systems enable you to work with apps and to monitor and maintain the functions of the computer or device. Whether you are purchasing a computer or mobile device, the choice of an operating system plays an important role.

Historically, the two types of operating systems have had different uses and capabilities. The differences are due in part to the disparity in screen size, keyboards, and processing power. Because of convergence, as well as the increased reliance on mobile devices for communications and productivity, the use and function of mobile and desktop operating systems are becoming more similar. The prevalence of web apps and cloud storage services enables users to access the same programs and files they work with on their desktop from a mobile device. Some developers now create operating systems that share code and have common features, regardless of whether they are installed on a computer or mobile device. Features, such as icons (typically used in mobile devices), make the transition between using a mobile device and computer easier. For example, mobile device operating systems include capabilities that allow users to take advantage of the touch screen displays. As more computer desktop monitors today are touch enabled, computer users can take advantage of this feature.

Differences exist in the way a user interacts with a mobile operating system, including:

- A desktop operating system may use menus, windows, and bars to run apps and to access features within apps. On a desktop, you can run multiple programs simultaneously and seamlessly due to the large screen and the use of pointing devices. This feature makes desktops more useful than mobile operating systems for productivity and multitasking.
- A mobile operating system may have one program running at a time with others running in the background, or it may provide a means for multiple apps to run simultaneously on the screen. Quick movements and gestures are often all that you need to perform tasks on a mobile device. Mobile operating systems use technologies such as cellular, Bluetooth, Wi-Fi, GPS, and NFC to communicate with other devices and to connect to the Internet. Mobile devices also typically include cameras, video cameras, voice recorders, and sometimes speech recognition.

Other Characteristics of Operating Systems

When purchasing a program or an application, you must ensure that it works with the operating system installed on your computer or mobile device. The operating system that a computer uses sometimes is called the platform because applications are said to run "on top of" it, or because the platform supports the applications. With purchased applications, their specifications will identify the required platform(s), or the operating system(s), on which they will run. A cross-platform application is an application that runs the same way on multiple operating systems.

Other questions to ask when considering an operating system include:

- **Who owns the code to the operating system's program?** Operating systems, like other types of software, can be open or closed source. **Closed source** programs keep all or some of the code hidden, enabling developers to control and profit from the program they create. Closed source programs have standard features and can be customized only by using the operating system's utilities. Microsoft Windows and macOS are examples of closed source operating systems. Open source programs and apps (including operating systems) have no restrictions from the copyright holder regarding modification and redistribution. Users can add functionality and sell or give away their versions to others. As previously discussed, Linux is an example of an open source operating system. Proponents of open source programs state that because the code is public, coders can examine, correct, and enhance programs. Some have concerns about unscrupulous programmers adding malicious code that can damage a user's system or be used to gather data without the user's knowledge. Whether you are choosing an open or closed source operating system, program, or app, be sure to research carefully and read reviews to ensure you are getting the highest quality program.
- **Will the operating system work on my new device?** Many of the early operating systems were device dependent and proprietary. A **device-dependent** program is one that runs only on a specific type or make of computer or mobile device. **Proprietary software** is privately owned and limited to a specific vendor or computer or device model. Some operating systems still are device dependent. The trend today, however, is toward **device-independent** operating systems that run on computers and mobile devices provided by a variety of manufacturers. The advantage of device-independent operating systems is you can retain existing applications and data files even if you change computer or mobile device models or vendors.

? Consider This

Open source or closed source — which is more secure?

Supporters of open source software maintain that this type of software enables developers to create high-quality programs. Source code, along with any changes, remains public, so communities of open source software developers can examine, correct, and enhance programs immediately when security issues arise. Developers of closed source operating systems, on the other hand, refuse to share some or all the code. They believe that companies and developers should be able to control, and profit from, the operating systems they create. Their philosophy may hinder third-party software developers who create programs and apps for the operating system. Fear of viruses and other security concerns can lead some to question about whether open source software is worthwhile. While dishonest and anonymous developers can use open source software to create programs that may actually be or may include malware, cryptography experts emphasize that Linux systems have fewer reported security exposures than Windows-based systems. Are the security concerns about open source software legitimate? Why or why not? Does the open source model lead to higher-quality software? Why or why not?

Ethics and Issues: Licensing an Operating System

When you purchase a new computer or mobile device, it typically has an operating system preinstalled. As new versions of the operating system are released, users often upgrade their existing computers and mobile devices to incorporate features of the new versions. Some upgrades are free; some offer an upgrade price that is less than the cost of purchasing the entire operating system.

As with any program or app, legally purchasing, or subscribing to, an operating system has many benefits both to you and to the technology industry, including:

- Benefits to you, the user, include continuity of service (no disruptions because you get cut off from using the software because it is improperly licensed) and security (you have access to the latest updates to known flaws or bugs).
- Benefits to the technology industry include antipiracy (keeping unlicensed products off the market) and innovation (incentivizing developers to continue to improve products).

New versions of an operating system usually are **backward compatible**, which means they recognize and work with applications written for an earlier version of the operating system (or platform). Newly developed applications may or may not be backward compatible; that is, they may or may not run on older operating systems. Further, an application may or may not be **upward compatible**, meaning it may or may not run on newer versions of an operating system.

OS Versions and Purchase Methods   To identify an operating system, you typically state its name and version number, such as Windows 11. Some software manufacturers are doing away with version numbers and instead are offering Software as a Service (SaaS). As with apps, SaaS operating systems are distributed online for a monthly subscription or an annual fee. Instead of releasing a new complete version of the program to purchase, the company will provide updates to its subscribers that include fixes for issues or additional functionality. For example, Microsoft plans to release Windows going forward as an SaaS-only model.

Other ways to purchase an operating system include being preinstalled on your computer or device, or as a paid download from the Internet.

Updating Operating System Software   By using properly licensed operating systems, you have access to all updates. Many software makers provide free downloadable updates, distributed in a service pack, to users who have registered and/or activated their software. Sometimes you will get a prompt when an update is available, which you need to authorize before the update is made. An operating system's automatic update feature can be configured to alert users when an update is available or to download and install the update automatically. These updates can include fixing program errors, improving program functionality, expanding program features, enhancing security, and modifying device drivers (Figure 8-8).

Figure 8-8   Windows Update window.

Source: Microsoft Corporation

Consider This

Automatic updates — safe or not?

The automatic update option occasionally has caused problems. In one case, people preparing their income tax returns were unable to print forms when a leading software company issued an automatic update one week before the filing deadline. In another situation, an automatic update was installed on all computers — even those with this feature disabled. The company claimed that the update was harmless and was for the benefit of its customers. Only later did some users realize that this secret update caused serious problems. One consequence of the ensuing outrage was that many people turned off the automatic update feature, fearing that future updates might cause even more damage. Is the automatic update feature enabled or disabled on your computer? Why? Should software companies be able to send automatic updates to your computer without your knowledge? Why or why not?

Manage Files and Folders

A **file** is collection of information stored on your computer, such as a text document, spreadsheet, photo, and song. Files are stored in folders. The file format determines the type or types of programs and apps that you can use to open and display or work with a file. Some files be opened only in the program with which they were created. Others, such as graphics files, can be opened in multiple programs or apps. A **file extension** is three- or four-letter sequence, preceded by a period, at the end of a file name that identifies the file as a particular type of document, such as .docx (Microsoft Word document), or .jpg (a type of graphic file). When you save a file, the program or app assigns the file extension (Table 8-6).

Table 8-6 Examples of File Extensions

File type	Extensions
Microsoft Office	.docx (Word), .xlsx (Excel), .pptx (PowerPoint)
Text file	.txt, .rtf
Webpage	.htm or .html, .xml, .asp or .aspx, .css
Graphics	.jpg, .png, .tif

You can manage files and folders on your computer or device in several ways. You can change or view the properties of a file, compress a file to save storage space, move or rename a file or folder, and organize your files. As cloud storage becomes more prevalent, and users rely more on their mobile devices, some of these tasks may not be ones you have encountered before. In an office setting or for your own personal use, however, they still are valuable skills to learn about and know. Operating systems include many utilities, also called tools, that enable you to perform file management tasks.

File Properties

Every file has properties, such as its name, type, location, and size (Figure 8-9). File properties also include metadata, including the dates when the file was created, modified, and last accessed. The modified date is useful if you have several versions of a file and want to identify the most recent version. The operating system assigns some properties to files, such as type or format, and updates other properties, such as date, size, and location. Some file types have unique properties. For example, an image might contain information about the dimensions (size) of the image, while a song or media file might include the artist(s) names.

Figure 8-9 Viewing a file's properties.
Source: Microsoft Corporation

Properties ˅	
Size	219KB
Pages	58
Words	14638
Total Editing Time	5999 Minutes
Title	Add a title
Tags	Add a tag
Comments	Add comments

Related Dates

Last Modified	Today, 4:02 PM
Created	2/10/2023 2:11 PM
Last Printed	

Related People

Author	A admin

File Compression

File size usually is measured in **kilobytes (KB)** (thousands of bytes of data), megabytes (MB) (millions of bytes of data), or gigabytes (GB) (billions of bytes of data). The more data, the larger the file, and the more storage space it takes up. For example, a simple text file with limited formatting may be several KB, a file containing a high-resolution graphic image could be several MB, and a movie-length video could be a GB.

You often need to compress files and folders before you share or transfer them. For example, by attaching a compressed file to an email message, the smaller file travels faster to its destination. Before you can open and edit a compressed file, you need to extract or uncompress it. Desktop operating systems offer utilities to compress and uncompress files. Mobile operating systems do not always include these by default, but you can install them.

To compress a file or folder, select it in your operating system's file management utility and then instruct the utility to zip or compress the file. To uncompress, double-click the file in the file management utility, and either drag selected files to another folder or instruct the utility to extract all files into a new folder.

Manage File Names and File Placement

Every file on a computer or device has a name. When you save a file, you must give it a name that follows rules called file-naming conventions. Each operating system has its own file-naming conventions. For example, Windows file names cannot include some symbols, such as asterisks or slashes. Only the colon (:) is a prohibited character in macOS. Some files are automatically given a default name when you create them, which you then can override. Most file names contain an extension that identifies its contents, such as the type of platform or app on which the file can be used. File name extensions are added automatically when you save a file, but you can change the extension in some cases.

A file name should identify the content and purpose of the file, as well as any other information, such as whether the file is a draft or final. A folder can only include one file with the same name of the same type. You can have multiple files of the same type with the same name only if they are in different folders. To differentiate a version of a file without overwriting the original, you could add additional characters such as numbers, the date, or the initials of the person who modified the file.

File saving controls let you specify where to store the file and what file name to use. You can save your file directly to a folder on your hard drive or device, upload it to the cloud, or save it to a storage medium, such as a flash drive. Files you work on using a web app, such as Google Docs or Office 365, save changes as you make them. You also can save a file with a new file name or on a new location so that you can reuse your work or keep track of document versions. To open a saved file, make sure you have access to its location.

To copy or move files from one location to another, you must first select the files. You can select them from a file management utility, the desktop, or another location. You can select multiple files at once or just a single file. One method of copying or moving files in Windows is to use the Clipboard, which saves the file or folder from the source file or folder until you paste it into the destination file or folder. Recall that the Clipboard is a temporary storage area that holds the selections you copy or cut so you can use them later. You also can drag files and folders between or within file management utility windows. Other operating systems have functions similar to a Clipboard, as well as other file management utilities.

Manage Folder Names and Folder Placement

An operating system utility allows you to create new, named folders; choose the location of folders; move files between folders; and create a folder hierarchy that includes subfolders (Figure 8-10). Every file you save will have a destination folder, and by choosing the correct folder or adding new folders, you can help keep your files accessible and organized.

Figure 8-10 Folder hierarchy.
grmarc/Shutterstock.com

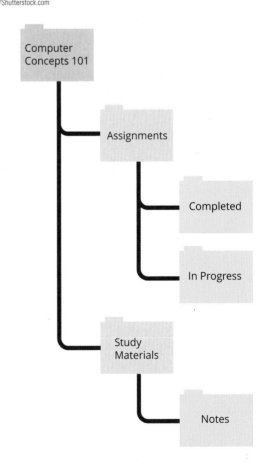

A **library** is a special folder that catalogues specific files and folders in a central location, regardless of where the items are actually stored on your device. Library files might include pictures, music, documents, and videos. Your operating system most likely comes with a number of libraries. You can customize your libraries to add additional folders and include files from the Internet or a network. Libraries are helpful to find all files of a certain type, no matter where they are located on your computer or device. Files you save on your mobile device may be saved automatically in a library by type, such as image or movie, or by the app used to create it.

When you create a folder, the folder may be given a default name, such as New folder, or you may be required to name it in order to save it. Folder names should identify the content and purpose of the folder, as well as any other relevant information. Within your file manager, you can move, copy, and delete folders. Moving or copying a folder affects all the contents of the folder. Deleting a folder moves it to the Recycle Bin or Trash folder, where you can permanently delete it or restore it to its original location if you change your mind.

Organize Files

You can use a file manager to reorder, move, or navigate between folders. The Windows file manager is called File Explorer (Figure 8-11), and the macOS file manager is called Finder. When you start the file manager, you have access to frequently or recently opened files and folders, favorite files and folders, and the main folders on your computer or device. You can use the search tool to locate files and folders by file name, content, date, and more. To navigate to a folder, you need to locate it using the search tool or by opening a main folder and then opening subfolders until you get to the folder in which the file(s) you need are located. By giving your files descriptive names and placing similar subfolders together in a folder, you can more easily locate the files and folders you need.

 **Consider This** ───────────────

Do operating systems encrypt data and files?

To protect sensitive data and information further as it travels over a network, the operating system may encrypt it. Recall that encryption is the process of encoding data and information into an unreadable form. Administrators can specify that data be encrypted as it travels over a network to prevent unauthorized users from reading the data. When an authorized user attempts to read the data, it is automatically decrypted, or converted back into a readable form. Do you know if your operating system uses encryption? How might you find out if you do not know? Is this important to you? Why or why not?

Use Operating System Management Utilities

Operating systems provide users with a variety of utilities related to managing your computer and devices, and its programs (Table 8-7). You can use a variety of administrative utilities to manage resources, monitor performance, and more. You also can customize your operating system and device to meet your needs. With any computer or device, you should know how to manage the program windows to work efficiently.

Use Administrative Utilities

An operating system controls your computer by managing its resources. The operating system tracks the names and locations of files, as well as empty storage areas where you can save new files. It alerts you if it detects a resource problem, such as too many programs or apps are running for the memory to handle, or the printer is not turned on, or your hard drive is out of space. To manage RAM resources, an operating system keeps track of the apps, processes, and other tasks the system performs. You can open your computer or device's version of the task manager to view running programs and see the percentage of RAM being used. You can shut down programs and apps in the task manager to free up RAM.

Figure 8-11 Windows File Explorer.
Source: Microsoft Corporation

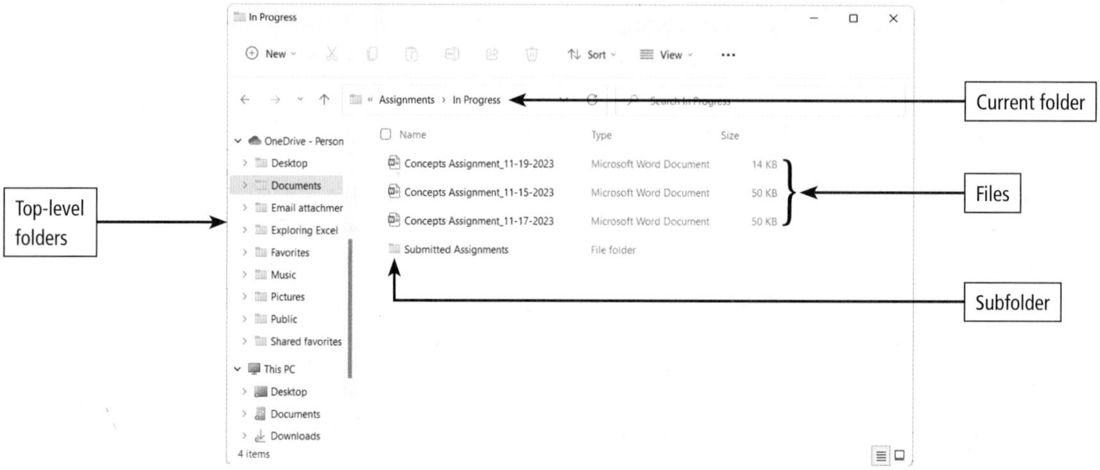

Table 8-7 Operating System Tools

Tool	Function
File management	Performs functions related to displaying files; organizing files in folders; and copying, renaming, deleting, moving, and sorting files
Search	Attempts to locate files based on specified criteria
Image viewer/Gallery	Displays, copies, and prints the contents of graphics files
Uninstaller	Removes a program or app, as well as any associated entries in the system files
Disk cleanup	Searches for and removes or archives unnecessary files
Lock screen	Causes a display's screen to require the user to sign in again if no keyboard or mouse activity occurs for a specified time
File compression	Shrinks the size of a file(s)
Maintenance	Identifies and fixes operating system problems, detects and repairs drive problems, and includes the capability of improving performance
Backup	Copies selected files or the contents of an entire storage medium to another storage location
Power management	Monitors battery usage

Adjust Power Settings   You might keep your computer or device running constantly, or you may choose to shut it down, either to save power or prevent it being shut down suddenly and unexpectedly, such as by a thunderstorm or battery issue. Operating systems provide shut down options so that you can exit programs and terminate processes properly. You can instruct the device to completely shut down, which closes all files and apps and then turns off the power. Some operating systems have a Sleep option to use low power instead of shutting down. Sleep stores the current state of open programs and files, saving you time when you resume using your device.

Because most users tend to keep their desktop computer or laptop plugged in while in use, battery life is a bigger concern with mobile devices. You can switch to a low-power mode, which limits data usage, dims the screen brightness, and makes other adjustments to slow down battery usage. You also can purchase a replacement battery to switch to when battery power gets low, or you can opt for a portable charger you can plug in with a USB cord to charge your device.

Using Diagnostic Utilities   Regardless of the operating system you are using, if your computer starts to slow down or act erratically, you can use a utility to diagnose and repair the problem. A common solution for Windows desktop systems is to run a **disk cleanup utility**, which finds and removes unnecessary files, such as temporary Internet files or files you have marked for deletion. Disk optimization utilities free up disk space by reorganizing data.

The Recycle Bin, or Trash folder, is another type of disk utility. This folder stores files you have designated to be deleted. When you move a file to the Recycle Bin or Trash, it still takes up storage space but no longer appears in the folder or location where it was created. The file is permanently deleted only when you empty the folder or run a disk cleanup utility.

Monitoring Performance   Operating systems typically include a performance monitor. A **performance monitor** is a program that assesses and reports information about various computer resources and devices. For example, users can monitor the processor, drives, network, and memory usage.

The information in performance reports helps users and administrators identify a problem with resources so that they can try to resolve any issues. If a computer is running extremely slow, for example, the performance monitor may determine that the computer's memory is being used to its maximum. You might then consider installing additional memory.

Customize an Operating System

When you start using a computer or device, the operating system and related software and hardware have default settings. Recall that default settings are standard settings that control how the screen is set up and how a document looks when you first start typing. As you continue to work with your computer or device, you may decide to customize the settings to be more productive (Figure 8-12). Operating systems allow you to make adjustments, such as connecting to a network, controlling sounds, allowing or preventing app notifications, changing the brightness or other screen display settings, changing the appearance of the home screen or lock screen, applying a theme to change the look and feel of the operating system elements, and setting lock screen settings. You also can use these utilities to uninstall apps, add accounts, and adjust privacy settings. In addition, you can create shortcuts that link to files and apps that allow you to access the object from the desktop.

Figure 8-12   Settings for an Android smartphone.
Source: Android/Google

Manage Desktop Windows

All operating systems include similar features. The desktop (Figure 8-13) contains icons for programs and files, as well as toolbars, taskbars, menus, and buttons you can use to start programs and apps. A notification area displays the date and time, as well as shortcuts to utilities such as audio controls and network connections.

In any operating system, a **window** is a rectangular-shaped work area that displays an app or a collection of files, folders, and utilities. You can use two types of windows on a computer's desktop: a **program window** displays a running program; a **folder window** displays the contents of a folder, drive, or device. Every time you open a new program or file, a new window opens. You can switch between windows to access different information or resources. When you open an app, file, or folder, it appears on the desktop in a window. Most windows share common elements (Figure 8-14).

These elements common to most windows include the following:

- The center area of the window displays its contents.
- The title bar at the top displays the name of the app, file, or folder shown in the window.
- On a computer, buttons enable you to maximize (make the window fill the screen), minimize (reduce it to a button on the taskbar without closing it), and resize the window.
- Some windows include a ribbon, toolbar, or menu bar that contains text, icons, or images you select to perform actions and make selections.
- Windows also can include vertical and horizontal scroll bars that you drag to display contents currently out of view.

Figure 8-13   macOS desktop.
Source: Apple Computer

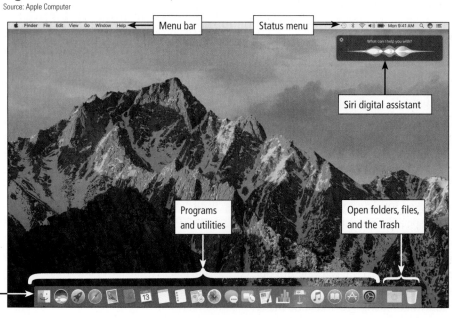

Figure 8-14   Common window elements.

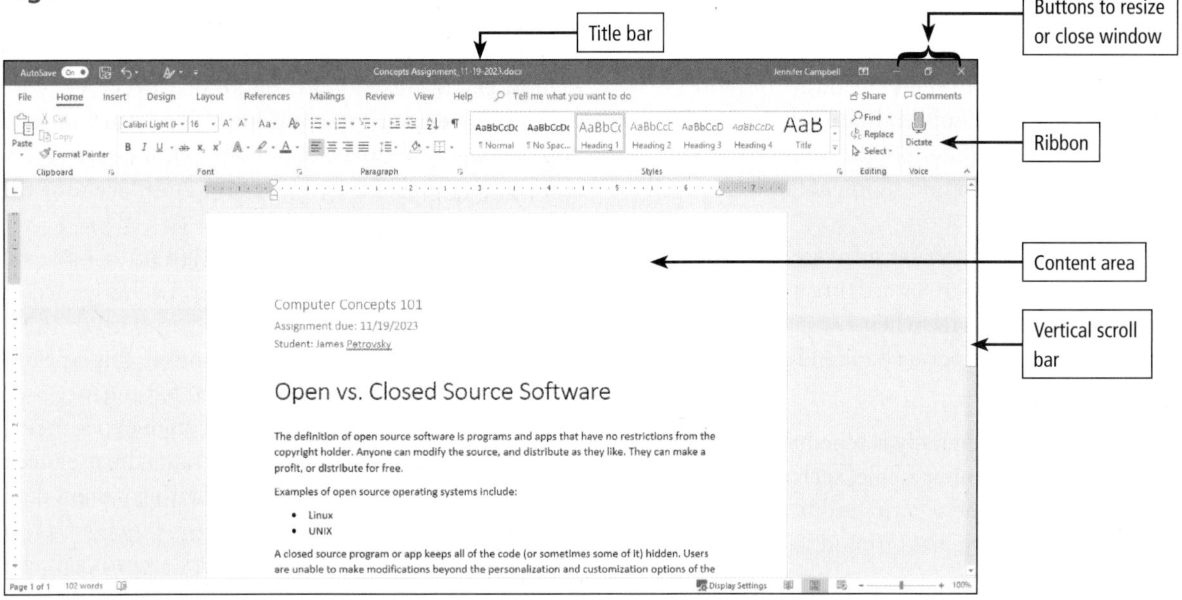

When you have multiple windows, files, and apps open at a time, the windows can appear side by side or stacked. Most mobile devices display only stacked, or tiled, windows. The active window is the window you are currently using, which appears in front of any other open windows. The steps to switch between windows depend on the type of device or operating system you are running. For example:

- On a mobile device, you might have a button near the Home button that displays all open windows in a stack. When you select it, it displays the stack of open windows and apps. You can select a window to make it the active window, close individual windows, or close all open windows.
- On a computer, you can click an icon on the Windows taskbar or the Dock on an Apple computer. You also can use keyboard shortcuts to cycle through **thumbnails** (a small version of a larger image) of open windows.

❓ Consider This

What is a natural user interface?

Just as you can customize your GUI-based operating system, a **natural user interface (NUI)** is an interface that enables you to train it to respond to your gestures and voice commands. Input methods for a NUI include voice (such as with Alexa or Siri), touch, and gestures. As you continue to interact with your NUI, it learns more about you, and you are able to accomplish more complex tasks. NUIs are especially helpful to those who require assistive technologies, because they do not rely on manipulation of a pointing device or using a keyboard to input or instruct. Have you ever used a NUI? What did/could you use it for? What type of input would you most like to train it to do? Why?

Secure IT: Securing an Operating System

Many of the security techniques you use to manage your device, apps, and online social media accounts apply to an operating system. In addition to using passwords or other authentication devices and other privacy settings, you can use utilities specific to the operating system to enable security settings for the device and its individual users. Network administrators, as well as owners of computers, typically have an administrator account that enables them to access all files and programs, install programs, and specify settings that affect all users on a computer, mobile device, or network.

Using an Operating System's Security Utilities

Security software must run constantly to protect against new viruses, malware, and spyware attacks. Operating systems can include the following security utilities, many of which you have already learned about, including:

- **Firewall:** Security experts recommend using a firewall and configuring it to turn on or off automatically.
- **Automatic updating:** Security updates are issued at least once daily, and other updates are generated on an as-needed basis. Many people enjoy the convenience offered by allowing these fixes to install automatically instead of continually checking for new files to download. Users can view the update history to see when specific updates were installed. If an update caused a problem to occur, a user can uninstall these new files.

- **Antivirus software:** Many operating systems include antivirus programs that are updated regularly. Some users mistakenly think they should install and run another antivirus program simultaneously for more protection. They should not run more than one antivirus program on a computer because multiple programs might conflict with one another and slow overall performance.
- **Spyware and malware detection software:** Because sophisticated spyware and malware threats are emerging at an unparalleled rate, comprehensive spyware and malware detection software is crucial to fend off attacks on the computer or device.

The operating system generally is scheduled to scan and update when the computer is idle, such as in the middle of the night. Overall, the security utilities should run constantly and quietly in the background to ensure a safe computing experience.

Manage User Accounts

For each user, the network administrator or computer owner establishes a user account and determines permissions settings. **User accounts** identify the resources, such as apps and storage locations, a user can access when working with the computer. Permissions define who can access certain resources and when they can access those resources.

User accounts protect your computer against unauthorized access. A user account includes information such as the username or ID and a password. You can set preferences for each user account on your computer or device, as well as set permissions to certain folders or files. A standard user account is designed for the everyday user who will be using the computer or device for work or recreation. Additional responsibilities associated with an administrator account include installing programs and apps, adjusting security settings, and managing network access. On a computer you use at your home, you likely will not have a separate administrator account — the main user account will have administrator capabilities. On a networked computer, such as at your school or workplace, you will not have access to the administrator account. If you want to provide someone temporary access to your computer, you can create a secure guest account that gives access to basic functions.

A user account enables a user to **sign in** to, or access resources on, a network or computer. Each user account typically consists of a username and password or PIN, but other methods, such as facial recognition, fingerprint, or a physical security key, can be required for enhanced security (Figure 8-15). If the user's information matches their security settings, the operating system grants the user access. If the entry does not match, the operating system denies access to the user.

The operating system on a network records successful and unsuccessful sign-in attempts in a file. This allows the network administrator to review who is using or attempting to use the computer. The administrators also use these files to monitor computer usage.

Figure 8-15   Adding security to a user's settings.
Source: Microsoft Corporation

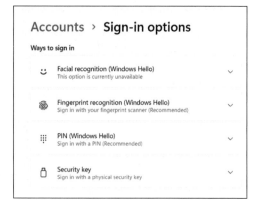

? Consider This ———————————————————————————————————

Should operating system manufacturers be liable for breaches due to security flaws?
If you purchase a household device with a warranty, you can hold the manufacturer responsible for replacing and fixing it. Some argue that the same product liability laws that protect consumers in other industries should apply to software. A flaw in an operating system can affect the performance of the computer or mobile device and subject data to corruption or unauthorized use. Operating system developers write code as securely as possible, but with the volume of code, mistakes are bound to occur. Users sometimes are unaware of their own role in infecting their own computer or mobile device.

Some argue that making software manufacturers responsible for flaws will inhibit innovation. If a company spends more time looking for potential security flaws, it has less time to spend enhancing the software. In addition, some of the same features that enhance an operating system, such as web integration, increase the software's vulnerability. Has your computer or mobile device become infected with malware due to a flaw in the operating system? How did you know? What responsibility does a software manufacturer have for preventing and fixing operating system flaws? Should users expect their software to be perfect? Why or why not?

How To: Use Virtual Machines

If you want to run multiple operating systems on the same computer, you could create a virtual machine. A **virtual machine (VM)** enables a computer or device to run another operating system in addition to the one installed. You might want to enable a virtual machine if you have an app that is incompatible with your current operating system, or if you want to run multiple operating systems on one computer. To run a virtual machine, you need a program or app that is specifically designed to set up and manage virtual machines. You also will need access to installation files for the operating system you want to run on the virtual machine. The virtual machine runs separately in a section of the hard disk called a partition. A **partition**, also called a volume, is a section of a hard drive that functions like a separate drive. You can only access one partition of a hard drive at a time.

Set Up and Use a Virtual Machine

To set up a virtual machine, you will need the required software, as well as installation media for the operating system you want to install in the virtual machine. The following steps describe how to set up a virtual machine:

1. Obtain and install an app that creates and runs virtual machines.
2. Run the app and select the option to create a new virtual machine.
3. Specify the settings for the new virtual machine.
4. If necessary, insert the installation media for the operating system you want to run in the virtual machine.
5. Run the virtual machine. Follow the steps to install the operating system in the virtual machine.
6. When the operating system has finished installing, remove the installation media.
7. While the virtual machine is running, if desired, install any apps you want to run.
8. When you are finished using the virtual machine, shut down the operating system in the same manner you would shut down your computer.
9. Exit the virtual machine software.

After you set up the virtual machine, you can use the virtual machine any time by performing the following steps:

1. Run the virtual machine software.
2. Select the virtual machine you want to run.
3. Click the button to run the virtual machine.
4. When you are finished using the virtual machine, shut down the operating system similar to how you would shut down your computer.
5. Exit the virtual machine software.

? Consider This

What security risks occur with virtualization?

With many companies allowing or requiring employees to work remotely, virtualization, such as use of VMs, has increased dramatically. Companies may enable temporary or contract employees to set up a VM on their own device, which may not be as secure as one that the company owns and manages. In addition, if VMs are set up for a specific purpose, such as a project, and then abandoned, the VM should be removed so as not to crowd the servers with unnecessary resources. VM management software can track access, permissions, and activity on a VM. Have you ever used a VM? What did/could you use it for? What precautions might you take as an employee or as an employer?

Study Guide

Instructions: The Study Guide exercise reinforces material you should know after reading this module. Answer the questions below using the format that helps you remember best or that is required by your instructor. Possible formats may include one or more of these options: write the answers; create a document that contains the answers; record answers as audio or video using a webcam, smartphone, or portable media player; post answers on a blog, wiki, or website; or highlight answers in the book/ebook.

1. Define the term, system software.

2. Name another term for an operating system. List common operating system functions.

3. Define the term, graphical user interface. List ways a user interacts with a GUI.

4. Define these terms: icon, button, menu, shortcut menu, and dialog box.

5. List dialog box controls.

6. Explain the purpose of a utility. List common utility types.

7. Describe how a user interacts with a command-line interface.

8. Define the term, resource.

9. Explain how an operating system manages memory.

10. Define the terms, page and thrashing.

11. Explain how an operating system manages input and output.

12. A(n) _____ is an area of memory that stores data and information waiting to be sent to in input or output device. Define the term, spooling.

13. Differentiate between single- and multitasking operating systems.

14. Define the terms, foreground and background, in a multitasking operating system.

15. Explain how an embedded computer uses an operating system.

16. Define the term, personal computer (PC) operating system. List examples of desktop operating systems.

17. Linux is _____, which means its code is provided free for use, modification, and redistribution.

18. Explain the role of a server operating system. List examples of server operating systems.

19. Define the term, virtualization.

20. Define the term, mobile operating system. List examples.

21. Differentiate between characteristics of mobile and desktop operating systems.

22. Explain considerations when deciding between closed and open source operating systems.

23. Define the terms, device-dependent, proprietary, and device-independent software.

24. New versions of an operating system usually are _____, which means they recognize and work with applications written for an earlier version.

25. List methods to purchase or license an operating system.

26. Explain the importance of enabling operating system updates, as well as the associated safety concerns.

27. Define the term, file. List types of file extensions.

28. List types of file properties.

29. List three ways file sizes are measured. Explain the purpose of file compression.

30. Define the term, library.

31. Explain why an administrator might enable encryption for a network.

32. List types of operating system management utilities.

33. Explain how an operating system manages resources.

34. Describe how you can manage power resources and use diagnostic utilities.

35. Explain the purpose of a performance monitor.

36. List methods to customize your operating system.

37. Explain how you can customize your hardware using system software.

38. Differentiate between a program window and a folder window. List common window elements.

39. Define the term, natural user interface.

40. List and describe common operating system security utilities.

41. Explain how you can manage user settings to improve security.

42. Explain who is responsible for issues caused by operating system flaws.

43. Define the terms, virtual machine and partition.

44. List steps to set up and use a virtual machine.

Key Terms

You should be able to define the Key Terms listed below.

background (8-6)
backward compatible (8-11)
buffer (8-6)
button (8-3)
Chromebook (8-8)
Chromebox (8-8)
Chrome OS (8-8)
closed source (8-10)
desktop operating system (8-7)
device-dependent (8-10)
device-independent (8-10)
dialog box (8-4)
disk cleanup utility (8-15)
file (8-12)

file extension (8-12)
folder window (8-16)
foreground (8-6)
graphical user interface (GUI) (8-3)
icon (8-3)
kilobyte (KB) (8-13)
library (8-14)
Linux (8-8)
macOS (8-8)
menu (8-4)
Microsoft Windows (8-8)
mobile operating system (8-9)
natural user interface (NUI) (8-17)

open source (8-8)
page (8-5)
partition (8-19)
performance monitor (8-15)
personal computer (PC) operating system (8-7)
program window (8-16)
proprietary software (8-10)
resource (8-5)
server operating system (8-8)
shortcut menu (8-4)
sign in (8-18)
spooling (8-6)

submenu (8-4)
system software (8-2)
thrashing (8-5)
thumbnail (8-17)
UNIX (8-8)
upward compatible (8-11)
user account (8-18)
utility (8-4)
virtual machine (VM) (8-19)
virtualization (8-9)
window (8-16)

Extend Your Knowledge

Instructions: The Extend Your Knowledge exercise expands on subjects covered in the module and encourages you to find the latest developments on these topics. Use a search engine or another search tool to locate news articles, blog entries, videos, expert discussions, or other current sources on the listed topics. List your sources, and write 3–4 sentences describing what you have learned to submit in the format required by your instructor.

- NUIs
- Virtualization
- SaaS operating system costs
- Operating system themes and wallpapers

What did you learn that helped you better understand the concepts in this module? Did anything surprise you? How will what you learned impact you?

Checkpoint

The Checkpoint exercises test your knowledge of the module concepts.

True/False   Mark T for True and F for False. If False, rewrite the statement so that it is True.

_____ 1. System software is the software that runs a computer, including the operating system.

_____ 2. Menus are windows with controls that let you tell the operating system how you want to complete a command.

_____ 3. Every program or app, including the operating system, requires RAM.

_____ 4. A spool is an area of memory that stores data and information waiting to be sent to an input or output device.

_____ 5. iOS is an example of a desktop operating system.

_____ 6. SaaS operating systems are distributed online for a monthly subscription or an annual fee.

_____ 7. When you save a file, the program or app assigns the file extension.

_____ 8. A program window displays the contents of a folder, drive, or device.

_____ 9. On a networked computer, such as at your school or workplace, you will not have access to the administrator account.

_____ 10. A partition is a section of a hard disk that functions like a separate disk.

Matching   Match the terms with their definitions.

_____ 1. virtual memory

_____ 2. resources

_____ 3. permissions

_____ 4. VM

_____ 5. library

_____ 6. upward compatible

_____ 7. Chrome OS

_____ 8. .jpg

_____ 9. virtualization

_____ 10. UNIX

a. the practice of sharing computing resources, such as servers or storage devices, among computers and devices on a network

b. will run on newer versions of an operating system

c. in the 1980s, its source code was licensed to many hardware and software companies to customize for their devices and applications

d. a type of graphic file

e. a special folder that catalogues specific files and folders in a central location

f. define who can access certain resources and when they can access those resources

g. enables a computer or device to run another operating system in addition to the one installed

h. Linux-based operating system designed to work primarily with web apps

i. the components required to perform work, including the processor, RAM, storage space, and connected devices

j. allows an operating system to temporarily store data on a storage medium until it can be swapped into RAM

Problem Solving

Instructions: The Problem Solving exercises extend your knowledge of module concepts by seeking solutions to practical problems with technology that you may encounter at home, school, or work. The Collaboration exercise should be completed with a team. You often can solve problems with technology in multiple ways. Determine a solution to the problems in these exercises by using one or more resources available to you (such as a computer or mobile device, articles on the web or in print, blogs, podcasts, videos, television, user guides, other individuals, electronics or computer stores, etc.). Is this a real issue you've encountered? Do you think you would be able to solve the situation if you encounter it? Describe your solution, along with the resource(s) used, in the format requested by your instructor (brief report, presentation, discussion, blog post, video, or other means).

Personal

1. **Difficulty Using a Guest Account**   You set up a guest account on your laptop so that your roommate can use it while theirs is in the shop; however, they complain that they cannot access the apps they need to based on the settings when you created the account. What are your next steps?

2. **Missing Customization Settings**   When you sign in to your operating system, your customized desktop background does not appear. Instead, the operating system displays the default desktop background. What might have happened?

3. **SaaS Not Available**   When you start your device, you get a message saying that your SaaS subscription has expired, and you no longer have access to your operating system. What are your next steps?

4. **Insufficient Access**   You are attempting to install a program on your computer and a dialog box appears informing you that you have insufficient privileges to install the program. What might be wrong?

5. **Missing Files**   You created a spreadsheet last semester to keep track of your grades. You know that you saved it to your hard drive, but you cannot remember where. What can you do?

Professional

6. **Virtual Machine Error**   You use virtual machines on your office computer so that you can run and test software in multiple operating system versions. When you attempt to run one of the virtual machines, you receive an error message that the virtual machine already is running. You are certain that the virtual machine is not running. What steps can you take to correct the problem?

7. **Missing Files and Settings**   When you sign in to various computers at work with the credentials assigned by your IT department, you typically see all your files. When you recently signed in to the computer in your office, however, you were unable to view your files. What are your next steps?

8. **Fingerprint Access Not Working**   Your employer requires you sign in to your company-issued laptop with a fingerprint. Recently, however, you cut the tip of your finger while cooking, and now the operating system is not recognizing it. What are your next steps?

9. **Mobile Device Operating System Upgrade**   A notification appears on your mobile phone stating that an operating system upgrade has been downloaded and is ready to install. Your company has provided the mobile phone to you for work-related business, and you are hesitant to install the upgrade. What are your next steps?

10. **Slow System Performance**   Your office computer has been running slow lately, and you are attempting to determine the cause. What steps can you take to determine what might be slowing your computer's performance?

Collaboration

11. **Technology in Meteorology**   Your environmental sciences instructor is teaching a lesson about how technology has advanced the meteorology field. Form a team of three people to prepare a brief report about how technology and meteorology are connected. One team member should research how meteorologists predicted weather patterns before computer use became mainstream. Another team member should create a timeline illustrating when and how technology was introduced to the meteorology field, and the third team member should research the technology that a network uses to broadcast and share the weather forecasts.

How To: Your Turn

Instructions: This exercise presents general guidelines for fundamental skills when using a computer or mobile device and then requires that you determine how to apply these general guidelines to a specific program or situation. You often can complete tasks using technology in multiple ways. Figure out how to perform the tasks described in these exercises by using one or more resources available to you (such as a computer or mobile device, articles on the web or in print, online or program help, user guides, blogs, podcasts, videos, other individuals, trial and error, etc.). Summarize your 'how to' steps, along with the resource(s) used, in the format requested by your instructor (brief report, presentation, discussion, blog post, video, or other means).

1 Configure Accessibility Settings

Most operating systems allow users to configure accessibility settings to make it easier for some individuals to interact with them. Accessibility features can perform functions such as enhancing the contrast between colors on the display device, narrating text that is displayed on the screen, and allowing the user to control the pointer using keys on the keyboard. Settings can assist users who have mobility issues, color blindness, or are Deaf or Blind. The following steps guide you through the process of configuring accessibility settings.

a. If necessary, sign in to your operating system.

b. Display your operating system's control panel, settings, or system preferences.

c. Select the command to display accessibility settings.

d. Select the accessibility setting you want to configure, and specify your desired settings.

e. Repeat the previous step for all remaining accessibility settings you want to configure.

f. When you have finished configuring the accessibility settings, save your changes and then close the window containing the control panel, settings, or system preferences.

g. If you no longer require the accessibility settings, display your operating system's control panel, settings, or system preferences, display the setting you want to disable, and then disable the setting.

Exercises

1. Accessibility settings are not only for people with impairments — these settings can make it easier for anyone to use a computer. Can you think of any accessibility settings that you might consider using to make it easier to interact with the computer? Are these available on your operating system?

2. Which third-party programs or additional hardware can provide additional features for accessibility?

3. Do you feel that the accessibility features in your computer or mobile device's operating system are sufficient? Why or why not? What would you add?

Internet Research

Instructions: These exercises broaden your understanding of module concepts by requiring that you search for information on the web. Use a search engine or another search tool to locate the information requested or answers to questions presented in the exercises. Describe your findings, along with the search term(s) you used and your web source(s), in the format requested by your instructor (brief report, presentation, discussion, blog post, video, or other means). Additionally, reflect on the process you used to complete this activity. How did you go about choosing the tool that you did and why? Would you do anything differently next time?

2 Making Use of the Web: Budget and Finance

Managing your money and keeping track of your budget are among the most important skills consumers need to master. Whether your financial institution is a retail bank, a virtual bank, or a credit union, you probably have access to an app with which you can monitor account balances, deposit checks, transfer funds, receive text message alerts, and pay bills. Other apps provide personal financial advice and calculators to help make saving, spending, and other planning decisions.

Research This: (a) Select two online banking apps. Compare the services and featured products. For example, do they offer bill payment, retirement accounts, and mobile banking apps? What fees are charged for these services? Which bank has the highest money market and certificate of deposit rates?

(b) Select two apps that that feature information about managing personal credit and debt. Read advice on managing student loans, credit card debt, overspending, or retirement planning. What background does the app give about the people who provide the advice content? What advice is given that can help you manage your expenses?

3 Security: Virus, Spyware, and Malware Protection

An operating system should include antivirus, spyware, and malware detection software to fend off intrusions. Major companies that provide this software often include information on their websites about recently discovered virus threats and hoaxes. They also track scheduled virus payload strikes and map global and regional virus attacks.

Research This: Visit at least two virus protection websites to obtain virus information. When were the latest active threats discovered and updated? What are their names and risk levels? When is the next virus payload strike scheduled? What type of malware is spreading via mobile device use? Which virus removal utilities and resources are available?

4 Social Media: Blogs

Operating systems constantly evolve as developers add new features, fix security issues, and modify functions. Computer and mobile device users need to stay abreast of these changes, especially when the updates affect performance and safety. Many blogs feature content about operating systems. Their posts cover industry news, photos, product reviews, previews of forthcoming software and hardware, and management changes. Most of these blogs are unofficial, meaning that the writers are not necessarily employees of the companies that develop the operating systems. The bloggers generally have extensive experience in the technology field and desire to share their expertise with others. Others are contracted or sponsored by operating system developers, who host blogs as part of their company's website.

Research This: Search online for a blog that tracks features or updates to a mobile, desktop, or other operating system that you use or about which you would like more information. Report the web address of the blog, along with a summary of the most recent blog post. What did you learn from the post? What qualifications did the author have? Where was the blog hosted?

Critical Thinking

Instructions: These exercises challenge your assessment and decision-making skills by presenting real-world situations associated with module concepts. The Collaboration exercise should be completed with a team. Evaluate the situations below, using personal experiences and one or more resources available to you (such as articles on the web or in print, blogs, podcasts, videos, television, user guides, other individuals, electronics or computer stores, etc.). Perform the tasks requested in each exercise and share your deliverables in the format requested by your instructor (brief report, presentation, discussion, blog post, video, or other means).

1. Migrating to an SaaS Operating System

You are the office manager at a social media consulting business. The office recently purchased several new computers. You now are running an operating system that requires a subscription for all machines, rather than a one-time license as you had the last time you purchased new computers. Your boss asks you to explain the benefits of the SaaS method and to evaluate long-term costs and benefits.

Do This: Use the web to learn more about SaaS operating system models. Which operating systems offer both a one-time and a subscription payment method? Which operating systems offer only one or the other? How do the costs compare? Read industry experts' reviews of each, and determine what benefits they cite for SaaS operating systems, as well as any disadvantages. Compile your findings.

2. Complete Security Solutions

Your neighbors started a new construction business. They would like to hire you to set up their new computers. Their business will use the Internet to communicate with clients via email, store backups of data, and access cloud-based accounting software. The office will include two networked computers, which will share a printer and an Internet connection. In addition, they will use a tablet so that they can access the cloud-based accounting software using Wi-Fi. Because of security concerns with using the Internet, they first would like you to install a program(s) designed to protect their computers from various security threats.

Do This: Use the web to find answers to the following questions. What types of security threats exist on the Internet that could impact their business? What types of security measures should they use? Evaluate two programs that provide a comprehensive security solution. What are the programs' functions? What are their costs? Do the services charge subscription fees in order to receive automatic updates? Which would you recommend? Why?

3. Case Study

Cooperative-Owned Farm Stand You are the new manager for a farm stand that is a cooperative effort, jointly owned by several local farmers. The owners have asked you to recommend options for new smartphones they are purchasing based on what operating systems would be the best fit.

Do This: Select two mobile operating systems to explore (such as Android, Windows (Mobile Edition), and iOS). Use the web to find industry experts' recommendations and user reviews for each operating system. Include the different device types for which each is available. Examine differences in security, features, speed, and reliability. What security concerns exist? What security features enable you to protect the smartphone and its data? Which mobile operating system offers the best features? Which is considered faster and/or more reliable? Your office computers run macOS. Do compatibility issues exist with any of the mobile operating systems? If so, what are the issues? Can you find solutions that would enable you to sync data? Compile your findings.

Collaboration

4. Desktop Operating Systems

You are an analyst for a marketing company. The company currently uses macOS on its 100 desktops. This year, the company plans to upgrade the operating system and, if necessary, its desktops. The company asks your team to compare the latest versions of the Windows, Mac, and Linux operating systems.

Do This: Form a three-member team and assign each member an operating system. Each member should use the web to develop a feature/benefit analysis and answer the following questions. What is the purchase or subscription cost per computer? What are the memory and storage requirements? Will the operating system require the company to purchase new computers? Which is best at protecting against viruses, spam, and spyware? Which support touch input? As a team, compile your findings and share your recommendation with the class.

Networks and Network Devices:
Communicating and Connecting

iStock.com/Metamorworks

Objectives

After completing this module, you will be able to:

1 Explain how a user interacts with a network
2 Identify types of network structures
3 Describe network standards and protocols
4 Explain how to use hardware to connect to a network
5 Explain how to set up a network
6 Identify network security tools
7 Describe the role of a network professional

How Do You Interact with a Network?

Wherever you go, you most likely will encounter and interact with some type of network. Whether it be a network that supports your cell phone, a wireless network at home, in a coffee shop where you browse the web and check your email, or an enterprise network connecting thousands of users, all networks have the same basic characteristics. Recall that a network is a system of two or more devices linked by wires, cables, or a telecommunications system. Networks allow computers to share resources, such as hardware, software, data, and information.

Different general types of networks exist, such as home networks, corporate networks, wireless networks, wired networks, cellular networks, and GPS networks. For a computer and device to communicate on a network, you must first connect to the network. In addition, the computer or device must be capable of communicating with the network using predefined standards and protocols.

A network requires a combination of hardware and software to operate. Smaller networks usually require simple hardware and can rely on the operating system's features to connect to other devices on the network, while larger networks typically require more sophisticated hardware and software.

Some networks provide connections to the Internet; this requires the services of an ISP. When a network is connected to the Internet, it enables the network to communicate with other networks that also are connected to the Internet, as shown in Figure 9-1.

Most of today's Internet connections are broadband connections, which are capable of transmitting large amounts of data across the network. Remember that with broadband connections, the computers and devices on the network are always connected to the Internet. Because of the risks associated with constant Internet connectivity, you should turn off computers and devices on your network when you are not using them for extended periods of time.

Networks as Communications Systems

Today, even the smallest computers and devices can communicate directly with one another, with hundreds of computers on a corporate network, or with millions of other computers around the globe — often via the Internet. Some communications involve cables and wires; others are sent wirelessly. The process in which two or more computers or devices transfer data, instructions, and information is known as digital communications.

All types of computers and mobile devices serve as sending and receiving devices in a communications system. For successful communications, you need the components shown in Table 9-1. This includes servers, desktops, laptops, tablets, smartphones, portable media players, handheld game devices, and GPS receivers. Communications devices, such as modems, wireless access points, and routers, connect transmission media to a sending or receiving device. Transmission media can be wired or wireless.

Figure 9-1   Networks can share resources and data.

istock.com/OnstOn; iStock.com/tlee000; iStock.com/Grassetto; iStock.com/Ra3rn; iStock.com/Bluebay2014; Blue Vista Design/Shutterstock.com; Ixpert/Shutterstock.com

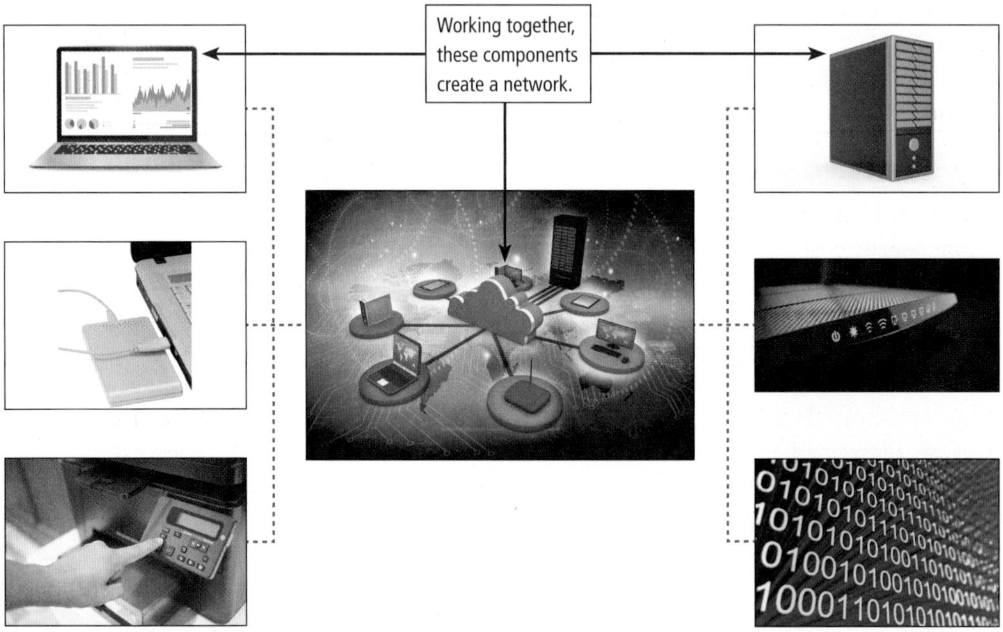

Working together, these components create a network.

Table 9-1 Communication System Components

Device	Purpose
Communications device	Connects the sending device to transmission media
Receiving device	Accepts the transmission of data, instructions, or information
Sending device	Initiates an instruction to transmit data, instructions, or information
Transmission media, or a communications channel	Means by which the data, instructions, or information travel

Network Uses

Networks serve many purposes and are used in more ways than you might imagine. Some common ways in which you will interact with a network include:

- **Facilitating communications.** Using a network, people communicate efficiently and easily via email, Internet messaging, chat rooms, blogs, wikis, online social networks, video calls, online meetings, videoconferences, VoIP, text messaging, and more. Some of these communications occur within an internal network. Other times, they occur globally over the Internet.
- **Sharing hardware.** Each computer or device on a network can be provided access to hardware on the network. For example, each computer and mobile device user can access a printer on the network, as they need it. Thus, home and business users create networks to save money on hardware expenses.
- **Sharing data and information.** Any authorized user can access data and information stored on a network. A large company, for example, might have a database of customer information. Any authorized employee can access the database using a computer or mobile device connected to the network.
- **Sharing software.** Users connected to a network can access software on the network. To support multiple users' software access, vendors often sell versions of their software designed to run on a network or as a web app on the Internet. These network and Internet subscription versions usually cost less than buying individual copies of the software for each computer. The license fees for these programs typically are based on the number of users or the number of computers or mobile devices attached to the network.
- **Sharing files.** A **peer-to-peer (P2P) network**, sometimes called a **file sharing network**, allows users to access one another's hard drives or cloud storage and exchange files directly via a file sharing program (Figure 9-2). As more users connect to the network, each user has access to shared files on other users' hard drives.

Figure 9-2 On a P2P network, each device shares hardware and software with other devices on a network.

Oleksiy/Shutterstock.com; iStock.com/123render; Alex Staroseltsev/Shutterstock.com; Sergey Peterman/Shutterstock.com

When users sign out of the network, others no longer have access to their hard drives.
- **Transferring funds.** **Electronic funds transfer (EFT)** allows users connected to a network to exchange money from one account to another via transmission media. Both businesses and consumers use EFT. Examples include wire transfers, use of credit cards and debit cards, direct deposit of funds into bank accounts, online banking, and online bill payment.

Home and Business Networks

Networks can be classified by their structure, standards, range, and more. Two basic categories of networks are home and business. Unlike other categories used to classify networks, home and business networks are differentiated by their purposes. Home networks typically exist within a single building, are easy to install and configure, and are accessed by only a few users. Networks at your business or school are meant to accommodate many users and large amounts of data and can be spread across many buildings.

Figure 9-3 Typical home network.

Norman Chan/Shutterstock.com; Zsolt Biczo/Shutterstock.com; Science Photo/Shutterstock.com; Source: Lenovo; Natalia Siverina/Shutterstock.com; Maxx-Studio/Shutterstock.com; Maxx-Studio/Shutterstock.com

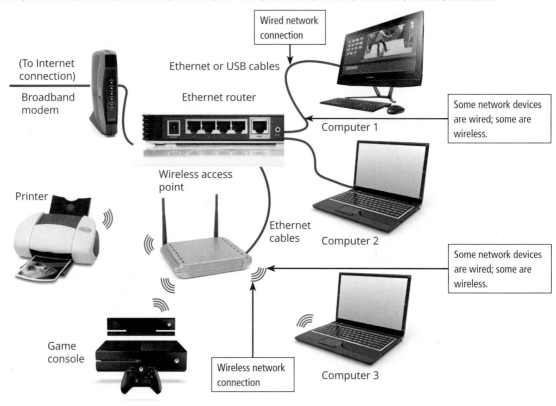

Home Networks   Home networks (Figure 9-3) provide home users with the following capabilities:

- Multiple users can share a single Internet connection.
- Files on each computer, such as photos, can be shared.
- Multiple computers can share a single hardware resource, such as a printer.
- Game consoles can connect to the Internet to facilitate online gaming.
- Voice over IP (VoIP) phone service provides voice communication without the need for traditional, copper telephone lines.
- Smart home devices, such as thermostats, light switches, smart speakers, and personal assistants, can connect to the Internet and to apps on your smartphone.

Business Networks   Business networks can be small or large and can exist in one or multiple buildings. Networks provide the following advantages to businesses:

- Facilitate communication among employees
- Share hardware, such as printers and scanners
- Share data, information, and software with one another
- Centrally store and back up critical information

Businesses use intranets, extranets, and VPNs (virtual private networks) to provide different services to employees

and clients. An **intranet** (intra means within) is an internal network that uses Internet technologies. Sometimes a company uses an **extranet** (extra means outside or beyond), which allows customers or suppliers to access part of its intranet. Organizations use intranets to communicate internally and can allow users to utilize a browser to access data posted on webpages. For example, an extranet might be used if a supplier needs to check a customer's inventory levels before deciding whether to ship additional product. A VPN can allow an individual to access an organization's network by using encryption and other technologies to secure the data transmitted along the path.

Wired and Wireless Networks

A **wired network** sends signals and data through cables, which may have to travel through floors and walls to connect to other network devices. Wired networks tend to be more secure and transmit data faster than wireless networks. A **wireless network** sends signals through airwaves and usually does not require cables. Wireless networks typically are more convenient and easier to set up than wired networks but can be less secure. Wireless networks make it possible to connect devices in locations where physical wiring is not possible or is difficult.

Cellular Networks

In addition to using their mobile phones to make and receive voice calls, millions of people use them to access the Internet. The use of mobile phones to access the Internet has become so popular that providers of mobile phone services continuously have to expand network capacity and support the latest cellular standards to keep up with demand. Various types of cellular networks are available, including 3G, 4G, and 5G. 3G and 4G (the G stands for generation) cellular networks have been the main providers of Internet services in most locations where cellular service is offered. 5G networks provide higher speed data transmission, making them more appealing to those requiring access to high-bandwidth content. 5G is not available everywhere yet, but as it rolls out, most carriers will be providing it as the standard. As cellular standards evolve, it is increasingly likely that home users may use a cellular provider for their Internet service, as opposed to relying on wired connections offered by other providers.

LTE (**Long Term Evolution**) is a network standard that defines how high-speed cellular transmissions use broadcast radio to transmit data for mobile communications. Developed by the Third Generation Partnership Project (3GPP), LTE has the potential of 100 Mbps **downstream rate** (receiving data) and 30 Mbps **upstream rate** (sending data). Based on the TCP/IP network standard, LTE supports data, messaging, voice, and video transmissions. Many mobile service providers, such as AT&T and Verizon Wireless, offer LTE service. Two competing standards for LTE are WiMax (Worldwide Interoperability for Microwave Access) and UMB (Ultra Mobile Broadband).

GPS

A **GPS** (**global positioning system**) is a navigation system that consists of one or more earth-based receivers that accept and analyze signals sent by satellites in order to determine the receiver's geographic location. Many mobile devices, such as smartphones, have GPS capability built into the device or as an add-on feature. Some users carry a handheld GPS receiver; others mount a receiver to an object such as an automobile, a boat, an airplane, farm and construction equipment, or a computer or mobile device. A GPS receiver is a handheld, mountable, or embedded device that contains an antenna, a radio receiver, and a processor. Many include a screen display that shows an individual's location on a map. Figure 9-4 shows how a GPS works.

Figure 9-4   How a GPS might work.

iStock.com/GeorgeManga; Tupungato/Shutterstock.com; Kaczor58/Shutterstock.com; iStock.com/Sebastien Cote; iStock.com/PhotoTalk; 3Dstock/Shutterstock.com; Lithiumphoto/Shutterstock.com; Evgeny Vasenev/Shutterstock.com; Courtesy of Garmin International; Courtesy of Garmin International; Mmaxer/Shutterstock.com; iStock.com/GeorgeManga

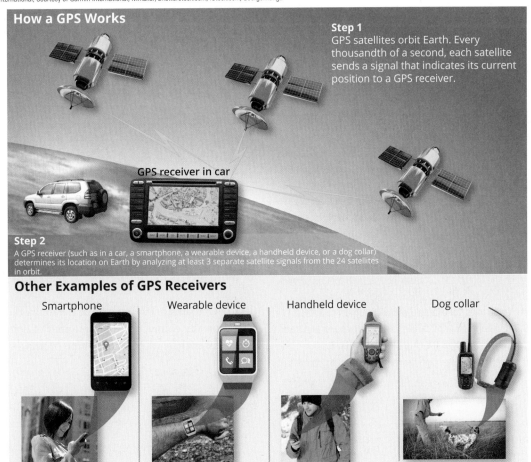

How a GPS Works

Step 1
GPS satellites orbit Earth. Every thousandth of a second, each satellite sends a signal that indicates its current position to a GPS receiver.

GPS receiver in car

Step 2
A GPS receiver (such as in a car, a smartphone, a wearable device, a handheld device, or a dog collar) determines its location on Earth by analyzing at least 3 separate satellite signals from the 24 satellites in orbit.

Other Examples of GPS Receivers

Smartphone   Wearable device   Handheld device   Dog collar

The first and most utilized application of GPS technology is to assist people with determining their location. The data obtained from a GPS, however, can be applied to a variety of other uses: creating a map, ascertaining the best route between two points, locating a lost person or stolen object, monitoring the movement of a person or object, determining altitude, and calculating speed.

Some GPS receivers work in conjunction with a cellular radio network. Parents, for example, can locate the whereabouts of a child who carries a mobile phone with GPS capability or other GPS-enabled device.

Communications Software

Communications software consists of programs and apps that:

- Help users establish a connection to another computer, mobile device, or network
- Manage the transmission of data, instructions, and information
- Provide an interface for users to communicate with one another

The first two often are provided by or included as tools with an operating system or bundled with a communications device. The third is provided by applications such as email, FTP, browsers, discussion boards, chat rooms, Internet messaging, videoconferencing, and VoIP.

Sometimes, communications devices are preprogrammed to accomplish communications tasks. Some routers, for example, contain firmware for various protocols. Other communications devices require separate communications software to ensure proper transmission of data.

❓ Consider This

What are the uses of an intranet?

Recognizing the efficiency and power of the Internet, many organizations apply Internet and web technologies to their internal networks. Intranets generally make company information accessible to employees and facilitate collaboration within an organization. Intranets are preferable when data being transferred should not necessarily reach the Internet. One or more servers on an intranet host an organization's internal webpages, applications, email messages, files, and more. Users locate information, access resources, and update content on an intranet using methods similar to those used on the Internet. A company hosts its intranet on servers different from those used to host its public webpages, apps, and files. Package shipping companies, for example, allow customers to access their intranet via an extranet to print air bills, schedule pickups, and track shipped packages as the packages travel to their destinations.

Network Structures

Home and business networks describe the main users of a network. In addition, networks can be classified by their **topology** (the method by which computers and devices are physically arranged on a network), **network architecture** (the logical design of all devices on a network), and geographic reach. Each of these categories describes a different type of network structure. The same network can be described differently using each of these categories. For example, topology describes the layout of network devices, architecture describes the role of servers and users, and the geographic span of a network determines how wide the network reaches. Networks also can be distinguished by whether or not they use wired cables or are for private or public use.

Network Topologies   Common network topologies include bus network, ring network, star network, and mesh network (Table 9-2). Each topology has its own advantages and disadvantages. Some topologies are more appropriate for small networks, while others might be more appropriate for large networks.

Network Architecture   Two common network architectures are client/server and peer-to-peer (P2P).

On a **client/server network**, one or more computers act as a server and the other computers on the network request resources from the server (Figure 9-5). Recall that a server controls access to hardware, software, and other resources. The server can also provide a centralized storage location that other computers on the network can access. A **client** is a computer or mobile device on the network that relies on the server for its resources. Clients on a client/server network often do not have equal permissions; that is, one client may be able to access certain files or resources on the server, while other clients may not have access to those same resources. Client/server networks often are controlled by a network administrator. An example of a client/server network might be in an organization where employees all have one or more computers or mobile devices that connect to one or more servers for the purpose of sharing files and other resources.

A peer-to-peer (P2P) network is a network architecture that typically connects a small number of computers, often fewer than 10. With this type of network, computers

Table 9-2   Network Topologies

Type	Description	Layout
Bus network	All devices attach to a central cable, called a bus, that carries the data. If the bus fails, the devices on the network will no longer be able to communicate.	
Mesh network	All devices interconnect with one another. If a single device on the network fails, the rest of the network will continue to function by communicating via an alternate route. Two types of mesh topologies are a full mesh topology (each device on the network is connected to every other device on the network) and a partial mesh technology (each device may or may not be connected to all other devices on the network).	
Ring network	Data travels from one device to the next in a sequential fashion. If one device on the network fails, communication on the network could cease to function. Ring networks are no longer common.	
Star network	Each device on the network is attached to a central device, such as a server or switch. If the central device fails, the other devices will be unable to communicate. If a connected device fails, all other devices will still be able to communicate. Two or more star networks may be joined together using a bus to form a tree topology. Tree topologies often are used in schools and businesses.	

communicate directly with one another and can share one another's resources. For example, one computer can use a printer connected to another computer while also requesting and downloading a file stored on a third computer. Because all computers on a P2P network are treated equally, a network administrator often is not required.

An **Internet peer-to-peer (Internet P2P) network** is a type of P2P network where users share files with one another over the Internet. The files in an Internet peer-to-peer network transfer directly from one user's computer to the other, without first being stored on a server. While Internet P2P networking itself is legal, it is illegal to share files or other resources that are protected by copyright.

Figure 9-5   Sample client/server network.

iStock.com/Scanrail; iStock.com/SKrow; iStock.com/Luismmolina; Oleksiy/Shutterstock.com; Anan Chincho/Shutterstock.com;

Geographic Reach   Networks are configured in all sizes and can be defined by not only the number of devices they connect or physical/logical arrangement but also by their geographic footprint. These networks include the following:

- A **local area network (LAN)** connects computers and devices in a limited area, such as a home, a school, or a small office complex (Figure 9-6). A **wireless LAN (WLAN)** is a LAN that uses wireless connections.
- A **wide area network (WAN)** is a network that connects devices in a large geographic region, such as a multinational company or national retail chain. The Internet is classified as a WAN.

- A **metropolitan area network (MAN)** is a type of wide area network that is operated by a city or county.
- A **personal area network (PAN)** connects personal digital devices within a range of approximately 30 feet, such as a smartwatch that connects to your cell phone. Devices on a personal area network typically are connected via Bluetooth, which can facilitate communication at a range of 30 feet/9 meters or less.
- A **body area network (BAN)** is a form of personal area network that consists of small, lightweight biosensors implanted in the body. These biosensors can monitor an individual's health or activity, and report statistics and results to a medical professional.

Figure 9-6   Sample LAN.
Xtuv Photography/Shutterstock.com

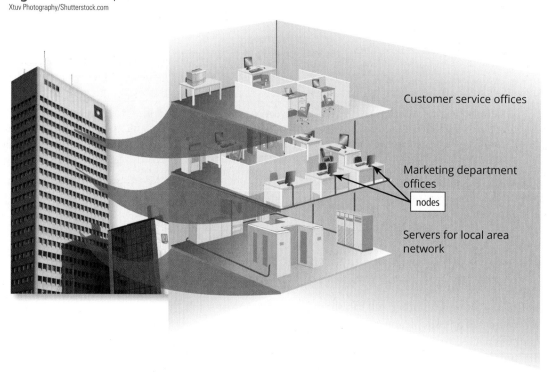

Customer service offices

Marketing department offices

nodes

Servers for local area network

? Consider This

What is a data plan?

A **data plan** specifies the amount of data your provider offers you per month. Your mobile device's data plan enables you to access the Internet through your mobile service provider's network when Wi-Fi is not available. Without a data plan, you must use Wi-Fi or a wired connection to access the Internet on your computer or mobile device. Some mobile service providers offer an unlimited data plan for your device, while many offer limited data plans. If you exceed your data limit in a given month, additional fees apply. By monitoring your data usage to see how much you use on average over a few months, you can decide on the best plan for you. Some carriers offer a shared data plan that provides an allotted amount of data to be shared across several smartphones, tablets, laptops, gaming devices, and mobile hot spots. Using Wi-Fi when available to access the Internet will save on data usage charges if you have a limited data plan.

Network Standards and Protocols

Networks connect terminals, devices, and computers from many different manufacturers across many types of networks. For the different devices to be able to communicate on various types of networks, the networks must use similar techniques of moving data from one application to another. To alleviate the problems of incompatibility and ensure that hardware and software components can be integrated into any network, various organizations, such as ANSI (American National Standards Institute) and IEEE (Institute of Electrical and Electronics Engineers), propose, develop, and approve standards.

Network standards define guidelines that specify the way computers access a network, the type(s) of hardware used, data transmission speeds, and the types of cable and wireless technology used. A protocol is a standard that outlines characteristics of how devices communicate on a network, such as data format, coding schemes, error handling, and the sequence in which data transfers over the network. Network standards and protocols often work together to move data through a network. Some of these standards define how a network is arranged physically, while others specify how messages travel along a network. Thus, as data moves through a network from one program to another, it may use one or more of these standards. Table 9-3 identifies some of the more widely used network communications standards and protocols for both wired and wireless networks.

Network Standards

For computers and devices to successfully communicate on a network, they must support the same network standards.

Hardware and software manufacturers design their products to meet the guidelines specified in a particular standard, so that their devices can communicate with the network. A network standard defines guidelines that specify the way computers access the medium to which they are connected, the type(s) of medium used, the speeds used on different types of networks, and the type(s) of physical cable and/or the wireless technology used.

The most common standard for wired networks is Ethernet. The Ethernet standard controls how network interface cards (NICs), routers, and modems share access to cables and phone lines, as well as dictates how to transmit data.

Most businesses use a standard, such as EDI (electronic data interchange), that defines how business documents travel across transmission media. For example, businesses use EDI to send bids and proposals, place and track orders, and send invoices.

Internet Protocols

A protocol may define data format, coding schemes, error handling, and the sequence in which data transfers over a network. One common family of protocols is TCP/IP (Transmission Control Protocol/Internet Protocol), which is a set of protocols that is used by all computers and devices on the Internet. TCP defines how data is routed through a network, and IP specifies that all computers and devices connected to a network have a unique IP address.

Two types of IP addresses exist: IPv4 (Internet Protocol version 4) and IPv6 (Internet Protocol version 6). IPv4 was the standard Internet protocol in use for many years, but the rapidly increasing number of computers and devices connected to the Internet demanded support for more IP

Table 9-3 Network Standards and Protocols

Name	Type	Sample Usage
Bluetooth	Protocol	Wireless headset
IrDA	Standard	Remote control
LTE	Standard	Mobile phones
NFC	Protocol	Mobile phone payment
RFID	Protocol	Tollbooth
TCP/IP	Protocol	Internet
Token ring	Standard	LAN
UWB	Standard	Inventory tracking
Wi-Fi	Standard	Hot spots

addresses. As a result, the IPv6 protocol was developed. The IPv4 protocol supports nearly 4.3 billion unique IP addresses, while the newer IPv6 protocol supports more than 340 undecillion (3.4×10^{38}) addresses.

Close-Distance Communications Protocols

Many network standards and protocols define the network type and purpose, some of which have already been discussed. In addition to network protocols for LANs, WANs, and MANs, other wireless protocols support close-distance communication. These standards include Wi-Fi, LTE, Bluetooth, UWB, IrDA, RFIC, and NFC. Table 9-4 summarizes these common close-distance network protocols.

Wi-Fi Computers and devices that have the appropriate wireless capability can communicate via radio waves with other computers or devices using Wi-Fi, which identifies any network based on the 802.11 standards. Developed by IEEE, 802.11 is a series of network standards that specifies how two wireless devices communicate over the air with each other. Common standards include 802.11a, 802.11b, 802.11g, 802.11n, 802.11ac, and 802.11ax, with data transfer rates ranging from 11 Mbps to 7 Gbps. Many devices support multiple standards. For example, a designation of 802.11 ac/b/g/n/ac/ax on a computer, router, or other device indicates it supports those six standards (ac, b, g, n, ac, and ax).

Wi-Fi sometimes is referred to as wireless Ethernet because it uses techniques similar to the Ethernet standard to specify how physically to configure a wireless network. Thus, Wi-Fi networks easily can be integrated with wired Ethernet networks. When a Wi-Fi network accesses the Internet, it works in conjunction with the TCP/IP network standard.

One popular use of the Wi-Fi network standard is in hot spots that offer mobile users the ability to connect to the Internet with their Wi-Fi-enabled wireless computers and devices. Many homes and small businesses also use Wi-Fi to network computers and devices wirelessly. In open or outdoor areas free from interference, the computers or devices should be within 300 feet of a wireless access point or hot spot. In closed areas, the wireless network range is about 100 feet. To obtain communications at the maximum distances, you may need to install extra hardware to extend or strengthen a wireless signal.

Bluetooth Bluetooth is a network protocol that defines how two Bluetooth devices use short-range radio waves to transmit data. The data transfers between devices at a rate of up to 3 Mbps. To communicate with each other, Bluetooth devices often must be within about 33 feet but can be extended to about 325 feet with additional equipment.

Most mobile devices and computers manufactured today are equipped with Bluetooth capability. One of the earliest and most popular uses of Bluetooth is to connect hands-free headsets to a mobile phone. Bluetooth has many additional uses, and device manufacturers are increasingly including Bluetooth technology.

A Bluetooth device contains a small chip that allows it to communicate with other Bluetooth devices. For computers and devices that are not Bluetooth-enabled, you can purchase a Bluetooth wireless port adapter that will convert an existing USB port into a Bluetooth port. Most current operating systems have built-in Bluetooth support. When connecting two devices using Bluetooth, the originating device sends a code to the connecting device. The codes must match to establish the connection. Devices that share a Bluetooth connection are said to be paired.

Table 9-4 Close-Distance Network Protocols

Network Protocol	Common Use
Bluetooth	Devices communicating with one another over a short range (usually less than 30 feet/9 meters)
IrDA	Remote controls or other data transmission within close proximity
LTE	Uses radio signals to communicate data over cellular networks
NFC (near field communication)	Used in credit cards, smartphones, and tickets to facilitate close-range communication
RFID (radio frequency identification)	Radio signals transmitted through antennas, often found in tollbooth transponders or embedded chips in animals
UWB	Low-energy radio technology for short-range, high-bandwidth communications
Wi-Fi	Hot spots and wireless home and small business networks using TCP/IP

You can use Bluetooth-enabled or Bluetooth-enhanced devices in many ways, including the following:

- Connect devices, such as mobile phones, portable media players, or GPS devices, with vehicle stereos, which use the vehicle's speakers to project sound (Figure 9-7).
- Use GPS receivers to send directions to a mobile phone or GPS-enabled device.
- Transfer photos wirelessly from a digital camera to a laptop or server.
- Play music on a smartphone through the speakers on a computer or other Bluetooth-enabled device.
- Send signals between video game accessories, video game devices, and a television.
- Establish a PAN.
- Allow communications between a computer and devices, such as a keyboard, printer, Smart TV, or mobile phone. Connecting these devices enables you to print documents, share calendar appointments, and more.
- Replace wired communications devices, such as bar code readers, with wireless devices to enhance portability.
- Transmit data from a medical device, such as a blood glucose monitor, to a mobile phone or other device.
- Change the channel, pause a program, or schedule a recording using a Bluetooth-compatible or Bluetooth-enabled television and remote control.
- Track objects that include tags or nodes used to send wireless signals read by a real-time location system.

UWB UWB (ultra-wideband) is a network standard that specifies how two UWB devices use short-range radio waves to communicate at high speeds with each other. At distances of about 33 feet, the data transfer rate is 110 Mbps. At closer distances, such as about 6.5 feet, the transfer rate is at least 480 Mbps. UWB can transmit signals through doors and other obstacles. Because of its high transfer rates, UWB is best suited for transmission of large files, such as video, graphics, and audio. Examples of UWB uses include locating and tracking inventory, equipment, or personnel (especially in remote or dangerous areas).

IrDA Some devices, such as television remote controls, use the IrDA (Infrared Data Association) standard to transmit data wirelessly to each other via infrared (IR) light waves. The devices transfer data at rates from 115 Kbps (thousand bits per second) to 4 Mbps between their IrDA ports. Infrared requires line-of-sight transmission; that is, the sending device and the receiving device must be in line with each other so that nothing obstructs the path of the infrared light wave. Because Bluetooth and UWB do not require line-of-sight transmission, these technologies are more widespread than IrDA.

RFID RFID (radio frequency identification) is a protocol that defines how a network uses radio signals to communicate with a tag placed in or attached to an object, an animal, or a person. The tag, called a transponder, consists of an antenna and a memory chip that contains the information to be transmitted via radio waves. Through an antenna, an RFID

Figure 9-7   Connecting your phone to your car's Bluetooth.

Adisa/Shutterstock.com; Vartanov Anatoly/Shutterstock.com; Pakhnyushchy/Shutterstock.com

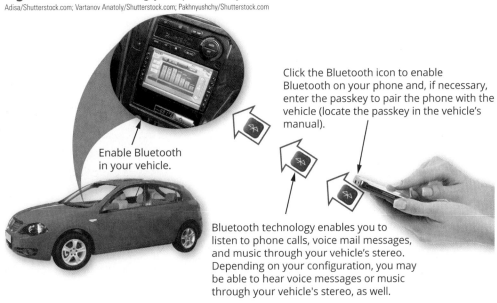

Enable Bluetooth in your vehicle.

Click the Bluetooth icon to enable Bluetooth on your phone and, if necessary, enter the passkey to pair the phone with the vehicle (locate the passkey in the vehicle's manual).

Bluetooth technology enables you to listen to phone calls, voice mail messages, and music through your vehicle's stereo. Depending on your configuration, you may be able to hear voice messages or music through your vehicle's stereo, as well.

Figure 9-8 How electronic RFID toll collection works.

iStock.com/Benkrut; Courtesy of Misty Vermaat; Courtesy of Misty Vermaat; Vibrant Image Studio/Shutterstock.com; iStock.com/Luismmolina

How Electronic RFID Toll Collection Works

Step 1
Motorist purchases an RFID transponder or RFID tag and attaches it to the vehicle's windshield.

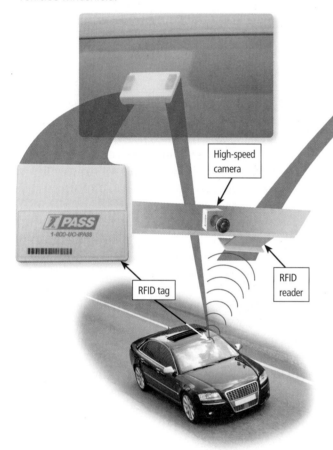

High-speed camera

RFID tag

RFID reader

Step 2
As the vehicle approaches the tollbooth, the RFID reader in the tollbooth sends a radio wave that activates the windshield-mounted RFID tag. The activated tag sends vehicle information to the RFID reader.

Step 3
The RFID reader sends the vehicle information to the lane controller. The lane controller, which is part of a local area network transmits the vehicle information to a central computer that subtracts the toll from the motorist's account. If the vehicle does not have an RFID tag, a high-speed camera takes a picture of the license plate and the computer prints a violation notice, which is mailed to the motorist.

reader, also called a transceiver, reads the radio signals and transfers the information to a computer or computing device. Depending on the type of RFID reader, the distance between the tag and the reader ranges from 5 inches to 300 feet or more. Readers can be handheld or embedded in an object, such as a doorway or a tollbooth (Figure 9-8).

NFC NFC (near field communications) is a protocol, based on RFID, that defines how a network uses close-range radio signals to communicate between two devices or objects equipped with NFC technology (Figure 9-9). Examples of NFC-enabled devices include smartphones, digital cameras, televisions, and terminals. Credit cards, tickets, and NFC tags are examples of objects that also use NFC technology. An NFC tag is a chip that can store small amounts of data. NFC tags are in a variety of objects, such as posters, ski lift tickets, business cards, stickers, and wristbands.

Figure 9-9 NFC communication examples.

Alexander Kirch/Shutterstock.com; iStock.com/Cheyennezj; iStock.com/Pierrephoto

NFC-enabled credit card

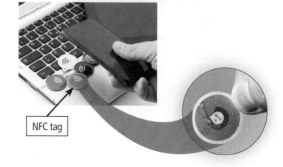

NFC tag

Consider This

What are the advantages and disadvantages of using Bluetooth technology?

Bluetooth has many advantages, including the following:

- If a device has Bluetooth capability, using Bluetooth technology is free.
- Although Bluetooth devices need to be near each other (approximately within 30 feet or 10 meters), they do not have to be in the same room, within the same line of sight, or facing each other.
- They typically require low processing power and use little energy, so using this technology will not drain a device's battery.
- Establishing a wireless Bluetooth connection requires only a few simple steps.
- Connections have low security risks.
- Bluetooth technology is standardized globally, meaning it can be used to connect devices that are not the same make or model.
- Connections have little risk of interference with other wireless networks, because the strength of the wireless signals is weak and because of frequency hopping, which changes frequency channels periodically.

Disadvantages of Bluetooth technology include:

- It has low bandwidth, which limits its range and capabilities.
- Its slow data transfer speeds mean Bluetooth technology is not an ideal solution for replacing a LAN.
- Bluetooth-enabled mobile payment services are new, which means they may invite security risks.

Most analysts agree that the advantages of Bluetooth technology far outweigh the disadvantages.

Network Connection Hardware

Nodes, or devices on a network, can be computers, tablets, mobile phones, printers, game consoles, or smart home devices. Other network elements that you have been introduced to that help facilitate communication include the following:

- Hubs provide a central point for network cables in a network and are used to transfer data to all devices.
- Switches, used more frequently than hubs, also provide a central point for network cables in a network; however, they transfer data only to the intended recipient.
- Routers, which connect two or more networks and direct, or route, the flow of information along the networks or to the Internet so that multiple users can share a connection.
- A modem connects a sending or receiving device, such as a computer, to a communications channel, such as the Internet. The modem connects your network to the Internet through an ISP.

Most modems are digital. A **digital modem**, also called a broadband modem, is a communications device that sends and receives data and information to and from a digital line. Three types of digital modems are cable modems, DSL modems, and ISDN modems. A **cable modem** uses a cable TV connection. A splitter connects one part of the cable to your cable box or device, and the other part to the cable modem. Figure 9-10 illustrates a typical cable modem installation. A **DSL modem** uses standard copper telephone wiring. Similarly, an ISDN (Integrated Services Digital Network) modem is a broadband modem that sends digital data and information from a computer to an ISDN line and receives digital data and information from an ISDN line. DSL and ISDN modems usually are external devices, in which one end connects to the phone line and the other end connects to a port on the computer. Figure 9-11 shows an example of a cable modem and a wireless router.

Figure 9-10 Typical cable modem installation.

iStock.com/Tiridifilm; Image100/Alamy Stock Photo; iStock.com/SKrow; Pablo Eder/Shutterstock.com

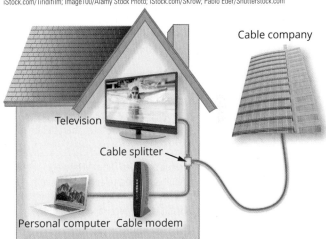

Figure 9-11 Cable modem and wireless router.

Norman Chan/Shutterstock.com

Communications Lines

A **dedicated line** is a type of always-on physical connection that is established between two communications devices. Businesses often use dedicated lines to connect geographically distant offices. Dedicated lines can be either analog or digital. Recall that analog devices read or produce physical signals in their original form, whereas digital devices use data that has been changed into a form that computers and other devices can use. **Multiplexing** is a process that combines multiple analog or digital signals into a single signal over a shared medium, such as a cable. Digital lines increasingly are connecting home and business users to networks around the globe because they transmit data and information at faster rates than analog lines.

Digital dedicated lines include cable television lines, DSL, ISDN lines, FTTP, T-carrier lines, and ATM (Table 9-5).

Table 9-5 Digital Dedicated Lines

Type	Description
Cable	The cable television (CATV) network provides high-speed Internet connections. The CATV signal enters a building through a single line, usually a coaxial cable, which connects to a modem that typically attaches to your computer via an Ethernet cable.
DSL, ADSL	DSL (Digital Subscriber Line) transmits on existing standard copper phone wiring. ADSL (asymmetric digital subscriber line) is a type of DSL that supports faster downstream rates than upstream rates.
ISDN	ISDN (Integrated Services Digital Network) refers to both a circuit-switched telephone network system and a set of communication standards used to transmit data, voice, and signaling.
FTTP	FTTP (Fiber to the Premises) uses fiber-optic cable to provide extremely high-speed Internet access to a user's physical permanent location. An optical terminal at your location receives the signals and transfers them to a router connected to a computer.
T-Carrier	Any of several types of long-distance digital phone lines that carry multiple signals over a single communications line. Digital T-carrier lines use multiplexing so that multiple signals share the line. T-carrier lines provide very fast data transfer rates. Only medium to large companies usually can afford the investment in T-carrier lines because these lines are so expensive. The most popular T-carrier line is the T1 line. Main users of T3 lines include large corporations, phone companies,

Type	Description
	and ISPs connecting to the Internet backbone. The Internet backbone itself also uses T3 lines.
ATM	ATM (Asynchronous Transfer Mode) is a service that carries voice, data, video, and media at very high speeds. Phone networks, the Internet, and other networks with large amounts of traffic use ATM.

❓ Consider This

How many connections can a router support?
Although a router may be able to connect more than 200 wired and/or wireless computers and mobile devices, the performance of the router may decline as you add connections. Some mobile service providers limit the number of connections to their mobile broadband wireless routers. For this reason, you should monitor the devices connected to your network, whether you have a home network or are a network administrator. Check the capabilities of your network and analyze whether it is sufficient for your current and future needs. For example, if you own a small business with plans to expand, it may be more cost-effective to purchase network equipment that will support your planned expansions.

How To: Set Up a Network

A home network enables you to use a common Internet connection among many computers and mobile devices. Other uses include connecting entertainment devices, such as digital video recorders (DVRs) and televisions, to the Internet and establishing a connection between devices in order to play multi-player games.

Before purchasing hardware or contracting a network expert to set up your network, consider how your network will be used and by whom. Ask yourself the following questions:

- What devices will connect to the network? The number of devices, as well as the operating system or platform on which the devices operate, will determine the speed and strength needed to run your wireless network.
- How wide of a range do you need, and where will most of the use take place? If you have a small apartment, your needs will differ from those with a large home.
- How many users typically will be using the network, how will they use it, and for what purposes? The number

of users affects the capabilities of the network and determines whether you need to define permissions for certain users or devices.

- How secure must your network be? Hiding the network name, requiring passwords, or having a user with network administration capabilities can help ensure your network is safe from unauthorized use.

Set Up a Home Wireless Network

A home network can be as simple as using a cable to connect two devices. More complex home networks include wireless technologies that connect several devices to one another and to the Internet. Hardware needed for a wireless, Internet-connected home network includes the following: a modem, a router, a wireless access point, and devices that you will connect to your network.

The steps required to install a home wireless network may vary depending on factors such as the type of wireless network hardware you purchase, the size of your home, and the devices you want to connect to the wireless network. The following general steps describe how to set up a home wireless network.

1. Purchase a modem or separate wireless router and connect it to your home's Internet service.
2. Review the documentation that came with your wireless modem or router to perform the following tasks:
   a. Enable the wireless network.
   b. Configure a name for the network.
   c. Configure a wireless network key.
3. For each device you want to connect to the wireless network, perform the following tasks:
   a. Enable the device's wireless functionality.
   b. Search for and connect to the name of the wireless network you specified in Step 2b.
   c. Enter the wireless network key you set in Step 2c.

Once you configure your wireless network, you can create usernames and user groups. Names and groups establish network users, who can share files (such as documents, music, and photos), as well as devices (such as printers) with others connected to the network.

Maintaining the network involves monitoring the security settings and network activity, establishing connections to new devices as needed, and enhancing the wireless signal if necessary. Wireless home network speeds and ranges vary. The strength of the wireless signal affects the range of the network.

Add a Printer to a Network

Adding a wireless printer to a home or small office network has several advantages. For example, multiple computers and mobile devices on the network can use the printer. You also can place the printer anywhere in the home or office, as long as it is within range of the wireless signal. For example, a wireless router can be on the first floor of your house, and a wireless printer can be on the second floor. Once the printer is installed on the network, you can download an app from the manufacturer to send documents to the printer from network-connected devices (Figure 9-12). The following steps describe how to add a wireless printer to a home/small office network:

Figure 9-12 Sending a document to a wireless printer.
iStock.com/Baloon111

1. Determine the location to install the wireless printer. This location must have an electrical outlet for the printer and also be within range of the wireless network. You can check the strength of wireless signals in your home or office by walking around with a mobile computer or device while connected to the network and monitoring the signal strength.
2. Be sure to place the printer on a stable surface.
3. Access the printer's settings and navigate to the network settings.
4. Connect to the wireless network in your home or small office. If necessary, specify the encryption key for your network.
5. Enter any remaining required information.
6. Install the printer app on the computer(s) and devices from which you want to print to the wireless printer.
7. Verify the devices are able to print successfully using the wireless printer.

Strengthen Your Wireless Signal

If you reside in a large apartment or house and use a wireless network, you may find that you either experience poor network performance or are unable to access the network in certain locations. These problems may be related to a weak wireless signal in your home. Various options are available to strengthen a wireless signal to increase network performance and ensure you have a wireless connection throughout your home. The following points describe how to strengthen a wireless signal:

- If your wireless router or wireless access point has an antenna(s), make sure the antenna(s) is extended completely.
- If you are able to remove the antenna(s) from your wireless router or wireless access point, consider replacing it with a wireless signal booster (Figure 9-13). Check your device's and the wireless signal booster's documentation to determine whether it will work with your device.

Figure 9-13   Wireless signal booster.

iStock.com/Lobro78

- If possible, position the wireless router or wireless access point in a central location of your home and away from appliances or other electronic devices that may degrade the signal.
- Purchase a **booster**, which is an amplifier used to improve reception and extend the range, for your wireless router or wireless access point. Boosters also are called **repeaters**. Some range extenders are compatible only with specific wireless routers or wireless access points, and others are universal. Make sure the range extender you purchase is compatible with your device. Once installed, follow the range extender's instructions to enable it on your network.

- If you still experience problems with the strength of your wireless signal after following the suggestions above, consider replacing your wireless router or wireless access point with a newer model.

❓ Consider This

Can IP addresses be used to determine a computer or device's location?

In many cases, you can determine a computer or a device's location from its IP address. For example, if an IP address begins with 132.170, a minimal amount of research will uncover that the University of Central Florida assigns IP addresses beginning with these numbers; however, additional research would be necessary to determine where the computer or mobile device is located on the network. Certain websites allow visitors to find a location by entering an IP address. Some web apps infer your approximate location from your IP address when GPS is not available in order to provide you with local information or nearby search results. Have you ever noticed on a website that it has detected your location? How did/could you tell? What concerns do you have about this? What advantages are there to having your location known?

Secure IT: Secure a Network

You should consider several risks when using a connected network, many of which you have been introduced to. Table 9-6 summarizes common network risks. Arguably, wireless networks can be the most vulnerable because it is easier to connect to wireless networks than wired networks. You have already learned about changing the default password for your wireless access point, changing the SSID name, using encryption, and enabling a MAC address. If you have set up a wireless network at your home, consider taking these additional safety precautions to keep it as secure as possible. Wireless network settings usually can be changed by accessing the wireless router with a web browser. Review the manual for your router for more information on changing settings.

- Regularly change your wireless network key.
- If possible, regularly review the number of devices that are connected to your wireless network. If the number of connected devices exceeds what you are expecting, you might need to change the wireless network key.
- Regularly check for and perform updates to your router's software to make sure you benefit from all security improvements and feature enhancements.
- Require authorization such as a username or password to sign in, so that only recognized individuals are able to connect to it and access the information stored on its devices, while at the same time keeping unauthorized individuals from connecting to it.
- Install a firewall to keep out unauthorized traffic.

Table 9-6 Common Network Risks

Risk	Description
Adware	Displays unwanted advertisements on your computer
Spyware	Tracks and transmits personal information from your computer or device without your knowledge
Virus	Damages data on your computer or device or changes system settings
Worm	Spreads throughout a computer and/or network without requiring user interaction
Trojan	Disguises itself as or hides itself in a legitimate file and then causes damage to programs and data when opened
Ransomware	Locks you out of programs and data on your computer until you pay a ransom to regain access
Rootkit	Gains administrator-level, or root-level, access to a computer or network without the system or users detecting its presence

Figure 9-14 shows examples of some of the methods you can use to secure a network.

Secure Network Data

Because data and information stored on computers or devices connected to a network may be accessible by other computers and devices on the network, it is important to secure the data to prevent access by unauthorized individuals. One way to store data on a network is by using network attached storage. Recall that network attached storage (NAS) devices are one or more hard drives that connect directly to a network and provide a centralized location for storing programs and data on large and small networks. On a home network, you might store family photos and videos so that they are accessible to all members of your family. On a larger, more complex network, you might store important company files that require accessibility by multiple employees.

When you store files on a network, you might have the ability to specify users who can view the files, as well as users

Figure 9-14 Securing a network.

Chaoss/Shutterstock.com; Bofotolux/Shutterstock.com; Beboy/Shutterstock.com; Nelia Sapronova/Shutterstock.com; Ymgerman/Shutterstock.com

Encryption scrambles or codes data as it is transmitted over a network.

Authentication identifies you to the network. The most common type of authentication is providing a username and password.

Firewalls create a blockade between corporate or personal networks and the Internet.

Biometric devices authenticate identity by scanning your physical characteristics, such as a fingerprint.

who can view and make changes to the files. For example, if a company's financial documents are stored on a network, you might choose to let all company employees view the documents but allow only executives and accounting personnel to make changes to the documents. Be careful not to grant individuals more permissions than necessary, as this inadvertently can lead to undesired changes to files.

Other measures you can take to secure network data includes using encryption and monitoring network traffic.

Encryption To further ensure network data is safe, you also should turn on network encryption so that information from files being transmitted on the network cannot be intercepted by others. If you are connected to a wireless network, make sure the network supports encryption so that your data cannot be intercepted easily by others.

Encrypted wireless networks often use a **wireless network key**, a series of numbers and/or letters sometimes also referred to as a network security key, to encrypt data sent between devices. Before you are able to use an encrypted wireless network, you must first enter the correct key. Both the sending and receiving device must know the key to communicate on the wireless network. When you attempt to connect to a wireless network requiring a wireless network key, you will be prompted to enter the key when you initiate the connection. If you connect to a wireless network that does not require a wireless network key, that often means the network is unsecure, and you should avoid transmitting private information. You can specify the type of encryption, as well as the desired wireless network key, through the wireless router's configuration utility that is often accessible using a browser.

Monitor Network Traffic Network monitoring software constantly assesses the status of a network and sends an email or text message, usually to the network administrator, when it detects a problem. These messages may state that an outage has occurred, the server's available memory space is near capacity, a new user account has been added, or some other critical event has developed.

Monitoring software can measure the amount of network traffic, graph network usage, determine when a specific program uses the network, and show the bandwidth used by each computer or mobile device. On networks that use the TCP/IP protocol, for example, **packet sniffer** software monitors and logs packet traffic for later analysis. Packet sniffing can detect problems, such as why network traffic is flowing slowly.

The software also can play a security role, including identifying unusual or excessive network activity. For example, it can flag a remote computer always connected to the network or someone making repeated attempts to sign in to an account. Hackers use packet sniffer software to hijack a computer, which means they capture a user's packets and then reconstruct the contents of webpages that were visited, obtain usernames and passwords, and trace photos and videos viewed.

Detecting an Intruder to a Network

One of the largest Internet security threats is **IP hijacking**, which occurs when cyberthieves tap into home routers or cable modems or other Internet access points to intercept a paid Internet service. Some cyberthieves use the connection to commit illegal acts; others just steal the Internet connection. The incidences of IP hijacking are growing, and catching thieves is a difficult task for law enforcement officials.

Unscrupulous people hijack Internet service in one of two ways. Either the network has no security, or the thieves determine the network name and password and then reprogram their modem's settings to duplicate the network's settings. Experts recommend using the following steps to determine if someone is accessing a wireless network without permission:

- **Sign in to the administrative interface.** The modem's user's guide will provide instructions to view wireless clients actively using a wireless access point.
- **Count the number of connected devices.** Each device connected wirelessly to the network should be displayed in a table that shows, at a minimum, the device's name, MAC address, and IP address. Wireless devices that might be connected to the network include smartphones, game consoles, DVD players, and other hardware. If the number of devices seems unusually high, use a MAC lookup website, which can help you to determine the manufacturer of wireless devices in the list.
- **Secure the network.** The router's manufacturer's website should provide instructions about upgrading the security strength. Change the default network name and password, and be certain to use the latest wireless encryption technology. Enable the router's firewall and, if possible, use "stealth mode" to make the network less visible to outsiders. Disable the feature that allows users to administer the router wirelessly, so that changes can be made only when using a physical connection with an Ethernet cable.

❓ Consider This

What is Bluebugging?

Although Bluetooth technology generally has low security risks, security experts have seen an increase in **Bluebugging**, which occurs when cyberthieves exploit Bluetooth devices that have been paired. Hackers can intercept the signals, then take control and read or download personal data, place calls, monitor conversations, review text and email messages, and modify contacts. To prevent Bluebugging, turn off Bluetooth capability if it is not required, and use a Bluetooth earpiece only when you need to be hands free. Avoid using your device in crowded areas, and pair your devices for the first time in a secure environment, such as your home. Ensure your device's visibility setting is hidden and all paired devices are set to unauthorized so that the user must authorize each connection request. Upgrade your phone, because older devices are more vulnerable to these intrusions. Have you or someone you know been a victim of Bluebugging? How did/would you know? What damages might you incur if you are a victim?

Ethics & Issues: Responsibilities of a Network Professional

The role of a network administrator is to plan, design, purchase equipment for, set up, secure, and maintain a network (Figure 9-15). A trained network professional will know how to accomplish these tasks using hardware and software and will be able to create a network that not only is usable, but one that protects the data, devices, and systems. The network administrator will be able to provide network access and accounts to remote and in-person users on a variety of devices.

Figure 9-15 A network administrator is in a position of trust.
iStock.com/Gorodenkoff

In the course of doing their job, network administrators have access to vast amounts of data that needs to be protected. That data can include sensitive company information, employees' personnel files, and communications among employees. Keeping this data secure from unauthorized access is one of the main responsibilities of a network administrator. Unauthorized access may not be just from hackers but also from users on the network whose account authorizations enable them to see information that they are not supposed to.

USENIX is a nonprofit organization that was founded in 1975 to support network and system engineers and operators in innovation and research. It developed a code of ethics for system operators that provides standards for network administrators. The code includes guidelines for professionalism, personal integrity, privacy, laws and policies, communication, system integrity, education, responsibility to computing community, social responsibility, and ethical responsibility:

Professionalism

- I will maintain professional conduct in the workplace and will not allow personal feelings or beliefs to cause me to treat people unfairly or unprofessionally.

Personal Integrity

- I will be honest in my professional dealings and forthcoming about my competence and the impact of my mistakes. I will seek assistance from others when required.
- I will avoid conflicts of interest and biases whenever possible. When my advice is sought, if I have a conflict of interest or bias, I will declare it if appropriate, and recuse myself if necessary.

Privacy

- I will access private information on computer systems only when it is necessary in the course of my technical duties. I will maintain and protect the confidentiality of any information to which I may have access, regardless of the method by which I came into knowledge of it.

Laws and Policies

- I will educate myself and others on relevant laws, regulations, and policies regarding the performance of my duties.

Communication

- I will communicate with management, users, and colleagues about computer matters of mutual interest. I will strive to listen to and understand the needs of all parties.

System Integrity

- I will strive to ensure the necessary integrity, reliability, and availability of the systems for which I am responsible.
- I will design and maintain each system in a manner to support the purpose of the system to the organization.

Education

- I will continue to update and enhance my technical knowledge and other work-related skills. I will share my knowledge and experience with others.

Responsibility to Computing Community

- I will cooperate with the larger computing community to maintain the integrity of network and computing resources.

Social Responsibility

- As an informed professional, I will encourage the writing and adoption of relevant policies and laws consistent with these ethical principles.

Ethical Responsibility

- I will strive to build and maintain a safe, healthy, and productive workplace.
- I will do my best to make decisions consistent with the safety, privacy, and well-being of my community and the public, and to disclose promptly factors that might pose unexamined risks or dangers.
- I will accept and offer honest criticism of technical work as appropriate and will credit properly the contributions of others.
- I will lead by example, maintaining a high ethical standard and degree of professionalism in the performance of all my duties. I will support colleagues and coworkers in following this code of ethics.

 Consider This

How else can a network administrator provide access?

Instead of using the Internet or investing in and administering an internal network, some companies hire a value-added network provider for network functions. A **value-added network (VAN)** provider is a third-party business that provides networking services, such as EDI services, secure data and information transfer, storage, or email programs. With EDI services, a VAN can enable users to exchange funds with other users or businesses without establishing a direct connection between the two accounts. The transaction takes place without security risk to the other party's funding source (such as a bank account or credit card). Businesses that use VANs rely on their security, accuracy, and efficiency. Some VANs, such as PayPal, charge an annual or monthly fee; others charge by the service used. What advantages could you see to using a VAN? What disadvantages might there be? Would you use a VAN? Why or why not? If so, for what purpose?

Study Guide

Instructions: The Study Guide exercise reinforces material you should know after reading this module. Answer the questions below using the format that helps you remember best or that is required by your instructor. Possible formats may include one or more of these options: write the answers; create a document that contains the answers; record answers as audio or video using a webcam, smartphone, or portable media player; post answers on a blog, wiki, or website; or highlight answers in the book/ebook.

1. Most of today's Internet connections are _____ connections, which are capable of transmitting large amounts of data across the network.

2. List the components you need for successful communications.

3. List ways a user interacts with a network.

4. Explain how P2P networks function, and describe the uses of P2P file sharing.

5. Define the term, EFT. List uses for EFT.

6. List capabilities of a home network.

7. Explain advantages to a business to using a network.

8. Define the terms, intranet and extranet. Explain how businesses use both.

9. Differentiate between a wired and wireless network.

10. Describe cellular networks. What is the advantage of 4G and 5G networks?

11. Define the term, GPS. Explain how GPS can be used.

12. List examples of uses of communication software.

13. Define the terms, topology and network architecture.

14. List examples of network topologies.

15. On a(n) _____ network, one or more computers act as a server and the other computers on the network request resources from the server. Define the term, client.

16. Differentiate among LANs, WLANs, WANs, MANs, PANs, and BANs.

17. Define the term, data plan. Explain how you can limit your data usage.

18. Define the term, network standard. Explain how network standards and protocols work together.

19. Define the terms, Ethernet and EDI.

20. Describe how TCP/IP is used on computers and devices on the Internet and networks.

21. List examples of close-distance communications protocols.

22. _____ is a series of network standards that specifies how two wireless devices communicate over the air with each other.

23. Differentiate between upstream and downstream rates.

24. Describe the uses of the following close-distance protocols: LTE, UWB, IrDA, RFID, and NFC. LTE stands for Long Term _____.

25. List uses of Bluetooth. Describe advantages of using Bluetooth.

26. List hardware devices required to set up a network.

27. Differentiate among digital, cable, and DSL modems.

28. Define the terms, dedicated line and multiplexing.

29. Explain considerations regarding the number of devices a router can support.

30. List questions to ask during the planning process of setting up a network.

31. List steps for setting up a home wireless network.

32. List steps for adding a printer to a home wireless network.

33. Explain methods to strengthen your wireless signal.

34. Explain considerations for using an IP address to determine a device's location.

35. List common network security risks.

36. Explain methods to secure your network.

37. Explain how to secure network data.

38. Define the term, wireless network key.

39. Explain the purpose of a packet sniffer.

40. Define the term, IP hijacking.

41. List steps to determine if someone is accessing a wireless network without permission.

42. Describe how to prevent Bluebugging.

43. Explain the responsibilities of a network administrator.

44. List guidelines network administrators should follow regarding professionalism, personal integrity, privacy, laws and policies, communication, system integrity, education, responsibility to computing community, social responsibility, and ethical responsibility.

Key Terms

You should be able to define the Key Terms listed below.

802.11 (9-10)
Bluebugging (9-19)
Bluetooth (9-10)
body area network (BAN) (9-8)
booster (9-16)
cable modem (9-13)
client (9-6)
client/server network (9-6)
communications software (9-6)
data plan (9-8)
dedicated line (9-14)
digital modem (9-13)
downstream rate (9-5)
DSL modem (9-13)

EDI (electronic data interchange) (9-9)
electronic funds transfer (EFT) (9-3)
Ethernet (9-9)
extranet (9-4)
file sharing network (9-3)
GPS (global positioning system) (9-5)
Internet peer-to-peer (Internet P2P) network (9-7)
intranet (9-4)
IP hijacking (9-18)
IrDA (Infrared Data Association) (9-11)

local area network (LAN) (9-8)
LTE (Long Term Evolution) (9-5)
metropolitan area network (MAN) (9-8)
multiplexing (9-14)
network architecture (9-6)
network standards (9-9)
packet sniffer (9-18)
peer-to-peer (P2P) network (9-3)
personal area network (PAN) (9-8)
protocol (9-9)
repeater (9-16)

TCP/IP (Transmission Control Protocol/ Internet Protocol) (9-9)
topology (9-6)
upstream rate (9-5)
UWB (ultra-wideband) (9-11)
value-added network (VAN) (9-20)
wide area network (WAN) (9-8)
wired network (9-4)
wireless LAN (WLAN) (9-8)
wireless network (9-4)
wireless network key (9-18)

Extend Your Knowledge

Instructions: The Extend Your Knowledge exercise expands on subjects covered in the module and encourages you to find the latest developments on these topics. Use a search engine or another search tool to locate news articles, blog entries, videos, expert discussions, or other current sources on the listed topics. List your sources, and write 3-4 sentences describing what you have learned to submit in the format required by your instructor.

- Internet P2P networks
- IPv4 and IPv6
- Bluebugging
- Network administrator ethics

What did you learn that helped you better understand the concepts in this module? Did anything surprise you? How will what you learned impact you?

Checkpoint

The Checkpoint exercises test your knowledge of the module concepts.

True/False   Mark T for True and F for False. If False, rewrite the statement so that it is True.

_____ 1. Smaller networks usually require simple hardware and can rely on the operating system's features to connect to other devices on the network.

_____ 2. Most of today's Internet connections are broadband connections.

_____ 3. A P2P network typically requires a network administrator.

_____ 4. Computers and devices do not have to support the same network standards to successfully communicate on a network.

_____ 5. You can use Bluetooth to establish a PAN.

_____ 6. A cable modem uses existing standard copper telephone wiring to send and receive digital data.

_____ 7. A dedicated line is a type of always-on physical connection that is established between two communications devices.

_____ 8. The number of devices, as well as the operating system or platform on which the devices operate will determine the speed and strength needed to run your wireless network.

_____ 9. Wireless network settings usually can be changed by accessing the wireless router with a browser.

_____ 10. USENIX developed a code of conduct for program developers.

Matching   Match the terms with their definitions.

_____ 1. network architecture

_____ 2. network standards

_____ 3. modem

_____ 4. EFT

_____ 5. protocol

_____ 6. intranet

_____ 7. booster

_____ 8. wireless network key

_____ 9. topology

_____ 10. value-added network (VAN)

a. allows users connected to a network to exchange money from one account to another via transmission media

b. the method by which computers and devices are physically arranged on a network

c. third-party business that provides networking services, such as EDI services, secure data and information transfer, storage, or email

d. specify the way computers access a network, the type(s) of hardware used, data transmission speeds, and the types of cable and wireless technology used

e. internal network that uses Internet technologies

f. connects a network to the Internet

g. an amplifier used to improve reception

h. the logical design of all devices on a network

i. a series of numbers and/or letters used to encrypt data sent between devices

j. common set of rules for exchanging information

Problem Solving

Instructions: The Problem Solving exercises extend your knowledge of module concepts by seeking solutions to practical problems with technology that you may encounter at home, school, or work. The Collaboration exercise should be completed with a team. You often can solve problems with technology in multiple ways. Determine a solution to the problems in these exercises by using one or more resources available to you (such as a computer or mobile device, articles on the web or in print, blogs, podcasts, videos, television, user guides, other individuals, electronics or computer stores, etc.). Is this a real issue you've encountered? Do you think you would be able to solve the situation if you encounter it? Describe your solution, along with the resource(s) used, in the format requested by your instructor (brief report, presentation, discussion, blog post, video, or other means).

Personal

1. **P2P File Sharing Restrictions**   You have been using a P2P file sharing network to exchange photos that you have taken with other amateur photographers. While the guidelines of the network state that files shared on it are fair use for others, you notice that one of your photos is on another user's blog without your credit line. How can you determine if this is legal, and what actions you might take?

2. **Cannot Connect to Hot Spot**   You have checked into a hotel that offers free Wi-Fi. When you search for available hot spots using your tablet after you check into your room, the hotel's hot spot does not appear in the list of wireless networks. What are your next steps?

3. **Paired Bluetooth Devices**   You and your brother each have your Bluetooth-enabled smartphones paired with your car so that you can talk through the car's microphone and listen through its speakers. When you and your brother are both in the car at the same time, his phone rings but it is not connected to the car's audio. Why might this be the case?

4. **Suspected Bluebugging**   You were using your smartphone and earbuds while walking through downtown yesterday. You now notice that messages on your phone were read that you did not open, and a friend tells you that you may have sent out a spam message. What might be the problem? How can you fix it?

5. **Wireless Network Coverage**   You installed a new wireless network in your house. You notice that you sometimes have trouble connecting to the network from certain locations in the house, but other times you can connect from the same location without issue. What might be causing the problem?

Professional

6. **Data Plan Limited**   You have been using your company-issued smartphone while travelling to another state. While you were there, you often did not have access to Wi-Fi. You think you may have used more data than your plan allows. How can you determine this? What could you do to fix it?

7. **Cannot Sign In**   Your corporate network requires you to sign in with a username and password as soon as your computer or mobile device connects. After entering your username and password, the computer still does not connect to the network. What might be the problem?

8. **Too Many Networks**   While attempting to connect to the wireless network at your job, you notice that five different wireless networks are available. How can you determine the network to which you should connect?

9. **No Network Connection**   You have unpacked, installed, and turned on a new computer at your desk. When the operating system starts and you start the browser to display a webpage, you receive an error message stating that you are not connected to the Internet. You check the network card on the back of the computer, and although the cable is plugged in, the lights next to the port are not flashing. What are your next steps?

10. **Connecting Corporate Email**   You are visiting your company's remote office for the day and realize that you do not have the necessary information to connect to its wireless network. Your boss has asked you to check your email messages throughout the day, so it is important that you connect to the Internet. What are your next steps?

Collaboration

11. **Technology in Agriculture**   Your employer owns hundreds of acres of soybean fields in an area without much rain. Your employer thinks that irrigation equipment can be used to monitor water levels in the soil and turn on sprinklers only as needed. This will save water, as well as time spent doing manual monitoring. Because you are a digitally literate employee of the organization, your supervisor asks you to research automated irrigation systems. Form a team of three people to research automated agricultural irrigation solutions. One team member should research automated irrigation systems that water only as needed. Another team member should research solutions that monitor soil water levels, and the third team member should create a list of reasons why these automated systems can decrease costs, bolster efficiency, and increase profit. Compile your findings and submit them to your instructor.

How To: Your Turn

Instructions: This exercise presents general guidelines for fundamental skills when using a computer or mobile device and then requires that you determine how to apply these general guidelines to a specific program or situation. You often can complete tasks using technology in multiple ways. Figure out how to perform the tasks described in these exercises by using one or more resources available to you (such as a computer or mobile device, articles on the web or in print, online or program help, user guides, blogs, podcasts, videos, other individuals, trial and error, etc.). Summarize your 'how to' steps, along with the resource(s) used, in the format requested by your instructor (brief report, presentation, discussion, blog post, video, or other means).

1 Test Your Internet Speed

Internet connection speeds will vary depending on the type of Internet connection you currently are using. If you believe your Internet speed is not what was promised by your Internet access provider, you can test your Internet speed to see how it is performing. The following steps guide you through the process of testing your Internet speed:

a. Turn off any computers or mobile devices that might be accessing the Internet, except for the computer on which you want to test your broadband speed.

b. If your CATV company provides your broadband Internet service, turn off all devices accessing the cable television. If you have cable boxes or converters, disconnect them from their power source so that they cannot communicate using the Internet connection while you are testing your broadband speed.

c. Start the browser.

d. Search for and navigate to a website that can test your Internet speed.

e. Click the button to start the test. The test may take up to one minute to complete before displaying results.

f. Internet speeds sometimes can vary with the time of day or day of the week. Repeat the previous steps to test your Internet speed at various times throughout the day, as well as on weekdays and weekends.

g. If you have any concerns regarding your Internet speed, contact your Internet access provider.

Exercises

1. What is the speed of the Internet connection on the computer or mobile device you currently are using?

2. Test your Internet speed while other computers and mobile devices also are using the Internet connection. How do the results vary from when your other devices are turned off?

3. Do you see differences in the Internet speed when you test it during the day versus at night? If so, what might explain these differences in speed?

Internet Research

Instructions: These exercises broaden your understanding of module concepts by requiring that you search for information on the web. Use a search engine or another search tool to locate the information requested or answers to questions presented in the exercises. Describe your findings, along with the search term(s) you used and your web source(s), in the format requested by your instructor (brief report, presentation, discussion, blog post, video, or other means). Additionally, reflect on the process you used to complete this activity. How did you go about choosing the tool that you did and why? Would you do anything differently next time?

① Social Media: Online Marketplaces

Using social media can be an excellent opportunity to unite with people who share similar interests. In some cases, local groups form for members to post items that they are willing to either sell, donate, or give to a user. These groups that offer items to sell may be called yard sales or marketplaces. Online social media platforms, such as Facebook, enable users to post items, prices, and conditions, such as delivery or pick-up instructions. Other groups freecycle, or give away items at no cost rather than taking them to a dump or putting them out for trash. These groups can be very helpful in finding unique or interesting items at no or low cost; however, risks are involved in putting information about yourself and your items online. Some cities and towns have safe spaces, such as the police department, for exchanges of items to occur. This eliminates the need to post your address or to meet someone at an unknown location.

Research This: Using a social media platform, search for a local social media marketplace and a freecycle group. How many members do they have? What conditions do they place on items that can be posted? What claims do their privacy statements make about not disclosing personal information? What policies are in place to report members who have acted inappropriately? In addition, determine if your area has a designated safe exchange site for items bought and sold using social media. If it does have such an site, what qualifies it as a safe site? What other precautions might you take to safely complete a transaction?

② Search Skills: Map Search

Search engines provide capabilities to search for maps, directions, and local attractions. Type search text in a search engine and then click the Maps link on a search engine's home page to see a map of locations for your search text. For example, type the search text, verizon wireless chicago, in the search box to find locations of Verizon Wireless stores in Chicago. Type the search text, cisco boston, to view the location of the Boston Cisco office on a map. To obtain directions, type the address to or from which to obtain directions, and specify walking, driving, or by public transportation. On mobile devices with GPS capability, you can specify to use your current location as a starting or ending location. You also can search near a location. For example, type the search text,

pizza near 125 high street boston, to display the names of pizza restaurants near that location. Some mapping search tools allow you to zoom, pan, and navigate a map in aerial view or street view, showing the location when looking from above or on the street.

Research This: Create search text using the techniques described above or in previous Search Skills exercises, and type it in a search engine to create maps that provide this information: (1) aerial and street view of your home, (2) directions to a local store that sells wireless networking equipment, (3) locations of your mobile service provider's retail stores in your current city, and (4) distance between Microsoft's headquarters in Redmond, Washington and Apple's headquarters in Cupertino, California. Take screenshots to capture and document your results.

③ Security: Online Dating Fraud

According to some online dating websites, 20 percent of people currently in committed relationships met online. While using these dating websites may result in a positive experience, the Better Business Bureau and other consumer-oriented organizations receive thousands of complaints each year about these services. Online dating fraud is rising, so security experts caution online dating members to follow safe practices, including the following:

- Compose a profile carefully, and be certain it reflects the image you want to portray. Do not post your full name, phone number, or home or work location.
- Use the service's messaging system before sending email or text messages or having a phone conversation.
- When arranging a first date, meet in a safe location, such as a restaurant during a busy time of the day. Share your plans with a friend, and keep a mobile phone handy.
- Trust your instincts. If you feel uncomfortable or threatened, leave the location and call a friend.

Research This: Visit at least two websites providing advice for online dating members. What guidance is provided in addition to the four safe practices listed above? What behaviors may signal potentially dangerous situations? Where can members verify other members' reputations? How can members report fraud and inappropriate behavior?

Critical Thinking

Instructions: These exercises challenge your assessment and decision-making skills by presenting real-world situations associated with module concepts. The Collaboration exercise should be completed with a team. Evaluate the situations below, using personal experiences and one or more resources available to you (such as articles on the web or in print, blogs, podcasts, videos, television, user guides, other individuals, electronics or computer stores, etc.). Perform the tasks requested in each exercise and share your deliverables in the format requested by your instructor (brief report, presentation, discussion, blog post, video, or other means).

1. **Transmission Media**

   You work as an intern in the IT department for a local newspaper. The newspaper's management team recently approved a budget for redesigning the interior of its century-old building as part of an urban rehabilitation project. Because the employees at the newspaper more often use mobile devices and laptops than desktops, the newspaper plans to set up a wireless LAN.

   Do This: Prepare information that summarizes the issues surrounding wireless network setup. Include the following information: What hardware is required for a wireless network? Could the thick walls in the building present a problem? If so, how can the issue be resolved? Does a wireless network present any health hazards? What security concerns exist for a wireless network? What advantages does a wireless network have over a wired network for the newspaper's needs?

2. **Wireless Networking Standards**

   Several networking standards exist for wireless networks, which were discussed in this module. You plan to install a wireless network in your house and want to ensure that you choose the standard that best meets your needs.

   Do This: Use the web to research the various wireless networking standards and answer the following questions: Which was the first developed standard? Are any of the standards more susceptible to interference from other wireless devices in your home, such as alarm systems and mobile phones? Which standard is the fastest? Is the fastest standard always the best, or do other factors on your wireless network or on the Internet affect performance? Is the equipment to support one standard more expensive than the equipment that supports the other standards? Which would you recommend? Why? Address the answers to those questions, as well as any other information you find pertinent. Compile your findings.

3. **Case Study**

   Cooperative-Owned Farm Stand   You are the new manager for a farm stand that is a cooperative effort, jointly owned by several local farmers. The co-op's office equipment consists of a few laptops and tablets, a printer, and several smartphones; it also utilizes a LAN. The owners have asked you to investigate how they might use Bluetooth technology to improve connectivity.

   Do This: Review the uses of Bluetooth technology discussed in this module. Which uses might apply to the farm stand? Can you think of other ways you might use Bluetooth technology? What are the advantages of using Bluetooth technology? Use the web to find industry experts' recommendations for Bluetooth use in a small business. What other wireless technologies might the farm stand use? Examine issues related to bandwidth, speed, and reliability. What security concerns exist? What measures should the shop take to prevent Bluebugging? Would you recommend the farm stand use Bluetooth? Why or why not? Should the farm stand replace its LAN with Bluetooth? Why or why not? Compile your findings.

Collaboration

4. **Network Security**

   You are a network administrator for a small security firm. The company's main office includes 20 workers, most of whom use laptops. This year, the company plans to upgrade the network. The company asks your team to create a list of common network security issues, to make recommendations for hardware and software, and to create guidelines to secure the network.

   Do This: Form a three-member team. As a team, list different networking security risks discussed in this module. Each member should choose a different risk to research. Members should do the following: Describe the risk. Find an example of an industry article or blog post describing an experience with the risk. What damage was done? What steps did the network administrator take to recover from the damage and/or prevent future attacks? What hardware or software can be used to safeguard against the risk? What guidelines for network users should be in place to help avoid the risk? As a team, compile your findings and share your recommendation with the class.

Databases: 10
Understanding Data Storage

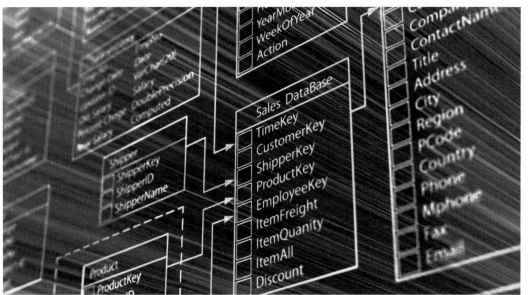

iStock.com/Enot-poloskun

Objectives

After completing this module, you will be able to:

1 Explain how to interact with a database
2 Identify database components
3 Identify database functions
4 Define relational databases
5 Discuss how to use a database system
6 Explain how to organize data in a database
7 Explain how to set up a database
8 Explain how to ensure database integrity
9 Discuss how to use data responsibly

Interacting with a Database

Chances are you have interacted with several databases today and did not know it. Did you check your email today, sign in to a social media account, buy anything online, or check your bank account balance? You do not even have to be on the Internet to interact with a database. If you filled your car with gas, bought a bus ticket, visited the drive-through for coffee or lunch, or used your credit card at a store, you used a database. These activities all require interactions with a database, either to pull information from the database (such as when signing into an account) or to add information to a database (such as when filling out a form). Recall that a database is a collection of data organized in a way that allows you to access, retrieve, and create reports of that data.

Computers process data in a database to generate information for users. Businesses use databases to track information over time. A retail business might use a database to store customer information, details on sales transactions, or an accounting of inventory in stock. A medical office might use a database to track patients' medical histories, appointments, test results, and doctor's notes. A database at a school, for example, contains data about its students and classes. Figure 10-1 shows an Access (Microsoft's popular database program) **navigation pane**, which is a pane in a program window that lets you move between objects (such as tables, queries, forms, and reports) in a database, for a community college.

When you are accepted to a school, you typically complete an online admission form that is displayed as a form in a browser or in an app. You enter your personal information in the form and sometimes upload a photo of yourself. Upon submitting the form, the page uploads your personal information and photo in a database on a server at the school. The school's admission system assigns an ID number to the student and stores it in the database. The system then sends the student an email message with advisor information. The student's photo and relevant information is sent to an ID card printer, where the student's photo, name, and student ID, as well as the date the card was issued, is printed on the front of the card, and the ID number is encoded on a magnetic stripe on the back of the card (Figure 10-2).

Figure 10-1 Navigation pane for a Student database.
Source: Microsoft Corporation

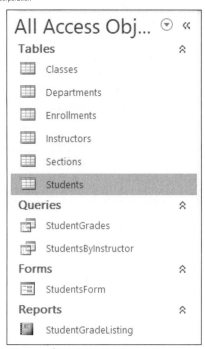

Figure 10-2 Creating a Student ID card from a database form.
Source: Microsoft Corporation, iStock.com/CiydemImages, iStock.com/Kuzmik_A

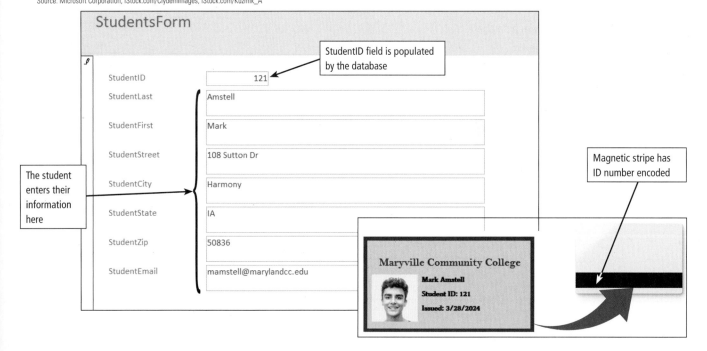

Why Use a Database?

Data is a crucial component of most organizations, and databases are relied upon to perform the critical job of organizing this data, making it easily accessible when needed, and ensuring the data is kept safe and secure. Because organizations have to store so many different kinds of information, one might wonder why they do not just create files in a word processing program or a spreadsheet application. Because those types of files can easily store information, why complicate things by using a database? While documents and spreadsheets do store information, generally that information is isolated from the information held in other documents or spreadsheets. Document and spreadsheet files are stored as unrelated objects in a file system; you can open one file and use it, but the data inside it is not connected in any way to data in a different file. Databases offer the advantage of showing connections between different sets of data.

Interact with Data

Data in a database is useful only if it can be organized and is easily accessible. This means users need to be able to add and delete data, sort and filter data, and analyze the data to detect patterns and gain other insights. A **database management system** (**DBMS**), or database program, is software that allows you to create, access, and manage a database. DBMSs offer several tools to help streamline these processes and get the most benefit from data stored in a database.

Sort and Filter Data   You can sort the records in a table according to the contents of one or more fields. For example, you could sort the records in a table alphabetically by last name, or numerically by ZIP code. You can choose to sort records in ascending order (A to Z, or lowest number to highest number) or in descending order (Z to A, or highest number to lowest number). You also can sort a table by its primary key. A **primary key** is a field that uniquely identifies each record in a table, such as Student ID. Figure 10-3 shows the Students table sorted alphabetically in ascending order by last name (StudentLast).

Figure 10-3   Students table sorted by StudentLast column.

Source: Microsoft Corporation

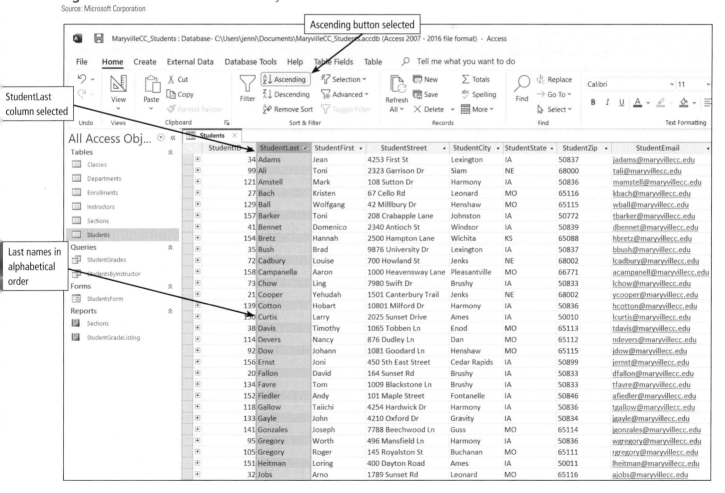

Figure 10-4 Students table filtered to show only records with StudentState as IA.

Source: Microsoft Corporation

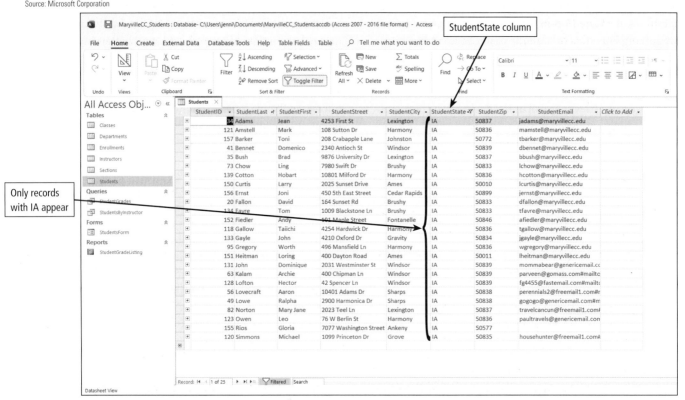

You might also want to temporarily hide some of the records in a table while you work with a few, specific records. To do this, you can apply a filter. For example, you might want to see a list of all students who live in Iowa (IA). To do this, you can filter the StudentState field for all records where the State equals IA so that all other records are hidden, as shown in Figure 10-4. The other records still exist; they are just temporarily not visible.

File Processing Systems and the Database Approach

In the past, many organizations exclusively used file processing systems to store and manage data. In a typical file processing system, each department or area within an organization has its own set of files. The records in one file may not relate to the records in any other file.

A database can be more complex than a file processing system. People with special training usually develop larger databases and their associated applications. Databases also require more memory and processing power than file processing systems.

File Processing System Weaknesses Many file processing systems have two major weaknesses: redundant data and isolated data.

- **Redundant Data:** Because each department or area in an organization has its own files in a file processing system, the same fields are stored in multiple files, creating redundancy. Data redundancy occurs when you store the same data in more than one place. It wastes space and can cause inconsistencies. Duplicating data in this manner can increase the chance of errors. If a student changes their address, for example, the school must update the address in each instance. If the Address field is not changed in all the locations where it is stored or is changed incorrectly in one location, then discrepancies among the files exist. This duplication also wastes resources, such as storage space and time. When new students are added or student data is modified, file maintenance tasks consume additional time because employees must update multiple instances of the same data.
- **Isolated Data:** It often is difficult to access data that is isolated, such as when it is stored in separate tables. Sharing data from multiple, separate files to generate a list in a file processing system often is a complicated procedure and usually requires an experienced programmer.

Almost all applications use the file processing approach, the database approach, or a combination of both approaches to store and manage data.

The Database Approach When an organization uses a database approach, many programs and users share the data in the database. A school's database most likely, at a minimum, contains data about students, instructors, schedule of classes, and student schedules. As shown in Figure 10-5, various areas within the school share and interact with the data in this database. The database does secure its data, however, so that only authorized users can access certain data items.

The database approach addresses many of the weaknesses associated with file processing systems. Advantages of the database approach include the following:

- **Reduced data redundancy:** Most data items are stored in only one file, which greatly reduces duplicate data. For example, a school's database would record a student's name and address only once. When student data is entered or changed, one employee makes the change only once.
- **Improved data integrity:** When users modify data in the database, they make changes only once. Thus, the database approach increases the data's integrity by reducing the possibility of introducing inconsistencies or errors.
- **Shared data:** The data in a database environment belongs to and is shared, usually over a network, by the entire organization. This data is independent of, or separate from, the programs that access the data. Organizations that use databases typically have security settings to define who can access, add, modify, and delete the data in a database.
- **Easier access:** The database approach allows nontechnical users to access and maintain data, provided they have the necessary privileges. Many computer users also can develop smaller databases themselves, without professional assistance.

- **Reduced development time:** It often is easier and faster to develop programs that use the database approach. Many DBMSs include several tools to assist in developing programs, which further reduces the development time.

Web Databases

Many websites you interact with use databases to provide searchable content. A database service, or a website that acts as a portal for a database, enables government agencies, schools, and companies to share information with a wide audience. Some web databases are accessible to the public. Examples of public databases include shopping and travel databases. Other databases contain information accessible only to authorized users. Examples of protected databases include certain government databases or entertainment and research databases that are subscription based.

- Government web database services can provide access to information about the government, as well as information created and used by government agencies. Some information that government agencies publish in databases is available to the public. Through these database services, for example, users can locate information about current laws. Other database services, such as those for criminal databases, allow access only to those individuals with the necessary clearance. Government database services also enable officials around the world to share data.
- You can search an entertainment web database service to find out who guest-starred on your favorite television program or locate video or audio clips. Using a subscription-based entertainment web database service allows you to access media content, such as music. These database services often enable you to create and share playlists. Entertainment professionals use subscription-based web databases to view and post casting notices or update artist profiles.

Figure 10-5 Networks can share resources and data.

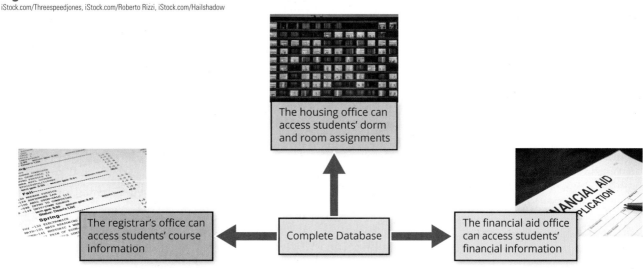

- Booking online travel through a travel web database service enables you to view multiple vendors and options. You can limit a search to desired locations and dates. These database services help you find deals on air travel, car rentals, hotel rooms, and vacation packages. Travel web database services can save your personal data and travel history. These services will send notifications about upcoming travel deals and communicate changes or updates to your travel plans.
- Shopping web database services enable you to locate the right size and color, sort by price or featured products, and more. Vendors can use a web database service to show photos of items they sell and to track inventory. Some shopping database services search for bargains, presenting a variety of purchasing options so that you can find the lowest price. These database services also use your search and purchasing history to suggest products in their databases that you may be interested in buying.
- You can interact with web databases to research product information when making a major purchase, such as a new appliance or car. Information accessible through these web database services includes costs, safety concerns, and industry and user reviews. Some research web database services provide financial information for potential investors, including company histories and stock analysis. Research web database services are available to help you find a college or university and then provide information about admission requirements, financial information, and application advice.
- Teachers can search education web database services to locate and share curricula, worksheets, and lesson plans. Schools use web database services to store and distribute student contact information and grades. Students interact with web database services when registering for their courses online. Using these services during enrollment helps a school to streamline its course selection process.

❓ Consider This

What is the advantage of a database over a spreadsheet?
You might have used a spreadsheet to track some basic information, such as a directory of contact information or expenses in a budget. While spreadsheets fill an important role, they are unable to perform the sophisticated manipulations that a database can. A spreadsheet is designed to store numbers, charts, and other data in a grid of cells where it can perform automatic recalculations as data changes. The data is organized in a grid of rows and columns; and while you can have multiple worksheets within a spreadsheet, these worksheets are not designed to fluidly interact with one another. In other words, the spreadsheet software is not capable of recognizing any significant relationships among each worksheet except in the form of performing calculations. Have you ever used a spreadsheet or a database? For what purpose have you used or would you use each? Can you think of examples of structured data, such as in a spreadsheet, that would be better suited to a database?

Database Components

Data is organized in levels. **Information technology** (**IT**) professionals classify data in a hierarchy. Each higher level of data consists of one or more items from the lower level. Depending on the application and the user, different terms describe the various levels of the hierarchy, as defined and described in the next sections.

A database contains a group of related data files. A **data file**, called a table in Access, is a collection of related records stored on a storage medium, such as a hard drive, or on cloud storage. A table contains records, a record contains fields, and a field is composed of one or more characters. The sample database shown in this module contains six tables: Classes, Departments, Enrollments, Instructors, Sections, and Students (shown in Figure 10-1).

- The Classes table contains records about the classes in which a student is enrolled for a given semester.
- The Departments table contains records about the departments' instructors and classes.
- The Enrollments table contains records about which students are enrolled in which classes.
- The Instructor table contains records about current instructors.
- The Sections table contains records about class offerings in a particular semester.
- The Student table contains records about enrolled students.

Elements of a Database

From smallest to largest, the parts of a database that store data are: character, field, record, and table. Other database objects, such as records, forms, and queries, are based on data stored in tables. As previously discussed, a bit is the smallest unit of data the computer can process. Eight bits grouped together in a unit constitute a byte. In the ASCII coding scheme, each byte represents a single **character**, which can be a number (4), letter (R), blank space (Spacebar), punctuation mark (?), or other symbol (&).

Fields Recall that a field is a combination of one or more related characters or bytes and is the smallest unit of data a user accesses. A **field name** uniquely identifies each field. Some database programs do not allow the use of the spacebar character in field names. For example, you may see the field for a last name written as LastName or last_name, with any descriptor (such as Student or Prof incorporated into the name). When searching for data in a database, you often specify the field name.

A database uses a variety of characteristics, such as field size and data type, to define each field. The field size defines the maximum number of characters a field can contain. For example, the InstructorID field (which is captioned as Instructor ID for when it appears in forms, etc.) contains 6 characters and, thus, has a field size of 6 (Figure 10-6).

Figure 10-6   Field properties for the InstructorID field.
Source: Microsoft Corporation

Field Size	6
Format	"999999"
Input Mask	999999
Caption	Instructor ID
Default Value	
Validation Rule	Between "30000" And "50000"
Validation Text	Please enter valid Instructor ID.
Required	Yes
Allow Zero Length	No
Indexed	Yes (No Duplicates)
Unicode Compression	Yes
IME Mode	No Control
IME Sentence Mode	None
Text Align	Center

Records   Recall that a **record** is a group of related fields. For example, a student record includes a set of fields about one student, including the primary key field. The data in a primary key is unique to a specific record. For example, a StudentID field uniquely identifies each student because no two students can have the same student ID. In some tables, the primary key consists of multiple fields, called a composite key. For example, the primary key for the Classes table could consist of the fields SemesterCode, ClassCode, and ClassSection, which together would uniquely identify each class listed in a schedule.

Tables   A table is the highest level in the data hierarchy, as it contains fields and records. A Student table at a school might consist of thousands of individual student records. Each student record in the table contains the same fields. Each field, however, contains different data. Figure 10-7 shows a small sample of the Student table that contains four student records, each with eight fields.

Queries   Sorts and filters are helpful when working with a single table; however, most of the work users perform in a relational database requires working across multiple tables. In fact, this is essentially the point of having the relationships among tables: you can find patterns and insights based on data held in various tables. To do this, you use queries. A query extracts data from a database based on specified criteria, or conditions, for one or more fields. For example, in the sample community college database, you could run a query that shows all the students taking any class taught by a particular instructor. Figure 10-8 shows the results of this query.

Figure 10-8   A query can use fields from multiple tables.
Source: Microsoft Corporation

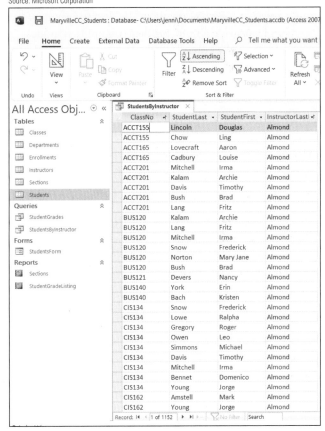

Figure 10-7   Tables organize records and fields in columns and rows.
Source: Microsoft Corporation

Each row in a table is record

Each column in a table is a field

	StudentID ▾	StudentLast ▾	StudentFirst ▾	StudentStreet ▾	StudentCity ▾	StudentState ▾	StudentZip ▾	StudentEmail ▾
⊞	34	Adams	Jean	4253 First St	Lexington	IA	50837	jadams@maryvillecc.edu
⊞	99	Ali	Toni	2323 Garrison Dr	Siam	NE	68000	tali@maryvillecc.edu
⊞	121	Amstell	Mark	108 Sutton Dr	Harmony	IA	50836	mamstell@maryvillecc.edu
⊞	27	Bach	Kristen	67 Cello Rd	Leonard	MO	65116	kbach@maryvillecc.edu

Forms   While you can enter data directly into a table, most database users are not given direct access to the DBMS in this way. Nontechnical users typically prefer a more user-friendly interface as they enter data. Think about the last time you created an account online. You did not see the underlying table with its records and fields. To reduce data entry errors, well-designed forms should validate data as it is entered. Instead, you entered data into a more visually appealing form, sometimes called a **data entry form**, where each field was spaced out on the screen to make it easier to interact with and understand.

Recall that a form is an object that provides an easy-to-use data entry screen that generally shows only one record at a time. Forms should be easy to use and navigate and provide relevant information about the data to be entered (for example, provide a note or other prompt that guides the user to enter the correct data in the correct format). This form might also have included instructions specific to each field if the information to be input is not obvious, such as "This field is required" or "Insert date in the format MM/DD/YYYY." At its core, a form provides a data entry screen that generally shows only one record at a time (Figure 10-9).

Reports   Database users often collect data from a database with the intent of communicating this information to other people, such as a project team or an advisory board. It is helpful to format this data in a way that is easy for people who are not familiar with the database to understand. You can do this by creating a report, which is a user-designed layout of database content (Figure 10-10). As is true of a form, you can add needed information to help clarify the purpose of the report and more easily draw attention to the most important pieces of information. Sometimes it is helpful to generate a report to a webpage for easy access via the Internet.

Figure 10-9   Forms are used for data entry.

Source: Microsoft Corporation

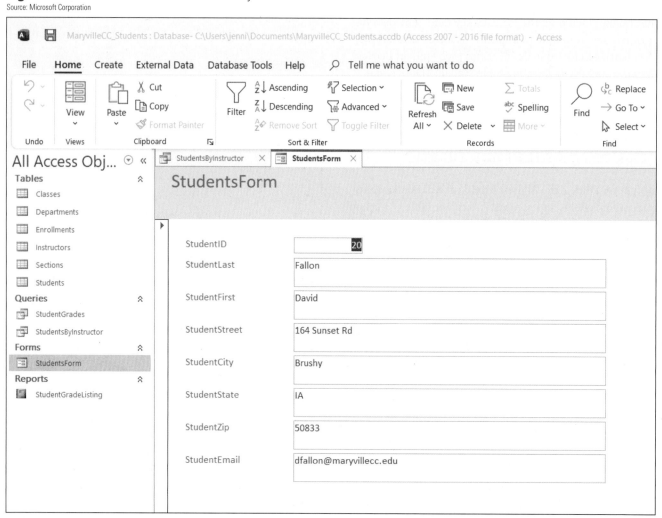

Figure 10-10   Reports show the result of a query or other database output.
Source: Microsoft Corporation

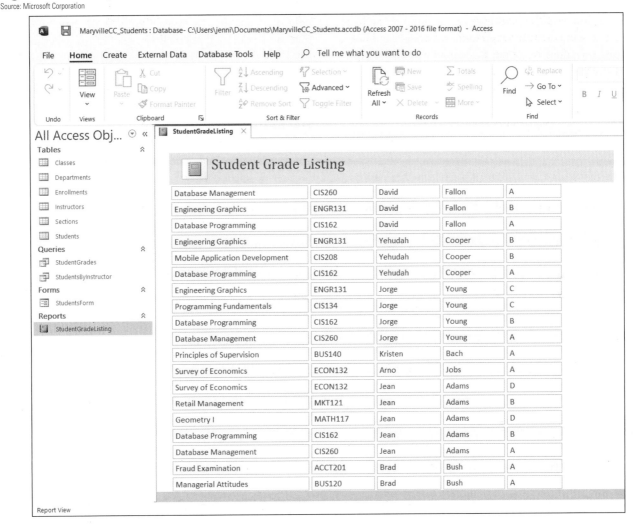

Data Type

In order to ensure that the data in a database has integrity, fields must have the correct data type. The **data type** specifies the kind of data a field can contain and how the field is used. Figure 10-11 identifies the data types for fields in the Enrollments table.

Figure 10-11   Data types in the Enrollments table.
Source: Microsoft Corporation

Field Name	Data Type
EnrollmentID	Number
SectionNo	Number
StudentID	Number
DateOfEnrollment	Date/Time
Grade	Short Text

Common data types include the following:

- **Text:** Letters, numeric characters, or special characters
- **Number:** Positive or negative numbers and the number zero, with or without decimal points; also called numeric values

- **AutoNumber:** Unique number automatically assigned by the DBMS to each added record, which provides a value that identifies the record (such as a student ID)
- **Currency:** Dollar and cent amounts or numbers containing decimal values
- **Date:** Month, day, year, and sometimes time; also called date/time
- **Memo:** Lengthy text entries, which may or may not include separate paragraphs; also called long text
- **Yes/No:** Only the values Yes or No (or True or False); also called Boolean
- **Hyperlink:** Email address or web address that links to a webpage on the Internet or document on a network
- **Object:** Photo, audio, video, or a document created in other programs or apps, such as word processing or spreadsheet, stored as a sequence of bytes in the database; also called BLOB (binary large object)
- **Attachment:** Document or image that is attached to the field, which can be opened in the program that created the document or image (functions similarly to email attachments)

Fields that contain numeric characters whose values will not be used in calculations usually are assigned a text data type. Some examples include phone numbers and ZIP codes. These numbers are representative of data and not values that would be useful in a calculation, unlike numbers that represent time, money, or size, for example.

❓ Consider This

How can you remember the purpose or use of database objects?
If you are new to using databases, it can be difficult to recall the difference between forms, tables, queries, and reports in Access. It is helpful to think of each object in terms of how it relates to the data in the database. A form is designed for easily entering data in a table. A table holds data. A query combines data from one or more tables. A report presents data in a visually appealing format. Can you think of specific uses of each of the database objects? What value does each object have?

Database Functions

DBMSs are available for many sizes and types of computers. Whether designed for a small or large computer, most DBMSs perform common functions, including creating a data dictionary, allowing table retrieval and maintenance, establishing user privileges, and backup and recovery of the database.

Data Dictionary

A **data dictionary**, sometimes called a **repository**, contains data about each table in the database and each field in those tables. For each table, it stores details such as the table name, a description, the table's relationship to other tables, and the number of records in the table. For each field, it stores details such as the field name, description, field type, field size, default value, validation rules (**validation** is the process of comparing data with a set of rules or values to determine if the data meets certain criteria), and the field's relationship to other fields.

A DBMS uses the data dictionary to perform validation checks to maintain the integrity of the data. When users enter data, the data dictionary verifies that the entered data matches the field's data type. For example, the data dictionary allows only dates to be entered in a DateAdmitted field. The data dictionary also can limit the type of data that can be entered, often allowing a user to select from a list. For example, the data dictionary ensures that the State field contains a valid two-letter state code, such as IA, by presenting a list of valid state codes to the user.

File Retrieval and Maintenance

A DBMS provides several tools that allow users and programs to retrieve and maintain data in the database. To retrieve or select data in a database, you query it. Recall that a query is a request for specific data from the database. Users can instruct the DBMS to return or store the results of a query. The capability of querying a database is one of the more powerful database features.

A DBMS offers several methods to retrieve and maintain its data. The more commonly used are query languages and query by example, and report writers. Another method is by importing data.

Query Language and Query by Example One of the most common database uses is to create simple queries; however, you can use queries for more than just pulling data from tables to see it. You can also edit records, add records, and delete records using query functions. This is commonly performed using a query language, such as Structured Query Language (SQL). **Structured Query Language** (**SQL** pronounced S-Q-L or sequel) is a popular query language that allows users to manage, update, and retrieve data. A **query language** consists of simple, English-like statements that allow users to specify the data they want to display, print, store, update, or delete. Each query language has its own formats and vocabulary.

SQL has special keywords and rules that users include in SQL statements. Figure 10-12 shows an SQL statement and its results. In addition, most DBMSs include **query by example** (**QBE**), a feature that has a graphical user interface to assist users with retrieving data.

Figure 10-12 A SQL statement and its results.
Source: Microsoft Corporation

```
SELECT CLASS_TITLE, CLASS_SECTION,
 MAXIMUM_ENROLLMENT - CURRENT_ENROLLMENT AS SEATS_REMAINING
FROM SCHEDULE_OF_CLASSES, CLASS_CATALOG
WHERE SCHEDULE_OF_CLASSES.CLASS_CODE = CLASS_CATALOG.CLASS_CODE
ORDER BY CLASS_TITLE
```

Class Title	Class Section	Seats Remaining
Intro to Computer Science	CIS-14	19
Marketing 101	BUS-09	4
Databases for the Web	CIS-19	20
Microeconomics	BUS-03	9

Report Writer   A **report writer**, also called a **report generator**, allows users to design a report on the screen, retrieve data into the report design, and then display or print the report (Figure 10-13). Unlike a form, you use a report writer only to retrieve data. Report writers usually allow you to format page numbers and dates; titles and column headings; subtotals and totals; and fonts, font sizes, color, and shading; and to include images. Some report writers allow you to create a report as a webpage.

User Privileges

Most organizations and people realize that data is one of their more valuable assets. To ensure that data is accessible on demand, an organization must manage and protect its data just as it would any other resource. For example, data in a database often is encrypted to prevent unauthorized users from reading its contents, and its access is restricted to only those who need to process the data. One method to accomplish this is to assign privileges to users that specify which database components they can read or edit.

A DBMS provides means to ensure that only authorized users can access data. In addition, most DBMSs allow different levels of access privileges to be identified for each field in the database. Access privileges define the actions that a specific user or group of users can perform on the data. For example, in the Classes table, the student would have read-only privileges. That is, the student could view the list of classes offered in a semester but could not change them. Department heads, by contrast, would have full-update privileges to classes offered during a particular semester, meaning they can view and modify the data. Finally, some users have no access privileges to the data; that is, they cannot view or modify any data in the database.

Backup and Recovery

Occasionally, a database is damaged or destroyed because of hardware failure, a problem with the software, human error, or a catastrophe, such as fire or flood. A DBMS provides a variety of techniques to restore the database to a usable form in case it is damaged or destroyed.

- A backup, or copy, of the entire database should be made on a regular basis. Some DBMSs have their own built-in backup tools. Others require users to purchase a separate backup program, or use one included with the operating system.
- More complex DBMSs maintain a **log**, which is a listing of activities that modify the contents of the database. If a registration department specialist modifies a student's address, for example, the change appears in the log.
- A DBMS **recovery utility** uses logs and/or backups, and either a rollforward or a rollback technique, to restore a database when it becomes damaged or destroyed. In a **rollforward**, also called forward recovery, the DBMS uses the log to reenter changes made to the database since the last save or backup. In a **rollback**, also called backward recovery, the DBMS uses the log to undo any changes made to the database during a certain period. The rollback restores the database to its condition prior to the failure. Depending on the type of failure, the DBMS determines which type of recovery technique to use.
- **Continuous backup** is a backup plan in which changes are backed up as they are made. This backup technique can cost more than other backup strategies but is growing in popularity for businesses whose data must be available at all times, because it provides recovery of damaged data in a matter of seconds. Organizations such as hospitals, communications companies, and financial institutions often use continuous backup.

Figure 10-13   A report being designed and the final result.
Source: Microsoft Corporation

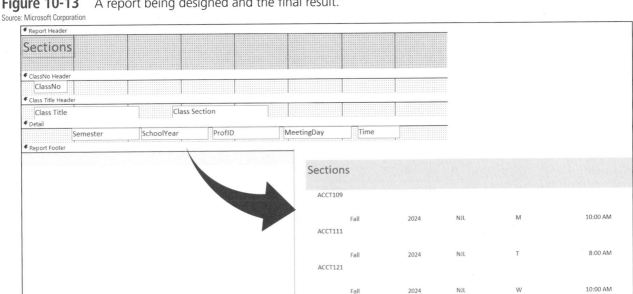

❓ Consider This

Should you delete records from a database?

DBMSs use a variety of techniques to manage deleted or obsolete records. Sometimes, the DBMS removes the record from the table immediately, which means the deleted record cannot be restored. Other times, the record is flagged, or marked, so that the DBMS will not process it again. In this case, the DBMS places an asterisk (*) or some other character at the beginning of the record to indicate that it was deleted. DBMSs that maintain inactive data for an extended period commonly flag records. For example, a school might flag courses no longer offered or former employees no longer employed. When a DBMS flags a deleted record, the record remains physically in the database, but is deleted logically because the DBMS will not process it. DBMSs will ignore flagged records unless an instruction is issued to process them. From time to time, users should run a program that removes flagged records and reorganizes current records. For example, the school may remove from the drive the names of applicants who chose to attend other schools instead. Deleting unneeded records reduces the size of tables, thereby freeing up storage space. Why might you flag a record instead of deleting it? Other than storage, what other advantage might there be to deleting obsolete records?

Relational Databases

A database can show relationships between tables. A **relationship** shows how data in one table relates to data in another table and is one of the main advantages of using a database. A relationship can streamline data entry. For example, a student's ID can be stored in the Students table. Each student in the Enrollments table can pull that information from the Students table when it is needed without having to store that information repeatedly for every order (Figure 10-14). This method reduces the quantity of data stored in a database by minimizing data duplication across multiple tables. This, in turn, reduces the chances for errors and inconsistencies. It also makes data updates, such as updating a student's information, much faster and easier to do.

The primary key in each table also enables relationships between tables. A **foreign key** is a field in one table that contains data from the primary key in another table. A table can have more than one foreign key from other tables.

The following list explains the three most common types of table relationships:

- A **one-to-many relationship** connects each record in one table to one or more records in another table. For example, most schools assign exactly one instructor to each course, and each instructor can teach many courses. This creates a one-to-many relationship, as shown in Figure 10-15.

Figure 10-15 A one-to-many relationship.

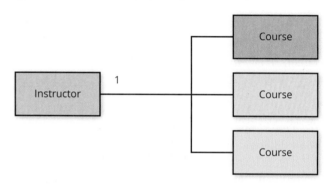

- A **one-to-one relationship** is restricted to exactly one record in the table on each side of the relationship. For example, a school's student council likely has only one president's position, and only one elected student can fill that position. This creates a one-to-one relationship as shown in Figure 10-16.

Figure 10-16 A one-to-one relationship.

Figure 10-14 Databases can establish relationships between tables.

Source: Microsoft Corporation

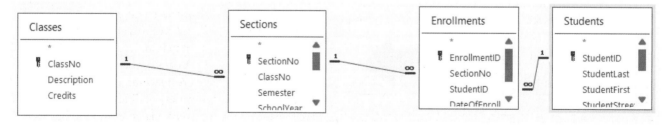

- A **many-to-many relationship** allows more than one record on the left side of the relationship to be connected to more than one record on the right side of the relationship. For example, each student at a school can take more than one course at a time, and each course will typically have more than one student in it. This creates a many-to-many relationship, as shown in Figure 10-17.

Figure 10-17   A many-to-many relationship.

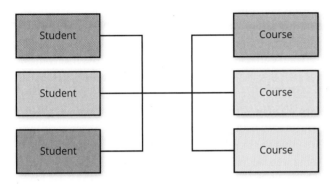

Nonrelational Databases

In many situations, the enforced consistency of a relational database (with the same kinds of information in every record in a table) is an advantage. This consistency, however, comes with the limitation that data must generally be represented by text or numbers rather than images, videos, or other table types. As the Internet — and particularly web applications — became more popular, this restriction led to the emergence of more powerful database technologies better suited to managing Big Data.

For example, **NoSQL databases** or **nonrelational databases** resolve many of the weaknesses of relational databases. NoSQL originally stood for non-SQL, but more recently has been called not-only SQL because some of these systems do support SQL-based languages.

These unstructured databases use a variety of approaches to store many kinds of data. One simple example is a key-value database. **Key-value databases** (also called key-value stores) create any number of key-value pairs for each record. A **key-value pair** consists of two related items: a constant that defines the set (the key) and a variable that belongs to the set (the value). For example, in a student database, you might store each piece of a student's contact information in a separate key-value pair in a list (Table 10-1).

Table 10-1   Sample Key-Value Database

Key	Value
Street Address	123 Artist Way
City	Martin
State	OH

Nonrelational databases do not offer the same kind of data consistency or validation as relational databases. They are, however, highly scalable, which means the resources available to the database can be increased to manage the massive volume of Big Data that continues to increase continually. This is possible because a nonrelational database can be distributed across multiple servers, which makes it easy to add more servers without compromising the database's design. Also, the data stored in a nonrelational database is more protected from loss due to a system or hardware failure, which is to say the database offers high availability. Many other types of databases exist, depending on the hardware architecture that supports the database, the kinds of data the database is designed to work with, and the ways data is organized within the database.

? Consider This

Which is better — a relational or nonrelational database?
Each database type has its strengths. For example, with a relational database your data is categorized and structured. Data is easy to navigate, and the input and meaning of the data is consistent. It is easy to define relationships between data points. With a nonrelational database, because data is not confined to structured groups, you can perform more flexible functions that allow your analysis to be more dynamic and varied. Choosing a database type is the first of many decisions you make when creating a database. What disadvantages can you see to each type? Can you think of examples when each type might be preferable? Which would you prefer to work with? Why?

Use a Database System

Microsoft Word is an application you use to open and work with a document that contains text or images. You could also open that document in Google Docs or a similar word processing application that can read a document file. Similarly, when you open a spreadsheet in Excel, the Excel application allows you to access the numbers and calculations contained within the spreadsheet. You could instead open the spreadsheet in Google Sheets or a similar spreadsheet application.

You can see a similar pattern with databases. The database itself contains the data records and fields. With a DBMS, users create a computerized database; add, modify, and delete data in the database; sort and retrieve data from the database; and create forms and reports from the data in the database. A variety of different DBMS options are available, many of which enable separation between the interface and the data itself and can support advanced queries.

Popular Database Management Systems

One common example of a DBMS is Microsoft Access, which is a part of the Microsoft Office suite of applications, along with Word, Excel, PowerPoint, and others. The screenshots in this module show a database in Access. Access is designed to work with relational databases, so it more specifically is called a **relational database management system (RDBMS)**, which is a software program in which data is organized as a collection of tables, and relationships between tables are formed through a common field.

Access is just one of many RDBMSs, but it is the one many users begin with as they are learning about database concepts. Other examples of RDBMSs that also use SQL include the following:

- Oracle Database is a proprietary RDBMS offered by Oracle.
- MySQL is an open-source RDBMS. Open source programs such as MySQL are often considered more secure because users can evaluate the source code of the software to ensure no loopholes are left open for attackers to exploit. Open source software also can be customized by technically skilled users.
- Microsoft SQL Server, like Access, is produced by Microsoft; however, it is designed to handle much higher volumes of data.
- MariaDB is a free RDBMS developed by the same people who built MySQL.
- PostgreSQL is another free and open source RDBMS.
- Amazon's Aurora is a **database as a service (DBaaS)**. This means the DBMS runs on servers owned by a cloud provider, and users access the database remotely through a browser.

You also can use other kinds of database management systems that rely on different kinds of technologies, so it sometimes is helpful to specify that a particular DBMS is designed to work with relational databases by using the more specific term, relational database management system (RDBMS). All the DBMS options in the preceding list are also considered RDBMSs.

Front-End and Back-End Databases

A DBMS is used to manage data in the database; however, most nontechnical users do not interact directly with the DBMS. For example, if you have a social media account like Facebook or Twitter, your account information is stored in a database. You can make changes to that information whenever you want even though you do not have direct access to the DBMS that manages the data. Instead, you sign in to your account through a browser and make changes on a user interface webpage.

Instead of working directly with the DBMS, some users interact with a front-end database, also just called a front-end. A **front-end database** is part of a split database that contains the user interface and other objects, but not the tables that are needed for an application. A front-end generally has a more user-friendly interface than the DBMS. For example, when you interact with your social media account on a website, you are using the front-end database user interface that is built using web languages such as HTML, CSS, and JavaScript. This interface is designed to be user friendly while also limiting and streamlining the kinds of tasks a user can complete within the database. This helps preserve the database's integrity and security, because, from a security standpoint, it would be unwise to give nontechnical users the ability to delete an entire table in the database. Interacting with the front-end interface also requires little to no understanding of the database's underlying structure, relationships, and format.

In contrast, database designers and administrators interact with the database's back-end. A **back-end database**, sometimes simply called the back-end, is part of a split database that contains table objects and is stored on a file server that all users can access. A back-end database might include the database server hosting the data, some aspects of the DBMS, and the database itself. Specially trained **database administrators (DBAs)** work with the back-end components to ensure a company's business data is safe, secure, and well-managed. Web developers also distinguish between the front-end and back-end portions of application development. With large, complex applications, some developers will specialize in back-end development while others focus more on front-end development.

 Consider This

Can databases help solve crimes?

Forensic databases are used to store data about crime, criminals, and suspects, in order to solve a variety of cases. The process of matching fingerprints is performed using systems such as the FBI's Next Generation Identification (NGI) System. Detectives scan fingerprints they find at crime scenes; the computer then will search the database of millions of fingerprints from criminal and civil subjects, as well as fingerprints of those in the military or other organizations, and attempt to find similarities in the loops, arches, and whorls. Some law enforcement agencies have added palmprints to their fingerprint database. This function gives criminal justice entities, such as law enforcement agencies and parole offices, updated status notifications of crimes committed by people holding positions of trust, such as caregivers and teachers. In addition, the Interstate Photo System (IPS) facial recognition service permits police to search photo images of people associated with criminal identities. What other data do you think exists in a forensic database? Is it ethical to keep information in these databases about the victims of a crime? Why or why not? How valuable do you think forensic databases are in solving crimes? Why?

Organize Data

Data in a database is organized to allow for quick searches and to support connections between data in relationships. While this organization can expand into a highly complex and intricate structure, basic concepts used throughout the structure help evaluate the data and ensure the data makes sense. Proper setup of tables is one way to ensure that your data is accessible and accurate. Keys and indexes help organize data more efficiently.

Primary Keys

Each record in a table must be unique in some way, different from all other records in the table. You might initially think that each student's name in the table would be unique; however, it is possible for two students to have the same name. For this reason, most tables include a primary key, which is a field that contains a unique series of characters of some kind, such as a student ID number. In Figure 10-18, the StudentID field is the Students table's primary key.

Typically, every table in a relational database has a primary key. If the information in a table does not naturally include a field with unique information, the database will assign an automatically generated number to each record that is unique and then use that number field as the primary key.

Indexes

The primary key helps improve database performance by creating an index for the table. An index is a database object that is created based on a field or combination of fields. The index speeds up searching and sorting records in a table. The index on the primary key field keeps a constantly updated list of all records in that table sorted in numerical order by those unique numbers. Even if users re-sort the records according to last name in alphabetical order or in chronological order by birthdate, the DBMS can always very quickly reorganize the records by the primary key because of the index on that field.

Other fields can be indexed, as well. Think about the index in the back of a book. It lists topics that are commonly searched in that book and cites one or more page numbers for each of those topics. A database index works in a similar fashion. It provides a presorted list of values in a particular field, which allows the database to quickly hone in on the information it needs. Imagine you are working with a table containing a million customer records, and you want the DBMS to find only the hundred or so records for customers who live in Chicago. If the DBMS already has an index of customers sorted by city, it will quickly be able to reduce that list to only the records you want. This is how an index speeds up data processes in a database. You can create an index for any field you search often.

Figure 10-18 A table's primary key is its unique identifier.

Source: Microsoft Corporation

	StudentID	StudentLast	StudentFirst	StudentStreet	StudentCity	StudentState	StudentZip	StudentEmail
	20 Fallon	David	164 Sunset Rd	Brushy	IA	50833	dfallon@maryvillecc.edu
	21 Cooper	Yehudah	1501 Canterbury Trail	Jenks	NE	68002	ycooper@maryvillecc.edu
	26 Young	Jorge	5050 Hummingbird Trail	Landis	NE	68001	rocketscientist@freemail1.cor
	27 Bach	Kristen	67 Cello Rd	Leonard	MO	65116	kbach@maryvillecc.edu
	32 Jobs	Arno	1789 Sunset Rd	Leonard	MO	65116	ajobs@maryvillecc.edu
	34 Adams	Jean	4253 First St	Lexington	IA	50837	jadams@maryvillecc.edu
	35 Bush	Brad	9876 University Dr	Lexington	IA	50837	bbush@maryvillecc.edu
	37 Mitchell	Irma	424 Cyclone Dr	Ovid	MO	65117	skithealps@tripmaker.com
	38 Davis	Timothy	1065 Tobben Ln	Enod	MO	65113	tdavis@maryvillecc.edu
	41 Bennet	Domenico	2340 Antioch St	Windsor	IA	50839	dbennet@maryvillecc.edu
	45 Snow	Frederick	42 Carthage Rd	Henshaw	MO	65115	birdwatcher@genericemail.co
	48 Rafi	Erica	4400 Galatian Dr	Siam	NE	68000	fantastic1@stopandgo.com
	49 Lowe	Ralpha	2900 Harmonica Dr	Sharps	IA	50838	gogogo@genericemail.com
	56 Lovecraft	Aaron	10401 Adams Dr	Sharps	IA	50838	perennials2@freemail1.com
	57 Lincoln	Douglas	4278 Webster Dr	Rhoads	MO	65118	floydman@genericemail.com
	63 Kalam	Archie	400 Chipman Ln	Windsor	IA	50839	parveen@gomass.com
	72 Cadbury	Louise	700 Howland St	Jenks	NE	68002	lcadbury@maryvillecc.edu

primary key (label pointing to StudentID column)

❓ Consider This

How are databases used in cryptocurrency?

Cryptocurrency is digital currency that uses encryption to protect against counterfeiting or double-spending. Cryptocurrency records are stored in a database called a blockchain. A blockchain is a series (or chain) of records stored in encrypted blocks across a network. Often, blockchains are stored across nodes on a peer-to-peer network. Each node follows protocols designed to validate a new block of data, as well as report its existence as part of the chain. A blockchain consists of infrastructure (hardware), network (nodes), consensus (validation), data (blocks), and an application so that users can modify and manage the blockchain. Besides cryptocurrencies, what other uses might blockchains have? Do you think a blockchain is secure? Why or why not? Have you ever used a blockchain?

How To: Set Up a Database

No matter how large or complex your database will be, the first step should be to create a plan for it. During the planning phase, you should establish the purpose of the database, what data it will store, how that data will be used, what elements you will need, and what relationships you will need to establish. Once you have answers to those questions, you can start by adding tables. Because all data is stored in tables, you will need to first create the tables you need by determining fields and their properties. Only after you have tables can you enter data and then use that data to create forms, queries, and reports. Although the steps and figures in this module use Microsoft Access, the process is similar to other programs you might use to create and manage a database.

Create a Table

To create a useful database table, you would start by determining exactly what information you want the table to hold, and then create all the necessary fields with the right data types and lengths before entering data. Choosing appropriate data types ensures that your database will work as efficiently as possible. And choosing appropriate field lengths helps protect the database from certain kinds of security risks.

A DBMS offers different ways to view a table, such as Datasheet view and Design view in Access. Datasheet view shows the table in a grid view with all its fields and records,

and is used to add, edit, and delete records, as well as add, edit, or rename fields. Design view shows the properties of the table, including all fields, the fields' data types, and any assigned field properties, but does not show the data itself. Datasheet view is used for structure and data entry, while Design view is used to set parameters for the table's data.

To create a table, you first start with creating a blank database, which you save with a descriptive file name. To create a new table in Access:

- Click the Table button on the Create tab on the Ribbon to create a blank table.
- Enter unique field names for the table, and make sure to break fields into the smallest logical unit. For example, a phone number would be one field, as there is no value in searching for and creating reports based on a portion of a phone number. A person's last name and first name should be two separate fields so that you can sort by either first or last name.
- Include at least one field that will be unique to each record. If you can identify no logical choice, such as a StudentID number, you can use an AutoNumber field that will assign a unique number for each record you create.
- Once the table is set up, switch to Design view (Figure 10-19). For each field, determine the property.
- Once all tables are created, you can establish relationships between fields in the tables.

Figure 10-19 A table in Design view.
Source: Microsoft Corporation

Field Name	Data Type	
StudentID	Number	Student's ID Number
StudentLast	Short Text	Student's First Name
StudentFirst	Short Text	Student's Last Name
StudentStreet	Short Text	Student's Street Address
StudentCity	Short Text	Student's City
StudentState	Short Text	State in which Student Lives
StudentZip	Short Text	Zip code for State in which Student Lives
StudentEmail	Hyperlink	Student's Maryville CC Email Address

General Lookup

Field Size	Double
Format	General Number
Decimal Places	Auto
Input Mask	
Caption	
Default Value	
Validation Rule	
Validation Text	
Required	Yes
Indexed	Yes (No Duplicates)
Text Align	General

Create Other Database Objects

When creating other database objects, you will be pulling information from tables, so you should understand the data in each table, as well as how the tables relate to one another. Consider the following:

- A form should include all the fields in the table that will store the data in a logical manner and can provide guidance when filling out the form. If the table contains many fields, you may want to split the form into multiple parts. Often, you will want to require that all fields be entered before submitting a form so that the data in your tables is complete and contains no blank fields.
- Queries can be as simple as finding all records that meet certain criteria, such as age or city, or as complex as creating a large list of records that can be sorted or filtered in several ways. Unlike a form, because a query is not used to enter data, a query does not have to include all the fields in a table.
- When creating a report based on a table or query, you should consider not only the table or query upon which to base the report and which fields to include, but also the layout and design of the form. A well-designed report will be easier to read and look more professional.

❓ Consider This

What is data visualization?

Data visualization is the process of presenting data graphically in the form of charts, maps, or other pictorial formats in order to understand the resulting information easily. As the size of databases grows, data visualizations make it possible to interpret complex data sets, find relationships among data items, and discover patterns that can provide useful information. Colors often are used to present contrasting data or to show relative data by using varying shades of the same color. Data visualization products often present multiple objects to show the data in different formats. For example, a table might list rainfall by county next to a map that shows rainfall using colors to indicate which counties have higher or lower rainfall amounts. What visualizations have you seen that help make sense of complex data sets? What format of visualization do you find most valuable? Why?

Secure IT: Database Integrity

Data in a database can be more vulnerable than data in a file processing system because it can store a large amount of data in a single physical file. Many users and programs share and depend on this data. If the database is not operating properly or is damaged or destroyed, users may not be able to perform their jobs. Further, unauthorized users potentially could gain access to a single database file that contains personal and confidential data. To protect their database resources, individuals and companies should establish and follow security procedures.

Managing a company's databases requires a great deal of coordination. The database administrator (DBA) is the person in the organization who is responsible for managing and coordinating all database activities, including development, maintenance, and permissions. One way the DBA ensures that the data in the database has integrity is to perform validation checks. The DBA also is responsible for securing, maintaining, and backing up the database and protecting its data.

Validating Data

Controlling a field's data type is an important part of the data validation process. Many programs perform a validity check that analyzes data, either as you enter the data or after you enter it, to help ensure that it is valid. For instance, when an admissions department specialist adds or modifies data in a student record, the DBMS tests the entered data to verify it meets certain criteria.

If the data fails a validity check, the computer either should not allow the invalid data to be stored, or it should display an error message that instructs the user to enter the data again. Validity checks, sometimes called validation rules, reduce data entry errors and thus enhance the data's integrity. Validation techniques include:

- **Alphabetic/numeric check:** An alphabetic check ensures that users enter only alphabetic data into a field. A numeric check ensures that users enter only numeric data into a field. For example, data in a phone number field should contain only numerals. Data in a Current Enrollment field should contain numerals.
- **Range check:** A range check determines whether a number is within a specified range. Assume the lowest per credit hour fee at the school is $75.00 and the highest is $370.75. A range check for the Credit Hour Fee field ensures it is a value between $75.00 and $370.75; any value entered that is less than $75.00 or greater than $370.50 would be considered invalid.
- **Consistency check:** This check tests the data in two or more associated fields to ensure that the relationship is logical and their data is in the correct format. For example, the value in a Date Admitted field cannot occur earlier in time than a value in a Birth Date field.
- **Completeness check:** A completeness check verifies that a required field contains data. For example, some fields cannot be left blank; others require a minimum number of characters. One completeness check can ensure that data exists in a Last Name field. Another can ensure that a day, month, and year are included in a Birth Date field.

- **Check Digit:** A **check digit** is a number(s) or character(s) that is appended to or inserted in a primary key value. A check digit often confirms the accuracy of a primary key value. Bank account, credit card, and other identification numbers often include one or more check digits.
- **Data type check:** Field data types ensure that the correct type of data is entered into a field. For example, a numeric data type will not allow alphabetic characters.
- **Presence check:** This check, when enabled, requires the user to add information to a particular field and will not allow the user to leave a field blank.
- **Field property check:** Some field properties can be used to validate data entry. For example, a maximum field length of 2 can be used on a state code field to prevent the entry of longer entries.
- **Uniqueness check:** This check, when enabled, requires the user to enter information unique to that record. For example, if someone has already created an account with a certain username, no one else can create another account with that same username.
- **Format check:** Access allows the use of an input mask to control how data is formatted in a field. An **input mask** is a field property that provides a visual guide for users as they enter data. Figure 10-20 shows the Input Mask wizard. (A **wizard** is a tool that guides you through the steps of a process or task by asking a series of questions or presenting options.) For example, an input mask might require that a ZIP code be entered using nine digits instead of five.

- **Multiple choice check:** This check can be enforced by using a data type that allows users to choose from a preexisting list, such as a list of days of the week. While these validity checks cannot guarantee that the data is accurate, they can serve as a guide to help database users notice if they are entering incorrect data. For example, if you start to type your street address into a phone number field, the database will alert you to the problem and ask for more appropriate information.

Table 10-2 lists some of the validity checks just discussed and shows valid data that passes the check and invalid data that fails the check.

Table 10-2 Sample Valid and Invalid Data

Validity Check	Field(s) Being Checked	Valid Data	Invalid Data
Alphabetic Check	City Name	Boston	1289#%
Numeric Check	Current Enrollment	24	s8q
Range Check	Per Credit Hour Fee	$220.25	$2,120.00
Consistency Check	Date Admitted, Birth Date	9/19/2019 8/27/2000	9/19/2019 8/27/2020
Completeness Check	Last Name	Gupta	
Other Check	Email Address	eg@earth.net	egearth.net

Secure a Database

As you can imagine, database security is a critical issue for companies that store highly sensitive and valuable data in their databases. Whether the database contains financial information, medical data, purchase transactions, or user passwords, the business has a responsibility to protect that information and ensure it does not fall into the wrong hands. A data breach can be costly in terms of negative media exposure, loss of trust with customers or business partners, and government fines or even criminal charges.

The following lists several best practices in database security:

- Users given access to the database should have a profile that includes a long, secure password for their account that must be changed periodically. Users should be given only the minimum access privileges required to do their job, such as the ability to view data but not change it or delete it.
- Web servers are designed to be accessible to the open Internet, but database servers should reside in more secure segments of the network behind a firewall.
- Sensitive data in a database should be encrypted. If a hacker manages to access a password database, for example, encryption can provide a last layer of defense

Figure 10-20 Access provides an Input Mask wizard.

Source: Microsoft Corporation

that might prevent the attacker from actually using the stolen information. Not all data in the database must be encrypted, as that could severely slow the database's overall performance. The data that indicates a person's identity (such as a name or Social Security number), contact information, or other personal information (such as medical records), though, should be encrypted. Any backup files also should be encrypted.

- Limit the number of unsuccessful sign-in attempts in a specified period, and record when users access the database.

Maintain a Database

Database maintenance starts as soon as the database is created and lasts as long as the database is used. One of the primary maintenance concerns is limiting the size of the database by including only the records and data that is currently relevant. For example, if the database contains a table that you do not need (and you do not foresee a future need for the data in that table), remove the table from the database. Periodically, you should evaluate the fields in all remaining tables and make sure they are assigned the proper data type, and remove fields you no longer need from the tables in your database. If the database contains a large number of records, consider deleting records you no longer need.

Back Up and Recover a Database

The backup process for a sizable database is not as simple as creating a second copy of a database file. Because the data in a database changes frequently, backups must be created or updated on a regular basis. For this reason, many DBMSs include built-in backup tools. These backups might include information about the state of the database at a particular point in time and a log of any changes to data since the previous backup, along with information about who made the changes and when. In some cases, the database is backed up continuously.

When needed, a database can be restored using the backup files. This recovery process might be applied to only a single object or record, or to the entire database, depending on the situation. This process is usually performed using a recovery tool, which can be part of the DBMS or part of a more complex backup program.

Protect Data

Not all threats to a database come from potential attackers. Ensuring that data is accessible when it is needed and that no one has made unauthorized changes are also key aspects of database security. In fact, a classic security model called the **Confidentiality, Integrity, and Availability (CIA) triad** (Figure 10-21) addresses these concerns directly, as described in the following list:

- Confidentiality implies the need to protect a database from unauthorized access, as discussed previously.
- Integrity refers to protecting data from unauthorized changes.
- Availability indicates the need to ensure that data is accessible by authorized users when needed.

Figure 10-21   The CIA triad is a classic security model for protecting data.
Source: Microsoft Corporation

Techniques to secure access to a database and encrypt sensitive data address the first two concerns, confidentiality and integrity. One way to address availability of data is to back up a database. This way, data is not lost in case of hardware failure, software problems, human error, or environmental threat (such as fire or flood). The database can be recovered, sometimes automatically, and data access can be restored with (hopefully) minimal disruption.

? Consider This ——

What is the principle of least privilege?

Many organizations adopt a principle of least privilege policy, where users' access privileges are limited to the lowest level necessary to perform required tasks to prevent accidental or intentional misuse of the data. This is accomplished by restricting users to accessing only the database tables and records that are necessary to perform their job function(s). For example, some organization grant only administrators the ability to create and delete tables and restrict typical users only to view records. What value can you see in the principle of least privilege? What disadvantages might be incurred with such a policy? If you use a database, what are your privileges? Are they sufficient? Why or why not?

Ethics and Issues: Using Data Responsibly

You have learned about how data is stored in databases and how to access that data. Data by itself, however, does not provide much meaning without context or organization. Raw and unorganized facts are not valuable to organizations. When data that has been collected and been processed in a way that reveals patterns, relationships, and other insights, it becomes information. Information is extremely valuable. All database users should know and understand how data is used, collected, and analyzed, especially on a large scale.

Big Data

To glean meaningful insights, you need a large volume of relevant data. Database technologies have evolved over the years to manage massive amounts of data. These large and complex data sources that defy traditional data processing methods are called Big Data. If you have posted information to a social media website, purchased an item based on a recommendation after online research, or clicked a targeted ad related to your search or web activity, you probably have witnessed what Big Data can do.

All these activities generate and interact with data that is stored, analyzed, and referenced when making business decisions. The massive volume of data kept by a typical organization complicates storage and analysis processes, especially when you consider that data is often not structured in a way that allows it to be stored in traditional relational database tables.

Other examples of Big Data use include the following:

- Data streams from Internet of Things (IoT) devices that monitor a passenger plane's engine performance
- Constantly changing ownership and valuations of stocks on the New York Stock Exchange
- Items purchased, coupon usage, type of checkout used, and payment types at every cash register of a grocery store chain
- Student responses and scores, attendance, time on task, and discussion board messages in a learning management system
- Biological data collected by wearable fitness trackers
- Posts, reactions, blocks, and account settings on a social media website or app
- Video footage from traffic cameras at intersections and along highways
- Historical, current, and forecasted weather and environmental data

This list shows only a few examples of the terabytes of Big Data (a terabyte is about a billion kilobytes) generated every millisecond on Earth. In fact, Big Data is often described according to the three Vs, which are:

- **Volume:** The massive amount of data that must be stored and analyzed
- **Variety:** The different formats in which this data can exist, such as music or video files, photos, social media texts, financial transactions, IoT sensor data, and more
- **Velocity:** The fact that this data is often generated and received at high speeds

Two additional Vs often used to describe Big Data include the following:

- **Value:** The helpfulness of the data in making strategic decisions
- **Veracity:** How accurately this data reflects reality

Sources of Big Data

One way that businesses generate Big Data is by capturing customer behaviors. For example, in addition to storing information about a customer's purchases, some shopping websites also gather data about how much time customers spend on a webpage, how many items they view before making a purchase, and which company website pages customers visited, in order to create a more customized experience. Amazon and other retailers compile data from customer purchases in a process called collaborative filtering to recommend related products. For example, Amazon recommends that customers who purchase a digital camera might also want to purchase a storage card or a camera case.

Government agencies generate large amounts of data in real time from satellite images, social media posts, and media. By analyzing this data, they can monitor transportation systems, dispatch first responders in emergencies, and provide consumers with information to make informed choices about healthcare, schools, and community services.

Temperature and barometric sensors, wearable devices, and buses and trains equipped with GPS capability all transmit data over the Internet to be used in a variety of web and mobile applications.

Business Intelligence

As you previously learned, data mining is the process of sifting through Big Data to find the important questions that will yield fruitful results. The analysis of Big Data benefits businesses by providing a bird's-eye view of how well the business is functioning and giving insights into how to improve business processes and increase productivity. The processes and technologies used to do this analysis are called **business intelligence (BI)**.

BI systems might collect data from existing databases (such as a product database) and from live data streams (such as an online transaction processing system) into a central repository called a **data warehouse**. While a data warehouse is a type of database — and most use tables, indexes, keys, and SQL queries — some significant differences exist between a data warehouse and the relational databases you have learned about so far. For example, data in a data warehouse comes from many sources, it interacts with many applications, and the structure is optimized for running complex queries. Basically, where traditional databases are designed primarily for storing data, a data warehouse is designed primarily for analyzing data.

Another option for BI systems is a **data lake**, which is a collection of both structured and unstructured data. Where data warehouses collect and analyze structured data, a data lake allows for more diverse data formats, including collecting raw data, such as video streams or IoT sensor data.

After data from a data warehouse or data lake is summarized and analyzed, it often is presented to decision-makers in **dashboards** that provide at-a-glance views, with live updates as data continues to pour in (Figure 10-22). Emerging patterns and insights from these **data analytics** processes help to inform business decisions and strategies. For example, a retailer can develop a more complete understanding of customer interests and preferences. The retailer might discontinue a product, reposition a product, or create new products based on this information. It also might adjust its marketing strategies, offer new financing options, fine-tune product or service pricing, or shift its customer service priorities.

Figure 10-22 Dashboards often update automatically as new data comes in.

iStock.com/SpiffyJ

❓ Consider This

What use of collected data is fair?

If you willingly purchase products at a store, can the business analyze your purchases to create a profile to use for marketing purposes? Can it sell that data to a third party? **Function creep** occurs when a company uses the technology intended for one purpose for an entirely different purpose. One example of function creep is when companies use or sell customer data collected through sales transactions using customer loyalty cards or other customer-tracking methods. While some companies use data for their own purposes, such as to plan inventory or identify sales trends, others sell to data brokers or businesses that perform marketing surveys or generate credit reports. Privacy advocates are concerned about any use of personal data for purposes other than what the customer intended; further, many consumers would like more control over their data. The FTC Fair Information Practices (FIP) guidelines attempt to address data privacy concerns. FIP states that companies must inform customers of their data use and must allow customers to allow or deny consent. Critics contend that the FIP guidelines are not legally binding, and that some countries include more restrictions that include laws for regulating data collection and usage. Have you experienced examples of a company using your personal data? For what purpose? Do you read a company's data privacy policy before using its website or service? Why or why not? How should the government enforce data privacy laws?

Study Guide

Instructions: The Study Guide exercise reinforces material you should know after reading this module. Answer the questions below using the format that helps you remember best or that is required by your instructor. Possible formats may include one or more of these options: write the answers; create a document that contains the answers; record answers as audio or video using a webcam, smartphone, or portable media player; post answers on a blog, wiki, or website; or highlight answers in the book/ebook.

1. List examples of how the following use databases: businesses, schools, retail business, and medical office.

2. Explain why you might choose a database over a spreadsheet.

3. Define the term, DBMS, and explain what it stands for.

4. A(n) _____ is a field that uniquely identifies each record in a table. Explain how sorting and filtering data can be helpful.

5. Define the term, file processing system. List some disadvantages to using a file processing system.

6. List advantages to the database approach.

7. List examples of the following uses of web databases: government, entertainment, travel, shopping, research, and education.

8. Define the term, data file. List another term for data table.

9. List the parts of a database from smallest to largest. Explain the purpose of each part.

10. Explain when you might use a query.

11. What is the purpose of a form?

12. Explain how a report is used.

13. Explain the purpose of a data type. List examples of common data types.

14. Explain why some numbers are not assigned a text data type.

15. Define the term, data dictionary. _____ is the process of comparing data with a set of rules or values to determine if the data meets certain criteria

16. List and describe common methods to retrieve and maintain data.

17. Explain the importance of assigning user privileges.

18. List common techniques to restore a database. Define the term, log.

19. List considerations when determining whether or not to delete records from a database.

20. Explain the importance of relationships. Define the term, foreign key.

21. Differentiate among one-to-many, one-to-one, and many-to-many relationships.

22. Define the terms, nonrelational database and key-value database.

23. Explain why you might choose a relational or nonrelational database.

24. List popular DBMSs. _____ DBMS runs on servers owned by a cloud provider, and users access the database remotely through a web browser.

25. Differentiate between a front-end and back-end database. What are users who work with a back-end component called?

26. Explain how databases are used in forensics.

27. Explain how a database uses primary keys and indexes to organize data.

28. Define the term, blockchain. Explain how cryptocurrency uses databases.

29. List steps to create a table using Microsoft Access.

30. List considerations when creating forms, queries, and reports.

31. Define the term, data visualization.

32. List types of validation techniques. A(n) _____ is a number(s) or character(s) that is appended to or inserted in a primary key value.

33. List methods you can use to secure a database.

34. Explain how to maintain a database.

35. Explain the importance of creating a backup of a database.

36. List methods to protect data. What does the CIA triad stand for?

37. What is the principle of least privilege?

38. List examples of uses of Big Data. What are the 3 Vs?

39. List sources of Big Data.

40. Explain how analysts use business intelligence processes and technologies.

41. Define these terms: data warehouse, data lake, and dashboard.

42. Define the term, function creep.

Key Terms

You should be able to define the Key Terms listed below.

back-end database (10-14)

blockchain (10-15)

business intelligence (BI) (10-20)

character (10-6)

check digit (10-18)

Confidentiality, Integrity, and Availability (CIA) triad (10-19)

continuous backup (10-11)

dashboard (10-21)

data analytics (10-21)

data dictionary (10-10)

data entry form (10-8)

data file (10-6)

data lake (10-21)

data redundancy (10-4)

data type (10-9)

data visualization (10-17)

data warehouse (10-21)

database administrator (DBA) (10-14)

database as a service (DBaaS) (10-14)

database management system (DBMS) (10-3)

file processing system (10-4)

foreign key (10-12)

front-end database (10-14)

function creep (10-21)

index (10-15)

information technology (IT) (10-6)

input mask (10-18)

key-value database (10-13)

key-value pair (10-13)

log (10-11)

many-to-many relationship (10-13)

navigation pane (10-2)

nonrelational database (10-13)

NoSQL database (10-13)

one-to-many relationship (10-12)

one-to-one relationship (10-12)

primary key (10-3)

query by example (QBE) (10-10)

query language (10-10)

recovery utility (10-11)

relational database management system (RDBMS) (10-14)

relationship (10-12)

report generator (10-11)

report writer (10-11)

repository (10-10)

rollback (10-11)

rollforward (10-11)

Structured Query Language (SQL) (10-10)

validation (10-10)

wizard (10-18)

Extend Your Knowledge

Instructions: The Extend Your Knowledge exercise expands on subjects covered in the module and encourages you to find the latest developments on these topics. Use a search engine or another search tool to locate news articles, blog entries, videos, expert discussions, or other current sources on the listed topics. List your sources, and write 3-4 sentences describing what you have learned to submit in the format required by your instructor.

- Web databases
- Forensic databases
- When to use a nonrelational database
- DBaaS options

What did you learn that helped you better understand the concepts in this module? Did anything surprise you? How will what you learned impact you?

Checkpoint

The Checkpoint exercises test your knowledge of the module concepts.

True/False   Mark T for True and F for False. If False, rewrite the statement so that it is True.

_____ 1. In a typical file processing system, each department or area within an organization has its own set of files.

_____ 2. Fields that contain numeric characters whose values will not be used in calculations usually are assigned a number data type.

_____ 3. A DBMS uses the data dictionary to perform validation checks to maintain the integrity of the data.

_____ 4. In a rollforward, the DBMS uses the log to undo any changes made to the database during a certain period.

_____ 5. Nonrelational databases are highly scalable, which means they can handle the demands of Big Data.

_____ 6. Amazon's Aurora is a free and open source RDBMS.

_____ 7. Typically, every table in a relational database has a primary key.

_____ 8. In Microsoft Access, Design view shows the table in a grid view with all its fields and records.

_____ 9. A check digit tests the data in two or more associated fields to ensure that the relationship is logical and their data is in the correct format.

_____ 10. Big Data is often described according to the three Vs: volume, variety, and velocity.

Matching   Match the terms with their definitions.

_____ 1. foreign key

_____ 2. front-end

_____ 3. data visualization

_____ 4. data lake

_____ 5. data file

_____ 6. report

_____ 7. validation

_____ 8. check digit

_____ 9. index

_____ 10. data dictionary

a. collection of related records stored on a storage medium

b. number(s) or character(s) that is appended to or inserted in a primary key value

c. contains data about each file in the database and each field in those files

d. process of presenting data graphically as charts, maps, or other pictorial formats

e. process of comparing data with a set of rules or values to determine if the data meets certain criteria

f. collection of both structured and unstructured data

g. part of a split database that contains the user interface and other objects

h. field in one table that contains data from the primary key in another table

i. user-designed layout of database content

j. database object that is created based on a field or combination of fields

Problem Solving

Instructions: The Problem Solving exercises extend your knowledge of module concepts by seeking solutions to practical problems with technology that you may encounter at home, school, or work. The Collaboration exercise should be completed with a team. You often can solve problems with technology in multiple ways. Determine a solution to the problems in these exercises by using one or more resources available to you (such as a computer or mobile device, articles on the web or in print, blogs, podcasts, videos, television, user guides, other individuals, electronics or computer stores, etc.). Is this a real issue you have encountered? Do you think you would be able to solve the situation if you encounter it? Describe your solution, along with the resource(s) used, in the format requested by your instructor (brief report, presentation, discussion, blog post, video, or other means).

Personal

1. **No Search Results** While searching a web database for a hotel room for an upcoming trip, a message is displayed stating that no search results match your criteria. What can you do to correct this problem?

2. **Incorrect Price** You are shopping for groceries and, after loading all items in your cart, it is time to check out. The cashier scans your items, but you realize that the register is not reflecting an advertised discount on one of the items. Why might this be happening?

3. **Database Connection Error** While interacting with a web app, an error message appears informing you that the web app is not able to connect to the database. What might be causing this?

4. **Inaccurate Credit Report** You have obtained a free copy of your credit report and notice that multiple companies are accessing your credit report without your knowledge or permission. Your financial records are very important, and it is troubling that other companies are accessing this information. Why might this be occurring?

5. **Function Creep** You recently performed a search in your browser for a recent illness you had. When you sign in to a shopping app that you frequently use, it is recommending several options to relieve the symptoms of your illness. How can this happen? What could you do to prevent this? Do you consider this to be an invasion of privacy?

Professional

6. **Data Entry Issues** You are in charge of adding student information to your school's database using a front-end. When you attempt to enter the street address for one of the students, the entire street name does not fit in the text box. What are your next steps?

7. **Incorrect Postal Codes** Your company's database stores information about its customers, including their names, addresses, phone numbers, email addresses, and order history. While reviewing the database to ensure data integrity, you notice that some of the postal codes, which should be a minimum of five digits, are only four digits. What might be wrong, and how can you fix it?

8. **Unclear Form** Your colleague designed a form for customers to enter their data in order to join your store's rewards program. They ask you to test it before rolling it out to the customers. You have a hyphenated last name, and both parts of it are eight characters. When you try to enter your last name in the field, you get an error message. What might be the problem, and how should your colleague fix it?

9. **Database Recovery** Your boss has informed you that the main customer database for your company has become corrupt. You believe you can use the recovery utility to salvage the data in the database, but when you attempt to recover the database, you receive an error message that the recovery has failed. What are your next steps?

10. **Report Feedback** You created a report that shows the results of a query you executed to reflect customers' shopping habits. You present the findings in a list and also sorted it by category; however, your colleagues do not seem to grasp the significance of the data you presented. How could you present the data differently in the report?

Collaboration

11. **Technology in Sports** You serve as an assistant coach for your former high school's baseball team. The head coach has been using several spreadsheets to keep track of players' statistics, contact information, payment records, and more. You suggest that a database would enable you to streamline the data, reduce redundancy, and limit errors. Form a team of three people to determine the requirements for implementing the database. One team member will create a list of suggested tables and relationships between them. One member will outline the types of reports and queries that can be run. A third member should make suggestions for the types of users and what their permissions levels should be.

How To: Your Turn

Instructions: This exercise presents general guidelines for fundamental skills when using a computer or mobile device and then requires that you determine how to apply these general guidelines to a specific program or situation. You often can complete tasks using technology in multiple ways. Figure out how to perform the tasks described in these exercises by using one or more resources available to you (such as a computer or mobile device, articles on the web or in print, online or program help, user guides, blogs, podcasts, videos, other individuals, trial and error, etc.). Summarize your 'how to' steps, along with the resource(s) used, in the format requested by your instructor (brief report, presentation, discussion, blog post, video, or other means).

1 Use a Research Database

Students often use one or more research databases to locate information about a particular topic. Research databases often can be accessed through a library's website or through a research database's website. The following steps guide you through the process of using a research database:

a. Locate and then navigate to the research database that contains the information you are seeking. If multiple databases that are specific to your search are available, select one and explain why you made the selection.

b. Determine whether you can access the research database. For instance, you may need to verify your identity as a library patron or a student. Some databases are available to the public at no charge or with no other restrictions.

c. Navigate to the research database you plan to use.

d. If the research database contains an option to perform an advanced search, click the option to perform the advanced search.

e. Use three search criteria. Note that not all research databases will request the same search criteria. The following list contains some common criteria:
   1. Keywords
   2. Author

3. Publication date
   4. Publication type
   5. Education level

f. Run the search.

g. Browse the search results and then click the search result that interests you.

h. Read the content in the search result. Does it provide the answer you were looking for?

i. Run the search again using two additional criteria. Compare the results.

Exercises

1. Why might you want or need to use a research database?

2. What research databases are available to you as a student at your school?

3. Evaluate three research databases that you may need to use throughout your academic career. Which one do you like the most? Why? Which one do you like the least? Why?

Internet Research

Instructions: These exercises broaden your understanding of module concepts by requiring that you search for information on the web. Use a search engine or another search tool to locate the information requested or answers to questions presented in the exercises. Describe your findings, along with the search term(s) you used and your web source(s), in the format requested by your instructor (brief report, presentation, discussion, blog post, video, or other means). Additionally, reflect on the process you used to complete this activity. How did you go about choosing the tool that you did and why? Would you do anything differently next time?

1 Making Use of the Web: Entertainment

Many people in the past few years have scaled back their away-from-home activities in favor of in-home entertainment. A number of services are available that you can use to stream music, podcasts, movies, and TV programs. All these programs use databases to store not only customer data but information about the available media options.

These services' databases enable you to search for media using a variety of keywords or criteria. For example, you can search a music streaming service for music by year, artist, or genre. You could search for podcasts that discuss a specific topic. You can look up all movies that feature a certain actor or those by a specific director.

Research This: (a) Locate a music streaming website or app. If you have a subscription to one, you can use that; otherwise, locate one that allows you to listen for free. Your library may also offer a music streaming service to patrons. Search for all music of a certain genre, then narrow your search to all music in that genre by a specific artist. How accurate are the results? Does the service offer the music you desire for free? What features might you be able to access with a paid subscription?

(b) Locate a podcast service or app. Search for podcasts on a specific topic, such as your favorite TV program. List the top results in the search results. Listen to one podcast. What information would be stored in the database that would enable your search to be accurate?

(c) Locate a TV or movie streaming website or app. If you do not have a subscription, services, such as IMDB, offer free programming with advertisements. Search for all programs or movies by actor, then narrow your search by selecting additional criteria until you have only a few options. What criteria did you select and why?

2 Social Media: Targeted Ads

Companies collect data as people browse websites. Just seconds after individuals visit a specific webpage, advertisements are displayed matching their shopping patterns and favorite products. This tracking is prevalent in online social networks, too, as marketers match users' profiles and other posted information, such as status updates, with specific businesses. Facebook, for example, allows retailers to upload their databases containing email addresses, phone numbers, and other personal facts. This data then is compared with the Facebook users' data. When a match is found, specific advertisements are displayed. Social media may charge the advertisers each time a user clicks an ad, called CPC (cost per click) or PPC (pay per click), which could range from a few cents to several dollars. Another option is to charge for a specific number of times an ad is displayed, called CPI (cost per impression).

Research This: Locate at least two articles discussing targeted ads on online social networks. How do businesses place their ads based on the users' online identities and profiles? What steps are taken to ensure the users' privacy? Should users expect companies to collect data about some of their online behaviors in return for using the websites at no charge?

3 Search Skills: Verifying Search Results

Even though a link to a website or other online resource may appear first in your list of search results, the information it presents may not be accurate. Several strategies exist to help you determine the credibility of search results. Verify the information you read by finding supporting information on other websites or by comparing search results from different search engines. Often authors will provide links to sources within or at the end of an article. Search for information about the author to help determine his or her credibility, authenticity, or objectivity. Some articles may present opinions, not facts.

If you do not recognize or have doubts about the domain name of a website you are reading, type the search text, whois, in a search engine to locate the WhoIs database. Then type the domain name of the website in question (such as cengagebrain.com) in the WhoIs search box to find its owner. You then can search for more information about the website's owner. If you are looking for time-sensitive information, check the date when the links or pages were updated. If a webpage is filled with ads or pop-ups, it may be a scam.

Research This: Use a search engine to answer these questions and report your findings. (1) Find an article on Wikipedia about web databases. What references reinforce the statements in the article? (2) Find a popular blog about web marketing and use WhoIs to determine the blog's owner. (3) Find two different publications (blog posts, articles, or videos) by the same author or on a similar topic. (4) Search for information about the author to determine their credentials.

Critical Thinking

Instructions: These exercises challenge your assessment and decision-making skills by presenting real-world situations associated with module concepts. The Collaboration exercise should be completed with a team. Evaluate the situations below, using personal experiences and one or more resources available to you (such as articles on the web or in print, blogs, podcasts, videos, television, user guides, other individuals, electronics or computer stores, etc.). Perform the tasks requested in each exercise and share your deliverables in the format requested by your instructor (brief report, presentation, discussion, blog post, video, or other means).

1. Online Movie Reviews

Information about movie titles and television shows is available from the web database IMDb (Internet Movie Database). Visitors can search IMDb using by title, cast member, year produced, characters, genre, awards, or other criteria. Each movie or show's listing offers a brief description and rating and includes links to such items as summary, trivia, reviews, quotes, and even streaming video options.

Do This: Visit imdb.com and search for both recently released and classic movies. Explain the steps you used to query the movie database. Assess how complete the information provided was. Who would benefit most from using the movie database? Why? Did the information provided differ when viewing recently released titles versus classic movies? What did you learn from your queries? Can you identify a few fields that are included in the records for each movie? What other searches can you perform on this site?

2. Spreadsheets versus Databases

Some individuals and small organizations prefer using spreadsheets instead of databases. People who use spreadsheets might argue that — similar to databases — spreadsheets have columns and rows, and you can keep track of different sets of data in individual worksheets. This is similar to how you would use tables in a database to store different data sets. In addition, some find it easier to install, use, and maintain spreadsheet software than database software. After reading this module, you are convinced that databases have additional advantages, such as the capability of storing more data and more quickly searching for data, as well as generating reports.

Do This: Prepare information aimed toward individuals who prefer spreadsheets to databases. Include reasons why it is not advisable to store large amounts of data in spreadsheets; also discuss why the reporting and querying capabilities of databases might be superior. Explain benefits for using a database for collaborating and sharing information among departments in a business.

3. Case Study

Cooperative-Owned Farm Stand You are the new manager for a farm stand that is a cooperative effort, jointly owned by several local farmers. The farm stand uses a database to store information about its inventory, prices, employees, customers, and special offers. The farm stand's website uses information stored in the database to display products, pricing, and sales. The owners have asked you to investigate how the farm stand should secure its database.

Do This: Using information learned in the module, as well as performing additional research, prepare information about securing a database. What risks exist for databases? Who should determine the security measures to take? What should you include in the database security policy? Include recommendations for backing up data, validation, maintenance, and assigning different access levels to employees and managers. Is the farm stand bound to uphold pricing mistakes that appear on its website? Why or why not? Compile your findings.

Collaboration

4. Using Big Data

You are a marketing intern at a firm that has a fast-growing online retailer as its client. The company collects a vast amount of data about its customers and has asked about the possible uses of it. Your team brainstorms several options, including targeted ads and selling the data to a data broker. Your boss asks you to research the legal uses of the data, as well as the responsibilities of the company to inform its customers about the uses of the data.

Do This: Form a three-member team. One member should find examples of company policies that outline use of their collected data. Another should research companies that assist websites with providing targeted ads and glean as much information as possible about fees, data access, and more. A third should research data brokers and what types of data are most valuable. As a team, discuss the legal and ethical concerns with each of the options, then compile your findings and share your recommendation with the class.

Program Development: 11
Creating Systems and Applications

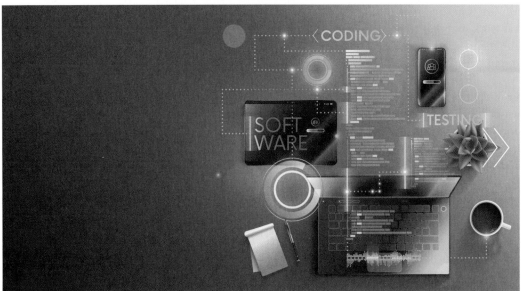

iStock.com/Andrey Suslov

Objectives

After completing this module, you will be able to:

1 Identify the role of a developer
2 Explain the methods of development
3 Describe the tools and strategies critical to system development
4 Identify other roles and tasks in development
5 Identify application development languages and tools
6 Identify strategies for designing secure systems and applications
7 Explain how to sell your app
8 Explain the importance of ethics in development
9 Apply decision-making strategies to solve problems

What Does a Developer Do?

Development is the process of creating information systems or programs and apps from the idea stage to distribution to users. Recall that programs and apps, also known as software, are coded instructions to control a computer or device, and that an information system is collection of hardware, software, data, people, and procedures that work together to produce information. During development, many steps and people are involved in programming, designing, coding, and testing.

Some general steps occur in the development cycle, and many similar roles must be filled, whether you are designing an information system or app. Knowing the basics of the development cycle can help you to understand and make choices about your system or app needs.

Developers follow three general guidelines:

- Group activities into phases, such as planning, analysis, design, implementation, security, and support.
- Involve users for whom the program is being developed. Customers, employees, data entry specialists, and accountants all are examples of users.
- Define the standards, or sets of rules and procedures, the developers should all follow to create a product with consistent results.

Reasons for Development

With all the products available to purchase, why would anyone go through the trouble of creating a new one? App developers usually focus on a new or developing need or service (such as ride-share apps) or to extend a product or company's existing offerings (such as to provide users with an app from which they can shop a website's products or order from a restaurant). Typically, apps are developed to provide income generation by selling the app, enabling in-app purchases, or selling advertising to other companies.

A user may request a new or modified information system for a variety of reasons. The most obvious reason is to correct a problem, such as an incorrect calculation or a security breach. Another reason is to improve the information system. Organizations may want to improve hardware, software, or other technology to enhance an information system.

Sometimes, situations outside the control of an organization require a modification to an information system. Corporate management or some other governing body may mandate a change. Mergers, reorganizations, and competition also can lead to change.

To start the development process, users write a formal request for a new or modified information system or app, which is called a project request or request for system services. The project request becomes the first item of documentation for the project. Documentation is a collection and summary of the data, information, and deliverables specific to the project. The developer can be involved in the request development or be asked to take on the project after the request is made.

Managing Development Changes

After a project's features and deadlines have been set, the developer, acting as the project leader, monitors and controls the project. Some activities take less time than originally planned; others take longer. The developer may realize that an activity is taking excessive time or that scope creep has begun. Scope creep, also called feature creep, occurs when one activity has led to another that was not planned originally; thus, the scope of the project now has grown. The scope of a project includes its goals, objectives, and expectations of the project.

Project leaders should use change management, which is the process of recognizing when a change in the project has occurred, taking actions to react to the change, and planning for opportunities because of the change. For example, the project leader may recognize the team will not be able to meet the original deadline of the project due to scope creep. Thus, the project leader may extend the deadline or may reduce the scope of the system development. If the latter occurs, the users will receive a less comprehensive system at the original deadline. In either case, the project leader revises the first project plan and presents the new plan to users for approval. It is crucial that everyone is aware of and agrees on any changes made to the project plan.

User Experience

The most important part of development is to consider how it will be used. User experience (UX) refers to the focus on the user's reaction to and interaction with a product, including its efficiency, effectiveness, and ease of use. UX comes into play during all aspects of the software development process. During the analysis phase, the needs of the customer help decide the scope of the project. A designer takes into account how the user will interact with the program to come up with a design that is appealing and easy to use. Programmers and testers work together to recreate and troubleshoot potential issues or areas of confusion. Designers use wireframes, which are blueprints of different aspects of the program that also indicate how a user gets from one area of the program to another (Figure 11-1).

Figure 11-1 UX designers plan a program's sequence, use of colors, and more.

iStock.com/YakobchukOlena

? Consider This

What is a macro?

A **macro** is a series of statements that instructs a program or app how to complete a task. Macros are simple programs that allow users to automate routine, repetitive, or difficult tasks in application software, such as word processing, spreadsheet, or database programs. You usually create a macro in one of two ways: (1) record the macro or (2) write the macro. A macro recorder is similar to a movie camera because both record all actions until turned off. Once the macro is recorded, you can run it any time you want to perform that same sequence of actions. When you become familiar with programming techniques, you can write your own macros instead of recording them. Have you ever used a macro? What did/could you use one for? What advantages and disadvantages can you think of to using macros?

Phases and Methods of Development

As previously stated, a project starts with a request or need for a new system or app, or enhancements to a current one. These requests may arise because new technology is available to improve an existing product or a need is identified. Regardless of how the need arises, you should view a project in terms of solving a problem. Part of forming a request for a project is to determine its description (what type of program is it, and how will it be created?), purpose (how will it be used?), and goals (what are the desired outcomes?). Another important determination is what type of data will the program collect and produce and what data type(s) are needed. Once the idea of a project is formed, the development can start. The set of activities used to build an app is called the **software development life cycle (SDLC)**.

The phases in the SDLC also can be applied to system development. Each activity, or phase, is a step in the life cycle. The goal in creating and using an SDLC is to produce the fastest, least expensive, and highest quality product. The steps can vary, and sometimes overlap, but most development processes include most or all of the following phases: planning, analysis, design, implementation, and support/security (Figure 11-2). System development also includes training users. To give context to each phase, consider the example of building a virtual reality app for firefighters to simulate fighting a fire in a high-rise building.

Figure 11-2 The SDLC.

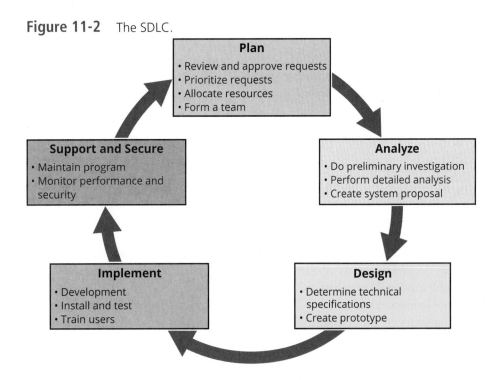

Planning Phase

The **planning phase** for a project begins with a request for the project and is triggered by the development of the project documentation. The request might come to a committee that authorizes development; that committee might consist of business managers, managers, and IT professionals. The committee performs four major activities, as follows:

- Review and approve requests.
- Prioritize project requests.
- Allocate resources such as money, people, and equipment.
- Form a project development team.

Analysis Phase

The **analysis phase** consists of two major components: conducting a preliminary investigation and performing detailed analysis. The preliminary investigation some-times is called a feasibility study. The goal of this part of the phase is to determine if the project is worth pursuing. **Feasibility** is the measure of the suitability of the development process to the individual project at any given time. This is a critical phase, as it provides the customer or client with a clear-cut plan for achieving the goals. If a program gets developed without a feasibility study, the work put into development could be wasted if stakeholders are not happy with the final product. Four general factors are used to determine a project's feasibility:

- Operational feasibility measures how well the product will work and whether it will meet the requirements of the users.
- Schedule feasibility determines if the deadlines for project phases are reasonable. Issues with schedule feasibility might lead to the project's timeline being extended or the scope of the features to be scaled back.
- Technical feasibility measures whether the developers have the skills and resources, as well as the number of programmers, to complete the features of the product.
- Economic (cost/benefit) feasibility determines whether the benefits (profits) will outweigh the costs of development and support.

Analysts conduct studies to reach a conclusion about whether or not the project should continue. This study might include interviewing the person(s) who submitted the initial request, reviewing existing documentation, and more. Detailed analysis produces an overview of the users' wants, needs, and requirements and recommends a solution. Once these steps are completed, if the committee or analysts determine the project should go forth, they produce a system proposal. The purpose of a **system proposal** is to use the data gathered during the feasibility study and detailed analysis to present a solution to the need or request.

Design Phase

The **design phase** is when the project team acquires the necessary hardware and programming tools, as well as develops the details of the finished product.

During the first part of the design phase, all technical specifications are determined, evaluated, and acquired. The team produces a list of requirements and sends out requests for solutions from potential vendors. Vendors submit back to the team proposals that include all estimated costs, as well as a timeline for completion. The team then makes decisions about how to best meet the technical needs of the project and accepts the proposals from vendors that meet those requirements.

The second phase outlines the specifications for each component in the finished project. This includes all input and output methods, as well as the actions a user can perform. During this phase, the analyst or developer will create charts and designs that show a mockup of the sample product. Other decisions that get made during this part of the phase include media, formats, data validation, and other factors developers use to create a prototype of the final product. A **prototype** is a working model that demonstrates the functionality of the program or app.

During this phase, the team working on the fire safety app chooses a designer from a short list of vendors who can meet the schedule and budget. The developer presents a chart of all the options and navigation methods of the training, as well as the technical specifications to complete the tasks. The team considers UX when designing with a prototype that includes the format, media, and sample data.

Implementation Phase

The purpose of the **implementation phase** is to build the product and deliver it to users. During this phase, the development team performs three major activities:

- Develop the product using programming tools or languages.
- Install and test the product, including each individual component and how it works with other programs and apps.
- Train users to use the new product, including one-on-one or group sessions, web-based tutorials, and user manuals.

In the case of a product that will be used on a network or system, such as a database, or an information system, the final step in the implementation phase is to convert to the new system. Conversion can happen all at once, in phases, or as a pilot program in one location or department.

- With **direct conversion**, the user stops using the old product and begins using the new product on a certain date. The advantage of this strategy is that it requires no transition costs and is a quick implementation technique. The disadvantage is that it is extremely risky and can disrupt operations seriously if the new product does not work correctly the first time.
- **Parallel conversion** consists of running the old product alongside the new product for a specified time. Results from both products are compared. The advantage of this strategy is that you can fix any problems in the new product before you terminate the old product. The disadvantage is that it is costly to operate two products or systems at the same time.
- In a **phased conversion**, each location converts at a separate time. For example, an accounting system might convert its accounts receivable, accounts payable, general ledger, and payroll sites in separate phases. Each site can use a direct or parallel conversion. Larger systems with multiple sites may use a phased conversion.
- With a **pilot conversion**, only one location in the organization uses the new product so that it can be tested. After the pilot site approves the new product, other sites convert using one of the other conversion strategies.

During this phase, the developers create the first versions of the finished app by using programming tools. They recruit users to install and test the product on various devices, and incorporate their feedback. Then they test the app with a wider audience, and train firefighters to use the app. The team also creates a user manual that is accessible from the app.

Support and Security Phase

During the **support and security phase**, the product receives necessary maintenance, such as fixing errors or improving its functionality. Analysts also monitor the performance to ensure efficiency.

One of the most important parts of development is ensuring security. All elements must be secure from hacking, or from unauthorized collection of data of its users. Security concerns are addressed through each phase of development, and apps are tested for reliability.

One of the ways developers ensure that their products work as intended is to test them thoroughly. During the **testing** process, each function is tested to ensure it works

properly. Testing starts at the first phases of development and continues throughout. **Quality assurance** testers perform the testing and report any issues to the developers.

Testers and developers include documentation in the code. Documentation involves adding notes to the code that explain and outline the intended function of sections or lines of code. During development, project members produce documentation. It is important that all documentation be well written, thorough, consistent, and understandable. Project managers distribute documentation guidelines to all project members to ensure that the documentation each produces will be complete and consistent. Documentation reflects the development process in detail. Developers should produce documentation during development, not after, in order to ensure its accuracy and thoroughness. Documentation also can be used as the basis for user manuals and instructions that help users learn how to use the product's features. Reputable developers include both testing and documentation for all of their products.

During this phase, the team continues to add different scenarios to the app, increasing the knowledge that can be gained by using it. Each new scenario is thoroughly tested before its release. The team also addresses any security issues that arise.

Development Methodologies

Several methodologies exist to guide the SDLC process. They can be broken down into two main categories. **Predictive development** uses a linear, structured development cycle. One example of predictive development is the waterfall method. The **waterfall method** takes each step individually and completes it before continuing to the next phase (Figure 11-3).

Figure 11-3 The waterfall method.

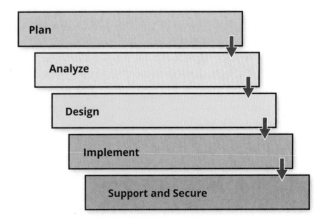

Figure 11-4 Agile development.

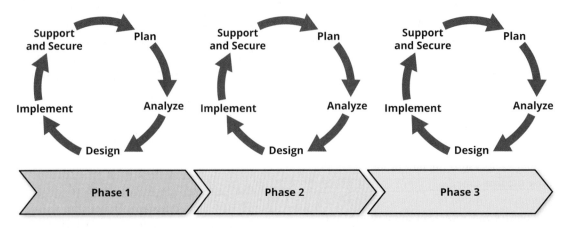

Agile development, also called adaptive development, incorporates flexibility in the goals and scope of the project. Agile projects may evolve in phases, releasing components as they are finalized and adding functionality as it is needed or requested by users (Figure 11-4). Agile development incorporates testing and feedback from users and stakeholders at all phases of the process, making it more responsive to rapidly changing technologies and markets.

Rapid application development (RAD) uses a condensed or shortened development process to produce a quality product. The team involved must be highly skilled at programming and development to ensure the quality of the code and instructions. RAD development is best for projects with a clear goal and limited scope. RAD projects can be lower in cost because of the shortened process and they work well for time-sensitive programs.

DevOps encourages collaboration between the development and operations. DevOps produces programs quickly and then offers continuous updates to increase the functionality of the program. While DevOps ensures frequent releases of fixes and enhancements, some users prefer to have a complete product from the start, without needing continuous updates.

The methodology chosen depends on several factors. If the project is based on previous known successful projects, predictive methods may be the best choice. For projects without a clear goal or whose scope may change, agile development works best.

System Development Tools and Strategies

One aspect of managing projects is to ensure that everyone submits deliverables on time and according to plan. A deliverable is any tangible item, such as a chart, diagram, report, or program file. Charts can help to create schedules and assign tasks. Developers also use project management software to assist them in planning, scheduling, and controlling development projects (Figure 11-5). Project management is the process of planning, scheduling, and then controlling the activities during system development.

Figure 11-5 Project management software is used to track the status of tasks.

iStock.com/AndreyPopov

 Consider This

How are projects prioritized?

The projects that receive the highest priority are those mandated by management or some other governing body. These requests are given immediate attention. Other project requests are evaluated based on their value to the organization. Some projects are approved, and others are rejected because of lack of time, money, or resources. Of the approved projects, it is likely that only a few will begin system development immediately. Others will have to wait for additional funds or resources to become available. Have you ever had to prioritize competing projects? What qualities might you use to evaluate whether a project has value and should continue?

During system development, members of the project team gather data and information. They need accurate and timely data and information for many reasons. They must keep a project on schedule, evaluate feasibility, and be sure the system meets requirements.

Gantt and PERT Charts

Popular tools used to plan and schedule the time relationships among project activities are Gantt and PERT charts (Figure 11-6).

- A **Gantt chart**, developed by Henry L. Gantt, is a bar chart that uses horizontal bars to show project phases or activities. The left side, or vertical axis, displays the list of required activities. A horizontal axis across the top or bottom of the chart represents time.
- Developed by the U.S. Department of Defense, a **PERT chart**, short for Program Evaluation and Review Technique chart, analyzes the time required to complete a task and identifies the minimum time required for an entire project.

PERT charts, sometimes called network diagrams, can be more complicated to create than Gantt charts, but are better suited than Gantt charts for planning and scheduling large, complex projects.

Select Project Management Software

Several project management programs and apps are available, some for free while others are fee based. These programs and apps are designed for projects of specific sizes, so be sure to research the various programs and apps on the market and choose one that best suits your needs. To manage a project using project management software, follow these steps:

1. Make sure you understand the project in its entirety, as well as the steps you must take to bring the project to completion.
2. Determine the date by which the project must be completed.
3. Verify you have the appropriate resources (people and materials) to complete the project. If you do not have the necessary resources, obtain them, if possible.
4. Determine the order of the steps that must be taken to bring the project to completion. Identify steps that must be taken before other steps, as well as steps that can be completed at the same time as other steps.
5. Verify the feasibility of the plan.
6. During the project, it will be necessary to update the progress and possibly adjust dates. Changes to the project and its dates should be communicated to the entire project team.

Figure 11-6   Sample Gantt and PERT charts.

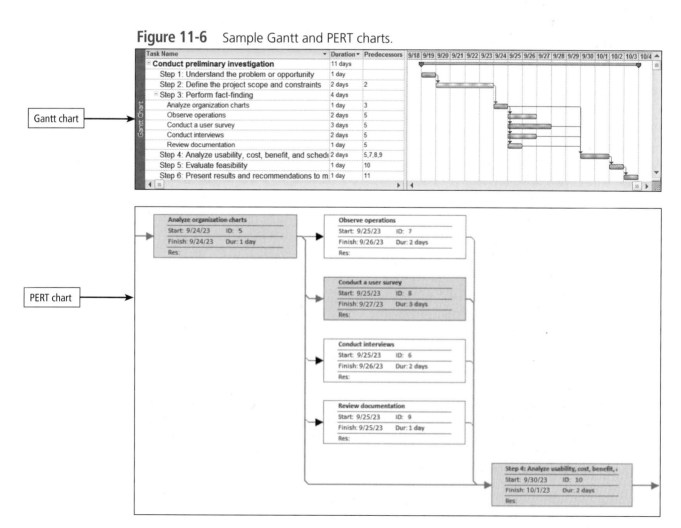

Data and Information Gathering Techniques

Systems analysts and other IT professionals use several techniques to gather data and information. They review documentation, observe, survey, interview, conduct joint-application design sessions, and research.

- **Review documentation:** By reviewing documentation, such as organization charts, memos, and meeting minutes, systems analysts learn about the history of a project. Documentation also provides information about the organization, such as its operations, weaknesses, and strengths.
- **Observe:** Observing people helps systems analysts understand exactly how they perform a task. Likewise, observing a machine allows someone to see how it works.
- **Survey:** To obtain data and information from a large number of people, systems analysts distribute surveys.
- **Interview:** The interview is the most important data and information gathering technique for the systems analyst. It allows the systems analyst to clarify responses and probe during face-to-face feedback.
- **JAD sessions:** Instead of a single one-on-one interview, analysts often use joint-application design sessions to gather data and information. A **joint-application design (JAD) session**, or **focus group**, consists of a series of lengthy, structured group meetings in which users and IT professionals work together to design or develop an application (Figure 11-7).

- **Research:** Newspapers, technology magazines and journals, reference books, trade shows, the web, vendors, and consultants are excellent sources of information. These sources can provide the systems analyst with information, such as the latest hardware and software products and explanations of new processes and procedures. In addition, systems analysts often collect website statistics, such as the number of visitors and most-visited webpages, etc., and then evaluate these statistics as part of their research.

❓ Consider This

How important is documentation?

The final information system should be reflected accurately and completely in documentation developed throughout the development project. During system development, project members produce a large amount of documentation. Maintaining up-to-date documentation should be an ongoing part of system development. Too often, project team members put off documentation until the end of the project because it is time consuming, but these practices typically result in lower-quality documentation. Documentation helps with large projects that involve multiple programmers to see what work others have done, what the status is of a section of code, and more. Documentation also can be helpful when a program is being updated by a new team of developers. If you were working on a large project, what types of things would you consider important to document? What would you like others to document? Think of a group project you have worked on, and what steps were/could have been helped by using documentation.

Figure 11-7 Focus groups provide valuable user feedback.
iStock.com/Monkeybusinessimages

System Development Tasks and Roles

The programmer might be the first person you think of when you consider a project's development; however, with a complex software product, many roles need to be filled. Some people may take on multiple roles, and other tasks might be so large that they require many individuals to complete. Whether you are one or one of many, some of the required software development roles are listed in Table 11-1.

System Development Participants

System development should involve representatives from each department in which the proposed system will be used. This includes both nontechnical users and IT professionals. Although the roles and responsibilities of members of the system development team may change from organization to organization, this module presents general descriptions of tasks for various team members. For each system development project, an organization usually forms a **project team** to work on the project from beginning to end. The project team consists of users, the systems analyst, and other IT professionals.

During system development, the systems analyst meets and works with a variety of people. A **systems analyst** is responsible for designing and developing an information system. The systems analyst is the users' primary contact person. Depending on the size of the organization, the tasks performed by the systems analyst may vary. Smaller organizations may have one systems analyst or even one person who assumes the roles of both systems analyst and software developer. Larger organizations often have multiple systems analysts who discuss various aspects of the development project with users, management, other analysts, database analysts, database administrators, network administrators, web developers, software developers, and vendors.

Project Leadership and Management

The goal of project management is to deliver an acceptable system to the user in an agreed-upon time frame, while maintaining costs. In smaller organizations or projects, one person manages the entire project. For larger projects, the project management activities often are separated between a project manager and a project leader. In this situation, the project leader manages and controls the budget and schedule of the project, and the project manager controls the activities during system development. Project leaders and/or project managers are part of the project team. The systems analyst either acts as the project manager or works closely with the project manager.

To plan and schedule a project effectively, the project leader identifies the following elements:

- Scope
- Required activities
- Time estimates for each activity
- Cost estimates for each activity
- Order of activities
- Activities that can take place at the same time

After these items are identified, the project leader usually records them in a project plan, often using project management software.

Obtain Hardware and Software

After the project is approved, the systems analyst begins the activity of obtaining additional hardware or software or evaluating cloud providers that offer the computing services to meet the organization's needs. The systems analyst may skip this activity if the approved solution does not require new hardware or software. If this activity is required, it consists of four major tasks: (1) identify technical specifications, (2) solicit vendor proposals, (3) test and evaluate vendor proposals, and (4) make a decision.

Table 11-1 Common Roles and Responsibilities of the Software Development Team

Role	Duties
Project manager	A person dedicated to coordinating project components and ensuring that each member is progressing as planned; oversees the product's team, budget, and schedule; reports to the development company's management
Designer	Develops the program's user interface, including colors, fonts, and layout
Programmer	Writes code or uses a product development app to create the program's specifications
Testers	Review every aspect and functionality of a program to ensure it works as intended
IT department	Interacts with customers and users of the product to assist them with any issues that arise

Identify Technical Specifications The first step in acquiring necessary hardware and software is to identify all the hardware and software requirements of the new or modified system. To do this, systems analysts use a variety of research techniques. They talk with other systems analysts, visit vendors' stores, and search the web. Many trade journals, newspapers, and magazines provide some or all their printed content online.

After the systems analyst defines the technical requirements, the next step is to summarize these requirements for potential vendors. The systems analyst can use three basic types of documents for this purpose: an RFQ, an RFP, or an RFI.

- A **request for quotation (RFQ)** identifies the required product(s). With an RFQ, the vendor quotes a price for the listed product(s).
- With a **request for proposal (RFP)**, the vendor selects the product(s) that meets specified requirements and then quotes the price(s).
- A **request for information (RFI)** is a less formal method that uses a standard form to request information about a product or service.

Solicit Vendor Proposals Systems analysts send the RFQ, RFP, or RFI to potential hardware and software vendors. Another source for hardware and software products is a value-added reseller. A **value-added reseller (VAR)** is an organization that purchases products from manufacturers and then resells these products to the public — offering additional services with the product.

Instead of using vendors, some organizations hire an IT consultant or a group of IT consultants. An **IT consultant** is a professional who is hired based on technical expertise, including service and advice.

Test and Evaluate Vendor Proposals After sending RFQs, RFPs, or RFIs to potential vendors, the systems analyst will receive completed quotations and proposals. Evaluating the proposals and then selecting the best one often is a difficult task.

Systems analysts use many techniques to test the various software products from vendors. They obtain a list of user references from the software vendors. They also talk to current users of the software to solicit their opinions. Some vendors will provide a demonstration of the product(s) specified. Others supply demonstration copies or trial versions, allowing the organizations to test the software themselves.

Make a Decision Having rated the proposals, the systems analyst presents a recommendation to the committee or person in charge of making a decision. Typically, those with decision-making responsibilities are part of an organization's management team and are in charge of setting a company's priorities and goals, securing funding, and ensuring that projects have the support that they need. The recommendation could be to award a contract to a vendor or to not make any purchases at this time. The recommendations should include information about the process taken in the first three steps, including the top proposals (if any) and reasons for making the recommendation.

If it is decided that a project will go forward, the development team will then start the technical work of coding and creating the project using a programming language and development tools.

 Consider This ———————————————

How can a program's performance be measured?
Sometimes it is important to know whether the software can process a certain volume of transactions efficiently. In this case, the systems analyst conducts a benchmark test. A benchmark test measures the performance of hardware or software. For example, a benchmark test could measure the time it takes a payroll program to print 50 paychecks. Comparing the time it takes various accounting programs to print the same 50 paychecks is one way of measuring each program's performance. What do you think would happen if a program failed its benchmark test? Who would be responsible for fixing the problem? Have you ever worked with a program that ran slowly or had problems when processing multiple requests? What would you, as a user, suggest to remedy the problem?

Development Languages and Tools

A **programming language** is a set of words, abbreviations, and symbols that a programmer or developer uses to create instructions for a program or app. Several hundred programming languages exist today. Each language has its own rules, or **syntax**, for writing instructions. Some languages are designed for a specific type of application. Others can be used for a variety of programs and apps. Because each language has its strengths and features, often developers use more than one language during development.

Programming Language Generations

With each generation of programming languages, the process became easier and more human-like. This progress has enabled high-quality programs to be developed in a shorter amount of time and with fewer errors. The first languages that were developed are considered low-level languages. Two types of low-level languages include machine and assembly languages.

- **Machine languages** are first generation language; their instructions use a series of binary digits (0s and 1s) (Figure 11-8). Coding in machine language is tedious and time consuming. Assembly languages are the second generation of languages.
- With an **assembly language**, the programmer uses symbolic instruction codes, such as A for add, M for multiply, and L for load. These languages can be difficult to learn. Procedural languages, such as C and Fortran, are the third generation of languages and are considered high-level languages.

Procedural languages use a series of English-like words to write instructions, such as ADD for addition, or PRINT for printing.

Fourth generation languages, or **4GLs**, provide a graphical environment in which the programmer uses a combination of English-like instructions, graphics, icons, and symbols to create code. Fifth generation languages, or **5GLs**, was an attempt to create programs that solve problems without requiring the programmer to write algorithms. This proved difficult to implement; many 5GLs on the market actually are 4GLs that include some automation.

Types of Programming Tools

Application development tools provide a user-friendly environment for building programs and apps. These languages provide methods to create, test, and translate programs and apps.

- A **source code editor** is a text editor designed for programming. When you enter code in a source code editor, the editor adds color-coding to highlight syntax to differentiate between types of code, indentation for substeps, autocompletion of common instructions, and the automatic addition of braces and other punctuation that separates code (Figure 11-9).

Figure 11-9 Editing source code.

iStock.com/Traffic_analyzer

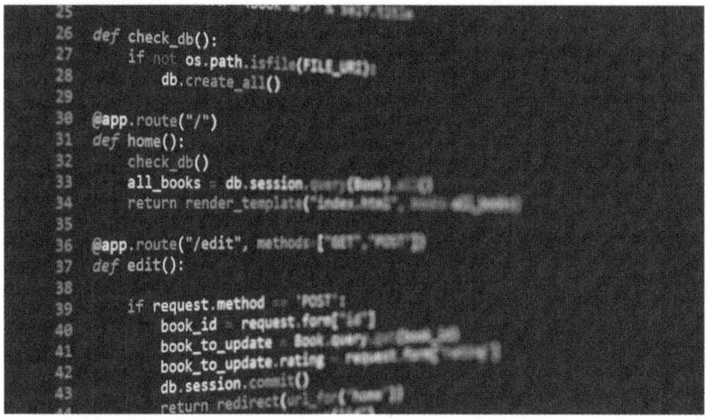

- Programmers also use **debuggers** to test code in one section, or an entire program, to determine any errors and provide suggestions to fix them. Debuggers often will stop running the code when an issue is detected in order to highlight exactly where in the code the error occurs. Some allow you to step through the code one instruction at a time to ensure each phase works as intended.

Assembly and procedural languages produce a program's source code. In order to run the program or app, the source code must be translated into machine

Figure 11-8 Translating text into binary code.

"Be the change that you wish to see in the world."
— Mahatma Gandhi

```
00100010 01000010 01100101 00100000 01110100
01101000 01100101 00100000 01100011 01101000
01100001 01101110 01100111 01100101 00100000
01110100 01101000 01100001 01110100 00100000
01111001 01101111 01110101 00100000 01110111
01101001 01110011 01101000 00100000 01110100
01101111 00100000 01110011 01100101 01100101
00100000 01101001 01101110 00100000 01110100
01101000 01100101 00100000 01110111 01101111
01110010 01101100 01100100 00101110 00011101
00100000 00001010 00010101 00100000 01001101
01100001 01101000 01100001 01110100 01101101
01100001 00100000 01000111 01100001 01101110
01100100 01101000 01101001 00100000
```

language, the 0s and 1s of binary code. The two tools that assist in translation are compilers and interpreters.

- A **compiler** is a separate program that converts the entire source program into machine language before executing it. The output from a compiler is the object code, which the compiler stores so that the program or app can be run. The compiler also produces a list of errors in the source code.
- An **interpreter** translates and executes one statement at a time. Interpreters do not produce or store object code. Each time the source program runs, the interpreter translates instructions statement by statement.

Programmers might use separate tools for each of these or use an **integrated development environment** (**IDE**). An IDE is an application that provides multiple programming tools in one environment. The benefit of an IDE is that you become familiar with one interface, and the tools can work together to automate and perfect your program.

To make creating programs and apps even easier, IDEs that use 3-D environments, such as Unity (Figure 11-10), enable developers to create and add code and visualize the effects at the same time. These environments combine code editors and graphical previews and enable the creation of a program that can run on multiple platforms.

A **software development kit** (**SDK**) is a set of programming tools that includes a programming interface, compiler, debugger, and more. Often, SDKs are proprietary and can be used to develop apps that run on that company's platform and device. For example, you cannot use an Android SDK to create an app that will run on Apple's iOS.

A **code repository** is another web-based tool programmers use to archive and host source code. Repositories are often used by open source projects so that developers can access the parts of the code they want to modify. Many code repositories include social aspects that enable programmers to connect with each other, comment on, and share code.

Object-Oriented Programming

A common method of programming is object-oriented. Software developers use **object-oriented programming** (**OOP**) tools to implement objects in a program. In programming, an **object** is an item that can contain both data and the procedures that read or manipulate that data. An object represents a real person, place, event, or transaction. A **class** is a type of object that defines the format of the object and the actions an object can perform. Each object in a class has the same format and can be used in the same way. A **method** defines the behavior of an object. Python (Figure 11-11) is an example of a high-level language that uses OOP and which is used for large-scale projects.

One benefit of OOP is the ability to reuse and modify existing objects. For example, a program developed for a human resources department might have a class called Employee, with objects for both part-time and full-time employees. Both objects can be used by the payroll program as well as the health benefits program. Developers can create programs and apps faster, because they design programs using existing objects.

Figure 11-10 Unity 3-D game development environment.
Source: Unity Technologies 2018

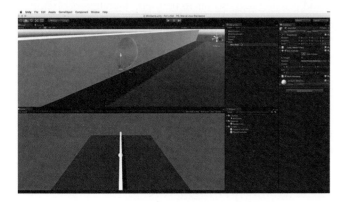

Figure 11-11 Python is a popular programming language.
Source: Python Software Foundation

When determining which OOP language or tool to use, developers rely on the following guidelines:

- Determine the device(s) on which the program or app will run. Some platforms, such as Apple devices, have limited languages and tools available.
- Explore the capabilities of each language or tool, as they vary greatly.
- Consider the speed at which programs and apps developed with a certain language or tool will run.
- Determine the type of environment the program or tool offers. Some rely only on text editors, while others provide graphical interfaces and text editors.

❓ Consider This

How do you determine which program or tool to use?
You, as a software developer, can choose from a variety of object-oriented programming languages and application development tools to write a program or app for a computer or mobile device. First, determine the types of devices on which your program or app will run. For example, if you are writing an app for a mobile device, limited languages and tools may be available for you to use. Determine the capabilities of the programming languages you are considering using, as some programming languages have greater capabilities than others. Consider the speed at which programs and apps run that are written in a particular programming language. For example, a program or app might run faster if it is written in one language as opposed to another. Consider whether you want to write a program using a text editor or an IDE. Solicit recommendations from other developers. Explain the type of program or app you plan to write and consider suggestions they might offer. What other criteria could you use to evaluate programs and tools? If you must write a program or app using a programming language with which you are not very familiar, what resources can you utilize to obtain assistance?

Secure IT: Designing Secure Systems and Applications

Security is part of development at all stages. Often it is the reason a new app or system is being created in the first place, as a response to evolving security threats from hackers who look for system flaws or to incorporate new security techniques and tools to create a more robust app or system. Questions to ask about security during development include:

- What security risks are known for the type of app or system you are creating? How will you address these issues?
- What logic errors might cause security flaws or other issues? How will you debug the program to ensure it meets the highest standards?
- How secure is the language or tool that is being used during development? What security flaws are known, and how will you work with them?

- What measures will you take during each phase to ensure security?
- How will you protect users' personal data during the lifetime of the product?
- How will you protect the code of your app or system from people trying to copy it for their own uses?
- At what point would you consider an update or revision to the product to be necessary?

You already have learned about the debugging process, which ensures that the code works as intended, and benchmark tests that determine the product's capabilities. Other tests exist that are used during development and implementation of an app or system, some of which are discussed in the following section.

Tests During Development

At each stage, and for more complex projects, multiple times during each stage, tests should be conducted that expose any security flaws so that they can be addressed and fixed before the product is launched. Often the quality assurance testers drive this process or are involved in some way. One method of testing is to use the program as intended, using appropriate input and steps to ensure that the outcome is as expected. Other methods include the following:

- A **security audit** looks at common security practices and ensures that the app or system meets the recommended criteria.
- With **penetration testing**, developers attempt to break into the app or system. These can involve trying to gain unauthorized access that can be used to pinpoint security vulnerabilities.
- **Fuzz testing** (also called fuzzing) uses automated tools that test a system by using unexpected input to ensure the app or system does not crash.

All these tests can point out security, performance, or quality gaps or issues before a product is launched.

Tests at the End of Development

At the late stages of development, prerelease versions of the product, called a **beta version**, may be released so that select users can start using the product to determine any additional work that is needed. An advantage of beta testing is that the product is being used by real users in the way that they actually will be using the final product. These users, called beta testers, often are selected or offered the opportunity to participate in the development of the new product in order to find errors in usage or security.

Other tests that the system analysts run include:

- A **unit test** verifies that each individual program or object works by itself.
- A **systems test** verifies that all programs in an application work together properly.

- An **integration test** verifies that an application works with other applications.
- An **acceptance test** is performed by end users and checks the new system to ensure that it works with actual data.

? Consider This

What consequences are associated with releasing a product with security flaws?

If you are selling your app or system, you rely on positive reviews of your product to ensure that users continue to purchase it. If a security breach occurs and users' personal data is stolen, the public relations efforts to combat the problem can be as expensive as the measures necessary to fix the problem. If your app or system will be used by an internal group, such as within your own company, the security risks mean that your customers' data — as well as your company's proprietary information — could be stolen. Stolen company information can mean that your financial information and future development plans can be made public along with your employees' data. Companies that have dealt with security breaches have been the targets of large, class-action lawsuits from customers whose data has been stolen. The expense of these lawsuits can cause a company to lay off employees or even declare bankruptcy. Have you ever been the victim of a security breach? What responsibility did/should a company take when this occurs? What security features do you look for when purchasing apps or systems for your own use?

How To: Place Your App in an App Store

Before you offer your app in an app store, you need to protect your creation. When you create a program or app, you are protected under copyright laws, even before you apply for them. Programs and apps are considered the intellectual property of the creator(s). As part of development, you should consider the type of license(s) you want to offer, or whether to distribute the program or app as open source. Recall that licenses are categorized by the number of allowed users: single user (also known as an end-user license agreement, or EULA), multiple users (specifies a limit to the number of users), and site license (enables an organization to provide access to as many users as it wants).

Websites exist that help developers acquire trademarks and copyrights, often for a fee. You also should secure a domain name for your company or product so that you can ensure you have a website to sell, market, and support the program or app. You may want to consider hiring an attorney who specializes in digital copyrights in order to protect against piracy and to develop your license agreements.

Using an App Store

Once you have a completed app that is secure, protected, and error-free, you are ready to share it with users. Depending on the platform on which the app was developed, you may be limited to one app store, such as Google's PlayStore. App stores may charge you a small one-time account setup fee to start using the app store, after which you can upload as many apps as you wish.

After you upload your app but before it is published, run additional tests within the device's environment to ensure that no additional security flaws are uncovered. You then will need to create a listing for your app. The listing should include an icon, screenshots, description, and demo videos. For each app you upload, you will need to fill out a ratings questionnaire that enables the app store to solicit, collect, and publish user reviews. This step is not optional, and by skipping it you run the risk of having your app removed from the play store. Once you have user ratings and reviews, you can include those in your listing. If you are selling your app, consider the price to set by looking at comparable apps. You may give your app away at no cost but charge advertisers to include ads in your app, or you might allow for in-app purchases that can be used to upgrade the app's features or enable boosters in a game.

Once your app is uploaded, you need to continue to monitor the ratings and reviews. It is good practice to react to negative reviews by posting a response or by fixing or updating the app if necessary (Figure 11-12). You also will need to continue to advertise the app on your website, by promoting it using paid ads in the app store, or by using targeted social media advertising.

? Consider This

Should you offer your app in multiple languages?

When you upload your app to an app store, you specify the language in which the instructions and other content are written, as well as what regions of the world in which your app should be sold and promoted. The default language is United States English, although your app can be in any language you choose. You might be tempted to use a quick translation service to convert any text to another language in order to reach a global audience; however, you might create unintended issues if you do not take the time to prepare a specific version of your app geared towards a culture or country. Some languages, such as Arabic, read right to left instead of left to right. Other cultures may find idioms or your choice of graphics hard to understand or even offensive. If you plan to offer your app in multiple languages, deciding to do so before development will enable you to take into consideration cultural and language preferences. Planning for releases in multiple languages also allows you time to translate documentation and any instructions, to ensure that the UX for your app will be positive for all versions. Have you ever used an app that seems like it was created for another language or by someone not a native speaker of your primary language? What types of issues did/might occur? As a developer, what do you see as the main challenge of creating apps that reach a global or cross-cultural audience?

Figure 11-12   You can manage your reviews using the Google Play Console.
Source: Google LLC

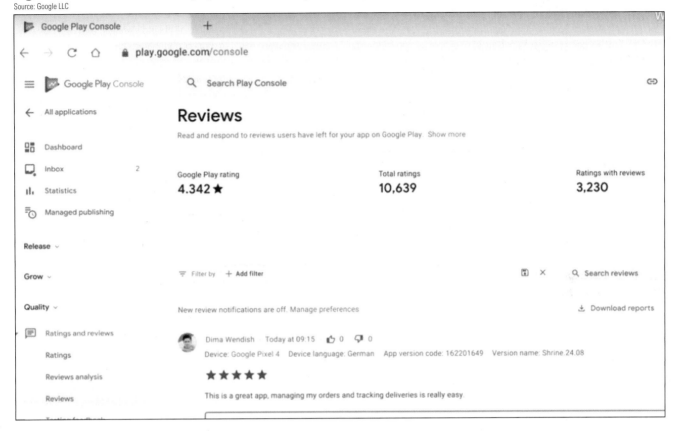

Ethics and Issues: The Social and Ethical Obligations of a Developer

Ethical decisions you make during development go beyond protecting your app or system's users' privacy. **Ethical design** is a set of evolving principles that developers should follow to enhance UX, to make data collection usage transparent, and to enable users to easily make choices that protect their privacy.

Some principles of ethical design include:

- Do not hide or obscure options that enable users to accept cookies, allow the app to access their location, or other options that may affect a user's privacy. The best policy is to ask permission before accessing a device's GPS or turning on its camera.
- Include an easily accessible statement that lists the privacy and security features of the app and a method of notifying users when the features change.
- Do not collect more data than is needed. If a user's account can be created using only a few pieces of information (such as email and username), do not ask for additional distinguishing information, such as address,

age, or income level, that may be of value to data brokers but does not increase the UX.

- Always request permission before sending the user push notifications. A **push notification** is an alert sent through the user's device's notifications, or by email or text, that may let users know about new features or remind them when a game booster is available. (The opposite of a push notification is a **pull notification**, which is sent in response to a user's actions or request).
- Clearly distinguish ads from app content. For example, in a travel app, let users know which search results are sponsored and separate those from results that might be more relevant to their needs.

Ethical design may also take into consideration technology addiction and the issues that arise when users spend too much time on their devices. Some app developers include time management options that disable an app during certain hours or after a specific time interval. Many games have stopped sending reminders to play the game periodically so as not to distract users.

How can you evaluate an app for ethical design?
You not only should recognize the signs of unethical design if you are developing an app, but you also should be able to identify it as a user. You can start the process before you even download or enable an app by reading its reviews, doing a search for known data breaches or security flaws, and reading its statement about privacy and data collection. If you download a free app, consider how the developers are making money on the app. Is it through advertising? Is it clear what is sponsored content? Might the app be selling your data to a data broker? One way to protect your data is to be aware of what information is required to create an account or register an app and enter only the minimum required data. If you discover that an app is misusing your data or accessing your location or camera without your permission, you should uninstall the app and report it to the app store. Have you ever used an app that used unethical design? How did/could you know? What other steps can you take to protect yourself?

Problem Solving and Decision Making

All apps and systems are developed to create a solution to a problem. Sometimes that solution is simply to provide a way for users to have fun by creating a game. Other problems require solutions that are more complex or even urgent. By thinking of development as problem solving, however, you gain a context that enables you to apply the methods and strategies you have learned to create solutions.

Common to all development are the following principles that enable decision making:

- First identify a problem's description, purpose, and goals. Determining these will enable you to create a solution. For example, a description might be an app that matches dog owners with local dog walkers, with the purpose of providing dog owners with scheduling and paying for people to take care of their dogs and for dog sitters to specify the scope of work, their price, and provide references. The goals of the app would be to make money through commission by charging users a fee to use and advertise on the app.

- Identify and use the appropriate data type with which to represent and classify the data in a program. Recall that data types can determine the use of, allowed input for, and length of data. For example, a phone number would be saved as short text, but a number that could be used in calculations would be saved numerically. Your data has more value if it is properly classified in order to be used as intended.

- Understand how to use algorithms to solve problems. An **algorithm** is a process or set of rules used in problem-solving, such as calculations. Algorithms specify the procedures and actions that a program uses to process input and create output.

- Understand that computer data is represented using the binary system. Recall that the binary system uses combinations of 0s and 1s to represent data. To count in the binary system, you alternate using zeroes and ones. For example, 1 in binary is 01. To continue counting, you add a digit for each number, so two is 1 0, three is 1 1, four is 1 0 0, and so on (Figure 11-13). You can convert digital numbers to binary, and vice versa, using formulas.

Figure 11-13   Converting numbers to binary.

Decimal	Binary
1	01
2	10
3	11
4	100
5	101
6	110
7	111
8	1000
9	1001
10	1010

- Use variables within a program. In programming, a variable is a named location in memory used to store information, such as a value, that is used in a program. Although the value of the variable might change, the program will perform the appropriate actions on the value because it uses the variable name in its code. For example, a program might include an instruction to calculate how many days are left before an event. Because the current date will continue to change, using a variable will allow the output to be accurate as the value changes.

- Use arithmetic operators to create mathematical expressions. You will need to understand not only what each is used for (addition, subtraction, multiplication, and division) but the order in which operations in complex calculations will occur. You also will need to ensure that the proper data type is used for numerical data. For example, data such as a phone number, which would not be used in a calculation, are assigned the text data type, and data such as hours an employee works are assigned the numeric data type.

- Understand how to use sequencing within a program. A sequence is a set of steps that must be completed in a certain order. For example, in storytelling or instructions, using an incorrect sequence will confuse the user.

- Use conditional statements to instruct the program to make decisions. Similar to Boolean operators, a condition is either true or false. Programs use If… Then…Else statements to determine the action to take (Figure 11-14).

Figure 11-14   Sample If…Then…Else statement.

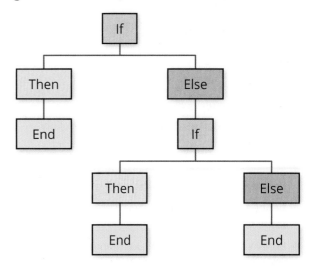

- Use iterations, which are repetitions of a sequence of instructions. An iteration can occur until a certain condition is reached, stop after a specified number of times, or occur until all items in a list have been through the sequence.

? Consider This

What is a sandbox?

A sandbox is an environment that allows software developers to test their programs with fictitious data without adversely affecting other programs, information systems, or data. Sandboxes are used for testing purposes both by developers and users. Developers use sandboxes to test code or sections of code. Often used for revisions, the sandbox environment will mimic the environment (system and network) into which the new code will be placed. Developers can see how the code affects the environment without impacting the actual system and users. Users often work with a sandbox to familiarize themselves with a new program or information system before they use it. Security experts also use sandboxes by trying to hack in or release malicious code to see how it would affect the system. Do you see any disadvantages to using a sandbox? If so, what? In what other situations might you use a sandbox?

Study Guide

Instructions: Answer the questions below using the format that helps you remember best or that is required by your instructor. Possible formats may include one or more of these options: write the answers; create a document that contains the answers; record answers as audio or video using a webcam, smartphone, or portable media player; post answers on a blog, wiki, or website; or highlight answers in the book/e-book.

1. Define the term, development.

2. List three guidelines developers generally follow.

3. Explain reasons why a new product may be developed.

4. _____ is a collection and summary of the data, information, and deliverables specific to the project.

5. Define the term, scope. Explain what occurs during scope creep.

6. Explain how project leaders use change management.

7. Explain the importance of UX.

8. Describe how macros are used and created.

9. List phases in the SDLC. During which phase would a committee review and approve requests and form a project development team?

10. _____ is the measure of the suitability of the development process to the individual project at any given time.

11. List the four factors that affect feasibility.

12. Explain the purpose of a system proposal.

13. Define the term, prototype. During which phase of the SDLC might a prototype be created?

14. Differentiate among direct, parallel, phased, and pilot conversion.

15. Who performs testing of a product?

16. Differentiate between predictive development and the waterfall method.

17. Describe how agile development is used.

18. What does RAD stand for?

19. What is an advantage of the DevOps approach?

20. Explain how projects are prioritized.

21. A(n) _____ is any tangible item, such as a chart, diagram, report, or program file.

22. Explain the project management process.

23. Describe how project managers use Gantt charts and PERT charts.

24. List steps to manage a project using project management software.

25. List techniques IT professionals use to gather data and information about a project. What is a JAD session?

26. Explain the importance of documentation.

27. Describe the role of, and participants in, a project team.

28. Describe the role of the system analyst.

29. List elements a project leader uses to plan and schedule a project effectively.

30. What major tasks occur if additional hardware or software is needed during development?

31. Differentiate among an RFQ, RFP, and RFI.

32. Define the term, VAR.

33. Explain how a systems analyst would test and evaluate the vendor proposals.

34. Describe how a benchmark test is used.

35. Each programming language has its own rules, or _____, for writing instructions.

36. Differentiate among machine, assembly, and procedural languages.

37. Describe characteristics of 4GLs and 5GLs.

38. Explain how each of the following is used: source code editor, debugger, compiler, and interpreter.

39. Define these terms: IDE, SDK, and code repository.

40. In terms of OOP, describe how objects, classes, and methods are used.

41. List security questions you might ask during development.

42. Describe the differences among the following types of tests: unit, systems, integration, and acceptance.

43. Explain the consequences of releasing a product with security flaws.

44. Describe steps you can take to protect your product before it is released.

45. Explain considerations for sharing your app using an app store.

46. Explain considerations when determining whether to produce your app in multiple languages.

47. Describe principles of ethical design. What is a push notification?

48. Explain principles that enable decision making. A(n) _____ is a process or set of rules used in problem-solving, such as calculations.

49. Define these terms: variable, sequence, conditional statement, and iteration.

Key Terms

You should be able to define the Key Terms listed below.

4GL (11-11)

5GL (11-11)

acceptance test (11-14)

adaptive development (11-6)

agile development (11-6)

algorithm (11-16)

analysis phase (11-4)

assembly language (11-11)

beta version (11-13)

change management (11-2)

class (11-12)

code repository (11-12)

compiler (11-12)

conditional statement (11-17)

debugger (11-11)

deliverable (11-6)

design phase (11-4)

development (11-2)

DevOps (11-6)

direct conversion (11-5)

documentation (11-2)

ethical design (11-15)

feasibility (11-4)

focus group (11-8)

fuzz testing (11-13)

Gantt chart (11-7)

implementation phase (11-4)

integrated development environment (IDE) (11-12)

integration test (11-14)

interpreter (11-12)

IT consultant (11-10)

iteration (11-17)

joint-application design (JAD) session (11-8)

machine language (11-11)

macro (11-3)

method (11-12)

object (11-12)

object-oriented programming (OOP) (11-12)

parallel conversion (11-5)

penetration testing (11-13)

PERT chart (11-7)

phased conversion (11-5)

pilot conversion (11-5)

planning phase (11-4)

predictive development (11-5)

procedural language (11-11)

programming language (11-10)

project management (11-6)

project management software (11-6)

project team (11-9)

prototype (11-4)

pull notification (11-15)

push notification (11-15)

quality assurance (11-5)

rapid application development (RAD) (11-6)

request for information (RFI) (11-10)

request for proposal (RFP) (11-10)

request for quotation (RFQ) (11-10)

sandbox (11-17)

scope (11-2)

scope creep (11-2)

security audit (11-13)

sequence (11-17)

software development kit (SDK) (11-12)

software development life cycle (SDLC) (11-3)

source code editor (11-11)

support and security phase (11-5)

syntax (11-10)

system proposal (11-4)

systems analyst (11-9)

systems test (11-13)

testing (11-5)

unit test (11-13)

user experience (UX) (11-2)

value-added reseller (VAR) (11-10)

variable (11-17)

waterfall method (11-5)

Extend Your Knowledge

Instructions: The Extend Your Knowledge exercise expands on subjects covered in the module and encourages you to find the latest developments on these topics. Use a search engine or another search tool to locate news articles, blog entries, videos, expert discussions, or other current sources on the listed topics. List your sources, and write 3-4 sentences describing what you have learned to submit in the format required by your instructor.

- Macro security issues
- 5GLs
- Ethical design
- Converting binary to digital code

What did you learn that helped you better understand the concepts in this module? Did anything surprise you? How will what you learned impact you?

Checkpoint

The Checkpoint exercises test your knowledge of the module concepts.

True/False   Mark T for True and F for False. If False, rewrite the statement so that it is True.

_____ 1. The scope of a project includes its goals, objectives, and expectations of the project.

_____ 2. Operational feasibility measures whether the developers have the skills and resources, as well as the number of programmers, to complete the features of the product.

_____ 3. Phased conversion consists of running the old product alongside the new products for a specified time.

_____ 4. A Gantt chart is a bar chart that uses horizontal bars to show project phases or activities.

_____ 5. A VAR is an organization that purchases products from manufacturers and then resells these products to the public.

_____ 6. A compiler translates and executes one statement at a time.

_____ 7. With penetration testing, developers attempt to break into the app or system.

_____ 8. When listing your app in an app store, filling out a ratings questionnaire typically is optional.

_____ 9. A push notification is an alert sent through the user's device's notifications, or by email or text.

_____ 10. In programming, a variable is named location in memory used to store information, such as a value, that is used in a program.

Matching   Match the terms with their definitions.

_____ 1. RAD

_____ 2. fuzz testing

_____ 3. documentation

_____ 4. deliverable

_____ 5. object

_____ 6. ethical design

_____ 7. iteration

_____ 8. benchmark

_____ 9. procedural language

_____ 10. system proposal

a. test that measures the performance of hardware or software

b. a collection and summary of the data, information, and deliverables specific to the project

c. any tangible item, such as a chart, diagram, report, or program file

d. an item that can contain both data and the procedures that read or manipulate that data

e. test that uses automated tools that test a system by using unexpected input to ensure the app or system does not crash

f. uses a series of English-like words to write instructions

g. data gathered during the feasibility study and detailed analysis used to present a solution to the need or request

h. repetition of a sequence of instructions

i. set of evolving principles that developers should follow to increase UX

j. uses a condensed or shortened development process to produce a quality product

Problem Solving

Instructions: The Problem Solving exercises extend your knowledge of module concepts by seeking solutions to practical problems with technology that you may encounter at home, school, work, or with nonprofit organizations. The Collaboration exercise should be completed with a team. You often can solve problems with technology in multiple ways. Determine a solution to the problems in these exercises by using one or more resources available to you (such as a computer or mobile device, articles on the web or in print, blogs, podcasts, videos, television, user guides, other individuals, electronics or computer stores, etc.). Describe your solution, along with the resource(s) used, in the format requested by your instructor (brief report, presentation, discussion, blog post, video, or other means).

Personal

1. **Poor App Sales**   You created an app and uploaded it to an app store. You created a simple listing that shows a screenshot and a one-paragraph description of the app. After all your hard work in development, you were hoping to make a profit, but you have sold only a few instances of the app. What else can you do to increase your sales?

2. **Push Notifications**   You downloaded a gaming app from an app store. Several times a day, you receive alerts on your phone reminding you to play the game. Is this ethical? What can you do to stop this from happening?

3. **Incorrect Calculations**   You have created a simple app that uses a few calculations. The calculations include several different operations, including addition, subtraction, and multiplication. You think that you entered all the steps the program should take to produce the right results, but the calculations are off. What might be occurring?

4. **Macro Issues**   You recorded a macro that enables you to print multiple copies of a report at once without you having to go through the steps every time. The next time you start your word processing app, you get an error message that there is a security issue related to your macro. What should you do?

5. **Missing Documentation**   You created an app that has met with some success. Now you have hired a small team to program updates and new versions of the app. The team, however, is having trouble understanding some of your code and asks you for the documentation, which you do not have. How should you proceed?

Professional

6. **Security Breach**   The system your team designed and which is being used by your company was hacked. Customers' data was stolen, and sensitive information was published. How should your company address the public relations issues?

7. **Project Proposal Rejected**   Your team has asked management for approval to create an app that will enable users to access your product on their mobile devices instead of strictly through the website. You created a proposal, but the management team rejected it. What can you do to convince them?

8. **Ethical Design Concerns**   You have been working on a fitness app that requires users to create an account to track their exercise, food and water intake, sleep, stress, and more. After you have created the form that asks for a username and email, your manager tells you to add questions to determine each user's location, age, and other demographics. Should you do this? Why or why not?

9. **Selecting Project Management Software**   Before you start a new, complex project that involves several people on your development team, you know that you need to select software that will help you track and schedule tasks. What criteria should you look for when selecting a program?

10. **Beta Release Issues**   You have performed some minimal testing as you develop a product for your company, but you are eager to get it into customers' hands to see how they like it. Before you have completed all the testing, you decide to release a beta version. Initial feedback is that the product has several flaws and crashes often. What should you do?

Collaboration

11. **Technology in Sports**   You serve as an assistant coach for your former high school's softball team. The coaching staff informs you that they would like to create an application that will keep track of the players' statistics. For instance, they would like to track each player's number of strikeouts, walks, hits, and home runs. Form a team of three people to determine the requirements for implementing this request. One team member will research the types of apps that can track this data, another team member will determine the specifications for a computer or mobile device capable of running the software and storing the data, and the other team member will determine the best way to collect the data during the game.

How To: Your Turn

Instructions: This exercise presents general guidelines for fundamental skills when using a computer or mobile device and then requires that you determine how to apply these general guidelines to a specific program or situation. You often can complete tasks using technology in multiple ways. Figure out how to perform the tasks described in these exercises by using one or more resources available to you (such as a computer or mobile device, articles on the web or in print, online or program help, user guides, blogs, podcasts, videos, other individuals, trial and error, etc.). Summarize your 'how to' steps, along with the resource(s) used, in the format requested by your instructor (brief report, presentation, discussion, blog post, video, or other means).

❶ List Your App in an App Store

The following steps guide you through the process of planning an app that can be listed in an app store.

a. Determine what type of platform you should use to create your app by considering the following:
   1. The platform should be reputable and have good reviews.
   2. Reviews should contain no indication that the platform has known security flaws.
   3. The platform should be easy to use.
   4. The platform will need to create an app that you know will work with Android devices.

b. Once the app is created, you need to create a developer account for the app store. Consider the following:
   1. Decide whether to use your own name and contact information or if it is best to create a separate account for your business.
   2. Research legal advice for protecting your work, and determine any additional steps you need to take.
   3. Determine if you should create a website for your app; if so, decide what to include on the website.

c. Test the features of the app to make sure it works as intended, making sure you consider the following:
   1. What testing tools does the app store console include?
   2. If your app fails any of the tests, what steps will you take?

d. Plan what a listing for the app should contain, including:
   1. Write a brief description of the app.
   2. Include any reviews you have received from users who have tested your app.
   3. Determine which graphics and media you should include.

e. Decide how your app will make money. For example, will you sell the app or solicit companies to place advertisements within the app?

f. Fill out the ratings questionnaire, and make a plan to address and respond to criticism of your app.

g. Determine any additional measures you should take to ensure your app succeeds.

Exercises

1. Have you ever created an app that you listed in an app store? What type of app did/would you create?
2. Evaluate at least two different app stores. Which has the best reviews from developers? Which do you think would be the best fit for your app?
3. What security measures does the app store include that help you protect your work and your customers' data?

Internet Research

Instructions: The Internet Research exercises broaden your understanding of module concepts by requiring that you search for information on the web. Use a search engine or another search tool to locate the information requested or answers to questions presented in the exercises. Describe your findings, along with the search term(s) you used and your web source(s), in the format requested by your instructor (brief report, presentation, discussion, blog post, video, or other means). Additionally, reflect on the process you used to complete this activity. How did you go about choosing the tool that you did and why? Would you do anything differently next time?

❶ Security: Selling Data

When you use apps and websites, businesses automatically store personal data about you, your transactions, and your preferences in their marketing databases. They often use this data to analyze sales, develop advertising campaigns, and solicit more business from you. Unbeknownst to many consumers, some companies also sell or rent this data to other businesses for the purpose of developing interest-based or online behavioral advertising. Consumers can refuse to receive targeted email messages and marketing materials, but they often must search the websites or paper forms for check boxes to indicate these opt-out preferences. Some consumer advocates view this practice as an invasion of privacy and urge businesses to default to not adding consumers' information to databases unless the consumer opts in to receive additional materials.

Research This: Read the privacy statements on two apps that you have installed. Do any include opt-in or opt-out provisions? What do they disclose about their use of collected data? Search for any known security breaches involving the apps. What steps can you take to protect yourself while using the apps? Which organizations help protect consumers and offer information on maintaining online privacy? Then, search for at least two marketing companies that provide online direct advertising campaigns. How do these companies use databases to match consumers' buying preferences with targeted offers?

❷ Making Use of the Web: Project Management Software

Using project management software can assist you in planning, scheduling, tracking, and controlling all aspects of a development project. Many options exist for this type of software, with a wide range of capabilities and price. Your needs depend on the complexity of your project and the number of people on your development team. Some advanced features include real-time chat with members of the project team and automated workflow plans.

Research This: (1) Use a search engine to find a list of the top-rated project management programs. Read the reviews of three to five of the options. List the features that they share and any unique capabilities that distinguish any of the programs. (2) Visit the websites of the three programs. Determine the costs for purchasing or subscribing. What types of licenses are available? If the program offers upgraded services, such as a premium option, what features are available and what is the additional cost?

❸ Search Skills: UX Trends and Jobs

UX is an evolving design and development area. Many criteria go into prioritizing an app or system's UX. As new technologies develop and user trends change, UX guidelines change. To be a UX designer, you need to keep current with these trends and know how to plan for them and incorporate them into a program's design.

Research This: (1) Use a search engine to find both a recent list of UX trends, as well as a similar list from two years or more prior. Compare the two, and list common criteria as well as differences. Why might one trend go out of fashion and another emerge? (2) Visit a job search website and search for entry-level jobs in UX. List the required education and experience. Determine what types of duties are required, along with the salary ranges. Would you consider a job in UX? Why or why not?

Critical Thinking

Instructions: The Critical Thinking exercises challenge your assessment and decision-making skills by presenting real-world situations associated with module concepts. The Collaboration exercise should be completed with a team. Evaluate the situations below, using personal experiences and one or more resources available to you (such as articles on the web or in print, blogs, podcasts, videos, television, user guides, other individuals, electronics or computer stores, etc.). Perform the tasks requested in each exercise and share your deliverables in the format requested by your instructor (brief report, presentation, discussion, blog post, video, or other means).

1. **Development Languages**

   Many development languages exist, and each has its own strengths and weaknesses. Some are recommended for large-scale projects, while others help you optimize your app or system for web-based or cloud delivery. Some development environments include additional tools that help complete a project.

   Do This: Visit a current website that rates programming languages. Review the credentials of the website or author to ensure that the website provides independent reviews and is not sponsored. Which languages are the easiest to use? Which languages include the most capabilities? What are the advantages and disadvantages of the top five rated languages? Find at least two other independent lists. How do the rankings differ? What languages are on all the lists?

2. **Program and System Testing Tools**

   You want your program not only to be secure but also to run without errors, slowdowns, or crashes. While you, and your quality assurance team, can run debugging tests during development to identify any bugs that you need to fix, you also can use tools and services for additional testing. Using outside testing services can be an advantage; because the people performing the tests and using the testing tools are not involved in development, they might identify issues your development team would overlook.

   Do This: Prepare information about available testing tools and services. Include reasons why it is advisable to use testing tools and services, and identify what issues may arise if your product ends up containing errors after release. Explain the costs and types of tests available.

3. **Case Study**

   Cooperative-Owned Farm Stand   You are the new manager for a farm stand that is a cooperative effort, jointly owned by several local farmers. The farmstand wants to create an app that vendors can use to coordinate and communicate among one another for scheduling, announcements, and help needed.

   Do This: Using information learned in the module, as well as performing additional research, prepare information about creating an app from scratch. What tools exist to create a simple app? Do any apps exist that might be suitable, eliminating the need to create a new app? What security concerns might arise from using the app? Who should be involved in determining whether the app should be created and what features to include? Include recommendations for tools, platforms, languages, and UX. Compile your findings.

Collaboration

4. **System Development Life Cycle**

   A major retail company has hired your team to create custom inventory-tracking software. Your team has several experienced members, as well as a few new programmers. You will use what you have learned about the system development life cycle (SDLC) to create a plan for the project.

   Do This: First, determine the project's description, purpose, and goals, as well as what problem it will solve. Assign SDLC steps to different teammates and compile a plan for each step. Share your findings. Does the plan contain gaps? Do any steps or tasks overlap? What guidelines should you follow during system development? What roles are needed? How might you use project management software? What data will you collect, and what data types should you assign the data? As a team, answer the following questions to share with the retail company: Would you use a compiler or an interpreter? Why? Would you use an object-oriented programming language? Why or why not? What types of information gathering techniques would be most effective? Why? Would you recommend outsourcing parts of the process? Why or why not? What is necessary to create a prototype of the project? Search for popular programming languages. Find industry experts' reviews of each language. Can you find an example of a program that uses each language? Which language might be best suited to this project? Why? As a team, compile your findings and share your recommendation with the class.

Web Development: 12
Creating and Publishing Online Content

iStock.com/JuSun

Objectives

After completing this module, you will be able to:

1. Identify steps to plan a new website
2. Discuss tools for developing a website
3. Explain how to use HTML to add content to a webpage
4. Explain how to use CSS to format content on a webpage
5. Describe website security techniques
6. Identify steps for publishing a website
7. Describe how to create accessible websites

Plan a Website

Many factors influence how you might develop a personal or professional website. Applying web technologies is only one part of what is required to produce a successful website: a website that effectively communicates, educates, entertains, or provides a venue for conducting business transactions also requires good web design. Web design does not refer only to choices of colors, fonts, backgrounds, and images; to make your design accessible to all devices, you must apply responsive web design (RWD) so that the website's content adapts appropriately to the size and orientation (portrait or landscape) of the display on any device (Figure 12-1). Once a website is published online, you can use analytics tools to monitor visitor behavior on the website.

Create a Design Plan

Before you begin to create a website, you must develop a solid, detailed plan for the website, called a **website plan** or **design plan**. This plan determines the purpose, audience, content, structure, navigation system, visual design, and publishing and maintenance strategy. Although you can create a plan using several methods, the six steps discussed in the next sections should be part of your overall plan.

Define the Website's Purpose and Audience   First, define the website's goals and objectives. **Goals** are the results you want your website to accomplish within a specific time frame. Goals might include sales, number of visitors, or social media interactions. **Objectives** are those methods you will use to accomplish the website's goals. A formal, written **purpose statement** summarizes your website's goals and objectives to ensure they meet the audience's expectations and needs. It is good practice for a website to include a call-to-action in its objectives list. A **call-to-action** (**CTA**) is a suggestion or offer that requires the website visitor to interact with the website by purchasing a product, following the company's social media account(s), making a donation, sharing or commenting on an article, requesting an appointment, signing up for an account, or registering for an event or program (Figure 12-2).

Recognizing the website's target audience, and knowing their wants, needs, and expectations, enables you to create a website that provides the most value for that particular audience. A **target audience profile** is a research-based overview that includes information about potential website visitors' demographic and psychographic characteristics. **Demographic characteristics** include gender, age group, educational level, income, location, and other characteristics that define who your website visitors are. **Psychographic characteristics** include social group affiliations, lifestyle choices, purchasing preferences, and political affiliations. These and other characteristics explain why visitors might want to access your website, as well as how they might interact with your website. A target audience profile is crucial when making decisions regarding **user interface** (**UI**) and user experience (UX).

Figure 12-1   RWD adapts screen content to fit the device's screen size.
Source: Expedia

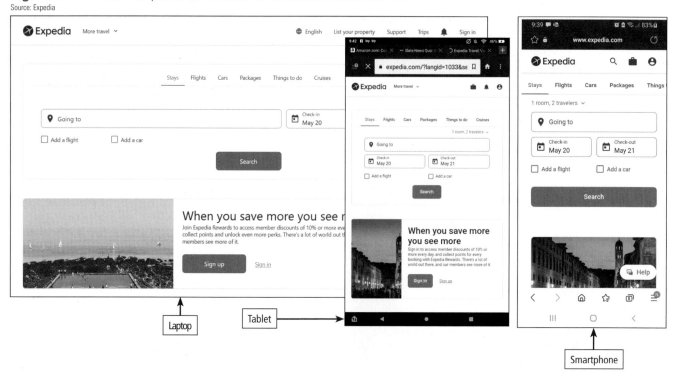

Laptop

Tablet

Smartphone

Figure 12-2   The Kiva website includes a CTA to give microloans.
Source: Kiva Systems, Inc.

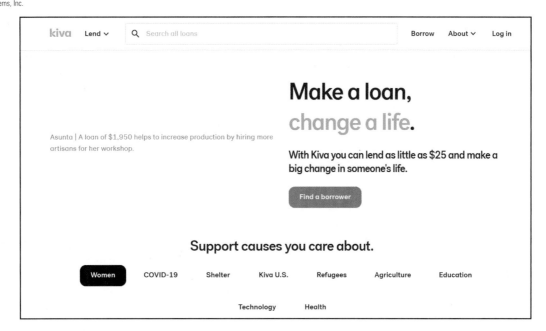

Determine the Website's Content   A website's content likely will consist of multiple webpages including a combination of text, images, audio, video, animations, and multimedia elements. Most websites consist of two types of webpages: a home page and subsidiary pages. The **home page** is the main webpage around which a website is built that opens every time you start a browser and is the anchor for the entire website (Figure 12-3), and the **subsidiary pages** provide detailed content and interest. Website visitors will access subsidiary pages using the navigation tools your website provides, a search box, or links from the home or landing page. Some websites also have a **landing page**, which is the page that a browser navigates to when you click a link in an ad, email message, or other online promotion from a different website.

In general, you should create original content elements prepared specifically for the web instead of choosing existing content elements designed for print. For example, a printed brochure for a new smartphone might include an image with several paragraphs of text. Information about the same smartphone on a webpage might include content in a bulleted list and use digital media, such as animations or graphics. You should be selective, basing your choice of elements on how effectively they will contribute to your website's message and purpose, as well as how your audience will benefit from the content. In general, website content includes less text and more visuals but might include links that users can click to find out more information, such as a smartphone's technical specifications. Content that furthers a website's purpose adds value to the website and does not just fill space on a page. **Value-added content** is information that is relevant, informative, and timely; accurate and of high quality; and usable.

Figure 12-3   The REI home page.
Source: REI

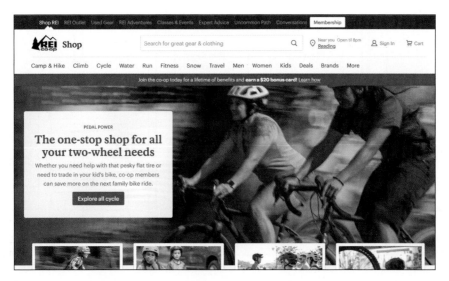

You might use different types of value-added content on your website, including text, images, audio, video, animation, multimedia, and dynamically generated content. Respect copyrights and give credit to content you repurpose from another source, where appropriate. Keep in mind that some users have visual, learning, or other differences that influence their website viewing experience. **Dynamically generated content**, unlike static information, updates periodically and can appear on a website's pages when triggered by a specific event, such as the time of day or by visitor request. Webpages that display dynamically generated content typically acquire the information from a database.

Search engine optimization (SEO) refers to tools to allow search engines to better find or index your website. The goal of SEO is to design a webpage in order to increase the likelihood that the webpage will appear high in a search engine's search results list, which, in turn, increases the likelihood of the webpage being visited. Content-related SEO tools include meta tags, descriptive page titles, relevant inbound links from other websites, and clearly written text. The webpage's title identifies the page and appears in a browser tab. **Meta tags** are HTML specification tags that tell search engines what data to use. Adding meta tags to your webpages and carefully wording each webpage title can increase the probability that your webpages will be included in many search engines' indexes and that your pages will appear in search results lists for important keywords and phrases.

You should take the time to familiarize yourself with legal and privacy issues related to publishing a website. For example, you might see an image on a webpage that would be perfect for your website. To use it, all you need to do is download a copy of the image to a storage device on your computer. Although it is relatively easy to copy an image, doing so potentially is illegal and definitely is unethical. By downloading and using the image without permission, you could violate the creator's copyright or ownership right to the image. You are responsible for obtaining all permissions for content on your website, and you can be subject to fines or prosecution for any violations.

Select the Website's Structure   A website's structure is the linked arrangement of pages. The website's structure should support the website's purpose and make it easy for visitors to find what they want at the website in as few clicks as possible. The website should use navigation, links, and other methods to show website visitors their location within the website; it also should clearly show how to return to the home page or previously visited webpages. Planning the website's structure before you begin creating its pages has several benefits, such as the ability to do the following:

- Visualize the organization of the website's pages and linking relationships.
- Organize the pages by level of detail.
- Follow the links between pages to make certain visitors can click through the website quickly to find useful information — fewer clicks mean more satisfied website visitors.
- Rearrange pages and revise linking relationships, identify missing elements or webpages, and then visualize the changes before you create the website.

An outline of a website's structure can serve as a blueprint and illustrate how visitors can follow links from page to page. Some designers use a text outline to plan a website's structure, whereas others use storyboards or flowcharts to create a visual representation of the website's structure. A **storyboard** is a series of pages originally developed to present scenes graphically for a movie or television program (Figure 12-4). A **flowchart** is a diagram that shows steps or processes and is used to determine the paths users will take to find subsidiary pages (Figure 12-5).

Figure 12-4   Sample storyboard for three pages of a website.

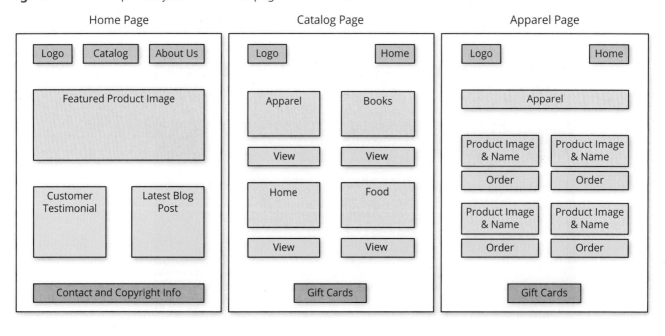

Figure 12-5 Sample flowchart for a website.

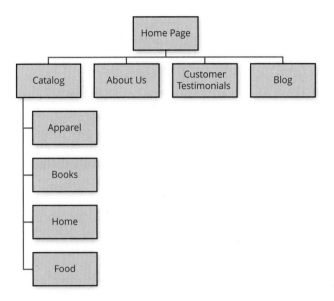

Specify the Website's Navigation System A navigation system that is easy for visitors to understand and follow will draw them deeper into your website to view subsidiary pages with content that can satisfy their needs and expectations. A website navigation system consists of different types of links: text links; hidden links; image links; related link groups presented as menus, bars, or tabs; and breadcrumb trails. Some content is linked using multiple methods. A breadcrumb trail shows a visitor the path from the home page to the currently viewed page. Websites often use a combination of these link types. A large website with many pages also should include a search capability, which allows visitors to search for content within the webpage.

General rules for links and other navigation tools include:

- **Text links:** A text link should clearly identify its **target**, which is the webpage or content to which the link points. Use formatting, such as color and bolding, to indicate a text link, rather than adding instructional text telling the user to click a link. Be consistent with how text links are treated throughout your website. Avoid using the same formatting you use for links to emphasize text.
- **Image links:** An image link assigns a link to a visual element, such as an illustration or a photograph. Often the logo of the company or organization of the website serves as the main link back to the website's homepage.
- **Navigation areas:** You should group related links into a navigation area to create an eye-catching design element and help visitors identify links to a website's major subsidiary pages quickly. Navigation areas can group links in menus, bars, tabs, or a combination of techniques. A **navigation menu** is a list of related links. A **navigation bar** generally uses graphic buttons to present links.
- **Search feature:** A **website search feature** is another popular navigation tool for websites with multiple pages. If you do not manage your own web servers, you can contract with a hosted website search provider to provide search services. A **hosted website search provider** is a third-party company that uses spiders or other tools to build a searchable index of your website's pages and then hosts the index on their servers. Some website development tools include a search feature option.

Figure 12-6 shows navigation features on a Cengage webpage.

Figure 12-6 A page on the Cengage website.

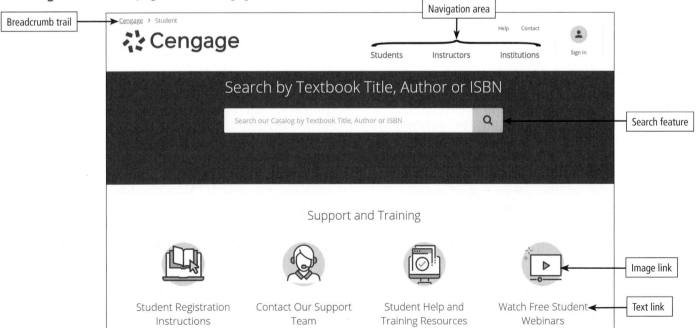

Design the Look of the Website   To promote uniformity and maintain brand identity across pages at your website, use visual consistency when choosing color and typeface, when positioning content across all pages at your website, and by repeating design features across all pages at a website, including:

- Font and typeface
- Content position
- Color scheme
- Placement of company or website name, logo, and navigational elements

As you consider color options for a website's pages, remember the power of color to influence moods, the cultural implications of color, and your target audience's expectations for the use of color at your website. Apply the same color scheme to the background, navigation and other visual elements, and text for all webpages to build visual consistency throughout your website. Choose background and text colors that provide sufficient contrast to enhance readability.

Test, Publish, and Maintain the Website   A complete web design plan includes details outlining how and when you will test the website, how you will publish the website, where you will host it, and the necessary measures to maintain and update the website. These factors affect the budget and timing of your website, as well as its ultimate success. Without testing, you cannot determine if your website will work properly, or if it contains errors or broken links. If you design a website that exceeds the limit of your host web server's allotted size, you cannot publish the website. Without a plan for updating content, your website will remain unchanged, giving visitors few reasons to return. Consider the following:

- **Testing:** A formal website **usability test** is an evaluation that generally takes place in a structured environment, such as a testing laboratory. During the test, usability and design professionals observe exactly how visitors use a website and then use the research to create a report containing design recommendations. Formal website usability tests can be very expensive and might exceed your budget. An informal usability test, however, involves using a team of friends, family members, coworkers, or other interested parties to test a website's navigation system or other website features and then report on their experiences. Testers should use a variety of devices, screen sizes, resolutions, and browsers to make the results more complete. Informal usability testing generally is very inexpensive, perhaps even free, but the feedback can be invaluable.

- **Planning to publish:** As part of your plan, you should ask yourself the following questions about when your website is published:
  - Will you host the website on an internal web server, or will you contract with an external vendor?
  - What size limits exist for the website?
  - What budget restrictions exist for publishing the website?
- **Maintaining the website:**
  - How often will you update the content?
  - Who updates the content?
  - What budget restrictions exist for maintaining the website?
  - How will you monitor your website to determine what changes, if any, need to be made?

❓ Consider This ———————————————

Does it matter where you place your content?
Another important UX issue to consider in content positioning is where visitors typically first look when viewing a webpage. **Eye-tracking** studies use various technologies to analyze the movement of visitors' eyes as they view a webpage and produce **heat maps**, an analytical tool that uses color to represent data. The resulting heat maps suggest that a website's visitors typically follow an **F-pattern**: they first look at the top of the page and scan from left to right (the top bar of the F), then move down slightly and scan left to right (the lower bar of the F). Finally, they look from the top to the bottom of the left side of the page (the vertical stem of the F). Eye-tracking studies add support to the concept of placing calls-to-action, visual identity content, and major links at or near the top and left side of a page to improve usability. Calls-to-action should be placed prominently to ensure visitors focus on them. Do you follow an F-pattern when viewing a webpage? What elements typically do you find in that space? Can you think of other placement considerations?

How To: Use Tools for Developing a Website

You can create a simple webpage by typing HTML tags and related text into a document created in a plain text editor, such as Notepad, which is the text editor available with the Windows operating system. A **text editor** is software used to create plain (ASCII) text files. Some web designers or programmers prefer to use an HTML editor to create webpages. An **HTML editor** is a text editor enhanced with special features that easily insert HTML tags and their attributes.

Many web designers use specific web development tools. Inserting and formatting text and inserting images or links in a webpage using a web development tool is similar to creating a document in a word processor, such as Microsoft Word. Additionally, using a web development tool to create webpages eliminates the need to learn a markup language, such as HTML. A **markup language** is a coding system that uses tags to provide instructions about the appearance, structure, and formatting of a document. The markup languages used to create webpages are HTML, XML, and XHTML. Using markup languages can involve complex coding procedures, because the web development tool automatically generates the underlying markup language tags as you insert and format text, images, and links. Most web development tools also allow you to view and manipulate the underlying HTML code, if desired. Additional benefits of using web development tools include the capability to create webpages rapidly.

An integrated development environment (IDE), such as WebStorm, is a powerful web development tool to create and manage complex, interactive, and animated webpages; it also includes website design, publishing, and management capabilities. Software vendors who create web development tools often provide additional support and resources at their websites, such as clip art and multimedia, training seminars, user forums, and newsletter subscriptions.

IDEs offer more support than text editors, including hints, preview features, line numbers, and color coding. Figure 12-7 shows a website code in Notepad and in the WebStorm IDE.

A **web template** is a predesigned model webpage that you can customize for fast website or webpage creation

and updating. Some web hosting websites provide web templates (in addition to hosting services) that make it quick and easy for small business owners to create their e-commerce websites, focusing on the webpage's content rather than on the design details.

Website Builders and Content Management Systems

To create a more complex website quickly without coding HTML, you can use a website builder or content management system. A **website builder** is a tool used to create professional-looking websites, by dragging and dropping predefined elements to their desired locations on a page, without coding. A **content management system** (**CMS**) is software that provides website creation and administrative tools that enable the management of web content development, including authoring, reviewing, editing, and publishing. Content providers working within a CMS use web templates, style sheets, and other administrative tools to efficiently create, manage, update, and upload webpage content. The templates, style sheets, and other frequently used content elements, such as a logo graphic, are stored in a database called a **content repository**.

These tools are useful to create a personal blog or website, or a website for an organization or small business. They provide a variety of templates or themes to design your website and a visual editor like a word processor, to enter website content. A variety of templates have responsive design and allow you to preview your website as it will appear on a

Figure 12-7   Comparing a text editor with an IDE.

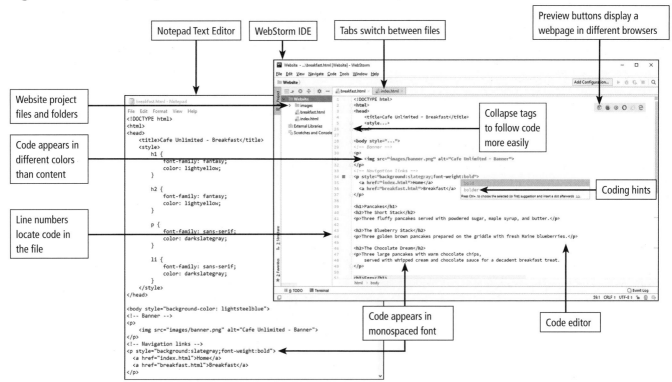

Table 12-1   Comparing Website Builders and Content Management Systems

	Website builder	**Content management system**
Examples	Google Sites, Wix, Weebly	WordPress, Drupal
Popular uses	Small businesses, personal websites, online stores	Blogs, websites for large businesses or organizations, online stores
Collaboration	Few contributors	Few or many contributors
Setup required	Little to none; can get a website up and running quickly	If self-hosted, need to manage and configure a web server and install software before designing the website, or use a fully hosted version for easier setup
Templates and themes	Available from provider	Available from provider or third-party designers free or for purchase
Ease of use	Enter content in a visual editor	Enter content in a visual or HTML editor
Customer support	Paid subscriptions provide tech support through chat or online forums	Self-hosted CMS users rely on a community of enthusiasts and online resources

mobile device. Many website builders and CMSs are web applications that present webpages containing forms where you can enter website content and settings. A database located on a server stores the structure, appearance, and the content of a website. The application obtains this information from the database and then assembles it to provide the code for a browser to display. Table 12-1 summarizes features of website builders and content management systems.

Use a Website Builder   You do not need to install or configure any software to use a website builder. Website builders provide a simple drag-and-drop editor, predesigned layout options, and business capabilities, such as shopping carts, online payments, product catalogues for online stores, photo galleries, and widgets. A **widget** is an object, such as a web app, that is embedded in a webpage and provides access to resources that are stored elsewhere. Examples of widgets include advertisements, as well as social media sharing buttons that users click to post your webpage content to their social media feed or send to another user via direct messaging. Some may offer apps for updating a website using a mobile device. Website builders often show sample demonstration websites to offer design ideas for your own website. Many website builders include SEO capabilities.

Because websites created with a website builder are stored in a database on the web host's server, moving the website later to a different web host or platform can be difficult. You are limited to the templates provided when selecting a design or layout for your site. Many website builders offer basic free hosting and services that are adequate for most personal sites, with advanced capabilities (such as using a custom domain name or increasing the amount of storage for site content) available for a fee.

Wix (Figure 12-8) and Weebly are popular website builders to create websites for individuals and small businesses. Both include hosting services, an easy-to-use drag-and-drop interface, and a variety of responsive themes and templates so that your website will appear correctly on any device. They also support online stores, SEO tools, adding your own domain name, and creating email marketing campaigns.

To create a website using a website builder:

1. Sign up for the service on the provider's website.
2. Select a template or design for your website.
3. Choose your website's domain name.
4. Set up SEO and other website options.
5. Design the website and enter the website content using a drag-and-drop interface and visual editor.

Figure 12-8   Creating a website using the Wix website builder.

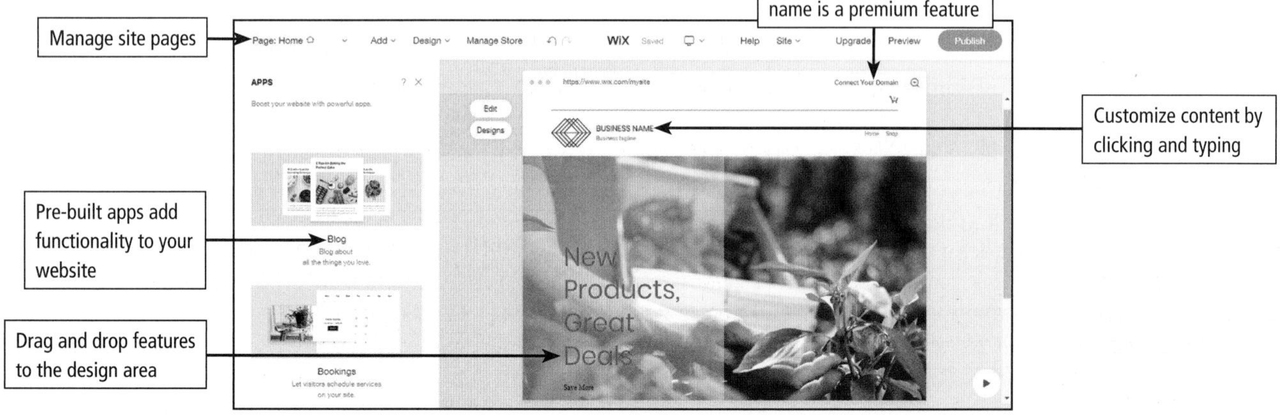

Manage site pages

Adding your own domain name is a premium feature

Customize content by clicking and typing

Pre-built apps add functionality to your website

Drag and drop features to the design area

Using a Content Management System Many CMSs are open source applications and offer regular updates, enhancements, plug-ins, and themes for download, often at no cost. A **plug-in** is a third-party program that extends the built-in functionality of an application or browser. Plug-ins for CMSs add capabilities such as displaying a slide show, providing a contact form, or accepting online payments.

CMSs require you to obtain web hosting services, set up a domain name for your website, and manage the content, contributors to the website, and their roles. You can sign in to your website on your browser and access the CMS through a dashboard page. The dashboard has options to add new pages, blog posts, images, and other content.

When working on websites with hundreds or thousands of pages, you often share the process of entering or updating content with others who are responsible for managing different pages of a website. Using a CMS, you often can restrict access to certain capabilities based on a contributor's role when working on the website. For example, an editor might be able to add or update content, while an administrator also might be able to add or remove users and change the website's theme.

WordPress is a popular, user friendly, open source CMS often used as a blogging platform and tool for creating small- to medium-sized websites (Figure 12-9). WordPress has many plug-ins and themes available free or for purchase from third-party developers, and the software has frequent updates.

For easy setup, you can subscribe to free or paid service plans from WordPress, which offer different features, storage, hosting, and customization capabilities. Advanced or professional users can install and configure the WordPress software on their own web servers. Many web hosts offer automatic installation tools to simplify the process of installing WordPress and creating its database.

Many large organizations use Drupal, another powerful open source CMS, for developing their websites. When designing a website using a CMS, you can select a theme, specify site navigation menus, and identify content to appear in the sidebars, header, or footer of each page. To create a website using the WordPress CMS:

1. Select a theme for your website.
2. Set up the theme in the dashboard, specifying fonts, colors, menu items, page header and footer content, and other settings.
3. Set up website options, including website name, description, and format of links.
4. Install plug-ins for SEO, website maintenance, managing access, and other functions.
5. Enter website content using a drag-and-drop interface and visual editor, or edit the HTML code for page content.

Figure 12-9 Creating a website using the WordPress CMS.

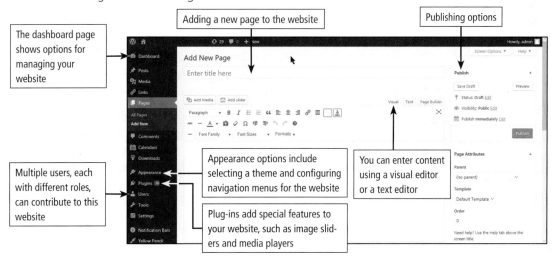

? Consider This

How can you use scripts?

A **script** is programming code that performs a series of commands and can be embedded in a webpage. **JavaScript** is a popular language for writing **client-side scripts**, that is, scripts that run in a browser to control a webpage's behavior and often make it interactive. When you complete a form in a browser, code written in JavaScript can check to make sure that you did not miss any of the required values. When a webpage displays a slide show of photos or images, JavaScript code probably controls it. When you can click a button to display the text on a webpage in a larger or smaller font size, or when a webpage displays the current date and time, JavaScript is making it happen.

Adding JavaScript to a webpage lets you code how you want the website to behave. JavaScript can perform simple actions, such as displaying an alert box if a required form field is empty or retrieving and displaying the current date and time, to more complex actions, such as performing calculations. In many cases, the JavaScript code appears between opening and closing `<script>` tags in the head section of an HTML document. In the body section, you can reference the JavaScript code to run. Do you know if you have ever come across a plug-in? What could a plug-in add to a website you visit frequently?

Use HTML and XML

A webpage uses codes, or **tags**, written in HTML to describe the content of information on a webpage. Webpages can contain headings, paragraphs, hyperlinks, lists, images, videos, forms, buttons, and other elements. You can create webpages for a website by writing HTML code manually or by using tools to assist you in this process.

When a webpage downloads to a browser, the browser reads and interprets the HTML tags to display the webpage with organized and formatted text, images, and links. In many browsers, you can view the underlying HTML, CSS, and JavaScript code for a webpage by right-clicking on the page and selecting the View Source or View Page Source option. Figure 12-10 shows a webpage as it appears in a browser, along with the corresponding HTML, CSS, and JavaScript source code.

Extensible Markup Language (XML) is a markup language that uses both predefined and customized tags to facilitate the consistent sharing of information, especially within large groups. Whereas HTML defines the appearance and organization of webpage content, XML defines the content itself. For example, using XML, a programmer can define the custom tag `<serialnum>` to indicate that the information following the tag is a product serial number. Table 12-2 compares HTML and XML.

HTML Syntax

As is true of programming languages, syntax, or rules, are important when coding in HTML. HTML tags are written in lowercase characters and are enclosed within angle brackets (< >). Almost all HTML tags appear in pairs, with an opening tag and a closing tag. An opening tag contains the tag name followed by any **attributes** or additional information needed to completely specify the tag. Each attribute is followed by an equal sign (=) and the attribute's value in quotation marks. A closing tag begins with a forward slash (/) followed by the tag name. For example, the `<form>....</form>` HTML tag pair indicates the beginning and the end of a webpage form, respectively.

The structure of a webpage coded in HTML contains the following elements (Figure 12-11):

- The first line of code contains the line `<!DOCTYPE html>`.
- The next line of code in a webpage file is always an `<html>` tag to indicate that the content is written using HTML. This is the opening `<html>` tag. The file ends with the corresponding closing `</html>` tag.
- The head section, located between the `<head>` and `</head>` tags, includes tags for the title of the webpage that appears in the browser tab displaying this webpage; it also may include styles and JavaScript.
- The body section, located between the `<body>` and `</body>` tags, contains the content of the webpage marked up with HTML tags. When tags enclose several lines of

Figure 12-10   A webpage and its source code.

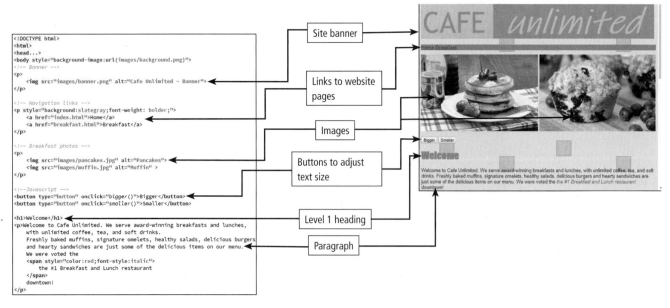

Table 12-2   Comparison of HTML and XML

HTML	XML
Describes content and how to present it in a browser	Describes data without specifying how it will be presented
Stores layout information in a text format for a browser to interpret	Stores data in a text format to share between applications
Predefined tags describe placement of content on a webpage as paragraphs, links, headings, images, and other elements	Customized tags describe data in context (LastName, FirstName, AnimalName, AnimalBreed, AnimalType)

content, you might indent content between the opening and closing tags so that they are aligned. This makes it easier to follow the HTML code when developing the webpage.

- The body area is marked with comments to indicate where the page content begins and ends. Comments look similar to HTML tags, except that they have an exclamation point and two dashes (!--) after the opening bracket and two dashes (--) before the closing bracket. Including comments makes it easier to read the HTML code as you work on it.

Figure 12-11   Structure of a webpage coded in HTML.

Format Page Content

Unformatted text in a website is not very useful or appealing. You need to organize and format it to convey the information you desire by including elements like headings, paragraphs, and line breaks.

- **Add Headings:** Headings indicate the different sections of a webpage. HTML supports six levels of headings. The `<h1>` tag displays text in the largest font size, and the `<h6>` tag displays text in the smallest font size (Figure 12-12).

Figure 12-12   Heading tags display headings in different text sizes.

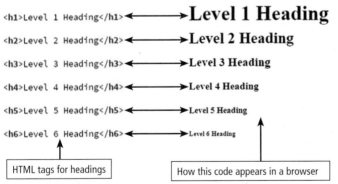

- **Add Paragraphs:** In addition to a title and headings, you need to identify paragraphs. The `<p>` and `</p>` tags identify the beginning and ending of paragraphs. If you have several paragraphs of text on your webpage, these tags will inform the browser to insert additional line spacing above and below the paragraph so that the text is easier to read. The browser ignores line breaks and line spacing in the HTML file, so it is important to properly define the paragraphs using the `<p>` and `</p>` tags. If you view the code in the index.html file in a browser before adding paragraph tags, the browser will display it as one

long paragraph, even though the HTML file appears to have several paragraphs. To display the text correctly in a browser, place `<p>` and `</p>` tags around each paragraph.

- **Add Line Breaks:** Add a `<br>` tag when you want to break a line with no white space before or after it. The `<br>` tag does not have a corresponding closing tag.

Webpage File Names

When you save the code for a webpage as a text file, choose a short but descriptive file name for the page. A good practice is to use lowercase letters, numbers, and underscores in webpage file names. Avoid using special characters and spaces in webpage names. The file extension for webpage files is usually .html. The .html file extension indicates to the browser that the file stores HTML code. The file name containing the content of a website's home page is often named index.html. You often can omit index.html when entering the address of a website's home page in a browser. Web servers will look for a page named index.html automatically if no page name is specified as part of a web address entered in a browser.

Add Links

A link, or hyperlink, can be text or an image in a webpage that you can click to navigate to another webpage, download a file, or perform another action, such as sending an email message. Including links to all the pages in your website makes it easy for visitors to navigate your website. In addition to providing links to pages in your website, you also can provide external links to other websites. Webpages always are stored as separate files, and hypertext references to the files appear in the HTML code using the `<a>` (anchor) tag. The `<a>` tag's href (hypertext reference) attribute often refers to the location of the file or webpage that you want to view or download. The `<a>` (anchor) tag specifies information about hyperlinks to display on a website. You must provide an attribute to reference the location of the linked page or document, and optionally can specify in which browser tab to display it.

The href attribute's value references a resource (usually a webpage, image, or file) using either a relative reference or an absolute reference. Relative references identify the location of resources in the current website. Absolute references identify the location of resources from other websites. An absolute reference includes the full path, including the protocol and domain name containing the webpage.

If your website has a broken link, the desired webpage, image, or file will not load correctly. Common causes of broken links include the following:

- The http:// protocol prefix is missing from an absolute reference.
- You did not upload a webpage, image, or file to the web server.
- You made an error when typing the resource referenced in the href attribute.
- The webpage, image, or file is not located in the directory referenced in the href attribute.

Although an absolute reference must include http://, some browsers may not display the http:// prefix in the address bar when navigating to a webpage. Most websites will display links to pages on other websites in a new browser tab or window to indicate that you are leaving the website you had been visiting.

Add Lists

Two types of lists that HTML supports are unordered lists and ordered lists. Unordered lists display a collection of items in a list format, with each list item preceded by a bullet symbol. Ordered lists, by default, precede each list item with a number. Displaying information in an unordered or ordered list makes it easier to follow than if it appeared in one long, multi-line paragraph. The `<ul>` and `</ul>` tags surround list items for an unordered list and precede each list item with a bullet. The `<ol>` and `</ol>` tags surrounds list items for an ordered list and precede each list item with a number. Specify each item between `<li>` and `</li>` tags.

Add Images

The `<img>` tag specifies information about an image to display on a website. You must include attributes to specify the location of an image file. Also keep in mind that visitors to your page who are visually impaired or visitors whose browsers are configured not to display images may be unable to view images on a page. Because of this, you should include alternative (alt) text that describes the image.

Banners often appear at the top of each page so visitors will recognize the website easily. Photos and graphics can make a website more attractive or help to deliver its message, but not all viewers may be able to see them. When identifying images to include on a webpage, choose images with appropriate dimensions for the webpage and relatively small file sizes. Images load at the same time as the webpage, so pages with several large images may cause the page to take a longer time to load, which can be annoying to users.

Most browsers can display images stored in JPEG, GIF, or PNG format (identified with .jpg, .gif, or .png file extensions). If you are trying to display photos from a digital camera or smartphone, you should use image-editing software to shrink the photos to an appropriate size, such as 300×400 pixels for a small image or 600×800 pixels for a medium-sized image, to display in a browser. Large images can take a long time to load, which may impact the performance of your website.

Add Multimedia

Adding multimedia content makes your website more engaging to visitors. Multimedia content can include audio, photos, or videos stored on media sharing websites; media content, such as online calendars, documents, and slide-shows; Tweets and social media posts; and maps positioned at preset locations. Some websites include audio, such as speech, music, or other sounds, and video, such as screen recordings, animations, and videos recorded with a video camera on a smartphone. When adding audio or video to a site, many developers include controls to adjust or mute the volume so that you can turn off the sound, if desired.

You can play your own audio and video files on your website without uploading them to a media-sharing site, such as SoundCloud (for audio files) or YouTube (for video files), by embedding them in your webpage. When you embed items on a website, you place a copy of an object created in a source file into a destination file so that a one-way connection to the source program becomes part of the destination file. Prior to HTML 5, and in older browsers (such as Internet Explorer version 8 and earlier), the only way to play audio or video on a website was to use a plug-in. HTML 5 introduced the `<audio>` tag to play audio files and the `<video>` tag to play video files. You can specify the audio or video file to play using the `<source>` tag.

Table 12-3 summarizes common attributes for the `<audio>` and `<video>` tags.

Table 12-3 Attributes for the `<audio>` and `<video>` Tags

Attribute	Description
autoplay	Include this attribute to play the audio or video automatically when the page loads (may not work on mobile devices)
controls	Include this attribute to display audio or video controls, such as play, pause, and volume; if you do not include this option, the only way to stop playing the audio is to close the page
width	Width of video player in pixels
height	Height of video player in pixels

Most media sharing sites, as well as mapping sites and social media sites, allow you to embed content posted on their website in your own. Look for a Share icon or an option often labeled Share or Embed. When you click Share, the webpage will display HTML code, usually containing an `<iframe>` tag, that you can copy and paste into your HTML file at the location where you would like the media to appear.

❓ Consider This

How can you check the validity of your HTML code?
The World Wide Web Consortium (W3C) oversees the specification of HTML standards, and as HTML evolves, the W3C identifies some tags as deprecated, or obsolete. As HTML evolves, some features are deprecated, rather than removed instantly when newer techniques are developed to accomplish the same tasks. For example, in earlier versions of HTML, you could use the `<font>` tag to specify the font or color of text on a webpage. With the development of CSS (cascading style sheets), the W3C has deprecated the `<font>` tag. While the `<font>` tag still may display text in a font correctly in some browsers, the preferred way to display text in a specific font is using CSS. When developers learn of deprecated features, they should begin to update webpages to follow the new standard. Deprecated features will still work in some browsers, but eventually may be unsupported. You can replace many deprecated tags with CSS. Most IDEs notify you if you use a deprecated tag. The W3C also provides an HTML 5 validator web app to ensure that a webpage's code follows the specifications, or rules, for HTML 5. Compare your experience with creating documents and using styles in word processing documents. Why might it be better to separate text from its formatting?

Use CSS

A cascading style sheet (CSS) uses rules to standardize the appearance of webpage content by defining styles for elements, such as font, margins, positioning, background colors, and more. Web designers store CSS specifications that will be applied to multiple webpages in a website in a separate document, called a **style sheet**. A web designer can attach the style sheet to multiple website pages; any changes made to the style sheet automatically apply to the associated webpages. For example, changing a heading font in the CSS automatically will update that heading font in all webpages associated with the CSS. Cascading refers to the order in which the different styles are applied.

A style is a group of formatting properties, such as bold, italic, font type, font size, or font color, applied as a group to selected text. When you use CSS, you create a style sheet containing style rules. **Style rules** are specifications that define one or more formatting properties and their values (declarations) for specific HTML tags (selectors).

The "cascading" part of CSS refers to how it prioritizes style rules to determine priority in case of conflicting rules. Style rules are applied in cascading order based on priority. The first priority is for specifications the author sets in the form of inline styles. The second priority includes internal and external style sheets. The lowest priority is default styles specified by the browser. Style sheets standardize formatting of a webpage, which saves time and simplifies the process of creating and modifying webpages. Using style sheets prevents you from having to insert HTML tag formatting attributes and values for individual elements. If you make a style change to the style sheet, such as changing the font color for all headings, the associated webpages update automatically. Using style sheets also helps you maintain visual consistency across all pages at your website.

Web design programs provide CSS tools you can use to create and edit style sheets and link style sheets to your pages. Web templates have style sheets already linked. You also can create style sheets using **CSS editor software**. While HTML helps to define the placement of items on a webpage, your webpages will look dull if you do not change fonts, font sizes, font styles, colors, backgrounds, borders, and other styles. CSS makes it easier to specify the appearance for each tag in the same webpage or same website.

Embedded and Inline Styles

You can code styles that apply to all tags of one type on the webpage as **embedded styles**, within `<style>` and `</style>` tags placed in the head section of an HTML document, or as an **inline style**, specified as a `style` attribute of most HTML tags within the body section. Individual webpages can reference a common style sheet to create a consistent appearance across all pages in a website. A style declaration contains the style name followed by a colon, followed by the value for the style. If more than one style is used, separate each style with a semicolon. Figure 12-13 shows an embedded style and an inline style.

Figure 12-13 Comparing embedded and inline styles.

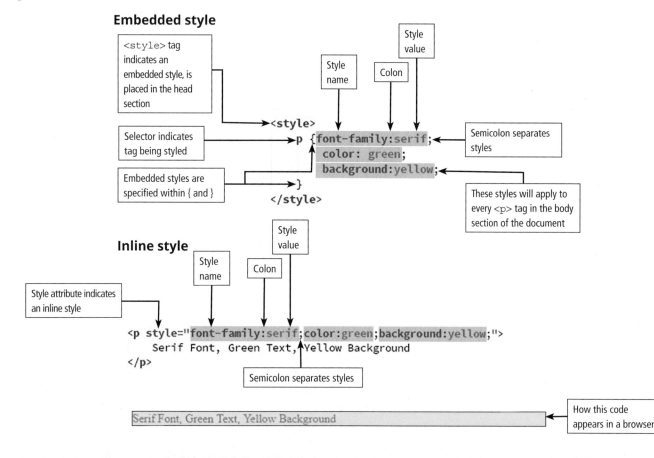

When you create an inline style, the style must be associated with a tag. If you are applying a style to a small section of a document that is not surrounded by its own tag, such as a few words or phrases, surround that content with a `<span>` tag and specify the style using a `style` attribute within the `<span>` tag.

A font is a set of letters, numbers, and symbols that all have the same style and appearance. A **font family** is a group of related fonts. When specifying fonts, you can specify a font family rather than a specified font. By using a font family, the browser will choose a font installed on the computer or device that most closely matches the specified font family. If you specify a font name that is not installed on the computer or device displaying the webpage, the page may not display correctly. Values for the font-family style include serif, sans-serif, monospace, cursive, and

fantasy. Browsers may choose different fonts to display for each font family. Table 12-4 shows font families in the Google Chrome and Microsoft Edge browsers.

Add Colors

Most browsers recognize common color names, such as red, orange, green, and blue, as well as other predefined color names, such as navy, lime green, chartreuse, and papayawhip. You can use the rgb() function to specify colors by providing their red, green, and blue components as numbers between 0 (absence of a color) and 255 (fullness of a color). You can use hexadecimal (base 16) numbers between 00 and FF to specify a color's red, green, and blue components. The color value is preceded by a #. Table 12-5 shows examples of colors and their RGB and hexadecimal color values.

Table 12-4 Font Families in Different Browsers

Code	Chrome	Edge
`<p style="font-family:serif">Hello!</p>`	Hello!	Hello!
`<p style="font-family:sans-serif">Hello!</p>`	Hello!	Hello!
`<p style="font-family:monospace">Hello!</p>`	Hello!	Hello!
`<p style="font-family:cursive">Hello!</p>`	Hello!	Hello!
`<p style="font-family:fantasy">Hello!</p>`	**Hello!**	Hello!

Table 12-5 Color Names with RGB and Hexadecimal Values

Color name	Sample	Values to use with rgb function	Hexadecimal color value	Comments
Black		rgb(0, 0, 0)	#000000	Black is the absence of color
Gray		rgb(128,128,128)	#808080	Same red, green, and blue values
White		rgb(255, 255, 255)	#FFFFFF	White is fullness of color
Red		rgb(255, 0, 0)	#FF0000	All red, no green, no blue
Navy		rgb(0, 0, 128)	#000080	No red, no green, 50% blue
Magenta		rgb(255, 0, 255)	#FF00FF	Combines red and blue

 Consider This ──

What are current web design trends?

Identifying and adopting trends in web design is an ongoing concern for developers. Trends might be use of bold colors and fonts or interactive features, such as chat. One year, developers may create websites that put all content in one (or a few) long webpages that users can scroll to read content without interruption. The next year, developers may break up content into short, navigable pages that decrease loading time. Trends fluctuate between sleek and modern, or vintage/retro design styles. Choosing to adapt to the trends is a choice designers need to make based on their style and brand. A rare bookstore might choose vintage rather than modern because it is a reflection of the content and purpose of the website. Use of 3-D, virtual reality, video, images only, text only, a blend of text and images, or other media and visual choices can affect the mood and experience of the user. What web design trends do you see? What trends appeal to you? Why? How do color and font choices influence your UX at a website?

Secure IT: Protect Your Website

Criminal activity based on identity theft is a major problem for both businesses and consumers. Depending on your website's focus, you may have access to vast amounts of data that you need to use responsibly. Like any digital content or entity, your website can be subject to hackers, malware, and other threats. As you have learned, one of the main reasons to address security issues is that they can result in loss or misuse of data (your company's or your customers').

Choices you make during development that affect security including choosing a reliable hosting company, using a CMS or other website tool that is known to address or prevent security flaws, and performing extensive testing. You also should keep your website and the technologies used to support it are up to date.

Hypertext Transfer Protocol Secure (HTTPS)

Hypertext Transfer Protocol Secure (HTTPS) is a protocol used to make a secure connection to a computer; identified by the https prefix in a URL and often used by banks and retail stores. HTTPS uses the protocol Transport Layer Security (TLS) to encrypt data that helps protect consumers and businesses from fraud and identity theft when conducting commerce on the Internet. TLS can encrypt communications, such as between your website and a browser accessing the website. TLS has many other uses and often is referred to by its predecessor, Secure Sockets Layer (SSL).

HTTPS benefits include:

- Authentication of a website
- Ensure integrity of data during web exchanges
- Protection against attacks such as eavesdropping and hacking

Website authentication is achieved by the use of digital certificates. A digital certificate is a technology used to verify a user's identity by using a digital key that has been "signed" by a trusted third party. This third party verifies the owner and that the key belongs to that owner. Digital certificates are issued by online providers called certificate authorities. A secure website is indicated by the HTTPS protocol in the URL shown in the browser's web address bar (Figure 12-14). Many browsers only will access websites that use HTTPS and will alert you if a website cannot be verified.

Other Security Techniques

The following are additional techniques you can practice to ensure your website's safety.

- **Use plug-ins strategically:** Plug-ins that enhance your website's UX and functionality also can open the website to security flaws. Ensure that any plug-ins you use are secure and that are used only when necessary. In addition, security plug-ins exist that can protect your website from hacking and malware. These may be purchased from a separate vendor or included in your CMS or other website tool.

- **Secure passwords:** It might seem obvious, but the passwords that you use to manage your website content should be kept secure and distributed only to those who need them. In addition, you can use different sign-ins for additional administrators of your website, each of which may have different capabilities and permission levels. Like with a database, this enables you to keep track of who makes what changes and limits the changes each user is permitted to make.

- **Install a web firewall:** A web firewall monitors the HTTP traffic to and from your web service and can alert you to any unusual activity. It can be instructed to block malicious requests for data or information automatically, thereby preventing hackers from accessing the underlying data in your website.

Figure 12-14 A secure website.

Source: Bank of America Corporation 2018

Lock icon indicates a secure connection

https in the URL indicates a secure connection

Click the name of the organization to display the website's digital certificate

? Consider This

What is an NFT?

A **non-fungible token** (**NFT**) is a certified, unique data file associated with a digital file. Digital art, memes (**memes** are video clips, animated GIFs, or digital images, often with humorous text added, that are spread by Internet users), assets in virtual games, and other media, such as video and music, can be traded as NFTs. NFTs can be traded like cryptocurrency and also are stored on a blockchain. Like cryptocurrencies, NFT trading can be risky because of issues surrounding authenticity, regulation, and fluctuations in value. Other issues surrounding NFTs include plagiarism, environmental impact (it takes a great deal of electronic activity to verify and trade an NFT), and money laundering. Have you ever traded an NFT? Why or why not? What issues can you see regarding NFTs and other digital currency-related trends?

Publish a Website

After creating a website or modifying a webpage, you must publish the page and any multimedia content it contains to a web server so that visitors can access it on the Internet. Your college or university may give you space on one of their web servers to host a website for your classes; when creating a personal or professional website, you can purchase hosting services from a web host. The server on which your website is located will have an **Internet Protocol** (**IP**) address, which is a unique number that identifies every computer on the Internet. You also will need to select a domain name for your website so that visitors can locate your website easily. A domain name is the portion of a URL or email address that identifies one or more IP addresses, such as cengage.com. Your web host may provide or allow you to specify a web address at their domain, or you can purchase a domain name from a **domain registrar**, which is an organization that sells and manages domain names. When choosing a domain name, select one that is descriptive of your website's purpose or reflects your business name.

Several factors are important to consider when selecting a web host:

- **Storage space:** If your website will contain many photos or videos, you will need a significant amount of space. If the web host provides storage on a server with a solid-state drive, the website performance may be faster than if storage is on an older hard disk drive.

- **Bandwidth:** Bandwidth is a term commonly used to describe the capacity of a communication channel. If you expect lots of traffic on your website, you might want to opt for a plan that offers unlimited bandwidth.
- **Reliability:** Uptime is a measure of a web host's reliability. It could be costly to you if your website goes down due to an issue with your hosting provider; many hosting companies will claim to offer 99% or 99.999% uptime.

Basic hosting packages are quite affordable and may include space on a shared server for one website, along with websites from other customers, and limited disk space. Higher-end packages are good choices for businesses and websites requiring additional bandwidth, processing, and speed for their websites, and storage on a dedicated server that you can administer. Read online reviews and do your research to find a hosting service that meets your needs. When you have finished testing the pages in your website, you are ready to publish them so that anyone can access them on a device connected to the Internet. Websites published on a web server are accessible online for all to see.

You can use FTP (File Transfer Protocol), which is an app you can use to upload the files from a local computer to a remote web server. FTP specifies rules for transferring files from one computer to another on the Internet. Many IDEs also include built-in FTP capabilities so that you can publish your website to a web server without having to use a separate application. Figure 12-15 shows the FileZilla app being used to upload webpages to a website.

Figure 12-15 Using FileZilla to upload website files to a web server.

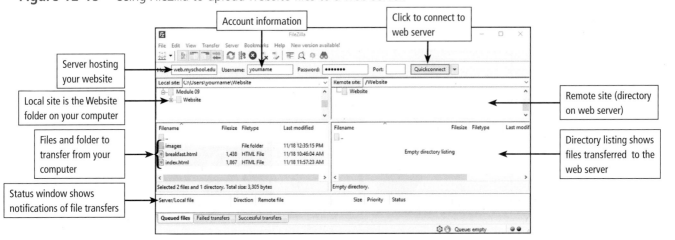

Web Analytics

Once your website is published, you can start tracking its usage. **Web analytics** involves collecting, measuring, evaluating, and reporting how your website is used. Website owners use analytics data to understand who their visitors are, where they are coming from, and how they interact with the website. By learning how visitors explore a website, businesses can reorganize information and website content so that the most requested information is easy to locate. Tracking website performance data — such as pages visited and how long it takes them to load — can help determine when to increase bandwidth or other hosting requirements. Google Analytics is a powerful free tool for capturing and reporting website analytics data (Figure 12-16).

You can use analytic tools to:

- Count visitors to your website, and distinguish between return and unique visitors using cookies, IP addresses, and other data to determine the size of your total audience and how many people return for subsequent visits.
- Determine users' activities on your website by tracking their **click path** or **clickstream**, which is the sequence of pages or activities the user performs on the website. This gives not only valuable information about your website's navigation, but also which pages are of most interest to users.
- Receive information about a user's time spent on a page or on the entire website, which helps to gauge the stickiness of your content. **Sticky content** gets users to spend long periods of time engaging and encourages them to return for future visits.

- See the number of times a sponsor's advertisement is interacted with or viewed. **Impressions** are the number of times an ad is visible to users on a webpage, regardless of whether the user clicks or interacts with the ad. An ad's **click-through** rate is the number of times users click the ad to go to the sponsor's website. Both impression and click-through rates are used to collect money and sell advertisements to sponsors.

Uploading Website Files

The computer that you use to edit your website is called your **local computer**. To transfer the files from your local computer to a **remote web server** (a web server on the Internet), you will need to connect to the remote web server using an FTP client. You also will need an account on a web server in order to publish a website. If your school provides you with space to host a website, ask your instructor for the settings to connect to your account on the school's web server. In general, you will need to know the host or web server name and your username and password to publish the files. You should publish only those files related to your website assignment on your school's web server. After the file transfer completes, check the time and date and the size of the files on the server. The sizes should match the sizes of the files on your local computer. A file's time and date shows the time and date that the web server received the file. View the website by entering the web address of the website's home page (on the server) in the browser's address bar to verify that the files uploaded correctly.

Figure 12-16 Google Analytics captures and reports web traffic.
Source: Google.com

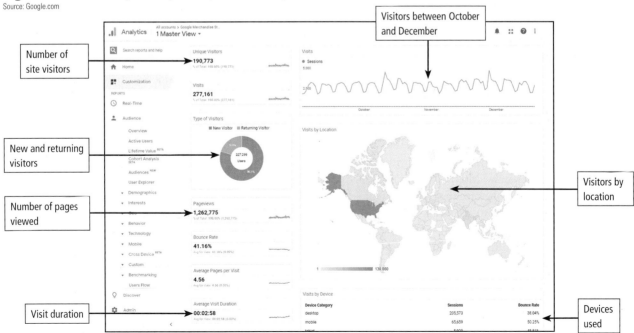

When you have finished transferring the files from your local computer to a web server, you can view the website on any device connected to the Internet by typing the absolute web address of the website's home page or any page on the website, in the address bar of a browser. An absolute web address begins with http:// and includes the website's domain name or the name of the server hosting the site. You should view the website online to make sure it is displayed as you intended and that the links work correctly.

? Consider This

What agreements should you make with advertising sponsors for your website?

Website owners, and especially bloggers, rely on sponsorships to make money from their website. If your website receives a lot of traffic, advertisers may approach you directly or be willing to discuss opportunities if you approach them. If you are using a CMS, it may have services that you can apply for, depending on your website traffic. In addition to selling ad space, you can make deals with vendors to promote their products by posting pictures or reviews or by talking about the product's benefits in your web content. An **affiliate agreement** with a vendor specifies that you receive commission on any sales that are generated by users of your website. The vendor can track your sales based on click-through rates or by a specific promotion code that is linked to your account for your users to include in their order entry. Are you a website or blog owner, or do you know one, who earns money through sponsorships? What kinds of responsibilities do website owners have to their audience to let them know when they promote a product using an affiliate agreement? If you had a product to advertise, what would you want to include in an agreement with a website or blog owner?

Ethics & Issues: Follow Accessibility Guidelines

Following guidelines that remove or ease barriers that limit access to your content to those with disabilities should be part of your content goals. In addition, you should consider those with socioeconomic restraints that may limit their web access to viewing websites with content that requires a lot of bandwidth. In addition to ensuring access, you also should make sure that your content feels inclusive to all and takes into account users' uniqueness, such as culture and identity.

The **Web Accessibility Initiative** (**WAI**) consists of groups of users and developers who create guidelines about usage, tools, and education regarding web accessibility. WAI was established by the W3C. The WAI develops guidelines to ensure all website visitors can access content on webpages, including the **Web Content Accessibility Guidelines** (**WCAG**).

WCAG guidelines include four principles of accessibility regarding information and user interfaces. The following lists the principles and examples of each:

- **Perceivable:** Presentable in ways that users can perceive using their available senses.
  - Non-text content must be available to be read or described by an e-reader or other adaptive technology and include captions and media alternatives for audio or video content.
  - Present related text in meaningful sequences or groups.
  - Distinguish text headings and sections using a combination of color, font size, text spacing, and contrast.
- **Operable:** Able to be used regardless of device or disability.
  - Provide alternative methods to navigate and provide input, including choices between using a keyboard or other device.
  - Consider those with seizure disorders when presenting images that flash or use animation.
  - Allow for adjustable timing, including the ability to pause any content that streams or repeats.
- **Understandable:** Using an uncomplicated interface and content that meets readability standards.
  - Content should not use overly complicated language, excessive use of idioms or unusual words, and abbreviations or acronyms that may not be familiar to all users.
  - Navigation should be predictable and consistent on all pages.
  - Include input assistance, including labels and instructions, as well as guidance when errors are input.
- **Robust:** Able to be interpreted in multiple ways, including assistive technologies, translation tools, and different devices.
  - Following CSS and HTML standards and practices when presenting content, including reading order of page elements or table content.
  - Include any helpful status messages that give guidance to those using assistive devices.

Web development tools often include accessibility checkers that point out potential issues, such as lack of alt text or inconsistent navigation. You also can purchase external tools that provide even more insight into the accessibility of your website. In addition, you should employ user testing that focuses on accessibility concerns, such as accessiBe (Figure 12-17).

Figure 12-17   Compliance report using the accessiBe accessibility checker.

Source: AccessiBe

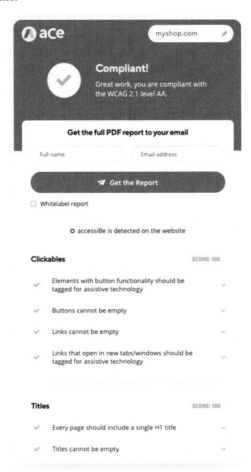

 Consider This

How can you determine which disabilities most need to be addressed?

More than fifteen percent of the world's population identify as having a disability. These users may require assistance or adaptive devices when accessing the web. Creating websites that enable them to view and interact with your content independently should be your goal. You should keep in mind that the range of disabilities users have is wide, and their needs vary. Users with visual disabilities include blind and low-vision users who may need e-readers or adjustable fonts, and those who are color-blind, who may be unable to interpret some contrasting color schemes. Users who are deaf or have hearing loss will need captions for any video or audio recordings that you include, a sign language interpreter, or a nonmedia alternative to the content. Motor disabilities include loss of limb or paralysis, which may mean that navigation and input methods need to be adaptive and obvious. If using speech as an input method, users who are unable to speak or who have speech impediments will need to be able to use a keyboard or other method. Users with cognitive conditions, including dyslexia, may require simple and straight-forward text and the ability to use an e-reader. Do you, or anyone you know, have any conditions that require adaptive devices or assistance when using digital and web content? What is the responsibility of the developer to provide solutions for these users? What consequences should there be for websites that do not comply with accessibility standards?

Study Guide

Instructions: The Study Guide exercise reinforces material you should know after reading this module. Answer the questions below using the format that helps you remember best or that is required by your instructor. Possible formats may include one or more of these options: write the answers; create a document that contains the answers; record answers as audio or video using a webcam, smartphone, or portable media player; post answers on a blog, wiki, or website; or highlight answers in the book/ebook.

1. Explain what a website plan determines. List six steps to consider when creating a website plan.

2. Differentiate between goals and objectives.

3. Define the term, CTA. Give an example.

4. Explain how demographic and psychographic characteristics are used to create a target audience profile.

5. Differentiate among a home page, subsidiary pages, and a landing page.

6. Define the terms, value-added content and dynamically generated content.

7. What does SEO stand for? Explain its purpose.

8. Define the term, storyboard. A(n) _____ is a diagram that shows steps or processes.

9. Describe the uses of the following: breadcrumb trail, text link, image link, navigation area, and search feature. What is a target?

10. List four design features that should be consistent across all webpages.

11. Explain the importance of website testing. Define the term, usability test.

12. Explain considerations when planning to publish your website.

13. Define the following: eye tracking study, heat map, and F-pattern.

14. Differentiate among a text editor, an HTML editor, and an IDE.

15. A(n) _____ is a coding system that uses tags to provide instructions about the appearance, structure, and formatting of a document.

16. Explain how a content provider works with a CMS. Define the term, content repository.

17. List features of website builders and content management systems.

18. List steps to create a website using a website builder.

19. Define the term, plug-in.

20. List steps to create a website using a CMS.

21. Define the term, script. What is a client-side script?

22. Explain the use of tags in HTML.

23. Differentiate between HTML and XML.

24. List elements in the structure of an HTML webpage. Define the term, attribute.

25. Explain how to use HTML to format titles, headings, paragraphs, and line breaks.

26. List concerns when naming webpages files.

27. Explain how to use links. Differentiate between relative and absolute references.

28. Explain how to use lists. Differentiate between unordered and ordered lists.

29. Describe considerations when adding images to a webpage.

30. List types of multimedia content you can add to a webpage. Define the term, embedding.

31. Explain issues surrounding the deprecation of HTML features.

32. Define the terms, style sheet and style rule.

33. Differentiate between embedded and inline styles. Define the term, font family.

34. Explain considerations when adding color to a webpage.

35. Explain why developers might or might not adopt current web design trends.

36. Explain how HTTPS and TLS can secure a website.

37. List other techniques you can use to ensure your website's security.

38. Define the term, NFT, and explain issues surrounding them.

39. Differentiate between and IP address and a domain name.

40. List factors to consider when selecting a web host. Explain the use of FTP.

41. Define the term, web analytics, and describe what information they provide.

42. Define the terms, click path, sticky content, impression, and click-through.

43. Describe agreements website owners can make with advertising sponsors.

44. Explain the role of the WAI in establishing the WCAG.

45. List the four principles of accessibility and give an example of each.

46. Explain website design considerations for different types of disabilities.

Key Terms

You should be able to define the Key Terms listed below.

absolute reference (12-11)
affiliate agreement (12-18)
attribute (12-10)
call-to-action (CTA) (12-2)
click path (12-17)
clickstream (12-17)
click-through (12-17)
client-side script (12-9)
content management system (CMS) (12-7)
content repository (12-7)
CSS editor software (12-13)
demographic characteristic (12-2)
deprecated (12-12)
design plan (12-2)
domain registrar (12-16)
dynamically generated content (12-4)
embed (12-12)
embedded style (12-13)
Extensible Markup Language (XML) (12-10)

external link (12-11)
eye-tracking (12-6)
F-pattern (12-6)
flowchart (12-4)
font family (12-14)
goal (12-2)
heading (12-11)
heat map (12-6)
home page (12-3)
hosted website search provider (12-5)
HTML editor (12-6)
impression (12-17)
inline style (12-13)
Internet Protocol (IP) (12-16)
JavaScript (12-9)
landing page (12-3)
local computer (12-17)
markup language (12-7)
meme (12-15)
meta tag (12-4)
navigation bar (12-5)
navigation menu (12-5)
non-fungible token (NFT) (12-15)

objective (12-2)
ordered list (12-12)
plug-in (12-9)
psychographic characteristic (12-2)
purpose statement (12-2)
relative reference (12-11)
remote web server (12-17)
script (12-9)
search engine optimization (SEO) (12-4)
Secure Sockets Layer (SSL) (12-15)
sticky content (12-17)
storyboard (12-4)
style rule (12-13)
style sheet (12-13)
subsidiary page (12-3)
tag (12-10)
target (12-5)
target audience profile (12-2)

text editor (12-6)
unordered list (12-12)
uptime (12-16)
usability test (12-6)
user interface (UI) (12-2)
value-added content (12-3)
Web Accessibility Initiative (WAI) (12-18)
web analytics (12-17)
Web Content Accessibility Guidelines (WCAG) (12-18)
web template (12-7)
website builder (12-7)
website plan (12-2)
website search feature (12-5)
widget (12-8)

Extend Your Knowledge

Instructions: The Extend Your Knowledge exercise expands on subjects covered in the module and encourages you to find the latest developments on these topics. Use a search engine or another search tool to locate news articles, blog entries, videos, expert discussions, or other current sources on the listed topics. List your sources, and write 3-4 sentences describing what you have learned to submit in the format required by your instructor.

- NFTs
- Memes
- Web design trends
- Social curation

What did you learn that helped you better understand the concepts in this module? Did anything surprise you? How will what you learned impact you?

Checkpoint

The Checkpoint exercises test your knowledge of the module concepts.

True/False   Mark T for True and F for False. If False, rewrite the statement so that it is True.

_____ 1. Objectives are the results you want your website to accomplish within a specific timeframe.

_____ 2. Meta tags are HTML specification tags that tell search engines what data to use.

_____ 3. In a CMS, the templates, style sheets, and other frequently used content elements, such as a logo graphic, are stored in a database called a content repository.

_____ 4. The <p> and </p> tags identify the beginning and ending of pages.

_____ 5. Absolute references identify the location of resources in the current website.

_____ 6. An inline style is specified as a style attribute within the body section.

_____ 7. A web firewall monitors the HTTP traffic to and from your web service and can alert you to any unusual activity.

_____ 8. A meme is a certified, unique data file associated with a digital file.

_____ 9. Uptime is a measure of a web host's reliability.

_____ 10. According to the WCAG, website content and interfaces should be perceivable, operable, understandable, and robust.

Matching   Match the terms with their definitions.

_____ 1. plug-in

_____ 2. content repository

_____ 3. domain name

_____ 4. psychographic characteristics

_____ 5. JavaScript

_____ 6. web template

_____ 7. XML

_____ 8. affiliate agreement

_____ 9. WCAG

_____ 10. demographic characteristics

a. a predesigned model webpage that you can customize for fast website or webpage creation and updating

b. a third-party program that extends the built-in functionality of an application or browser

c. used to write scripts that run in a browser to control a webpage's behavior and often make it interactive

d. defines the content of a webpage

e. database that stores templates, style sheets, and other frequently used content elements

f. social group affiliations, lifestyle choices, purchasing preferences, and political affiliations

g. gender, age group, educational level, income, location, and other characteristics

h. specifies that you receive commission on any sales that are generated by users of your website

i. guidelines to ensure all website visitors can access content on webpages

j. the portion of a URL or email address that identifies one or more IP addresses

Problem Solving

Instructions: The Problem Solving exercises extend your knowledge of module concepts by seeking solutions to practical problems with technology that you may encounter at home, school, or work. The Collaboration exercise should be completed with a team. You often can solve problems with technology in multiple ways. Determine a solution to the problems in these exercises by using one or more resources available to you (such as a computer or mobile device, articles on the web or in print, blogs, podcasts, videos, television, user guides, other individuals, electronics or computer stores, etc.). Is this a real issue you have encountered? Do you think you would be able to solve the situation if you encounter it? Describe your solution, along with the resource(s) used, in the format requested by your instructor (brief report, presentation, discussion, blog post, video, or other means).

Personal

1. **Deprecated Feature**   While testing your website before you publish it, the report from your CMS indicates that several of your features have been deprecated. What does that mean, and should you fix it?

2. **Blog Advertisers**   The blog you have been working on for over a year that focuses on clothes you have gotten from vintage and consignment shops has gotten a wide distribution. How can you attract advertisers to sponsor you, and what measures can you take to ensure that your sales are credited correctly?

3. **Unsecured Website**   While trying to access a website, your browser notifies you that the website's certificate cannot be verified. What might be causing this? Should you access the website in spite of the warning? Why or why not?

4. **NFTs**   You won a few hundred dollars in a raffle recently. Your friend tells you to invest in NFTs. You find an online vendor that sells NFTs, but you have concerns. Do the risks outweigh the rewards of purchasing NFTs?

5. **Website Too Large**   A website you created for a small landscaping business with your friend has grown quite large and experienced an increased in visitors. You started with just a few webpages, including a home page, a list of your services and references, and a contact form. Now you have added a blog, a gallery of photos of completed jobs, and a sales page for tools and plants. You are finding it difficult to determine how the pages should be linked. What tools can you use to evaluate the website's structure to create a better plan?

Professional

6. **Target Audience Profile**   You are trying to get investors and partners in your new business. You have created a website plan that lists the pages, contents, and links and have selected a CMS to use. A potential partner asks you what type of characteristics your audience has, but you are not sure. How can you determine this, and why is it important?

7. **Selecting a Development Tools**   You used a free web template to create a website but now are frustrated with the lack of flexibility to customize the colors, fonts, and layout. You decide to research other methods to create a new website into which you can insert the content you already created. What features should you look for in a web design tool? What might be best for you and your abilities?

8. **Securing a Website**   You know that using a digital certificate is an important part of securing your website and assuring your audience of the website's safety. You, however, do not know how to go about securing one or how to make sure it is visible to your users. What resources might you be able to use to obtain a certificate?

9. **Disappointing Analytics**   Your company's website analytics show that several pages on the website get very little traffic; it also reveals that most visitors do not return after the first visit. What might the problem be? How can you use this data to improve your website?

10. **Website Does Not Meet WCAG Guidelines**   You ran your website through the accessibility checker that came with your CMS when you first created it. After a recent resign, however, your company received some complaints from users that the navigation is difficult for those using assistive technologies. What is your responsibility? How can you fix this issue?

Collaboration

11. **Technology in Nonprofits**   You recently joined a nonpartisan organization that encourages diversity in candidates for local elections. You have volunteered to create a website that can contain candidate profiles, accept donations, and solicit volunteers to collect signatures and display campaign signs for candidates. Form a team of three people to determine the requirements for implementing the website. One team member will create a suggested structure for the webpage and create a storyboard for at least three pages. One member will make a list of graphics and multimedia that might be helpful to the website, as well suggest as how to ensure accessibility with the graphics and media. A third member should create a sample target audience profile, including suggestions for how to attract those users.

How To: Your Turn

Instructions: This exercise presents general guidelines for fundamental skills when using a computer or mobile device and then requires that you determine how to apply these general guidelines to a specific program or situation. You often can complete tasks using technology in multiple ways. Figure out how to perform the tasks described in these exercises by using one or more resources available to you (such as a computer or mobile device, articles on the web or in print, online or program help, user guides, blogs, podcasts, videos, other individuals, trial and error, etc.). Summarize your 'how to' steps, along with the resource(s) used, in the format requested by your instructor (brief report, presentation, discussion, blog post, video, or other means).

1 **Create a Website**

Many tools are available to help you create a website, even if you are not experienced with HTML, CSS, and other web technologies. The following steps guide you through the general process of creating the homepage for a simple website.

a. Download and install an IDE, such as WebStorm, or use a text editor to edit the website files.

b. Create a folder that will contain all the files and folders used in your website project.

c. Open a code editor or IDE, locate the project folder, and create a new HTML 5 file inside your Website folder called index.html.

d. Enter `<body>` and `</body>` tags, then type home page text between the body tags, including at least one line that will be a heading and another that will be a paragraph.

e. Type your website's title content between the `<title>` and `</title>` tags in the head section to set the title of the page.

f. Place `<h1>` and `</h1>` tags around the heading(s) and `<p>` and `</p>` tags around the paragraph(s).

g. Enter contact information at the bottom of the page, and type `<br>` after each line to include a line break.

h. Save the file and preview it in a browser.

i. Make a list of graphics, links, widgets, and other page elements you could add to your home page.

Exercises

1. What other pages should you add to your website?

2. Create a list of formatting you will specify using CSS.

3. What links should you include for subsidiary pages from the home page?

4. List criteria you should use to determine a website host. Would you need to make further adjustments to your website to fit the host's specifications?

5. Will you include social media sharing buttons? If so, for what social media platforms will you provide sharing buttons? How will you locate the necessary widgets to embed the button?

6. What steps will you take to ensure that your website meets accessibility criteria?

Internet Research

Instructions: These exercises broaden your understanding of module concepts by requiring that you search for information on the web. Use a search engine or another search tool to locate the information requested or answers to questions presented in the exercises. Describe your findings, along with the search term(s) you used and your web source(s), in the format requested by your instructor (brief report, presentation, discussion, blog post, video, or other means). Additionally, reflect on the process you used to complete this activity. How did you go about choosing the tool that you did and why? Would you do anything differently next time?

❶ Making Use of the Web: Identifying Calls-To-Action

As discussed earlier in this module, every website should include a call-to-action (CTA). How does that requirement factor into creating a website that meets its goals and objectives? Sometimes the CTA is an obvious part of the website's purpose, such as for a nonprofit that solicits donations, or an e-commerce business that wants users to purchase products. Other times, you might have to think about what function the CTA serves.

Research This: Using your browser history, load the four websites you most recently visited in different browser tabs. For each website, jot down info about the CTA. Describe how the CTA is formatted, where it is located, and how obvious it is to you. Think about what the website's goals and objectives are. How does the CTA help the website meet the goals and objectives? Do any of the websites have multiple CTAs? Can you think of other CTAs that the website might use?

❷ Social Media: Embed Social Media in Your Website

In addition to a website, most businesses have active social media accounts on multiple platforms, such as Instagram and Facebook. These platforms enable them to engage with their customers, advertise products and events, and gauge opinions based on comments, likes, shares, and other interactions. Many business websites embed their social media accounts in their website so that visitors can see the latest Tweet or post and then click it to interact with it on a social media platform.

Research This: Find two websites that include their social media feeds on their websites. Where in the website or on the homepage is the feed located? What platform(s) feeds are shown? How does the embedded social media feed enhance the existing webpage content? Visit two social media platforms and find out how to embed your feed onto a webpage. How easy do you find this? Do you need any additional tools? If so, what?

❸ Search Skills: Discover How Businesses Use Web Analytics

You have learned that analytics can be used to determine data and trends, as well as monitor engagement. In the real world, businesses take the data they receive from web analytics very seriously, because it can reflect issues with customer satisfaction, problems with a website's functionality, or determine whether or not a product is popular. Companies often prepare reports for investors or contract with companies that can interpret a website's analytics to help a company use that data to improve or make changes.

Research This: Find an example of a publicly traded company's annual report. View the report to see what types of analytics it contains and whether the company views these statistics as successful or not. If you are unable to find a report, list five categories of analytics that a report might include, and make a list of what would indicate success or failure in those categories. Then, find a company that offers analytic services, including monitoring and review. What specific services does the company provide? What would be the advantages of hiring such a company?

Critical Thinking

Instructions: These exercises challenge your assessment and decision-making skills by presenting real-world situations associated with module concepts. The Collaboration exercise should be completed with a team. Evaluate the situations below, using personal experiences and one or more resources available to you (such as articles on the web or in print, blogs, podcasts, videos, television, user guides, other individuals, electronics or computer stores, etc.). Perform the tasks requested in each exercise and share your deliverables in the format requested by your instructor (brief report, presentation, discussion, blog post, video, or other means).

1. Responsive Web Design

When smartphones and tablets first became popular, website developers could create separate mobile versions of their websites, which meant managing two separate websites. Responsive web design (RWD) technologies enable the developer to create one website that presents differently, depending on the device, platform, and even the screen orientation. Websites developed today typically employ a mobile-first strategy, in which they first consider the smallest screen size when determining layout and content. The goal of RWD is to create a website that has a positive UX, regardless of who is using the website and on which device.

Do This: Visit a website on at least two devices that have different screen sizes (or refer to Figure 12-1 in this module). Make a note of the differences on each for content, media, and navigation. In what ways did the website designer employ a mobile-first strategy? Is the website easy to use on all devices? Which do you prefer? Why?

2. Plug-Ins

Many websites use plug-ins to enhance interactivity and functionality. Plug-ins can be used to manage contact forms, provide enhanced analytics tools, improve SEO, send communications to subscribers, and more. Web development tools often include plug-ins to purchase; some are offered at no cost. Other plug-ins are available from third-party vendors or from the developers themselves. As with any technology, it is important to evaluate the source of a plug-in before installing or downloading it.

Do This: Make a list of popular types of plug-ins. Choose one CMS, such as WordPress. What types of plug-ins do they offer? How do they ensure the plug-ins are secure? What plug-ins might you use on a website you create for a club or organization with which you are involved or in which you are interested? Are these available in WordPress? If so, are they free or for a fee? Do alternatives exist outside of WordPress? If so, how reliable are these?

3. Case Study

Cooperative-Owned Farm Stand   You are the new manager for a farm stand that is a cooperative effort, jointly owned by several local farmers. The farm stand's website has not been updated in several years. The owners have asked you to investigate what the farm stand needs to do to make sure its website meets current accessibility standards.

Do This: Using information presented in the module, as well as performing additional research, prepare information about creating an accessible website. What is the responsibility of the website owner? What could be the consequences if the website is not compliant with accessibility standards? What tools are available that can help developers check their website for accessibility guidelines? Include recommendations for how to address several different disabilities. Compile your findings.

Collaboration

4. Creating a Target Audience Profile

You are a marketing intern at a firm that has a fast-growing online retailer as its client. The company's product offerings started in a niche market, appealing to users interested in archery in the Midwest. Now, however, it offers other outdoor sporting equipment and has a global audience. Your boss asks you to research how to create a new target audience profile that can help the company make adjustments to its content and branding.

Do This: Form a three-member team. One member should find and evaluate companies that provide target audience profiles as a service. Another should research templates and guidelines companies can use to create a target audience profile by themselves. A third should find case studies of companies that made decisions based on a target audience profile. As a team, discuss the options available to the company, generate recommendations, then compile and share your findings with the class.

Technology Careers:
Exploring and Preparing for Opportunities

13

iStock.com/Metamorworks

Objectives

After completing this module, you will be able to:

1 Identify the opportunities available in technology careers
2 Identify roles in the technology industry
3 Describe various information systems used in an enterprise
4 Identify security jobs
5 Describe the general areas of technology certifications
6 Explain how to be a successful telecommuter
7 Explain how to use resources to find a job

Careers in the Technology Industry

Nearly every job requires you to interact with technology to complete projects, exchange information with coworkers, and meet customers' needs. Business and government organizations of all sizes use a variety of computers, mobile devices, and other technology. Most use networks to ensure seamless communications among employees, vendors, and customers. They also use webpages, email, mobile apps, online social networks, and more to communicate with the public. Larger organizations use computers and other technology to answer and route phone calls, process orders, update inventory, and manage accounts receivable, accounts payable, billing, and payroll activities. To stay connected with employees and customers, they use mobile devices, web conferencing, and VPNs (virtual private networks). Even if you are not pursuing a career in technology, you will be using technology and relying on your colleagues who work in information technology (IT) to prepare and equip you for the technology necessary to do your job.

The technology industry has created thousands of high-tech career opportunities, even in organizations whose primary business is not technology related. Many opportunities exist for people of all skill levels, education, and interests, and a demand for computer professionals continues to grow. As new technologies emerge, organizations look for potential employees who possess skills and a desire to learn and who are comfortable using all types of technology.

Technology careers exist in many areas, including IT departments, technology equipment manufacturing, software and apps, technology service and repair, technology sales, educational training and support, and IT consulting.

IT Departments IT department staff are responsible for ensuring that all the computer operations, mobile devices, and networks run smoothly. They also determine when and if the organization requires new hardware, systems, or software. Usually, these jobs are divided into the following areas:

- **Management:** directs the planning, research, development, evaluation, and integration of technology.
- **Research and development:** analyzes, designs, develops, and implements new information technology and maintains and improves existing systems.
- **Technical services:** evaluates and integrates new technologies, administers the organization's data resources, and supports the centralized computer operating system and servers.
- **Operations:** operates the centralized computer equipment and administers the network, including both data and voice communications.

- **Training and support:** teaches employees how to use components of the information system or answers specific user questions.
- **Information security services:** develops and enforces policies that are designed to safeguard an organization's data and information from unauthorized users.
- **Marketing strategy:** directs and implements Internet and social media marketing.

Technology Equipment Manufacturing The technology equipment field consists of manufacturers and distributors of computers, mobile devices, and other hardware, such as hard drives, monitors, printers, and communications and networking devices. In addition to the companies that make end-user equipment, thousands of companies manufacture components used inside a computer or mobile device, such as chips, motherboards, cables and connectors, and power supplies.

Available careers in this field include positions with companies that design, manufacture, and produce computers and input, output, communications, mobile, and networking devices. Careers include designing and manufacturing computer chips and circuit boards (Figure 13-1), testing internal components, assembling computers and devices, and packing finished products.

Figure 13-1 Worker manufacturing a circuit board.
iStock.com/Arijit_Mondal

Software and Apps The software and apps field is comprised of companies that develop, manufacture, and support a wide range of software and apps for computers, the web, and mobile devices. Some companies specialize in a particular type of app, such as productivity software or tools; others might focus on a device type. Other companies produce and sell many types of software that work with both computers and mobile devices and may use Internet services to sync data among devices or provide collaborative features.

Some employees develop desktop, cloud, web, and mobile apps, such as productivity software, games, simulations, and more; some might develop operating systems and related tools.

Technology Service and Repair

The technology service and repair field provides preventive maintenance, component installation, and repair services to customers (Figure 13-2). Some technology service technicians possess general knowledge that enables them to work with a variety of devices from different manufacturers. Other technicians receive training and certifications directly from manufacturers to specialize in devices from that manufacturer. This work is best suited for those individuals who like to troubleshoot and solve problems and who have a strong background in electronics.

Figure 13-2 Technicians can install and fix internal components.
iStock.com/D-Keine

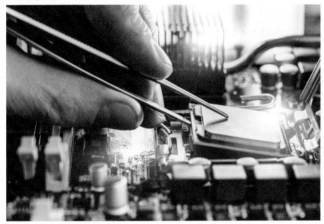

Many technology equipment manufacturers include diagnostic software with their computers and devices that assists technicians in identifying problems. Today's technology also allows technicians to diagnose and repair software problems from a remote location; that is, the technician accesses the user's hard drive or smartphone from a different location.

Technology Sales

Technology salespeople must possess a general understanding of technology and a specific knowledge of the product they are selling. Strong people skills are important, including a keen ability to understand the users' needs and relay a useful solution. Technology salespeople generally determine buyers' needs and direct buyers toward devices, computers, and apps that meet their needs.

Some salespeople work directly for technology equipment manufacturers, mobile device manufacturers, or software manufacturers. Others work for resellers, including retailers that sell personal computer products. The technology salesperson in a retail store often is a suitable entry-level job for students working toward a certificate or degree in computer-related fields. Before assuming the opinion of a salesperson is correct, be sure to independently research the product so that you can better determine whether answers to your questions are unbiased.

Technology Education, Training, and Support

Schools, colleges, universities, and private companies all need qualified educators to provide technology-related education and training. The high demand in this field has led to a shortage of qualified instructors at the college level as instructors increasingly move to careers in private industry, which offers the promise of higher pay. To teach in a university computer science program, you likely would need an advanced degree, such as a doctorate in computer science, which can require many years of study. A college or university computer science instructor might teach an entry-level course that covers the basics or could specialize in a single area, such as security, networking, programming, and more. You can compare the courses available at your school to see other areas in which an instructor might focus.

Corporate trainers teach employees how to use software and apps, design and develop systems, write programs, integrate and sync data from apps used on multiple devices, and perform other technology-related activities. Many large companies use their own training departments. Corporations usually do not require the rigorous educational backgrounds for trainers that educational institutions do for instructors.

In less formal setting, a help desk specialist answers hardware, software, and networking questions in person, over the phone, or electronically via email or a chat room. Educational requirements for help desk specialists are less stringent than they are for other careers in the technology field. The help desk specialist position is an ideal entryway into the IT field.

IT Consulting

Technology professionals sometimes become IT consultants after gaining experience in one or more technology-related areas, such as software development, systems analysis and design, network configuration, developing mobile devices, using social media, or web development. **IT consultants**, typically hired based on expertise, provide technology services to clients. Large enterprises often hire teams of consultants to offer advice about technology-related concerns. IT consultants must possess strong technical skills in their specialized area and must be able to communicate effectively to clients.

Consider This

How do you determine which education opportunities to pursue?

Most two-year and four-year colleges and universities offer degrees in computer science. A basic **computer science** program includes the study of computers and technology and how they are used. A more advanced degree in computer science also may also include the study of engineering, logic, and theory. Some programs allow you to focus on a specific area of computer science, such as artificial intelligence, programming, security, networks, or databases. Many factors go into selecting the right school for you, including geography, flexibility in scheduling, and costs. While some larger programs and schools might be more well-known and be regarded (fairly or unfairly) as more prestigious, they might not offer the convenience of a program that allows you to work full- or part-time, take classes online, is a short commute from your home, and costs less. Are you pursuing, or might you pursue, a degree in computer science? Why or why not? What type of degree program would best fit with your situation and needs? What aspects of computer science most interest you?

Technology Job Titles and Descriptions

The following sections briefly describe some of the more popular technology-related job titles for several categories of IT careers, including system development; technology operations; web marketing and social media; data storage, retrieval, and analysis; and app development and mobile technologies.

System Development   Careers in system development require you to analyze or create software, apps, databases, websites and web-based development platforms, and networks. Some careers are listed in Table 13-1.

Table 13-1   System Development Jobs

Job Title	Job Description
Cloud Architect	Identifies business requirements, strategies, and solutions for cloud storage and services that meet a company's goals or needs
Cognitive Engineer	Develops artificial-intelligence-based machines and programs based on data analysis to mimic human thought processes
Database Designer	Specifies the structure, interface, and requirements of a large-scale database; determines security and permissions for users
Program and App Developer	Specifies, designs, implements, tests, and documents programs and apps in a variety of fields, including robotics, operating systems, animation, and applications
Systems Analyst	Works closely with users to analyze their requirements, designs and develops new information systems, and incorporates new technologies
Systems Programmer	Installs and maintains operating system software and provides technical support to the programming staff
Web Designer	Designs the layout, navigation, and overall appearance of a website with a focus on user experience; specifies a website's appearance using HTML 5, JavaScript, CSS, media, and other web design technologies
Web Developer	Analyzes, develops, and supports the functionality of a website, including applications that often interact with databases or other online resources

Technology Operations   Careers in technology operations require you to have knowledge about how hardware, software, and network function. Some careers are listed in Table 13-2.

Table 13-2   Technology Operations Jobs

Job Title	Job Description
Computer Technician	Installs, maintains, and repairs hardware and servers; installs, upgrades, and configures software; troubleshoots hardware problems
Help Desk Specialist/Help Desk Technician	Answers technology-related questions in person, on the phone, or via email or an online chat room
Network Administrator/ Engineer	Installs, configures, and maintains LANs, WANs, wireless networks, intranets, Internet systems, and network software; identifies and resolves connectivity issues
Technical Project Manager	Guides design, development, and maintenance tasks; serves as interface between programmers/developers and management

Web Marketing and Social Media   Careers in web marketing and social media require you to be knowledgeable about web-based development platforms, social media apps, and marketing strategies. Some careers are listed in Table 13-3.

Table 13-3   Web Marketing and Social Media Jobs

Job Title	Job Description
Customer Relationship Management (CRM) Specialist	Integrates apps and data related to customer inquiries, purchases, support requests, and behaviors in order to provide a complete application that manages a company's relationships with its customers
Internet/Social Media Marketing Specialist	Directs and implements an organization's use of Internet and social media marketing, including Facebook pages, Twitter feeds, blogs, and online advertisements
Search Engine Optimization (SEO) Expert	Writes and develops web content and website layouts so that they will appear at the beginning of search results when users search for content
User Experience (UX) Designer	Plans and designs software and apps that consider a user's reaction to a program and its interface, including its efficiency, its effectiveness, and its ease of use

Data Storage, Retrieval, and Analysis   Careers in data storage and analysis require you to be knowledgeable about collecting, analyzing, and reporting data from databases or the web. Some careers are listed in Table 13-4.

Table 13-4   Data Storage, Retrieval, and Analysis Jobs

Job Title	Job Description
Data Scientist	Uses analytics and other Big Data techniques to interpret a company's data from a variety of sources to better understand its performance, make recommendations for improvement, and predict future outcomes
Database Administrator	Creates and maintains the data dictionary; monitors database performance
Database Analyst	Uses data modeling techniques and tools to analyze and specify data usage
Digital Forensics Examiner	Collects and analyzes evidence found on computers, networks, mobile devices, and databases
Web Analytics Expert	Collects and measures Internet data, such as website traffic patterns and advertising, and develops reports that recommend strategies to maximize an organization's web presence

App Development and Mobile Technologies   Careers in app development and mobile technologies require you to have knowledge about trends in the desktop and mobile app market, as well as the ability to develop secure apps for a variety of computers and mobile devices. Some careers are listed in Table 13-5.

Table 13-5   App Development and Mobile Technologies Jobs

Job Title	Job Description
Desktop or Mobile Application Programmer/ Developer	Converts the system design into the appropriate application development language, such as Visual Basic, Java, C#, and Objective C, and toolkits for various platforms
Games Designer/ Programmer	Designs games and translates designs into a program or app using an appropriate application development language
Mobile Strategist	Integrates and expands the company's initiatives for mobile users
Mobile Technology Expert	Develops and directs an organization's mobile strategy, including marketing and app development
Virtual Reality Engineer	Designs applications that incorporate technologies (such as VR and 3-D) with tools (such as Google Cardboard) to create storytelling tools and apps

Consider This

Is outsourcing jobs wrong?
Companies have a long history of **outsourcing**, or relying on outside companies to perform certain tasks. Outsourcing enables companies to find workers with specialized experience and to control costs. When a company sends jobs overseas, outsourcing becomes **offshoring**. To remain competitive, many companies have chosen to send computer jobs abroad to countries where salaries are typically lower. Opponents say that offshoring results in unemployment and harms the economy. Others argue that foreign economies benefit when companies hire and pay workers a fair wage and provide benefits and consumers benefit from the reduced cost of goods. Should companies receive criticism for outsourcing jobs? Why or why not? What are some possible alternatives to outsourcing that would help to keep a company competitive?

Information Systems in the Enterprise

Businesses, and their employees, use many types of systems. **Enterprise computing** refers to the use of technology by a company's employees to meet the needs of a large business. A system is a set of components that interact to achieve a common goal. A billing system, for example, allows a company to send invoices and receive payments from customers. Through a payroll system, employees receive paychecks — often deposited directly into their bank accounts. A manufacturing system produces the goods that customers order. Very often, these systems also are information systems. As you have learned, an information system is a set of hardware, software, data, people, and procedures that work together to produce information. Information systems support daily, short-term, and long-range information requirements of users in a company.

Ensuring Information Has Value

To assist with sound decision making, information must have value. For it to be valuable, information should be accurate, verifiable, timely, organized, accessible, useful, and cost effective.

- Accurate information is error free. Inaccurate information can lead to incorrect decisions. For example, consumers assume their credit reports are accurate. If your credit report incorrectly shows past-due payments, a bank might not lend you money for a vehicle or a house.
- Verifiable information can be proven as correct or incorrect. For example, security personnel at an airport usually request some type of photo identification to verify that you are the person named on the ticket.
- Timely information is useful only within a specific time period. A decision to build additional schools in a particular district should be based on the most recent census report — not on one that is 10 years old. Most information loses value with time. Some information, however, such as information about trends, gains value as time passes and more information is obtained. For example, your transcript gains value as you take more classes.
- Organized information is arranged to suit the needs and requirements of the decision maker. Two different people might need the same information presented in

a different manner. For example, an inventory manager may want an inventory report to list out-of-stock items first. The purchasing agent, instead, wants the report alphabetized by vendor.
- Accessible information is available when the decision maker needs it. Having to wait for information may delay an important decision. For example, a sales manager cannot decide which sales representative deserves the award for highest annual sales if the December sales have not been entered in the database yet.
- Useful information has meaning to the person who receives it. Most information is important only to certain people or groups of people. Always consider the audience when collecting and reporting information. Avoid distributing useless information. For example, an announcement of an alumni association meeting is not useful to students who have not graduated yet.
- Cost-effective information should provide more value than it costs to produce. An organization occasionally should review the information it produces to determine if it still is cost effective to produce. Some organizations create information only on demand, that is, as people request it, instead of on a regular basis. Many make information available online so that users can access it as they need it.

Typical Enterprise Information Systems

An enterprise requires special computing solutions because of its size and geographic distribution. A typical enterprise consists of a wide variety of departments, centers, and divisions — collectively known as functional units. Examples of functional units include human resources, manufacturing, and customer service.

Some information systems are used exclusively by only one type of functional unit within the enterprise. For example, marketing departments use market research systems to analyze data gathered from demographics and surveys, and social media marketing systems that analyze that data from email campaigns, online social networks, and content viewed and time spent on webpages.

Table 13-6 lists some of the more common information systems that are used by functional units in a typical enterprise.

Table 13-6 Information Systems Used Exclusively by Functional Units in an Enterprise

Functional Unit	Information System
Human Resources (HR)	• A **human resources information system** (**HRIS**) manages one or more administrative human resources functions, such as maintaining and managing employee benefits, schedules, and payroll.
Engineering or Product Development	• **Computer-aided engineering** (**CAE**) aids in the development and testing of product designs, and often includes CAD (computer-aided design).
Manufacturing	• Computer-aided manufacturing (CAM) controls production equipment, such as drills, lathes, and milling machines. • **Material Requirements Planning** (**MRP**) monitors and controls inventory, material purchases, and other processes related to manufacturing operations. • **Manufacturing Resource Planning II** (**MRP II**) is an extension of MRP that also includes product packaging and shipping, machine scheduling, financial planning, demand forecasting, tracking labor productivity, and monitoring product quality.
Sales	• **Salesforce automation** (**SFA**) helps salespeople manage customer contacts, schedule customer meetings, log customer interactions, manage product information, and place customer orders.
Customer Service	• **Customer relationship management** (**CRM**) manages information about customers, past purchases, interests, and the day-to-day interactions, such as phone calls, email messages, web communications, and Internet messaging sessions.

Other information systems that support activities of several functional units include:

- **Enterprise Resource Planning (ERP):** Enterprise Resource Planning (ERP) integrates MRP II with the information flow across an organization to manage and coordinate the ongoing activities of the enterprise, including product planning, manufacturing and distribution, accounting and finance, sales, human resources, and customer support. Advantages of ERP include complete integration of information systems across departments, better project management, and improved customer service. Complete integration means information is shared rapidly, and management receives a more complete and timely view of the organization through the information. Figure 13-3 illustrates how ERP encompasses all major activities of an enterprise.

Figure 13-3   ERP encompasses all the major activities throughout an enterprise.
iStock.com/Courtneyk, iStock.com/Insta_photos, iStock.com/Ergin Yalcin, iStock.com/Baona

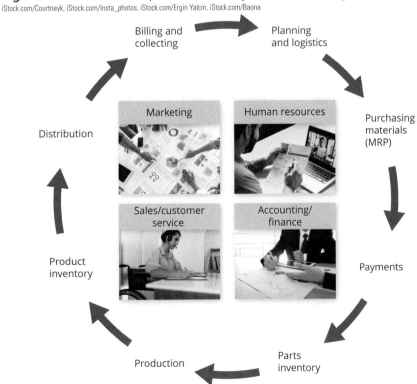

- **Document Management Systems:** A document management system (DMS) allows for storage and management of a company's documents, such as word processing documents, presentations, and spreadsheets. A central library stores all documents within a company or department. The system supports access control, security, version tracking of documents, and search capabilities; it also gives users the ability to check out documents to review or edit them and then check them back in when finished. Users are granted access to certain parts of the repository, depending on their needs.

- **Transaction Processing Systems:** A transaction processing system (TPS) is an information system that captures and processes data from day-to-day business activities. Examples of transactions are deposits, payments, orders, and reservations. When you use a credit card to purchase an item, you are interacting with a transaction processing system. Information systems use batch or online transaction processing systems (Figure 13-4). With batch processing, the computer collects data over time and processes all transactions later, as a group. With online transaction processing (OLTP), the computer processes each transaction as it is entered. For example, when you book a flight on the web, the airline probably uses OLTP to schedule the flight, book the flight, and send you a confirmation message. Most transaction processing systems today use OLTP because users need information immediately. For some routine processing tasks, such as printing monthly invoices or weekly paychecks, they use batch processing.

- **Management Information Systems:** A management information system (MIS) is an information system that generates accurate, timely, and organized information, so that managers and other users can make decisions, solve problems, supervise activities, and track progress. Management information systems often are integrated with transaction processing systems and focus on creating information that managers and other users need to perform their jobs. A management information system creates three basic types of reports: detailed, summary, and exception. A detailed report usually lists only transactions. A summary report consolidates data usually with totals, tables, or graphs, so that managers can review it quickly and easily. An exception report identifies data outside of a normal condition. These out-of-the-ordinary conditions, called the exception criteria, define the normal activity or status range.

- **Decision Support Systems:** A decision support system (DSS) helps users analyze information and make decisions. Some decision support systems are company specific and designed solely for managers. Others are available to everyone on the web. Programs that analyze data, such as those in a decision support system, sometimes are called online analytical processing (OLAP) programs. A decision support system uses data from internal and external sources. Internal sources of data might include databases, sales orders, MRP and MRP II results, inventory records, or financial data from accounting and financial analyses. Data from external sources could include interest rates, population trends, or raw material pricing.

Figure 13-4 Transaction processing systems.

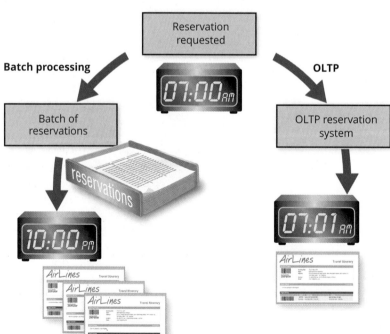

- **Expert Systems:** An expert system is an information system that captures and stores the knowledge of human experts and then imitates human reasoning and decision making. Expert systems consist of two main components: a knowledge base and inference rules. A knowledge base is the combined subject knowledge and experiences of the human experts. The inference rules are a set of logical judgments that are applied to the knowledge base each time a user describes a situation to the expert system. Expert systems help all levels of users make decisions. Enterprises employ expert systems in a variety of roles, such as answering customer questions, training new employees, and analyzing data. Expert systems also successfully have resolved such diverse problems as diagnosing illnesses, searching for oil, and making soup.
- **Supply chain management:** A supply chain management (SCM) system manages the flow of goods and services of a business, including purchasing of materials, inventory planning, manufacturing, and order fulfillment and tracking. An SCM helps the various functional units that plan, produce, and sell a company's products and coordinate activities between them.

❓ Consider This

How do enterprises use a CMS?

Recall that a content management system (CMS) enables and manages the publishing, modification, organization, and access of various forms of documents and other files, including media and webpages, on a network or the web. CMSs include information about the files and data (metadata). For example, the metadata for a company's employee manual may include the author's name, revision number, a brief summary, and last revision date. A CMS also provides security controls for the content, such as who is allowed to add, view, and modify content and on which content the user is allowed to perform those operations. Publishing entities, such as news services, use CMSs to keep websites and web feeds up to date. As news or information is published, it is categorized and updated on the appropriate sections of the website. Have you used a CMS for web publishing or other uses? What other uses can you think of for businesses to use a CMS?

Secure IT: Careers in Security

Security is a concern for all aspects of technology, including app usage, programming, web development, databases, networks, and more. Cybersecurity is a term used to encompass protection of systems and networks from hacking, data theft, viruses, and other issues that disrupt services. Cybersecurity is an important, and ever-evolving, industry. Companies prioritize security expertise when hiring for technology jobs at all levels.

Careers in information and systems security require you to be knowledgeable about potential threats to a device or network, including viruses and hacking. Security specialists need to know the tools and techniques to protect against threats.

Security jobs include:

- **Computer Security Incident Responder:** Creates logs, documentation, and recovery plans based on cybersecurity threats and incidents
- **Computer Security Specialist/Mobile Security Specialist:** Responsible for the security of data and information stored on computers and mobile devices within an organization
- **Digital Forensics Analyst:** Inspects electronic data to recover documents and files from data storage devices that may have been damaged or deleted, in order to use them as evidence in a crime investigation
- **Network Security Administrator:** Configures routers and firewalls; specifies web protocols and enterprise technologies
- **Security Analyst:** Implements security procedures and methods, looks for flaws in security of a company's devices and networks, works with and trains employees at all levels, and assigns permissions and network settings
- **Security System Project Manager:** Develops and maintains programs and tools designed to provide security to a network

❓ Consider This

What security issues are associated with drones?

Also known as an unmanned aerial vehicle (UAV) or unmanned aerial system (UAS), a drone is an aircraft that operates by an onboard computer and GPS, a remote control device, and/or an app on a computer or mobile device. Most are equipped with autopilot, a high-resolution camera, and real-time video. The drone pilot, or operator, manages the controls from the ground and can watch the drone by viewing a display attached to the base station. Insurance companies use drones to survey storm damage to buildings and property. Farmers create aerial maps to manage crop watering and fertilizing. Military uses of drones include surveillance of areas into which it would be unsafe to send personnel, to supply deliveries to combat areas, and even to detonate weapons.

Drones have been cited in instances where a person's privacy is invaded, as a drone can look through a window or over a person's yard in ways that may be hard to detect or notice. The Federal Aviation Administration (FAA) regulations limit the height a drone can fly, and state that the drone must stay within the operator's line of sight; further, it cannot venture over airports or populated areas. Have you ever used a drone? If so, for what purpose? To what extent should the FAA regulate drone usage? Why? What security concerns are associated with drone usage?

Technology Certifications

As you learned, a certification demonstrates your knowledge in a specific area to employers or potential employers. Organizations often require technology certification to ensure quality standards and to confirm their workforce remains up to date with respect to technology. When you earn a certification, you can include it on your print resume, as well as use a digital badge issued by the exam provider or a third-party organization on your personal website, blog, or LinkedIn page.

Application Software Certifications

Although numerous types of application software exist, several programs have achieved national recognition for use as business and graphics tools. Most sponsors of application software certifications have a partner training program and encourage computer-training centers to be authorized training representatives. A popular application software certification includes Microsoft Office Specialist (Figure 13-5), which tests a user's skills of Microsoft Office programs.

Figure 13-5 Microsoft Office Specialist (Fundamentals level) badge.
Source: Microsoft Corporation

As with most other certifications, vendor-authorized testing facilities take registrations and administer the certification test. People with the following jobs may be interested in application software certification:

- Corporate trainers
- Help desk specialists
- Office managers/workers
- Technology sales representatives
- Technology teachers

Data Analysis and Database Certifications

Data analysis certifications focus on the discovery, collection, and analysis of evidence on computers and networks. These certifications often contain the word, forensics, in their title. Database certifications cover the tasks required to support a database management system. If you are interested in working with data analysis or database certifications, you also may benefit from certifications in hardware, networking, programming, and security.

People with the following jobs may be interested in data analysis and database certification:

- Data scientist
- Database administrators
- Database analysts
- Digital forensics examiners

Hardware Certifications

Hardware certifications vary in scope from a narrow focus with an emphasis on the repair of a specific device to an integrated hardware solution that addresses a company's current and future technology needs. Obtaining an advanced certification in hardware implies that you have achieved a standard of competence in assessing a company's hardware needs, and you can implement solutions to help the company achieve its IT goals. A popular hardware certification includes CompTIA's A+ (Figure 13-6), which tests knowledge of computer setup, configuration, maintenance, troubleshooting, basic networking skills, and system software.

Figure 13-6 CompTIA A+ certification badge.
Source: CompTIA, Inc.

People interested in hardware certifications also may benefit from networking and operating system software certifications, which are closely tied to advanced hardware knowledge. People with the following jobs may be interested in hardware certification:

- Cable installation technicians
- Computer repair technicians
- Corporate trainers
- Help desk specialists
- IT consultants
- System engineers and administrators

Networking Certifications

Network expertise is acquired through years of experience and training because so many variables exist for a total network solution. Obtaining an advanced certification in networking implies that you have achieved a standard of competence, enabling you to address the complex issues that arise when planning, installing, managing, and troubleshooting a network. Cisco, CompTIA, and others offer certifications that test knowledge of installing, configuring, operating, and administering networks.

People in the following careers may be interested in network certification:

- Hardware service technicians
- IT consultants
- Network managers
- Network engineers
- System administrators

Operating System Certifications

Several options for various knowledge levels are available to those seeking operating system certifications. These certifications focus on particular skills of the user, the operator, the system administrator, and the software engineer. Microsoft, RedHat (Figure 13-7), and others offer certifications that test knowledge of their operating systems.

Figure 13-7   RedHat Certified Specialist badge.
Source: Red Hat, Inc.

If you are interested in an occupation as an operating system administrator or software engineer, you also may benefit from certifications in networking or hardware. These additional certifications are closely linked to the operating system and serve to broaden expertise in that area. People with the following jobs may be interested in a certification in operating systems:

- Hardware technicians
- Help desk specialists
- Network administrators
- IT consultants
- System administrators

Programmer/Developer Certifications

Various certifications are available in the programmer/developer area. These certifications usually are supported with training programs that prepare applicants for the certification test. A popular specific programmer/developer certification includes Google Apps Certified Specialist, which tests a user's skills of administering, selling, and deploying Google Apps. A broader development certification includes Project Management Professional (PMP), which tests knowledge of tasks required during system development (Figure 13-8).

Figure 13-8   PMI's PMP certification badge.
Source: Project Management Institute, Inc.

If you are interested in developing applications, you also may benefit from certifications in networking and courses in web design. These certifications are closely tied to programming and may broaden employment opportunities. People with the following jobs may be interested in a programmer/developer certification:

- Game developers
- IT consultants
- Mobile application developers
- Project leaders/managers
- Systems analyst
- Web developers

Security Certifications

Security certifications measure a candidate's ability to identify and control security risks associated with any event or action that could cause a loss of or damage to computer hardware, software, data, information, or processing capability. While some security certifications focus solely on network and Internet security, others include measures to secure operating systems, application programs, and information systems, as well as the physical facility and its people. A popular specific security certification includes Certified Information Systems Security Professional (CISSP), which tests in-depth knowledge of access control methods, information systems development, cryptography, operations security, physical security, and network and Internet security. Some security certifications relate specifically to the area of digital forensics.

People in the following careers may be interested in security certification:

- Information security officers and managers
- Law enforcement officials
- Military intelligence officers
- Network administrators
- Wireless network administrators
- Network security specialists
- Security administrators

❓ Consider This

How do you prepare for and take a certification exam?

Certifications cost time and money. Read evaluations of the certification to determine its value in the industry you have chosen. Examine employment projections and available job opportunities to determine if it is worth obtaining the certification. For most certification programs, courses are not provided. Test results alone determine certification. Few professionals, however, have the experience and skill set to take a certification exam without preparation.

To assist in preparing for a certification exam, several training options are available: self-study, online training, instructor-led training, and web resources. Authorized testing centers provide most certification exams for a fee. The exam sponsor's website typically lists testing centers near you. On the website, you can schedule and pay for your exam.

Guidelines for taking an exam include:

- Before leaving to take a certification exam, read the instructions provided by the testing center to ensure you bring all necessary supplies, equipment, or technology.
- Print a copy of the directions in case your GPS device or app fails.
- Arrive early and silence or turn off your mobile devices.
- Know approximately how long the exam will take so that you can use your time wisely.
- Some tests are in a multiple-choice format. Others are skill based.

You likely will know before you leave the testing center whether you passed the examination. If you do not pass an exam, you may have to pay the fee again to retake it. Have you ever taken a certification exam? Which exam did/would you choose? How did/might an exam help you with your chosen career?

How To: Create an Office for Telecommuting

Telecommuting, or working from home, can mutually benefit employers and employees. Employers do not have to pay for the physical infrastructure (including office space and parking) for the employee, and telecommuters often work more hours than those who physically commute to an office. Employees benefit from not having to commute and from having a comfortable work environment. Telecommuting also increases the pool of available jobs and applicants if employers and employees know that they can rely on telecommuting. In recent years, many companies have resorted to full telecommuting for all staff or have staggered days in which employees are in the office.

The following guidelines describe how to set up your home office for telecommuting:

- Choose a location in your home that is free from noise and distractions. If your home is occupied by others during the hours you plan to telecommute, your office should be located away from potentially noisy areas. For example, an office next to a room where someone else is watching television may not be an ideal choice.

Figure 13-9   Telecommuter with a treadmill desk.
iStock.com/Martin-dm

- Make sure your office has a comfortable desk and chair, or purchase a standing or treadmill desk (Figure 13-9). Although it may be tempting to sit on your couch with your laptop while you work, having a professional workspace will increase productivity.
- Consider acquiring a second monitor in order to multitask or increase your viewing space.
- Consider how you will store important documents: as paper copies in a file cabinet or digital documents on the cloud.

- If required, verify your office has a sufficient Internet connection. Be certain your wireless network is encrypted. Consider setting up one network for business or, if available, use your company's VPN, and have another network for personal use for business.
- Make sure your phone can receive a strong signal and has a conveniently located charger and power outlet.
- Use a headset with your phone to minimize background noise.
- Obtain supplies that typically are found in an office setting if you need them, such as a printer, writing utensils, paper, tape, a stapler, paper clips, and sticky notes.
- If your employer does not provide a computer for your use, ensure your computer is sufficiently equipped to complete your job tasks.
- Choose a background for web conferencing that is neutral. Consider using a background filter on the web conferencing app. If that is not an option for you, make sure that personal information, and anything that might be considered unprofessional, is not shown in the background area that shows on your screen.

❓ Consider This

Is telecommuting good or bad for business?

Although employees may view working from home as an ideal situation, some bosses do not agree. Supporters cite reduced pollution and commuting time. Other benefits include increased productivity due to lack of office gossip and politics. Many feel that they could not be as dedicated to their jobs without telecommuting because of the flexible hours and closeness to home. Others feel that trusted employees should have the privilege if they earn it. Companies benefit by saving on resources, such as office space.

Opponents claim that some lack the self-discipline to work remotely. Employees may be distracted more easily without direct management supervision. Some workers have difficulty setting appropriate boundaries regarding childcare or other family obligations. Additionally, productivity actually may decrease if employees stagger work hours to fit their schedule, limiting times when employees can schedule meetings.

Many experienced workers agree that telecommuting cannot replace valuable face-to-face time with coworkers, vendors, and customers. Some workers fear telecommuting because they feel that the lack of a personal relationship with managers puts them at the top of the list for downsizing. Is telecommuting good or bad for business? Why? Are some businesses or positions better suited for telecommuting? If so, which ones? Do some people lack the self-discipline to be productive while telecommuting? If so, how should managers determine whether to allow this practice and who may participate?

Ethics & Issues: Using Your Available Resources to Find a Job

Many job opportunities may exist in your industry, so it is important to narrow down the available jobs to ones for which you are qualified and in which you are interested. Tools at your disposal include the career service department at your school, career planning websites, and online social networks.

If your school has a career center or alumni network, take advantage of these valuable resources. Visit career services websites hosted by your college or university. These websites often contain information about career fairs, resume planning workshops, and campus recruitment activities. Career counselors and experienced alumni can help you prepare for and secure an interview in your chosen field. They also might provide references to potential employers.

Your instructors may be helpful resources when you are looking for a job. Because of their professional experience, they may be able to connect you with potential employers, recommend classes you should take, or suggest internship opportunities.

Career Websites

Whether you are seeking a new job or currently are employed, you may find a career website useful. Career websites often allow you to post your resume online or enter your resume information in a form at the website for potential employers to review. A resume often is your opportunity to make a good first impression to potential employers. It should be well-organized and free of errors. You can use a resume template or hire a professional resume writer to help create a resume. You can add notifications that indicate you are looking for work. Employers search for those notifications to find people who might match with an opportunity they have to offer. Examples of popular career websites include LinkedIn, Dice, and Monster.

You also can use a career website to upload, or link to, an online portfolio. While a resume lists your accomplishments, skills, employment history, and education, a **portfolio** shows examples of your work. Graphic artists and other digital media producers may use a portfolio to demonstrate their abilities, style, and past work (Figure 13-10).

Figure 13-10   Sample online portfolio.
iStock.com/Milindri

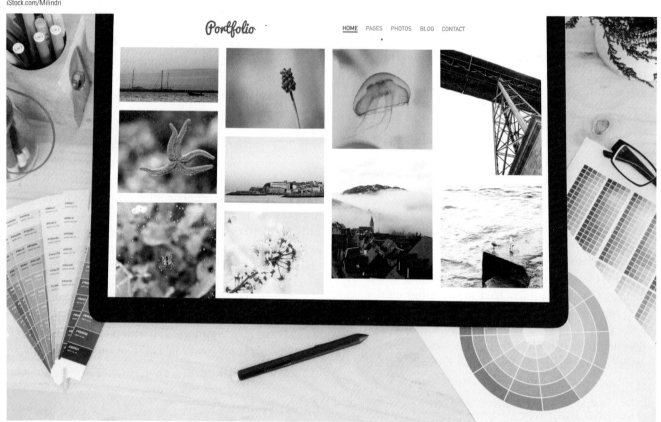

Start Your Job Search Online

Starting your job search online enables you to locate available jobs in which you are interested and determine ahead of time if you are qualified for the position, all before spending time applying.

Begin your job search by reviewing the information on online social networks, job search websites, and organizations' websites. On these websites, you can learn about career opportunities and prepare for an interview.

Research a company's online activity to become familiar with some of the products, services, and opportunities that they provide.

Use the employment database to learn about career opportunities. View a job listing to find the name of the person who posted the job and to determine the connections between you and those members you might want to contact in order to learn about a company or open jobs.

 **Consider This**

How can career websites further assist your job search?

You can perform many activities besides looking for a job and uploading your professional information on a career website. Other helpful actions might include:

- Follow companies' accounts to stay informed of job openings.

- Recommend colleagues and coworkers to recognize their skills and areas of expertise.

- Join groups of people with similar interests or experiences, for example, your school's alumni group or people who work at the same company.

- Consider expanding your network by connecting with your contacts' connections. If you invite an extended contact to connect, be sure to include a note that introduces yourself and indicates your professional reason for connecting.

    Have you used a career website? What did/would you use it for besides looking for a job?

Study Guide

Instructions: The Study Guide exercise reinforces material you should know after reading this module. Answer the questions below using the format that helps you remember best or that is required by your instructor. Possible formats may include one or more of these options: write the answers; create a document that contains the answers; record answers as audio or video using a webcam, smartphone, or portable media player; post answers on a blog, wiki, or website; or highlight answers in the book/ebook.

1. List ways in which companies use technology.

2. Explain areas in which IT jobs are divided.

3. List careers available in the technology equipment field.

4. Describe different opportunities in the software and apps field.

5. Describe how technology service and repair professionals use diagnostic software.

6. Explain the skills needed to be successful in the technology sales field.

7. Explain the role of a corporate trainer.

8. Define the term, IT consultant.

9. Describe considerations when selecting a computer science educational program.

10. List and describe system development jobs.

11. Differentiate among the following technology operations jobs: computer technician, help desk specialist/technician, network administrator/engineer, and technical product manager.

12. Explain the role of a CRM specialist.

13. List and describe jobs in the data storage, retrieval, and analysis field.

14. List and describe jobs in the app development and mobile technologies field.

15. Define the terms, outsourcing and offshoring, and explain considerations with these practices.

16. ___ computing refers to the use of technology by a company's employees to meet the needs of a large business.

17. List and describe characteristics of valuable data.

18. Define the following information systems: HRIS, CAE, CAM, MRP, MRP II, SFA, and CRM.

19. List advantages of ERP.

20. Explain how companies use a DMS.

21. List examples of uses of a TPS. Differentiate between batch processing and OLTP.

22. Describe the purposes of an MIS and a DSS.

23. Explain how an expert system uses a knowledge base and inference rules.

24. List the uses of an SCM.

25. Explain how an enterprise uses a CMS.

26. ___ is a term used to encompass protection of systems and networks from hacking, data theft, viruses, and other issues that disrupt service.

27. List types of security jobs.

28. Explain security concerns that exist with drone usage.

29. List types of people who may be interested in application software certification.

30. List types of people who may be interested in data analysis and database certification.

31. Explain what the A+ exam tests for. List types of people who may be interested in hardware certification.

32. Explain what an advanced networking certification can demonstrate. List types of people who may be interested in networking certification.

33. List types of people who may be interested in operating system certification.

34. Explain what the PMP exam tests for. List types of people who may be interested in programmer/developer certification.

35. Describe different focuses of security certifications. List types of people who may be interested in security certification.

36. Explain considerations when preparing for and taking a certification exam.

37. Explain benefits of telecommuting.

38. List guidelines to set up a home office for telecommuting.

39. Explain concerns associated with telecommuting.

40. Explain how to use a career center or your instructors in your job search.

41. Describe the role of a career website. Define the term, portfolio.

42. Explain how to use online resources to prepare for your job search.

43. List ways to use a career website.

Key Terms

You should be able to define the Key Terms listed below.

batch processing (13-8)

computer-aided engineering (CAE) (13-7)

computer science (13-4)

customer relationship management (CRM) (13-7)

cybersecurity (13-9)

decision support system (DSS) (13-8)

document management system (DMS) (13-8)

drone (13-9)

enterprise computing (13-6)

Enterprise Resource Planning (ERP) (13-7)

expert system (13-9)

human resources information system (HRIS) (13-7)

inference rules (13-9)

IT consultant (13-3)

knowledge base (13-9)

management information system (MIS) (13-8)

Manufacturing Resource Planning II (MRP II) (13-7)

Material Requirements Planning (MRP) (13-7)

offshoring (13-6)

online analytical processing (OLAP) (13-8)

online transaction processing (OLTP) (13-8)

outsourcing (13-6)

portfolio (13-13)

salesforce automation (SFA) (13-7)

supply chain management (SCM) (13-9)

telecommute (13-12)

transaction processing system (TPS) (13-8)

Extend Your Knowledge

Instructions: The Extend Your Knowledge exercise expands on subjects covered in the module and encourages you to find the latest developments on these topics. Use a search engine or another search tool to locate news articles, blog entries, videos, expert discussions, or other current sources on the listed topics. List your sources, and write 3-4 sentences describing what you have learned to submit in the format required by your instructor.

- Drone security
- Telecommuting trends
- New careers in technology
- Certification preparation

What did you learn that helped you better understand the concepts in this module? Did anything surprise you? How will what you learned impact you?

Checkpoint

The Checkpoint exercises test your knowledge of the module concepts.

True/False   Mark T for True and F for False. If False, rewrite the statement so that it is True.

_____ 1. Today's technology allows technicians to diagnose and repair software problems from a remote location.

_____ 2. A cognitive engineer develops artificial-intelligence-based machines and programs based on data analysis to mimic human thought processes.

_____ 3. A CRM specialist directs and implements an organization's use of Internet and social media marketing, including Facebook pages, Twitter feeds, blogs, and online advertisements.

_____ 4. CAM controls production equipment, such as drills, lathes, and milling machines.

_____ 5. With batch processing, the computer processes each transaction as it is entered.

_____ 6. A digital forensics analyst inspects electronic data to recover documents and files from data storage devices that may have been damaged or deleted, in order to use them as evidence in a crime investigation.

_____ 7. Popular networking certifications include CompTIA's A+.

_____ 8. PMP tests knowledge of tasks required during system development.

_____ 9. Telecommuters typically work fewer hours than those who physically commute to an office.

_____ 10. Dice and Monster are examples of popular career websites.

Matching   Match the terms with their definitions.

_____ 1. digital forensics examiner

_____ 2. MRP

_____ 3. SFA

_____ 4. CRM

_____ 5. MIS

_____ 6. inference rules

_____ 7. portfolio

_____ 8. expert system

_____ 9. DMS

_____ 10. IT consultant

a. a set of logical judgments that are applied to the knowledge base each time a user describes a situation to the expert system

b. manages information about customers, past purchases, interests, and the day-to-day interactions, such as phone calls, email messages, web communications, and Internet messaging sessions

c. collects and analyzes evidence found on computers, networks, mobile devices, and databases

d. an information system that generates accurate, timely, and organized information, so that managers and other users can make decisions, solve problems, supervise activities, and track progress

e. helps salespeople manage customer contacts, schedule customer meetings, log customer interactions, manage product information, and place customer orders

f. examples of work

g. typically hired based on expertise, provides technology services to clients

h. an information system that captures and stores the knowledge of human experts and then imitates human reasoning and decision making

i. allows for storage and management of a company's documents, such as word processing documents, presentations, and spreadsheets

j. monitors and controls inventory, material purchases, and other processes related to manufacturing operations

Problem Solving

Instructions: The Problem Solving exercises extend your knowledge of module concepts by seeking solutions to practical problems with technology that you may encounter at home, school, or work. The Collaboration exercise should be completed with a team. You often can solve problems with technology in multiple ways. Determine a solution to the problems in these exercises by using one or more resources available to you (such as a computer or mobile device, articles on the web or in print, blogs, podcasts, videos, television, user guides, other individuals, electronics or computer stores, etc.). Is this a real issue you have encountered? Do you think you would be able to solve the situation if you encounter it? Describe your solution, along with the resource(s) used, in the format requested by your instructor (brief report, presentation, discussion, blog post, video, or other means).

Personal

1. **Finding References**   As you near graduation, you start applying for jobs. Many of the applications you fill out ask for recommendations. You have had several jobs, but none in your field. What resources might your instructors and school have to help you determine the best people to ask?

2. **Online Job Search**   Having decided to work in the computer equipment field, you begin your job search online. In addition to looking on job search websites for available positions, what else should you research?

3. **Creating an Online Portfolio**   You are preparing your resume to submit for an entry-level web marketing job. While in school you helped several local businesses with their marketing and want to create a portfolio. What technology will you need? How can you let potential employers know about your portfolio?

4. **Contemplating a Job Offer**   After graduating with a degree in computer science, you send your resume to several companies. Almost immediately, you receive a job offer as a help desk specialist in a midsized organization. How can you find information about employee satisfaction with the company in order to determine whether or not to take the job?

5. **Appropriate Certification**   Because you hope to pursue a career as a system administrator, you would like to obtain a certification. Many certifications are available, but you want to choose the one(s) that will best prepare you for your future career. Which certification(s) will you consider?

Professional

6. **Staying Current with Technology**   Having accepted a job as a computer salesperson, you now realize the importance of staying up to date with the latest technologies and products. What are three ways that you can stay current in the technology field while working full time?

7. **Outsourcing IT Positions**   As the chief information officer for a large organization, you consider outsourcing various positions within your department to save money. What are some types of positions that can be outsourced easily? What positions might be difficult to outsource? Why?

8. **Preparing to Telecommute**   Your new job offers you the flexibility to work from home three to four days per week. While you work from home, you will need to participate in multiple web conferences each day, plus get your other work done. How can you avoid distractions when working from home? What equipment or devices should you ask your company to provide for you?

9. **Tough Decision**   Two top candidates who applied for a job within your organization have interviewed well, and you are having difficulty selecting which candidate should be offered the job. One candidate has several certifications and only two years of job-related experience, while the other candidate has six years of experience, but no certifications. What decision will you make, and why?

10. **Training Decision**   Your boss has allocated money to allow everyone in the IT department to attend training related to their job responsibilities. While researching the training available for your job as a system administrator, you learn that you either can take a semester-long course at a local university or attend an accelerated one-week, forty-hour training course. At the end of each training session, you will be ready to become certified. Which type of training will you choose? Why?

Collaboration

11. **Technology in Architecture and Design**   As a student in a drafting class, your instructor has challenged you to design your dream home by using programs and apps wherever possible. Form a team of three people to determine how to accomplish this objective. One team member should compare and contrast two programs or apps that can be used to create a two-dimensional floor plan, another team member should compare and contrast two computer-aided design programs or apps that can create a more detailed design of the house, and the third team member should compare and contrast two programs or apps that can assist with other aspects of the design process, such as landscaping and interior design.

How To: Your Turn

Instructions: This exercise presents general guidelines for fundamental skills when using a computer or mobile device and then requires that you determine how to apply these general guidelines to a specific program or situation. You often can complete tasks using technology in multiple ways. Figure out how to perform the tasks described in these exercises by using one or more resources available to you (such as a computer or mobile device, articles on the web or in print, online or program help, user guides, blogs, podcasts, videos, other individuals, trial and error, etc.). Summarize your 'how to' steps, along with the resource(s) used, in the format requested by your instructor (brief report, presentation, discussion, blog post, video, or other means).

1 **Conduct an Effective Interview**

Gathering information is an important task, whether you are trying to assess whether a job candidate would be a good fit for an open position, or if you need to compile feedback about a new system you are developing. An important means of gathering information is the personal interview. Interviews must be thorough and comprehensive. Prior to conducting an interview, you must determine that an interview is the best means for obtaining the information you seek. You have learned a variety of ways to obtain information, and you should use each of them appropriately. Because an interview may interrupt a person's schedule and takes time, you must be sure the information gained in the interview justifies this interruption. Once you have determined you should conduct an interview to gather information, plan to ask questions that will generate useful answers. The following steps guide you through the process of conducting an interview that ultimately will generate useful answers.

a. Your questions should directly address the goals of the interview. Do not expect the person being interviewed to provide a tutorial. Your questions must generate answers that supply you with the information you need to make a decision.

b. Your questions should be thought-provoking. In general, do not ask questions requiring a yes or no answer. Your questions should not lead the interviewee to an answer — rather, the questions should be open-ended and allow the person to develop the answer. As an interviewer, never argue with the person being interviewed, do not suggest answers or give opinions, ask straightforward questions rather than compound questions, never assign blame for any circumstance that might come up in the interview, and never interrupt while the person is talking. Finally, you, as the interviewer, should not talk much. Remember, you are conducting the interview to gain information, and it is the person you are interviewing who has that information. Let them talk.

c. Pay attention carefully, with your ears and your eyes. What you hear normally is most important, but body language and other movements often convey information as well. Concentrate on the interviewee — expect that you will make much more eye contact with the person than they will with you. Allow silences to linger — the normal impulse in a conversation is to fill the silence quickly; in an interview, however, if you are quiet, the person being interviewed might think of additional information.

d. As you listen, concentrate on the interviewee. When points are being made, do not take notes because that will distract from what the person is saying; stay focused. Once the information has been conveyed, jot down a note so that you will remember.

e. Throughout the interview, offer reinforcing comments, such as, "The way I understand what you just said is …" Make sure when you leave the interview that no misunderstandings exist between you and the person you interviewed.

f. Before you conclude the interview, be sure all your goals have been met. You may not have another opportunity to interview the person, so ensure you have asked sufficient questions to gain the information you need to make a decision.

g. After the interview, it is recommended you send a follow-up email message or letter to the person you interviewed to review the information you learned. This message or letter should invite the interviewee to correct any errors you made in summing up your findings. In addition, for all the people you interview, keep a record of the time and place of the interview. In this way, if any questions arise regarding the interview, you will have a record.

Interviewing Online

If you are not in the same physical location as the people you want to interview, it may be better to conduct the interview online. If you plan to conduct the interview online, consider the following advice:

• Plug in the computer or device so that you do not have to rely on battery power. If you must rely on battery power, be sure that the battery is fully charged.

• Use a wired Internet connection, rather than connecting to a wireless network, to minimize the risk of losing Internet connectivity during the interview.

• Select a location for the video call that has a neutral background and is free from distractions.

- Know how to initiate or receive a video call.
- Exit your email, chat, and other unnecessary applications during the interview so that you are not distracted or interrupted by alerts and notification messages.
- Test the videoconferencing software in advance to ensure the configuration works.
- Adjust the microphone, webcam, and speakers before the actual interview to ensure optimum call quality.
- Practice switching between the videoconferencing app's chat window and your desktop or a browser window, in case you want to share a link, send a file, or type a message during the interview.
- Keep your eyes focused on the webcam so that you will appear attentive.

Exercises

1. Think about the last time you were involved in an interview (either as an interviewer or an interviewee). What types of questions were you asked? Do you feel the questions solicited useful answers?

2. If you were to interview a candidate for a technology-related position, what types of questions would you ask?

3. What advantages do open-ended questions have? When might a question requiring a brief answer be appropriate?

Internet Research

Instructions: These exercises broaden your understanding of module concepts by requiring that you search for information on the web. Use a search engine or another search tool to locate the information requested or answers to questions presented in the exercises. Describe your findings, along with the search term(s) you used and your web source(s), in the format requested by your instructor (brief report, presentation, discussion, blog post, video, or other means). Additionally, reflect on the process you used to complete this activity. How did you go about choosing the tool that you did and why? Would you do anything differently next time?

❶ Social Media: Corporate Policies

Companies have created policies that employees must follow when participating in social media and online social networks. One company, for example, considers participation in social media to be an opportunity, not a right, and requires its employees to disclose their identity, protect the company's confidential and classified information, and use common sense when writing and airing opinions. Another company's employees are urged to use good judgment when using online social networks and are barred from discussing the company on their own websites and from commenting on or posting messages regarding the company and its products on any related websites.

Research This: Locate at least two corporate policies for social media participation and summarize the requirements. Do you agree with the companies' guidelines? Are the policies too lenient or too strict? What actions are taken if an employee fails to abide by the policies? In what ways may policies differ among various fields, such as in health care and education?

❷ Search Skills: Using the Web for Research

A search engine may provide targeted results from news websites, blogs, corporate websites, and other sources. In addition, research websites, digital libraries, and specialized search engines can provide valuable information when using the web for research.

Your college or university library's website may list links to online journals, magazines, films, and books that will be helpful resources. It may make available links to online research databases, such as Gartner, Factiva, LexisNexis, and ProQuest, that offer IT professionals' press releases, analysis, and case studies about companies, technologies, and industries. These sources often present valuable background information, and they offer IT professionals relevant business information to guide their decision making.

Academic search engines, such as Google Scholar, and digital libraries, such as JSTOR (Journal Storage), provide access to academic journals and conference publications that can be useful when doing academic research. Navigating to these websites from campus may give you additional access to online research databases to which your library has a paid subscription.

Research This: Complete these tasks and report your findings. (1) Use your school library's website to find articles in online newspapers about information literacy. (2) Use a research database available from your school library's website to find an article about the fastest-growing IT careers. (3) Use a research database available from your school library's website to find an article about a company or career discussed in this module. (4) Find a recent scholarly publication about rapid application development.

❸ Cloud Services: Enterprise Software Apps

Many companies make use of enterprise software apps to manage customer relationship management (CRM) and Enterprise Resource Planning (ERP). The rise of cloud computing in enterprises has resulted in these and other enterprise software apps being hosted and managed on the cloud, rather than being purchased and installed in-house. SaaS (software as a service), a service of cloud computing, provides the delivery of software applications that are stored and deployed from servers on the Internet.

Enterprise software applications are popular SaaS offerings because IT departments do not need to install the software or manage the servers on which they run; instead, they can concentrate on configuring and specifying the services that these apps provide. Their "pay as you go" model, where customers are charged only for the capabilities they use, make SaaS apps attractive from a financial perspective. Users always interact with the most up-to-date version, and because the apps are accessed in a browser, it is easy to maintain the app across large organizations.

Research This: (1) Read about Salesforce, a pioneer in cloud-based CRM applications. What services does Salesforce provide? Find a case study about Salesforce, and describe how Salesforce's cloud solutions met one of its customer's needs. (2) Read about enterprise SaaS offerings to manage business operations and customer relations. Select or compare cloud services from companies such as SAP, Microsoft, and Oracle, and prepare a summary of their offerings. What are advantages and disadvantages to companies running these apps on the cloud?

Critical Thinking

Instructions: These exercises challenge your assessment and decision-making skills by presenting real-world situations associated with module concepts. The Collaboration exercise should be completed with a team. Evaluate the situations below, using personal experiences and one or more resources available to you (such as articles on the web or in print, blogs, podcasts, videos, television, user guides, other individuals, electronics or computer stores, etc.). Perform the tasks requested in each exercise and share your deliverables in the format requested by your instructor (brief report, presentation, discussion, blog post, video, or other means).

1. Cybersecurity Threats

After a few years working in network management, you have realized that you are more interested in a career in cybersecurity. You want to find out what types of risks you might be expected to address if you were a cybersecurity specialist, and what technology exists that helps secure against threats. You hope that you are able to convince your company that it is worthwhile to support you in your training.

Do This: Research current cybersecurity threats, recent cybersecurity attacks, cybersecurity software, and cybersecurity training and certifications. Address the following questions: What new types of threats have recently emerged? What do you think is the motive behind the perpetrators? In a recent cybersecurity attack, what were the negative outcomes to the company or organization affected? Were the perpetrators caught? If so, what was their punishment? Do you think it was adequate? Why or why not? What new or enhanced software or apps are available to address cybersecurity threats? Are certifications available in cybersecurity? What training would you need to prepare for the exam? Do you think this is a worthwhile career move? Why or why not?

2. Training for a New System

Your company is in the process of converting its database system to a completely new platform. The new program will allow for greater security and better data analysis, as well as being more user friendly. The currently used program has been in service for six years, and the employees who use it are nervous about the transition. It is in the company's best interest to keep the employees happy and provide them with resources to ensure the transition is a smooth one. You have been asked to gather information about how to train users on a new system.

Do This: Research tips from other database professionals on how to make a system transition. What recommendations require outside resources? What recommendations can easily be done with a company's existing resources? Find websites for corporate trainers who specialize in database transitions. What services do they provide? What are the costs? Find a website for a large database system developer, and determine what resources it provides when you purchase the system. Do they offer training? Are user manuals provided?

3. Case Study

Cooperative-Owned Farm Stand   You are the new manager for a farm stand that is a cooperative effort, jointly owned by several local farmers. The farm stand wants to hire someone to manage its technology but does not believe it needs anybody full time. The owners have asked you to investigate what the costs are for hiring an IT consultant and what types of services they provide.

Do This: Make a list of three tasks an IT consultant might perform that would benefit the farm stand. Why are these tasks more suitable for a professional to execute and not someone with basic computer skills? Find profiles on a career website for IT consultants in your area. Make a list of services they provide. Find one who could help with the three tasks you identified. What are the costs, and how are they determined (i.e., by project or hourly)? Is a minimum number of hours specified for which you must hire the person? Would you recommend this service to the farm stand? Why or why not?

Collaboration

4. Job Search

You work in the human resources department of a network security company. You currently have several openings for positions, including a network administrator, a security expert, and a help desk technician.

Do This: Form a three-member team and have each team member choose a different position. As a team, discuss any common requirements or background necessary for all the positions based on the needs of a network security company. Each team member should list the educational background, available certifications, and other requirements for the position, and research and compare computer science programs at the university level that would prepare someone with the necessary skills for the position. Find listings for similar jobs in your area. What responsibilities are listed for the position? What salary information can you locate? Create a list of information potential employees should have as part of their online profile. As a team, meet to discuss and compile your findings.

Appendix – Technology Acronyms

Acronym	Description	Page	Module
2FA	two-factor authentication	5-18	5
3GPP	Third Generation Partnership Project	9-5	9
4G	fourth generation	2-9	2
4GL	fourth generation language	11-11	11
5GL	fifth generation language	11-11	11
ADA	Americans with Disabilities Act	1-20	1
ADSL	Asymmetric Digital Subscriber Line	9-14	9
AI	artificial intelligence	4-33	4
AIFF	Audio Interchange File Format	4-24	4
ALU	arithmetic logic unit	3-2	3
AMOLED	active-matrix OLED	6-19	6
ANSI	American National Standards Institute	9-9	9
AOL	America Online	1-26	1
AR	augmented reality	4-31	4
ARPA	Advanced Research Projects Agency	2-2	2
ASCII	American Standard for Information Interchange	3-11	3
ATM	automated teller machine	1-6	1
ATM	Asynchronous Transfer Mode	9-14	9
AUP	acceptable use policy	1-16	1
B2B	business-to-business	2-17	2
B2C	business-to-consumer	2-17	2
BAN	body area network	9-8	9
BBS	Bulletin Board System	1-26	1
BD	Blu-ray Disc	3-20	3
BI	business intelligence	10-20	10
BIOS	basic input/output system	3-3	3
BLOB	binary large object	10-9	10
BYOD	bring your own device	1-9	1
C2C	consumer-to-consumer	2-17	2
CA	certificate authority	5-19	5
CAD	computer-aided design	4-20	4
CAE	computer-aided engineering	13-7	13
CAM	computer-aided manufacturing	1-10	1
CAPTCHA	Completely Automated Public Turing test to tell Computers and Humans Apart	5-18	5
CARS	credible, accurate, reasonable, supportable	2-31	2

Acronym	Description	Page	Module
CATV	cable television	9-14	9
CC	Creative Commons	2-32	2
CCFL	cold cathode fluorescent lamp	6-19	6
CDP	continuous data protection	5-12	5
CIA	Confidentiality, Integrity, and Availability	10-19	10
CISSP	Certified Information Systems Security Professional	13-11	13
CMOS	complementary metal-oxide semiconductor	7-17	7
CMS	content management system	12-7	12
COPPA	Children's Online Privacy Protection Act	5-21	5
CPC	cost per click	10-27	10
CPI	cost per impression	10-27	10
CPU	central processing unit	3-2	3
CRM	customer relationship management	13-7	13
CRT	cathode-ray tube	6-24	6
CSA	Cloud Security Alliance	5-14	5
CSS	cascading style sheets	2-5	2
CTA	call-to-action	12-2	12
DaaS	data as a service	3-34	3
DBA	database administrator	10-14	10
DBaaS	database as a service	10-14	10
DBMS	database management system	10-3	10
DDoS	distributed DoS	5-8	5
DHC/ OCIA	Department of Homeland Security's Office of Cyber and Infrastructure Analysis	6-30	6
DMCA	Digital Millennium Copyright Act	5-21	5
DMS	document management system	13-8	13
DNS	domain name system	2-7	2
DoS	denial of service	5-8	5
dpi	dots per inch	6-18	6
DRAM	dynamic RAM	3-3	3
DRM	digital rights management	2-32	2
DSL	digital subscriber line	3-22	3
DSS	decision support system	13-8	13
DV	digital video	6-9	6
EB	exabyte	7-3	7
EDI	electronic data interchange	9-9	9
EFT	electronic funds transfer	9-3	9

Appendix

Acronym	Description	Page	Module
ENIAC	Electronic Numerical Integrator and Computer	1-4	1
EPS	Encapsulated PostScript	4-23	4
ERP	enterprise resource planning	13-7	13
EULA	end user license agreement	4-11	4
FIP	Fair Information Practices	10-21	10
fps	frames per second	4-28	4
FTP	File Transfer Protocol	2-23	2
FTTP	Fiber to the Premises	9-14	9
GB	gigabyte	2-8	2
GBps	gigabytes per second	7-3	7
GHz	gigahertz	3-24	3
GIF	Graphics Interchange Format	4-23	4
GPS	global positioning system	9-5	9
GPU	graphics processing unit	6-20	6
GUI	graphical user interface	8-3	8
HD	High Definition	4-27	4
HDD	hard disk drive	3-20	3
HDTV	high-definition television	6-20	6
HRIS	human resources information system	13-7	13
HTML	Hypertext Markup Language	2-5	2
HTTP	Hypertext Transfer Protocol	2-6	2
https	Hypertext Transfer Protocol Secure	2-18	2
IaaS	infrastructure as a service	6-30	6
IDE	integrated development environment	11-12	11
IDEA	Individuals with Disabilities Education Act	1-20	1
IEEE	Institute of Electrical and Electronics Engineers	9-9	9
IETF	Internet Engineering Task Force	2-4	2
IoT	Internet of Things	1-4	1
IP	Internet Protocol	2-6	2
IP	intellectual property	5-5	5
IPC	instructions per cycle	3-16	3
IPS	Interstate Photo System	10-14	10
IPv4	Internet Protocol version 4	9-9	9
IPv6	Internet Protocol version 6	9-9	9
IR	infrared	9-11	9
IrDA	Infrared Data Association	9-11	9
ISDN	Integrated Services Digital Network	9-13	9
ISP	Internet service provider	2-3	2
IT	information technology	5-31	5

Acronym	Description	Page	Module
JAD	joint-application design	11-8	11
JPEG	Joint Photographic Experts Group	4-23	4
JSTOR	Journal Storage	13-21	13
KB	kilobyte	7-3	7
KBps	kilobytes per second	7-3	7
LAN	local area network	9-8	9
LCD	liquid crystal display	6-19	6
LED	light-emitting diode	6-19	6
LMS	learning management system	1-10	1
LTE	Long Term Evolution	9-5	9
M2M	machine-to-machine	1-10	1
MAC	Media Access Control	5-14	5
MAN	metropolitan area network	9-8	9
MB	megabyte	2-8	2
MBps	megabytes per second	7-3	7
MFD	multifunction device	3-14	3
MFP	multifunction printer	6-16	6
MG	megabyte	7-3	7
MICR	magnetic-ink character recognition	6-13	6
MIDI	Musical Instrument Digital Interface	4-25	4
MIS	management information system	13-8	13
MRAM	magnetoresistive RAM	3-3	3
MRP	material requirements planning	13-7	13
MRP II	manufacturing resource planning II	13-7	13
ms	milliseconds	6-19	6
NAS	network attached storage	7-13	7
NFC	near-field communications	1-5	1
NFT	non-fungible token	12-16	12
NGI	Next Generation Identification	10-14	10
NIC	network interface card	3-22	3
NUI	natural user interface	8-17	8
OCR	optical character recognition	6-12	6
OLAP	online analytical processing	13-8	13
OLED	organic LED	6-19	6
OLTP	online transaction processing	13-8	13
OMR	optical mark recognition	6-12	6
OOP	object-oriented programming	11-12	11
OS	operating system	8-2	8
P2P	peer-to-peer	9-3	9
PaaS	platform as a service	7-9	7

Acronym	Description	Page	Module
PAN	personal area network	9-8	9
PB	petabyte	7-3	7
PC	personal computer	1-4	1
PERT	Program Evaluation and Review Technique	11-7	11
PIN	personal identification number	5-17	5
PNG	Portable Network Graphics	4-23	4
POS	point of sale	6-8	6
POST	power-on self test	3-3	3
PPC	pay per click	10-27	10
ppm	pages per minute	6-14	6
PSK	preshared key	5-13	5
PTI	Public Technical Identifiers	2-7	2
PUE	power usage effectiveness	5-6	5
QBE	query by example	10-10	10
QR	quick response	6-12	6
RAD	rapid application development	11-6	11
RAID	redundant array of independent disks	7-13	7
RAM	random access memory	3-2	3
RDBMS	relational database management system	4-18	4
RF	radio frequency	3-19	3
RFI	request for information	11-10	11
RFID	radio frequency identification	6-13	6
RFP	request for proposal	11-10	11
RFQ	request for quotation	11-10	11
ROM	read-only memory	3-3	3
rpm	revolutions per minute	7-6	7
RSI	repetitive strain injury	3-25	3
RTOS	real-time operating system	8-7	8
RWD	responsive web design	2-5	2
SaaS	software as a service	4-8	4
SAN	storage area network	7-13	7
SCM	supply chain management	13-9	13
SD	Standard Definition	4-27	4
SDK	software development kit	11-12	11
SDLC	software development life cycle	11-3	11
SecaaS	security as a service	5-30	5
SEO	search engine optimization	12-4	12
SFA	sales force automation	13-7	13
SNP	sip-and-puff	6-22	6
SQL	Structured Query Language	10-10	10
SRAM	static RAM	3-4	3

Acronym	Description	Page	Module
SSD	solid-state drive	3-20	3
SSID	service set identifier	2-10	2
SSL	Secure Sockets Layer	12-15	12
STaaS	storage as a service	7-9	7
SVG	Scalable Vector Graphics	4-23	4
TB	terabyte	7-3	7
TCP/IP	Transmission Control Protocol/Internet Protocol	2-6	2
TIF	Tagged Image File Format	4-23	4
TLD	top-level domain	2-7	2
TLS	Transport Layer Security	2-19	2
TPS	transaction processing system	13-8	13
UAS	unmanned aerial system	13-9	13
UAV	unmanned aerial vehicle	13-9	13
UHD	Ultra High Definition	4-27	4
UI	user interface	12-2	12
UNIVAC	Universal Automatic Computer	1-4	1
UPS	uninterruptible power supply	3-17	3
URL	uniform resource locator	2-6	2
USB	universal serial bus	7-7	7
UWB	ultra-wideband	9-11	9
UX	user experience	11-2	11
VAN	value-added network	9-20	9
VAR	value-added reseller	11-10	11
VM	virtual machine	8-19	8
VoIP	voice over Internet Protocol	2-23	2
VPN	virtual private network	5-10	5
VR	virtual reality	4-31	4
W3C	World Wide Web Consortium	2-4	2
WAI	Web Accessibility Initiative	12-18	12
WAN	wide area network	9-8	9
WAP	wireless access point	2-10	2
WAVE (or WAV)	Waveform Audio	4-24	4
WCAG	Web Content Accessibility Guidelines	12-18	12
WLAN	wireless local area network	3-19	3
WMA	Windows Media Audio	4-24	4
WPA2	Wi-Fi Protected Access 2	5-13	5
WPS	Wi-Fi Protected Setup	5-13	5
XML	Extensible Markup Language	12-10	12
YB	yottabyte	7-3	7
ZB	zettabyte	7-3	7

Index

Note: **Bold** page numbers indicate key terms.